*Tench Coxe
and the Early Republic*

Tench Coxe. Engraving by Samuel Sartain of a 1795 painting by J. Paul. (Courtesy of the Historical Society of Pennsylvania, Philadelphia.)

Tench Coxe
and the Early Republic

Jacob E. Cooke

Published for the Institute of Early American History and Culture
Williamsburg, Virginia
by The University of North Carolina Press
Chapel Hill

The Institute of Early American History and Culture is sponsored jointly by The College of William and Mary in Virginia and The Colonial Williamsburg Foundation.

Both the initial research and the publication of this work were made possible in part through grants from the National Endowment for the Humanities, a federal agency whose mission is to award grants to support education, scholarship, media programming, libraries, and museums, in order to bring the results of cultural activities to a broad, general public.

A modified version of chapter 10 was published under the title "Tench Coxe, American Economist: The Limitations of Economic Thought in the Early Nationalist Period," in Pennsylvania History, XLII (1975), 267–289. A modified version of chapter 11 was published under the title "The Collaboration of Tench Coxe and Thomas Jefferson," in the Pennsylvania Magazine of History and Biography, C (1976), 468–490.

Library of Congress Cataloging in Publication Data

Cooke, Jacob Ernest, 1924–
   Tench Coxe and the early Republic.

   Bibliography: p.
   Includes index.
   1. Coxe, Tench, 1755–1824. 2. Politicians—United States—
Biography. 3. Merchants—United
States—Biography. 4. American loyalists—Biography.
5. United States—Politics and government—1783–1865.
I. Institute of Early American History and Culture,
Williamsburg, Va. II. Title.
E302.6.C74C66   973.4'092'4 [B]   77-28832
ISBN 0-8078-1308-7

TO JEAN

Contents

Preface

Upon his death in July 1824 Tench Coxe left thousands of valuable historical manuscripts. Thrown into large tin boxes, for the most part unsorted and unlabeled, they passed, along with the property he had amassed during a lifetime of land speculation, to his children. The papers remained in the possession of his descendants for well over a century, during which time the manuscripts of Coxe's more prominent correspondents were gradually turned over to public repositories. By the mid-twentieth century Coxe's papers, still in the possession of his descendants, constituted one of the few, and indisputably the most important, untapped manuscript sources for the Revolutionary and early national periods of American history.

The historical consciousness and scholarly commitment of Daniel M. Coxe has at long last made his great-great-grandfather's papers available to scholars. In 1964 Mr. Coxe, having secured the consent of 102 heirs scattered throughout the United States and Europe, gave the Tench Coxe Papers to the Historical Society of Pennsylvania. To the deed of gift, however, there was one proviso: it was stipulated that the opening of the collection should await the preparation of what Daniel Coxe described as a "definitive, though not a commissioned biography." For this purpose I was for a number of years given exclusive access to the collection. The present volume is the result.

Coxe was apparently incapable of throwing away a single piece of paper. The sixty thousand manuscripts he left include doodles, recipes, receipts, checkbooks, household accounts, seemingly random quotations and research notes, broadsides, newspaper clippings, fragments of articles, and jottings of now meaningless figures. He also preserved documents of incalculable historical importance—including copies of his business correspondence with tory merchants during the American Revolution, the voluminous letterbooks of the Philadelphia mercantile firm of which he was senior partner during the Confederation era, official documents and correspondence accumulated during his long and varied career as a public servant, and, above all, the tens of thousands of letters sent to him by relatives, friends, prominent statesmen, congressmen, state and national political allies, fellow land speculators, and literary associates.

Unfortunately for his biographer, Coxe did not make copies of most of his own personal correspondence; all that remains are the rough drafts of letters (some virtually indecipherable) that to him warranted unusually careful composition. At the outset I was thus confronted not only with the task of cataloging a virtually chaotic mass of manuscripts and separating the consequential from the trivial but also with the problem of inferring the contents of most of Coxe's letters from the replies of his correspondents. The Coxe collection, in other words, might have better served as a source for the history of Coxe's time than for his biography.

Nevertheless, the Coxe papers reveal a man far more historically significant than has been previously recognized. Coxe either participated in or expressed his views on most of the major events in state and national history from the American Revolution to the 1820s. More important, his career embodies a large number of the significant themes of his time—the position of an aristocrat in the world's most democratic nation, the cruel choice of loyalties that confronted men of aristocratic status in 1776, the career of an American tory during the Revolution, the plight of a recreant loyalist in the new Republic, the profits reaped and perils encountered by an American merchant during the period of economic adjustment in the 1780s, and the lure and hazards of land speculation, that era's economic extravaganza. He is also representative of the nexus of nationalists whose publications promoted the adoption of the federal Constitution and the band of able public officials who helped to assure its success. As the second-ranking official in the Treasury Department and as an unofficial assistant to the secretary of state, Coxe was considerably more consequential in the early history of the new nation than historians have realized.

The same can be said of his career in party politics. As a Federalist apostate, Coxe was typical of a small but historically significant wing of his party—found in commercial centers like Philadelphia—that enthusiastically endorsed the fiscal policies of Hamilton while championing the commercial policies of Thomas Jefferson. Like other such quasi-Federalists, Coxe in time gave his undivided allegiance to Jefferson, the paragon of the Democratic Republican party; unlike most others, Coxe openly became one of the Virginian's most active and influential political supporters, as a state party leader, a national campaign coordinator, and a partisan polemicist. As the numerous papers and newspaper articles of that day not previously attributed to Coxe abundantly attest, Tench Coxe is the forgotten man in the early history of American political parties. In viewing partisan service as a stepping-stone to high (or at least remunerative) political office, he was also characteristic of his time, and in his relentless pursuit of office is reflected the early history of the spoils system. But Coxe's case is the more interesting because it is ironical.

All his life Coxe aspired to fame as a distinguished public official, never realizing that instead he was winning posthumous recognition with his pen. Although Coxe is generally recognized by historians as one of the foremost political economists of his day, neither the range nor the volume of his writings has been fully appreciated. Numerous drafts and fragments of articles in his papers provided the initial clues from which many of his anonymous publications could be identified; letters acknowledging receipt of one or another article provided additional leads, and newspaper files of the period uncovered still others. At one time or another virtually coeditor of three of Philadelphia's more prominent newspapers, Coxe was a prolific journalist whose interests were as broad as the events and problems of his day. But his major concern, his idée fixe, was the development of a balanced national economy, and his perception of the transforming effects of economic growth nurtured by industrialization was atypically astute and prescient. His writings also mirror the intellectual presuppositions and convictions of his time, among them a perfervid patriotism that often was more reflexive than reflective, a racy optimism cushioned by the belief in axiomatic progress, and a materialistic philosophy underpinned by the near-worship of technology. Thus far his biography is a chapter in American intellectual history of the early national period.

Just as Coxe's papers reveal his contributions to the formative years of our history, so they also pose the tantalizing oddity of the stymied career of an unusually gifted man in a society presumably receptive to talent. There was some truth in his comment that "the road open before him" at the outset of his public career appeared to lead "to the highest honors of the State."[1] But that road was blocked, and to Coxe, battered by the frustration of political ambition and by financial crises, his life must have seemed, if not a failure, a succession of frustrations. By more objective criteria, his experiences raise the question of why so able a man was relegated to relatively subordinate positions: that is, how did this aristocrat of acknowledged charm and administrative expertness manage to antagonize members of his own family (including his long-indulgent father), business allies (a listing of

1. *Aurora General Advertiser* (Philadelphia), Nov. 19, 1800.

whom would constitute a Who's Who of early American capitalists), and political associates (notably Hamilton, Jefferson, and John Adams)? Critical estimates of him, contemporary and posthumous, are suggestive. Hamilton called him "too cunning to be wise." John Quincy Adams wrote in his diary that Coxe was a "wily, winding, subtle, and insidious character"; the historian Richard Hildreth observed in the 1850s that he was "a mousing politician and temporizing busybody, though a man of considerable financial knowledge and ability." Coxe's "long and tragic record," comments a distinguished historian of our own day, "seems to render" as "a just estimate" Jefferson's "*implicit* appraisal that placed Coxe—talented, industrious, and informed as he was—among the sycophants and the office-hungry cormorants."[2]

Such uncomplimentary assessments of a man of uncommon ability and conspicuous accomplishments present a paradox that can be resolved only by an understanding of Coxe's complex and multifaceted personality. As is often true of historical figures, however, the material needed for a satisfactory personality profile is absent—no reminiscences of childhood, almost no records of private family life, no personal reflections, no private diary or journal, and only the sparsest remnants of personal letters (as distinguished from professional and business correspondence). Nevertheless, I have attempted in the pages of this book, for the most part implicitly, to explain Coxe's enigmatic personality by relying principally—as I believe any twentieth-century biographer should—on well-known psychoanalytic postulates. At the same time, recognizing the perils of lay analysis, I have tried to tell Coxe's story objectively, in the sense of setting forth the "facts," and have thus left readers free to interpret the record in the light of their own theories.

My emphasis throughout is on Coxe's public rather than his personal life. Even to recount his public life in detail would require a volume too bulky to meet either the financial exigencies of publishing or the endurance threshold of all except the most intrepid readers. I have accordingly focused on those aspects of Coxe's varied career that have the greatest intrinsic historical interest—his experience as a tory, his voluntary services as an adviser to members of the First Congress, his official partnership with Hamilton and his unofficial collaboration with Jefferson, his role as a party leader and partisan publicist, his administrative trials and achievements from 1803 to

---

2. Alexander Hamilton to Oliver Wolcott, Jr., Aug. 5, 1795, Oliver Wolcott, Jr., Papers, Connecticut Historical Society, Hartford; Charles Francis Adams, ed., *Memoirs of John Quincy Adams*, IV (Philadelphia, 1875), 370; Richard Hildreth, *The History of the United States of America* . . . , V (New York, 1851), 378; Julian P. Boyd et al., eds., *The Papers of Thomas Jefferson* (Princeton, N.J., 1950–), XIX, 127, italics added, hereafter cited as Boyd *et al.*, eds., *Jefferson Papers*.

1812 as purveyor of the United States (the official primarily responsible for equipping military forces), and, above all, his accomplishments as a political economist. By the same token, I have paid considerably less attention to Coxe's business career (as Philadelphia merchant and as buccaneer in land speculation), to his voluminous writings on diplomatic affairs during the Jefferson era (writings that did not, except in a few instances, influence public policy), or to his commendable administration of the Pennsylvania Land Office. On these, as well as other subjects, Coxe's manuscripts contain thousands upon thousands of pages, which should someday provide a major source for many monographs.

Over the years that I spent on this biography, I benefited from the aid of many librarians, the advice of other scholars, the support of foundations, the encouragement of friends and colleagues, and the invaluable help of a few selfless co-workers. While collecting Coxe material from libraries and archives across the country, I was uniformly accorded courteous cooperation by many people—unfortunately too many to list here. I am most particularly indebted to the staff, past and present, of the Historical Society of Pennsylvania—to John Platt, Conrad Wilson, Vilma Halcombe, Peter Parker, and Lucy West, and particularly to the society's director emeritus, Nicholas B. Wainwright. I also received many favors at the society's next-door neighbor, the Library Company of Philadelphia. I was spared much travel and research by Julian P. Boyd, editor of *The Papers of Thomas Jefferson*, who kindly allowed me to make copies of the Coxe-Jefferson correspondence. For working arrangements that were conducive to the research and writing of this book, I extend my thanks to associates at Lafayette College—its administrative officers, library staff, and my history department colleagues—most especially to K. Roald Bergethon, Robert S. Chase, Jr., George G. Sause, Clyde L. Haselden, Albert W. Gendebien, and Richard E. Welch, Jr. I also thank Mary Lou Millar, who typed successive drafts of my manuscript, and I owe an especial debt of gratitude to Hilda Cooper, on whose secretarial expertness I heavily relied during the years that I was writing this book. I am also greatly indebted to Lucy Trumbull Brown, manuscript editor at the Institute of Early American History and Culture, for the extended time and editorial expertness that she bestowed on this biography. This volume was made possible not only by the support of Lafayette College but also by the generous aid of two foundations. In the 1968/1969 academic year I was awarded a Guggenheim Foundation fellowship, which permitted me to launch the Coxe project by spending the requisite time at the Historical Society of Pennsylvania. In 1972 a grant from the National Endowment for the Humanities made possible the completion of a first draft of this biography, which does not necessarily represent the views of the Endowment. I am also grateful to the late Daniel M. Coxe for the free hand, the assistance, and the encouragement that he provided, and to Dorothy Weld Coxe for her warm interest.

Above all, I wish to express my gratitude to the two people who contributed most to the research and writing of this biography: my student assistant for three years, Alan D. Wrigley, and my wife, Jean. Mr. Wrigley assisted me in sorting and cataloging the Coxe collection, transcribing many of its seemingly indecipherable items, and helping to track down Coxe's anonymous newspaper articles. The dedication to my wife inadequately conveys my appreciation for her inspiration, her sacrifices, and her indispensable assistance. Whatever merit this book may have is owing to her expert and scrupulous scholarship; without her patience and encouragement this work probably would not have been completed.

*Tench Coxe
and the Early Republic*

1 ⚜

Forebears and Youth

"My great grandfather Dr. Daniel Coxe was principal proprietor" of colonial New Jersey, and "our Carolana claim, was the largest proprietarship ever held by one family in our country," Tench Coxe wrote to President James Monroe in 1822.[1] Tench Coxe's own career was decisively molded by the achievements and aspirations of this English forebear.

Dr. Coxe and his great-grandson had much in common. The Englishman was an able scientist, his American descendant an economist of repute, and both earned considerable acclaim for their publications. Dr. Coxe won the support of members of the royal household, even the king; his great-grandson earned the confidence of influential men in public life, including presidents. To neither were the rewards of profession and public life sufficient. Both dreamed of carving vast empires from the American wilderness and attempted to do so with a single-mindedness that bordered on mania. Both secured hundreds of thousands of acres of virgin land and, unable to resist the urge to buy still more, jeopardized peace of mind and material comfort by yielding to temptation. Yet their personal sacrifices handsomely benefited their posterity: just as Daniel provided his American heirs with vast landholdings that rendered them independently wealthy, so Tench Coxe purchased and held onto lands that eventually enriched his descendants.

Daniel Coxe, the oldest of thirteen children, was born in 1640 and educated at Cambridge, where in 1669 he became an "M.D., *per literas regias*."[2] A scientist of note, he published a study on the effect of nicotine

1. Tench Coxe to James Monroe, Sept. 9, 1822, Tench Coxe Papers, Historical Society of Pennsylvania, Philadelphia, hereafter cited as Coxe Papers.
2. Dr. Daniel Coxe's father, also named Daniel, was a resident of Westminster. In 1648 he was granted a coat of arms and two years later acquired an estate at Stoke Newington.

upon animals and conducted other chemical experiments that were published in the *Philosophical Transactions* of the Royal Society. His distinction
was recognized by membership in England's most prestigious learned societies, the Royal Society and the Royal College of Physicians of London, and
by appointment as physician to the courts of Charles II and Anne. But for
Dr. Coxe, as for his great-grandson, his accomplishments paled in contrast
to his fantasies of owning vast landed estates. The actualization of this
dream was owing less to royal patronage than to an advantageous marriage.
His wife, Rebecca, the only surviving child of John Coldham and Rebecca
Dethick (daughter of London's lord mayor), was an heiress. As was the
custom of the day, she put her fortune at her husband's disposal.[3]

Thanks to this financial backing, Dr. Coxe was able to indulge his
appetite for land speculation. He began in 1687 by purchasing most of the
province of West Jersey, presumably also acquiring the right of government.
Easily exchanging the role of court physician for that of chief proprietor and
ruler of a colony, Coxe promptly began making arrangements to sail for the
New World to assume personal control of his propriety. His plans did not
materialize, however, and he was obliged to govern through a deputy.[4]
Since his principal concern was not political power but profits, it was an
agreeable arrangement to Coxe. To encourage prospective emigrants to buy
or lease his lands, he commissioned enticing and somewhat disingenous
prospectuses and himself wrote a promotional piece entitled "Dr. Daniel
Coxe His Account of New Jersey."[5]

In 1690 Dr. Coxe estimated his property in West and East Jersey at
around a million acres, a domain including "a plantacion att Cape May
made by a very skilfull French Gardiner who is there resident" and who
"hath planted some thousand fruit Trees of divers and the best sorts."
Owning such an imperial estate temporarily soothed Coxe's speculative

---

3. On May 12, 1671, Dr. Daniel Coxe married Rebecca, daughter of John Coldham of Toot-
ing Graveney near London. Coldham, an alderman of London, was apparently a man of considerable property, most of which went to his only surviving child, Rebecca, upon his death in
1696. Brinton Coxe to Charles E. Coxe, Sept. 10, 1871, Coxe Papers.

4. According to John Oldmixon, "Dr. Daniel Coxe . . . took the Government into his own
Hands; but being then in very great Business in his Profession, he did not think fit to leave it for
the Profits of his Province, and govern'd the Colony always by a Deputy. In the year 1690, his
Practice diminishing in England, he resolved on a Voyage to his American Territories, and was
actually gone as far as Salisbury, on his way to Plimouth to embark there for this Country, but
he was disswaded by a friend from the intended Voyage." [Oldmixon], *The British Empire in
America* . . . , I (London, 1708), 147.

5. "Dr. Daniel Coxe His Account of New Jersey," Rawlinson Manuscripts, Bodleian Library,
Oxford, hereafter cited as Daniel Coxe, "Account of New Jersey." According to John Edwin
Pomfret, the leading authority on the history of colonial New Jersey, "for some time Coxe had
been contemplating the sale of the lands and government of West Jersey. Indeed his 'Account of
New Jersey,' written in 1690, was in large measure addressed to a potential buyer." Pomfret,
*The Province of West New Jersey, 1609–1702: A History of the Origins of an American Col-
ony* (Princeton, N.J., 1956), 171.

itch, and he assumed the fulltime role of American colony-builder. "I have at the Expence of above Three thousand pounds," he wrote in 1688, "setled a Towne and Established a fishing for Whales which are very numerous about Cape may both within the Bay and without all along the sea coast which I am assured if well mannaged will bring in above 4000 £ per Annum all charges Defrayed."

These were not the only commercial possibilities Coxe envisioned for his New World possessions. He pointed to many other opportunities—the logging of timber for shipbuilding, the cultivation of hemp for cordage, the mining of "mineralls of diverse sorts," and the construction of iron works. Other possibilities that Coxe noted were the production of wine and brandy from the "multitude of wild Grapes," the manufacture of china and cooking utensils (for which he had by 1685 erected a pottery at Burlington), the promotion of the fur trade, and the establishment of a "Magazine or Storehouse in Delaware River" to serve as an entrepôt for European commodities exchangeable for American commodities that could be exported to the West Indies.[6]

In March 1692 Dr. Coxe, discouraged by the crown's attitude toward the Jerseys and with his sights on more lucrative speculations, sold the lion's share of his New Jersey property, along with his presumed governmental prerogative, to the West Jersey Society, a group of forty-eight investors, of whom the majority were London merchants. The price agreed upon was £9,800, for that date a handsome sum. Now was the time, Coxe decided, to acquire most of the North American continent rather than a mere province. Captive of the vision that would continue to inspire Americans for two centuries, he turned his attention to the boundless and virtually unsettled lands of the south and west, and though he never left England, "in imagination he stood tiptoe upon his Jersey hills and strained his eyes westward."[7] There he figuratively saw millions of acres of available land, the possession of which a monarch might have envied. Fortunately for Dr. Coxe, the patent for the province of Carolana-Florida—a staggeringly enormous expanse of territory—was for sale.

The proprietorship of Carolana dated back to 1629, when Charles I granted to Sir Robert Heath an area encompassing the entire North American continent between the thirty-first and thirty-sixth parallels and stretching westward from the Carolinas and Georgia to the Pacific Ocean. In June 1696 Coxe purchased the territory from Sir James Shaen, knight and baronet.[8] Promptly acquiring every available scrap of printed material on the

6. Daniel Coxe, "Account of New Jersey."
7. Verner W. Crane, *The Southern Frontier, 1670–1732* (Philadelphia, 1929), 49.
8. "Abstract of title of Dr. Coxe to Carolana," 1700, C.O. 5/1259, p. 453, Public Record Office.

transappalachian region, Coxe began to plan for the development and settlement of his empire. As he pored over his large collection of pamphlets, books, and maps, his vision of incalculable riches grew brighter, his plans for exploiting this princely domain ever grander. In a remark that might also have been applied to Tench Coxe, Francis Nicholson, governor of Virginia, wrote of Coxe: "I believe he is an honest Gentleman and a very good Doctor, by what he told me concerning his ill success of his Jersey proprietorship, I thought he had done with such prospects, but I am afraid several people have abused the Doctor's good nature and generosity by telling him of Strange Countries and giving him Mapps thereof."[9] Whether credulous or not, Coxe was among the first of his countrymen to envisage English control and colonization of the American west—a prescience that his great-grandson, although in a different context, would share a century later. Just as "by his propaganda" Dr. Coxe "helped to spread" the "momentous idea" that "the destiny of the English in America embraced more than the settlement and exploitation of the Atlantic seaboard," so his descendant Tench would help to spread the eventful idea that the American future embraced the factory, as well as the farm.[10]

Dr. Coxe's most ambitious project was the formation of what he called a "New Empire," for the settlement and development of which he proposed the organization of a joint-stock company capitalized at some £400,000 and consisting of fourteen "original proprietors" and one thousand associates, from whom were "to be chosen several committees," including ones for religion, law, charitable uses, and the natives.[11] To settle this empire Coxe organized and supervised the emigration of about five hundred French Protestant refugees, who, financed by a grant of £3,000 from William III, planned to sail from England to the Gulf of Mexico. Had the times been more auspicious, his audacious plans might have succeeded, as had similar ones launched during earlier decades of the seventeenth century. As it was, the commander of an exploratory expedition that Coxe had sent to the Gulf of Mexico reported that the French had a strong foothold in the area and, even more disheartening, that the doctor's grant did not extend that far south. Coxe was not to be stopped; in 1700 he redirected the settlers to the county of Norfolk in Virginia. But like the Jamestown settlers a century earlier, the transplanted Europeans found it difficult to cope with the new environment.[12] Coxe appealed to the crown for support, but his

9. Francis Nicholson to Lords of Trade, Aug. 27, 1700, C.O. 5/1312 (pt. 1), pp. 44–48, Public Record Office.

10. Crane, *Southern Frontier*, 50.

11. Coxe assigned the task of drawing up the charter and bylaws to an assistant, James Spooner. The latter's "Draught of a Scheme I drew for Dr. Daniel Coxe . . . for the settlement which we called 'the New Empire'" is in the Rawlinson MSS, Bodleian Library, Oxford.

12. Coxe claimed the county of Norfolk through a grant that had been made by Sir John

project was foiled by the death of his patron, William III. Although he attempted to revive his colony during the reign of Queen Anne, the wars then raging "prov'd, excessive chargeable" and, in the words of the doctor's son, "employ'd the whole Thoughts and Attention of the Ministry," obliging Coxe to desist "from any further Prosecution of That Affair, till a fitter Opportunity should offer itself."[13]

The opportunity to revive his project never came. But Dr. Coxe did not abandon his ambitious plans, much less surrender his claim to Carolana;[14] a century later his design for building a new commonwealth on the cornerstone of a great land company provided the inspiration for Tench Coxe's attempt to establish a model town in the vast wilderness that he had acquired in western North Carolina. Upon Daniel Coxe's death in 1730, his lands passed to his heirs, who held them until 1769.

Carolana's magnificent resources and its consequent suitability for émigrés were the themes of a promotional book compiled by Dr. Coxe's son, Colonel Daniel Coxe. *A Description of the English Province of Carolana*, first published in London in 1722, was largely composed "out of Memoirs, which the present Proprietor of Carolana, my honour'd Father, had drawn from several English Journals and Itineraries Taken by his own People, whom he had sent for Discovery."[15] But Coxe's *Description of Carolana* was something more than a travel book. In a long preface to the documents the colonel recounted "the vast Trouble and Expence" of his father in his strenuous attempts to explore and colonize Carolana and called on the crown to secure for England the diplomatic, military, and economic advantages certain to accrue from the exploitation and settlement of the area. Conversely, he pointed to the alarming possibility of Britain failing to make good its claim. If this happened, the vast North American interior might fall by default to its powerful antagonists, the French, "who all the

---

Harvey, governor of Virginia, to Lord Maltravers in 1637. W. Noel Sainsbury *et al.*, eds., *Calendar of State Papers, Colonial Series* (London, 1860–), XVIII (*America and West Indies, 1700*), nos. 143, 146. The papers describing the French emigration are in the Bodleian Library. Dr. Coxe was also one of the promoters of a company chartered in 1703 for procuring "naval stores to be made and produced in New England." The project is described in the manuscripts of Henry Newman, New Hampshire's colonial agent, Rawlinson MSS, Bodleian Library.

13. Daniel Coxe, *A Description of the English Province of Carolana. By the Spainards call'd Florida, and by the French, La Louisiane*, 4th ed. (London, 1741), the preface (pages unnumbered). Coxe sent many memorials to the Board of Trade trying to revive the project; one of these written after 1702 and probably in 1719 is found in Additional Manuscript 15903, fol. 116, British Library.

14. Crane states that "after 1700 his [Dr. Daniel Coxe's] sole significance was a voice warning England against French encirclement in North America." Crane, *Southern Frontier*, 59–60. The warning was reechoed by Benjamin Franklin in the Albany Plan of Union in 1754.

15. Daniel Coxe, *Description of Carolana*, preface. Subsequent editions were published in 1726, 1727, and 1741.

World acknowledge to be an Enterprizing, Great and Politick Nation" willing to "use all manner of Artifices to lull their Neighbours a sleep . . . whilst they cunningly endeavour to compass their Designs by degrees." If France were thus placed in a position to seize the valuable fur trade of the west and to imperil the security of England's colonists, then these colonists, fettered by provincial ties and loyalties, could not be expected to put up any united resistance—"regardless of the General or Common Danger, . . . they feel not the immediate Effects of it" or realize that "what happens to one Colony to Day, may reach another to Morrow."[16]

Colonel Coxe, convinced that "a Wise Man will not stand with his Arms folded, when his Neighbours House is on fire," proposed, "with the utmost Deference to His Majesty and His Ministers," a scheme of confederation remarkably similar to the famous Albany Plan of Union that Benjamin Franklin would offer three decades later. "A Coalition or Union of this Nature," Coxe insisted, would, "in all probability, lay a sure and lasting Foundation of Dominion, Strength, and Trade, sufficient not only to Secure and Promote the Prosperity of the Plantations, but to revive and greatly increase the late Flourishing State and Condition of Great Britain, and thereby render it, once more, the Envy and Admiration of its Neighbours." More than that, the English colonies in America, thus "joyn'd in one Common Interest . . . under one Gracious Sovereign," would be able not only to "provide for and defend themselves against any troublesome Ambitious Neighbour, or bold Invader" but also to exploit this New World cornucopia, whose contents Colonel Coxe described with the same obvious relish and lavish detail that would characterize the writings of his grandson.[17] It was, then, not only the exploits of Dr. Daniel Coxe, the greatest English land buccaneer of his day, that dazzled Tench Coxe;[18] he was also influenced by the literary achievement of his grandfather, whose style, approach, and emphasis (even his defects as a literary craftsman) were mirrored in many of his descendant's voluminous publications. The complex relationship of an individual to his own and his family's past is always difficult to unravel, but it is clear that in Coxe's case his forebears, as much as the proverbial child, were father of the man.

In addition to literary inspiration, Colonel Daniel Coxe provided his grandson with the example of a prominent political career fraught with illustrations of what an ambitious politician should avoid doing. Tench

16. *Ibid.*
17. *Ibid.*
18. Besides the Jersey and Carolana lands Dr. Daniel Coxe had acquired "200,000 acres on the Merrimac River, a region that was being rapidly settled, where lands were selling for £10 per 100 acres. . . . He also owned a tract of 5,000 acres of meadowland near Huntington, Long

chose not to learn from his grandfather's example; his own stormy role in Pennsylvania politics would duplicate in a democratic setting the part that his grandfather had played in the royal colony of New Jersey a half century earlier. Colonel Coxe had come to America in 1701 or 1702, perhaps in the entourage of Jersey's first royal governor, Edward Hyde, Lord Cornbury, a cousin of Queen Anne's who earlier had also been appointed governor of New York. The purpose of Coxe's trip was to oversee the lease and sale of the New Jersey lands his father had retained in 1692 and of the extensive tracts his father had assigned to him. The younger Coxe, next to William Penn the largest single shareholder in the province, could rightly expect to exercise considerable influence on the West Jersey Council of Proprietors, which, over succeeding decades, he managed to dominate high-handedly and to mulct of enormous holdings. He also became the storm center of the faction-ridden politics of early eighteenth-century New Jersey. Colonel Coxe, described by the usually forbearing William Penn as "one of the falsest of men" and by Jersey's Royal Governor Robert Hunter as "a noisy old fool," occupied at one time or another most of the high offices of the colony, while energetically following his father's favorite occupation of land speculation.[19]

There was, however, a romantic side to Colonel Coxe's nature. According to family tradition, his marriage on May 8, 1707, to a girl half his age was a model of melodrama: though he was an intolerant spokesman of the colony's anti-Quaker party, Coxe "eloped with a maiden of that faith and was married at three o'clock in the morning under the trees, by firelight, by Cornbury's chaplain." Devout Quaker or not, Sarah Coxe was a suitable wife for the political boss of New Jersey. She was the daughter of John Eckley, a former member of the Pennsylvania Provincial Council and judge of that colony's supreme court.[20] The Coxes settled in Burlington, the provincial capital, where Mrs. Coxe, until her untimely death in 1725, dutifully

---

Island . . . and a similar sized tract in Harlem township. With others he purchased a tract of 150,000 acres in Pennsylvania from William Penn, his share of which amounted to 10,000 acres." Pomfret, *Province of West Jersey*, 164.

19. "Letter of William Penn to James Logan, 1702," *Pennsylvania Magazine of History and Biography*, XXXVI (1912), 305–306; John E. Pomfret, *Colonial New Jersey: A History* (New York, 1973), 136. The cause of Penn's comment was Coxe's claim to land in Salem, which conflicted with William Penn's own plans. In the exchange of letters between Logan and Penn, Col. Coxe is referred to as "young Dr. Coxe." Edward Armstrong, ed., *Correspondence between William Penn and James Logan and Others, 1700–1750* (Historical Society of Pennsylvania, *Memoirs*, IX–X [Philadelphia, 1870–1872]), I, 174, 230.

20. Alexander Du Bin, *Coxe Family* . . . (Philadelphia, 1936), 13; Lewis Townsend Stevens, *The History of Cape May County, New Jersey, from the Aboriginal Times to the Present Day* . . .(Cape May City, N.J., 1897), 62. The tale related in the text doubtless is apocryphal. The couple apparently were married with her father's blessings, which the rites of the Church of England required. Du Bin, *Coxe Family*, 13.

attended the Church of England, played a social role befitting the wife of a New World seigneur, and gave birth to at least four children.

Upon the colonel's death in 1739 his estate went to his four legitimate children (one of whom was William, Tench Coxe's father),[21] and to three others who were the colonel's natural offspring by "Mary Johnson of Trenton, spinster" (some forty years later the daughter of Mrs. Johnson's son Charles Coxe would become Mrs. Tench Coxe).[22] To these legatees Daniel Coxe left extensive property holdings in New Jersey (including ironworks and gristmills), as well as lands in New York and Massachusetts.[23]

Goodly inheritance though this was, it paled alongside the promise of Carolana, and for three decades the colonel's heirs employed all the legal resources they could muster and all the influence they could command to validate their claim to this imperial domain.[24] In 1763 they turned to Benjamin Franklin, requesting that he recommend to them some suitable person in England "to solicit their Claim to that Country, and obtain for them either a Renewal of the Grant, or a Grant of some other Territory in Lieu of it, or an equivalent Sum as a Compensation for the Expences of the Family in the Discovery and Attempts of Settlement in that Country, which were frustrated by the French." Franklin, who indicated that he would like an opportunity to invest in Carolana should the family's claims be validated, was obliging. In March 1763 he wrote to his close friend and legal adviser Richard Jackson, the new English agent for Pennsylvania, recommending the Coxes "and their Interests to you most cordially and warmly, as they are good Friends of mine and Persons of Worth, Candor and Honour."[25]

21. The four children were John (d. 1753), a member of the New Jersey bar and a royal councillor; Daniel (1710–1757 or 1758), an English-educated barrister and by royal appointment one of Trenton's burgesses; Rebecca (1716–1802), who according to family legend was once betrothed to one of Jersey's royal governors, but who broke the engagement and "retired from the world although beautiful and wealthy" (Du Bin, *Coxe Family*, 14); and William. Neither John nor Rebecca married or had issue. Daniel had two children—Daniel, who married Sarah Redman, and Grace, who married John Tabor Kempe, the royal attorney general of New York.

22. To his illegitimate children Charles, Thomas, and Mary Coxe, Col. Coxe bequeathed 350 acres of land in Hunterdon County, N.J. But "the stone house in Trenton wherein Mary Johnson lived" was left to William Coxe. According to a codicil to Col. Coxe's will, "Mary, daughter of Mary Johnson . . . died since date of will." William A. Whitehead *et al.*, eds., *Archives of the State of New Jersey*, 1st Ser. (Newark, N.J., 1880–1928), XXX, 118–119, hereafter cited as *N.J. Archives*.

23. The will was dated Mar. 21, 1737, and was proved on Apr. 30, 1739. *Ibid.*

24. William Alexander Duer, *The Life of William Alexander, Earl of Stirling . . .* (New York, 1847), 89. Stirling did attempt to aid William Coxe and the other heirs by asking a prominent solicitor in London "to be a friend of this worthy man." See Stirling to Henry Wilmot, Dec. 16, 1767, to John Tabor Kempe, Dec. 16, 1767, *ibid.*, 91–93. The living heirs of Col. Daniel Coxe were in 1769 William Coxe and Rebecca Coxe and their nephew Daniel Coxe and niece Grace Coxe Kempe.

25. Benjamin Franklin to Richard Jackson, Mar. 8, 1763, Leonard W. Labaree *et al.*, eds., *The Papers of Benjamin Franklin* (New Haven, Conn., 1959–), X, 213, hereafter cited as Labaree *et al.*, eds., *Franklin Papers*.

For a year Franklin and Jackson busied themselves in support of the Coxe claim, but after a diligent search failed to uncover the original grant to Dr. Daniel Coxe by William III, their interest waned. The Coxe family's sustained effort to win royal recognition of their title to Carolana finally ended in 1769 when the Privy Council decided that the claim was invalid, largely because of the long interval since the original grant was made and the interim settlement of the area. All was not lost, however; in return for formal relinquishment of the claim, the Privy Council agreed to award the family one hundred thousand acres in Oneida County, New York.[26] It was a good bargain, but to the Coxes it was a comedown. "Let us," Colonel Daniel Coxe had once written, "consider the Fall of our Ancestors and grow wise by their misfortunes."[27] Tench Coxe refused to heed this advice and instead fell heir to the land mania of his ancestors.

Tench's father, William, though a large landowner, chose a new type of career for an American Coxe. He left Burlington as a young man and established himself as a merchant in Philadelphia. There, on April 10, 1750, he married Mary Francis, daughter of Elizabeth Turbutt and Tench Francis. Tench Coxe was born on May 22, 1755, the third of William and Mary's thirteen children. Of the ten who lived to maturity, only four had any appreciable effect on or intimate relationship with Tench—Sarah (1751?–1825), who at the age of seventeen married Andrew Allen, Pennsylvania's attorney general; John D. (1752–1824), a future Philadelphia lawyer and judge; William, Jr. (1762–1831), by turns merchant, gentleman farmer, pomologist, and federal congressman from New Jersey; and Daniel W. (1769–1852), a successful international merchant and the sibling to whom Tench was closest.

The importance of Tench's mother goes beyond the influence of child raising. As a Philadelphia aristocrat, she counted among her close relatives distinguished Englishmen like Sir Philip Francis and a good number of Pennsylvania's first families, including the Tilghmans, Willings, Shippens, Binghams, Mifflins, Chews, and Burds.[28] Such aristocratic lineage added luster even to a Coxe, thus assuring Tench of an unassailable social position

---

26. See Franklin to Jackson, Apr. 17, Sept. 22, Dec. 19, 1763, Mar. 14, 31, May 1, June 25, 1764, Jackson to Franklin, Nov. 12, Dec. 27, 1763, Apr. 13, Aug. 11, 1764, *ibid.*, 254–255, 341–342, 369–371, 404, 413–414, XI, 107, 152, 175–176, 185, 238, 311. For the actions of the Privy Council, see W. L. Grant and James Munroe, eds., *Acts of the Privy Council, Colonial Series . . .* , V (London, 1811), 140–142.

27. Daniel Coxe, *Description of Carolana*, preface.

28. Many of these relationships were brought about by the marriages of seven of the children of Tench Francis, Sr.: Mary Francis married William Coxe, Anne Francis married James Tilghman, Tench Francis married Anne Willing (sister of Thomas Willing), Elizabeth Francis married John Lawrence, Margaret Francis married Edward Shippen, Rachel Francis married John Relfe, and Turbutt Francis married Sarah Mifflin.

that had a decisive effect on his career, though he seldom acknowledged its influence. It was the more important because Philadelphia, capital of one of the most democratic of the American colonies, was itself a stronghold of aristocracy. Class stratification was never more marked, the elite more aloof and more powerful, than during Coxe's youth, when "inheritance and breeding had come to be considered almost as important as wealth as a basis for social standing."[29] Heir to both, Coxe remained secure in his social status throughout a long career of political rebuffs and financial setbacks. While he would in time rail against class privilege, denouncing aristocrats as monarchists all, he remained at heart a Philadelphia aristocrat. The city, then the largest in North America, was as important as the status, for Philadelphia always seemed to him the most cultured, the most beautiful, the first city in America.

William Coxe's mercantile activities were profitable owing to influential connections and business acumen and by 1762 had so expanded that he took on a partner, Moore Furman. Formerly the head of a Trenton, New Jersey, mercantile firm, Furman, like Coxe, was also a successful land speculator, having acquired acreage in Jersey, New York, and Pennsylvania.[30] The firm of Coxe and Furman flourished for the next decade and a half and was terminated only when the outbreak of the Revolution rendered the partnership of a passive tory like William Coxe and an ardent whig like Furman impossible.

In the interim Coxe assumed the public stations that accrued as if by right to a wealthy Philadelphia merchant of distinguished lineage. A member of the Proprietary Party, which was centered in Philadelphia and led by men of wealth and prestige like William Allen, Coxe was appointed a city alderman in 1758, served on official investigatory committees, was made a trustee of the College of Philadelphia in 1759, and on two occasions refused to accept the mayorship of Philadelphia.[31] He might have been better off to have also refused the post of stamp distributor for New Jersey, an appointment made pursuant to the famous Stamp Act of 1765 on the recommendation of his friend Benjamin Franklin. Like other unsuspecting appointees,

29. Ethel E. Rasmusson, "Capital on the Delaware: The Philadelphia Upper Class in Transition, 1789–1801" (Ph.D. diss., Brown University, 1962), 23.

30. *Letters of Moore Furman, Deputy Quarter-master General of New Jersey in the Revolution* (New York, 1912), vii–viii.

31. On May 5, 1758, William Coxe was appointed an alderman. He also sat on a committee with Henry Harrison and Samuel Rhoads to investigate the wharves. This information was contributed by Mrs. J. Hubley Schall of Harrisburg, Pa., from an original document in her possession. On Coxe's role as trustee, see Thomas Harrison Montgomery, *A History of the University of Pennsylvania* . . . (Philadelphia, 1900), 343. On Coxe's refusal to serve as mayor, see William Nelson, ed., *New Jersey Biographical and Genealogical Notes* (New Jersey Historical Society, *Collections*, IX [Newark, N.J., 1916]), 87.

however, Coxe did not anticipate the violent nature of the colonial reaction to the act and was no doubt dazed by the public outcry against those who had accepted offices under it. Appointed late in May 1765, he was soon confronted with what his fellow agent in Pennsylvania called "a Sort of Frenzy or Madness" that possessed "People of all Ranks." Bowing to public clamor and personal threats, Coxe resigned the office on September 3, much to the anger of royal officials like William Franklin, New Jersey's governor.[32] It was an experience that Coxe did not wish to repeat and that was in part responsible for the cautious stance of neutrality he would adopt during the American Revolution.

In 1765 Tench was only ten years old, and the reverberations of the Anglo-American dispute that over the next decade jolted Philadelphia patricians like his father and numerous kinsmen, could have had only the most tangential effect on the boy. The influences that decisively affected his later career can only be conjectured. But surely during these years were planted the seeds of character traits that would bedevil him throughout his adult life—his deviousness, obsequiousness to those with political power and prestige, naive faith in business associates he should have mistrusted, intemperateness in his attacks on political opponents, lack of prudence in personal financial affairs, and unrealistic political ambition. At this time, too, the foundations of personal qualities that made him one of the most influential publicists of his day were formed—his unflagging intellectual curiosity, desire to excel, remarkable industry, and contagious optimism.

The nature of Coxe's education and the quality of his school performance are as open to conjecture as the formative influences of his childhood. When he was six years old, he entered the academy division of the Philadelphia College and Academy, where he was annually enrolled until the spring of 1771, the eve of his sixteenth birthday.[33] More than fifty years later Coxe wrote that "in the course of my collegiate education, I was bred in the theory and practice of surveying, and the relative sciences," but his matriculation record suggests rather that whatever his course of study may have included, he attended the college for only a brief period, if at all.[34] And the infrequency with which in later life he mentioned his schooling

32. John Hughes to Benjamin Franklin, Sept. 8, 1765, Labaree *et al.*, eds., *Franklin Papers*, XII, 264. See also William Coxe to William Franklin, Sept. 3, 1765, William Franklin to William Coxe, Sept. 4, 1765, *N.J. Archives*, 1st Ser., IX, 497–498. William Franklin wrote to Benjamin Franklin about William Coxe on Sept. 7, 1765: "The Person appointed Distributor of Stamps has, however, thought proper to resign his Office, owing chiefly, I am convinced, to his timid Disposition, and the Sollicitations of his Friends in Pennsylvania." Labaree *et al.*, eds., *Franklin Papers*, XII, 260–261.

33. College Tuition Book, 1757–Oct. 17, 1769, Accounts of Tuition and Fees, July 1767–Oct. 1779, University Archives, University of Pennsylvania, Philadelphia.

34. Coxe to James Monroe, Sept. 9, 1822, Coxe Papers.

suggests the minimal importance he attached to it. Like many of his contemporaries, Coxe was essentially self-educated, but not poorly educated. Despite his skimpy schooling, he acquired a close familiarity with the classics in philosophy, history, and political theory. The mastery was not publicly unveiled until his debut as a political economist in the mid-1780s, but the preparation must have begun during his school days and early manhood.

Coxe was, in sum, a precocious youngster, recognized as such and encouraged by his parents—particularly his father, whose high estimate of his son's ability was presumably responsible for the imperturbable indulgence he displayed toward Tench for four decades. The other Coxe children (except Molly, who was apparently mentally retarded) seem to have been expected to make their own way, with perhaps an occasional parental prod or gift, but Tench, through whatever vicissitudes he experienced, was always serenely sure that his father's approval, like his purse, was bottomless. Not until the eve of William Coxe's death in the late 1790s was Tench confronted with the cruel fact that even parental forbearance can be strained. But the awareness came too late: persuaded of his personal invulnerability, Coxe had long since come to expect from others the indulgence displayed by his doting father. The result was a public career soured by unrequited claims on Alexander Hamilton, John Adams, and Thomas Jefferson, to name only the more prominent. That career demonstrated, in the end, how inflated expectations could frustrate the success of an uncommonly talented public servant.

In any event, sometime during 1772 he went into business for himself (doubtlessly prompted by his father, who was grooming Tench for a partnership in the family firm).[35] Coxe's occasional and small-scale business transactions occupied only a fraction of his time, some of which he spent reading and studying, thus enlarging the knowledge of economics, history, and related subjects that would characterize his later writings. There was also time to spare for Philadelphia's lively social life.

The blocks surrounding the Coxe home on Walnut Street were crowded with the residences of scores of friends and relatives—his uncle James Tilghman (whose son William had already established what would be a life-long intimacy with Tench), the Shippens, and the Galloways. Nearby were former schoolmates like Moses Franks and Moses Levy, and friends like William Hamilton (Philadelphia's closest approximation to the dandyism of London society) and Dr. Benjamin Rush (who had joined the faculty of the College of Philadelphia in 1769 and at whose wedding in January 1776 Coxe served as a groomsman).[36] Although Coxe obviously relished

---

35. These ventures were undertaken in cooperation with two friends residing on the island of St. Croix: Francis Markoe, a member of a prominent Philadelphia family, and Benjamin Yard, a nephew of Moore Furman. Both men would remain close friends with Coxe for many years.
36. Benjamin Rush to Coxe, Oct. 20, 1800, Coxe Papers.

the Philadelphia social whirl, he also enjoyed the meetings of a discussion group organized at his initiative, which included such close friends as Tilghman and Rush. The latter's participation, if Coxe's aunt is to be credited, must have been particularly animated. Commenting on Tench's "new coterie," Abigail Coxe wrote: "Dr. Rush I am well acquainted with. He does not want sense, but his Fire and Vivacity is ready to run away with him and I us'd to tell him that he is 'tremblingly alive all o'er.' "[37] Coxe's enthusiastic participation in the wide-ranging debates of his talk club, as well as his extensive reading and independent study, was a significant part of his self-education and indicated the broad interests of the prominent political economist he would become. More suggestive yet was his membership in the United Company of Philadelphia for Promoting American Manufactures, "one of the earliest joint stock manufacturing undertakings of the country," which he joined in 1775.[38] Thus, at the outset of his career there were intimations of the man to be.

Just as Coxe constantly was in the company of former schoolmates and relatives, so he was in frequent communication with those who had left Philadelphia, among them his brother John, who was in London to read law at the Temple; John Pringle (of South Carolina), who in December 1774 sailed for England for the same purpose; Samuel Hanson of Maryland; and John Smith, now residing on the West Indian island of Tortola. Another important correspondent was Edward Goold, a New Yorker and a partner in Beekman, Goold, and Company. Coxe had met Goold in the spring of 1774, and an enduring friendship and an eventual business partnership developed between the two men.

Coxe's most faithful correspondents were two political extremists, his Aunt Abigail Coxe, a committed monarchist and the mother of Daniel Coxe of Trenton, and James Wilkinson, an ardent American patriot during the Revolutionary period. With the latter Coxe enjoyed a friendship as close as it was brief. Wilkinson, whose later notoriety makes Coxe's subsequent reputation appear spotless by comparison, enrolled in medical school in Philadelphia in 1773 and remained there until 1775.[39] The two ostensibly ill-sorted young men were soon constant companions and were deeply attached to each other. Addressing Coxe as "my dear Portius" and designating himself "Marcus," Wilkinson wrote from Maryland in the spring of 1775 that Tench's letters "are a *healing Balsam*, a *restorative Cordial* to the droop-

37. Abigail S. Coxe to Coxe, Mar. 10, 1775, *ibid.*
38. Joseph Stancliffe Davis, *Essays in the Earlier History of American Corporations* (Cambridge, Mass., 1917), I, 355. See also Coxe's certificate of membership, Nov. 8, 1775, Coxe Papers.
39. Thomas Robson Hay and M. R. Werner, *The Admirable Trumpeter: A Biography of General James Wilkinson* (Garden City, N.Y., 1941), 1–5.

ing Spirits of the once Gay, the once lively Marcus. . . . When I every day enjoyed the Company and was happy in the Conversation of my Portius, I knew not how dear He was to me. . . . Be cautious my Portius how you mention our mutual Friend Barclay with such affectionate warmth lest you plant in my Bosom that Enemy to human repose, Jealousy. . . ."[40] But the yet undeclared Anglo-American war, which commenced a month after this letter, quickly revealed that their friendship, however close, was not strong enough to withstand political differences. Commenting on Coxe's caution about "the disagreeable consequences which Politicks, when introduced into a Private Correspondence, are likely to produce," Wilkinson observed that "I should at any other time carefully avoid a Subject too interesting, at this unhappy juncture of Affairs, for our Silence or inattention." Although Coxe also supported the American cause, he surely did not share the bellicose views of Wilkinson, who boasted in October 1775 that "I wear my Regimentals, Sword etc. Strut and look Big in hopes of exciting the Wit or Satire of some Tory." Nor was Tench receptive to the Marylander's invitation that Coxe join him on "the Field of War" in defense of American rights.[41]

Coxe's reaction to the events of the turbulent years that preceded Independence is not known. Although he must have written a good many letters, none has been preserved. It is reasonable to assume, however, that the protective shell of his fundamentally pro-English relatives alienated him from the larger American society of that day. Nevertheless, in 1774 and 1775 he, like many other members of his family, supported colonial resistance to England's more coercive policies.[42] "No man knows better than you," he wrote some twenty-five years later to Benjamin Rush, "how much I felt the first injuries of this country, how much I deplored the seemingly unfavorable division of the empire."[43] If so, he must have followed with sympathetic interest the deliberations of the First Continental Congress in September 1774, though certainly his views would have been closer to the moderate than the more radical members.

In March 1775 he wrote to John Pringle, lamenting that a great many people in Pennsylvania "do not assert the Cause of American Freedom, with the warmth and earnestness that every man of a disinterested free

40. James Wilkinson to Coxe, Mar. 15, 1775, Coxe Papers. The reference is to Thomas Barclay, whom Coxe had presumably met on his trip to New York City in 1774. Barclay was a tory who, after the confiscation of his property, joined the British Army. At the end of the war he fled to Nova Scotia. He returned to New York City in 1799 as British consul.

41. Wilkinson to Coxe, 1775, and Oct. 8, 1775, Coxe Papers.

42. Coxe's father and his partner Furman, for example, "appear as signers of the non-importation Act in 1775." *Letters of Moore Furman*, viii.

43. Coxe to Benjamin Rush, Oct. 20, 1800, Coxe Papers.

spirit would wish to see prevail through all the Colonies."[44] Yet to him this freedom did not entail independence. Committed to reconciliation rather than to revolution, he believed, like other colonial moderates, that petition and protest would persuade the king and his ministers of the essential loyalty of their American subjects. Coxe accepted the middle ground that, as he failed to realize, is often untenable in an era of revolutionary upheaval.

That his position was untenable was brought home to Coxe by the events of the summer and fall of 1775. The Second Continental Congress, though it expressed no overt intention of establishing an independent nation, was obliged to assume responsibility for the militia besieging Boston, to issue paper money to support its troops, and to begin negotiations with foreign countries. For their part, the English appeared intent on a showdown. In August, George III issued a proclamation declaring that the colonies were in a state of rebellion, and four months later Parliament interdicted American trade and subjected American ships and goods to confiscation. To all but the most purblind reconciliationists, it was becoming clear that the success of the patriot cause required the driving force of independence.

Still Coxe clung tenaciously to the hope that the rupture could be healed, while sharing the sentiments of Edward Goold, who wrote that "unless some more conciliating measure should be adopted by the Colonies I really look upon the prospect with horror." It may also well be that to Coxe, as to Goold, such anxiety was based in part on practical considerations. The prospect was especially disturbing, Goold explained, because "a large part of our property" is "afloat."[45]

If Coxe shared such apprehensions, he did so because of his formal debut in the spring of 1775 as a Philadelphia merchant. Since his older brother, John, was preparing for a legal career at the Inns of Court,[46] Tench, who had been trading on his own since 1772, was next in line to join the family firm. And William Coxe, Sr., made no secret of his opinion that "it would afford me pleasure . . . to be one of the first of a house that would continue for ages." Some weeks before his twentieth birthday on May 20, 1775, Coxe acceded to his father's wishes. "Tenny seems rather inclinable to go into business than to travel," William Coxe wrote to his partner, Moore Furman, on April 10. "He may judge right, as joining a house is not like setting off alone, and I am willing to forward him . . . and fix a new plan for our future pursuit." Although William Coxe hoped that the new partnership would begin in October 1775, this was not possible, largely because of his insistence that arrangements be made for his withdrawal from active

---

44. John Pringle to Coxe, Apr. 22, 1775, *ibid.*, quoting a remark by Coxe.
45. Edward Goold to Coxe, Jan. 24, 1775, *ibid.*
46. John D. Coxe to Tench Coxe, Aug. 20, Sept. 24, 1774, *ibid.*

participation in the firm and for his move to a "place of retreat" in Sunbury, near Burlington.[47]

Finally, in May 1776, on the eve of the Declaration of Independence, the plans were completed, and the firm of Coxe and Furman became Coxe, Furman, and Coxe. Because of the extreme uncertainty of business conditions, no formal agreement was signed,[48] but Tench was informally given "a fair and equal third," as well as "an Annual Allowance for the Entertainment of Company," in return for which he was "to stand by the laboring Oar." "My father promises that he will make every thing easy," he confided to his cousin William Tilghman. It was indeed a generous paternal gesture, for despite the sharp decline in profits caused by the British interdiction of American trade, the firm, in Tench's words, continued "even at this distressing and unsettled hour" to yield "much more than the calls" of the "numerous families" of its partners required. Young Coxe was grateful. "I am singularly blest in my father," he remarked, "whose Behavior to me in this whole affair has rivetted my very Soul to his."[49]

The events of the first six months of 1776 had brought Tench and the members of his immediate family, as well as the Tilghmans, Chews, and Allens, closer and closer to the critical choice of allegiance. The Second Continental Congress responded to the exigencies of war by assuming more and more power and during the first half of 1776 increasingly gave the appearance of an independent national government. In March it authorized privateering against British ships. In May it recommended that the colonies throw off what little royal authority was still exercised and create governments based on popular consent. Independence now awaited only a formal baptism by Congress. The rites began on June 7 when Richard Henry Lee, delegate from Virginia, rose and moved "that these colonies are, and of right ought to be, Free and independent states"; they were concluded on July 4 when the members of Congress, having approved Lee's motion two days earlier, signed the Declaration of Independence.

Its adoption confronted Coxe, then twenty-one years old, with one of the most difficult, and surely the most consequential, single decisions of his career. Despite the successive political crises he had witnessed during his youth, he had remained confident that the pattern of his life—his mercantile career, his social position—was securely set. Now all was in jeopardy; now his future hinged on his decision whether perhaps to risk all by joining the patriots or maybe to save much by siding with the king. Since he was not

47. William Coxe, Sr., to Moore Furman, Apr. 10, 1775, *ibid.*
48. "Memorandum," n.d., *ibid.*
49. Coxe to William Tilghman, Oct. 7–8, 1776, *ibid.*

passionately committed to either side, his resolution of the problem depended on a divination of events that he could not possibly foresee. So here he was, a politically unsophisticated and ambitious young man required to gamble all on one decision.

"The fact would seem to be," an anonymous critic charged many years later, that Coxe "determined upon the Declaration of Independence to oppose it."[50] Although Coxe never explicitly confirmed the allegation, it is rendered plausible by an admission wrung from him many years later by an insistent journalistic antagonist. In the summer of 1776, Coxe conceded, "he had resigned . . . by letter to Col. Thomas McKean . . . the subalterns commission he had held" in the Fourth Pennsylvania Regiment.[51] In any event, it seems clear that once American independence was proclaimed, Coxe determined to remain neutral if possible but to side with England if forced to make a choice. It was a decision conveniently assisted by innate cautiousness, but one that was also forged by familial respect and precept.

Most members of his immediate family and many of his relatives were either passive or active tories. Some, like his father, adopted a cautious stance of neutrality, doubtlessly motivated by a desire to escape the consequences of the war unscathed and with the family fortune intact, no matter which side won. Others, like his brother-in-law Andrew Allen, sided with England partly because of their attachment to the crown, partly because of their horror, as James Allen put it, at "the Mobility Triumphant; . . . the madness of the multitude."[52] In June 1776 Andrew Allen, sensing the inevitability of independence, resigned his seat in the Continental Congress, attached himself to the British army, and in the winter of 1779/1780 sailed for England, leaving behind his children and his wife, Sarah. Other relatives, such as the Tilghmans, were of divided loyalties. Tench's uncle James sought to maintain prudent neutrality by isolating himself in the country. Entrusting his Philadelphia business affairs to Tench, Tilghman, accompanied by his wife and a number of his children (including William, Coxe's most constant wartime correspondent), retired in the autumn of 1776 to Chestertown, Maryland. Two of Tilghman's sons, Richard and Philip, elected to join the British, while another, Tench, joined the Continental army and became one of George Washington's most trusted aides-de-camp. As with the Tilghmans, so with the Coxe clan—Tench's first cousins Daniel Coxe of Trenton and Grace Kempe of New York became tories, but most, like Tench's three brothers,

---

50. *Aurora*, Aug. 8, 1804.
51. *Ibid.*, Aug. 24, 1804; *Freeman's Journal and Philadelphia Daily Advertiser*, Aug. 27, 1804.
52. "Diary of James Allen, Esq., of Philadelphia, Counsellor-at-Law, 1770–1778," *Pennsylvania Magazine of History and Biography*, IX (1885), 186.

maintained a discreet silence that passed for commitment to the patriot cause.

Coxe himself strove for awhile to remain publicly uncommitted (as he, in fact, may privately have been), but by electing to stay in Philadelphia instead of joining his family in Sunbury he rendered a perch of neutrality precarious. This was tellingly demonstrated by military developments during the late summer and autumn of 1776. In mid-September the British army, fresh from its victories on Long Island, swept the American troops from New York City. A short time later Washington was leading his ragged and defeated army from New York across New Jersey to the rolling countryside west of Philadelphia. From Pittstown, Moore Furman, now a deputy quarter-master general, reported to Coxe. Apparently unaware that his Philadelphia business partner might not share his anxiety or endorse his terminology, Furman wrote that "our Enemies are Stealing upon us, and will at last get too great Advantages for us to make proper terms—they have now full Possession of Long Island and will no doubt fix themselves Strongly there . . . when they are quite Ready will then attack again."[53] That the Continental army, weakened by desertion and captures, could withstand such an attack seemed less and less likely as the weeks went by. And the British, flushed with victory, appeared certain to resume the offensive.

"Something of consiquence will soon happen between the two ar-meys," a tory correspondent wrote to Coxe from New Brunswick on October 13, 1776. If the British "can give Gen'l. Washington a Gen'l. defeat you'l see them at Philadelphia this fall—don't be unprepared for such an event."[54] Coxe was better prepared for this than for the patriot assault upon British sympathizers that engulfed Philadelphia four weeks later. In the meantime he stuck to his desk at Coxe, Furman, and Coxe, seemingly unperturbed, even confident that the course of the war would bring riches rather than reprisal. Far from having "apprehensions about a genteel subsistence," he wrote Tilghman in October, he planned on expanding his activities and "making money out of the immediate line of my profession by employing a Sum of money in two other Branches of business."[55] Such optimism at a time when the British army was already nearby was caused by something more than merely a sanguine temperament or youthful exuberance.

"She who was ever the Idol of my soul consents to make me happy," he informed Tilghman on October 7. "Scarce have I entered into life, when I am surrounded with those Joys which hope . . . and the livliest imagina-tions have set before me."[56] The inspiration for this bombast was Catherine

53. Furman to Coxe, Sept. 9, 1776, Coxe Papers.
54. Christopher Miller to Coxe, Oct. 13, 1776, *ibid*.
55. Coxe to William Tilghman, Oct. 7–8, 1776, *ibid*.
56. *Ibid*. See also Daniel Coxe to Coxe, Oct. 16, 1776, *ibid*.

McCall, to whom Coxe would be married fifteen months later. For the time being, the engagement not only reinforced his complacency about the future but also spurred his already well-developed acquisitive instinct. As demand and prices soared in the autumn of 1776, so did profits. "The prices of all kind of Goods are Extremely high here," he wrote on November 19. But no matter how inflated the price of goods or costly their transportation, "They have a handsome profit if they arrive safe."[57] For Coxe to avail himself of such opportunities, however, he now would have to accept what he presumably had determined to oppose some five months earlier—American independence.

As the Continental army moved toward Pennsylvania and as rumors spread that Sir William Howe was approaching Philadelphia, military preparations and martial fervor took on a new urgency. Almost overnight Philadelphia became an army post—recruits drilled in the streets; strict military regulations were imposed; and self-constituted vigilantes, expecting the British army momentarily to besiege the city, turned fiercely on the suspected enemies within the gates. Early in December, James Allen recorded in his diary that "a persecution of Tories" had begun, "(under which name, is included every one disinclined to Independence tho' ever so warm a friend to constitutional liberty and the old cause). . . . Houses were broken open, people imprison'd without any colour of authority by private persons, etc." As panic grew, shops and schools were closed, and the cobbled streets were crowded with wagons carrying household goods and business wares to places of safety and with carriages carrying tories and suspected tories away from the wrath of superpatriots.[58]

Some of the wagons contained property belonging to Coxe, Furman, and Coxe, and one of the carriages carried Tench Coxe. His exit on December 2 was not voluntary, however. "He was driven by the violence and threats of a body of armed men, when a boy, to the British army," Coxe recalled a decade later, an accurate explanation if qualified by the reminder that Coxe, then twenty-one, had passed boyhood.[59] Whether his initial plans were to follow other members of his family to England or to establish himself in business in British-occupied New York is not clear. In any event, he went first to New Jersey, where a majority of citizens were sufficiently indifferent to the outcome of the war to render tories comparatively safe, and then to New York City, where he spent the next six or seven months.

In New York any misgivings he may have had about siding with the

57. Coxe to James Kennedy, Nov. 19, 1776, *ibid.*
58. Three Allens were included in this flight. "Diary of James Allen," *PMHB*, IX (1885), 193.
59. *Federal Gazette, and Philadelphia Evening Post*, Nov. 22, 1788. The date of Coxe's departure from Philadelphia is given in the Coxe, Furman & Coxe Letterbook, Coxe Papers.

crown were dispelled by the unreserved loyalty of relatives, longtime friends, and new acquaintances who warmly greeted him. Edward Goold, described by Coxe as his "dearest best beloved friend," freely opened both his house and his purse. His first cousin Grace Coxe Kempe, whose husband was attorney general of New York, welcomed him cordially. So too did his father's old-time business associates, Abraham Cuyler, Daniel Ludlow, Isaac Low (who showed particularly "genteel attention"), and Colburn Barrell.[60] To Coxe this reassuring reception must have compensated for the disappointment and disapproval with which patriot friends greeted his flight to the enemy. "I . . . must confess," John Pringle wrote from Paris, that Tench's explanations of his decision "were not satisfactory to me." Convinced that his former schoolmate "acted honestly upon erroneous principles," Pringle observed that Coxe had "suffer'd" himself "to be misled by paying too great regard to old prejudices," as he in fact had. From St. Croix, Benjamin Yard, Moore Furman's nephew and Tench's good friend, reported that even at such a distance newspapers had carried news "of the step you had taken and the Printers have been very liberal of their Abuse on the Occasion." Coxe's conduct, Yard said, was "rash and imprudent."[61]

With its senior member in retirement and its junior partner in exile,[62] Coxe, Furman, and Coxe limped along under the management of Moore Furman, whose support of the American side, though surely dictated by conscience, proved an expedient and prudent business decision. As a deputy quartermaster general, Furman was in an advantageous position both to sell the firm's inventory and to safeguard its capital, of which Furman and the elder Coxe had already withdrawn "no less than £11,000 in specie."[63] The transportable possessions, including account books and other records, had been hastily packed by Tench during the last hectic days before his flight from Philadelphia and shipped to Furman in Pittstown.[64] The firm's holdings of gold and silver, by far its most valuable asset, were, however, "delivered" (presumably by Tench himself) to William Coxe, Sr., at Sunbury.

60. Coxe to Goold, June 17, 1778, to Isaac Low and Abraham Cuyler, Dec. 16, 1777, to Goold, Dec. 19, 1777, to Low, Apr. 1, 1778, Colburn Barrell to Coxe, Nov. 9, Dec. 15, 1777, June 17, 1778, Coxe Papers.

61. Pringle to Coxe, Aug. 29, 1778, Yard to Coxe, Nov. 2, 1777, *ibid.*

62. William Coxe was not completely retired from business, however. With Edward Goold he made plans for a future partnership and even managed to make "conditional" purchases of goods in Philadelphia for the joint account of Goold and himself. The plan apparently fell through because the British commander-in-chief refused to grant the "general permission to ship," which Coxe had counted on. William Coxe to Robert Wigram, Jan. 24, Mar. 23, 1778, *ibid.*

63. Coxe to Furman, Dec. 19, 1788, *ibid.*

64. Coxe to Miller, July 4, 1785, to David Beekman, Apr. 16, 1779, *ibid.* Coxe apparently left a chest containing his own money in Philadelphia, presumably in the custody of a relative or friend. Furman to Coxe, Dec. 10, 1784, *ibid.*

Furman quickly "sold off the little Stock on hand" and prudently invested the firm's sizable sum of Continental money in loan office certificates.[65] Although Coxe and his father would subsequently wrangle with Furman for more than a decade over the manner in which he had managed their affairs, they were at the time happy that they were being handled at all.

During his months of involuntary leisure Tench Coxe must have followed military operations with intense interest. From the vantage point of New York City, where British warships rocked gently in the harbor and thousands of Redcoats paraded in the streets, he surely felt confident that he had chosen the winning side. The depleted patriot army in winter headquarters at Morristown—lacking adequate medical supplies, food, and clothing —appeared no match for their well-trained, well-supplied, and numerous opponents. Even the eight thousand recruits who flocked to the Continental standard with the onset of mild spring weather seemed incapable of preventing an American collapse. Or so it appeared to General Howe, who began to make preparations for an invasion of Pennsylvania, where he expected to proclaim the news of a British triumph from his headquarters in America's first city. While Howe proceeded at his characteristic snail's pace, in May 1777 Washington moved his army from Morristown to Middlebrook, a more advantageous spot for thwarting British attacks and for blocking the anticipated advance of the British toward Pennsylvania. Over the next two months Howe tried to force the Americans into battle by deceptive troop movements, but his clever feints resulted only in indecisive minor skirmishes. At the close of June the British commander was back in New York, where tory exiles, Coxe among them, impatiently awaited the launching of his Pennsylvania campaign. Of its success and an ultimate English victory, however, Coxe was a good deal less sanguine than the British commander. In mid-July, agonizingly uncertain about his future in his own country, he made tentative plans for exile in England.[66] But he soon recoiled from such a drastic step and chose instead to risk his future on the ultimate triumph of British arms.

By the end of July 1777 his decision appeared a safe gamble. On July 23, 260 ships carrying an army of about fifteen thousand men sailed out of

65. Furman to Coxe, May and May 17, 1779, *ibid*. The amount purchased on behalf of Coxe, Furman & Coxe was $12,500. Furman to Coxe, May 17, 1779, *ibid*. An additional number of certificates was invested in a farm, which Furman subsequently sold for £700. Furman to Coxe, Mar. 7, 1794, *ibid*. Furman's major and most irksome task, however, was fending off importunate creditors. See Coxe, Furman & Coxe Letterbook, Jan.–Feb. 1777, *ibid*. After February there are no entries in the letterbook until the end of May, when Furman returned to Philadelphia. He had stayed there only a short time because "the two Armys begin to be restless." Furman to Benjamin Andrews, May 29, 1777, *ibid*.

66. Coxe described his plans in a letter to Yard of July 14, 1777. See Yard to Coxe, Nov. 2, 1777, *ibid*.

New York harbor on the first leg of a journey that Howe confidently assumed would end with the capture of Philadelphia. Accompanying the army were a number of tory refugees, eager to return in triumph to a city from which they had ignominiously been expelled. Among them was Tench Coxe.[67] On July 29 the British fleet reached Delaware Bay, then turned about and sailed into the Chesapeake; the troops disembarked at Head of Elk. However circuitous their route, British troops were by late August marching northward toward Philadelphia, near which the Continental army had assembled. When the armies met on September 10 and 11 at Brandywine Creek, Howe emerged the victor in a pitched battle that ended with the Americans fleeing in confusion. Washington was determined not to abandon the field without another fight, but a driving two-day rainstorm compelled him to withdraw across the Schuylkill River. The road to Philadelphia was now open for the British.

67. This can be inferred from Coxe's own letters of this period. See especially Coxe to Wigram, July 24, 1778, *ibid*.

2

The Tory

On the morning of September 26 an advance guard of three thousand British troops commanded by Lord Cornwallis marched into Philadelphia accompanied, a youthful bystander reported, "by Enoch Story, Jos. Galloway, Andw. Allen, William Allen and others."[1] Tench Coxe was among the "others." He "triumphantly" entered the city, so a hostile witness alleged, "crowned as a victor, at the head of an enemy, yet reeking with the blood of his countrymen." Critics later had a field day with the manner of his return. He accompanied Howe's troops, a representative newspaper attack remarked in 1804, "with laurel in his hat"—an accusation that Coxe denied, thus leaving himself fairly open to the reply that he "may have worn hickory leaves or a pine branch, and be within the letter of his quibble."[2]

Such verbal sport aside, some newspaper accounts of Coxe's return home, though written much later, have the ring of authenticity. So it is with William Duane's description, published in 1804, which depicts Coxe, "while riding along the streets addressing himself to Cornwallis," as commenting: " 'My lord this is Second and the next my lord is Third st., and that, my lord, gaol at the corner, and that three story brick house, with the conductory on the chimney, my lord is where old Franklin lived'—and then my lord would say—thank you Mr. Coxe, thank you, ha ha—pon my word, hah Mr. Coxe, very useful information, heh—heh—thank ye, Mr. Coxe—and then Capt. Ross, his aide de camp would ask—and pray Mr. Coxe which

1. "The Diary of Robert Morton," *PMHB*, I (1877), 7.
2. *Gazette of the United States, and Philadelphia Daily Advertiser*, Sept. 4, 1799. An entry in the Coxe, Furman & Coxe Letterbook reads: "I arrived in Philadelphia on Friday the 25th of September 1777 after having been absent near ten months from the 2nd Decr 1776. Tench Coxe." Coxe Papers. Coxe was in error as Friday was Sept. 26, 1777.

are the best quarters. And of course as he knew the best houses he was as polite as possible. . . . This information to be sure was not describing the *best roads*—but the best houses—not how to avoid ravines or ambuscades, but how to avoid bugs and confined air."[3]

Coxe, whether or not "with a British officer locked in his arm," entered a quiet and sparsely populated city, where stores had been left empty by departing whig merchants and the population consisted largely of women, children, and Quaker pacifists.[4] "Philadelphia is rather a lovely city of considerable size. . . . The public squares are beautiful. . . . The City is very charmingly situated in level fertile country," a Hessian commander wrote on the day of the occupation. To Coxe, happy to be "safely home after so many fatigues and perils," it doubtlessly appeared even more beautiful than it did to its invaders.[5] His return was a symbolic vindication of the wisdom of his commitment to the English.

The half-deserted city was quickly transformed. Other tory exiles returned, English and Scotch merchants arrived aboard British transports, business resumed, and Philadelphia again became the busy commercial hub and lively social center with which Coxe was familiar. The presence of British nobles and British officers dazzled the local tories, the circulation of British gold appeased the neutrals, and the superior power of the British army silenced the secret patriots. The winter social season of 1777/1778 was one of the liveliest in memory, so convivial that Benjamin Franklin was led to remark that Philadelphia had taken Howe. More likely, the general and his staff beguiled the city's elite, who, perhaps dimly aware that the glittering new social order might not last, abandoned themselves to a season of gaiety. Weekly balls at the City Tavern, theatrical performances by British officers at Southwark Theater, official receptions, public spectacles, and private parties allowed the Philadelphians to "forget there is any war, save that it is a capital joke."[6]

Certainly Washington's ragtag army offered no discernible threat to the British occupation. A week after Howe's triumphant conquest of Philadelphia the Americans challenged him at Germantown, ten miles outside the city, where most of the British troops were quartered. Washington's audacity

---

3. *Freeman's Jour.*, Aug. 27, 1804; *Aurora*, Aug. 29, 1804.

4. *Aurora*, Aug. 23, 1804; Ellis Paxson Oberholtzer, *Philadelphia: A History of the City and Its People: A Record of 225 Years* (Philadelphia, n.d.), I, 268.

5. Bernhard A. Uhlendorf and Edna Vosper, eds., "Letters of Major Baurmeister during the Philadelphia Campaign, 1777–1778," Pt. I, *PMHB*, LIX (1935), 413–414; Colburn Barrell to Coxe, Nov. 8, 1777, Coxe Papers, quoting Coxe to Barrell, Oct. 22, 1777.

6. "Extracts from the Letter-Book of Captain Johann Heinrichs of the Hessian Jäger Corps, 1778–1780," *PMHB*, XXII (1898), 139. See Fred L. Pattee, "The British Theater in Philadelphia in 1778," *American Literature*, VI (1935), 381–383; Oberholtzer, *Philadelphia: A History*, I, 272–273.

was no match for British numerical superiority, and in the confused battle that ensued the American commander lost a thousand men, twice as many as his adversary. Repulsed but undaunted, Washington continued to harass Howe's forces as they sought to clear the Delaware River for the British fleet commanded by Admiral Lord Richard Howe, who impatiently waited to sail up the bay and join the army in Philadelphia. Resistance proved futile, and by December the British were in secure control of the Delaware forts. Cast down by the defeats of Brandywine and Germantown, Washington now went into winter quarters on a bleak plateau at Valley Forge, scarcely twenty miles from Philadelphia, where he strove merely to keep his wretched, starving, and freezing army intact. Howe, snug and secure in Philadelphia, did not even bother to attack. But to those Philadelphia tories not blinded by self-interest, the seemingly impregnable British position in Philadelphia was offset by the most important American victory of the war. On October 17, 1777, the British were stunningly defeated at Saratoga, where General Burgoyne surrendered his entire army, five thousand strong, to General Horatio Gates. That Coxe's own correspondence contains only laconic comments on what to him must have been a disquieting development was the result of his agreement with the viewpoint expressed in a letter from his friend Edward Goold: "I shall make no Reflections upon this melancholy affair. I expect our Turn will come next."[7]

The dispatch with which Coxe and Goold took advantage of the opening of the Philadelphia market suggests their eagerness to store up profits while the British remained. As Coxe put it: "If we must suffer misfortunes, we ought to draw all the good from them possible." During his months of idleness in New York he had discussed with Goold his plans to resume business in Philadelphia, and the two had agreed on an informal partnership, including "a recommendation of each other to our respective friends."[8] In a gesture that revealed both his respect for the reputation Coxe and Furman still enjoyed in the Caribbean and his fondness for Tench, Goold persuaded his partner, Gerard Beekman, to recommend himself and Coxe "mutually throughout all the Islands" of the West Indies, averring that "it was equally the same whether the Cargoes" were shipped to one or the other.[9] Once his friend was safely back in Philadelphia, Goold seized the first opportunity to ship goods the two had jointly purchased the previous summer. "I hope you have got our Things," he wrote on October 26. "If Philadelphia is to be head Quarters I think they will be safest there. . . . Turn

7. Edward Goold to Coxe, Oct. 26, 1777, Coxe Papers.
8. Coxe to Goold, Feb. 7–Mar. 1, Mar. 17, 1778, *ibid*.
9. Goold to Coxe, May 6, 1778, *ibid*.

them into Cash as soon as possible and Remit the Net proceeds in good Bills."[10]

Coxe, believing it improper "to use as heretofore the names of our late W. C. and M. Furman," now launched his own firm. "Tench Coxe has for sale at the house of Mrs. Ford in Walnut Street, next door to the corner of Second Street," an advertisement of October 25 read, "cotton counterpanes . . . pearl necklaces . . . brocades, satin . . . silk-knee garters" and a "few boxes of Keyser's pills" for venereal disorders, rheumatism, asthma, dropsy, and apoplexy.[11] During subsequent weeks he was able to offer more of the same, as well as other articles. Goold not only sent additional consignments himself but also persuaded other New York merchants to make Coxe their agent.[12] Since Coxe sold on a commission basis—usually receiving 5 percent on all goods sold—his profits were exactly proportional to the size and value of the cargoes his business associates consigned to him. And his New York friends were in a position to ship in quantity. In early November, for instance, Goold procured for him "a very Large Consignment from Mr. Isaac Low and Mr. Abraham Cuyler to the amont of . . . near £3,000 Stg."[13]

By the same conveyance Coxe also received a rich cargo from Colburn Barrell, with whom, as with Goold, he had made arrangements during his exile in New York for an informal business partnership once the British were in control of Philadelphia.[14] Over the next seven months Barrell consigned to Coxe numerous and valuable cargoes, and as their mutual profits increased so too did the warmth of their friendship.

The smooth and successful resumption of trade offered great promise of larger profits to Coxe. Consignments from his New York correspondents arrived at a market that, due to the combined needs of the British army and Philadelphia's steadily growing population, was particularly favorable—one characterized by soaring prices that often produced speculative windfalls.[15] Certain that he would reap his share, Coxe began looking for larger quarters and in mid-December moved to a new store, "one of the best" in the city, "it being within call of the Coffee House."[16]

10. Goold to Coxe, Oct. 26, 1777, *ibid.* The first ships arrived from New York carrying supplies and provisions about four weeks after the British occupation. See Willard O. Mishoff, "Business in Philadelphia during the British Occupation," *PMHB*, LXI (1937), 167.

11. Coxe to William Ballyn, Mar. 14, 1778, Coxe Papers; *Pennsylvania Evening Post* (Philadelphia), Oct. 25, 1778. The ad was repeated on subsequent days.

12. Among the merchants for whom Coxe was agent were Stephen Skinner, Richard Yates, Robert Watts, Daniel Ludlow, Gerard Beekman, Isaac Low, and Abraham Cuyler.

13. Goold to Coxe, Nov. 10, 1777, Coxe Papers.

14. Barrell to Coxe, Nov. 8, 1777, *ibid.*

15. Coxe to Skinner & Yates, Dec. 20, 1777, to Watts & Kearney, Dec. 20, 1777, *ibid.*

16. Coxe to Barrell, Dec. 15, 1777, *ibid.*

To a more cautious businessman expansion of any kind might have appeared ill advised. Philadelphia's trade was subject to the vagaries of winter weather, then imminent, and to the decisions of British officials, who only a week before had imposed severe restrictions on certain forms of commercial activity. The avidity with which New York merchants took advantage of the higher prices in Philadelphia ("Some people will burn their fingers, thro' this Rage for Shipping hither," Coxe commented) prompted General Howe to take swift action to obviate the possibility of both shortages in New York and an overstocked market in Philadelphia. On December 5 he accordingly ordered that "no more Vessels than those already cleared should be permitted to go to Philadelphia."[17] However, Coxe's confidence in the continued expansion of his business activities was not altogether misguided. Just as British officials could regulate and even prohibit trade, so also could they lighten restrictions or lift bans. Much depended on the amount of influence a merchant had with British officials, and few merchants were in a better position than Coxe to secure favors.

Coxe's emphatic affirmation many years later that "I never was in any employment whatever under Great Britain or her Governors, Generals, Admirals" was indisputably correct, and he scarcely can be blamed for failing to add that, though not thus employed by the English, he was their firm ally.[18] His correspondence (despite the many statements on the subject he subsequently excised) clearly reveals that he was, in fact, on close terms with high-ranking British officials, whose cooperation he solicited and whose patronage and support he enjoyed. Nor did he admit that he sought and was awarded contracts for the supply of the British army and navy.[19] Coxe's subsequent disclaimers were perhaps attributable to other, more irresponsible charges leveled against him. He was repeatedly accused in later years, for example, of having been a member of "the *Board of Refugees* that was established for the trial of the unfortunate Americans who fell into the hands of the British General." There is no reason to doubt his indignant rejoinder that this was "a most dangerous and criminal falsehood."[20] Nor is

17. Coxe to Goold, Dec. 19, 1777, Goold to Coxe, Dec. 6, 1777, *ibid*.

18. *Aurora*, Oct. 8, 1800.

19. This is clearly demonstrated by his own letterbook, as well as by letters from his business correspondents. "I did nothing in that way on my Arrival" in Philadelphia, Coxe wrote months later. Coxe to Robert Wigram, May 22, 1778, Coxe Papers. But by mid-December 1777 he had entered into an "engagement" with James Thompson of New York "for business to be done for the Contractors." Coxe to Goold, Dec. 19, 1777, *ibid*. He subsequently sold woolen goods, among other items, to the British army (Coxe to Low & Cuyler, Jan. 24, 1778, Barrell to Coxe, Mar. 25, 1778, *ibid*.) and sought an appointment from naval officials in New York as agent for the sale of prizes in Philadelphia. Coxe to Thompson, Apr. 1, 1778, *ibid*.

20. The charge was printed in the *Gaz. of U.S.*, Sept. 29, 1800; Coxe's rejoinder was in the *Aurora*, Oct. 9, 1800. Presumably the writer who made the charge confused Tench with his

there conclusive evidence to support the charge, made time and again by his political opponents, that he marched "arm in arm" with British officers "into the gaol to insult the Whigs confined there." To one such prisoner, Jacob Bright, previously a member of the Pennsylvania Council of Safety, Coxe purportedly remarked that Bright would "be kept in prison till he should rot." Far from being vindictive toward imprisoned whigs, Coxe insisted that he "gave donations of provisions and cash, and offered, voluntarily, loans of money to the prisoners."[21]

However charitable, Coxe was an active loyalist on intimate terms with British officers, who repaid his civilities with numerous favors on which his prosperity was based. And with British soldiers quartered over his own store,[22] Coxe scarcely could have been unaware of either the extent of British power or the advantages of a cordial relationship with influential officials. His assiduous cultivation of them was totally in character, revealing a trait that time would enhance. Nor was his success lost on his New York correspondents. Soliciting his agency in recovering £200 imprudently advanced to a British army officer, Edward Goold reflected the viewpoint of these correspondents when he alluded to the confidence reposed in Coxe by the commanding general.[23]

But official control of commerce in British-occupied America was dictated by the exigencies of the British war effort as a whole, not by the interests of tory merchants, however well favored. Regulation was accordingly strict. By the terms of a proclamation issued by Howe on December 4, 1777, all merchants' ships were required to make entry of vessels and to submit accurate manifests of their cargoes.[24] Any goods not so declared or landed without a license were subject to seizure and forfeiture. Even after acquiring the requisite licenses, importers of rum, spirits, molasses, and salt were subject to close surveillance and regulation. These products were required to be stored in the owner's or importer's warehouses, to be available for inspection by British officials, and to be sold only with official permission.[25] Similar restrictions were imposed on vessels leaving Philadelphia

---

cousin Daniel Coxe of Trenton, N.J., who was a member of the board of directors of Associated Loyalists.

21. *Aurora*, Aug. 29, 1804; *Freeman's Jour.*, Aug. 23, 1804.

22. Joseph Sherwell to Coxe, May 15, 1779, Coxe Papers.

23. Goold to Coxe, Feb. 7, 1778, *ibid*.

24. An earlier proclamation, dated Nov. 24, 1777, stated that in view of the "evil consequences" of an "unrestrained trade in spiritous liquors," all masters of merchant ships must report to British officials the amount on board and be granted a permit before landing it. *Pa. Eve. Post*, Nov. 25, 1777.

25. *Ibid.*, Dec. 4, 1777. A proclamation of Dec. 9 imposed additional regulations specifying the conditions under which the city's citizens might purchase certain enumerated articles. *Ibid.*,

—shipmasters were required, under penalty of forfeiture of goods and imprisonment, to submit sworn manifests "specifying the quantity and quality of the goods, and by whom shipped, together with the permission granted for the loading of the vessel." Nor could vessels in ballast depart without permission. Such regulations applied to all shipping, domestic and foreign, out of Philadelphia.[26]

It was this situation that made Coxe's assistance even more valuable to his New York correspondents. As early as December 6, 1777, for example, Richard Yates consigned to Coxe a cargo aboard his "Armed Schooner Reed," requesting him to secure a permit "either from Lord or General Howe" to send the ship to Grenada for a cargo to be shipped to New York. "It being a point of the last consequence," Coxe reported, "I waited on Capt McKenzie," secretary to Lord Howe. "He informed me that Capt. Hammond was the Admiral's chief Agent here and that he would make it a point to do every thing with him to obtain the necessary permit. . . . I . . . shall leave nothing neglected which may tend to the accomplishment of this important point." Nor did he. Five days later he had "the very great pleasure" of informing Yates that "I have this Inst [ant] a note from Head Quarters" granting the *Reed* a license to go to Grenada.[27] As if to prove that one good turn from Hammond deserved another, Coxe at the same time successfully solicited the captain's aid in securing compensation for Abraham Cuyler, whose snow, the *Sir William Johnston*, was lost near Cape Henlopen, en route from New York to Philadelphia with a consignment for Coxe. "I will endeavor to make it appear that the Snow was *plundered and destroyed* which . . . must have really been the Case," Coxe reported. He was successful. By order of Captain Hammond, who willingly came to Coxe's aid, the commander of H.M.S. *Lizard* gave the requisite certificate.[28]

Not every Philadelphia merchant, however exalted his social position,

---

Dec. 9, 1777. For a description of the specific procedures, see Coxe to Tennant, Ross, Kennedy & Morrice, Apr. 30, 1778, Coxe Papers.

26. *Pa. Eve. Post*, Dec. 20, 1777. In mid-Jan. 1778 British authorities imposed still stricter rules on the activities of merchants. A proclamation issued by Joseph Galloway, superintendent general, on Jan. 17 forbade the sale of any goods by public vendue except by license from the city police and under strict regulations, including payment of a fee to be appropriated "for the public uses of the city of Philadelphia and its environs." *Ibid.*, Jan. 17, 1778.

27. Richard Yates to Coxe, Dec. 6, 1777, Coxe to Skinner & Yates, Dec. 15, 20, 1777, Coxe Papers. Specifically, Yates had instructed Coxe to secure a cargo in Philadelphia to the value of £1,500 and if unsuccessful to deliver that sum in gold to the captain of the *Reed*, who was "to Purchase the Goods we have directed him to Procure" in Grenada "and Ship us agreeable to the directions we have given him." Yates to Coxe, Dec. 8, 1777, *ibid*. Even the patronage of the Howes was no guarantee of success. As it turned out, the *Reed* was captured by an American privateer.

28. Coxe to Low & Cuyler, Dec. 16, 1777, to Cuyler, Dec. 23, 1777, to Capt. McKenzie, Dec. 19, 1777, *ibid*.

had ready access to the close advisers of both the commanding general and Admiral Howe, to men like McKenzie and Hammond, or to officers like Commissary General Daniel Wier, who had lucrative contracts to award. The major reason Coxe was favored with this preferred position is suggested by the large number of Coxe's relatives who held prominent positions during the British occupation. Clearly the most influential was Joseph Galloway, the most powerful civilian official in Philadelphia. Although Coxe's kinship to Galloway was distant,[29] standards of a society that counted relatives three or four times removed as cousins dictated that their relationship be acknowledged, and in view of the authority invested in Galloway by the British commander this could not fail to be important. Galloway was only the most prominent of Coxe's many relatives and acquaintances who occupied important offices or enjoyed the confidence of the Howe brothers. Coxe's friend David Franks was "agent for the contractors for victualling His Majesty's troops at Philadelphia" and also, for a time, commissary of prisoners.[30] Andrew Allen, Tench's brother-in-law, was on intimate terms with the British commander, who four months before the occupation had appointed Allen to run the state as lieutenant governor during Governor Penn's exile. Another of Tench's brothers-in-law, George McCall, was married to the daughter of Daniel Chamier, British commissary general in North America. Coxe's first cousin Daniel Coxe, who successfully had raised the West Jersey volunteers for royal service, came to British-occupied Philadelphia, where Howe promptly appointed him "one of the magistrates to Govern the civil affairs within the lines."[31]

Even such powerful connections could not prevent the sharp decline of Coxe's profits in January 1778. Both nature and man were responsible. A severe cold spell early in January "froze the Schuylkill over solidly and the Delaware from the banks nearly to the middle," and General Howe decided to forestall severe shortages of goods by imposing an embargo on all shipping in the city's port.[32] According to "positive instructions" issued on December 23 to Galloway, the superintendent general, no goods were to be shipped to Great Britain, Ireland, or the West Indies, and no goods to any

29. Jane Galloway Shippen, Coxe's aunt, was Galloway's niece.

30. Daniel Chamier to David Franks, Feb. 8, 1776, Coxe Papers. See also Edward E. Curtis, *The Organization of the British Army in the American Revolution* (New Haven, Conn., 1926), 173–175.

31. For Andrew Allen, see "Diary of James Allen," *PMHB*, IX (1885), 425; William Allen Benton, *Whig-Loyalism: An Aspect of Political Ideology in the American Revolutionary Era* (Rutherford, N.J., 1969), 201. On George McCall, see Coxe to Goold, Mar. 17, 1778, Coxe Papers. On Daniel Coxe, see Coxe to William Ballyn, Mar. 14, 1778, *ibid*.

32. Goold to Coxe, Mar. 13, 1778, *ibid*; Bernhard A. Uhlendorf and Edna Vosper, eds., "Letters of Major Baurmeister during the Philadelphia Campaign, 1777–1778," Pt. II, *PMHB*, LX (1936), 51.

part of the American continent occupied by the King's troops, "but by a Spe [cial permit] to be obtained from the General himself."[33] Howe was not particularly lavish with permits, and for a time, as Coxe remarked, "the Embargo and the Ice together we might have supposed would have stop'd the navigation."[34] That the embargo did not stop the shipping was due to the ingenuity of Coxe's New York consignors, notably Goold. Royal transports and the British packet still sailed, weather permitting, between New York and Philadelphia, and Goold had discovered even before the embargo that clandestine shipments might easily be arranged through compliant officials. Thus, in mid-November he had persuaded Captain Waddy of the ship *Adventure* to hide some chests of tea, a scarce and expensive commodity in Philadelphia, in his cabin. Informing Coxe that the captain would find a way to evade diligent customs officers, Goold cautioned his agent not to mention the shipment "where it might prejudice him."[35] What commenced so promisingly in November continued during succeeding months, thanks largely to Coxe's success in disposing of contraband goods.

"I wish every one of your Correspondents here were as well pleased with you as I am—and I have the pleasure to tell you the generality of them are very well satisfied," Goold wrote to Coxe on March 25. They should have been. The "prevalence of the partiality" in favor of Coxe made him the ideal business ally, endearing him to the New York business associates whose pockets he was lining.[36] Nevertheless, tory merchants, including Coxe, continually deplored "this vicious rebellion" that occasioned such burdensome restrictions on trade. Peace, whether the result of a British or an American victory, would, in their view, bring stable trading conditions and surer, if smaller, profits. Indeed, the swiftness and willingness with which many of them—Goold, Thomas Atwood, Richard Yates, Daniel Ludlow—later switched to the American side suggests that their first loyalty may all along have been to the pocketbook rather than to the king. As one of Coxe's business partners remarked with unconscious mockery, "War or Peace, all serves the purpose of some."[37] In their defense, however, it should be observed that they undoubtedly sincerely subscribed to Adam Smith's comment that he had "never known much good done by those who effected to trade for the public good. It is an affectation, indeed, not very common among mer-

---

33. Coxe to Goold, Dec. 19, 1777, to Robert Wigram, Jan. 24, 1778, to Gerard Beekman, Dec. 23, 1777, *ibid.*

34. Coxe to Terrill & Kearney, Jan. 23, 1778, *ibid.*

35. Goold to Coxe, Nov. 15, 1777, *ibid.*

36. Goold to Coxe, Mar. 25, 1778, Barrell to Coxe, Apr. 9, 1778, *ibid.* The phrase, quoted by Barrell, was Coxe's.

37. Goold to Coxe, Apr. 2, 1783, *ibid.*

chants, and very few words need be employed in dissuading them from it."[38]

Many of these tory merchants and the cream of British officialdom, as well as many of Coxe's relatives and friends, must have attended Tench's wedding on January 14, 1778, making it one of the highlights of the city's social season. The bride was Catherine McCall, daughter of Anne Searle and Samuel McCall, a Philadelphia merchant, both of whom were deceased. Like Coxe, she was a member in good standing of the tightly knit Philadelphia elite.[39] Tench's own happiness, however, must have been tinctured by anxiety about her poor health, which perhaps stemmed from tuberculosis. But, for the moment, he probably shared the view of a relative that "every thing is gay, and happy and it is likely to prove a frolicking winter."[40]

The news of the Franco-American treaties of commerce and alliance of February 1778 made it seem likely that this might be the last such "frolicking" season under British auspices. This "unnatural alliance" between "French Royalty and American Liberty" promised to provide the embattled Americans with the military assistance essential to their success.[41] Coxe did not record his reaction to the momentous French commitment to join forces with the Americans until independence had been achieved, but the irony of an alliance between Washington's depleted, ragged, and hungry army and the military forces of a great world power could scarcely have escaped his notice.

During the spring of 1778 Coxe, discounting rumors that the British might soon abandon Philadelphia, confidently made arrangements for again enlarging his trading activities. Considering his similar plans for business expansion virtually on the eve of his departure from Philadelphia fifteen months earlier, it is apparent that he had a peculiar penchant for launching ambitious operations just at the moment when he should have been intent on consolidating what he already possessed. In any event, on March 19, 1778, he sent out a circular letter offering the former clients of Coxe, Furman, and Coxe his own services in conducting their business affairs in America during "this confused time," as well as after "this unhappy contest is settled." Although ostensibly designed "to secure all the old friends of our

38. Adam Smith, *An Inquiry into the Nature and Causes of the Wealth of Nations* (New York, 1937 [orig. publ. London, 1776]), 423.

39. Coxe to Thomas Attwood, Mar. 3, 1778, Coxe Papers. For information on the McCall family, see Gregory B. Keen, "The Descendants of Jöran Kyn, The Founder of Upland," *PMHB*, V (1881), 452–453; Margaret L. Brown, "Mr. and Mrs. William Bingham of Philadelphia: Rulers of the Republican Courts," *PMHB*, LXI (1937), 287; and Richard Willing to Coxe, Mar. 3, 1824, Coxe Papers.

40. "Diary of James Allen," *PMHB*, IX (1885), 432.

41. Albert J. Beveridge, *The Life of John Marshall*, II (Boston, 1916), 2.

house and give them an opportunity of introducing me to New ones," the real purpose of the circular was to assure customers that if Coxe were obliged to discontinue his mercantile house, then one of its predecessors, either Coxe and Furman or Coxe, Furman, and Coxe, would resume business.[42] With Tench a tory, his father a neutral, and Moore Furman a patriot, the former partners apparently were playing a clever game of heads I win, tails you lose. The rules were perhaps dictated by William Coxe: "My father," Tench wrote a St. Croix friend, "is desirous of making a final Settlement of all our late Concerns that we may be ready either to begin together or separately as may be hereafter agreed on among Us."[43] To Tench present prospects were more important than plans for the future.

During the weeks immediately following his circular letter Coxe's optimism appeared justified. "The number of Inhabitants, Refugees, and Military being great," he explained, the opportunities afforded by the Philadelphia market were virtually limitless.[44] He congratulated himself that he was in a position to meet the demand. His various correspondents "having shipt largely to this port," he observed on March 25, "I have had my hands extremely full"; a month later he estimated that over recent weeks he had received from New York, Madeira, Great Britain, and the West Indies consignments totaling £30,000.[45] "I . . . must think myself well off with my present good Fortune," he on one occasion boasted to Goold. "Very few indeed of my fellow citizens have been as much favored."[46]

He was indeed favored, not only in fortune but also by those whose patronage made it possible. Although by the spring of 1778 British trade regulations were becoming increasingly stringent, they could still be evaded by merchants who were familiar with the law's loopholes or who enjoyed the confidence of port officers and contractors. Trade with the British West Indies was a case in point. Although it was already subjected to particularly rigorous rules, Coxe learned in March from his friend Commodore Hammond that General Howe "is determined to knock up all speculations from that way." In passing on this information to a New York correspondent, Coxe noted a significant exception: "He wishes to see the Army, Navy and inhabitants supplied nevertheless, and intends to grant special licences for that purpose to persons in whom he can confide." The result was that Coxe and a few other merchants who had ready access to the commanding gen-

42. Circular letter from Coxe, Mar. 19, 1778, Coxe to Goold, Mar. 17, 1778, Coxe Papers.
43. Coxe to Benjamin Yard, Mar. 14, 1778, *ibid.*
44. Coxe to Terrill & Kearney, Apr. 10, 1778, to Isaac Low, Apr. 1, 1778, *ibid.*
45. Coxe to Pennington & Biggs, Mar. 25, 1778, to Isaac Hartman, Apr. 26, 1778, *ibid.* In Apr., Coxe sold merchandise valued at £2,100 for Barrell alone. Coxe to Barrell, May 20, 1778, *ibid.*
46. Coxe to Goold, Mar. 31, 1778, *ibid.*

eral's deputies were given a virtual monopoly. So long as they received some licenses the precise number was of no great consequence, for, as Coxe explained, if only a few were issued, "the quantities imported will be small" and "there will be no difficulty in making the prices anything that the holders of the Commodities may choose."[47]

Such monopolistic ventures seemed only to sharpen Coxe's acquisitive instinct; the profits of illegal trade were even greater than those of government-sponsored transactions. The precise extent of his own clandestine operations during the British occupation cannot be known, if only because they necessarily were kept as secret as possible. But as his correspondence reveals, he did participate. The most conspicuous incident occurred toward the end of April. Coxe received a consignment from Alexander Kennedy and Company, a partnership of St. Croix merchants, aboard the sloop *Lord Howe*, which had come by way of the British island of Tortola. In addition to a quantity of sugar, the cargo included muskets, rum, and gin, among other items, the importation of which was forbidden except under the most stringent regulations. Apprehensive that his attempts to dispose of contraband goods (especially the guns) "might lead to dangerous enquiries," Coxe cautioned his temporary partners not "to hazard a cargo of this nature." But either loyalty to them or his own avarice outran discretion and, assuring the St. Croix merchants that "these things are managed in some Instances," he agreed to handle the consignment.[48] His initial fears were justified; just after the *Lord Howe* was unloaded at his wharf, Coxe was obliged to direct her captain to pull up anchor and to depart "without loss of Time on account of an information which had been most cruely Lodged against the Sloop for importing Arms." The worst was yet to come. A day later Galloway "ordered the arms Seized . . . in my store; my Clerk Sleeps there, and [I] being out at the Time he had the key; this being mentioned Mr. G. directed his Deputy to Brake Open the Door." Coxe was shocked and angry at what he regarded as "a Step So indecent and cruel." "If I ever forget," he wrote on May 8, "it must be because my senses and feelings are impaired by Time and I hope to remember it in the day when I can punish him for it without fear of his Patron."[49] That Galloway had done only what his official duty required was no excuse to Coxe, who no doubt

47. Coxe to Low, Mar. 1778, *ibid*. Not only was Coxe himself awarded a goodly number of special licenses (Samuel Herv & Co. to Coxe, Feb. 19, 1778, Coxe to Barrell, Mar. 23, 1778, to Thompson, Mar. 1778, to Goold, Apr. 11, 1778, *ibid*.), but he willingly offered "my little influence" to obtain them for some of his New York correspondents. Coxe to Stephen Skinner and Richard Yates, Apr. 4, 1778, *ibid*. See also Goold to Coxe, Mar. 25, Apr. 24, 1778, Coxe to Barrell, Stoughton & Davis, Apr. 12, 1778, *ibid*.

48. Coxe to Tennant, Ross, Kennedy & Morrice, Apr. 30, 1778, *ibid*.

49. Coxe to James Bruely, May 3, 1778, to Skinner, Yates & Van Dam, May 5, 1778, *ibid*.

shared the viewpoint of Edward Goold, who asked, "Why this Severity?" "I am as much prejudiced against smugling as any Man can be—but—I cannot at present look upon this thing in that light."[50]

Coxe attributed such setbacks to Lord Howe's withdrawal of his favor—a withdrawal reflected in the sudden coolness of subordinates, like Galloway, who had previously been so obliging. It was not only upon Coxe that the commanding general suddenly ceased to smile but also upon other formerly favored merchants. The explanation, as Coxe correctly perceived, was Howe's firm resolve not "to do any other but absolutely necessary Business" pending the expected arrival of his replacement, Sir Henry Clinton.[51] What Coxe did not know was that the new commanding general was bringing with him the king's orders to abandon Philadelphia. Even after Clinton's arrival on May 8, Coxe, preoccupied by concern for his wife's health, refused to believe rumors that the new commander planned to evacuate the city. He remained confident that the British were in Philadelphia for a long stay.

On May 18 General Howe's staff officers honored the retiring commander by inviting some 750 guests to a fête that climaxed a season of lavish entertainment. Designated the "mischianza," the festival opened with a "grand regata" along the Delaware. English officers and their wives, along with their more socially prominent Philadelphia sympathizers, were transported in brightly decorated boats and were cheered by thousands of spectators who lined the docks. Disembarking at Walnut Street wharf, the guests walked between columns of grenadiers standing rigidly at attention to the elegant Wharton mansion, where a triumphal arch had been erected. Here there was a "tilt or tournament," sprightly band music, a grand ball, rockets and fireworks—all climaxed by a midnight banquet in an elegant saloon, where tables "were loaded with 1,040 plates, dishes, etc.," and a host of servants, who "satisfied every desire before one could express it," served the guests. Those invited included a good number of Coxe's relatives and friends —the Chews, the Redmans, the Bonds, the Shippens, the Franks—and perhaps Tench himself.[52]

Although blithely unaware that the extravaganza symbolized the end of an era, Coxe was disturbed by the "confused state of affairs" occasioned by the change of command. By the second week of May official permissions for the clearance of ships were scarce. Philadelphia's harbor was crowded

50. Goold to Coxe, May 6, 1778, *ibid.*
51. Coxe to Tennant, Ross, Kennedy & Morrice, May 2, 1778, *ibid.*
52. Oberholtzer, *Philadelphia: A History*, I, 274–276; Uhlendorf and Vosper, eds., "Letters of Maj. Baurmeister," Pt. II, *PMHB*, LX (1936), 179–180. See also *Royal Pennsylvania Gazette* (Philadelphia), May 26, 1778.

with idle ships that could not be loaded; nor could their cargoes be sold. The revival of trade depended on Sir Henry Clinton, who was, as Coxe commented, so "totally engaged in receiving the returns and making the new arrangements" that the prospect appeared poor.[53] Coxe was further discouraged by the frosty reception he continued to receive from British officials. By mid-May 1778 he believed that he was being subjected to systematic harassment by Galloway, whose behavior he described as "uncommonly malevolent." But he could at least console himself that a few influential British officers, like Commodore Hammond and Daniel Wier, still professed their willingness to promote his interests.[54]

Coxe did not realize that neither Howe nor Clinton was likely to issue licenses to supply a city they planned to turn over to the enemy. Instead, he mistook the stirring of military activity by the British, preparing to leave Philadelphia, as the beginnings of a campaign to crush the American army. The British were planning to take the offensive, he wrote on May 22, and "are throwing out every Thing that Can Induce the people out of the Lines to believe they are going to Evacuate the City. Their view is probably to bring Gen Washington as near the city as possible and so push into his rear and force him to a General Action."[55]

Early in June the illusion was shattered, and the blow was the more stunning to Coxe because it was so unexpected. Coxe, like all other Philadelphia merchants, received from British headquarters an order to ship out all goods on hand. Having repeatedly discounted the warnings of his New York friends to stand ready for such an event, he now energetically, almost frantically, took measures to assure the safety of their goods. Fortunately for him, two idle brigs belonging to New York business associates were anchored in Philadelphia harbor. Not even taking time to prepare bills of lading or separate invoices, Coxe and his four clerks had the vessels loaded with most of the goods in his well-stocked warehouse.[56] Within five days, after a scene "the most confused ever I was in," the job was done, and on June 4, 1778, the two brigs sailed down the river, carrying away the rich cargo.[57] Although gratified by his success, Coxe was exhausted. "O God my dear friend," he confided to Goold, "what with hurry, Business and Anxiety, I am almost jaded to Death. Such another week as the Last would have put

53. The more so in view of an embargo that was imposed on May 9, 1778. Coxe to Goold, May 9, 1778, to Barrell, May 20, 1778, *ibid*.

54. Coxe to Goold, May 9, 1778, to Barrell, Stoughton & Davis, May 9–12, 1778, to Bruely, May 2, 1778, *ibid*.

55. Coxe to Wigram, May 22, 1778, *ibid*.

56. See Coxe to Aduljo & Maitland, Sept. 24, 1785, to Barrell, June 8, 1778, *ibid*. See also Coxe to Goold, June 4, 1778, *ibid*.

57. Coxe to Yates, June 3, 1778, *ibid*.

an End to my Existence. To increase my Distress Mrs. Coxe is extremely ill."[58]

During the following days, as the British completed preparations for evacuating the city, Coxe's apprehension about his wife's health rose steadily. He stifled it as best he could in order to concentrate his attention and energy on what, for the moment, was "the most important point"—the collection of the large sums of money owed to his correspondents and himself. Because many of his creditors were hastily packing up for departure with the British from a city that, in the words of a Hessian officer, resembled "a fair during the last week of business," it was apparent that what he did not immediately garner might be lost irretrievably. Obliged in some instances to take goods in payment, Coxe also managed to collect well over £9,000, even though he insisted that all "except really good men" had to give him "securities . . . payable in Bills of Exchange in London," preferably paymaster's bills.[59] Simultaneously, he also attempted to sell such goods as had not been shipped to New York on June 4 and, despite "a great glut" on the market, managed during the week preceding the evacuation to sell merchandise belonging to Cuyler and to Barrell for the sums of £2,600 and £8,000 respectively.[60]

Even with these business successes it was a time of "distress and trial," the more poignant because of his wife's illness. "Mrs. Coxe continues extremely ill," he lamented. "Heaven only knows what will be the Event—I dare not begin to fear for her."[61] To add to his burden the departing British army treated him no more kindly than had the patriot vigilantes eighteen months earlier: muskets stored in his warehouse were seized on orders of the commander in chief, lumber on hand was confiscated for the use of the British armory, and a departing British officer stole valuable furniture from a house on Front Street of which Coxe was custodian. "The British Army have used me in such a way that I must not trust myself to speak of their Conduct," he angrily complained on June 10. The worst was yet to come. On the eve of the evacuation British soldiers quartered above Coxe's store broke open a first-story window and wrecked and plundered its contents.[62]

The evacuation began when British troops moved across the river

---

58. Coxe to Goold, June 3, 1778, *ibid*.

59. Coxe to Barrell, June 3, 1778, *ibid*; Uhlendorf and Vosper, eds., "Letters of Maj. Baurmeister," Pt. II, *PMHB*, LX (1936), 175; Coxe to Barrell, June 3, 1778, to Aduljo & Maitland, Sept. 24, 1785, to Barrell, Low, Goold & Attwood, June 16, 1778, to John Coxe, June 10, 1778, Coxe Papers.

60. Coxe to Attwood, June 3, 1778, "Account with Abraham C. Cuyler," June 1778, Coxe to Barrell, June 17, 1778, Coxe Papers.

61. Coxe to Barrell, June 17, 1778, to Goold, June 4, 1778, to Goold and others, June 17, 1778, to Skinner, Yates & Van Dam, June 16, 1778, *ibid*.

62. On the furniture stolen, see John Smith to Coxe, May 22, 1778, Coxe to Mrs. Wood, June 1778, to John Coxe, June 10, 1778, to Goold, June 16, 1778, *ibid*. For Coxe's complaint,

into New Jersey on June 17, and royal transports, carrying heavy guns, auxiliary troops, and a large retinue of loyalists, sailed out of the harbor. Just after dawn on June 18 the rear guard departed, encountering on their way an American patrol entering the city. Some shots were exchanged, but the Redcoats marched on, leaving behind them a city in ruins—houses wrecked, "trees destroyed . . . churches and public buildings defiled. . . . Camp litter and filth everywhere; fences broken; . . . gardens and orchards trampled up and ruined."[63] It was the most desolate day of Coxe's life. His world was in shambles—his wife slowly dying, his well-calculated plans destroyed, and his property, repute, and safety in jeopardy. His last letter before the British departure mirrored his despair: "And now my dearest best Friend," he wrote to Goold, "I am to bid a long adieu. I ask Mrs. Goold to receive my tender love. . . . Shall I ever sufficiently thank you for your innumerable unparalleled acts of Kindness, Friendship and Generosity towards me. This American World will not Afford you happiness sufficient for the goodness of your excellent Heart. . . . I bid you a long and tender farewell earnestly beseeching the god of all mercies to preserve protect and defend you. . . . Kiss your dear little Children for me."[64] Whatever his fears and perhaps his plans for departing "this American World," such melodramatic phrases accurately portrayed his belief that his happiness and security were now at an end. "Farewell," he hastily scrawled on his letterbook as he closed it on the evening of June 17th, and then, in large letters, merely "Fare!"

Although depressed and apprehensive, Coxe could take some comfort in the hope that his highly placed whig acquaintances and connections might rescue him from the lash of patriot retaliation, just as influential friends and relatives had smoothed the road to his business success during the British occupation. The possibility of assistance from his cousin Colonel Tench Tilghman, Washington's trusted aide-de-camp, already had been attested by Tilghman's offer to forward letters addressed to Coxe by Edward Goold in New York;[65] the strong support of his close friend David S. Franks, aide-de-camp to General Arnold, was certain; and the aid of prominent whigs like Benjamin Rush and Thomas McKean could be relied on. But as Coxe soon realized, even influential allies might not be able to thwart the determination of an angry patriot legislature bent on retaliation against tories, especially those as exposed as he was.

---

see Coxe to John Coxe, June 10, 1778, *ibid.* On the plundering of Coxe's store, see Joseph Sherwell to Coxe, May 15, 1779, *ibid.*

63. Oberholtzer, *Philadelphia: A History*, I, 281.
64. Coxe to Goold, June 17, 1778, Coxe Papers.
65. *Ibid.*

On May 21, 1778, Coxe's name had appeared on a "Proclamation of Attainder" issued by the Supreme Executive Council of Pennsylvania "against certain persons adjudged guilty of High Treason."[66] Two days later, acting quickly to forestall conviction, he had taken the patriot oath of allegiance, which the Pennsylvania legislature had prescribed in June of the previous year.[67] Whether such a simple act of repentance revealed an absence of commitment to either side, a flexible conscience, or a desperate effort to salvage his fortune, and perhaps his neck, cannot be known. But if Coxe believed that this alone would avert his conviction, he was being fanciful. Something more than an oath was needed, as was demonstrated by the fate of other prominent tories, among them Joseph Galloway, members of the Allen family, and business associates like David Sproat and Samuel Kirk— all of whom were accused of treason and had their property subsequently confiscated.[68] A symbolic reminder of the threat Coxe faced was the civilian tenant of Galloway's former mansion, George Bryan, acting president of the state's Supreme Executive Council. Even more ominous was the popular wrath that soon erupted against those who had collaborated in the alleged barbarities of the British invaders, an eruption that must have been a chilling reminder to Coxe of his experience in December 1776 when angry patriots had driven him from the city.

These, then, were weeks of frustration, humiliation, and despair. The proclamation of attainder and treason was distressing enough; anxiety over his wife's fatal illness would have been painful at any time. Combined, they rendered this brief period one of unparalleled anguish. It must also have been a time, for Coxe unique, of self-appraisal and of anxious speculation about his future. The old authorities were gone; the old landmarks were disappearing. How could one whose loyalty to Britain's monarchy had overridden affection for his fellow countrymen now side with republicans to whom aristocracy and caste were remnants of a rejected past, to whom the authority of all rulers—even popularly elected ones—was but a vestige of royal authority? To Coxe it must have seemed a leap into the unknown. As his career demonstrates, he came to grips with the new order and eventually became one of its leading proponents. But this early crisis may also account

---

66. Samuel Hazard *et al.*, eds., *Pennsylvania Archives*, 1st–6th Ser. (Philadelphia and Harrisburg, Pa., 1854–1907), 4th Ser., III, 676, hereafter cited as *Pa. Archives*. The proclamation was printed in the *Pennsylvania Packet, or the General Advertiser* (Philadelphia), June 3, 1778.

67. Although how he managed to secure a pass or how he could have safely traveled outside British lines without one is not clear, Coxe presumably left Philadelphia on May 22 to seek out a Pennsylvania notary, before whom he took the oath of allegiance. This may account for a five-day gap, May 22–28, 1778, in his letterbook. Coxe preserved a copy of the oath in his papers. See the Coxe Papers.

68. See Lorenzo Sabine, *Biographical Sketches of Loyalists of the American Revolution, with an Historical Essay* (Boston, 1864), I, 158, 453–457, II, 324–325, 541.

for some of the traits that were so marked during his subsequent tenure in the Treasury Department: an unwillingness freely to offer again the loyalty he had mistakenly bestowed on the king and a deviousness he perhaps acquired from knowledge that his survival might depend on his willingness and readiness to shift allegiance.

Whatever the effect of this brief but critical period, Coxe's seemingly inexorable fate was reversed neither by his repentance nor by introspection but rather by the influence of William Coxe, Sr. Assurances "from my father soon put the danger of personal confinement or Injury out of the question," he wrote to William Tilghman in mid-July.[69] The danger presumably was removed by one or several of William Coxe's influential friends or relatives who had farsightedly opted for the American cause and could command the ear of Pennsylvania's chief justice, Thomas McKean, himself a Coxe family friend. "The chief justice has been sitting at the city courthouse for several days past," the *Pennsylvania Evening Post* announced on July 9, in order "to hear the charges against Tories accused of joining and assisting the British Army."[70] During this time Coxe appeared before him. "His behaviour," Tench reported to William Tilghman, "was much more friendly than I could have expected and perfectly genteel." Although Coxe was required to give bond for his impending trial, he came away from the conference convinced that "no proofs" would "be laid" before the grand jury against himself or other prominent loyalists and that "we shall in general be dismissed."[71] Such confidence could only have been based on McKean's assurances. Twenty years later one of Coxe's partisan critics succinctly described the situation. Although "proscribed . . . as a traitor," Coxe had escaped severe punishment "only from compassion to his youth and the worth of some of his relatives." The "man who saved him whose influence protected him," another political enemy pointed out, was McKean.[72] Certainly his conversation with the chief justice transformed Coxe. Momentarily forgotten were the preceding harrowing days; gone was the despair of the man who had scribbled "Farewell" in his letterbook. "I should prefer," he complacently wrote his cousin, a general dismissal of the charges rather than an

69. Coxe to William Tilghman, July 13, 1778, Coxe Papers. According to Coxe this statement was made to his wife, but Tench himself obviously received the same assurances.

70. *Pa. Eve. Post*, July 9, 1778. McKean was distantly related to Coxe by marriage. Tench Coxe wrote to Jefferson in 1801 (1802?) that his friendship with McKean began "in the year 1775 before I was of age." Coxe to Jefferson, n.d., Appointment Papers, R.G.59, National Archives.

71. Coxe to Tilghman, July 13, 1778, Coxe Papers.

72. *Gaz. of U.S.*, Sept. 4, 1799; *Aurora*, Aug. 29, 1804. On the other hand, a writer in the *Philadelphia Gazette and Daily Advertiser*, Oct. 14, 1800, asserted that "it is worthy of remark, that the attainder was taken off and Mr. Coxe saved from an ignominious punishment by the friendly exertions of Dr. Benjamin Rush." The same assertion was made by a writer in the *Aurora*, Aug. 30, 1804.

act of oblivion "because I see no necessity for an oblivion of a man's conduct whose intentions, at least, were not criminal and who can only be rendered offensive by an ex post facto law." He received the treatment that he preferred, for, as he explained many years later, when "he submitted himself to legal investigation," he "was informed that there were enough of witnesses in his favor, but none against him."[73] The manner of his rescue from conviction of treason and attainder left an indelible imprint on Coxe. It reaffirmed his emphasis on the importance of "connections" and influence, a characteristic discernible throughout his long career and revealed particularly in the assiduity with which he later cultivated men of political prominence. It perhaps was also a basis of his lifelong conviction, though often proved false, that highly placed friends or patrons would rescue him from the effects of bitter political battles—even those of his own making.

Soon after his interview with the chief justice, Coxe escaped the heat of the city and the "filth, stench and flies" by renting "a little retirement . . . for the Summer at the falls of Schuylkill."[74] The change would not only make his wife more comfortable but, he ardently wished, perhaps even restore her health. This, he soon painfully learned, neither climate nor medicine could do. Two weeks later, on July 22, she died.[75] Coxe was again cast into deep gloom. Two months of anguish ensued, relieved only by the news of dismissal of the charge of high treason.[76] But youth has its own amazing resilience, and three months later, after a visit with his parents in September, Coxe, displaying once again his characteristic optimism, was ready to resume his mercantile business. It was now his job to pick and choose from his past in order to master his future. "I am (if permitted)," he said, "likely to become a good American."[77]

73. Coxe to Tilghman, July 13, 1778, Coxe Papers; *Aurora*, Aug. 25, 1804. The absence of adverse witnesses is perhaps explained by the observation of a writer in the *Pa. Eve. Post*, July 18, 1778, that many Philadelphia whigs were indebted to some of the accused tories, men of former "office and power," for previous favors. Moreover, "those Whigs who left the City, could not possibly be acquainted with facts but by information" and were reluctant to offer hearsay evidence acquired from an "informer," a species of person who "heretofore has been held in high obloquy and reproach."

74. Oberholtzer, *Philadelphia: A History*, I, 281; Coxe to Tilghman, July 13, 1778, Coxe Papers.

75. Keen, "The Descendents of Jöran Kyn," *PMHB*, V (1881), 458.

76. *Pa. Archives*, 4th Ser., III, 938, 6th Ser., XIII, 475.

77. Coxe to John Coxe, June 10, 1778, Coxe Papers.

3

An American on Trial

Tench Coxe's career during the remaining years of the Revolution is witness to Henry James's remark: "It's a complex fate, being an American." For the time being, however, his rehabilitation seemed almost easy, especially considering the hostility of many Pennsylvania patriots toward renegade tories.[1] His friends and business acquaintances, choosing to overlook what Coxe later described as merely "one youthful indiscretion,"[2] sought to lighten his trial of starting anew. Tench was, after all, a member in good standing of a cosmopolitan community that was composed of men of social rank and economic status, bonds that not even the hatreds of war could dissolve.

The favorable reception accorded Coxe was also partly due to his modesty and discreetness. Having once gambled and lost, he resolved to bury his English past by fully committing himself to the American present. Commenting on an inquiry into his conduct that had uncovered "nothing very offensive," Coxe confided to his London banker that he expected "to be very quiet here." Convinced that he had meant "no injury to any private man, or public body," he was nevertheless relieved by the absence of rancor or recriminations and pleased by the continued affection and esteem of former schoolmates like Samuel Hanson of Maryland, who wrote that "the Impression which a Man of Virtue makes on my Heart is not to be effaced by any difference in political Sentiments."[3] The testimonial of the highest executive officer of the state of Pennsylvania was even more gratifying.

1. See Oberholtzer, *Philadelphia: A History*, I, 282–284.
2. *Fed. Gaz.*, Nov. 22, 1788.
3. Coxe to Robert Wigram, Nov. 16, 1778, to Benjamin Yard, Nov. 29, 1778, Samuel Hanson to Coxe, Apr. 1, 1779, Coxe Papers.

"You would do me much Injustice if you do not believe that upon all Occasions I have endeavored to palliate the Inadvertency and remove the Inconveniences into which you may have fallen," wrote Joseph Reed, president of the Supreme Executive Council. "And I do not speak my own Sentiments only, but those of many others, when I say that the Propriety, Modesty, and Prudence of your Conduct will probably in a little Time wholly remove the Impressions which have been made and fully restore you to your Friends and Country."[4] Such reassurances from so influential an official might well have inspired complacency in even a pessimistic man. Fortunately at that time Coxe could not know that his "one youthful indiscretion" would pursue him through life and beyond the grave. Yet he would soon learn what a gossamer thing tolerance of dissent in wartime is.

In the meantime, Coxe threw himself energetically into shoring up his mercantile business, which had collapsed following the British evacuation of Philadelphia. Its revival was not an easy task. Correspondents to replace his New York loyalist associates had to be found; customers to replace the British army were needed; and the confidence of merchants whom he had previously traded with had to be regained. To these ends he wrote friendly letters to former correspondents and obligingly performed the many favors they requested of him. Whatever his difficulties, Coxe at least had ample capital. In addition to the specie taken when he had hurriedly left Philadelphia in December 1776 and the horde of gold amassed during the British occupation, he also had large credits on the books of his London banker, Robert Wigram,[5] and of merchants at home and abroad. He also enjoyed the advantages of the business repute and, when necessary, the financial support of his father, who, though the war had somewhat impaired his fortune, still had a substantial income based on real and personal property.

Coxe's most promising business opportunity was a renewal of trade with St. Croix, where former business correspondents like Benjamin Yard and Nicholas Cruger were eager both to assist him and to regain for themselves a share of the profitable Philadelphia market. Yard, despite his strong disapproval of Coxe's collaboration with the British, labored to promote his friend's interests. However, the West Indian trade was fraught with risks, which island merchants sought to diminish by dividing cargoes and shipping them in as many vessels as might be available. To supplement caution, subterfuge was often employed, as when Nicholas Cruger, seeking to escape capture of one of his brigs by a privateer, arranged that the vessel, contain-

---

4. Joseph Reed to Coxe, Jan. 29, 1779, *ibid*. Reed's solicitude was not singular. Coxe wrote to Edward Goold on Oct. 20, 1778, that he had "experienced much kindness and indulgence from the gentlemen in office particularly." *Ibid*. See also James Wilson to Coxe, Nov. 23, 1779, *ibid*.

5. Coxe to Wigram, Nov. 16, 1778, *ibid*.

ing a consignment of goods to Coxe, be commissioned by St. Croix officials "under Pretense of her being bound to St. Thomas."[6]

Coxe also renewed trade with other West Indian islands, with Europe, and with Boston, Providence, Baltimore, and elsewhere. In reviving connections with his fellow Americans, however, he obviously concluded that candor was not the better part of business. To Benjamin Andrews of Boston, a former correspondent of Coxe, Furman, and Coxe, he explained his long silence by stating that "no opportunity" had "offer'd for your place for a long time" and that a "heavy domestic stroke" had "intirely deprived me of all Communication with friends." To another New England merchant he reported that he had "been long absent till July last."[7] Such evasiveness was unexceptionable; there was no particular reason why he should have confided to business associates his activities during the British occupation of Philadelphia. But from the standpoint of his career as a whole, one detects a trait, more pronounced with the passage of time, that would decades later render his veracity suspect to opponents and friends alike. In 1778 and 1779, however, Coxe heartily endorsed the comment of a friend that "there is something strangely illiberal in the Idea of estimating a Man's Merit by the Conformity or Non-Conformity of his political Opinions with One's Own."[8]

Despite the hazards of wartime trade and his own equivocal political position, Coxe's mercantile prospects superficially seemed brighter than he had expected. "The present State of our market," he informed a West Indian correspondent in December 1778, "is Such [that] No voyages planned by a person with the least mercantile knowledge can fail, provided they are fortunate in the point of Arrivals." Confident of his ability and counting on good luck, he promptly made plans to greatly expand his business activities and, to that end, announced early in January 1779 his decision "to go on under the old firm of C, F and C."[9] This was made possible by an arrangement with his father and Moore Furman, who agreed that their property might "be employed by the House of Coxe, Furman and Coxe" under Tench's "Care and management in Trade" at his "Discretion and the Net profits on which to be Equally Divided to the three partners Share and Share alike." William Coxe and Furman consented, moreover, to allow Tench "out of their Shares the Salary of a Clerk, and the rent of a Counting House and such Stores" as he might find necessary.[10] They were not being merely disinterestedly generous, however, for Coxe was taking on the difficult and

6. Cruger, Kennedy & Yard to Moore Furman, Dec. 23, 1778, *ibid.*
7. Coxe to Benjamin Andrews, Nov. 20, 1778, to Nathaniel Carter, Apr. 13, 1779, *ibid.*
8. Hanson to Coxe, Apr. 1, 1779, *ibid.*
9. Coxe to Tennant & Ross, Dec. 17, 1778, to Yard, Jan. 1779, *ibid.*
10. Furman to Coxe, Jan. 4, 1779, *ibid.*

time-consuming task of winding up the tangled affairs of both Coxe, Furman, and Coxe and its predecessor, Coxe and Furman. He attempted to collect the sizable debts outstanding, to pay the balances due creditors, to remit arrears of interest on loan office and other certificates, to satisfy the importunate demands of correspondents for exact statements of goods sold in 1776 and earlier (which he had to do before he could prepare a final settlement), and to arrange for the appraisal and occasional sale of lands owned singly or collectively by the firm's partners.[11] Coxe's tory record was an embarrassing handicap in the more delicate arrangements, such as negotiations to secure compensation for property confiscated by the state, notably a valuable stockpile of bar iron at Germantown. When he unofficially asked his friend Joseph Reed for assistance, Reed advised Coxe not to play an open part in the matter "for obvious reasons," suggesting instead that Furman, a consistent patriot, was better suited for such political negotiations.[12]

It was not only Coxe's reputation as a tory that limited his ability to conduct the affairs of the firm, but also, as Coxe soon learned, England's naval superiority, which rendered perilous even the limited foreign trade of Philadelphia merchants. By late March 1779 it appeared, as he remarked in explanation of his refusal to load a ship then anchored in Delaware Bay, "infinitely hazardous to keep any Concern in shipping just at this time."[13] Nor did prospects improve during the spring and summer. As prices soared and trade languished, Coxe, no doubt expressing the attitude of many other merchants, lashed out at "this tedious continuance of the War"—a statement suggesting that in 1779, as in 1776 and 1778, he was more deeply opposed to the war itself than he was ideologically devoted to the triumph of either Britain or America.[14]

Certainly the treatment meted out to him by his countrymen did nothing to strengthen his attachment to their cause. Within six months his satisfaction at the warm welcome accorded him upon his return to the whig fold had been replaced by the discovery that disloyalty during wartime is neither easily nor quickly forgiven. The Pennsylvania legislature remained steadfastly committed to enforcing its test laws; superpatriots remained intent on ferreting out and punishing disloyalty; and, like other reformed tories, Coxe soon found himself subject to both personal harassments and

---

11. See Furman to Coxe, Dec. 7, 1778, May 17, 1779, Nov. 22, Dec. 9, 1780, Nathaniel Carter to Furman, May 14, 1778, Coxe to Nicholas Cruger, Mar. 28, 1782, *ibid.*

12. Furman to Coxe, Jan. 20, 1779, *ibid.*

13. Coxe to Yard and Thomas Stevens, Mar. 26, 1779, *ibid.* Coxe went on to explain that "it is computed that theres 130 sail of cruisers on this coast at present from N. Hampshire to Georgia, besides those with which your seas swarm. Not more than half a dozen Vessels have got into the ports of Pennsylvania, and N. Jersey since the first of January when we suppose at least 60 sail might have been expected. The Trade of Chesapeak has suffered equally."

14. Coxe to Tennant & Ross, Apr. 13, 1779, *ibid.*

public attacks on his fickle loyalties. "I have no idea that the delicacy of my Constitution will be able to stand the political heat of this Climate," he wrote to his loyal confidant William Tilghman in April. "Yours is a *pretty retirement*." Even the routine protection of his business interests could be difficult. In a legal battle over the sale of Coxe and Furman's ship, the *Fame*, Coxe reported to Benjamin Yard that his opponents had "lately gone so far as to mention me in a political light" and surely had it in their "power to do anything with a Man in my Circumstances." Although it appeared increasingly likely that his toryism might be a virtually insuperable liability, he at first resolved "to ride out this unhappy Storm, having learned such a Lesson of Prudence from the Scenes I have already gone through."[15]

The resolve was short-lived. Weary and depressed by poor health, by the vicissitudes of business, and by renewed attacks on his loyalty, he reluctantly decided that he should leave Philadelphia, perhaps permanently. In anticipation of his possible exile, he began in April 1779 to lodge bills of exchange with George Clifford and Company of Amsterdam. But he soon decided that a visit with relatives in Maryland would be better than a trip to Europe. After a month or so with the Tilghmans in Chestertown and a few days with the Hemsleys in Queen Annes County, his health was restored, and his somewhat petulant reaction to personal attacks and business setbacks replaced by his more characteristic optimism.[16]

His posture of despair was, in any event, at odds with his active social life. Invitations to parties, suppers, and balls poured in just as they had during the lively social season of the British occupation. He was often entertained at Woodlands, the elegant country house of his friend Billy Hamilton, who like Coxe had been accused but acquitted of treason in 1778. He also frequently dined with the Chews, the Lewises, and the Shippens. "I heartily wish you were here to partake a little of the pleasure of our Evening Circles," he wrote to William Tilghman in October 1779. "They are now extremely agreeable."[17] Yet a lingering grief for his wife often left Coxe dispirited, and the company of the belles of the city did little to dispel her memory. "In truth," he caustically remarked, "I do not think" the quality of Philadelphia ladies rises "proportionately with the depreciation of money."[18] But time attenuated grief over the loss of his wife, and the city's social life became more and more alluring. "My expectation of happiness" must include "a proper share of the amusements of the World, and I am not so rigid as to suppose that these are improper," he wrote to Tilghman in January 1780.[19]

15. Coxe to William Tilghman, Apr. 21, 1779, to Yard, Aug. 17, 1779, to David Beekman, Apr. 16, 1779, *ibid.*
16. Coxe to Goold, Apr. 1, 1779, *ibid.* See also Coxe to Tilghman, Aug. 4, 1779, *ibid.*
17. Coxe to William Tilghman, Oct. 3, 1779, *ibid.*
18. Coxe to William Tilghman, Apr. 21, 1779, *ibid.*
19. Coxe to William Tilghman, Jan. 15, Apr. 18, Sept. 19, 1780, *ibid.*

But Coxe's plunge into the Philadelphia social whirl could not altogether dispel the dark cloud of political retaliation that hovered over him. Continued popular resentment against loyalists was demonstrated by the successful effort to strengthen the Test Act in September 1779, and neither news from the battlefield nor developments in Pennsylvania politics promised any abatement of the furor. A sense of crisis spread throughout Pennsylvania after the legislature, on June 1, 1780, adopted a resolution authorizing the Supreme Executive Council to impose martial law during any legislative recess—a sweeping grant of power of which President Joseph Reed took full advantage. Although Coxe was not directly affected, he could scarcely ignore either the public attitude that made possible such drastic legislation or the renewed clamor for the proscription of former tories and present neutrals. Philadelphia, William Tilghman cautioned Coxe, "is engaged in heats and animosities" of such intensity as might endanger even a prudent neutral like himself, not to speak of a former tory like Tench.[20]

As it turned out, Coxe was put to a different and unexpected kind of test: conscription. Early in July 1780 he was placed in a decidedly "unpleasant situation" when he received "a printed note to hold myself in readiness for marching, if farther advices should make it necessary." Although he reported a few days later to Tilghman, with obvious relief, that "the storm has blown over with no more than alarm," his escape was short-lived. On August 3 he received another notice, this one stating, "You being drawn in the 2d class of Captain M'Lane's Company, and Colonel James Read's Battalion are hereby desired to . . . march to the Support of the Continental Army the 10th instant, with your arms and accoutrements in good order."[21] Since Coxe's commitment to the patriot cause did not encompass a willingness to fight, it was fortunate for him that his induction notice included an escape clause in the form of a postscript: "An appeal will be held," it read, "at the state-house the 16th instant, at ten o'clock in the forenoon."[22] That he appeared and made a successful appeal seems certain. Although neither the precise nature of the appeal nor the basis for its acceptance are known, a

---

20. William Tilghman to Coxe, Jan. 24, 1780, *ibid*.
21. Coxe to William Tilghman, July 14, 1780, Samuel McLane to Coxe, Aug. 3, 1780, *ibid*. See also *Pa. Archives*, 6th Ser., I, 85.
22. Coxe's unwillingness to fight was expressed in a letter from Tilghman to Coxe, Aug. 24, 1780, Coxe Papers. This interpretation is at odds with the "General Return" of the Philadelphia militia, dated Aug. 10, 1780, which records that Coxe was called into active duty and was subsequently paid for his service. *Pa. Archives*, 6th Ser., I, 89. This return, as indicated, was dated six days before the date designated for an appeal, and there is, moreover, no evidence in Coxe's papers that he ever went on active duty. It should be noted, however, that he was listed in 1785, 1787, and 1789 on the rolls of the Philadelphia Militia's First Battalion successively as a private in the fifth, seventh, and third companies. In 1788 he was listed as a private in the Second Battalion. *Ibid.*, III, 959, 985, 995, 1045. On Coxe's opportunity for appealing his call to arms, see McLane to Coxe, Aug. 3, 1780, Coxe Papers.

casual comment by William Tilghman to Coxe a week later is suggestive: "Your militia fines would be an ugly pile to such a poor fellow as myself. You gentlemen in trade swallow them like nothing."[23]

If Coxe believed that this call to bear arms in support of American independence suggested official absolution for his past mistakes, he soon learned that what one group of his townsmen might grant, another could easily revoke. In October 1780 he was made the victim of guilt by association in a type of smear campaign of which, ironically enough, he himself would prove to be a skilled practitioner two decades later. It is doubly ironic that a cousin, a young lady of eighteen whom he knew only casually, should have provided the occasion.

In April 1779 Peggy, daughter of Coxe's uncle Edward Shippen, a former chief justice of Pennsylvania and prominent neutralist, had married General Benedict Arnold, a man twenty years her senior, the wounded hero of the Saratoga campaign, and the officer who in June 1778 had been appointed military commander of Philadelphia. Establishing himself in the grand Market Street house of Richard Penn and casting himself to play the role of Philadelphia's grand seigneur, Arnold succumbed to his avariciousness and fondness of luxury and society—behavior that was objectionable to the commonalty of Philadelphia because of his visits to tory families and his conspicuous consumption. To maintain this extravagant style of living, he engaged in high-handed and illegal business deals, in comparison to which the earlier corrupt practices of British officials seemed mere peccadillos. When news of his illegal activities reached the Pennsylvania Supreme Executive Council in January 1779, that body publicly denounced him, and Arnold, following the advice of Washington, requested a court-martial. In December 1779, after a long delay, Arnold was tried, found guilty of two of the lesser offences charges against him, and reprimanded.

Angered by the accusations of Pennsylvania officials and eager to escape the large debts he had recklessly incurred, Arnold had already sold out to the British and since May 1779 had been passing important military secrets. The general, who in the summer of 1780 had successfully contrived to be appointed commander of West Point, offered to hand over this key American military post guarding the Hudson River Valley to England's Sir Henry Clinton for a reward of £20,000. His treasonable negotiations were discovered in September 1780 when the Americans captured Clinton's emissary, Major John André, carrying letters that incriminated the American general.

The shock of Arnold's perfidy was the greater because it came at a

---

23. Coxe was willing to give his money if not his services. He averred many years later that he had contributed "£100 in specie toward the defense of the U.S." *Aurora*, Aug. 23, 1804.

time when the prospects of the patriot cause seemed unrelievedly bleak. The year 1780 had already been one of successive setbacks for the Americans—the loss of Charleston in May and General Horatio Gates's defeat by the British at Camden in August—and now the shock of treason in high places. Nowhere were its repercussions more pronounced than in Philadelphia, where sturdy patriots, recalling that the traitor had been lionized by the city's elite (many of whom were related to Arnold through his marriage to Peggy Shippen), determined to unmask other secret enemies within the gate. "Suspicion flies like Wildfire among his Connexions," Coxe wrote on September 28, some days after Arnold had fled to British-occupied New York.

As a close relative of the Shippens and one whose own tory record was public knowledge, Coxe could scarcely expect to escape suspicion and could only hope that, as in the past, influential officials might shield him from the fury of the mob. He was right on both counts. "On my going home to dinner" in midafternoon on September 27, he reported to William Tilghman, "I found the Vice President, Ch[ief] Justice and Sherriff at my house, wither they had come on a Suggestion of my being" Arnold's "Agent and correspondent. I made so firm and positive an assertion of my having no political or other connexions with him, and demanded to see my accusers with so much composure, that they were immediately satisfied."[24] Had he been less preoccupied with his own behavior, he might well have acknowledged that the "satisfaction" was due to their predisposition as much as to his own composure. Nevertheless, he resolved anew to assure his safety by being as inconspicuous and quiet as possible. "I know you will of Course write nothing criminal to me in these Times," he cautioned Tilghman, "but do not put anything on paper which might give offence, if seen by any Body."[25] Such circumspection and precaution made it easier for prominent officials, already favorably inclined, to certify his bill of patriotic health.

Nevertheless, Coxe was aware that his hard-earned immunity from retribution would not be secure until peace should resolve the animosities of war. During the remaining years of the Revolution his letters were characterized by such caution that one who now reads them might forget, as Coxe perhaps tried to do, that British and American troops were engaged in a see-saw war on whose outcome hinged the fate of an empire and the future of a new nation. The letters contained only the most casual references to such epochal events as the arrival of Rochambeau and French troops at Newport in May 1780; the rout of the Americans at Camden and the British defeat at King's Mountain in August and October of the same year; the battles of Cowpens, Guilford Court House, and Green Spring Farm during the first

24. Coxe to William Tilghman, Sept. 27–28, 1780, Coxe Papers.
25. Coxe to William Tilghman, Oct. 10, 1780, *ibid.*

six months of 1781; the subsequent march of Washington's army to Virginia; and the critical engagement between the French and British fleets that paved the way for the decisive victory of American and French forces at Yorktown. It was as if all these momentous developments were transpiring on a distant continent. "I am so hurt at the long continuance of this . . . War and its innumerable wretched Consequences," Coxe remarked in a moment of atypical candor, "that I could wish to keep the subject forever away from me."[26]

One way for Coxe to ignore the war was to focus attention on his mercantile business, which had no place to go but up after the setbacks of 1779 and 1780. By September 1780 he had decided to enhance the possibility of profits by trading independently. "I have just made a material Alteration in my affairs in Business," he wrote to Tilghman on September 19. "The Concern between my father and Mr. Furman will be immediately settled and I shall begin the world on my own Bottom entirely. I have a clear little capital of about 1000 Guineas of my own earning, a good education both as a gentleman and a Merchant and I trust shall make my Way in the World." On December 20, 1780, public notice was given "that the partnerships of Coxe and Furman, and Coxe, Furman and Coxe are dissolved."[27] That he delayed two years longer before publicly announcing the formation of his own firm was owing to his own rather cloudy reputation as a fair-weather ally of the Americans, as well as to his desire to await both the end of the continued trade barriers and the arrival of more propitious business conditions. But he did continue to operate a countinghouse, from which he cautiously expanded trading activities with other American cities, with the West Indies (until that trade all but ceased in 1782), and particularly with Europe.

One of Coxe's first moves after the dissolution of Coxe, Furman, and Coxe was to open a correspondence with Jonathan Nesbitt and Company of L'Orient, France. The firm, "composed of Mr. R. Morris of this city, Col. Barmister of Virginia, and our old acquaintance Mr. Nesbitt," was particularly active in the American trade and, despite the restrictions and dangers of transatlantic shipping during the Revolution, apparently prospered.[28] Nesbitt wrote to Tench early in January 1781 that he would "be happy on all occasions to promote Consignments to you, without any prospect of advantage to myself, except the pleasure of serving a Gentleman for whom I have the greatest Esteem and friendship." Whether or not he was quite so

26. Coxe to William Tilghman, Sept. 19, 1780, *ibid.*
27. *Ibid.*; *Pa. Jour.*, Dec. 20, 1780.
28. Coxe to William Tilghman, July 11, 1781, Coxe Papers.

selfless, Nesbitt did exert himself to promote his friend's interest.[29] Some months later Coxe entered into another advantageous business association with an American merchant resident in France, Jonathan Williams of Nantes, Benjamin Franklin's nephew. Pleased with such promising arrangements for the Franco-American trade, he was even more gratified at his success in concluding an informal trade agreement with three of his countrymen, Charles Sigourney, Henry Bromfield, and Duncan Ingraham, then in partnership in Amsterdam.[30]

As a supplement to the European branch of his business and as a compensation for the stagnation of commerce with the West Indies, Coxe could count on a sizable trade with merchants from Boston to Savannah. This internal trade was handicapped by tariffs imposed by the individual states, but not until later years, when these tariffs became burdensome enough to choke the greening of the American economy, did Coxe find them particularly bothersome. For now Coxe conducted a brisk business in flour and tobacco with his longtime friend William Hemsley of Queen Annes County, Maryland, as well as with other planters; he consigned blankets to Clark and Nightingale of Providence; he received consignments of French brandy, "the best Malaga Wine," and lemons from Boston; he shipped tea for sale on commission to merchants in other cities; and with his father's old friend and agent in Trenton, Abraham Hunt, he dealt in iron, sugar, and many other products. But his most important and valuable business associate was Edward Goold, his former tory partner, who still flourished in British-occupied New York, and with whom in 1782 alone he transacted business totaling about £3,500.[31]

Such a volume of trade, when added to his other extensive ventures,[32]

---

29. Nesbitt & Co. to Coxe, Jan. 12, Mar. 23, 1781, *ibid*. Coxe traded not only on his own account but also in partnership with other Philadelphia merchants. For example, he was interested with Edward Shippen, Jr., in a cargo from L'Orient that was shipped aboard the *St. James*. Nesbitt & Co. to Coxe, Jan. 13, 1782, *ibid*.

30. For his association with Jonathan Williams, see Williams to Coxe, Nov. 19, 1781. See also David S. Franks to Coxe, Aug. 19, 1781, Jan. 25, June 5, 6, 1782, *ibid*. Charles Sigourney and Henry Bromfield were from Boston, and Duncan Ingraham, with whom Coxe previously had been acquainted, was from Philadelphia. Bromfield returned to the United States in 1781, and Sigourney in 1782. Sigourney to Coxe, Oct. 9, 1782, Sigourney, Bromfield & Ingraham to Coxe, Sept. 12, 1781, *ibid*.

31. William Hemsley to Coxe, Mar. 31, June 17, July 25, 1781, Clark & Nightingale to Coxe, Nov. 26, 1781, Samuel Goold to Coxe, Aug. 15, 1782, Nathan Levy to Coxe, Oct. 12, 1782, Abraham Hunt to Coxe, June 28, 1782, *ibid*. For business with Goold, see account dated Apr. 2, 1784, *ibid*. Precisely how Coxe and Goold arranged such a volume of trade between Philadelphia and British-occupied New York is uncertain. One possible means was for British West Indian merchants to ship cargoes intended for Coxe to Goold in New York. See, for example, Tyler & Mumford to Coxe, Sept. 4, 1783, *ibid*. But the question of how Goold managed to get the goods to Coxe remains unanswered.

32. For appraisals of Coxe's property, see *Pa. Archives*, 3d Ser., XV, 246, 266, 739. Lambert

bears out Coxe's own complacent boast in June 1782 that the assured profits of his countinghouse were "like a public office without the Dependency of it." This happy situation he attributed to his "close application," "knowledge of Business," and cautious avoidance of imprudent speculation. Coxe showed his disdain for rash speculation when he commented on the ventures of a fellow merchant, Nicholas Low, a New York business acquaintance: "He has been speculating in Virginia in everything but the ladies. I fancy he does not think there is any profit in them, or he would not be able to keep his hands clear of them."[33]

In January 1782 Coxe married Rebecca, the eighteen-year-old daughter of Rebecca Wells and Charles Coxe, thus ending three years of speculation about his future domestic life. Since Charles Coxe was the natural son of Colonel Daniel Coxe and his mistress, Mary Johnson, Rebecca and Tench were first cousins. On this subject neither the newlyweds nor their numerous relatives ever wrote a single word, a silence no doubt dictated by a determination to obliterate the fact of Charles Coxe's illegitimacy. This had not, however, proved a barrier to Charles's success. He had conducted a profitable mercantile business in Philadelphia until 1766, when he purchased and removed to a 1,200-acre estate in Hunterdon County, New Jersey, where he also owned land bequeathed to him by his father. There he lived over the succeeding half century as a country gentleman in retirement. In the village of Sidney, a few miles from Flemington, he built a handsome home and became largely identified with the economic interests of the neighborhood, promoting projects as varied as the establishment of a woolen factory and the construction of a canal. His neighbors—apparently rather less snobbish than Charles Coxe himself—overlooked his maternity and accepted him as a member in good standing of the squirearchy of West Jersey, where he was repeatedly appointed justice of the peace and served on the legislative council.[34] He was, it seems, on close terms with his stepbrother William, who lived in nearby Sunbury, where Tench was a frequent visitor. It was on one of these visits that Tench proposed to Charles Coxe's pretty young daughter, who, presumably with the blessings of the related families, accepted.

On February 17, 1781, William Tilghman, having just heard gossip that his cousin was paying "devoirs to Miss R. Coxe" (and perhaps feigning

---

Cadwalader of Trenton referred to Coxe as "the first Man in Trade in Philadelphia." Cadwalader to Coxe, June 10, 1782, Coxe Papers.

33. Coxe to William Tilghman, June 29, 1782, Tilghman Papers, Hist. Soc. Pa., Philadelphia; Coxe to William Tilghman, Apr. 2, 1779, Coxe Papers.

34. *Letters of Moore Furman*, 95.

ignorance of a kinship the Coxes themselves chose to ignore), demanded to know, "Who is this little beauty?"—a question Coxe formally answered a few weeks later when his engagement to Rebecca was announced.[35] Tench insisted, however, that the nuptials be postponed until the following year. "Few Young Men," as a Maryland friend commented, "would postpone the greatest of all earthly Happiness from prudential Motives";[36] but Coxe, as cautious in love as he was at this time in politics and business, was determined to wait until his ship literally came in—in this instance the arrival of a valuable cargo from Europe.

On February 4, a day "cold . . . enough to freeze any heart," the wedding took place and was followed by a month-long honeymoon.[37] By March 7 Coxe, who had previously arranged for the decoration of a new house, wrote with obvious complacency that he was happily seated by *"my own Fire Side* with my wife . . . by me."[38] It was the beginning of the happiest relationship of his life, one that provided essential solace during a stormy career battered by the frustration of political ambition and by financial crises. As he would write soon after Rebecca's death twenty-five years later: "Our principles, upon all important subjects were the same. We loved the same pursuits—the same friends—our mutual confidence knew no bounds."[39]

With his newly found marital euphoria having blanketed the painful recollection of his first wife's long illness and premature death, Coxe longed for the war's end, confident that it would bring both the interment of his tory past and the expansion of his mercantile activities. His business was already fluctuating with the rumors of peace, which, beginning in the spring of 1782, dominated the talk of Philadelphia merchants daily gathered at the coffeehouse and, more important, governed the number of cargoes consigned to the city's port by merchants in the West Indies and Europe. The obvious explanation was offered by Jonathan Nesbitt and Company of Nantes, who informed Coxe that reports of a British withdrawal had prompted the withholding of goods already earmarked for shipment to the United States and remarked that "we apprehend the rumor of a Peace will lower the prices

---

35. William Tilghman to Coxe, Feb. 17, 1781, Hemsley to Coxe, Mar. 5, 1781, Coxe Papers.
36. Hemsley to Coxe, July 8, 22, 1781, *ibid.*
37. William Tilghman to Coxe, Feb. 28, 1782, *ibid.*
38. Coxe to William Tilghman, Mar. 7, 1782, *ibid.* Forty years later Charles Coxe's heirs alleged that upon the marriage of Rebecca to Tench, Charles Coxe had "advanced" the couple £1,000. This was denied by the children of Tench and Rebecca, who asserted that as a dowry Charles Coxe had given their parents certain lands in Pennsylvania that had formerly belonged to the Penn family. Because of title conflicts, Tench's children averred, these lands never actually passed to their father. "Affidavit of children of Tench and Rebecca Coxe," July 7, 1823, Charles Coxe Papers, Hist. Soc. Pa., Philadelphia.
39. Coxe to John Vaughan, Mar. 10, 1806, Coxe Papers.

considerably with you." Such caution caused severe shortages and erratic business conditions in the United States. In Philadelphia during the last days of June, for example, there was an unexpected "run against the merchants." Although Coxe was happy to report that in this instance he did "not . . . suffer at all," his luck soon deserted him.[40] In mid-August, shortly after arriving in Sidney, New Jersey, where Rebecca was vacationing for the summer with her family, he heard rumors of peace that sent him scurrying back to Philadelphia, where he found "all confusion and alarm" and "Goods of all kinds . . . dead and totally unsaleable." This stagnation was especially deplorable because "I have near four thousand pounds value by me the property of myself and friends."[41] In an effort to forestall the consequences of an even more depressed market, which definite news of a peace treaty would certainly occasion, he began to dispose of his stock on hand as rapidly as possible and to cancel shipments of goods previously ordered from Nesbitt. The latter understandably complained, "We find to our cost that it is become a very general mode in Philadelphia, first to order Goods, and then on the least appearance of a Change in affairs to Countermand these orders," a practice that "renders the Trade very disagreeable and precarious."[42]

Although such indignation may have been justified, Coxe and other American merchants had correctly foreseen the approaching end of the war. On November 30, 1782, the preliminary peace treaty was signed in Paris. Six days later Jonathan Williams, having heard in Nantes reliable rumors of peace, hurriedly wrote Coxe a letter including in lieu of a signature the statement: "You must guess my name by my handwriting." His purpose was twofold: to afford Coxe an opportunity personally to "make the best use of the information" and to urge that goods of his own consigned to Tench aboard the *Intrepid* "be disposed of at all Events if possible before the news is publicly known" in exchange "for everything that will not diminish in price at a Peace."[43] Whatever advantages Coxe may have gained from the advance knowledge of peace, they were small compared to his joy at the long-awaited opportunity for a fresh start in his own country, now cleared, so he hoped, of the mean spirit of war-bred divisiveness.

"On a peace I shall have no idea of being anything less than a very independent man in my Business, and in a course of Time, in my property

---

40. Nesbitt & Co. to Coxe, Mar. 23, 1782, William Tilghman to Coxe, July 12, 1782, *ibid*; Coxe to William Tilghman, June 29, 1782, Tilghman Papers.
41. Coxe to Thomas Riché, Aug. 13, 1782, Coxe Papers.
42. Nesbitt & Co. to Coxe, Sept. 28, 1782, *ibid*.
43. Williams to Coxe, Dec. 6, 1782, *ibid*.

also," he boasted to William Tilghman in June 1782.[44] The Anglo-American treaty, negotiated during the autumn of 1783, not only afforded Coxe such personally pleasing prospects but also signaled a new era of American commercial freedom. Freed from the straitjacket of Britain's navigational system and encouraged by war-spawned trading concessions from other foreign countries, the new nation could now, he believed, trade with countries the world over, guided only by mutual needs and the possibility of profits.

Coxe, like many other American merchants, eagerly laid plans for reaping the benefits of such promising business opportunities. On January 1, 1783, two months before news of England's formal acknowledgment of American independence reached Philadelphia, he dispatched a circular letter to business correspondents in Europe, the West Indies, and the states announcing his "intention to prosecute business on my own account." He assured each of them that "my connexions . . . enable me to procure for you a safe and able correspondence in any of our parts."[45] The hundreds of favorable replies that poured into Coxe's quarters on Front Street were to him gratifying reassurance that a period of sustained economic expansion was at hand. His confidence was justified, for the American Revolution, as a recent historian has remarked, did appear to foreshadow "the dissolution of mercantilism and the liberalism of trade, together with a new openness, trust, and pacific temper in the international community."[46]

Although the rosy dawn of unfettered and prosperous commerce proved false, Coxe and other American merchants briefly basked in its glow. During the first nine months of 1783 English traders, taking advantage of generations of experience in conducting the American trade and superior knowledge of American tastes, quickly sent out cargoes of manufactured goods carefully selected to satisfy an appetite sharpened by years of wartime fasting. The British products were eagerly bought up by Americans who ignored the potentially harmful side effects. The danger was that this lavish consumption, made possible by the generous extension of credits, would last only as long as the English merchants had confidence in the ability of their customers to pay.

Although Coxe eagerly took part in this British trade, he was far more enticed by the rich profits he expected to earn from the revival and expansion of commerce with the West Indies. His optimism was misplaced. Most English officials remained convinced that their nation's prosperity and power depended on maintaining inviolate their traditional mercantile sys-

---

44. Coxe to William Tilghman, June 1782, Tilghman Papers.

45. Printed circular, n.d., Coxe Papers. The date of Jan. 1, 1783, is given in the numerous replies Coxe received. On Apr. 25 and June 20 he sent out similar circulars.

46. Merrill D. Peterson, *Thomas Jefferson and the New Nation: A Biography* (New York, 1970), 289.

tem. This belief was strengthened by the earl of Sheffield, who in his influential *Observations on the Commerce of the American States* pointed to the ease with which the Americans could be held in commercial vassalage. Urging a policy of confrontation rather than conciliation, Sheffield recommended that Britain exploit the weakness of the new nation by rigorously enforcing its acts of trade and navigation, above all, the stipulation closing the British West Indies to foreign ships.[47] By providing a rationale for Parliament to do what it would probably have done anyway, Sheffield's pamphlet helped to shape English policy and had an important impact on many Americans. No one was more affected than Coxe, who over succeeding decades would verbally spar with Sheffield while seeking to vindicate his own faith in American economic independence. For the moment, however, Coxe's patriotic ardor was overshadowed by his practical concern over the effects of Britain's affirmation of her traditional commercial policies.

On July 2, 1783, the foundation on which Coxe and other American merchants had hoped to raise a new structure of commercial freedom and prosperity was removed. An order-in-council provided that certain enumerated American articles (naval stores, all types of lumber, horses and other animals, and all grains) could be shipped from the United States to the West Indies only "in British built ships owned by His Majesty's subjects and navigated according to law." Other goods (notably, salted fish and meats) could not be sent there at all.[48] The great expectations of those who had hoped for a commercial union between the United States and Great Britain were thus shattered by the ministry's firm conviction that "His Majesty's Dominions in the West Indies" were "the principal source of the national opulence and maritime power."[49] The dismay with which merchants in the United States greeted news of the decree was matched by that of Britain's West Indian planters. As one of Coxe's Jamaican friends lamented, "All our prospects of Trade are done away."[50] Yet Coxe's business records reveal that the outlook was by no means so bleak, at least not for merchants who,

47. [John Baker Holroyd, first earl of Sheffield], *Observations on the Commerce of the American States* . . . (London, 1784). This work was first published in Sept. 1783. It was advertised for sale in the *Pa. Gaz.*, Jan. 21, 1784. For a succinct description of Britain's alternatives in 1783, see Jerald A. Combs, *The Jay Treaty: Political Battleground of the Founding Fathers* (Berkeley, Calif., 1970), 3.

48. Grant and Munroe, eds., *Acts of the Privy Council, Colonial Series*, V, 530. Major West Indian products like rum, sugar, molasses, and coffee, however, could be shipped to the American states on the same terms as to a British colony. The order-in-council reached the United States in September and was printed in the *Pa. Gaz.*, Sept. 13, 1783.

49. Quoted in Francis Armytage, *The Free Port System in the British West Indies: A Study in Commercial Policy, 1766–1822* (London, 1953), 1.

50. Mumford to Coxe, Oct. 8, 1783, Coxe Papers. Mumford also observed that "in consequence of this new regulation Lumber etc. and Flour have rose 50%." See also Philip Philip Livingston to Coxe, Oct. 15, 1783, *ibid*.

like himself, could find ways to elude Britain's often-relaxed patrols and somnambulant customs officials.

For the moment, however, Coxe was preoccupied with rescue measures to assure the success of a large-scale domestic speculation he had undertaken soon after launching his own mercantile firm in January 1783. The opportunity had been provided by his friend Jacob Broom, merchant of Wilmington, Delaware, who had offered Coxe and David S. Franks shares in a business deal he was then hatching with the French commissariat. Both eagerly accepted. Accordingly, in mid-April, Broom, on behalf of the partnership, signed a contract with Chesnel, commissary general of war for the army of the comte de Rochambeau, for the purchase of French property—horses and stables—in Wilmington. Although the partnership sold the property at an ostensibly satisfactory profit, its disposal led to legal tangles that would require decades to unravel, the first of the many major litigations that make it appear as if Coxe's life were lived on the field of legal battle. At the time, however, the apparent success of one such venture prompted Coxe to join Broom and others in seeking additional war surplus contracts. The result was the purchase of gunpowder, lead, linen bags, and gun carriages stored in the French armory at Baltimore. Once again the contracts with the French commissary general presented more problems than profits and led to protracted litigation.[51]

Despite the demands of his countinghouse, where he was assisted only by a chief clerk and a few apprentices, Coxe found time to conduct the business affairs of friends and relatives, more often than not without pay. Placing personal loyalty above the risk of public censure, he freely offered his assistance to tories, many of whom had been close business associates in 1777 and 1778. Included among these were Philip Kearney, who had been arrested by order of General Washington and whose New Jersey estates had been confiscated; Henry White, a prominent New York loyalist; Samuel

---

51. There are hundreds of documents in the Coxe Papers dealing with the Broom-Coxe-Franks partnership. The detailed story of the sale of the French horses and stables can be followed in undated "notes" by Coxe, "Messrs. Coxe and Franks in a/c with Jacob Broom," Apr. 28, 1783–Aug. 25, 1783, submitted Feb. 17, 1796, "Accounts of Sales of Horses," Apr. 30, 1783–May 15, 1783, submitted Dec. 12, 1785, Broom to Coxe, June 1783, July 26, 1783, Aug. 20, 25, 31, 1783, Jan. 10, 16, Feb. 4, 1788, "Accounts of Coxe and Jacob Broom with David S. Franks," Jan. 4, 10, 1788, *ibid*. For information on the purchase of French equipment stored in Baltimore, see Chesnel to Coxe, June 7, Aug. 7, 1783, Broom to Coxe, May 15, Aug. 17, 20, 22, 1783, Coxe to Chesnel, Aug. 26, 1783, Thomas Russell to Coxe, June 14, July 28, Sept. 6, 30, Oct. 7, Nov. 1, 15, 22, 1783, *ibid*. The lead and bags eventually were shipped to other places, mainly Philadelphia and Wilmington, but because of their defectiveness they led to renewed litigation. Such gun carriages as were salable were disposed of in the South, where they were used on plantations. Some of the lead eventually found its way to China aboard the *Canton*, in which Coxe owned a part interest. See "Accounts," Jan. 5, 1784–1786, Broom to Coxe, Dec. 3, 1783, Jan. 2, 1786, "Arbitration," Nov. 12, 1783, *ibid*.

Kirk, a former tory associate in Philadelphia now in exile on Nova Scotia; John Stoughton, who had consigned to Coxe so many rich cargoes during the British occupation and who was now at Cap-Français; and James De Lancey, a New York tory who was on close terms with the Allens in London.[52] But he did not confine his assistance to tories. He also came to the aid of patriot refugees.[53]

Coxe was the most generous when loyalist relatives needed favors. For his uncle James Tilghman, who in 1777 had left the political heat of Philadelphia for the comparative safety of rural Maryland, he handled personal affairs (providing financial and other assistance to the two Tilghman sons who had sided with the crown) and also managed a variety of business matters (including the rental of Tilghman's handsome Philadelphia town house, the purchase of stock in the Bank of North America, and advice on other investments). Coxe also obligingly handled the Pennsylvania estate of his uncles, Turbutt Francis, who had died on July 30, 1777, and Sir Philip Francis, who was living in England; and he served, along with Thomas Mifflin and Sarah Francis, as guardian for Turbutt Francis's children. Above all, he dedicated himself to the interests of his sister, Sarah Allen, who on May 1, 1783, embarked for England to join her husband, Andrew.[54] The separation was as painful for Tench as for Sarah, who "felt more in parting"

52. Philip Kearney to Coxe, Aug. 8, 1783, Henry White to Coxe, May 10, 1783, Samuel Kirk to Coxe, June 8, 12, July 1, Sept. 13, Nov. 4, 1783, John Stoughton to Coxe, July 21, 1783, James De Lancey to Coxe, June 10, 1783, *ibid.*

53. Coxe subscribed $30 to aid South Carolinians who in the wake of the British victories in their state sought refuge in Philadelphia. Mabel L. Webber, ed., "Josiah Smith's Diary, 1780–1781," *South Carolina Historical and Genealogical Magazine*, XXXIII (1932), 79–84, XXXIV (1933), 139–146. A friendly editor (or perhaps Coxe himself) less than a decade later recalled other services Coxe had made to the patriot cause: "I am well assured, that in 1779 and 1780, he loaned money to the United States: that he became further interested in our funds: that he purchased in 1779 and 1780, real estates from the most active whigs—thereby placing his estate and theirs on the same foundation—the issue of the war. In 1778 also he contributed his share to the circulation of the bills of exchange of the United States and of the officers of the French army and Navy, to the amount of above two hundred and fifty thousand livres by which bills, the supplies of the allied armies of America and France were procured. . . ." *Independent Gazetteer: or the Chronicle of Freedom* (Philadelphia), Nov. 25, 1788.

54. On Coxe's aid to Tilghman's sons, see Coxe to Benjamin Andrews, Nov. 20, 1778, Andrews to Coxe, Dec. 10, 1778, Tench Tilghman to Coxe, Aug. 2, 1780, Coxe to William Tilghman, Nov. 4, Dec. 22, 1779, July 14, 1780, Coxe Papers. On Coxe's management of Tilghman's business matters, see James Tilghman to Coxe, Apr. 27, May 18, 27, June 30, July 7, 27, Dec. 29, 1783, *ibid.* On his aid to the Turbutt children, see Richard Tilghman to Coxe, July 24, 1783, Coxe to William Tilghman, Mar. 7, 1782, to Sir Philip Francis, June 20, 1787, *ibid.*; Sir Philip Francis to Coxe, May 30, 1783, Cadwallader Colden Collection, Hist. Soc. Pa., Philadelphia. On Coxe's aid to his sister Sarah, see Goold to Coxe, Apr. 30, 1783, Coxe Papers. On Apr. 14, 1783, Sarah Allen, through the agency of Abraham Kintzing, wrote John Dickinson, president of Pennsylvania, informing him that "with his approbation" she planned to join her husband in England. She was accompanied by her daughter, Margaret, and her son, Andrew. See also William Coxe, Sr., to Coxe, Mar. 31, 1783, *ibid.*

from him than from any other relative and who wrote him a letter expressing devotion that was, she said, "founded upon a sympathy of Souls."[55] Coxe shared with his parents the custodianship of his sister's two daughters, who temporarily remained in Philadelphia, and he also worked diligently to protect the American property interests of her husband. Although Andrew Allen's own property had been confiscated, Coxe skillfully managed to salvage that considerable part of the Allen family's Pennsylvania estate the commonwealth had left untouched—an immunity that was due to the foresight of William Allen (Andrew's father), who devised his property to his grandchildren.[56]

Even had Coxe not been the active head of a prominent mercantile firm, he would have been a busy man. In addition to the assistance he rendered to relatives and friends, he performed a variety of services for business associates in America, the West Indies, and Europe. He served as their real estate agent, both selling and renting houses; he performed the duties of a collection agency, dunning their Philadelphia debtors, often as hard to find as they were unwilling to pay; he arranged for them the sale or purchase of personal property, as varied as furniture and ships; he saw to the acceptance and discounting of bills of exchange and other financial transactions, domestic and international; he obliged some of them by undertaking the complicated and speculative disposal of paper money issued by the American states; he offered advice on the comparative soundness of securities in which they proposed to invest; and he arranged, when necessary, for legal aid, so essential in an age when the conduct of trade was more litigious than it was predictably profitable.[57] It was too much for one man, and by midsummer 1783 Coxe was casting about for a junior partner.

55. Sarah Allen to Coxe, n.d., *ibid.*

56. Sarah Allen to Coxe, Jan. 3, Mar. 12, 1784, Andrew Allen to Coxe, Aug. 11, 1786, Jan. 20, June 28, 1787, July 9, 14, 1795, *ibid.* By a codicil of Dec. 1, 1779, to his will, William Allen devised his property to his son's children in order to assure its retention by his family. He also deeded the lots he owned in the central part of Philadelphia "for divers good causes and considerations" to Edward Shippen, Jr., and Tench Coxe, with a life interest vested in himself. Charles S. Boyer, *Early Forges and Furnaces in New Jersey* (Philadelphia, 1931), 235. Coxe remitted money to his brother-in-law whenever possible (Coxe to William Tilghman, July 14, 1780, Coxe Papers) and promoted as best he could Allen's attempt to secure compensation from the British for his confiscated lands. Allen to Coxe, Sept. 14, 1783, *ibid.* The Pennsylvania Supreme Executive Council, to Coxe's disappointment and Allen's dismay, refused to grant the requisite documents. Allen to Coxe, Dec. 16, 1783, *ibid.*

57. See, for example, Cadwalader to Coxe, May 15, 1783, Yard to Coxe, June 1, 1783, Samuel Griffin to Coxe, Dec. 2, 1783, Goold to Coxe, Sept. 4, 16, 1783, Tyler and Mumford to Coxe, Sept. 24, Nov. 27, 1783, *ibid.*

4

Philadelphia Merchant

"All persons having accounts unsettled with Tench Coxe or Nalbro Frazier," the *Pennsylvania Packet* announced on January 1, 1784, "are requested to adjust them with Coxe and Frazier . . . at the late Counting house of Tench Coxe on Front Street." This partnership, which was arranged some months previously and announced in a circular letter of November 29, 1783, was the most important of Coxe's mercantile career.[1] Frazier was a New Englander who had brought letters of introduction to Coxe while visiting Philadelphia on a business trip in 1783. By this date Coxe had decided that his own business was "too various and Extensive to admit of his doing Justice to it alone," and he proposed that the Bostonian join his firm.[2] Both men subscribed to a capital stock that was enlarged by a loan from William Coxe, Sr.; three-fifths of the profits were to go to Coxe (who brought to the new firm "the Capital and Connexions of the House of C and Furman"), and two-fifths to Frazier.[3] This alliance between prominent merchants from two of the country's leading commercial centers was underpinned by their expectation of capturing a sizable share of trade between the

---

1. Premord & Son to Coxe, Feb. 29, 1784, Gannon & Co. to Coxe, Aug. 10, 1784, Philip Philip Livingston to Coxe, Dec. 22, 1783, Coxe Papers.

2. The most notable of Nalbro Frazier's letters of introduction was from Charles Sigourney, to whom Frazier was related. See Sigourney to Coxe, July 31, 1783, *ibid*. See also Davis, *History of American Corporations*, I, 141, 215, 243, 255, 258, 259, 309; Frazier to Coxe, June 7, 1784, Coxe Papers. On Coxe's decision to go into partnership, see Coxe & Frazier to Lane, Son & Fraser, Apr. 24, 1784, Coxe Papers. The partnership was to expire on Jan. 1, 1788. Coxe to David S. Franks, Nov. 26, 1787, *ibid*. It was renewed at that time and dissolved when Coxe was appointed assistant secretary of the Treasury in May 1790.

3. Coxe & Frazier to Lane, Son & Fraser, Apr. 24, 1784, Coxe to Frazier, May 24, 1790, *ibid*.

middle and New England states—an expectation attested to by Frazier's departure for Boston, only a few days after the formal inauguration of the new firm, to survey the state of commerce in that and other cities.[4]

Despite the cloudy future of American commerce, 1784 opened auspiciously. To many Philadelphians, Coxe among them, this hopeful beginning was symbolized by congressional ratification on January 14 of the definitive peace treaty and by the "public demonstration of joy" held in America's capital city of Philadelphia a week later, for which a triumphal arch, decorated by Charles Willson Peale, was erected and an impressive display of fireworks was prepared. Although cynics like Gouverneur Morris considered such an "exhibition . . . perfectly ridiculous," the occasion was appropriately symbolic.[5] It signalized the formal launching of the new nation, and the years of crisis ahead were anticipated when flaming lamps ignited a wooden stage and panic ensued.

Economic gauges clearly indicated that the independence of America was no guarantee for commercial success. The problems encountered by Coxe and Frazier during the rest of the decade had been adumbrated by Coxe's own experience in 1783. Restrictions on West Indian trade, dwindling markets abroad, and the burden of mounting debts at home combined to make this an era of difficulty for American merchants and the country's economy, though it is questionable whether or not the times were as perilous as historians have usually depicted them.[6]

To a casual observer the bustle and business activity of the capital of the new nation would have suggested a boom and not a depression. Philadelphia was the metropolis of the United States, a commercial center that, as Coxe remarked years later, conducted "much more trade, both external and internal . . . than any other port."[7] "The capital activity and connexions" of its business leaders "being much beyond" those of any other place in the country made "this city . . . a Magazine for the produce of many places," domestic and foreign. That he and his partner were counted among its leading merchants was due primarily to Coxe's "connexions" and to their

4. See Frazier to Coxe, Jan. 14, 1784, in which Frazier, writing from Boston, speaks of observations he would send to Coxe from that city and from other places he planned to visit on his return trip to Philadelphia, *ibid.*

5. *Pa. Archives*, 1st Ser., X, 149; Gouverneur Morris to Alexander Hamilton, Jan. 27, 1784, Harold C. Syrett *et al.*, eds., *The Papers of Alexander Hamilton* (New York, 1961–1976), III, 499, hereafter cited as Syrett *et al.*, eds., *Hamilton Papers*.

6. For an example of the historical controversy over economic conditions during the "Critical Period," see John Fiske, *The Critical Period of American History, 1783–1789* (Boston and New York, 1888); Merrill Jensen, *The New Nation: A History of the United States during the Confederation, 1781–1789* (New York, 1950); and Douglass C. North, *The Economic Growth of the United States, 1790–1860* (Englewood Cliffs, N.J., 1961).

7. Coxe, *A View of the United States of America . . .* (Philadelphia, 1794), 488. For full bibliographical information, see chap. 10, n. 29.

own capital. "The old and respectable houses which you find in this town have entirely engrossed the field here," he wrote to a West Indian correspondent, implicitly acknowledging the advantage accruing from the reputation established by Coxe and Furman and its successor. But not all was in a name, and to succeed as an international merchant one needed reliable correspondents, as well as business shrewdness and an intimate familiarity with world markets. As Andrew Allen reminded Coxe, "an honest industrious merchant" is "truly a citizen of the world and at home in every country where trade is known."[8] It was a demanding occupation, but one that carried with it compensatory rewards in profits and in status, for just as the nineteenth century was dominated by the manufacturer, so the eighteenth century in America and England was dominated by the merchant.

From their countinghouse on Front Street, Coxe and Frazier conducted a far-flung trade requiring an extensive knowledge of ships and shipping, credit standings of dozens of foreign correspondents, banking and currency conditions at home and abroad, the complexities of international exchange (including the labyrinthian credit procedures involving bills of exchange), the terms and procedures of insurance brokerage, trade rules and regulations everywhere (as well as ways to evade them), and the state and prospect of the economies of other nations. All this entailed a staggering amount of paper work—letterbook transcriptions of every letter sent, the preparation of invoices and bills of sale, the keeping of cashbooks, general profit-and-loss ledgers, and separate accounts for each correspondent —which was carried on with the assistance of five clerks, most of them apprentices who were the sons of friends and of whose welfare Coxe was commensurately solicitous.[9] Cargoes were unloaded onto their wharf on the Delaware, from which sales were made when possible; the remainder was stored in their warehouse in order to sell "to best advantage . . . when a better Market may be expected." Like Coxe, Furman, and Coxe, the new firm charged a commission of 5 percent on all goods consigned or purchased on order, and since this was their principal source of income, a good reputation was the surest means of retaining desirable customers and consignors. Their success in achieving this end depended both on taking prompt advan-

8. Coxe & Frazier to Thomas Potts, Apr. 7, 1784, Coxe & Frazier to James Taggert, Sept. 24, 1784, Andrew Allen to Coxe, Aug. 11, 1786, Coxe Papers.

9. Among their clerks were Tench's brother Daniel, the young son of Coxe's friend Abraham Kintzing, John Stille, Jr., Samuel Wilcox ("our cash and bookkeeper"), Archibald McCall, Jr. ("who was bred with us"), and William McIlwaine, the son of an Irish business correspondent. Coxe & Frazier to Arthur & Co., July 7, 1786, to William McIlwaine, Dec. 22, 1789, to Hope & Co., Oct. 21, 1787, *ibid.*; Coxe & Frazier to Edward Burd, July 12, 1786, Society Miscellaneous Collection, Hist. Soc. Pa., Philadelphia. They were also obliged to employ a clerk who knew French, the language of Continental traders. Coxe & Frazier to Daniel Major, July 27, 1784, Coxe Papers.

tage of the best possible prices and on making "quick remittances," which, as they said, were "the life of Business and essential to the honor" and prosperity of the merchant.[10] Conversely, of course, the profitability of their own consignments depended on the business acumen and reliability of their occasional partners and their correspondents.

When Coxe and Frazier was launched in January 1784 its partners sanguinely expected to seize a profitable share of Philadelphia's trade. Discounting the economic barometers that pointed to a deepening of the depression already underway, they confidently made plans for business expansion with the arrival of spring weather. "After a most tedious winter we have at length got our River opened," they reported on March 17. "Several vessels are come up."[11] Although unable to "get any English bottom to go to Jamaica," they hoped that if their own new brig could find some way to "be admitted" to that island, "it would give us a fine chance among our Neighbours"—a chance that would be particularly advantageous if, as they had predicted, the price of both West Indian and Philadelphia produce would fall, thus encouraging more trade.[12]

Most of Coxe and Frazier's trade was with the British islands. The possible returns from this commerce were worth its hazards to them, as well as other American merchants, largely because of the high prices prevailing in the islands for North American produce. Through the 1780s the cost of such articles rose steadily, in some instances to five times their prewar level, and at times of acute distress in the islands, as following devastating hurricanes in 1784, 1785, and 1786, they rose more sharply yet.[13] The bulk of Coxe and Frazier's West Indian trade was carried on legally in British-owned and -manned vessels (although some prohibited cargoes were shipped in this manner in counterfeit containers). Yet it was more profitable, although patently illegal, to employ their own vessels—an opportunity Coxe and Frazier did not pass up—and they occasionally had as many as three ships regularly plying the waters between Philadelphia and the Caribbean, a feat that was accomplished primarily by securing British ship registers.[14]

The story of their brig *Betsy* illustrates how this was done and sug-

10. Coxe & Frazier to William Arthur, Mar. 22, 1788, to James O'Neale, July 25, 1784, Coxe Papers. Coxe & Frazier's advertisements of goods for sale appeared frequently in Philadelphia newspapers. For a sampling, see *Pa. Packet*, June 6, 1785; *Pa. Gaz.*, May 24, 1786, Apr. 12, 1788; *Fed. Gaz.*, Mar. 27, 1790.

11. Coxe & Frazier to George Munro, Mar. 17, 1784, to Major, Mar. 5, 1784, Coxe Papers.

12. Coxe & Frazier to Major, Mar. 17, 1784, to John Moore, Mar. 17, 1784, *ibid.*

13. J. H. Parry and P. M. Sherlock, *A Short History of the West Indies* (London, 1956), 140.

14. Although they may have owned a whole or a part of other vessels, Coxe & Frazier did own at one time or another, as their letterbooks make clear, the following brigs: the *William Coxe*, the *Philadelphia*, the *Franklin*, the *Molly*, the *Betsy*, and the *Polly*. The latter two were apparently kept in operation for most of the decade.

gests the ease with which clandestine trade was contrived at a time when business ethics were not always clear or enforceable. The *Betsy* was a "handsome Vessel" of 170 tons burden, "18 months or 2 Years old, Yellow sides, white bottom, figure head and quarter pieces carved," suitable "either for freight or passengers." She was acquired by Coxe and Frazier in 1784 at a cost of £3,262 and was promptly "absolutely sold and conveyed to Moses Franks Esq of the City of London," whose American business affairs Coxe had handled for some years.[15] The sale was a paper transaction only. Coxe and Frazier, acting ostensibly as the Londoner's agents, thus managed to acquire an English register for a vessel that they used for trade on their own account and for their own profit. While the financial return, if any, that Franks received is unknown, he was listed as putative owner along with Thomas Torver, an English merchant on Tortola (where the vessel was officially registered).[16]

Although the *Betsy* "appears by her register the property of Moses Franks . . . and T. Torver," Coxe and Frazier explained to a West Indian correspondent, their own close friend "Mr. Lynch who knew her as the *Margaritta* can tell you what she really is."[17] She really was, of course, the illegal means by which Coxe and Frazier sought to tap the forbidden trade of the British islands. To render their profits the more secure, the Philadelphians devised additional maneuvers calculated to throw suspicious customs officials off the scent. For the Jamaica trade, they arranged to have the ownership of the *Betsy* transferred to Bell and La Touche of that island and requested them to "immediately take out a new register in your own names and give her the name of '*the West Indian.*' " "We have much real confidence in you," Coxe and Frazier assured their Kingston-based, secret partners, "and hope this vessel may be put into a good profitable line between your port and ours." Bell and La Touche were also reassured that "there can be no danger . . . as our conveyance is legal under our powers . . . and the property of the Brig is absolutely vested in you," even though (and the fact did not need to be made explicit) not a nickle would change hands.[18]

And so it went. The risks were great but so were the returns: "The

<hr />

15. Coxe & Frazier to Stuart & Blake, May 19, 1785, to Benjamin Yard, May 7, 1784, to Bell & La Touche, Jan. 28–29, 1785, to Yard, May 26, 1784, to Premord & Sons, Sept. 4, 1784, Coxe Papers.

16. Coxe & Frazier to Bell & La Touche, Sept. 24, 1784, *ibid*. In May 1784, before the arrangement with Franks was made, Coxe & Frazier had sent the brig, then named the *Margarita*, to Tortola, where a British register was procured through the agency of their friend Thomas Torver, who was instructed that "if you cannot continue to have her registered so New as 1783 then register as a prize which upon the whole may be best." Coxe & Frazier to Torver, May 25, 1784, *ibid*. Concerning the official register of the *Betsy*, see Coxe & Frazier to Bell & La Touche, Aug. 26, Sept. 24, 1784, to Torver, June 16, 1784, *ibid*.

17. Coxe & Frazier to Bell & La Touche, Aug. 26, 1784, *ibid*.

18. Coxe & Frazier to Bell & La Touche, Sept. 25, 1784, *ibid*. Bell & La Touche were also

circumstance of lying at the mercy of every Seamen, passenger etc. in these Vessels is so great," Coxe and Frazier commented in August 1785, "that immence profits should be made to render them an object." The joint venture with Bell and La Touche had presumably yielded just such profits. In January 1785 Coxe and Frazier asked another Jamaican firm, James and John Dick, if they would "take a half concern in the Brig . . . to keep her running to your address." Three months later Thomas Torver accepted Coxe and Frazier's proposal that "the part which belonged to Franks . . . be duly assigned to you," and that Torver (whose name, they admitted a few years later, "was really made use of as a cover") take "out a new register entirely in your name."[19]

Despite these and similar stratagems, Coxe and Frazier's hopes for a brisk trade with the British West Indies were eventually frustrated by the unexpected vigilance of local customs officials.[20] But stricter law enforcement was not alone responsible. From the outset Coxe and Frazier's ambitious plans had been largely thwarted by an economic decline at home, most particularly falling markets and a scarcity of money. As early as April 1784 the Philadelphians complained that the arrival of twelve vessels from the British islands "has glutted us with Rum and Coffee and Cocoa"; two weeks later the firm of Coxe and Frazier was obliged to inform Caribbean correspondents that, despite their earlier optimism, "the present State of our Markets here is not encouraging."[21] And the situation in 1784 forecast that of the rest of the decade.

While Coxe and Frazier tried by means fair and foul to brave the economic storm of the postwar years, they could not altogether escape its devastation. The woeful tale of ever-deepening depression and steadily stagnating trade is told by random excerpts from their letterbooks for 1785—on March 9 to a London correspondent: "The flood of goods brought out, . . .

---

called on from time to time to take the necessary precautions to prevent the vessel's seizure. See, for example, Coxe & Frazier to Bell & La Touche, Feb. 14, 1785, *ibid*.

19. Coxe & Frazier to Stephen & William Blackett, Aug. 22, 1785, to James & John Dick, Jan. 22, 1785, to Arthur, Sept. 30, 1789, to Thomas Torver, Apr. 18, 1785, *ibid*. On May 9, 1785, Coxe & Frazier sent Torver "a Bill of Sale for Mr. Franks part to you. . . . The bonds for her old register we presume cancelled and therefore the loss of her old register [in a manner not specified] may be omitted to be mentioned. The Officers in the English Islands are so suspicious now that even your property may be brought in question and delay and difficulty given. . . . " *Ibid*.

20. For other stratagems, see, for example, Coxe & Frazier to Benjamin W. Blake, Dec. 16, 26, 1785, *ibid*. See also Coxe & Frazier to Stephen & William Blackett, July 4, 1785, to Torver, July 7, 1785, *ibid*. On the vigilance of customs officials, see James Clark to Coxe, Feb. 20, 1786, Coxe & Frazier to Thompson, Campbell & McNeal, Apr. 18, 1786, *ibid*. Coxe & Frazier finally worked out arrangements for sale of the *Betsy* (by that time named the *Peggy*) in May 1786. Coxe & Frazier to Yard, May 20, 1786, to Blake, Dec. 16, 26, 1785, *ibid*.

21. Coxe & Frazier to Stephen & William Blackett, Apr. 20, May 10, 1784, *ibid*.

the purchases and immediate forced sales of swindlers, and other circumstances have contributed to render the American markets bad and the Philadelphia market the worst in the world"; on April 6 to a St. Croix merchant: "We have not been able to make sales" of West Indian products "without giving them away"; on May 13 to an English agent: "We cannot perform impossibilities nor could any man make even tolerable Sales, or remittances thro such a Season as we have experienced"; on June 4 to a London firm: "The Commerce of this Country . . . is at present so unsettled that little satisfaction is experienced in adventuring or transacting it"; on July 8 to Coxe's longtime friend Benjamin Yard: "You have no idea of the perplexed state of things here. The rage of party . . . the stagnation of trade . . . create great confusion"; and on August 26 to a London correspondent: "We are *extremely* distressed at the hardships which have fallen on those who have dealt with America." The quantities "of goods which have come out to this Country . . . are continuing our distress."[22]

By December 1785, however, Coxe and Frazier were convinced that the worst of the depression was over, a belief they shared with business correspondents during the winter and spring of the ensuing year. Their optimism was premised on both an expected fall in produce prices on the Philadelphia market and a concurrent steep rise in the demand and price of West Indian articles. The island products, they commented on November 30, 1785, are so "exceedingly scarce and high" that "we think the first importations in the Spring will command a great price."[23] Market conditions, which were only conjecturable in the winter season, seemed to bear out such predictions, and with the rather early arrival of mild weather and the opening of the Delaware during the first week of March 1786, their confidence mounted.[24] So far as imports from the Caribbean were concerned, this optimism was justified, but otherwise they were grievously mistaken.[25] "Everything" in Philadelphia "still wears the same stagnate appearance," Samuel Wilcox informed Coxe (then attending the Annapolis Convention) in September 1786. Despite plentiful crops, the price of local produce remained high, and, as the Philadelphia partnership complained, specie was so scarce that they dared not "ship goods on Credit or on an advance."[26]

22. Coxe & Frazier to Robert Wigram, Mar. 9, May 13, Aug. 26, 1785, to Yard, Apr. 6, July 8, 1785, to Cologen, Pollard & Cooper, June 4, 1785, *ibid.*

23. Coxe & Frazier to William D. Hall, Nov. 30, 1785, *ibid.* On hopes for the Philadelphia market, see Coxe & Frazier to Garnet & Swasey, Dec. 2, 1785, *ibid.*

24. See, for example, Coxe & Frazier to William Ashton & Co., Jan. 18, 1786, to John Gay, Jan. 25, 1786, to Yard, Feb. 20, 1786, to Christopher McEvoy, Mar. 8, 1786, *ibid.*

25. As Coxe & Frazier observed to Hoare of Honduras Bay on Sept. 6, 1786, "Our market for W. Indian produce has been very tolerable this season." *Ibid.*

26. Samuel Wilcox to Coxe, Sept. 7, 1786, Coxe & Frazier to Wilkinson & Cooke, Sept. 7, 1786, to Torver, May 11, 1786, *ibid.* "Our port has been so crowded with vessels this fall and

This stagnation was not offset by an enlargement of Coxe and Frazier's European trade.

Their initial belief following the Peace of Paris that trade with England would flourish had not been unrealistic. The direct trade between the two countries remained on the same footing as in colonial days: Great Britain continued to permit the duty-free importation of nonmanufactured goods from the United States, even when carried in American ships. But Britain deluged the American market between 1783 and 1784, and the consequent fall in prices, limitation of credit, and reduction of profit margins quickly dampened the enthusiasm of more prudent merchants like Coxe and Frazier. By the fall of 1784 they had resolved that "the very Great Quantity of Dry Goods which have been imported into this Country . . . had determined us to withhold all orders . . . till we see some Greater probability of . . . success."[27] It was a decision as wise as it was well timed, for two years later the partnership was still lamenting that commerce with England remained in a state of such "confusions" as to "render every prudential caution highly proper."[28]

Trade with the Continent did not offer compensatory advantages. Convinced that "the late revolution of these states will not prove more important to France in a political than in a commercial light," Coxe and Frazier originally had "views of connecting ourselves throughout the Capital Ports of France where we are not already known."[29] But such optimistic plans miscarried. Most French merchants, strangers to American markets and tastes, were unwilling to extend credits to American importers and made only the paltriest effort to seize a commerce long monopolized by Britain. Nor did Coxe and Frazier's trade with other European nations yield the profits they had expected in 1784. Although they did some business with allied merchants in Sweden, Holland, Spain, Portugal, and elsewhere, their

---

summer," Coxe & Frazier wrote on Oct. 31, 1786, to John Moore & Co., "that we have not a bble [barrel] of pork, beef, hams, fish or half a cargo of corn in the place nor indeed in the country." *Ibid.*

27. Coxe & Frazier to Blanchard & Lewis, Sept. 30, 1784, *ibid.* See also Coxe & Frazier to Wigram, Apr. 23, July 3, Oct. 7, 1784, to William Price & Co., July 30, 1784, *ibid.*

28. Coxe & Frazier to James Baille & Co., Oct. 10, 1786, *ibid.* Coxe & Frazier wrote to Wilkinson & Cooke on Sept. 7, 1786, that "dry goods still continue very dull, very little progress has been made in the sale of yours since our last, you may depend however upon our exertions to dispose of them." *Ibid.* Two weeks later they informed Robert Wigram that "the American markets continue to be a scene of the most injudicious speculations. Larger quantities of goods than we can consume are brought in among us." Coxe & Frazier to Wigram, Sept. 22, 1786, *ibid.*

29. Coxe & Frazier to Deleport & Co., Oct. 8, 1784, to John Lambert, Sept. 9, 1784, *ibid.* See also Coxe & Frazier to Marion & Brillantor Marion, Sept. 6, 1784, to Premord & Son, Sept. 4, 1784, to Daniel Crommelin & Sons, Mar. 17, 1785, to Barton, Johnson & Barry, Oct. 25, 1786, *ibid.*

ledgers demonstrate that if large profits were to be made, they must be sought elsewhere.[30]

One possibility was the domestic market. From the date of their partnership Coxe and Frazier had attempted to exploit the domestic sources of supply and potential markets outside Pennsylvania. Although they managed to conduct a somewhat sporadic and occasionally profitable trade with merchants in the middle and northern states, they were primarily intent on seizing a large share of the profits they believed could be garnered from the exchange of southern staples for American and European manufactures. But almost from the beginning their efforts to grasp this trade (including the negotiation of arrangements with "the first connections in the Capital Towns" of the South) were stymied by imports into that region directly from Europe and by the fall in foreign demand for articles such as tobacco, rice, and naval stores, as well as by the reluctance of Coxe and Frazier to extend the long-term credits to which Southerners were accustomed.[31] This was all for the better, as they soon realized; by May 1786 economic reports from the South were "miserable and such indeed as we could not have expected." That section, they explained to a London business associate, "is an opulent and thriving part of our Country," but the extensive and easy credit granted by English merchants had "enabled the planters to involve themselves too deeply." Recognizing their inability to compete successfully with British rivals, Coxe and Frazier virtually withdrew from business in the South by announcing at the end of 1786 that "numerous disappointments . . . have determined us to decline advancing" to correspondents in that section.[32]

So long as the American states were unable or unwilling to adopt a national commercial system, the economic affairs of each state were subject to the whims of foreign merchants, as well as to the restrictions of other nations. Commercial regulation, when attempted, was imposed by the individual states, and with scant success. Coxe did what he could to promote the

30. For an explanation of the French reluctance, see especially Gannan & Co. to Coxe & Frazier, Aug. 10, 1784, *ibid.* For Coxe & Frazier's trade with Spain and Portugal, see John Bulkeley & Co. to Coxe & Frazier, May 18, 1784, Charles Walsh to Coxe & Frazier, Aug. 15, 1784, Coxe & Frazier to John Bulkeley & Co., Jan. 20, 1785, to Shirley Banger & Co., April 11, 1785, to Strange, Dowell & Co., July 8, 1789, to Cologan, Pollard & Cooper, July 13, 1789, *ibid.* For their trade with Holland, see Coxe & Frazier to Daniel Crommelin & Sons, July 1, 1785, Apr. 7, 1786, to Wilhelm & Jan Willink, Nov. 19, 1785, Cornelius Schenkhouse to Coxe & Frazier, Aug. 6, 1784, May 4, 1787, *ibid.* For their Swedish trade, see Coxe & Frazier to Wahrendorf & Co., Lars Rejmer Psn. & Schon & Co., Mar. 30, Apr. 7, 1785, *ibid.*

31. For an especially glowing account of the opportunities of the southern trade, see John Coxe to Tench Coxe, Dec. 1, 1784, *ibid.* Concerning the failure to make connections with the "Capital Towns," see Coxe & Frazier to Wigram, Apr. 23, 1784, *ibid.*

32. Coxe & Frazier to Wilkinson & Cooke, May 6, 1786, to Thomas Cummings, Nov. 24, 1786, *ibid.*

adoption of effective tariff laws, for, particularly in Pennsylvania, he was convinced that partial retaliation was far better than no retaliation at all. The Pennsylvania law, which the legislature enacted in September 1785 at the behest of artisans and mechanics and over the opposition of many merchants, not only was representative of tariff legislation in other states, notably New York and Massachusetts, but also served as the prototype for the first federal tariff of 1789. Designed as "an act to encourage and protect the manufactures of this state," the Pennsylvania measure imposed specific duties on a long list of enumerated articles, ad valorem rates on others, additional duties on rum imported in foreign bottoms, and a levy of seven shillings and sixpence "upon every ton of shipping belonging in whole or in part to any foreign nation or state whatever," except those having treaties with the United States.[33] The two latter provisions were added largely at the insistence of Coxe, who as principal lobbyist for Philadelphia's mercantile community, worked chiefly through Charles Pettit, a member of the assembly and a prominent Philadelphia merchant.[34]

Coxe's endorsement of Pennsylvania's tariff marked the beginning of his life-long advocacy of protectionism and navigation acts. Although conceding that "it is not our interest perhaps to manufacture" articles produced more cheaply elsewhere, Coxe defended the retaliatory features of the Pennsylvania law on the grounds that they "will lead us to encourage" such domestic manufactures as are "perfectly in our power." America's "own Interests must be our principal rule," he wrote in April 1786, adding (as he would not always later do) that "in pursuing them, moderation with regard to other powers must be kept in view." Although his growing commitment to economic nationalism occasionally clashed with his pursuit of private profit, he had already embraced a number of controlling and enduring assumptions.[35] "As individuals, we have warm affections toward many valuable friends and relations in G. Britain," he on one occasion remarked, but "as citizens of America . . . we apprehend from weighty considerations that we must from interest, œconomy, and necessity take measures as a

---

33. "An Act to encourage and protect the manufactures of this state, by laying additional duties on the importation of certain manufactures which interfere with them," James T. Mitchell and Henry Flanders, comps., *The Statutes at Large of Pennsylvania from 1682 to 1801 . . .* (Harrisburg, Pa., 1896–1911), XII, 99–104, hereafter cited as *Pa. Statutes at Large*. The act was published in the *Pa. Packet*, Sept. 22, 1785. It also imposed a discriminatory duty on rum imported in foreign vessels—a duty that was repealed in 1786, at which time the duty of 7s 6d on foreign tonnage was lowered to 2s 6d. *Pa. Statutes at Large*, XII, 233–235.

34. Coxe to Charles Pettit, 1785, Coxe Papers.

35. Coxe & Frazier to James Warrington, Sept. 2, 1785, to John Dunlap, Apr. 15, 1786, *ibid.* Coxe did not in the mid-1780s, for example, consistently endorse legislation of the type he would later ardently support: apropos of the extra duty on foreign tonnage imposed by the Pennsylvania assembly, he and Frazier wrote that "we confess we think it very far from being proper." Coxe & Frazier to Stephen Blackett, May 14, 1787, *ibid.*

country that will be unfavorable" to that nation. Because of "the Universal restrictions," particularly those of England, "with regard to the commerce of America," he asserted, "it will be necessary to adopt economical manufacturing."[36] In time the qualification would disappear, and manufacturing would appear an end in itself, an economic summum bonum, but the principle of commercial reciprocity would remain a fixed article of his creed.

By the mid-1780s Coxe was an influential spokesman of the city's mercantile community, a role he exercised most conspicuously as a member of the "Committee of Merchants and traders of the City of Philadelphia." Formed early in 1784, the committee was appointed by the city's more prominent businessmen to devise measures to promote the "usefulness" of commerce "both to the Nation and to Individuals." Coxe served as secretary of the organization. Its most important function was lobbying. On matters of common concern the committee, with Coxe usually as its spokesman, petitioned the assembly, which listened sympathetically, thanks in part to committee members in that body. It was a request from the committee that moved the legislature to ask the Confederation government to take action to prevent continued depredations upon American vessels by the Barbary pirates. So it also was with alterations in the state's tariff and navigational legislation.

But the members of the committee, and none more than Coxe, were aware that only unified action on the part of all the states could provide commercial regulation effective enough to command the attention and respect of European nations. In his efforts to further this prospect Coxe was tireless. His first act as secretary of the committee was to dispatch a circular letter to merchants in other parts of the country soliciting their cooperation in a concerted effort to remove the disadvantages under which American commerce was then conducted. Coxe was particularly disturbed by the refusal of European powers to grant the United States commercial reciprocity. Speaking for the Philadelphia committee, he called on fellow traders to "look to the judicious Exercise of our Rights for the Attainment of those Advantages and reciprocal Benefits in Commerce to which our Situation and Circumstances fairly entitle us." However, on the important question of precisely how those rights were to be protected and such benefits secured, Coxe was inexplicit, merely expressing the committee's willingness to "harmonize" with the other states "in whatever measures may be adopted."[37]

Pondering the dismal state of American commerce, Coxe concluded that its improvement demanded a yet stronger organization of Philadelphia

36. Coxe & Frazier to Moore, Sept. 14, 1785, to James & John Dick, June 20, 1785, *ibid.*
37. "Circular Letter to the Merchants of the Trading Places in the United States," Jan. 3, 1784, *ibid.*

businessmen and closer cooperation with merchants elsewhere. These ideas were the basis of a newspaper article published anonymously in the *Pennsylvania Packet* in November 1784. Here Coxe proposed and submitted the draft of a constitution for "A Chamber of Commerce for the State of Pennsylvania." To assure the freedom won in the Revolution, Coxe argued, it was necessary "to draw forth the power and resources of our country, the cooperation and hearty support of the different class of citizens," particularly the merchants and traders, whose activities gave them "a fund of knowledge superior to that of any other body of citizens." For the knowledge of merchants and traders to be given "due weight and consequence in the affairs of the state," collective action was of major importance. To this end, Coxe proposed the organization of a Chamber of Commerce and the inauguration of regular correspondence between the chamber and similar organizations in the nation's other leading seaports. Through such communication and through meetings of deputies of the several chambers of commerce, cooperative policies might be pursued, and solidarity on important questions of public policy "involving our best commercial interests" might be secured. In attempting to remedy the defects of the Confederation, Coxe was recommending a powerful pressure group that "would form a new and powerful tie of friendship to bind the United States together." But his plea for class solidarity and special interest politics, along with his proposal for a new organization to make these effective, was passed over in silence.[38]

However, the Committee of Merchants did try to achieve by informal cooperation that which Coxe had recommended be done by incorporation. The Philadelphia merchants were convinced, as were merchants elsewhere, of the necessity for measures designed to protect and enhance American commerce, and increasingly they supported the imposition of national retaliatory legislation, including an act confining the exportation of domestic produce to American-owned vessels.[39] Since any effective measure would obviously need the approval of all the states, Coxe, on behalf of the committee, corresponded with nationalist-minded groups in other states. Although those to whom he wrote were presumably already persuaded, he may well have added some slight momentum to the mounting demand for a new government with powers adequate to safeguard and to promote national commerce. In the meantime, the prosperity of his own mercantile

38. "To the Merchants and Traders of Philadelphia," *Pa. Packet*, Nov. 11, 1784. For Coxe's authorship, see Daniel Major to Coxe, Jan. 12, 1785, Coxe Papers. The article was also published in newspapers of other cities. See Lawrence & Morris to Coxe, Nov. 18, 1784, *ibid.*

39. "The memorial of the committee of merchants and traders of the City of Philadelphia," Apr. 6, 1785, in *Pa. Packet*, June 2, 1785. There is a copy of the memorial in the hand of a clerk and with the endorsement of Coxe in the Coxe Papers. It was republished probably at Coxe's request in the *American Museum*, I (1787), 313–314.

firm hinged on exploiting trading ventures that did not demand the aegis of a restructured and more powerful Union. The Orient offered enticing prospects.

"America must trade as much as She possibly can, *directly to the original markets*, or her commerce must be lost," Coxe and Frazier wrote in May 1786. "A direct trade with money or our produce must take place with India, China . . . or other Countries which used to be carried on thro the medium of England, Holland, France and Spain." The profits that such a direct trade might yield to American merchants had been demonstrated by the voyage of the *Empress of China*, which had been dispatched in March 1784 to Canton by a consortium of Boston, New York, and Philadelphia merchants.[40] The ship returned to New York in May 1785 laden, so the *Pennsylvania Packet* reported, "with a full cargo of such articles as we generally import from Europe," thus presaging "a future happy period . . . of our rising empire, and future happy prospects of solid greatness."[41]

The 25 percent profit garnered by *Empress*'s promoters aroused the envy of other merchants, among them Coxe and Frazier, who announced with obvious relish late in October 1786 that "we are part proprietors and agents for one of the India Companies which are now attempting the second Experiment in the trade to China."[42] The other proprietors were well-to-do Philadelphia merchants, and the joint agents were Donnaldson and Coxe, a firm in which Tench's younger brother William was a partner. The "experiment" was to be carried out in the *Canton*, "a fine vessel of 310 tons . . . launched in 1785" and commanded by Captain Thomas Truxtun.[43] The firm of Coxe and Frazier was in an excellent position to garner not only a sizable commission for "half the Agency, which alone is a handsome profit," but also on a good return on their own investment of £800 in the voyage.[44]

By January 1786 the *Canton* was ready to sail. Insurance on the vessel had been arranged through Wakefield and Bell in London; John Frazier

40. Coxe & Frazier to James Wilkie, Oct. 17, 1786, Coxe Papers. Coxe noted that he was intimately acquainted with these merchants, as well as with the ship's captain, and he would (had he not delayed too long) have sent letters of introduction for them to his English correspondents concerned in the China trade. Coxe & Frazier to Wigram, Apr. 23, 1784, *ibid.*

41. *Pa. Packet*, May 16, 1785. For an account of the voyage, see Foster Rhea Dulles, *The Old China Trade* (Boston, 1930); Samuel W. Woodhouse, "The Voyage of the Empress of China," *PMHB*, LXIII (1939), 24–30.

42. Coxe & Frazier to McIlwaine, Oct. 30, 1786, Coxe Papers; Marion V. Brewington, "Maritime Philadelphia, 1609–1837," *PMHB*, LXIII (1939), 114.

43. Coxe & Frazier to Hope & Co., Oct. 21, 1787, *ibid.* According to Eugene S. Ferguson, the *Canton* was originally the *London Packet*, which was owned by Donnaldson & Coxe. Ferguson, *Truxtun of the Constellation: The Life of Commodore Thomas Truxtun, U.S. Navy* (Baltimore, Md., 1956), 62–63, 271.

44. Coxe & Frazier to John and Robert Barclay, Feb. 17, 1787, Coxe Papers.

(a younger brother of Nalbro Frazier) and Truxtun had been designated supercargoes; letters of introduction to English, French, Dutch, and Swedish factors had been prepared; and Truxtun had been supplied by the Continental Congress with a recommendation to the "most serene and most puissant, high, illustrious, noble, honorable, venerable . . . Emperor" and other exalted dignitaries.[45] On January 4 Coxe drafted detailed instructions for Frazier and Truxtun, offering advice on a myriad of anticipated problems, limiting their credit "absolutely to Seven Thousand pounds Sterling" and cautioning them again and again that "as the Ship goes out upon a very small capital . . . the most strict œconomy and frugality" are "indispensibly necessary."[46] The ship was loaded at Coxe and Frazier's wharf with a cargo of ginseng (prized by the Chinese as a restorer of virility to the aged) and assorted articles, and a few days later it dropped down the river, the second American vessel to go to the Orient.

When the *Canton* returned, anchoring in the Delaware on Sunday, May 19, 1787, within sight of the wharves, a crowd of well-wishers gave Captain Truxtun three rousing cheers as he emerged on deck. Once on shore, the captain, so he later recalled, was greeted by "Messrs. John Pringle, John Donnaldson, and Tench Coxe . . . in that kind of way, which affected my very Soul, and at once made me forget, the fatigues I had undergone in the prosecution of so long, tedious, new and hazardous a voyage." None of the "encomiums bestowed on Me," Truxtun related, were more lavish than those of Coxe, who "day after day" continued "paying me the Most profuse Compliments," to which "I could not but think myself intitled."[47] The compliments Truxtun received were indeed deserved. Thanks to his negotiation of credits totaling well over $30,000, he had managed to fill the *Canton* with a cargo (consisting primarily of teas) that "turned out to good profit" —all this despite the modest capital invested by the voyage's backers.[48]

45. For the *Canton's* insurance, see Coxe & Frazier to Wakefield & Bell, May 18, 1787, to John & Robert Barclay, Feb. 17, 1787, *ibid*. For the letters of introduction, see Coxe & Frazier to Wigram, Feb. 25, 1786, *ibid*. See also Coxe & Frazier to Lane, Lance & Fitzhugh, Jan. 3, 1786, to John Henry Coxe, Jan. 3, 1786, to Messr. Dumoulin, Jan. 4, 1786, *ibid*. For the recommendation to the emperor, see Oberholtzer, *Philadelphia: A History*, I, 315. For Coxe & Frazier and Donnaldson & Coxe's memorial of Dec. 22, 1785, to Congress for sea letters for the *Canton*, see Worthington Chauncey Ford *et al*., eds., *Journals of the Continental Congress, 1774–1789* (Washington, D.C., 1904–1937), XXIX, 909, XXX, 5–6.

46. Coxe & Frazier and Donnaldson & Coxe to John Frazier and Thomas Truxton, Jan. 4, 1786, Coxe Papers. Truxtun related that the "whole Capital engaged in the Expedition" was only "35,000 dollars, 17½ Shares of 2000 dollars." "Truxtun's Narrative," May 1, 1789, *ibid*. For his purchases in China, however, a £7,000 credit was, as stated above, authorized. Coxe & Frazier and Donnaldson & Coxe to Frazier and Truxtun, Jan. 4, 1786, *ibid*.

47. "Truxtun's Narrative," May 1, 1789, *ibid*. For Truxtun's account of his activities in Canton, see his letters to Coxe & Frazier, Nov. 15, Dec. 5, 1786, *ibid*.

48. Coxe & Frazier to Hope & Co., Oct. 21, 1787, to Wakefield & Bell, May 26, 1787, *ibid*.

Responding to Coxe's boasts about the money he had made, a Baltimore merchant addressed "my Friend Tenche Coxe Esqr., notwithstanding his *Asiatic* adventures . . . Bravo. 2500£ per annum. It is too much for any man in a FREE Republican Government." Elated by the *Canton*'s venture, which was "more profitable than our most sanguine expectations," Coxe and Frazier, along with the vessel's other backers, promptly decided that "we shall send her again to the same place this season."[49]

By December 1787 a larger group of investors (or ship's "husbands," as they were then called) had subscribed to an expanded capital, Coxe and Frazier once again had been appointed agents, and all was in readiness for a second voyage. The *Canton* refitted at a cost of £3,000, weighed anchor on December 11.[50] Seventeen months later it returned to Philadelphia with a cargo of "teas, nankeens, Canton Cloths . . . Japan ware, Chine Ware, Silks, etc.," with which, according to Coxe, "the owners" were "well-pleased."[51]

---

49. James Buchanan to Coxe, Apr. 29, 1788, Coxe & Frazier to Charles Sigourney, June 23, 1787, *ibid*.

50. The owners were Archibald McCall, Coxe & Frazier, Donnaldson & Coxe, J. Tidball, Keely & Jenkins, and R. James. "Meeting of Owners of Ship Canton," Aug. 10, 1787, *ibid*. There were 23½ shares in the partnership. Coxe & Frazier jointly with William Coxe, Sr., invested about £1,900, one-tenth of the vessel's capital. Coxe & Frazier to Warder, Dearman & Co., Dec. 15, 1787, to Hope & Co., Oct. 21, 1787, *ibid*. Insurance on their own investment was secured from Warder, Dearman & Co. in London. Coxe & Frazier to Warder, Dearman & Co., Dec. 15, 1787, *ibid*. Coxe & Frazier were again joined as agents by Donnaldson & Coxe. The payment allowed them was "a Commission of 2½ per Cent on the amount" of the disbursements for the vessel and the same sum for "goods shipt by her." "Meeting of the Owners of the Ship Canton," June 20, 1787, *ibid*. For the refitting costs, see Coxe and Frazier to Warder, Dearman & Co., Dec. 15, 1787, *ibid*. For date of departure, see Coxe & Frazier to Hope & Co., Dec. 12, 1787, *ibid*.

This time the *Canton* carried as supercargoes two young men from Coxe & Frazier's countinghouse, Samuel Wilcox and Archibald McCall, Jr. Captain Truxtun, who had at first enthusiastically endorsed the two, became disenchanted. "Truxtun's Narrative," May 1, 1789, *ibid*. In appointing the two young men, Truxtun complained, Coxe, on behalf of the ship's agents, not only failed to consult him but reneged on a previous promise that Truxtun himself should be one of the supercargoes, a position he wanted because of the 3% commission allowed. Worse yet, from Truxtun's viewpoint, was a section in his private instructions directing him to take orders from the two young men and "not to let a package come into, or go out of this ship without their written order"—provisos that the captain interpreted as a lack of confidence. Truxtun also claimed that Wilcox and McCall "most cruelly and egregiously Ill used" him. *Ibid*.

Truxtun complained even more about the treatment that he had received from Coxe. In July 1787, six months before the *Canton*'s second venture, Truxtun loaned one Joseph Harrison £1,000 on the basis of Coxe's assurances. *Ibid*. Upon his return from China in 1789, the captain discovered that Harrison was insolvent and blamed Coxe. Coxe to Daniel Ludlow and William Seton, Nov. 23, 1789, *ibid*. Truxtun, represented by William Lewis, Jared Ingersoll, and William Rawle, instituted a suit against Coxe to recover damages. Truxtun to Coxe, Aug. 3, 1789, *ibid*. The litigation dragged on for two years and was decided in Coxe's favor. William Coxe, Jr., to Coxe, Nov. 20, 1791, *ibid*.

51. Coxe & Frazier to Stephen Blackett, June 8, 1789, *ibid*; Coxe to Jeremiah Wadsworth, June 5, 1789, Wadsworth Papers, Connecticut Historical Society, Hartford.

They were, however, far less pleased than they had been with the vessel's first voyage, for, as Coxe explained, "the quality of the Teas" brought "cannot be called the very first," due, he believed, to the fact "that adulteration is practiced with great Skill in China." Even had they been of superior quality, however, they would not have commanded the profits earned on the teas imported two years earlier, for the domestic market was already stocked and several other cargoes from China had arrived simultaneously.[52] What had proved a lucrative trade for Coxe and Frazier had also attracted other American merchants, some of whom, Coxe said in October 1788, "were retired in the War" but "are now coming forward into the India trade with fresh funds and the best Credit," while yet others, among them "those who make the greatest figures in trade," had accumulated large "Capitals in the West India Trade which they cannot now do."[53] So Coxe and Frazier bowed to the dictates of the marketplace and left the China trade to those rich enough to better withstand its risks.

Coxe and Frazier might have counted themselves among those wealthy enough to risk the China trade had they been more careful about the company they kept. Instead, they found themselves in the red due to evasive and sometimes elusive trading partners to whom they had injudiciously extended credits. By the beginning of 1787 business conditions had improved decidedly, and by midsummer it appeared that the possible new government, then being hammered out by the Constitutional Convention in Philadelphia, might usher in a period of booming prosperity. Despite the shaky financial position of Coxe and Frazier, the partners were optimistic about the future. "Our commerce," they commented in the spring of 1787, "is undergoing a revolution which we think will be favorable to the Country and to the people," and, they might have added, to themselves.[54] The revolution was only a fantasy, but commercial conditions were in fact auspicious and, despite an alarming slackening of business activity in 1788, were even more

---

52. Coxe & Frazier to Gelton & Saltonstall, Aug. 22, 1789, Coxe Papers. Coxe & Frazier estimated the number of other ships at three or four. Coxe & Frazier to Stephen Blackett, June 8, 1789, *ibid.* Nevertheless, Coxe & Frazier were convinced that their inventory of £4,000 in teas would "prove a good Speculation." Coxe & Frazier to Gelton & Saltonstall, Aug. 22, 1789, *ibid.*

53. Coxe & Frazier to Wigram, Oct. 22, 1788, *ibid.*

54. Coxe & Frazier to Daniel Crommelin & Sons, Jan. 17, 1787, to Hope & Co., Mar. 15, 1787, *ibid.* In the winter of 1787 Coxe & Frazier reported that sugar commanded "an excellent price" in America and in their view would continue to do so "for a long time, and indeed always hereafter." Coxe & Frazier to Cornelius Hendrickson & Yard, Mar. 12, 1787, to Robert Thomson [Thompson], Jan. 6, 1787, *ibid.* Cotton, they said, was bringing "a noble price," which "must make it a great object." Coxe & Frazier to Hendrickson, May 26, 1787, *ibid.* As with these foreign articles so with local produce. "Our Crops continue to promise capitally," they wrote to Firebrace & Reed on June 25, 1787. *Ibid.* Indeed, all the expenses of business in America, they commented in July, "are reduced above one half since the close of the

favorable in 1789.[55] Coxe and Frazier were by no means laggard in taking profitable advantage of these conditions; the problem was that not even more-than-ordinarily high profits were able to offset the debts due them. Chief among their creditors was the Charleston firm of Scarborough and Cooke, with whom Coxe and Frazier had trustingly offered credit for a joint speculation, expecting to make a quick fortune.[56] When Coxe and Frazier tried to collect the money due them, Scarborough and Cooke managed to evade even the payment of interest and proved singularly adept at avoiding lawyers and lawsuits.[57] Other firms, though owing less, were equally resourceful.[58] As early as the summer of 1786, having some months earlier recklessly executed "orders to the amount of 2/3rds of our Capital," the firm of Coxe and Frazier was aware of financial storm clouds, though unprepared for the forthcoming deluge. "Our" Tench Coxe, the firm wrote to a London creditor in July, "has now . . . above £4,000 of monies due him on open accounts since 1782 and 83 and he cannot collect as much as will pay a

War." Coxe & Frazier to John Ross, July 31, 1787, *ibid.* The upsurge in foreign commerce was owing to enlarged trade with the islands of St. Croix, St. Eustatius, and the French Islands (Coxe & Frazier to William Barton, Aug. 26, 1787, to Hendrickson, June 16, 1787, *ibid.*) rather than with the British colonies. Coxe & Frazier to Torver, July 31, 1787, *ibid.*

55. Although Coxe & Frazier asserted that 1788 "was *not* a favorable year," exports of flour from the port of Philadelphia nevertheless increased. In 1786 they reported that 150,000 barrels of flour were exported; in 1787, 200,000; and in 1788, 220,000. Coxe & Frazier to Strange, Dowell & Co., July 8, 1789, to Stephen Blackett, June 22, 1789, to Cologan, Pollard & Cooper, July 13, 1789, *ibid.*

56. For many possible examples of Coxe & Frazier's descriptions of their terms of trade, see Coxe & Frazier to George Seiben, Sept. 25, 1784, to Hope & Co., Oct. 3, 1784, to Dillworth & Baines, Apr. 6, 1785, to Bruily & Harrigan, May 9, 1785, to Woolrich & Gillon, June 11, 1785, to William Arthur & Co., Sept. 15, 1785, to Blake & Stuart, Sept. 16, 1785, to Thomson [Thompson], Aug. 9, 1786, to Adam Sobother, May 26, 1787, to John Monro, June 27, 1787, to William Barton, Aug. 31, 1787, to Robert D. Holliday, Mar. 21, 1788, to Benjamin Hunting, Nov. 18, 1789, *ibid.*

57. There are scores of pages devoted to this protracted and complicated affair in Coxe & Frazier's and in Coxe's own letterbooks. The story was, in brief, this: Coxe & Frazier and Scarborough & Cooke in 1784 had signed a contract for the delivery of dry goods valued at £7,000. Soon thereafter the two firms entered into an agreement for a joint speculation in tea, valued at £3,600. When news of a sharp drop in the price of tea being auctioned at the L'Orient market reached the U.S., the two firms hastily amended their contractural arrangements. Instead of paying the agreed-upon deposit of £3,500 on the dry goods, William Cooke (the London representative of the firm of Scarborough & Cooke) proposed that that sum immediately be raised and spent for the purchase of the tea at L'Orient. Coxe & Frazier accepted the proposal. Coxe & Frazier to Lane, Son & Frazier, Aug. 17, 1784, *ibid.* But Cooke's financial position was so shaky that he could not secure the loan, and the teas were sold. Now Scarborough & Cooke were unwilling to pay the £7,000 due for dry goods. Under the pressure of a lawsuit instituted by Coxe & Frazier's attorneys in 1787, the Charleston merchants did assign to them certain bonds, but these turned out to be worth considerably less than purported, and in 1794, a decade after the original contract, some $10,000 remained unpaid. Coxe & Frazier to Moses Levy, Oct. 30, 1794, *ibid.* Nor, so far as Coxe's accounts reveal, was it ever paid.

58. For information on debts owed to and by Coxe & Frazier, see Coxe & Frazier to Patrick

baker's bill." In April 1787 Coxe and Frazier complained that "the difficulty of collections in this Country and the delay of our remittances from almost every part of the West Indies have plagued us exceedingly thro' the last year"; six months later they confided to their New York partners, Ludlow and Goold, that although they had "made money in business" and their "Commission business remains valuable beyond any former times," they found themselves "more pressed for money than has ever been the case." By January 1789 Frazier wrote to Coxe, then in New York as a delegate to the Continental Congress: "How we shall get through our money engagements I am sure I cannot tell . . . nor do I see any probability of collecting anything shortly."[59] In view of their own debts and depleted capital, it was imperative that they collect at least some of the "£11,000 outstanding in what we consider the best hands."[60] The effort must have been unsuccessful. Most of the money due the firm was still in the hands of their debtors when Coxe left the partnership in May 1790 to assist Alexander Hamilton in devising ways to pay the nation's public creditors.

Coxe would have left his countinghouse a rich man had it not been for bad debts; instead he left a well-to-do one. If he had chosen to continue his mercantile ventures rather than enter a public career, he would have made much more, given the flush times the country enjoyed in the 1790s and the early nineteenth century. As it was, he convinced himself that he could serve the public and get rich too. Land speculation was to be the means.

Although Coxe had contracted his forebears' land fever, his preoccupation with land speculation was too typical of his day to be attributed merely to that contagion. Land speculation was almost the only outlet for savings besides trade, and few men with capital to spare failed to participate

Lynch, Aug. 28, 1786, to Bell & La Touche, Aug. 29, 1786, to Elliot & Maurery, Jan. 8, 1787, to John and Robert Barclay & Co., Jan. 20, 1787, to Herriot & Tucker, Mar. 13, 1787, to Thomas Dickerson, Mar. 13, 1787, to Crockett & Harris, Apr. 12, 1787, to Dillworth & Baines, Dec. 22, 1787, to Arthur & Co., Mar. 22, 1788, Nov. 23, 1789, to Wigram, Oct. 22, 1788, to James Kingston, Dec. 1, 1788, to Jonathan O'Donnell, Jan. 16, 1790, to Josiah Parker, Feb. 1, 1790, to William Blake, Mar. 20, 1790, to Gelston & Saltonstall, Feb. 6, 1791, William Tilghman to Coxe, Feb. 4, 1787, Nalbro Frazier to Coxe, Jan. 15, Feb. 15, 1789, Wakefield & Bell to Coxe & Frazier, Jan. 7, 1790, Wigram to Coxe, Mar. 1, 1790, William Coxe, Jr., to Coxe, Mar. 9, 1790, Goold to Coxe & Frazier, Oct. 6, 1790, *ibid.*

59. Coxe & Frazier to Thomas Woolrich, Jr., May 13, 1786, to Thomas Dickerson, July 20, 1786, to Arthur & Co., Apr. 2, 1787, to Ludlow & Goold, Oct. 27, 1787, Frazier to Coxe, Jan. 15, 1789, *ibid.*

60. Coxe & Frazier to Yard & Hennen, Feb. 25, 1788, *ibid.* See also Coxe & Frazier to Julines Herving, Apr. 7, 1788, to Cornelius Hendrickson, May 20, 1788, to Wakefield & Bell, Nov. 15, 1788, *ibid.* In a letter written in Dec. 1788, Coxe & Frazier explained their situation as follows: "Various very large sums of Money are due to us from persons, who live in States

in this period's economic extravaganza. Coxe was not only cast in this role by family tradition but also prepared by an apprenticeship as his father's land agent. In addition to his share of the New York estate granted to the Coxes in exchange for relinquishment of the Carolana claim, William Coxe, Sr., had acquired extensive landholdings in Pennsylvania, which upon his retirement from business he entrusted to the management of his son. Tench also served as American agent for Sir Philip Francis, for Andrew Allen, for David Franks, and for others.[61]

Coxe's own career as a land speculator was given a boost by his father-in-law, Charles Coxe, who had provided as his daughter's dowry a share of a large land purchase he had recently made in Pennsylvania. From that beginning Tench cautiously began during the 1780s to establish what in time would be a landed empire. In 1782 he purchased a farm, Pidgeon Run, in Delaware, near New Castle; in 1783 he acquired a tract of land on the road from Philadelphia to York and with Benjamin Rush bought adjoining lands elsewhere in Pennsylvania. In 1784 his purchases included eight thousand acres of land in the western part of the commonwealth and, in partnership with his brother John, an extensive area in New York state between the Mohawk and Susquehanna rivers. Sometime during the decade he also acquired a sizable farm near Hartford, Maryland, a number of lots on Primrose Alley in Baltimore, and, by means of a complicated business transaction, a mortgage (held with other Philadelphia creditors of Joseph Harrison, an insolvent) on fifty-five thousand acres of land in Virginia.[62] Most gratifying

---

where the Laws are badly executed. In the fall of 1787 we had every reason to expect large and constant payments and remittances. We therefore went on as usual discounting at Bank bills of exchange and Notes for Goods, and paying and remitting even before hand, for before November 1787 we are bold to say our Correspondents always had advances equal to one fifth of our Commissions reckoning the simple Interest. Then we found, or rather in January, and February large Sums were delayed and little of them yet received and then for the first time began to fear we should not make our payments as we wished, but yet you will find offered to remit in produce. . . ." Coxe & Frazier to Hendrickson, Dec. 5, 1788, *ibid.*

61. See Coxe to Benjamin Andrews, Dec. 16, 1778, Enoch Edwards to Coxe, Oct. 7, 1779, *ibid.*

62. The dowry lands were located in the Tuscarora region of Pennsylvania. See Richard Peters to Coxe, Feb. 28, 1782, John Coxe to Coxe, Mar. 5, 1782, Charles Coxe to Coxe, Apr. 10, Aug. 18, 1782, *ibid.* For the Pidgeon Run lands, see Thomas Montgomery to Coxe, Mar. 9, Apr. 17, 1782, Forman & Chambers to Coxe, Dec. 2, 1782, *ibid.* For Coxe's 1783 purchases, see Charles Young to Coxe, Mar. 17, 1783, Jonathan Williams to Coxe, June 27, 1783, *ibid.* For his 1784 purchases, see "Inventory of Land," Apr. 1789, "Schedual [sic] of Pennsylvania Land," Oct. 1, 1789, *ibid.*; Warrantee Lists, *Pa. Archives*, 3d Ser., XXIV, 655, XXV, 68, 151, 303. Since land was not always purchased directly by the prospective owner, the name on the warrantee list was often of an intermediary. In this case a portion of the land was warranted to Ball, Stigafoose, and perhaps Gartly for Coxe, Stedman, and Jackson. For Coxe's New York lands, see John D. Coxe to Coxe, Nov. 29, 1784, Coxe Papers. Some of Coxe's New York land was later sold by William Cooper for £8,000. William Coxe, Jr., to Coxe, Aug. 21, 1790, *ibid.*

of all for Coxe was the opportunity to join other speculators in snapping up a large chunk of valuable land in the Wyoming Valley, recently opened to public purchase by a liberal land law passed in 1784.

Among his speculator partners in the Wyoming Valley transaction were Coxe's close friends Timothy Pickering and Samuel Hodgdon, Pickering's business partner. In April 1785 these three men and their associates contracted for sixty-three thousand acres located on the west bank of the Susquehanna River in what was then Luzerne and Lycoming counties. Coxe's share of about eight thousand acres cost roughly $4,000, which he paid in public securities. Despite the unsettled conditions in the Wyoming country, occasioned by the land war between the Connecticut settlers and the state of Pennsylvania, lands in the area appeared to Coxe and his partners worth the risks involved. In 1787 Coxe, Pickering, and Hodgdon (this time in company with another group of speculators) purchased an additional twenty thousand acres, of which Coxe acquired about five thousand. The lands, larded with minerals, were of incalculable value, and Coxe, aware of their potential, held onto his for a lifetime. Although these lands eventually contributed to making him land-poor, they made his descendants coal-rich.[63]

During the remaining years of the decade, Coxe gradually enlarged his landholdings in the Wyoming Valley and in other sections of Pennsylvania, notably in Bedford and Northampton counties. His interest in these lands and the realization that internal improvements would enhance their value encouraged him to support the construction of roads and canals in the northeastern corner of the commonwealth and elsewhere. He was one of the state commissioners responsible for building roads in Northampton and Luzerne counties, a member of the Pennsylvania Society for the Improvement of Roads and Inland Navigation, and, in Benjamin Rush's words, an instigator "of a scheme of rendering the Susquehanna navigable," proposing "to defray the expenses of it by means of an incorporated company."[64]

For Coxe's Maryland purchases, see Daniel W. Coxe to Coxe, Aug. 31, Sept. 20, 1790, *ibid.* There are also a number of undated surveys and maps of this Maryland farm in the Coxe Papers. For Coxe's ownership of the city lots, see Coxe to William Cooke, Aug. 12, 1815, *ibid.* For the entangled affairs dealing with Coxe's Virginia purchase, see the papers involving Henry Charton, Albert Gallatin, Joseph Harrison, Truxtun, Jean Savary de Valcoulon, Coxe & Frazier, and Tench Coxe for the years from 1784 to 1797, *ibid.*

63. See "Declaration, Articles of Agreement, and Deed" between Coxe, Timothy Pickering, and Samuel Hodgdon, Apr. 6, 1785, "rough calculation of the lands of Pickering, Hodgdon, Coxe, Ingraham & Co.," May 1785, "List of Certificates Paid Land office May 10, 1785—paid for Lands with Potter, Pickering, Fisher, Ingraham, Hodgdon, and Wikoff," "Account of Certificates delivered in to the Land Office, May 10, 1785 . . . ," John Young to Coxe, July 22, 1787, *ibid.*

64. See *Minutes of the Supreme Executive Council . . . (Colonial Records of Pennsylvania* [Harrisburg, Pa., 1853]), XV, 425, 445; Coxe to Andrew Craige, Apr. 3, 1788, to Picker-

Despite his mounting enthusiasm for land speculation, however, Coxe remained during the 1780s a prudently cautious investor, largely because he still had most of his money invested in trade. As he commented in January 1787, obliquely referring to the profitability of both regular and clandestine trade, "Several new objects produced by the Revolution have presented themselves to our monied men, and engage their Funds which were formerly" invested in lands.[65] As time would tell, his own money might more prudently have been applied to these "new objects" rather than to land speculation.

---

ing, May 22, 1788, to John Nicholson, Aug. 6, 1788, Robert C. Livingston to Coxe, Oct. 23, 1788, Coxe Papers; Norman B. Wilkinson, "Land Policy and Speculation in Pennsylvania, 1779–1800" (Ph.D. diss., University of Pennsylvania, 1958), 130–131; Benjamin Rush to Pickering, Jan. 29, 1788, [Octavius Pickering] and Charles W. Upham, *The Life of Timothy Pickering* (Boston, 1867–1873), II, 373–374; Charles Coxe to Coxe, Mar. 20, 1788, Furman to Coxe, Apr. 5, 1788, Coxe Papers.

65. Coxe & Frazier to John Barnes, Jan. 22, 1787, Coxe Papers.

5

Publicist and
Political Economist

Of all the decades in American history, an ambitious, upper-class man would perhaps have found the 1780s most propitious. To Coxe it was the happiest period of his life. Not only did he exude confidence and optimism about his own and his country's future, but he was also a contented family man. He was deeply attached to Rebecca—once described by Richard Tilghman as "the handsomest Woman in America"—as he was also to his three children born during this decade, Ann Rebecca, Tench, Jr., and Francis Sidney.[1] The Coxes' life was a comfortable one. By the time Tench celebrated his thirtieth birthday on May 22, 1785, he had acquired rather more than that "genteel subsistence" that a decade earlier he too modestly had said was the limit of his ambition. He was thus able to live in a style befitting a successful merchant, though not on the scale of Philadelphia tycoons like William Bingham, from whom Coxe rented a large house at the corner of Front and Pine streets.[2] The family did have enough servants to permit Rebecca Coxe to share with her husband the pleasures of Philadelphia society.

That the social life of the city's elite was, as befitted the new nation's principal metropolis, now much more republican in tone was suggested by Coxe's reputed comment "that on a survey of . . . Philadelphia, after the

1. William Tilghman to Coxe, July 24, 1783, Coxe Papers.
2. Charles Coxe to Coxe, Apr. 11, 1785, *ibid*. According to the tax records of Philadelphia County, in 1783 Coxe paid an "Effective Supply Tax" on 4 acres of land; this must have been the property on which his countinghouse was situated, plus additional land owned by him. *Pa. Archives*, 3d Ser., XVI, 610.

Revolutionary War, . . . not a single native American was found in livery." Although aristocratic trappings may have disappeared, upper-class society was still largely confined to successful merchants, large land owners, wealthy Quakers, and well-to-do Anglicans like Coxe, who was a pewholder and warden at St. Peter's Church.[3]

The social scene was active enough to satisfy the most intrepid party-goer. Winters were brightened by suppers, soirees, and balls, many of which the Coxes attended.[4] They were a handsome pair—Rebecca's short stature and dark hair offered a striking contrast to Tench, who was lean and tall, his sandy hair lightly powdered. Rebecca, an especially talented musician at a time when society ladies were expected to be at least proficient ones, was a welcome addition to the city's more elegant drawing rooms. Tench also adorned society, displaying an uncommon adeptness at flattery, even in an age when it was the common coin of conversation.[5] However, the Coxes' social life was not confined to the small circle of Philadelphia's elite. They frequently entertained friends and relatives from New York, Maryland, and Delaware and merchants from the West Indies, as well as foreigners like Jacques Pierre Brissot de Warville and members of the city's tiny diplomatic community, including Phineas Bond, the English consul, and Louis Guillaume Otto, the French envoy.[6] Summers were relieved by vacations at the homes of their parents in Sunbury and Sidney—visits prompted not only by familial loyalty but by a desire to escape the searing city heat and the dreaded yellow fever that periodically struck Philadelphia in late summer and early fall. Although Coxe was usually able to stay away from his countinghouse for only a few weeks, his wife and young children remained in the country from June to October, much to the joy of the grandparents, especially Charles Coxe, who viewed Rebecca's residence in Philadelphia as something of an exile.

One unsatisfactory feature of Coxe's otherwise comfortable personal life was the absence of the Tilghmans and the Allens, families that included relatives of whom he was fondest. He continued frequently to exchange letters with William Tilghman, who, having sat out the war in rural Maryland and having now qualified for the bar in that state, found himself a vic-

3. "Memoirs of a Senator from Pennsylvania, Jonathan Roberts, 1771–1854," *PMHB*, LXII (1938), 242; C. P. B. Jefferys, "The Provincial and Revolutionary History of St. Peter's Church, Philadelphia, 1753–1783," *PMHB*, XLVIII (1924), 355. See also William White to Coxe, May 29, 1781, Coxe Papers.

4. Coxe was a manager of the Dancing Assembly. Daniel W. Coxe to Coxe, May 12, 1790, Coxe Papers.

5. Observing that all people are receptive to "Genteel Flattery," Coxe's friend James Buchanan of Baltimore said that "few men can administer a more palatable Dose than Mr. T. C. —Our Friend Doctor Rxxx excepted." Buchanan to Coxe, Aug. 3, 1788, *ibid.*

6. Chaumont to Coxe, Sept. 2, 1788, Louis Guillaume Otto to Coxe, June 22, 1784, *ibid.*

tim of the war's backlash, struggling "even for the liberty of exercising" his profession. Coxe, distressed by such "cruel" attacks, implored his cousin to escape the fury of the storm by moving to Philadelphia.[7] He also urged his sister Sarah Allen and her family to return there from England, but Andrew Allen, having once made the decision to flee what he termed "the mischiefs and Distresses" of an independent America, was not receptive. For her part, Sarah Allen, concerned more about her favorite brother's secure future than his country's prospects, insisted that Coxe steer clear of politics, contenting "himself with being as I know he is an ardent well wisher to the interests of America."[8]

That Coxe did manage to remain aloof from politics must have required (at least in the light of his intense partisan involvement during subsequent decades) a herculean effort of will. His success doubtless reflected a keen awareness that to enter the political arena would be to invite a bright spotlight on his tory past. Nevertheless, he was an avid spectator of the partisan battles of the 1780s, from which he learned some of the techniques he himself would later employ. It was during this period that he came to see politics as a game of attack and counterattack, innuendo and slander, to which the code of a Philadelphia gentleman was inapplicable.

Pennsylvania politics were ill suited to those who clung to the punctilios of the gentry. The state constitution of 1776 was the most democratic in America, incorporating the familiar eighteenth-century standards of ultrademocracy: a single legislature, a plural executive, a judiciary with limited tenure, and, its most controversial feature, a council of censors designed to take cognizance of legislative breaches of the organic law. Largely because of its "radical" provisions, the constitution itself was the basic issue—the touchstone of state politics—during the Confederation era as it had been during the Revolution. Those who supported it were known as "Constitutionalists," a group that included Benjamin Franklin, George Bryan, John Bayard, Timothy Matlack, John Smilie, and William Findley. Opponents of the constitution were designated "Anti-Constitutionalists," though they preferred the label "Republicans," and included George Clymer, Benjamin Rush, James Wilson, and Robert Morris, men who by later terminology would have been termed conservatives. These men argued that the constitution lacked adequate checks and balances and a proper distribution of power; the Constitutionalists countered that it was an exemplary democratic document to which only aristocrats could possibly object. Coxe did not say

---

7. James Tilghman to Coxe, Feb. 1, Aug. 14, 1783, *ibid.*; Coxe to William Tilghman, May 4, 1784, Tilghman Papers, Hist. Soc. Pa., Philadelphia. James Tilghman informed Coxe on Apr. 27, 1784, that "Billy has triumphed over his Enemies and has obtained a Mandamus from the Supreme Court to restore him to his practice." Coxe Papers.
8. Sarah Allen to Molly Coxe, Jan. 30, 1789, *ibid.*

where his sympathies lay, insisting that "I am of no party" and avowing, with pardonable exaggeration, that he had "the supreme felicity of being friends with all."[9] Nevertheless, by instinct, principle, and preference, as well as by the company he kept, it seems reasonable to assume that on most issues he favored the Republicans.

Although Coxe eschewed direct participation in politics, he exercised no similar restraint in speaking out on the leading economic issues of the time.These were, of course, also political questions, but his arbitrary distinction reflected Coxe's increasing interest and expertness in manufacturing, agriculture, trade, money, and banking. It was, appropriately enough, a politically inspired dispute surrounding the Bank of North America that prompted him to break his self-imposed ban of silence on controversial issues. Designed to shore up the new nation's crumbling financial situation, the bank had been proposed by Robert Morris, superintendent of finance under the Confederation, and had been incorporated by the Continental Congress on December 31, 1781.[10] It was capitalized at $400,000 (subscribed in specie) and authorized to issue notes receivable in payment of duties and taxes. Located in Philadelphia and also chartered by Pennsylvania, the bank, under the direction of Coxe's brother-in-law Thomas Willing, served the fiscal needs of both nation and state. To merchants like Coxe, an original subscriber of four shares at $400 each and a large depositor, it afforded a chance for a profitable investment and met important needs of the mercantile community.[11] Yet the Bank of North America, like the First and Second Banks of the United States, was unpopular, and for similar reasons. Its purportedly excessive capital, small number of directors, and unspecified duration led to the charge that it wielded a degree of power intolerable in a democratic state, and its opponents (prefiguring the subsequent reactions of the Jeffersonians and Jacksonians to the Bank of the United States) made its reform, or else its abolition, a cornerstone of their political program. So it was that the Constitutionalists, in the words of a prominent nineteenth-century historian, "began a mad assault upon the institution. . . .

9. Coxe to David S. Franks, Nov. 26, 1787, *ibid.*; Coxe, *Cool Thoughts on the Subject of the Bank. Addressed to the Honorable the Representatives of the Freemen of the Commonwealth of Pennsylvania in General Assembly* ([Philadelphia], 1786), 3.

10. Bray Hammond, *Banks and Politics in America from the Revolution to the Civil War* (Princeton, N.J., 1957), 48–50.

11. Lawrence J. Lewis, *A History of the Bank of North America: The First Bank Chartered in the United States* (Philadelphia, 1882), 133. Coxe had also arranged purchases of bank stock for his uncle James Tilghman, who owned a sizable block of 13 shares. *Ibid.*, 134. As to Coxe's own deposits, a writer in the *Independent Gaz.*, Nov. 25, 1788, asserted that "when the Bank of North America was established and was considered essential to the payment of our army, he [Coxe] deposited with them in the first year fifty-eight thousand dollars in specie."

Its wealth, its political influence, its opposition to paper money marked it for destruction."[12]

In the meantime, another group of Pennsylvanians, of which Coxe was the leader, was making plans of a different kind. Accepting the Bank of North America as a viable and desirable institution, they wished only to destroy its monopoly by establishing another bank. They were not so much opposed to all banks as to the special advantages and limited number of shareholders of one bank. Ironically enough, their program of opposition was launched immediately after an announcement on January 12, 1784, that stock of the Bank of North America would be increased by one thousand shares at $500 a share.

Speaking of the proposed rival institution, the bank's official historian commented that a "number of influential citizens saw and envied the success of the Bank of North America" and "were anxious to participate in the profits of so lucrative a business" without paying so high a price for its shares.[13] More likely, Coxe's group wished for an opportunity to participate in the ownership and direction, as well as the benefits, of a new institution.[14] Some years later a newspaper critic wrote that "it is well known in the City" that Coxe in company "with some others projected the establishment of another" institution "in opposition" to the Bank of North America because he had not been "honored with a place in the direction."[15] In any event, the proposal for a rival institution was launched in January 1784 with a "Plan for Establishing a New Bank in the City of Philadelphia, by the name of the Bank of Pennsylvania," drafted by Coxe and published at his instigation in the *Pennsylvania Packet*. The promoters, keenly aware of the manifest "utility" of the Bank of North America, were prompted, Coxe explained, only by the wish to found another institution "as nearly similar to it as shall be found proper, in order that the benefits arising therefrom may be extended to a greater length than one institution of that kind can be expected to reach to." Coxe's "Plan for Establishing a New Bank" called for the issuance of shares of stock at $400 each and stipulated that whenever

12. Oberholtzer, *Philadelphia: A History*, I, 320.

13. Lewis, *Bank of North America*, 51.

14. Janet Wilson in her authoritative article on the Bank of North America correctly perceived that "support for the new organization [the proposed Bank of Pennsylvania] was evidently drawn from those who had no grievances against the Bank of North America but thought that competition was good for any business" and "those who wanted to invest in a cheaper bank stock than one at $500 a share." But in view of the economic status of the incorporators of the Bank of Pennsylvania (as described in the text above), she is surely mistaken in saying that its promoters "thought they discerned a menace to agrarian democracy in the Bank of North America." Wilson, "The Bank of North America and Pennsylvania Politics, 1781–1787," *PMHB*, LXVI (1942), 4.

15. *Independent Gaz.*, Nov. 26, 1788.

seven hundred should be sold, the subscribers should meet, adopt a constitution, and elect officers.[16]

Far from being "rising entrepreneurs" or "men on the make" (terms recent historians have applied to the early nineteenth-century advocates of state banks as rivals to the Bank of the United States), the promoters of the Bank of Pennsylvania were, like Coxe, well-established businessmen, including "some of the wealthiest Merchants." The list included eminent whig merchants like Samuel Powel, John Bayard, George Emlen, Jared Ingersoll, Jr., and George Meade, as well as former tories or "neutrals" like Coxe, Archibald McCall (Coxe's relative by marriage), Edward Shippen (Tench's uncle), and Samuel Pleasants. It also included a good number of men who were also stockholders in the Bank of North America—Tench himself, Emlen, Meade, Powel, Shippen, John Pringle, and John B. Church, one of its largest shareholders.[17] Although some joint subscribers, like Church, may merely have been running with the hares and hunting with the hounds, such an interlocking ownership and directorate clearly indicates that the sponsors of the new bank were not motivated by hostility to the older institution but rather by the wish to profit from an extension of banking facilities.

By January 31 subscriptions to the new bank had exceeded seven hundred shares, and the stockholders were requested to attend an organizational meeting at the City Tavern on February 5. At this meeting a constitution, presumably drafted by Coxe, was adopted.[18] Thirteen directors —among them Coxe and such large investors as McCall, Powel, John Steinmetz, Emlen, and Pleasants—were chosen, and a petition to the state assembly praying the incorporation of a new bank with a capital of $280,000 was agreed to and signed. The same day the new directors elected Edward Shippen president, appointed Coxe secretary, and authorized the employment of a cashier and the purchase of a bank building.[19] Whether or not he was the prime instigator of the new institution (and he appears to have been), Coxe shouldered the major share of the work involved in launching it. He carried on the search for a cashier, maintained lists of stockholders,

16. *Pa. Packet*, Jan. 22, 1784. The advertisement also appeared in other issues of that newspaper. See "Account," Jan. 22–Mar. 13, 1784, Coxe Papers.

17. John Chaloner to Alexander Hamilton, Jan. 21, 1784, Syrett *et al.*, eds., *Hamilton Papers*, III, 497; Lewis, *Bank of North America*, 133, 135.

18. *Pa. Packet*, Jan. 31, 1784. In Coxe's papers there is a copy of the constitution, in the hand of a clerk and endorsed "this Copy not right" by Coxe.

19. "Minutes of Stockholders Meetings," Feb. 5, 1784, "Minutes of the Board of Directors," Feb. 5, 21, 1784, Coxe Papers. See also John Thom Holdsworth, *Financing an Empire: History of Banking in Pennsylvania*, I (Chicago, 1928), 55; Lewis, *Bank of North America*, 52. Coxe's minutes of 5 meetings of the directors are in the Coxe Papers. Since the board met 16 times from Feb. 5 to Mar. 20 (see "List of Expenses at City Tavern," Coxe Papers), Coxe presumably misplaced the remaining minutes.

solicited subscriptions from friends and relatives far and near, and was instrumental in a concerted effort to enlist the aid of Philadelphia's members of the state assembly in support of the proposed charter.[20] This support was presumably secured, and, promptly upon presentation on February 10, the petition for the new bank was referred to a committee, dominated by its supporters, who two weeks later reported favorably.[21]

That such well-laid plans went awry may be attributed to the shrewd maneuvers of the directors of the Bank of North America. Their first step, taken on February 26, 1784, was a counterattack: a petition to the assembly "praying that they might be heard, by council, for the purpose of shewing Reasons why this Bank ought not to be incorporated."[22] Their second move, taken on March 1, was one of conciliation: an offer to increase the stock of the older bank by four thousand shares and to reduce the price per share to $400 in order to give rivals an opportunity to partake of the bank's privileges and profits. The scheme was an unalloyed success. The stockholders and directors of the Bank of Pennsylvania, Coxe included, eagerly swallowed the proffered bait, withdrawing the petition for a charter and avidly purchasing shares in the Bank of North America.[23]

In the politically charged atmosphere of 1784 and 1785 prudence would have dictated that the wealth and power of that bank be cloaked, not advertised. It was a time of acute depression and of sharp partisan rivalry, and the bank, controlled by the richest group in the Republican (Conservative) party, was highly vulnerable. The bank was also on shaky ground because of its firm opposition to a state emission of paper money, which the Constitutionalists saw as a panacea for the economic troubles of the 1780s. In firm control of the assembly, the Constitutionalists saw only one stumbling block to success: the unwillingness of the Bank of North America to accept paper on the same terms as specie. That institution's insistence on dealing only in specie was strongly supported by a committee of twelve prominent Philadelphia merchants (many of them friends of the bank), who in March 1785 drew up a petition describing the perils of a paper issue and

20. See "Minutes of the Board of Directors," Feb. 5, 9, 18, 1784, Nathaniel Banks to Coxe, Feb. 9, 1784, B. Fuller to Coxe, Feb. 5, 1784, Edward Goold to Coxe, Feb. 7, 1784, James Tilghman to Coxe, Jan. 30, 1784, William McIlwaine to Coxe, Feb. 17, 1784, Walter Livingston to Coxe, Apr. 4, 1784, Coxe Papers.

21. *Minutes of the Second Session of the Eighth General Assembly of the Commonwealth of Pennsylvania* (Philadelphia, 1784), 123–124, 149.

22. "Minutes of the Board of Directors," Feb. 26, 1784, Coxe Papers.

23. *Minutes of the Eighth General Pennsylvania Assembly,* 186. Coxe, for the joint account of himself and his business partner, Nalbro Frazier, purchased 2 shares, Joseph Swift 5 shares, Samuel Howell 27 shares, John Steinmetz 30 shares, and Jeremiah Warder 4 shares. The business partnership of Tench's brother William—Donnaldson & Coxe—purchased 20 shares. Lewis, *Bank of North America,* 140–147.

urging the state assembly to eschew fiscal irresponsibility. Coxe, as consistent a critic of paper currency as he was scornful of quasi-public banks that served only private interests, was among the petitioners.[24]

However well-intentioned Coxe and his fellow merchants were, their memorial was impolitic and predictably futile. The legislature, dominated by Constitutionalists, considered such support of the bank's position as a demonstration of that institution's subservience to the rich and influential mercantile interest, and it responded by promptly authorizing an issue of £150,000 in paper bills of credit. The victorious majority now moved to punish its powerful antagonist by voting on September 13, 1785, to repeal the bank's charter.[25] While the crippled institution continued to limp along under its congressional charter, its supporters castigated the action of the legislature as an unwarranted invasion of the rights of private property and an unconstitutional impairment of an inviolable contract. Their only recourse, however, was to accept the tactics of their opponents and to restore the charter by winning control of the legislature. They appeared to have done just this the following year when, after an election in which the recharter of the bank was a major issue, a committee of the assembly, responding to a deluge of probank petitions, recommended revocation of the repeal. When the legislature rejected the proposal on the eve of its adjournment on April 1, 1786, the probank forces reinforced an appeal to the courts with a pamphlet addressed to the state's electorate.

Coxe, foreseeing "a deal of confusion and difference" in Philadelphia over the controversy, initially "determined to keep clear of it."[26] But having persuaded himself that resolution of the issue depended neither on repeal nor on replication (as its intractable detractors and supporters variously contended) but on reform, he decided to publish his views. Since the authorship of anonymous articles was usually no secret to the city's cognoscenti, it was an act of personal courage in the sense that it jeopardized the continued support of influential acquaintances (among them Thomas Willing, James Wilson, and Thomas FitzSimons) who were either directors or ardent supporters of the bank. His *Thoughts concerning the Bank of North America* was published on December 6, 1786, and (forecasting the prolixity that in the future would mar even his finest performances) two other pamphlets followed in quick succession—*Further Thoughts concerning the Bank* and *Cool Thoughts on the Bank*.[27] Coxe took the position that a bank "wisely

---

24. The petition was printed in the *Pa. Gaz.*, Mar. 2, 1785.

25. *Minutes of the Second Session of the Ninth General Assembly of the Commonwealth of Pennsylvania* (Philadelphia, 1785), 13, 333–370. A good account of the legislative fight against the bank can be found in Wilson, "Bank of North America," *PMHB*, LXVI (1942), 6–9.

26. Coxe to unknown recipient, Jan. 13, 1786, Coxe Papers.

27. [Coxe], *Thoughts concerning the Bank of North America; with some facts relating to*

and justly constructed, would be a public good." The legislature, he said, had been ill advised in destroying an institution that it should have regulated. To provide the assembly with some historical perspective for judging the operations of the Bank of North America, Coxe compared it with other banks, ancient and modern, concluding that the "bank of England is better worth our attention than any which has ever existed, whether we consider it with regard to the prodigious aids it has afforded to the government, or its usefulness to the commercial and manufacturing interests and, through these, to the cultivators of the soil." To what extent was the Philadelphia bank subject to the same type of public control exercised over the English institution? Coxe took issue with those who argued that the bank was merely a trading company and therefore not a proper object of legislative surveillance and regulation. Rather, he believed, the bank should properly be viewed "as a branch of the political economy, important in its magnitude and in its operations and effects." Incorporated banks, he said, arise from "public occasions, and have been instituted to answer public ends." Paradoxically enough, the United States was the only free government to "have endowed a wealthy corporation with powers and privileges opposed to freedom and equality," and this in the face of the examples to be drawn from the history of other nations.[28]

Coxe's biting arraignment of the corporate offenses and public irresponsibility of the Bank of North America was accompanied by recommendations for its reform. Let the legislature restore the bank, he said, but let the new charter be something more than a patchwork reform merely limiting the institution's duration and the amount of its stock. He suggested that the bank "be new modelled, so as to harmonize with the Government of this country, and with the present state of trade and commerce" and proposed that the new plan for the Bank of North America be "substantially the same as that of the Bank of England."[29] While probank pamphleteers like Thomas

---

such establishments in other countries, respectfully submitted to the honorable the General Assembly of Pennsylvania, by one of their Constituents ([Philadelphia?], 1786); [Coxe], Further Thoughts concerning the Bank, respectfully submitted to the Honorable the General Assembly of Pennsylvania, by one of their Constituents (n.p., 1786); Coxe, Cool Thoughts, probably published in Philadelphia on Dec. 11 or 12, 1786. On Dec. 13 the Pa. Gaz. announced that "Cool Thoughts" is "just published by Charles Cist in Race Street."

28. [Coxe], Thoughts concerning the Bank of North America, 1, 2, 5, 4.

29. Coxe, Cool Thoughts, 16; and [Coxe], Further Thoughts concerning the Bank, 7. The same opinion was expressed in a petition to the Pennsylvania General Assembly by a group of "Subscribers, Stock-holders in the Bank of North America." An undated draft of the petition in the Coxe Papers, in the hand of a clerk and including a number of deletions, suggests that Coxe was its author. The petition stated that "your Petitioners have considered the Constitution of the Bank of England and are inclined to believe that the Public Credit of that Nation . . . is principally owing to the wise regulations of their Bank, wherefore they would recommend to the

Paine, James Wilson, and Pelatiah Webster exercised considerable influence on public opinion, Coxe was the ablest of the bank's critics.[30] Many of the reforms he recommended were incorporated into the recharter bill that passed the assembly by a vote of thirty-five to twenty-eight and became law on March 21, 1787. The corporate existence of the bank, now closely remodeled on the Bank of England, was limited to fourteen years, its capital was limited to $2,000,000, and its activities were restricted—all proposals that Coxe had convincingly propounded.

By this time Coxe not only was one of Philadelphia's most influential merchants but also was well on the way to becoming one of that city's most prominent public-spirited citizens. He joined the leading humanitarian organizations of the city and willingly gave his time to the direction of their affairs. One of his interests was the "Philadelphia Society for alleviating the miseries of public prisons." Launched in May 1787, this society was the first effective reform organization of its kind in the country. Along with the familiar offices of such associations, the constitution of the society provided for the establishment of an "Acting Committee" to visit the public prisons weekly in order to "enquire into the circumstances of the persons confined" and "to report such abuses as they shall discover, to the officers of the government who are authorized to redress them." Coxe, a charter member of the society, was one of the original six members of this committee and, after the expiration of his term of office, was chosen a member of the society's electing committee.[31]

Just as he was concerned by the barbarous treatment of prisoners, he was also indignant at the inhumane treatment of slaves. Many Philadelphians, including a number of Coxe's relatives, had long objected to slavery and particularly to the practice of reenslaving free blacks by kidnapping or by shady legal maneuvers. In April 1775 America's first abolitionist society, the "Society for the Relief of Free Negroes unlawfully held in Bondage," had been organized in Philadelphia, but the work of this group was disrupted by years of war and readjustment to peacetime conditions. Revived in 1784,

Honble House a particular Attention to the System of Laws concerning the Bank of England." The recommendations were substantially the same as those proposed by Coxe in his several pamphlets on the subject.

30. See Thomas Paine, "Dissertations on Government; the Affairs of the Bank; and Paper Money," in Moncure Daniel Conway, ed., *The Writings of Thomas Paine*, II (New York, 1894), 182; Hammond, *Banks and Politics*, 60; [James Wilson], *Considerations on the Bank of North-America* (Philadelphia, 1785); Peletiah Webster, "An Essay on Credit . . . ," Feb. 10, 1786, in Webster, *Political Essays on the Nature and Operation of Money, Public Finances, and Other Subjects . . .* (Philadelphia, 1791).

31. *American Museum*, I (1787), 455, 456; *Pa. Gaz.*, Jan. 16, 1788.

the organization limped ineffectually along until April 1787, when it was renamed the "Pennsylvania Society for Promoting the Abolition of Slavery" and was remodeled by the adoption of a new constitution and the election of new officers. Benjamin Franklin was chosen president; Coxe and Benjamin Rush were designated secretaries of the society, whose membership included a number of Coxe's friends and business associates, as well as his brother John.[32] The bulk of the society's paper work was handled by Coxe, who more than any other individual deserved credit for the accomplishments of the group. It was successful not only in building up public sentiment and in promoting official action for abolition of the slave trade and slavery (to this end a petition condemning the institution was presented to the Constitutional Convention) but also in providing legal aid for the country's free Negroes. Nearer home, the members worked to improve the lot of the three hundred Negro families then living in Philadelphia.[33] One measure of the society's success was the inspiration it offered for the organization of similar societies in other states. It was also influential in securing the passage by the Pennsylvania assembly in 1787 of a measure strengthening earlier antislavery legislation. By 1800 there were less than two thousand slaves left in the state.[34]

Coxe's views on slavery were for his time relatively enlightened, though, as was the case with many of his fellow abolitionists, there was considerable disparity between principle and practice. His occasional cooperation in arranging for the return of slaves requested by his correspondents in the West Indies may be explained as an unwillingness to offend business associates, and his purchase of slaves for William Hemsley of Maryland may be attributed to his desire to assist a longtime friend.[35] But, so far as

32. Jensen, *New Nation*, 135; *American Museum*, I (1787), 460–462. See also Edward Raymond Turner, "The Abolition of Slavery in Pennsylvania," *PMHB*, XXXVI (1912), 129–142. The full name of the reorganized society was the "Pennsylvania Society for Promoting the Abolition of Slavery, the Relief of Free Negroes Unlawfully Held in Bondage, and for Improving the Condition of the Colored Race." Coxe continued as secretary of the society until 1789, when he resigned to attend the Continental Congress in New York. *Aurora*, May 21, 1799.

33. Coxe's role is attested by the papers of the society in the Historical Society of Pennsylvania. For an account of those papers, see Norman B. Wilkinson, "Papers of the Pennsylvania Society for Promoting the Abolition of Slavery," *PMHB*, LXVIII (1944), 286, 288.

34. Allan Nevins, *The American States during and after the Revolution, 1775–1789* (New York, 1924), 450; Jensen, *New Nation*, 135. One of Coxe's many acts on behalf of the society was to write to all the governors and to correspond with sympathetic foreigners. Coxe to Benjamin Franklin, Mar. 1788, June 9, 1787, Benjamin Franklin Papers, American Philosophical Society, Philadelphia.

35. For examples of Coxe's cooperation in the return of slaves, see Coxe & Frazier to Stephen and William Blackett, Mar. 8, May 10, 1784, to Isaac Hartman, Nov. 20, 1786, to Stephen Blackett, May 22, 1787, to Benjamin Yard, Aug. 27, 1787, to William Blackett, Apr. 8, 1788, Thomas Roker to Coxe, Jan. 7, 1787, Feb. 27, 1788, Coxe Papers. For Coxe's purchase of slaves, see William Hemsley to Coxe, Nov. 22, Dec. 13, 1779, Apr. 14, 1781, *ibid*.

the records reveal, in neither instance was he troubled by conscience. Nor did he then or in subsequent years, when he consistently opposed the institution of slavery, manage to resolve the tension between his humanitarian instincts and a strong and ineradicable racial bias.

The assumption that the black man was innately inferior eroded Coxe's otherwise sincere commitment to the abolition of slavery. He insisted that "the tranquility of the United States" rendered "the steady use of efficacious *alternatives* preferable to the immediate application of more strong remedies, in a case of so much momentary and intrinsic importance." By "more strong remedies" he obviously meant immediate emancipation. The "efficacious" alternative he proposed was not colonization but containment: encircle and choke the institution of slavery by gradual emancipation, terminate the slave trade, and greatly increase the South's white population by offering inducements to immigrants from the northern states and Europe. The pursuit of such a program, Coxe confidently predicted, would have the happy effect of reducing the proportion of "those unhappy, and once dangerous people, to a very safe point indeed." Safety for the whites was to him the desideratum; to engulf black men in a sea of white settlers was the solution. As he wrote to Madison some decades later, agricultural diversification and its attendant immigration were the sure means by which the South might rid herself of an evil institution.[36]

Despite what appears to the present-day reader as shockingly stark racism, Coxe and his like-minded "abolitionists" must be judged by the standards of their time or else a whole generation of well-intentioned reformers must be gratuitously indicted. Coxe did perceive that the denial of freedom in one section of the Union made it difficult to achieve equality in the others, and his participation in the abolition society does, at the least, indicate that he was seriously concerned. Though he was incapable of facing unflinchingly the dilemmas of a society professing freedom and countenancing slavery, he, like other reformers of the day, deserves credit for perceiving, however dimly, that the thrust of modernity was (in Tocqueville's phrase) toward an ever-enlarging "equality of condition."

Coxe's selection as a representative of the Union's leading commercial state to the Annapolis Convention attests that by the mid-1780s he had earned the confidence of fellow merchants and public officials. His appointment, so he recalled many years later, resulted from "the vote and nomination of Dr. Franklin," then president of the Supreme Executive Council.[37] It

---

36. Coxe, *View of the U.S.*, 437, 505.
37. Coxe to Jefferson, Sept. 28, 1807, Coxe Papers. According to Robert L. Brunhouse, Charles Biddle, the council's vice-president, was "instrumental in appointing Tench Coxe."

was also due to his well-earned standing as a prominent spokesman of Philadelphia's mercantile community, for the Supreme Executive Council (interpreting literally the statement that the purpose of the convention was "to take into consideration the Trade of the United States" and to consider a "uniform system in their commercial Regulations") chose a delegation dominated by merchants. In addition to Coxe, Robert Morris, George Clymer, and Thomas FitzSimons were chosen.[38]

Despite the failure of past efforts to secure interstate cooperation, Coxe was optimistic that the "jealous disposition" of the states might be overcome and that the outcome "of the business, it is hoped, will be the Investment of Congress with some new and wholesome powers for Commercial purposes."[39] As the spring and summer months before the convention passed, however, the apathy demonstrated by many states and the tardiness of others in appointing delegates gradually undermined his confidence. To him, as to his former business partner Jacob Broom, a Delaware merchant and fellow delegate to the Annapolis Convention, it seemed evident that if only a few states appointed representatives, "all this parade would appear merely" ridiculous.[40] His optimism was also dampened by a persuasive letter from Andrew Allen reminding him that even if the convention paved the way for national action, the retaliatory trade legislation on which Coxe set such store was unlikely to be effective. The adoption of general commercial regulations, Allen asserted, would have no effect upon the determination of the English government "to exclude Aliens of all denominations from a participation of the commercial advantages reserved to British subjects—particularly as America had no equivalent to offer for any such advantages."[41]

Whatever his misgivings about the convention's success, Coxe was flattered by the appointment, pleased at the prospect of meeting prominent public figures from other states, and excited by the possibility that this might be the debut of a distinguished public career. He must have been in a cheerful mood when in early September he stepped into his chaise for the journey to Maryland. He traveled alone. His fellow delegates tarried in Philadelphia awaiting the arrival of the New England representatives, a futile vigil that prevented their attendance at the convention. Stopping over

---

Brunhouse, *The Counter-Revolution in Pennsylvania, 1776–1790* (Harrisburg, Pa., 1942), 194.

38. *Pa. Archives*, 1st Ser., XI, 521, 522. The fifth delegate was John Armstrong, Jr., secretary of the Supreme Executive Council.

39. Robert C. Livingston to Coxe, July 4, 1786 (quoting from an unfound letter from Coxe of June 14, 1786), Coxe to Hope & Co., Apr. 7, 1786, Coxe Papers.

40. Jacob Broom to Coxe, Aug. 4, 1786, *ibid.*

41. Andrew Allen to Coxe, Aug. 11, 1786, *ibid.*

in Baltimore for a few days, Coxe attended to business affairs and enjoyed "the amusement of the Theatre— . . . the Tragedy of Alexander and a musical Entertainment"[42] and by September 9 was on the road to Annapolis. He arrived with time to spare before the opening session of the convention on September 11.

Only twelve delegates, representing five states—New York, New Jersey, Pennsylvania, Delaware, and Virginia—were present. Among them, however, were men with whom Coxe's career would be inseparably connected: Alexander Hamilton of New York, John Dickinson of Delaware, and James Madison of Virginia. Dickinson was elected chairman, and Coxe was designated secretary of the convention. The members immediately "entered into a full communication of Sentiments and deliberate consideration of what would be proper to be done,"[43] including a discussion of a "little enquiry into our commerce" by Coxe, which was printed and distributed to the delegates. The theme of this essay was the contrast between the liberal trade policies of Pennsylvania and the selfishly provincial restrictions followed by several of the other states. The latter, Coxe asserted, had enacted laws "opposed to the great principles and spirit of the union," while Pennsylvania had acted with a laudable "regard for the general commerce of the nation," behavior that he believed the convention should emulate.[44]

Whatever they may have thought of Coxe's proposal (and it did reveal, paradoxically, how strong the ties of state loyalty were even among those who advocated a closer union), the delegates quickly decided that with so few states represented, there was no point in debating or recommending measures for a uniform commercial system. Instead, a committee was appointed to prepare an "Address" to the several states. Drafted by Hamilton and adopted on September 14, it was a masterly maneuver by which ultimate success was plucked from apparent failure. Asserting that the commercial powers of Congress could not be altered without taking

42. Coxe to Rebecca Coxe, Sept. 8, 1786, *ibid*.

43. "Minutes of the Annapolis Convention," Sept. 11, 1786, *ibid*. The copy of the minutes (one of only two extant copies) in the Coxe Papers has a notation in Coxe's handwriting: "The original minutes, containing the above report [the Address of the Convention], at length, was signed by all the Commissioners." Although this suggests that Coxe was the secretary of the convention, minutes of the convention were apparently also taken by Egbert Benson. See Thomas A. Emmet, *Annapolis Convention Held in 1786 with the Report of the Proceedings Represented to the States by President John Dickinson* (New York, 1891).

44. Coxe to Madison, Sept. 9, 1789, Madison Papers, Lib. of Cong. Coxe must have been referring to a letter on trade between Pennsylvania, Maryland, and Virginia that he wrote to the Virginia commissioners, with whom he had been authorized to confer, and to the Maryland commissioners. "Letter from Tench Coxe, esq. one of the commissioners from the state of Pennsylvania, at the Annapolis convention, in Sept. 1786, to the commissioners from the state of Virginia," *American Museum*, VII (1790), 293–294. Since Coxe's letter was dated Sept. 13, 1786, it must have been presented to the second meeting of the convention that was held on that date.

other matters into consideration as well, the document recommended that the states appoint commissioners to meet in Philadelphia the following May. The purpose, in Hamilton's phrase, was "to devise such further provisions as shall appear to them necessary to render the constitution of the fœderal Government adequate to the exigencies of the Union."[45] By also sending a copy of the address to the Continental Congress, the delegates to the Annapolis Convention implicitly invited that body to sign its own death warrant, an invitation Congress was obliged to accept. Deeming "capital alterations in our general government indispensably necessary," Coxe joined his colleagues in signing the "Address," though he believed himself "unauthorized by my powers" to do so.[46]

Coxe went to Annapolis a firm supporter of commercial reform; he left an ardent advocate of a remodeled and stronger union. "The picture of our country drawn at the Annapolis Convention alarmed me," he wrote to Madison years later, and "public life became my principal engagement."[47] To Coxe, as to other nationalists, the central problem of the time was now clear. It was not, as historians were later to claim, primarily to fashion a government that would serve their own business or political interest, nor was it to abort the growth of democracy by imposing a coercive government characterized by minority rule. "The problem," to borrow the words of a distinguished twentieth-century historian, "was to find a method, if union was to subsist at all, for overcoming the difficulty" caused by the irresponsibility of the states: to find "some scheme or plan of organization wherein there would be reasonable assurance that the states would fulfill their obligations and play their part under established articles of union and not make mockery of union by willful disregard or negligent delay." To Coxe the solution was adumbrated by the Annapolis Convention. From the date of that assembly until the ratification of the Constitution, he wrote to Madison in 1789, "I . . . deemed capital alterations in our general government indispensably necessary."[48]

After the convention Coxe traveled to Baltimore, where he tarried to write a lecture to the Maryland legislature on the desirability of reforming its laws discriminating against the commerce of other states.[49] Sharing his

45. Syrett *et al.*, eds., *Hamilton Papers*, III, 689.
46. Coxe to James Madison, Sept. 9, 1789, Coxe Papers.
47. Coxe to Madison, June 11, 1801, *ibid.*
48. Andrew C. McLaughlin, *A Constitutional History of the United States* (New York, 1936), 146; Coxe to Madison, Sept. 9, 1789, Madison Papers, Lib. of Cong.
49. Coxe to Samuel Chase, Peregrine Leatherbury, William Smith, Samuel Hughes, and William Hemsley, *Pa. Archives*, 1st Ser., XI, 61. A draft is in the Coxe Papers. This letter, addressed to the Maryland commissioners for presentation to the state legislature, was essentially the same as the communication made to the Virginia delegates on Sept. 13. The major difference was the inclusion of a section setting forth Maryland's discriminatory laws.

carriage with James Madison, he returned by September 19 to Philadelphia, where he promptly submitted a report on his activities at the convention to President Franklin of the Pennsylvania council.[50] Coxe was "openly attacked" for supporting the "bold and necessary measure" to call a new convention with general powers, Coxe recalled with pride many years later, but "the confidence which Dr. Franklin reposed in him, and the decision and good management of that venerable patriot, procured an immediate approbation of the measure, and, of course, of Mr. Coxe's conduct by the executive and legislature."[51]

Such official approbation dispelled Coxe's fears that the glare of publicity might illuminate his war record; he was thus free to support publicly a restructured and strengthened Union. He also emerged as a leading advocate of a national economy nourished particularly by the encouragement of manufactures. His transition from a merchant preoccupied primarily with profits to a prominent publicist was rapid, though explicable. Although his formal schooling was skimpy, he had educated himself, acquiring for that purpose a large library on a variety of subjects from philosophy and history to grammar and agronomy.[52] But his speciality was political economy, and though he was familiar with economic theory, his expertness was in what is now termed "applied economics." His mastery largely stemmed from his experience as a merchant whose worldwide business transactions required a close knowledge of sources of supply in America, Europe, the West Indies, and the Orient; a familiarity with trade conditions (including trade laws, prices current, the quantity of exports and imports at various ports, shipping conditions, and credit transactions); and an understanding of money and banking. Coxe's preference for the practical over the theoretical—his fondness for statistics and discrete facts—rendered him an apt pupil, though it also served to circumscribe the horizons of his thought. Yet it was, in Leo Marx's phrase, "precisely the narrow prudential quality of his mind that made him responsive to the forces which were to determine the main line of national development."[53] Coxe was also one of the few businessmen of his

50. Coxe to Madison, May 5, 1807, Madison Papers, Lib. of Cong.; *Pa. Archives*, 1st Ser., XI, 60–61. Coxe received a little over £14 for his "pay as a Commissioner at the Commercial Convention at Annapolis." *Minutes of Supreme Executive Council*, XV, 135.

51. *Aurora*, Nov. 4, 1800.

52. For a description of Coxe's library, see Ezekiel Forman to Coxe, Apr. 6, 1800, Coxe Papers. For listings of books Coxe ordered from British book dealers, see "Invoice," Feb. 2, 1792, William Cass to Coxe, July 23, 1791, James Phillips to Coxe, July 26, 1791, Coxe to Phillips, May 16, 22, 1791, Coxe Papers.

53. Leo Marx, *The Machine in the Garden: Technology and the Pastoral Ideal in America* (New York, 1964), 151.

time intellectually agile enough to scale the walls of his countinghouse in order to prescribe for the economic problems of the nation.

Coxe's abilities were demonstrated at the first meeting of the Philadelphia Society for Political Inquiries, an organization of fifty members of the city's intellectual establishment, held at Benjamin Franklin's house on May 11, 1787.[54] His subject, one that reflected the interest sparked by the Annapolis Convention, was *An Enquiry into the Principles on which a Commercial System For the United States . . . should be Founded*.[55] Based on the premise that the United States had reached a period of crisis "when exertion or neglect must produce consequences of the utmost moment," Coxe's *Enquiry into a Commercial System* set forth a means of overcoming a "wanton" consumption of imported luxuries, a fluctuating paper money, a circumscribed foreign commerce, and an "ineffectual and disjointed" federal government.[56] His somewhat impassioned insistence that these problems could be surmounted may have been partly attributable to his determination to discredit the views of his brother-in-law Andrew Allen, who over the years had regularly included in his letters to Tench aspersions on the future of American commerce. "The commercial prospects of america do not to me wear that bright aspect as to hold certainly flattering encouragement," the exiled tory wrote in a characteristic letter. To Allen it was "more than probable, that for many years to come the trade of the American states, must be more and more contracted." Where could the Americans, now deprived of the sure protection and inestimable benefits of membership in the British Empire, find "the springs which are to set the commercial machine a going?" Allen asked. They would find them, Coxe answered in his *Enquiry into a Commercial System*, in the two most important economic enterprises in the United States—agriculture and commerce.[57]

Forecasting a major theme of Hamilton's Report on Manufactures, to which he would substantively contribute five years later, Coxe began his argument with an elaboration of the then-current truism that agriculture was the nation's "leading interest," the "great source of our commerce and

54. J. Thomas Scharf and Thompson Westcott, *History of Philadelphia, 1609–1884*, I (Philadelphia, 1884), 445. The organization's full title was "The Society for Political Enquiries, for Mutual Improvement in the Knowledge of Government, and for the Advancement of Political Science."

55. [Coxe], *An Enquiry into the Principles on which a Commercial System For the United States of America should be Founded; to which are added Some Political Observations connected with the subject* (Philadelphia, 1787). Mathew Carey published the essay in the *American Museum*, I (1787), 432–444. It was also incorporated by Coxe in his *View of the U.S.*, 4–33.

56. [Coxe], *Enquiry into a Commercial System*, 5–6.

57. Andrew Allen to Coxe, Aug. 11, 1786, Coxe Papers; [Coxe], *Enquiry into a Commercial System*, 7.

the parent of our manufactures." Attuned to the rural pieties of his day, Coxe emphasized the then virtually axiomatic idea that commerce was the "handmaid of agriculture." He cautioned that any system of commercial regulation "prejudicial to this great mass of property, and to this great body of the people" would irreparably damage the national interest. Having acknowledged the primacy of agriculture (an essential gesture in a country in which nine-tenths of the population were farmers, and a preeminence to which Coxe, as a member of the Philadelphia Society for Promoting Agriculture, was committed), Coxe argued that sound policy also required the encouragement of commerce and "its connections." To this end he offered recommendations that, as time would reveal, bore a close affinity to Thomas Jefferson's views and that would remain for decades fixed canons of Coxe's own commercial policy. The proposals included (1) the restriction of navigation between the ports of the nation to American vessels, (2) the encouragement of the fisheries, most notably by prohibiting competitive foreign articles, (3) the confinement of foreign imports "to the bottoms of the country producing them, and of their own citizens," a proposal modeled on British trade laws, and (4) the prohibition of foreign articles made from American raw materials.[58]

Coxe asserted that manufactures should be encouraged and protected where they existed, as in Massachusetts, but not artificially promoted in areas where agriculture was more suitable, as in the slave states. Instead, southern produce should be exchanged, free of duty, for articles manufactured in the North, where the multiplication of factories should be pushed "with industry and spirit." Coxe did not propose to encourage manufacturing by the imposition of additional import duties but rather by "a proper use of the natural advantages of the country." These, if fully utilized, would allow his fellow citizens to manufacture their own goods, especially cotton, and thus to pocket the 25 percent markup on European articles. "Here," he said, "is a solid premium, operating like a bounty," that costs the consumer nothing.[59]

The vision of national wealth and power, created by abundant natural resources and a great common market, that Coxe shared with his audience was alluring, one that would in the future become reality. At the time, however, it was as insubstantial as his roseate picture of the current state of the nation's economy. Something more than immutable economic laws or confident nationalism (as Alexander Hamilton was to argue in his Report on Manufactures, with which Coxe would by then agree) was needed

58. [Coxe], *Enquiry into a Commercial System*, 7, 9, 10, 13, 14, 16, 48. See also Peter DeWitt to Coxe, May 11, 1790, Coxe Papers; Coxe to William Tilghman, July 15, 1785, Tilghman Papers.

59. [Coxe], *Enquiry into a Commercial System*, 20, 22, 31, 25.

to establish flourishing manufactures in an overwhelmingly agrarian society. Coxe's optimism and confidence, however appealing to many of his country-men, might well have been tempered by the caustic comments of Andrew Allen. In an oblique reference to his kinsman's *Enquiry into a Commercial System*, Allen remarked that while the Americans might well "retrieve their character as a People which has brought upon them the Dislike and Con-tempt of Europe," they could become a "great People" only if "they remain at Peace amongst themselves" and "make those gradual Advances towards Wealth and Consequence which other Nations have done before them. If they aim suddenly at great Things," Allen admonished, "they will be apt to realize the fable of Phaeton."[60]

To Coxe, contrarily, the Americans had nothing to fear from the scorn of Europeans and little to learn from their history. Like Madison and Jefferson, he saw America as an innocent new nation happily isolated from the corrupt Old World beyond the seas. Prefiguring the theme of separation and disengagement from the affairs of Europe, which was to be a major prop of United States foreign policy for well over a century, Coxe wrote: "Having no foreign colonies whose situation and weakness would subject them to their attacks, and having all our resources at hand to defend our coasts, and cut up their trade in its passage by our doors, no European power will be inclined to insult or molest us." On the other hand, a neutral and geographically isolated America could only benefit from a war between foreign powers. "Our ships would carry for them, or instead of theirs, and our lands and manufactures would furnish the supplies of their fleets and islands in the West Indies," Coxe wrote in a passage that remarkably fore-cast the effect of the wars resulting from the French Revolution a few years later.[61]

For the moment, Coxe believed that the sole impediment to the enjoyment of the "substantial blessings" of that national wealth, whose foundations he believed to be already firmly established, was "a weak and half-formed federal constitution." The urgent and indispensable need, he wrote in italics, was *a system which will promote the general interests without the smallest injury to particular ones*," a system that must, above all, include the restoration of public credit at home and abroad by payment of the public debt. Prefiguring a program that some years later he would help to shape, Coxe wrote that "the general impost . . . the sale of the lands and every other unnecessary article of public property . . . would put the sinking and funding of our debts within the power of all the states."[62] More

---

60. Andrew Allen to Coxe, Nov. 13, 1787, Coxe Papers.
61. [Coxe], *Enquiry into a Commercial System*, 34.
62. *Ibid.*, 45, 46–47, 49, 50.

immediately, it was within the power of the states, whose delegates were then meeting in Philadelphia, to structure a new government that would not only promote fiscal responsibility but also provide the essential political framework for his program of economic nationalism. "For the sake of diffusing his ideas," Coxe dedicated his pamphlet to the federal convention and saw to it that "every member was presented with a copy, that it might be carried into various parts of the States."[63]

Coxe's *Enquiry into a Commercial System* is significant both as a contribution to American political economy and as a guide to his own intellectual biography. Not only did he have an atypically astute (though at that time necessarily dim) perception of the transforming effects of economic growth nurtured by industrialism, but his pamphlet also announced themes that Coxe would continue to elaborate on for the next thirty years—the promotion of manufactures as the means of achieving a balanced economy and greater national self-sufficiency, the desirability of the cultivation of cotton in the South and of its manufacture in the North, the essentiality of a system of sound public credit, and the separation of America from the affairs of the Old World. In short, Coxe proposed the securing of domestic prosperity and tranquility through economic growth based on the country's isolated position and vast natural resources. It was an ennobling vision and in the end overshadowed the petty squabbles and partisan rancor that temperament consigned to him.

For the moment, Coxe was intent on fostering an organization designed to further his increasingly ardent advocacy of accelerated industrialism—the Pennsylvania Society for the Encouragement of Manufactures and the Useful Arts, of which he was a charter member and for which he more than any other individual provided the inspiration. The "most important" of several similar organizations launched in the 1780s, the Pennsylvania society was formed in response to what Coxe later described as "the distresses which had resulted from a long revolutionary struggle, and from the commercial and manufacturing derangements produced by excessive importations from 1783 to 1787."[64]

The society was first proposed on July 26, 1787, at a meeting, attended by Coxe and other prominent Philadelphians, that was called "to take into consideration the most effectual means of encouraging useful arts and manufactures in this country." The group appointed a committee (of which Coxe was a member) to draft a constitution and to report at a second meeting to be held two weeks later. The constitution, presumably drafted by

63. *Intelligencer, and Weekly Advertiser* (Lancaster, Pa.), Apr. 19, 1803.
64. Davis, *History of American Corporations*, II, 257–258; *Philadelphia Evening Post*, Mar. 13, 1804.

Coxe, provided that any citizen of the United States might join the new society, which was to be governed by a president, four vice-presidents, and a board of twelve managers.[65] Those on the board of managers, to which Coxe was elected, were the most important officers. They were authorized to direct the day-to-day affairs of the organization, to allocate its funds (including the granting of premiums), to gather and disseminate useful information, and to investigate modes of manufacturing. The most novel feature of the society (and one that foreshadowed the Society for Establishing Useful Manufactures, of which Coxe would also be a leading promoter years later) was the creation of a "manufacturing fund" to be raised by individual subscriptions of not less than £10 and to be used (under the direction of a twelve-man committee annually elected by shareholders) for the establishment of experimental factories.

On August 12 a "numerous meeting" of Philadelphia friends of domestic manufacturers assembled at the University of Pennsylvania to consider the proposed federal constitution and to hear an address by Coxe. The occasion was a milestone in the nation's economic history, according to Coxe; until "sound policy and public spirit gave a late, but auspicious birth to this Society," the promotion of manufactures had had "but a few uncontested friends." This was largely the result of a number of public misconceptions, among them "want of skill in business" by Americans, the allegedly harmful effects of manufacturing on the health of workers, and the scarcity and high cost of labor. Coxe centered his attention on refuting the misconception that labor problems would defeat plans for American manufacturing. He pointed to the advantages of utilizing "water-mills, wind-mills, fire, horses," and, most particularly, "machines ingeniously contrived." The latter had already born out the expectations of "the most visionary enthusiast on the subject" and were demonstrably adaptable to American conditions. The further introduction and improvement of such machines was assured, Coxe insisted, both by the discoveries of European inventors, which the United States "may certainly borrow," and by the technological skill of his countrymen. Moreover, Europe would assist in alleviating America's labor shortage by providing thousands of workers determined to flee their "oppressors" of the Old World in order to enjoy the "blessings of civil and religious liberty" in a new nation, "this asylum for mankind."[66]

65. Draft of "The Constitution of the Pennsylvania Society for the Encouragement of Arts and Domestic Manufactures," Coxe Papers. The presence of a draft of the constitution in the Coxe Papers (though in the unidentified handwriting of a clerk) suggests Coxe's authorship. It differs in minor particulars from the plan as published in the *American Museum*, II (1787), 167–169. A printed copy of this is also in the Coxe Papers.

66. *An Address to an Assembly of the Friends of American Manufactures, Convened for the Purpose of establishing a Society for the Encouragement of Manufactures and the Useful Arts . . . 9th of August 1787, by Tench Coxe* . . . (Philadelphia, 1787). This address was also pub-

Following a literary pattern that was de rigueur for the generation's advocates of industrialism, Coxe next turned to a discussion of the circumstances favoring domestic manufactures. He ticked off the familiar ones: (1) an abundance of raw materials such as flax, hemp, wool, and, most important, cotton, a staple that southern planters could cultivate profitably and on which "the best informed manufacturers calculate the greatest profit"; (2) the great expense entailed in importing European manufactures; (3) the employment of those otherwise without work; (4) the boon to agriculture offered by an increased work force; and (5) the assurance of requisite manufactured goods in time of war.

Having disposed of objections to the introduction of manufactures and discussed their advantages, Coxe, tailoring his essay to the specifications he would in the future employ time and again, outlined measures for more effective encouragement of manufactures. Although repeating some of the arguments set forth three months earlier in his *Enquiry into a Commercial System* (especially the proposed enactment of a navigation act similar to England's), Coxe now centered his attention on the efficacy of premiums for mechanical inventions and technological improvements, whether made by Americans or introduced from abroad. He also recommended an active recruitment program, proposing that a committee of the society visit every ship entering an American port from a foreign country "in order to enquire what persons they may have on board, capable of constructing useful machines" or "qualified to carry on manufactures." Finally, in a plea that would later become capsulated in the phrase "Buy American," Coxe argued that the purchase of American manufactures "would wean us from the folly" of an "absolutely wanton" and extravagant purchase of European finery and "would produce, *in a safe way*, some of the best effects of sumptuary laws."

Coxe's conclusion was designed to answer the question, "What benefits will accrue from the encouragement of manufactures?" Among the many benefits he mentioned, he chose (no doubt because he was aware of the receptivity of an urban audience to such an appeal) to focus on "the employment in manufactures of our poor, who cannot find other honest means of

---

lished in the *American Museum*, II (1787), 248–255, the *Pa. Packet*, Aug. 11, 1787, the *Pennsylvania Herald* (York), Aug. 7, 1787, and the *Pa. Jour.*, Aug. 15, 1787. Copies of Coxe's address "were presented to general Washington, and the other members of the federal convention, then sitting in Philadelphia." [Coxe], *A Memoir, of February, 1817, Upon the subject of the Cotton Wool Cultivation, the Cotton Trade, and the Cotton Manufactories of the United States of America*, (n.p., n.d.).

subsistence." He buttressed his argument with that litany of eighteenth- and nineteenth-century economic thought: "A man oppressed by extreme want, is prepared for all evil; and the idler is ever prone to wickedness: while the habits of industry, filling the mind with honest thoughts . . . do not leave leisure for meditating or executing mischief."

It would be misleading to overemphasize Coxe's repetition of familiar ideas. Leo Marx, one of the two modern American scholars to place Coxe in the first rank of American political economists, has concluded that his achievement was, for its time, uniquely creative. Confining his analysis of Coxe's ideas to the two essays he published in the summer of 1787, Professor Marx contends that at the outset this then virtually unknown publicist boldly contested "the whole body of respectable economic theory" that denied the practicality of American manufactures. And this he accomplished with extraordinary effectiveness, largely because he tailored his program of industrialism to the needs of a predominantly rural society that subscribed to an agrarian ethos. According to Marx, "the culminative effect" of Coxe's emphasis on laborsaving machinery was "to undermine most prevailing expectations about the future of the American economy." Once Coxe brought the new technology into the picture, the prospect changed completely, for he alone among the political economists of his day recognized that what others saw as impediments to America's economic growth were actually stimulants, in the sense that, paradoxically enough, the abundance of land and the dearness and scarcity of labor in America lent "a unique significance to the machine." Coxe resisted the temptation to which Hamilton would succumb and did not reject the then-popular notion that the primacy of agriculture was attributable to the inseparable relationship of farmers to the soil; instead he set forth a comparable claim for manufacturing.

Convinced that the adoption of machine technology would mold the nation's future, Coxe not only made a place for it in a preponderantly agricultural nation but also more than any other man of his time pointed out to his fellow citizens the virtually limitless power of mechanization. The power need not have the disrupting social and human effects it had produced in Europe because, Coxe believed, as did Jefferson at a later date, the New World milieu would purify the factory system, cleansing it of "its unfortunate feudal residues." And while Coxe was by no means the only publicist of his day to recognize both the importance of technological innovation and its suitability to the American environment, his view that the American promise would be actualized by machine production did become a national cliché by the middle of the nineteenth century. Professor Marx thus only pardonably exaggerates when he concludes that "the speeches of Tench Coxe in the summer of 1787 prefigure the emergence of the machine as an American cultural symbol, that is, a token of meaning and value recognized by a large part of the population."[67]

At the time, Coxe was confident that the Pennsylvania Society for the Encouragement of Manufactures would demonstrate in practice what he advocated in theory. As a member of both the board of managers and the manufacturing committee, he was strategically situated to assure that it did. He was also in a position to advise sister societies in other states, the launching and organization of which was a constitutionally avowed objective of the Pennsylvania group.

The promotion of a national network of societies was a congenial task for Coxe, and he undertook it through correspondence with leading proponents of manufacturing like Jeremiah Wadsworth of Connecticut, Morgan Lewis and Walter Rutherford of New York, and a group of Virginians interested in "carrying on the manufactory of cotton in Williamsburg."[68] Coxe was especially interested in textile production, and his unswerving advocacy of the cotton industry deserves the praise of an authoritative mid-nineteenth-century economic historian who wrote that Coxe's "unwavering perseverence, in the . . . promotion of the growth of cotton" and his "commencement and forwarding the cotton manufacture under every disadvantage and embarrassment" entitle him to appear at "the head and front" of an industry that in time "whitened the fields of the South" while bringing the North "alive with the busy hum of industry."[69] In 1787 Coxe was eager for the society promptly to begin to manufacture cotton, as well as other textiles. Such operations, he argued in a newspaper article published in mid-August, required only the raising of a small capital, which then could be profitably employed in erecting factories. The result would be jobs for the idle, including women and children, "who might otherwise be a burden." More important yet, such enterprises would serve as pilot projects, providing indispensable information on modes, costs, and techniques of manufacturing for similar societies in other states, whose concerted activities "would

67. Marx, *Machine in the Garden*, 158, 163. The other historian to rank Coxe highly as a political economist is Joseph Dorfman, who depicts Coxe as one of the most original and persuasive economic writers of the early national era. See Joseph Dorfman, *The Economic Mind in American Civilization, 1608–1865*, I, II (New York, 1946).

68. Coxe to Jeremiah Wadsworth, June 5, 1789, Wadsworth Papers, Conn. Hist. Soc., Hartford; Wadsworth to Coxe, May 31, June 27, 1789, Apr. 4, 1790, Morgan Lewis to Coxe, July 29, 1788, Walter Rutherford to Coxe, May 4, 1789, Edmund Randolph to Coxe, Sept. 10, 1788, Andrew Van Bibbler to Coxe, May 3, June 16, Sept. 3, 1789, William Cooper to Coxe, Aug. 20, 1789, Coxe Papers.

69. George S. White, *Memoir of Samuel Slater, The Father of American Manufactures. Connected with a History of the Rise and Progress of the Cotton Manufacture in England and America . . .* (Philadelphia, 1836), 47, 49.

raise the national strength to a higher point than any thing else that is within our power."[70]

Believing that the one factor missing in his equation for rapid industrialization was the introduction of laborsaving machinery, Coxe promptly made arrangements to copy some designs of England's textile machinery—machinery that was primarily responsible for that country's position as the world's leading manufacturer of textiles. For this purpose he had for some time been on the lookout for a reliable agent. In July or August 1787 he chose Andrew Mitchell, an English citizen then living in western Pennsylvania, who Hugh Henry Brackenridge, Pittsburgh's most prominent lawyer and literary figure, had recommended as a "man of taste, . . . with . . . some knowledge of the world." On August 9 Coxe and Mitchell agreed to a plan "to procure for their joint and equal benefit and profit, and for the good of the United States of America models and patterns of a number of machines and engines now used in the Kingdom of Great Britain . . . for manufacturing cotton."[71] Only an experienced agent, skilled in subterfuge, could have carried off such an audacious plan. Mitchell was not such an agent. In March 1788 customs officials seized a trunk containing Mitchell's pirated models of English machinery; he rescued them, or so he told Coxe, at the cost of a large bribe. Two months later Mitchell reported that the valuable trunk had been entrusted to a friend of his in London for safekeeping and requested that Coxe designate a third party, unsuspected by British officials, to arrange for its transportation to Philadelphia. By the early summer of 1788 Mitchell had fled England and, according to William Temple Franklin, who at Coxe's request investigated the matter, "was settled at Copenhagen, and had a Place in the Dock Yards there." The mysterious—and perhaps mythical—trunk, which purportedly contained "a set of complete brass models of Arkwright's machinery," was never found.[72]

Although deprived of the coveted textile machinery Coxe had tried to secure, the Pennsylvania society had in the meantime gone ahead with its plans to inaugurate manufacturing operations. By early April 1788 Coxe finally witnessed the commencement of the "cotton manufactory" he had so determinedly promoted. Within only a few months the society's managers could gratifyingly report that the factory established on Market Street was

70. *Independent Gaz.*, Aug. 14, 1787.

71. Hugh Henry Brackenridge to Coxe, Mar. 18, 1790, "Contract: Coxe and Andrew Mitchell," Aug. 9, 1787, Coxe Papers.

72. Mitchell to Coxe, Feb. 1, Mar. 7, May 4, 1788, Franklin to Coxe, Apr. 7, 1791, *ibid.*; J. Leander Bishop, *A History of American Manufactures from 1608 to 1860 . . .* , 3d ed. rev., I (Philadelphia, 1868 [orig. publ. 1861]), 397. According to a mid-19th-century historian who was uncommonly familiar with Coxe's career, the trunk containing the models was seized by British officials. White, *Memoir of Samuel Slater*, 71.

"in a very flourishing condition" and that its future seemed more promising yet.[73] Such optimism was misplaced. It soon became obvious that despite timely assistance from the state legislature, domestic manfactures of cotton were unable to compete with English imports.[74] Whether or not this handicap could have been surmounted became a moot point in March 1790 when the factory was burned to the ground, the result, Coxe charged many years later, of "foreign Jealousy and contrivance."[75]

Coxe was disappointed that manufacturing operations were not promptly resumed in the society's factory, but he remained confident that the experiment of the Pennsylvania society was a success. It had, he boasted, "eminently contributed" to a "safe and correct legislative encouragement of numerous manufactures, . . . to the diffusion of useful knowledge upon the subject of manufactures," and "to exciting a patriotic spirit on the subject," thus enabling the friends of American manufactures "to form some safe opinions of our future prospects." These prospects, despite the failure of many of "our sanguine expectations," appeared bright.[76] The more so, Coxe believed, because of the national economic planning made possible by a new federal constitution.

73. *American Museum*, III (1788), 286, II (1787), 265, IV (1788), 406–409. See also "Report of George Clymer and Tench Coxe," *ibid.*, II (1788), 406.

74. In Mar. 1789 the state assembly subscribed 100 shares to the manufacturing fund of the Pennsylvania society. *Pa. Statutes at Large*, XIII, 239–240. J. Franklin Jameson, ed., "Letters of Phineas Bond, British Consul at Philadelphia, to the Foreign Office of Great Britain 1787, 1788, 1789," I, American Historical Association, *Annual Report for the Year 1896* (Washington, D.C., 1897), 552–554, 652–656.

75. Coxe to William Findley, 1816, Coxe Papers. For Coxe's account of the fire, see *A Communication from the Pennsylvania Society for the Encouragement of Manufactures and the Useful Arts* (Philadelphia, 1804).

76. *Aurora*, July 24, 1802.

6

Champion of the Constitution

Coxe's burgeoning repute as a political economist coincided with the Constitutional Convention that met in 1787. The possibility that the gathering would provide for a "firm and steady government" affording a national sphere of operations for aspiring statesmen was to Coxe, by now transparently eager to move outside the comparatively narrow circle of his Philadelphia mercantile and fraternal associates, a "happy prospect."[1] In an obvious reference to himself he remarked to his cousin William Tilghman that the current exigencies of public affairs made it "of the utmost importance that men of real Virtue, knowledge, and clear property . . . should be forced into public life." "So strongly am I impressed with these Sentiments," he added, that "I have withdrawn myself entirely from Scenes of pleasure, and make the study of our Affairs the amusement of those hours I can spare from . . . my profession."[2]

Personal considerations aside, Coxe hoped that the convention would vest the Union with powers he had long viewed as indispensable prerequisites to a national economy. His great expectations were in direct proportion to his low regard for government under the Confederation. Like other proponents of a strong central government, he deplored the discordant, conflicting, and misguided economic policies of thirteen virtually independent states, policies that undermined the realization of his own proposals for an unhampered common market at home and an expansion of American trade abroad. "A weak and relaxed civil Authority and a very sparse and extending population," he wrote to Madison sometime later, "presented to my

1. Coxe, "Thoughts on the present situation of the united states," *American Museum*, IV (1788), 402.
2. Coxe to William Tilghman, Feb. 8, 1787, Tilghman Papers, Hist. Soc. Pa., Philadelphia.

mind no prospect of the restoration of order among ourselves, or of confidence among our foreign friends."[3] Particularly pernicious, to his mind, were the fiscal and monetary policies of the states—"instalment laws" and "other invasions of the rights of property" like the issuance of paper money (a practice, Coxe insisted, that was contrary to "all the ordinary ways and means of established nations," one that had subjected the Americans to "danger and Dishonour"). Similarly unfortunate had been the refusal of the states either to impose on themselves or to authorize federal imposition of regulations on foreign commerce, a situation that had "contributed greatly to the disorders of our country" by rendering American commerce subject to the whims of other nations.[4]

These were some of the many impediments to order and prosperity that Coxe was confident would be removed by the convention. He sought to influence its secret proceedings by conversing with delegates he knew, by assiduously circulating among them his own writings on commerce and manufactures, and (demonstrating that his commitment to governmental reform overrode his humanitarian impulses) by preventing the presentation to the convention of a possibly divisive memorial denouncing the slave trade that had been drawn up by his fellow members of the Pennsylvania Abolition Society.[5]

No American of his day more enthusiastically and uncritically endorsed the famous document that was signed on September 17 in Philadelphia's Old State House than Coxe, and few of its many proponents wrote more tirelessly or more voluminously in its defense. "You may judge of my anxiety upon the subject of the Constitution," Coxe later wrote to James Madison, "when I assure you that I got thru near thirty lengthy publications before the expiration of a year."[6] Although many of his articles were redun-

---

3. Coxe to James Madison, Sept. 20, 1789, Madison Papers, Lib. of Cong.

4. Coxe, "Thoughts on the present situation," *American Museum*, IV (1788), 401–404.

5. Coxe to Madison, Mar. 31, 1790, Madison Papers, Lib. of Cong. No corroborative evidence has been found for John Bach McMaster's statement that Coxe "stood up before the Federal Convention and begged southern delegates to go home and urge their people to cultivate it [cotton]." McMaster, *A History of the People of the United States, from the Revolution to the Civil War*, I (New York, 1887), 297. Certainly in private conversation, however, Coxe urged those whom he knew to do so.

6. Only a fraction of the 30 articles have been identified. Consistent with the policy followed elsewhere in this book, I have attributed to Coxe only those articles for which there is concrete evidence of his authorship. It appears certain, however, that he wrote a good many of the articles appearing in the *Pa. Gaz.* and most particularly the *Fed. Gaz.*, and it is likely that many of those signed by his favorite pen names—"An American," "Philodemos," "Columbus," "A Freeman," and "A Pennsylvanian"—were from his pen.

Coxe's major essays are cited in the notes below. Among the other articles he contributed to the debate over the Constitution were the following: "Queries to the Honorable George Bryan, one of the Justices of the Supreme Court of Pennsylvania," *Pa. Gaz.*, Apr. 2, 1788; "To the People of the United States," *Pa. Gaz.*, Apr. 30, 1788; "Address to the printers of newspapers

dant and verbose, flat and uninspired, they were no more so than hundreds of others, both for and against the Constitution, that filled the pages of practically every American newspaper from September 1787 to midsummer of the following year. This journalistic outpouring stands today as a monument both to the extent to which literate Americans were involved in the outcome of an issue they recognized as momentous and to their extraordinary immunity from boredom. Of the scores of articles on the new Constitution, only *The Federalist*, written by Alexander Hamilton, James Madison, and John Jay, has endured, and it (despite the same redundance and prolixity that marred other similar literature) is justifiably recognized as America's most original contribution to the theory and practice of republican government. Although Coxe's essays were not in the same literary league, they perhaps were contemporaneously more influential, precisely because they were less scholarly and thus easier for most readers to follow. He was, in any event, surely justified in recalling two decades later that "*at least as to industry*, no one did more" to secure ratification. And though he exaggerated when he told Madison that "his health was nearly sacrificed" because of the "sedentary habits" he thus was led into, it was true that his "exertions in favor of this great cause . . . injured my private interest materially."[7] As Madison, Rush, and other contemporaries recognized, Coxe's writings, though ungraced by concinnity, contributed materially to the Constitution's adoption. His essays were circulated throughout the Union, not only by newspaper republication but also through the medium of the widely read *American Museum*. They included commentaries on virtually every clause of the Constitution and, taken together, reflected his vision of a national economy cemented by a strong and effective political union.

Coxe's debut as a Federalist pamphleteer occurred toward the end of September 1787. On September 18 the new Constitution was read to the Pennsylvania legislature, meeting in a room above that in which the recent convention had sat; the next day it was published in the Philadelphia press. A week later Coxe, appointed along with James Wilson and Benjamin Rush "a member of the general federal committee of the state to carry the adoption of the federal constitution," published the first of a series of articles in defense of that document. These were designed to neutralize the Anti-

throughout the united states: written by Tench Coxe, esq.," *American Museum*, IV (1788), 181–182; "To the Inhabitants of the Western Counties of Pennsylvania," *Pa. Gaz.*, July 23, 1788; "To the People of the United States, and particularly to the Independent Electors of Pennsylvania," *Pa. Gaz.*, Sept. 10, 1788; "Address to the friends of religion, morality, and useful knowledge," *American Museum*, IV (1788), 228–232, 338–341.

7. Coxe to Madison, Aug. 5, 1808, italics added, Sept. 9, 1789, Madison Papers, Lib. of Cong.; Coxe to Benjamin Rush, Feb. 12, 1789, Rush Papers, Hist. Soc. Pa., Philadelphia.

federalist propaganda in the backcountry of Pennsylvania. "My object has been to remove apprehensions and to obviate popular reasonings drawn from the public feelings," he explained to Madison, and for that reason neither the substance nor language of his essays were those he would have used "if I had addressed a philosophic mind."[8]

Focusing on anticipated objections, Coxe, in "An Examination of the Constitution," was more concerned with dispelling presumed prejudices than with affording an analysis, "philosophic" or otherwise.[9] Instead, he presented a disquisition on comparative government, taking as his central theme the superiority of the proposed Constitution to the government of England. Driven to the New World by the "want of charity in the religious systems of Europe, and of justice in their political governments," the Americans had established the freest government in world history, and it was this rather than the inherent defects of the English constitution that had compelled the colonists to declare their independence. Once independence was secured, the Americans had sought to maintain their freedom by devising a federal constitution altogether devoid of the coercive features of European governments. But the Articles of Confederation were so *"universally admitted to be inadequate to the preservation of liberty, property, and the union"* that the states had cooperated *"to amend and supply the evident and allowed errors and defects of the federal government."* Happily for them, the new Constitution, far from duplicating the "much boasted British form of government," was, like the United States itself, sui generis, a free government for a free people.[10]

Although there was considerable merit in the observation that one who read "An Examination of the Constitution" attentively would "find that it does not tell us what the new constitution is, but what it is not . . . and extols it on the ground that it does not contain all the principles of tyranny with which the European governments are disgraced," Coxe's fellow proponents of the Constitution were complimentary.[11] His essays would

8. *Aurora*, Oct. 9, 1800; Coxe to Madison, Sept. 27, Oct. 21, 1787, Madison Papers, Lib. of Cong.

9. As initially published in the *American Museum*, Coxe's articles, four in number, were entitled "On the federal government"; the first two articles were unsigned, while numbers three and four were signed "An American Citizen." *American Museum*, II (1787), 301–306, 387–391. The first three essays were dated Sept. 26, 28, and 29, respectively; the fourth essay was undated. The essays also appeared in the *Pa. Gaz.*, Oct. 24, 1787. In 1788 they were anonymously published in pamphlet form under the title *An Examination of the Constitution for the United States of America, submitted to the people by the general convention, at Philadelphia, the 17th. day of September, 1787, and since adopted and ratified by the conventions of eleven states, . . . By an American Citizen. To which is added, a speech of the Honorable James Wilson, Esquire, on the same subject* (Philadelphia, 1788).

10. Coxe, "On the federal government," *American Museum*, II (1787), 301.

11. "To the Citizens of Philadelphia," signed "An Officer of the late Continental Army," *Independent Gaz.*, Nov. 6, 1787.

"satisfy the most scrupulous and jealous citizens" that the Constitution was "not chargeable with a similitude to real monarchy or aristocracy," remarked James Madison, who was sufficiently impressed by Coxe's commentaries to arrange their republication in Virginia.[12] Pennsylvania Federalists (including Wilson and Rush) also extracted material from Coxe's writings for distribution in that state's western counties, where politicians were purportedly acting in concert with leaders of the state's Constitutionalist party to defeat ratification.[13]

The Pennsylvania Constitutionalist party's chances of defeating the federal Constitution were slim, and even before Coxe completed the last number of his "An Examination of the Constitution," that party suffered a significant defeat in the assembly. In the early afternoon of September 28 the Federalists had adopted by a vote of 43 to 19 a motion, offered by Coxe's friend George Clymer, authorizing a ratifying convention to meet in Philadelphia. This was done on the day preceding adjournment of the assembly and before the Constitution had been formally submitted to the legislative body. Having laid the groundwork for victory in the face of determined Antifederalist (Constitutionalist) opposition, the Federalists voted to adjourn until four o'clock in the afternoon, at which time they planned to work out detailed arrangements for the convention. The sequel is too well known to bear retelling except in the most cursory way. The Antifederalist minority (hoping that the approaching general election would make them a majority) decided to absent themselves from the assembly, thus preventing a quorum. Their stratagem appeared successful when their absence obliged the late afternoon session to adjourn. When the assembly reconvened on the morning of September 29, however, the indignant Federalists instructed the sergeant at arms to round up the still absent minority and to escort them to the state house. With the help of an obliging mob, two of the nineteen were seized, "dragged . . . through the streets to the State House, and thrust . . . , with clothes torn and faces white with rage," into the assembly chamber, where they were physically restrained while the triumphant majority pushed through a resolution designating the first Tuesday in November for the election of delegates to a convention in Philadelphia on November 21.[14] Coxe, though "sorry for anything that appears irregular," was obviously delighted

12. Madison to Coxe, Oct. 1, 1787, Madison Papers, Lib. of Cong. Madison wrote to Coxe some months later that Coxe's first three articles "were published in Richmond in a pamphlet with one or two other little pieces, and that they had a very valuable effect." The fourth article, Madison said, was "circulated in the newspapers." Madison to Coxe, Jan. 3, 1788, *ibid*. At Coxe's request, Madison also gave Hamilton copies of the articles. See Madison to Coxe, Oct. 26, 1787, Coxe Papers.

13. Coxe to Madison, Oct. 21, 1787, Madison Papers, Lib. of Cong.

14. For a detailed discussion, see John Bach McMaster and Frederick D. Stone, eds., *Pennsylvania and the Federal Constitution, 1787–1788* (Philadelphia, 1888), 3–5, 27–72.

by the likely result of such strong-arm tactics. He informed Madison that he had "no doubt of a large majority of the Convention adopting this new frame of government in toto," and he complacently anticipated that this would tear "this Constitutional party to pieces."[15] It did so only temporarily, of course, and there is at least some element of irony in the fact that the ultimate success of the Antifederalist, renamed the Republican, party would be measurably owing to Madison and to Coxe himself. In 1787, however, the two men unreservedly united with other nationalists to assure adoption of an instrument they believed indispensable to the survival of the Union.

During the weeks that preceded the state convention in November, Coxe strove to assure Pennsylvania's ratification, an event on which he believed the fate of the Constitution hinged. Not only was Pennsylvania one of the large states whose support was crucial, but also, so Coxe believed, Pennsylvania would carry the neighboring states of Delaware and New Jersey. Although it appears retrospectively that the issue was never in doubt, Coxe and fellow Federalist leaders believed otherwise. As they saw the situation, the opposition was led by proven vote-getters like George Bryan, William Findley, John Smilie, Robert Whitehill, and a host of other politicians whose popular appeal was such that not even the eloquence of James Wilson, the grandiloquence of Benjamin Rush, or the mountainous publications of Coxe could easily counter it.

Coxe, Rush, and Wilson were the principal organizers of a meeting attended by "a very great concourse of people" and held at the state house on the evening of October 6, 1787, a few days before scheduled elections for the state assembly. Coxe was secretary, and Wilson and Rush the main orators. After Wilson had delivered "a long and eloquent speech upon the principles of the federal Constitution," Rush "addressed the meeting in an elegant pathetic style, describing our present calamitous situation, and enumerating the advantages which would flow" from the adoption of the Constitution.[16] The meeting launched an initially vigorous and fiercely contested campaign. Federalist rallies were succeeded by rallies of the Antifederalists, whose leaders persuasively replied to the "eloquent" and "elegant" addresses of champions of the Constitution. The articles with which the Federalists, Coxe among them, filled the pages of the *Pennsylvania Packet* and the *Pennsylvania Gazette* were matched by the rejoinders that dominated Ebenezer Oswald's *Independent Gazetteer*.

The parameters of the debate that occupied Coxe and countless other publicists well into the summer of 1788 were set during these weeks preced-

15. Coxe to Madison, Sept. 28–29, 1787, Madison Papers, Lib. of Cong.
16. *Pa. Packet*, Oct. 10, 1787. See also *Independent Gaz.*, Oct. 9, 1787.

ing the meeting of the Pennsylvania convention. Although the issues introduced were wide-ranging and the quality of the arguments uneven, the constant themes played by the Antifederalists, who called the tune to which the Federalists for the most part merely responded, were these: the Constitution created a "consolidated" union, not an acceptable confederation of states but a coercive government over individuals that would undermine and eventually destroy the state governments; it vested the power of "direct" taxation in Congress, a power certain to be abused; and it eliminated annual elections, the guarantee against legislative usurpation. The Constitution also failed to prohibit a "standing army," that bugaboo of eighteenth-century liberal thought; it undercut the prerogatives and power of state courts by establishing a federal judiciary; it conferred on Congress the power to impose commercial regulations injurious to the interest of some states; and, most lamentable of all, it included no bill of rights guaranteeing freedom of speech, freedom of the press, freedom of religion, trial by jury, and other traditional safeguards against tyranny. To these objections Coxe, like dozens of other Federalist pamphleteers, devoted article after article.

The state ratifying convention that assembled in Philadelphia on November 21 was dominated from first to last by the Federalists, who had won a decisive victory in a somewhat listless election held two weeks previously. Although suspense was lacking, the delegates engaged in three weeks of spirited debate. Finally, on the evening of December 12, as Coxe happily reported to political allies in other places, the convention "adopted and finally ratified the federal Constitution by a Majority of 46 to 23," thus becoming the second of the nine states needed for the inauguration of the new government.[17] He surely must have been among those who witnessed on the following day the triumphant procession of the delegates, who, joined by the state's president and vice-president, the faculty of the University of Pennsylvania, city officials, and militia officers, marched to the courthouse, where the public announcement of ratification was greeted by the firing of cannon and the ringing of bells.[18]

A superficial reading of the convention debates and the accompanying polemical journalism in Pennsylvania, as elsewhere, might bear out the contention of historians who for roughly the first half of the present century followed the lead of Charles A. Beard. This group viewed the debate over ratification as a battle between rival economic interests subsumed in the political sphere under the familiar antagonism of "aristocracy versus democracy." More recent scholarship suggests otherwise. The position of a good many leading Antifederalists was dictated by nothing more ennobling

17. Coxe & Frazier to Buchanan & Robb, Dec. 13, 1787, Coxe Papers.
18. McMaster and Stone, eds., *Pennsylvania and the Constitution*, 426–428.

than a desire to hold onto the power and perquisites of state office. Certainly in Pennsylvania the most prominent opponents of the Constitution were state officeholders, lending credence to the conclusion of the most authoritative recent study that "the Constitutional battle in Pennsylvania can . . . be best understood as essentially an 'outs' versus 'ins' controversy which revolved around the stakes and division of political power between the state and national government."[19] Such an interpretation can also be drawn from Coxe's writings, but his major preoccupation was to persuade readers that the critical state of the country's economic and political affairs rendered the adoption of the Constitution an imperative prerequisite to national prosperity and strength. He addressed his arguments to the voters or convention members of other states, as well as to Pennsylvanians who might yet, he feared, impede ratification of the Constitution by demanding its prior amendment.

The subsequent activities of the Antifederalist minority in the Pennsylvania convention gave some basis to Coxe's fears. The day the Constitution was ratified, the dissenters, hoping to pluck victory from defeat by consolidating their support in the central and western parts of Pennsylvania and by uniting with Antifederalists in other states, published their "Address and Reasons of Dissent."[20] Harping on the theme that the Constitution was the work of conspirators intent on thwarting the popular will—"a few men of character, some more noted for cunning than patriotism"—the dissenters trotted out the familiar arguments against adoption. Thomas Hartley expressed the reaction of the Federalists when he wrote to Coxe that "the Designs of the Leaders in the Minority were to inflame the Minds and imbark the Passions of the People of the Country against the New Constitution." In view of such nefarious plans, he cautioned, the Federalists "ought not to be sunk into a State of Security" but should immediately launch a "Winter Campaign." He left it to Coxe "to determine how this Business should be managed."[21]

At no loss as to how to do so, Coxe published several "hastily written" rejoinders.[22] His first reply, under the signature "Philanthropos," asked how, in view of the widely different grounds of opposition taken by such prominent critics as Elbridge Gerry of Massachusetts and George Mason of Virginia, both of whom differed with the Pennsylvania minority, a second

19. Roland M. Baumann, "The Democratic-Republicans of Philadelphia: The Origins, 1776–1797" (Ph.D. diss., Pennsylvania State University, 1970), 81.
20. "The Address and Reasons of Dissent of the Minority of the Convention of the State of Pennsylvania to their Constituents," *Pa. Packet*, Dec. 18, 1787. It was signed by all but two of the 23 members of the minority.
21. Thomas Hartley to Coxe, Jan. 11, 1788, Coxe Papers.
22. Coxe to Madison, Jan. 23, 1788, Madison Papers, Lib. of Cong.

convention could be expected to turn out a document more acceptable than the proposed Constituion.[23] Coxe's second effort, a series of articles addressed "To the Minority of the Convention of Pennsylvania," examined what he regarded as the opposition's most effective and popular issue, the allegation that the Constitution threatened the annihilation of the states by providing for the "consolidation of the united states into one government." Coxe argued that the Constitution provided for a carefully delineated division of sovereignty between the states and the Union and, far from threatening the continued existence of state governments, made them "absolutely necessary to the . . . execution of the federal constitution itself." The whole issue, moreover, was a red herring—under the Confederation there had in fact been a division, though an unsatisfactory one, of sovereign powers; under the Constitution the states retained extensive powers. The much-touted phrase "We the People" with which the new Constitution opened was not proof of intended consolidation, Coxe claimed, but referred to the people "in their capacities as citizens of the several members of our confederacy."[24]

In another series of articles, addressed "To the People of the United States" and signed "A Pennsylvanian," Coxe charged that the leaders of the Pennsylvania Antifederalists "were all of what is here called the Constitution Party, or supporters of the present constitution of this state."[25] He thus pinned the label of "party" men on the Antifederalists *qua* Constitutionalists and accused them of fidelity to a constitution less democratic than the one proposed by the federal convention. He then turned to an exegesis of the "Address . . . of the Minority" of the Pennsylvania ratifying convention and provided a lengthy rebuttal to almost every point there made. Congressional "command over the purse of America" did not, he said in a representative argument, jeopardize the essential taxing powers of the states, which remained virtually intact. The states had a concurrent power in some instances, exclusive power in others, and through their own representatives might prevent the imposition of any direct tax. What of the argument that Congress would exercise "the power of the sword"? It was patently fallacious, Coxe replied; the power resided with the state militia, which when combined would form an army "tremendous and irresistible," a sure safeguard against federal usurpation. The argument that the national judiciary would overawe or undermine state courts was also mistaken, according to Coxe. It

---

23. "To the People of the United States," dated Jan. 15, 1788, appeared in the *Independent Gaz.*, Jan. 16, 1788. This was followed by an "Address to the minority of the convention of Pennsylvania," which appeared in the *Pa. Gaz.* in three parts on Jan. 23, 30, and Feb. 6, 1788. It was reprinted in the *American Museum*, III (1788), 158–161, 242–245, 365–367.

24. "Address to the minority," *Pa. Gaz.*, Jan. 23, 30, 1788.

25. "To the People of the United States," signed "A Pennsylvanian," appeared in four essays in the *Pa. Gaz.*, Feb. 6, 13, 20, 27, 1788.

was based on neglect of the essential fact that the great majority of litigation would be cognizable only by state courts. To the assertion of the Constitution's naysayers that the existence of coordinate sovereignties would be "a solecism in politics," Coxe's rejoinder was atypically concise and remarkably prescient: "The Federal government and the state governments are neither coordinate, co-equal, nor even similar. . . . They are of different natures. The general government is federal, or an union of sovereignties, for special purposes. The state governments are social, or an association of individuals, for all the purposes of society and government."[26]

Apropos of the contention that the Constitution imperiled civil rights by neglecting to guarantee their exercise—which many regarded as the strongest argument in the Antifederalists' arsenal—Coxe had little to say, probably because he believed such rights were adequately protected by state constitutions. What he wrote of liberty of conscience certainly also applied to other basic freedoms. Since the federal government was not invested with any authority to interfere in religious affairs, he argued, it was reasonable to assume that the members of the Constitutional Convention had by silence expressed their disapproval of "the interference of human authority in forming laws concerning matters of conscience." Writing as "Publius," Alexander Hamilton more concisely expressed the same idea when he remarked that the inclusion of a bill of rights in a government possessing only delegated powers would have been a redundancy.

The articles signed "A Pennsylvanian" were Coxe's most noteworthy contribution to the ratification debate and invite comparison to the best of the literature spawned by that controversy, including the *Federalist* essays, which Coxe approvingly quoted and to which his work was superior in its treatment of some subjects. His status as an influential polemicist during the ratification debate would have been the same and perhaps greater had he written no others.

By the time Coxe completed the more than eight-thousand-word disquisition of "A Pennsylvanian" in late February 1788, six states had ratified the Constitution, and he was confident that the others would soon give "unequivocal proofs of the same disposition." Over the preceding two months he had closely followed the results of each state convention, sharing with Madison and other correspondents his anxieties, exulting with each new accession to the Union, and cooperating with fellow Federalists elsewhere to secure success. He had been particularly concerned about the outcome in Massachusetts, where the prospect of a Federalist victory appeared especially dim. He did what he could. Copies of the debates in the

26. "To the People of the United States," *Pa. Gaz.*, Feb. 13, 20, 27, 1788.

Pennsylvania convention (sketchily reported though they were) went to Madison, then in New York, with a request that they be forwarded to Rufus King for distribution among the delegates to the Massachusetts convention. Coxe also sent copies of his own articles directly to King. His pamphlets, merely joining as they did the flood of literature poured on the delegates, probably had scant effect on the work of that convention, in which, as Madison told him, Federalist "hopes and apprehensions were pretty nearly balanced by the sum of probabilities on each side."[27] The suspense ended on February 6 when the Massachusetts convention approved the Constitution by a majority of nineteen, making that state the sixth to enlist under the federal banner.

Though it appeared likely that the favorable decision of the three additional states necessary to launch the new government would be forthcoming, Coxe, along with most other nationalists, viewed the accession of Virginia, the nation's most populous state, as indispensable to the success of the Union. To promote this prospect, he sent a good many of his articles to Madison, who, convinced that they "would have a very valuable effect," arranged for their circulation throughout the state.[28] Aware at the same time that what he had written for a Pennsylvania audience might not appeal to a southern one, Coxe decided early in January 1788 to address the Virginia electorate directly.

His appeal took the form of a public letter to Richard Henry Lee, Virginia's most influential Antifederalist pamphleteer, who in *Letters from the Federal Farmer to the Republican* had written a cogent and popular indictment of the Constitution.[29] Coxe had been told by James Wilson and Benjamin Rush that of all Lee's arguments, his charge that the congressional commerce power would benefit the northern and injure the southern states was doing "the greatest mischief in Virginia." He thus elected to reply to a widely reprinted letter that Lee had written to Governor Edmund Randolph, in which that accusation was more pointedly made than in the Virginian's *Federal Farmer* essays.[30] Taking as his text Lee's remark that the provision of the Constitution allowing a majority to control commerce opened the

27. Coxe to Madison, Jan. 16, 23, 1788, Madison to Coxe, Jan. 30, 1788, Madison Papers, Lib. of Cong.

28. Madison to Coxe, Jan. 3, 1788, *ibid.* See also Madison to Coxe, Oct. 1, 26, 1787, Coxe Papers; Coxe to Madison, Dec. 28, 1787, Feb. 25, 1788, Madison Papers, Lib. of Cong.

29. See Paul Leicester Ford, ed., *Pamphlets on the Constitution of the United States, Published during Its Discussion by the People, 1787–1788* (Brooklyn, N.Y., 1888), 277–325. Lee's pamphlet was so popular that it went through four editions.

30. Coxe to Madison, Dec. 27, 1787, Madison Papers, Lib. of Cong. Coxe's "A Letter to the Hon. Richard Henry Lee, Esq.," signed "An American," appeared in the *Pa. Packet*, Jan. 2, 1788, and in the *Pa. Gaz.*, Jan. 16, 1788. It was reprinted in the *American Museum*, III (1788), 78–83.

way for the several commercial states of the North to dominate the agricultural states of the South, Coxe replied that since a number of northern states (notably New Jersey and Delaware) were also primarily agricultural, the Virginian's argument was based on a faulty premise. Even in the principal commercial states (Pennsylvania, New York, and Massachusetts), he added, "the comparative weight of their merchants" was slight "when opposed to their country gentlemen." The bulk of Coxe's letter, however, was designed to reassure Lee and other southern planters that agriculture was "the great leading interest of America," the "spring of our commerce, and the parent of our manufactures"—an assertion Coxe had persuasively presented in his *Enquiry into a Commercial System* of the previous May, from which he now quoted in extenso. Madison considered Coxe's letter to Lee a fine performance, one that "must be satisfactory to the writer himself [Lee] . . . , if he can suspend for a moment his preconceived opinions." Alexander Hamilton greeted the letter with "pleasure and approbation," and the approval of other Federalists was attested by republication of the letter in "the country newspapers of New York and New England," as well as in southern journals.[31]

Coxe's letter may have been effective, but its influence was weakened by its appearance more than six months before the Virginia convention, which met on June 2, 1788. During the weeks preceding, Madison, who had returned home from New York, continued to share his views of both the local and national scenes with Coxe, who for the moment was preoccupied by correspondence with relatives and friends about the ratification debate in Maryland.[32] When that state ratified on April 28, Coxe once again turned his attention to the battle taking place in Richmond. "The fate of the new Constitution is now hastening to a crisis," he wrote to Madison on May 19. All depended on Virginia, he believed; if she rejected the Constitution, the outcome in New Hampshire and New York would be "extremely uncertain." Coxe's reaction to such an ominous possibility was "once more to attempt some observations not so much on the Constitution itself as on its relation to the Prosperity of Virginia and the United States."[33]

In his "Address to the . . . members of the Convention of Virginia,"

31. Madison to Coxe, Jan. 3, 1788, Coxe to Madison, Dec. 28, 1787, Madison Papers, Lib. of Cong.

32. Coxe's part in the Maryland ratification debate can be inferred from the following letters: William Tilghman to Coxe, Nov. 25, 1787, Jan. 2, Feb. 11, Apr. 6, 11, 20, 1788, Hartley to Coxe, Feb. 15, 1788, Samuel Smith to Coxe, Apr. 13, 1788, Alexander C. Hanson to Coxe, Mar. 27, 1788, Buchanan to Coxe, Apr. 22, 1788, Coxe Papers.

33. Coxe to Madison, May 19, 1788, Madison Papers, Lib. of Cong.; Irving Brant, *James Madison: Father of the Constitution, 1787–1800* (New York, 1950), 194. See also Coxe to Timothy Pickering, May 2, 1788, Pickering Papers, Massachusetts Historical Society, Boston.

he abandoned the exaggerated courtesy and obliqueness that had characterized many of his other articles on the Constitution.[34] Answering the argument of some Virginia critics that their "extensive state" would not be
properly represented in the proposed Congress, Coxe asserted that they
could not expect to have their cake and eat it too: since Virginians refused
to take black men into consideration in electing their own legislature, it was
extraordinarily inconsistent for them to insist that the citizens of the United
States do so in electing federal representatives. In any case, the Constitution
generously included a provision that allowed three-fifths of a state's unfree
citizens to be counted when apportioning representatives, a proviso that
gave Virginia five and a half votes for her 168,000 slaves. Nor did Coxe
believe that any credit should be given to the claim that property should be
represented: it was inadmissible to all "friends of equal liberty among the
people" and was tantamount to objecting to the Constitution because it
secured "the equal liberties of the poor." Coxe's impatience with those
whom his friend Thomas Hartley termed Antifederalist "Nabobs" was manifest.[35] Forgo selfish and petty concern with local and state interests, he in effect advised the Virginia Antifederalists. Adopt the Constitution now, amend
it later if necessary.

In a letter acknowledging copies of Coxe's "Address to the Convention of Virginia" and announcing that he had distributed them "in the
manner most likely to be of service," James Madison confirmed the Philadelphian's fears. Madison warned that the Virginia convention might reverse
Coxe's recommendation by demanding amendments before adoption or by
contriving "to procrastinate the debates till the weariness of the members
will yield to a postponement of the final decision to a future day."

As Madison and other Federalists labored in the extreme heat that
enveloped Richmond, Coxe turned his attention to the New York ratifying
convention, scheduled to assemble on June 17 in Poughkeepsie. He reported
to Madison that "the course of things" there "has proved very unfavorable."
A reversal of this trend might be brought about either by news of Virginia's
ratification or by the "Virtue, Knowledge and Abilities" of Federalist delegates "to work such Conversions as were effected in Massachusetts."[36] The
conversion of such staunch Antifederalists as Melancton Smith and Gover-

---

34. "Address to the honourable the members of the Convention of Virginia," signed "An
American," appeared in the *Pa. Gaz.*, May 21, 28, 1788. It was reprinted in the *American
Museum*, III (1788), 426–433, 544–548. From New York, William Bingham wrote to Coxe
that since he was "of opinion" the Virginia address "may operate a very good Effect on the
Minds of the People of this State," he would have it republished there. He also turned over a
copy to Hamilton. Bingham to Coxe, May 25, 1788, Coxe Papers.
35. Hartley to Coxe, Jan. 11, 1788, Coxe Papers.
36. Coxe to Madison, June 11, 1788, Madison Papers, Lib. of Cong.

nor George Clinton, however, did not appear to be within the power even of debaters as persuasive and eloquent as Robert R. Livingston and Hamilton, the most conspicuous Federalist leaders at the Poughkeepsie convention.

Although presumably aware that his pen was unlikely to accomplish what the debate could not, Coxe nevertheless decided to lend his assistance. In an article addressed to the New York convention, he staged a parade of horribles that would follow that state's rejection of the Constitution. Neighboring states would be in a position to cripple the New York economy by the imposition of import duties and other hampering trade restrictions. Just as his address to the Virginia convention had emphasized the Constitution's utility to the agricultural interest, so his New York pamphlet stressed its importance to government stockholders and to merchants. Some states were paying no interest on the public debt, while others were paying it in depreciated paper money, Coxe reminded New York business leaders. "How stands private faith, and the obligations of contract?" he asked the merchants. In some states creditors were unable to collect money due them, and in all the states there was an alarming trend inexorably leading "to the utter subversion of common honesty, and the rights of property."[37]

Having done all within his power to secure adoption of a new government, of which his expectations by now bordered on the messianic, Coxe impatiently awaited the national verdict. The suspense was brief and the result gratifying: New Hampshire ratified on June 21, 1788, making the Constitution the law of the land; then on June 26 came a narrow victory in Virginia, the tenth state to ratify; and next, and most unexpected of all, New York ratified on July 26.[38]

Weeks before then, on July 4, Philadelphia had celebrated what in the jargon of the day was termed "the completion of the Federal edifice." It was the greatest celebration the city had witnessed since the lavish "mischianza" honoring Lord Howe in 1778, an analogy that, if Coxe allowed himself to make it, would have been a gratifying reminder of how far his country had traveled in only a decade and of his share in the progress. The five thousand paraders (including representatives of virtually every occupation, profession, association, and religious denomination, and almost every politician, high and low, in Philadelphia) assembled at eight in the morning at the corner of South and Third streets. Coxe marched as one of six members of the city's committee of merchants and traders, whose "standard

---

37. "To the Honorable the Convention of the State of New-York," signed "A Pennsylvanian," appeared in the *Pa. Gaz.*, June 11, 1788. Coxe sent copies of the address to William Bingham, who presented them to Hamilton and Jay. Bingham to Coxe, June 12, 1788, Coxe Papers.

38. See Morgan Lewis to Coxe, July 29, 1788, for a discussion of why New York, "contrary to all expectations," ratified. Coxe Papers.

was the flag of a merchant ship of the united states . . . on one side of the flag a ship, the Pennsylvania, with the inscription, '4th July 1788.' On the reverse of the flag a globe, over which was inscribed, in a scroll, '*par tout le monde.*'" The mile-and-a-half-long patriotic procession wound through the city's streets, ending, ironically enough, at the estate of a former tory, William Hamilton, who "kindly offered the spacious lawn before his house at Bush-Hill for the purposes of the day." There under bright canvas awnings the celebrants were treated to "a cold collation" and, though the subject must by this time have been somewhat frayed, to an address on the merits of the Constitution by James Wilson, orator laureate of the Philadelphia Federalists.[39]

By this time Coxe had, in effect, gained his own newspaper, the *Federal Gazette and Philadelphia Evening Post*. The city's most ardent champion of the Federalist cause, the *Federal Gazette* was edited by Andrew Brown, a native of Dublin whose earlier career included serving first in the British and then in the American army, running a girls' academy in Philadelphia, and editing a newspaper in New York. His establishment of the *Federal Gazette* on March 8, 1788, was made possible by Benjamin Rush, whose purse soon turned out to be too slender for continued support.[40] Although Brown was obliged to suspend publication on April 24, 1788, he succeeded sometime during the next few months in finding another patron from among Rush's circle of intimate friends. Coxe offered to furnish the money necessary for the resumption of the paper's publication, taking as security a lien on the editor's presses and type. By the terms of their conditional contract ("conditional," so Coxe explained, in the sense that he reserved the right to annul it at his convenience) Coxe also promised to publish his own writings in the *Federal Gazette*, a commitment that he did not always honor.[41] Nevertheless, in view of Coxe's characteristically heavy journalistic output, it is plausible to assume that the *Federal Gazette*, relaunched on October 1, 1788, included many of his anonymous articles. These continued to appear even after Coxe, angered by Brown's continued

39. The celebration was reported in detail by the Philadelphia press. The above account is based on the report in the *Pa. Packet*, July 4, 1788, and on Francis Hopkinson's "Account of the grand federal procession in Philadelphia, July 4, 1788," *American Museum*, IV (1788), 57–75 (Hopkinson was chairman of the arrangements committee).

40. Vernon O. Stumpf, "Eleazer Oswald: Politician and Editor" (Ph.D. diss., Duke University, 1968), 252–253.

41. The terms of the contract can be inferred from Coxe to Andrew Brown, June 10, 1790, Daniel W. Coxe to Coxe, June 14, 1790, Coxe Papers. In order to assist Brown, Coxe was obliged to turn down Mathew Carey's "offer of a double interest" in the *American Museum*. Coxe to Mathew Carey, Oct. 4, 1788, Coxe Papers. See also Daniel W. Coxe to Coxe, June 14, 1790, *ibid*.

demands for money, exercised in the summer of 1790 his option to revoke their contract.

It was well that Coxe had a newspaper, since he and his fellow Federalists intended to assure that the implementation of the Constitution be entrusted only to its proven friends. In September 1788 the Pennsylvania Assembly would elect two United States senators, and during subsequent months the people would choose a new state legislature, eight federal congressmen, and ten presidential electors. Determined to leave as little as possible to chance, the Federalists in their first campaign gambit attempted to rig the electoral process in such a way as to utilize the majority they were sure they commanded. To curtail the strength of the Antifederalists in backcountry areas, a law was enacted providing that members of the House of Representatives and presidential electors would be chosen on a statewide rather than a district basis, as had previously been done. No such stratagems were necessary for the election of suitable senators, since the Federalists were in sure control of the legislature. The identity of these senators was another matter. During the preceding weeks a spirited contest had developed among the proponents of one or another available candidate—George Clymer, for whom Coxe attempted to round up support months before the Constitution was ratified; John Armstrong, Jr., Revolutionary War general and author of the Newburgh Address of March 1783, whose friends, Coxe reported to Madison, were "strenuous and apparently determined"; William Maclay, a lawyer and land speculator from the Harrisburg area, who, Coxe said, was much better read "than the country Gentlemen . . . usually are"; Robert Morris, who to Coxe was "an able man in commerce, finance" and (in an oblique reference to Morris's leadership of the so-called Philadelphia junto) "some other very important matters"; and William Bingham, of whom not much was said after Morris's candidacy gained momentum.[42]

Despite backstairs maneuvering that appeared to put the issue in doubt, Coxe's prediction that "Morris and McClay will be the men" was borne out.[43] To the Federalists their election, coupled with passage of the general ticket election bill, presaged even greater party triumphs. Coxe and the inner circle of Philadelphia leaders attempted to consolidate their gains by the appointment of a committee (composed of Coxe, James Wilson, Rush, Maclay, Samuel Miles, and William Nichols) to correspond with fellow partisans elsewhere in the state. In a circular letter, written in part by Coxe, county leaders were urged to work for the election of an assembly that would defeat the expected Antifederalist attempt to delay launching the

42. Hartley to Coxe, Mar. 3, 1788, Coxe Papers; Coxe to Madison, Sept. 10, 26, Oct. 22, 1788, Madison Papers, Lib. of Cong.

43. Coxe to Madison, Sept. 26, 1788, Madison Papers, Lib. of Cong.

new government until certain constitutional amendments were adopted.[44] To the Philadelphia committee these delaying tactics might be successful in view of the "injurious impressions" that the Federalists' opponents "may have . . . clandestinely made on the minds of the people." That the secret power of the opposition was exaggerated became clear when the friends of the Constitution won a smashing victory. Dominating the assembly by a two-to-one majority, the Federalists promptly ordered that elections for Congress be held on the last Wednesday in November. Although Coxe and his friends expressed alarm at the "extraordinary conduct" of the Antifederalists in presuming to recommend candidates for state and federal office, the Federalists adopted the same strategy. Coxe himself drafted a circular letter calling for the selection of delegates to a nominating convention in Lancaster on November 3.[45]

It appeared likely that Coxe's name would be placed in nomination by his Philadelphia friends. State leaders Thomas Hartley and William Maclay so predicted, and Charles Smith of Sunbury proposed to nominate Coxe himself if the Philadelphians did not.[46] On October 18 during a public meeting held at the state house, it was recommended that the city's delegates to the Lancaster convention nominate Coxe, Samuel Powel, Benjamin Chew, Thomas FitzSimons, William Bingham, and George Clymer. The proposal was heatedly challenged by "two ambitious lawyers," William Lewis and William Jackson, who charged that the slate had been drawn up by the "junto" without consulting other Federalists. When the subject was reconsidered at a meeting on October 25, backcountry politicians successfully insisted that the names of Powel, Coxe, and Chew be dropped, the last two presumably because their tory backgrounds were too well known.[47] It was, as William Shippen commented, "too soon for such characters to fill our first places." Whether he agreed or not, Coxe, who was "surprized to find my name upon the list," had planned voluntarily to withdraw.[48]

44. *Aurora*, Sept. 30, 1799. In the Coxe Papers there is a draft of the circular written in an unknown hand, dated "September 1788," and carefully edited by Coxe. For mention of other circulars and newspaper articles that Coxe wrote on this subject, see James Campbell to Coxe, Oct. 7, 1788, Charles Smith to Coxe, Oct. 18, Nov. 14, 1788, Coxe Papers. Coxe's authorship of additional though unidentified articles is also attested by the assertion of "Civis," who stated that Coxe disseminated "his political papers through the country, addressed to the influential characters of each county." *Independent Gaz.*, Nov. 21, 1788.

45. An undated draft of the circular by Coxe is in the Coxe Papers. A copy, dated Oct. 2, 1788, signed by 13 Federalists, including Coxe, is in the Pickering Papers.

46. Hartley to Coxe, Oct. 6, 1788, William Maclay to Rush, Oct. 18, 1788, Smith to Coxe, Oct. 18, 1788, Coxe Papers.

47. *Pa. Packet*, Oct. 18, 1788; *Pa. Jour.*, Oct. 22, 1788. The three men were replaced by Henry Hill, Hilary Baker, and John M. Nesbitt.

48. William Shippen to T. L. Shippen, Nov. 26, 1788, Shippen Family Papers, Lib. of Cong.; Coxe to Madison, Oct. 22, 1788, Madison Papers, Lib. of Cong.

At the Lancaster convention, which convened as scheduled on November 3, Coxe "was very warmly advocated" by both Charles Smith, his devoted political fan, and John Arndt, Northampton County political leader. Smith assured him that he had the support of other "very *particular* friends," but his nomination was opposed by most of the Philadelphia delegates.[49] With or without Coxe the Federalist ticket seemed assured of success on November 26. On that blustery and rainy day the Federalist nominees—Thomas FitzSimons and George Clymer, the Philadelphia candidates, along with representatives of the "country" interest and the German population—triumphed, though by the unexpectedly slim vote of eight thousand to six thousand. Having already received a consolation prize, Coxe could accept without resentment the preferment of men he regarded as less able than himself.[50]

Coxe's award was an appointment on November 14, 1788, as one of Pennsylvania's delegates to the Continental Congress. Although he was flattered, the appointment was a somewhat dubious honor, in view of the scheduled extinction of the Congress only a few months later. In any event, it was appropriate that his nomination as "the sole commercial" delegate (the other delegates were John Armstrong, Jr., and James R. Reid) should have been made by George Clymer, a fellow merchant and close associate in the Pennsylvania Society for the Encouragement of Manufactures. Clymer's recommendation was readily endorsed by an assembly controlled by Federalists who felt obliged to recognize a fellow partisan, even a former tory, who had contributed so heavily to the ratification of the Constitution.[51] The expression of gratitude, though token, also required a spark of courage, for no other Pennsylvania appointment or nomination at the time provoked more vitriolic condemnation.[52]

49. *Aurora*, Sept. 30, 1799; Smith to Coxe, Nov. 14, 1788, Coxe Papers. Smith pointed in particular to the support Coxe received from delegates from Northampton, Cumberland, Allegheny, Bucks, Berks, Montgomery, and Huntingdon counties. Coxe asserted that his nomination was unsuccessful because either he or Clymer had to give way, and Clymer refused to do so. Coxe to Timothy Pickering, Dec. 17, 1788, Pickering Papers.

50. See Coxe to Pickering, Dec. 17, 1788, Pickering Papers.

51. Coxe to Jefferson, Sept. 28, 1807, Coxe Papers; Coxe to Madison, Sept. 17, 1789, Madison Papers, Lib. of Cong.; *Aurora*, Nov. 4, 1800. A copy of the assembly resolution, dated Nov. 14, was transmitted to Coxe by Richard Peters in a letter of Nov. 15, 1788. Coxe Papers. Coxe accepted the appointment on Nov. 17, 1788. He later said that he was appointed "as a person on whom a reliance was placed, that no manœuvre should be practiced to prevent or defeat . . . the new government." *Aurora*, Nov. 4, 1800.

52. According to Rush, "Major J____" was responsible for the public attacks on Coxe. Rush was presumably referring to Maj. William Jackson, who had opposed Coxe's inclusion on the Philadelphia slate of congressional candidates a month earlier. Rush to Coxe, Feb. 5, 1789, Coxe Papers.

"It is high time for the whigs to open their eyes," admonished an anonymous polemicist on November 19. "The junto at the helm have thrown off the mask, and tories are openly brought forward to the highest places of trust and profit." Coxe's appointment was condemned as a profanation of "that glorious cause" for which our "illustrious martyrs" of the Revolution had "bled and died." If those members of the assembly thus willing "to trample upon the blood" of American patriots were not checked, Pennsylvanians would "before long find Galloway and Arnold in the list of our principal magistrates."[53] This attack was followed by another, this time much more dispassionate and thus more effective. The anonymous critic, identifying himself as "Civis," a whig "of a moderate cast of character," argued that full civil rights should be restored to former tories who had taken an oath of allegiance and that those who had remained largely inactive during the Revolution should be allowed to hold public office, however exalted. But to "Civis" charity had limits and should not be extended to "characters whose conduct during the war has designated them as objects of peculiar and pointed detestation." One such character was Coxe, who "like a PARRICIDE joined the councils of the enemy." If England had won, Coxe "would have been now basking in the sunshine of *British* favor," a "prudent deserter," who having once enjoyed the patronage of the enemy was now intent only on "enriching himself with the spoils of his fellow citizens." There was more in the same vein, all questioning whether "perseverence," "plausible manner," and "affected concern for the public good" were enough "to expiate an intended patricide." Was a man of such "pretentions" entitled to the "honors of that government which he sought to destroy?"[54]

Other opponents were little more than character assassins. "Semper Idem," charged that Coxe, "hungry and voracious," was in "search of some fruit of a more *fattening* quality than the *manufacturing* fund" and described him as "*a supple, fawning, smiling* PROTEUS, *ready to fetch and carry* as his masters bid him," a man to whom Lord Chesterfield's maxim that "a talent for pimping insures the fortune of the possessor" was particularly apposite.[55] Such slander was strong meat even in newspapers that reeked of scurrility, but it merits repetition because it represents the kind of abuse that would litter the path of Coxe's political career, whether on the ascendancy in 1788 or on the decline fifteen years later. It serves, moreover, as a timely reminder that the essence of a historical character is sometimes as well captured in the strictures of his enemies as in his self-appraisal or in the praise of friends. Why were words like "deception," "duplicity," "dis-

53. *Independent Gaz.*, Nov. 19, 1788.
54. "Civis to Mr. Oswald," *ibid.*, Nov. 21, 1788.
55. *Independent Gaz.*, Nov. 26, 1788.

simulation," or "deceit" (to use only a single letter of the alphabet) much more often applied to Coxe than to other contemporary victims of political abuse? Either they were to some extent appropriate, or a long list of traducers coincidently chose the same language, or the vocabulary of the day was remarkably limited.

The problem for Coxe and his political allies was a practical one—how to defend him against both character assassination and the valid charge that he had been a tory. The most effective approach and also a squarely honest one was taken by "A Citizen," probably Benjamin Rush, who argued that whatever Coxe's mistakes as a youth his subsequent career had proven him to be a loyal and dedicated American, one who had labored tirelessly and selflessly for his country's well-being, as attested by his public-spirited activities in Philadelphia, his attendance at the Annapolis Convention, and his influential publications on American commerce and manufactures."[56] Although Coxe himself feigned imperviousness to the assaults on him, he must have shared the indignation expressed by friends and by relatives. His sister Sarah Allen wrote from London that Tench would be happier if he "steered clear of politics," otherwise he would invite opponents "to scan what is past," which, in turn, would "lead him into difficulties" or "at least effectually destroy his peace of mind." Coxe rather thought it better to harbor "no resentment" and "to set out quietly to attend my duty."[57]

Early in January 1789 he boarded the stage that daily left Philadelphia for New York, where (after an overnight layover in Newark) he arrived on the following day. He need not have hastened, for a good number of congressional delegates, presumably adverse to participating in a death watch, never arrived at all. Although a new federal year had commenced in November 1788, no quorum was yet present, nor would there be until January 21. Coxe, having settled in at the boardinghouse of Mrs. Dorothy Elsworth, attended Congress on January 10 and presented his credentials.[58] Such formalities were virtually the extent of the official duties required of him, for, as Nicholas Eveleigh of South Carolina remarked, those who watched over the Continental Congress during its final months had nothing to do but "to adhere steadfastly to each other and to the old constitution as long as it would support us," while remaining "very friendly to the stranger that was

---

56. Reprinted from the *Fed. Gaz.* in the *Independent Gaz.*, Nov. 25, 1788.

57. Coxe to Pickering, Dec. 17, 1788, Pickering Papers; Sarah Allen to Molly Coxe, Jan. 30, 1789, Coxe Papers. One part of Coxe's duty, as he saw it, was to continue his writings in defense of the Constitution. He did so in a series of articles entitled "Thoughts on the subject of Amendments to the Federal Constitution," signed "An American Citizen," *Pa. Gaz.*, Dec. 3, 10, 24, 31, 1788. Coxe identified himself as the author in a letter to Pickering of Dec. 17, 1788, Pickering Papers.

58. Frazier to Coxe, Jan. 15, 1789, Coxe Papers; Ford *et al.*, eds., *Journals of the Continental Congress*, XXXIV, 605.

preparing to oust us."[59] For his part, Coxe assisted John Nicholson, the state comptroller general, in preparing documentary evidence of Pennsylvania's claims against the Union, which, according to Nicholson, amounted to more than five million dollars. He also sought to further Pennsylvania's attempt to purchase the Erie Triangle, an extensive tract of land located on the south of Lake Erie, to which the state had acquired a shaky title from representatives of the Six Nations in January 1789, and he corresponded with state officials on public affairs.[60]

But such tasks were not time-consuming, and he was free to spend long hours with his close friend Edward Goold, to renew other acquaintances (particularly with the Livingston clan), and to make new ones, among them John Dawson of Virginia, Colonel William S. Smith, John Adams's son-in-law, and Jeremiah Wadsworth of Connecticut. If the many social engagements (which, he complained, scarcely left him time to write letters) could have been transferred to Philadelphia, his pleasure would have been unmarred. As it was, he was certain that it would "take New York half a century to equal" Philadelphia "in the sensible modes of life and in politics and science, even if we stand still." Nevertheless, as he wrote to Dr. Rush, whose letters of introduction had helped to assure a warm reception, he was flattered by the "polite, respectful and very cordial" attention given him by the first-rate citizens of a second-rate city. "Tench Coxe is a moving common place book of knowledge"; his "integrity is equal to his talents as a politician," Rush wrote to Alexander Hamilton, who, having transacted legal affairs for the Coxes and having met Tench at the Annapolis Convention, needed no introduction. John Jay, in reply to a similar letter from Rush, had described Coxe as a man of " 'manners'—'talents,' and 'information.' "[61]

As Rush's comments indicate, the relationship between him and Coxe —both politicians, both, in time, federal officeholders, both controversial —was remarkably warm and close. Their pre-Revolutionary friendship had deepened over the years. The numerous letters they exchanged during the brief period that Coxe was in New York reveal their common interest in a wide range of subjects, from the deficiencies of Pennsylvania politicians to the value of Sunday schools. Had only a handful of prominent Pennsylvanians shared Rush's estimate of Coxe's virtuous character and unusual

59. Nicholas Eveleigh to Coxe, Mar. 24, 1789, Coxe Papers.

60. Nicholson to Coxe, Jan. 12, Feb. 4, 1789, *ibid.*; Coxe to Nicholson, Jan. 31, 1789, Lafayette Manuscripts, Indiana University, Bloomington, Ind.; *Pa. Archives*, 1st Ser., XI (1855), 537–543.

61. Coxe to Rush, Jan. 13, Feb. 2, 1789, Rush Papers; Coxe to Madison, Jan. 27, 1789, Madison Papers, Lib. of Cong.; Rush to Hamilton, Jan. 5, 1789, Syrett *et al.*, eds., *Hamilton Papers*, V, 242–243; Rush to Coxe, Jan. 31, 1789, Coxe Papers.

talent, Coxe would have forged ahead in politics despite the incubus of toryism that, as Rush lamented on one occasion, had "*cooled* the zeal of some of" his "best friends."[62]

For the moment, thanks to Rush's letters of introduction and to the cordiality of longtime New York friends, Coxe was kept busy enough to overlook both the handicaps to his future political career and the futility of his attendance at a Congress that had nothing to do. There was plenty of time, however, to try to assure that the new government would. Since the new House and Senate appeared certain to be safely controlled by friends of the Constitution, Coxe focused his attention on the imminent balloting of the electoral college, seeking in particular to assure a unanimous vote for Washington, as well as for John Adams's election as vice-president. The electors, having been chosen by the voters in January, were scheduled to assemble on February 4 at designated places throughout the country. Although Washington's election was certain, Adams's selection was rendered doubtful, or so it appeared to Coxe and other Federalists, by maneuvers of the opposition to win the second spot for New York's Governor George Clinton or some other prominent Antifederalist leader, by the machinations of Federalists in some states to secure the place for a favorite son, and by the scattering of "second votes" to obviate a tie.

Among Adams's most enthusiastic boosters was Benjamin Rush, who in letter after letter to Coxe sang the New Englander's praises—"a collossus of wisdom and virtue," he described him in one letter. Coxe, a receptive listener, promised that though he wished "to be *perfectly* unknown and unobserved" in New York, he would promote Adams as best he could. This he did in conversations with political leaders gathered in New York and by correspondence with influential state leaders elsewhere, particularly in New Jersey, Maryland, and Virginia. "Mr. Adams," he wrote to James Madison, "is esteemed by the people, has high ideas of Government, is a friend to property, will take the feelings of New England with him, has been used to the forms of legislature and diplomatic business, he is a man of a pure private character, and has knowledge and abilities beyond the proper duties of a V.P."[63] Coxe also kept abreast of the situation in Pennsylvania by the exchange of letters with Rush, James Wilson (who, if Rush's letters are to be credited, was then the Federalist boss of the state), William Bingham, and others.[64]

The votes cast by Pennsylvania's ten electors foretold the election

---

62. Rush to Coxe, Feb. 5, 1789, Coxe Papers.
63. Rush to Coxe, Feb. 14, 1789, *ibid.*; Coxe to Rush, Jan. 13, 1789, Rush Papers; Coxe to Madison, Jan. 27, 1789, Madison Papers, Lib. of Cong.
64. Rush to Coxe, Jan. 19, 1789, William Bingham to Coxe, Feb. 23, 1789, Samuel Pleasants to Coxe, Feb. 18, 1789, Hartley to Coxe, Jan. 12, 1789, Coxe Papers.

results nationally. Washington was chosen unanimously, while the vice-presidential vote was scattered, with Adams receiving a plurality. More gratified by the former than disturbed by the latter, Coxe exulted in the confidence reposed in Washington by the "united voice of free people—a transcendent honor infinitely beyond the proudest triumphs of ancient times." Rush was less enthusiastic. He thought it a national disgrace that Adams had not been given "a more united vote" and feared that the demonstration of "idolatrous and exclusive attachment . . . to General Washington" proved "that monarchy is natural to the americans."[65] Seven years later Coxe would reverse Rush's argument by maintaining that to support Adams was to endorse monarchy, but in 1788, convinced of Washington's preeminent virtue and of Adams's commitment to republicanism, he refrained from commenting on his friend's remark, surely attributing it to Rush's penchant for overstatement.

For his own part, Coxe believed that he was riding the wave of the future, and he no doubt subscribed to Rush's reassuring belief that within a year none of his critics would "dare to lisp a word" to his "disadvantage."[66] He returned to Philadelphia on March 4, 1789, persuaded that his service in the Continental Congress was only the beginning of a distinguished political career. Coxe had every reason to be complacent about the future. Having accumulated, so he told Madison in April 1789, a capital of £30,000, his financial status (even though he may have neglected to subtract his debts from his assets) was now such that he could afford to accept whatever calls might be made on him for public service.[67] And he was confident that such calls would come. Was he not, as Rush often reminded him, one of Pennsylvania's inner circle of influential Federalists? Was he not one of his state's best-known political economists? Had he not also earned the esteem of men who were likely to play leading roles both in the Congress and the executive department? Considering himself thus favorably circumstanced, Coxe eagerly awaited the inauguration of the new government and an invitation to assist in making it an instrument for concretizing his own program of economic nationalism.

65. Coxe to Rush, Feb. 12, 1789, Rush Papers; Rush to Coxe, Feb. 14, 1789, Coxe Papers.
66. Rush to Coxe, Feb. 5, 1789, Coxe Papers.
67. Coxe to Madison, Apr. 5, 1789, Madison Papers, Lib. of Cong. Coxe received £93 for his services as a delegate to the Continental Congress. See account for £50 dated Feb. 23, 1789, Benjamin Franklin Collection, Sterling Library, Yale University, and a second account for £43 dated Mar. 19, 1789, in the Gratz Collection, Hist. Soc. Pa., Philadelphia.

7 ✦

Congressional Gray Eminence

Could Coxe have had his wish, he would have served in the First Congress. But the scathing personal attacks occasioned even by his nomination to the defunct Confederation Congress obliged him to accept his tory cross. Acknowledging the improbability of an elective office, he hoped instead for an appointive one. If industry or talent had been the principal criterion for a high federal post, his wish would have been granted, for a good number of influential congressmen could have testified both to his ability and to his constructive influence on affairs of state. Indeed, he might be termed the gray eminence of the First Congress; no other private citizen exercised a greater influence on its deliberations and decisions.

That his role has gone so long unrecognized is a result of the previous inaccessibility of certain records. His own letters, except those to Rush and Madison, have long since disappeared. His papers do include, however, extensive correspondence from members of the Pennsylvania delegation to Congress and from congressmen from other states—prominent New Englanders like Benjamin Goodhue, George Thatcher, Nicholas Gilman, and William S. Johnson, and southerners like James Jackson, William Grayson, and James Madison. A cynic might plausibly contend that this correspondence, whether consciously so or not, was self-serving. But although Coxe in time would be a perennially avid aspirant for public office, his overriding interest in 1789 and 1790 was the public weal, not private advantage; convinced that the decisions made by the new government would decisively affect the lives of subsequent generations, he was primarily concerned with the successful implementation of the Constitution, which he had so tirelessly labored to get adopted.

Coxe corresponded with many congressmen, and the letters he received from Pennsylvania's representatives show that they were convinced that Coxe's concern for the welfare of the United States was sincere. Coxe was in frequent communication and on politically intimate terms with Frederick and Peter Muhlenberg, and especially with George Clymer, Thomas Hartley, and Thomas FitzSimons, all of whom were longtime friends.[1] Coxe was also Senator William Maclay's unofficial Philadelphia adviser, at least in 1789, before Maclay's dogged and inflexible opposition to what he construed as the inequities and monarchical tendencies of Hamilton's fiscal policies became so obsessional that the senator neither sought nor wished advice. In sum, the number and substance of Coxe's letters lend credence to the remark of a later critic that a congressman from Pennsylvania did not need to know how to write because Coxe "can write enough for them both, . . . and if the member can sign his name, this is all that will be required of him."[2]

Members of the Pennsylvania delegation welcomed Coxe's prolificness. "I shall be much obliged for your Communications which I will always Reply to," FitzSimons wrote soon after the First Congress assembled. Coxe readily complied, sometimes writing as often as three times a week. FitzSimons, in turn, not only kept his Philadelphia adviser fully informed on the progress of legislation before the House but urged him to transmit information on a variety of subjects, particularly statistics on manufacturing and commerce. Hartley, Clymer, and Maclay also asked Coxe for advice. "I wish your opinion on the impost," Maclay wrote in a representative letter, "as well as every other if you have leisure to communicate it."[3] Although gratified by such displays of confidence, Coxe was even more flattered by the receptivity of congressional correspondents from other states, especially Madison, the most commanding and influential figure in the House.

The range of subjects on which Coxe offered advice was as broad as the issues confronting the First Congress. He discussed relations with other nations; the "affairs of the Western Country," including internal improvements, which in his view would strengthen the bonds of union, would allow the West "to send us their produce," and would "enable us to send them our manufactures and importations"; the question of salaries for congressmen

1. Coxe to James Madison, Sept. 17, 1789, Madison Papers, Lib. of Cong. In the same letter Coxe also wrote that Sen. Robert Morris requested "me to correspond with him at New York, and his gentlemanly stile of treating that correspondence has shown his confidence and his good dispositions." In a characteristic vein Morris had acknowledged Coxe's advice on Aug. 6, 1789, saying, "I shall always receive your Communications with pleasure and give them that Candid consideration you would wish." Coxe Papers.

2. *Aurora*, Aug. 28, 1804.

3. Thomas FitzSimons to Coxe, Apr. 25, 1789, William Maclay to Coxe, May 16, 1789, Coxe Papers. See also, for example, FitzSimons to Coxe, Apr. 1790, Thomas Hartley to Coxe, Mar. 16, 1789, George Clymer to Coxe, Jan. 18, 1789, *ibid.*

and other public officials; the adoption of titles, forms, and ceremonies consonant with what Maclay called "republican plainess";[4] the establishment of a federal judiciary; the provision of a bill of rights; and the adoption of sound policies respecting the removal power of the president. But he was primarily interested in two other problems that dominated the work of Congress's first session: the enactment of tariff legislation and the site of the national capital.

The tariff was the first major item on the congressional docket. Coxe showered counsel on his friends (particularly Madison, Clymer, and Fitz-Simons) that was consistent with his advocacy of the encouragement of domestic manufactures, and the measure Congress finally adopted did incorporate a number of his proposals. On April 8, 1789, three weeks before Washington's inauguration, a Committee of the Whole had begun debate in the House on a measure for levying imposts. Its sponsor and the leader in debate was Madison, to whom Coxe had sent "a few notes on some points which appear necessary to be considered in forming our System of impost." Coxe's major recommendation was a drawback on all foreign articles exported to any place outside the United States. If this were done, Coxe wrote, the impost would be, in effect, a "consumption duty," and "this happy circumstance results—that while it is *virtually* an excise it is not chargeable with those invidious objections which usually attend that species of revenue."[5] Madison, already persuaded that tariff and tonnage duties were necessary to remedy "the deficiency in our Treasury" and thus "to revive those principles of honor and honesty that have too long lain dormant," was receptive to such views.[6]

Coxe's advocacy of high tariff protection for infant industries was far less congenial to Madison. The Virginian recommended instead a measure that, in calling for specific duties on a small number of enumerated articles and ad valorem duties on all others, was essentially a revenue tariff. The navigation system Madison proposed did, however, reflect Coxe's insistence on commercial reciprocity. Madison unsuccessfully urged Congress to levy discriminatory tonnage duties designed to bolster American trade, as well as to favor those countries that had made reciprocal commercial arrangements with the United States while penalizing those, like Great Britain,

---

4. On relations with other nations, see Coxe to Madison, June 18, Sept. 20, 1789, Madison Papers, Lib. of Cong. On internal improvements, see Coxe to Madison, Apr. 21, 1789, *ibid.* Concerning "republican plainess," see Maclay to Coxe, Apr. 15, May 16, 1789, Arthur Lee to Coxe, May 12, Aug. 4, 1789, Coxe Papers.

5. Coxe to Madison, Mar. 24, 1789, Madison Papers, Lib. of Cong. An incomplete copy of the enclosure in the hand of a clerk is found in the Coxe Papers.

6. [*Annals of the Congress of the United States*]: *The Debates and Proceedings in the Congress of the United States, 1789–1824* (Washington, D.C., 1834–1856), I, 102, hereafter cited as *Annals of Cong.*

that had imposed restrictions on American shipping. Since the bulk of the new nation's foreign trade was still with England, the proposal for discriminatory duties implicitly raised the question of the proper orientation of American foreign policy, a question soon to become a major partisan issue.

For the time being, the development of parties could no more be foreseen than the European war, which in only a few years would render the nation's commercial policy an issue of central importance. Nevertheless, Madison's bill brought to the fore the clash of sectional and group interests that members of Congress had hoped to reconcile. Madison himself argued that the welfare of the Union must take precedence over sectional interests and pled for mutual concessions. To a number of other congressmen, however, forbearance ended where the issue of protection began. The Massachusetts delegation, for example, doggedly championed the demand of New England rum distillers for a lower rate on molasses, while the Pennsylvania representatives insisted on protection for a variety of manufactures that, thanks in part to the encouragement given by the Pennsylvania Manufacturing Society, of which a number of Pennsylvania delegates were active members, were yearly increasing.

On March 16, two weeks before there was a quorum in the House of Representatives, Hartley, already on hand in New York, wrote to Coxe suggesting that, "as the great Subject of Imposts will come before Congress, . . . it would be very well for your Society to examine what Articles we can raise or manufacture in America." A short time later, Clymer, in order to "shew that Congress are not watering a barren soil," called on his fellow Philadelphian for "a clear representation of the actual condition of manufactures in our state." For his part, FitzSimons acknowledged the reliance he placed on Coxe's correspondence by lamenting that while the representatives from other states, particularly New York and Massachusetts, "have all the Assistance and Information the Commercial people possess—not a Merchant in Philadelphia except Yourself has ever taken the trouble to write a line upon the Subject."[7]

FitzSimons, determined to retain for his constituents the advantages gained by Pennsylvania's tariff of 1785, assumed the leadership of the protectionist group opposed to the free-trade drift of Madison's proposals. On April 9, the day following the introduction of the Virginian's resolution on the tariff, FitzSimons offered a counterproposal that called for a system of permanent duties "adequate to our present situation, as it respects our agriculture, our manufactures, and our commerce."[8] The success of his proposal

7. Hartley to Coxe, Mar. 16, 1789, Clymer to Coxe, Apr. 20, 1789, FitzSimons to Coxe, Apr. 25, 1789, Coxe Papers.
8. *Annals of Cong.*, I, 106.

was jeopardized, FitzSimons reported to Coxe, by the "great Jealousys" that "have obtained in the minds of the Members of the Southern states Who take for Granted that they are not and will not be Manufacturers and that every duty Layd for the Encouragement of them will be paid exclusively by themselves. Tho this is by no Means the fact—they either cannot or will not be Reasoned out of it."[9] It was soon apparent, however, that votes might accomplish what reason could not. On April 11, following the defeat of Madison's proposition, a Committee of the Whole began debate on the measure proposed by FitzSimons.

The bill was tailored to Coxe's specifications. Convinced that genuinely protective schedules were essential to the realization of national independence and economic growth, Coxe impressed his views in letter after letter on one or another congressman. Frederick A. Muhlenberg, for example, found Coxe's remarks so important that he passed them on "not only to the Pennsylvania Delegation but also to the Gentlemen from the Eastward, who in general are in favour of Manufactures," all of whom were "much pleased with them." Coxe's congressional friends were obviously receptive to his ideas, for they sometimes used his arguments during the course of debate. FitzSimons wrote on May 3, 1789, for example, that Coxe's "observations respecting the Effect of Manufactures on the interest of the Southern states have on different Occasions been urged, but as men are not easily convinced against their will they have rather Sought for plausible reasons for Opposition than for Information to convert them."[10]

The result of this conflict between the advocates of a protective tariff and those who favored a tariff for revenue only was a compromise. Coxe was disappointed that Congress turned down his pet proposal for the duty-free importation of cotton. "Tis the only article," he explained to Madison, "to which labor saving Machines can be applied and it may be increased by the planters and importers to any quantity." At the same time he was pleased by the protectionist features of the impost bill that became law on July 4. Speaking for the merchants of Philadelphia, he assured Madison "that little either of clamor or argument has appeared against the duties proposed."[11]

During the protracted deliberations on tariff and tonnage legislation Coxe had also carefully followed congressional debate on adoption of a bill of rights to be submitted to the states. Only a year earlier he had ridiculed

---

9. FitzSimons to Coxe, Apr. 25, 1789, Coxe Papers.

10. Frederick A. Muhlenberg to Coxe, May 3, 1789, FitzSimons to Coxe, May 3, 1789, *ibid.*

11. Coxe to Madison, June 18, 1789, Madison Papers, Lib. of Cong.; "An Act for Laying a Duty on Goods, Wares, and Merchandises imported into the United States," July 4, 1789, *The Public Statutes at Large of the United States of America* (Boston, 1845–1942), I, 24–27, hereafter cited as *U.S. Statutes at Large.*

the Antifederalists' demand that amendments safeguarding traditional civil liberties be added to the Constitution. The document was silent on subjects such as liberty of the press and personal rights, he had argued, "because they are already provided for by the state constitutions."[12] The Constitution did not protect the privilege of eating and drinking, Coxe observed in a far-fetched analogy, but few men would seriously contend that their right to dine was thereby endangered. As ratifying convention after convention demanded the adoption of a bill of rights, however, he came to the conclusion that such an inclusion would give the Constitution "an honest Triumph over the disingenousness of those who have opposed it on that score against their better knowledge." Some weeks before the meeting of the First Congress he accordingly wrote to Madison: "I have reflected since I had the pleasure of seeing you on the form of a declaration to be introduced into the constitution in favor of religious liberty, and I think the Idea of extending the powers of the union to an interposition between the state legislatures and their respective constituents might be accomplished, to universal satisfaction. . . ." Madison agreed. Among the amendments he recommended to Congress on June 8, 1789, was a declaration that "no State shall violate the equal rights of conscience, or the freedom of the press or the trial by jury in criminal cases."[13]

Madison's proposals, compiled from the propositions recommended by the Virginia ratifying convention, as well as those submitted by other state conventions, included the first ten amendments that would constitute the federal Bill of Rights. As debate on the Virginian's widely publicized amendments proceeded, Coxe was one of many correspondents who expressed approbation. "The most ardent and irritable among our friends are well pleased with them," he wrote, while those who "have hitherto been silent . . . are stript of every rational, and most of the popular arguments they have heretofore used." Believing, nevertheless, that "a few well tempered observations on these propositions might have a good effect," Coxe wrote two articles, initially published in Philadelphia and reprinted in New York, explaining and defending each of Madison's proposals. Taken together, he concluded, the proposals "manifest an attentive regard to the convenience, and a virtuous solicitude for the safety and happiness of the people, while they leave unimpaired those wholesome and necessary powers which *the freemen* of the United States have wisely granted to their national government." His essays, published under the name "A Pennsylvanian," were sent to Madison, who commented that although the success of his "experi-

12. [Coxe], "On the federal government," *American Museum*, II (1787), 387–391.

13. Coxe to Madison, Mar. 18, 1789, Madison Papers, Lib. of Cong.; *Annals of Cong.*, I, 431–432.

ment" in reconciliation of the "discontented part of our fellow Citizens" was "wholly uncertain," it "is . . . already indebted to the co-operation of your pen."[14]

Coxe was also consulted by his congressional acquaintances about other important measures before the House, including the removal power of the president and the judiciary bill. The former issue arose on May 19 when Madison included in his proposal for the creation of executive departments a motion that department heads were "to be removable by the President." This "very interesting question," he wrote Coxe, "has grown out of the silence of the constitution with regard" to the subject. Madison reported that the House had accepted the argument that the removal power, "being of an Executive nature and not taken from the President by the exception in favor of the Executive agency of the Senate, . . . remained to him by virtue of the general clauses vesting him with the Ex power." Madison had persuasively defended this position during the House debate, and Coxe expressed his full "approbation."[15] Coxe also endorsed and, through letters of advice to Senator Maclay, helped to shape the judiciary bill of 1789—the basic charter of the federal court system and, from the perspective of the present, the single most important measure of the First Congress.[16]

The congressional issue that most concerned Coxe, however, was more parochial—the location of the national capital.[17] His preoccupation was not singular, for the question was of overriding importance to the great majority of politically involved Pennsylvanians, as well as to congressmen from other states who hoped to capture this highly valued prize. Although historians have duly chronicled the heated controversy and backstairs maneuverings occasioned by the debate over the site of the federal city, the impression is frequently left that, compared to the tariff, the Bill of Rights, or the public debt, the issue was inconsequential. In any account of the

14. Coxe to Madison, June 18, 1789, Madison to Coxe, June 24, 1789, Madison Papers, Lib. of Cong.; Coxe, "Remarks on the . . . Amendments to the Federal Constitution moved on the 8th instant, in the House of Representatives," *Fed. Gaz.*, June 18, 30, 1789.

15. *Annals of Cong.*, I, 371, 456–585; Madison to Coxe, June 24, 1789, Madison Papers, Lib. of Cong. See also Hartley to Coxe, Aug. 5, 9, 1789, Coxe Papers.

16. See Maclay to Coxe, June 16, 1789, *ibid.* On July 4, 1789, Maclay acknowledged to Coxe "most hearty thanks for the communications which you have favored me with respecting the Bill for establishing the Judiciary." *Ibid.*

17. For Coxe's earlier preoccupation with the subject, see Coxe to James Tilghman, Aug. 6, 1788, Tilghman Papers, Hist. Soc. Pa., Philadelphia; Coxe to William Irvine, Mar. 13, 1789, Irvine Papers, Hist. Soc. Pa.; Coxe to Rush, Feb. 2, 1789, Rush Papers, Hist. Soc. Pa.; Coxe to Madison, July 23, Sept. 10, 1788, Madison to Coxe, July 30, 1788, Madison Papers, Lib. of Cong.; James R. Reid to Coxe, Aug. 20, 26, 1788, Morgan Lewis to Coxe, Sept. 10, 1788, Arthur Lee to Coxe, Aug. 4, 1788, William Bingham to Coxe, July 21, Aug. 25, 1788, Coxe Papers.

famous "compromise of 1790," of course, it bulks large, but few historians emphasize that in the presumed bargain between Hamilton's financial program of assumption and the location of the nation's capital, the latter was of primary importance to a great many, perhaps a majority of, congressmen. As Thomas FitzSimons, a persistent promoter of Philadelphia's claims, remarked, there was no more important subject before the First Congress than the permanent residence. "It was a question," he said, "in which the people of every part of the Union were deeply interested."[18]

From the day the First Congress convened in April 1789, the New Yorkers were determined that the capital stay where it was, while the Pennsylvania delegates were just as intent that it be removed to Philadelphia or to some other site in their state. For their part, the Virginians had tried for almost a decade to locate the capital on the Potomac River. Their glowing descriptions of that location prompted Fisher Ames to observe that they seemed "to think the banks of the Potomac a paradise, and the river an Euphrates." Ames and his fellow New Englanders did not agree. "It is the opinion of all the Eastern States," said Theodore Sedgwick, "that the climate of the Potomac is not only unhealthy, but destructive of northern constitutions. . . . Vast numbers of Eastern adventurers have gone to the Southern States, and all have found their graves there; they have met destruction as soon as they arrived." From the vantage point of the mid-twentieth century, the issue may appear of small importance, but in that day of poor roads, slow travel, inadequate inns, and, above all, strong local attachments, no question was of more immediate concern. "The place of the seat of government," as James Jackson of Georgia remarked, "might be compared to the heart of the human body; it was the centre from which the principles of life were carried to the extremities, and from these it might return again with precision."[19] Just as a half century later cities in the Mississippi Valley would vie with one another to become the eastern terminus of a transcontinental railroad in the belief that growth and prosperity would ensue, so in the 1790s states and cities sought to secure the first national capital in the belief that it would promote commercial prosperity.

Many congressmen also believed that the location of the capital would affect public policy. This was particularly true of Virginians, who believed that the Potomac site would make the government more susceptible to southern influence. Since there was general agreement that the capital must be centrally situated, all of the locations proposed were necessarily confined to the area between the Potomac and New York City. But the exact location, as Edmund Burnett remarked of the similar debate that had raged

18. *Annals of Cong.*, I, 787.
19. *Ibid.*, 858, 847–848, 789.

since 1783 in the Continental Congress, "became a bone of contention, and the struggle accompanied by not a little angry growling" went on "sometimes with one pack in possession of the bone, sometimes another."[20]

Months before the First Congress assembled, the Pennsylvania congressmen were mapping out strategy for what they were sure would be a vigorously contested battle, and their letters to Coxe over succeeding months help to throw light on what Fisher Ames described as the "dark intrigues" and "nearly impenetrable" designs that characterized congressional behavior on the subject. One of the first maneuvers was to try to make Philadelphia so attractive to the moribund Continental Congress that it would rescind its resolution of the previous September designating New York City as the first meeting place of the new government. This decision, the Pennsylvanians well knew, had been reached only after weeks of acrimonious debate between the advocates of the chief rivals, Philadelphia and New York, as well as among the proponents of the Potomac and lesser contenders such as Baltimore, Annapolis, and Wilmington. The decision had been reached, in James Madison's words, only because its opponents were forced to the alternative of yielding or "strangling the Government in its birth."[21] To the Pennsylvanians, however, acquiescence was viewed as a tactical retreat, not as a surrender. The New Yorkers' strategy, George Clymer told Coxe, was to place Congress "in too delicate a predicament to hazard so invidious and violable a step as a removal." To keep Congress in their state, he said, members of the New York legislature were willing to resort to the most extreme measures: "They freely give their money for a magnificent house and a library forsooth to the Congress—And what is more propose for the first time in their history, and in spite of fashion and inclination to become readers themselves."[22]

As the Pennsylvania delegates assembled in New York City to await the opening of Congress, they professed to see all about them an implacable hostility to what they regarded as the superior claims of their own state. Senator Maclay was sure that Coxe could "scarce conceive the rancor and Malevolence that is uttered against Pennsylvania in this place, but against Philadelphia in particular." Thomas Hartley, who was somewhat more restrained, reported that although the citizens of New York seemed "very polite to the Pennsylvanians," they also appeared to be "rather suspicious." In a clear, if unintended, demonstration that the suspicions were well founded, Hartley went on to say that "we must wait for a favourable Moment to Endeavour to move the Seat of Government to a more Central Situation. I

20. Edmund Cody Burnett, *The Continental Congress* (New York, 1941), 712–713.
21. *Ibid.*, 719.
22. Clymer to Coxe, Jan. 1789, Coxe Papers.

hope that most of the Virginians will be with us." To Frederick A. Muhlenberg even the fireworks and parades on the day of Washington's inauguration were suspect. "The Yorkers know the Impressions these things will have," he informed Coxe, "and no Doubt they will make use of them when the propriety of a Removal comes to be considered." Two weeks later, on the eve of the opening of Congress, Hartley found that "all is still Maneouvring about the Seat of Congress," and he cautioned Coxe that "when we write upon this Subject" it be "done under strict Confidence because the too free Communicating to others may be injurious to our Wishes in the Main Object."[23]

Given the machinations of Hartley's colleague, Senator Maclay, such secrecy was in order. On a blustery Sunday late in March, Maclay devoted "a few leisure moments" to drafting a "sham Petition" on the removal of Congress to Philadelphia. Although doubting that "we can with safety attempt a removal before the end of the first Session," Maclay believed that "the sham on our side will . . . have no ill effects." Insisting that "there can be no necessity of my name being known as the Author . . . ," he successfully urged Coxe to publish the fake petitions in Philadelphia newspapers and to "send me inclosed 2 or 3 of them."[24]

Once Congress convened, the location of the capital continued to dominate the correspondence between Coxe and the Pennsylvania delegation. If that correspondence is a reliable gauge, Pennsylvania congressmen shared James Jackson's exaggerated fear that upon the solution to the residence question "depended the existence of the Union."[25] Coxe was a tireless and influential champion of Philadelphia's claim. He not only contrived "sham" petitions with Maclay but also supplied him and other Pennsylvanians with descriptions and drawings of buildings, like the state courthouse, that might be suitable for federal offices.[26] He was also their unofficial and unpaid, but energetic and effective, "public relations" agent in Philadelphia. Congressman Hartley's injunction was characteristic: "Your attention in Philadelphia to the Gentlemen of the South as they come on will certainly have a good Effect and is *certainly* necessary." Coxe scarcely needed to be reminded of the importance of cultivating possible congressional allies, northern as well as southern. To George Thatcher, congressman from Mas-

23. Maclay to Coxe, Mar. 30, 1789, Hartley to Coxe, Mar. 16, 30, 1789, Muhlenberg to Coxe, May 3, 1789, *ibid.*

24. Maclay to Coxe, Mar. 30, 1789, *ibid.* The sham petition entitled "To the Honorable and Right Honorable Members of the Congress of the United States of America, now convened at New York" was subtitled "The Remonstrance, Memorial and humble Petition of the Inhabitants of Rh*** I*l**d" and signed "Y. Z. X. W. etc. etc." It was published in the *Fed. Gaz.*, Apr. 3, 1789.

25. *Annals of Cong.*, I, 789.

26. See, for example, Maclay to Coxe, Mar. 30, 1789, Coxe Papers.

sachusetts, for example, he described Philadelphia's two public libraries "containing about 13,000 Sets of books," casually mentioning that "such a collection would have a great Convenience and would save the heavy expense of purchase to the Gentlemen in Congress."[27]

By late August the Pennsylvanians had concerted plans for forcing a decision in favor of their state, either as temporary or permanent capital.[28] Their strategy, not so subtle as they believed, was revealed on August 27 when Thomas Scott introduced a motion that if adopted would commit Congress to a removal either to Pennsylvania or to the Potomac. After a brief debate it was agreed that Scott's motion should be taken up on September 3.[29] The Pennsylvanians were playing a shrewd game—if the Potomac were chosen as the permanent location, Philadelphia would be selected as the interim capital. The bargain underlying their strategy was revealed by Thomas Hartley: "The most of our Delegation," he told Coxe, "have engaged with the Gentlemen of the South to vote with them for Potomack and they say they will adjourn to Philadelphia."[30]

The bargain was not so uneven as it superficially seemed, however, for to some members of the Pennsylvania delegation gaining the temporary capital was the desideratum. The advantages of Philadelphia were so great, they believed, that once Congress moved there it would be unwilling to leave. The alliance of Pennsylvanians and southerners was thwarted when a countercoalition of New England and New York congressmen proposed

27. Hartley to Coxe, Mar. 16, 1789, *ibid.*; Coxe to George Thatcher, Apr. 8, 1789, Independence Hall Collection, Philadelphia.

28. On Aug. 23, four days before a motion was introduced in Congress, Hartley informed Coxe that a motion for "fixing the federal Seat" had been prepared. Coxe Papers. It was the intention of the Pennsylvania delegation to obtain a decision in the first session of Congress. Their reason, as FitzSimons explained, was "that their weight at present either in the house of Representatives or senate is greater than it Can be when No. Carolina and Rhode Island are Represented—besides that the longer Congress sit here the Greater will be the difficulty of Removal." FitzSimons to Coxe, Sept. 6, 1789, *ibid.*

29. *Annals of Cong.*, I, 786, 792.

30. According to Hartley, the Pennsylvanians turned down a last-minute offer from "the New Yorkers and Eastern people" to vote immediately for a removal to Trenton because "our Gentlemen had gone too far with the Southern Men." Hartley to Coxe, Sept. 2, 1789, Coxe Papers. The Pennsylvanians, according to FitzSimons, had earlier attempted to strike a bargain with the New Englanders by offering that if "any part of Pennsylvania was fixed on to support it and to remain here till Accomodation should be provided." But the New Englanders were persuaded by the New Yorkers to postpone a decision until the next session. It was only then, FitzSimons explained to Coxe, that "we declared that we would Join the southern interest." FitzSimons to Coxe, Sept. 6, 1789, *ibid.* The bargaining between the Pennsylvanians and the New Englanders was not a well-kept secret. Madison, for one, described it to Alexander White on Aug. 24, 1789. Madison Papers, New York Public Library, New York City. Nor was the subsequent agreement between the South and Pennsylvania unknown to other congressmen. Fisher Ames, for example, described it to George R. Minot on Sept. 6, 1789. Seth Ames, ed., *Works of Fisher Ames. With a Selection from His Speeches and Correspondence*, I (Boston, 1854), 71.

that the permanent capital be on the Susquehanna River, and the temporary capital in New York.[31] The maneuver was a shrewd one. Tempted by the prospect of winning the grand rather than the consolation prize, the Pennsylvanians divided on the issue, abandoned their southern cohorts, and agreed to a decision that temporarily knocked Philadelphia and the Potomac out of the race. As Virginia congressman Josiah Parker wrote to Coxe, the solemn oath between the Pennsylvanians and the southerners could only "be compared to Lord Mansfield's to the late pretender."[32]

It was thus with the acquiescence of the Pennsylvanians and in the face of opposition by many southerners that a bill designating a site on the banks of the Susquehanna passed the House of Representatives a week before adjournment. But the Senate, largely because of the backstairs negotiations of Robert Morris, substituted Germantown (a stone's throw from Philadelphia), and in the ensuing parliamentary wrangle Pennsylvania's opponents managed to table the bill until the next session. To Coxe it was an unseemly example of the victory of parochialism over the national interest, which in this case he identified with Pennsylvania's interest, and he doubtless agreed with his friend John Dawson, who wrote from Richmond, "I . . . sincerely wish that a veil could be thrown over the whole of that transaction."[33]

Although disappointed that Philadelphia had not won the coveted prize, Coxe could take satisfaction in the knowledge that his ideas had influenced other measures of the first congressional session. He was far less pleased that his contributions had been behind-the-scenes and that his assiduous quest for public office had been unsuccessful. He was entitled to be puzzled, for among his strong supporters could be counted virtually the entire Pennsylvania delegation, as well as such notables as the Lees of Virginia and James Madison. Nor had he been backward in pressing his claims.

Madison had scarcely had a chance to recover from his long journey to the new capital before he received a letter from Coxe. The Virginian had only to read its opening sentences to know what his correspondent wanted: "I am very much at a loss how to address you on the subject which has induced me to trouble you with this letter," Coxe wrote. "It would have the complexion to most men of mere private gratification and advantage." Dispensing lengthily with the other pro forma disclaimers of office seekers of that time and averring that his own search had been prompted by the insistence of friends, Coxe got to the point: "As your Opinion must have frequently weight and as *I would sincerely wish for no employment which you*

---

31. The prize was handed to the Pennsylvania delegates by the New Yorkers, who, Fitz-Simons said, "obtained an Agreement of all the Eastern Members to Vote for Susquehana." FitzSimons to Coxe, Sept. 6, 1789, Coxe Papers.
32. Josiah Parker to Coxe, Sept. 8, 1789, *ibid*.
33. John Dawson to Coxe, Oct. 26, 1789, *ibid*.

might consider as improper for me . . . I have thought it not improper . . . to communicate to you . . . my not being averse to the Ideas suggested to me." He firmly insisted that no reply to his letter was necessary, and Madison obliged. Other congressional acquaintances were more cooperative, even eagerly so. To Frederick A. Muhlenberg his friend's wish for a public office was "perfectly agreeable to my Wishes," and he assured Coxe that "it had been the Subject of Conversation amongst Your friends here and unanimously approved of."[34] Their approval, Coxe disappointedly learned, did not assure an appointment. Nor were Coxe's chances enhanced by a brief trip to New York in May, during which he undoubtedly set forth his qualifications to congressional friends.

Similarly unrewarding were his not-too-subtle efforts to make certain that Washington knew of his authorship of an address submitted to the president by a convention of the Episcopal church that had met in Philadelphia in August. The convention's "Address" to the president expressed joy at "the election of a civil ruler, deservedly beloved, and eminently distinguished" and was in this and every other way characteristic of the many bombastic and laudatory messages that rained on Washington. Its presentation, at Coxe's behest, was arranged by Senator Robert Morris, the brother-in-law of Bishop William White of Pennsylvania, who in mid-August agreed to "muster as many respectable Pennsylvania Episcopalians" as he "could find in this City to attend" Bishop Samuel Provoost of New York "at the Time of Delivery to the President" in late August.[35]

Two weeks later Coxe's hopes for joining the Washington administration soared. On September 15, the day the bill for creating the post office passed the Senate, his friend Arthur Lee hastily advised him to lose no time in rounding up support for appointment as postmaster general. Although he promptly did so, the post went instead to a former Antifederalist, Samuel Osgood of Massachusetts, whose selection was due, so Arthur Lee explained, to the president's belief that the New Englander "had pretensions" Washington "thought he could not get over."[36] Coxe's own disappointment was

---

34. Coxe to Madison, Apr. 5, 1789, Madison Papers, Lib. of Cong.; Muhlenberg to Coxe, May 3, 1789, Coxe Papers.

35. Coxe, "Address of the convention of the protestant episcopal church, in the states of New York, New Jersey, Pennsylvania, Delaware, Maryland, Virginia, and South Carolina, held at Philadelphia; To the president of the united states," Aug. 7, 1789, in *American Museum*, VI (1789), 104–105; Robert Morris to Coxe, Aug. 15, 1789, Coxe Papers. For Coxe's efforts to make certain Washington knew of his authorship, see Coxe to Madison, Sept. 20, 1789, Madison Papers, Lib. of Cong.; Morris to Coxe, Aug. 15, 1789, Coxe Papers.

36. Lee to Coxe, Sept. 15, 26, 1789; Muhlenberg to Coxe, Sept. 21, 1789, Coxe Papers; Coxe to Madison, Sept. 17, 1789, Madison Papers, Lib. of Cong. See also Hartley to Coxe, Sept. 21, 1789, Arthur Lee to Coxe, Sept. 22, 1789, Coxe Papers. The other leading contenders for the post were Ebenezer Hazard, Richard Bache, and William S. Smith, John Adams's son-in-law.

assuaged, as he told Madison, by the knowledge that his "exertions in the federal cause" had won him the confidence and support of so many of its more politically powerful proponents.[37] Decorum forbade him to add that he also believed he had suffered only a minor setback in a quest in which he confidently expected those friends to assure success.

The second session of the First Congress began on January 7, 1790. The fiscal fate of the nation was in its hands, and Coxe, like other advocates of a sound financial system, anxiously awaited the first major report of the secretary of the Treasury. In naming Alexander Hamilton to that post four months earlier, Washington, on whose staff the young New Yorker had served during the Revolution, realized that he was tapping the best financial talent the country could offer. The president's satisfaction was the greater because, along with most public figures of the time, he recognized that the Treasury Department would be the nerve center of his administration. Fiscal ineptitude had been in large measure responsible for the series of events that had toppled the Confederation government and led to the adoption of the Constitution. Among the most important provisions of that document was the pledge that "all debts contracted and engagements entered into before the adoption of the Constitution shall be as valid against the United States under this Constitution as under the Confederation." The most pressing problem of the new government was the fulfillment of this pledge, and it fell to Hamilton to propose the ways and means. His recommendations created the most bitter controversy of the first decade of the nation's history.

On September 21, 1789, the House of Representatives, mindful that "an adequate provision for the support of the public credit" was "a matter of high importance to the national honor and prosperity," had directed the newly appointed secretary of the Treasury to "prepare a plan for that purpose." The financial chaos Hamilton was asked to reduce to order was complex enough to tax the skill of the most resourceful financier. By mid-January 1790 he had submitted to Congress his detailed plan for handling the national debt, one that was also a carefully sketched blueprint for national strength and prosperity. Since time was needed to digest the report and to work out its implications for the new government, the sweep of Hamilton's proposals was not at first apparent. But within a few weeks they sparked a debate that was to absorb Congress for the next six months.

In his report Hamilton divided the public debt, including accrued interest and principal, into three parts: first, the foreign debt totaling about $11,700,000; second, the nation's domestic debt amounting to $40,400,000; and third, the debts of the states, which he approximated at $25,000,000.

37. Coxe to Madison, Sept. 28, 1789, Madison Papers, Lib. of Cong.

He recommended the payment of the foreign debt and the interest thereon in full; the payment of both principal and interest of the domestic debt but with a reduction of the interest rates pledged by the Confederation government (specifically, a rate of 4 percent for long-term government bonds and a rate of 6 percent for short-term bonds); the inauguration of a sinking fund designed both to manage the government's savings or surplus and through stock purchases to maintain the price of public securities; and the assumption of state debts on equal terms with public securities but with interest payments postponed until January 1, 1792. Some parts of his report were unexceptionable; other parts aroused intense opposition. There was little dispute, for example, on his proposal for handling the foreign debt, for it was agreed that national honor and the successful financial operations of the government dictated that it be paid in full. There was also agreement that the domestic debt be funded at par, though there were differences about who should receive the money. The sinking fund was accepted as a prudent fiscal expedient. More controversial was Hamilton's recommendation for the assumption of state debts.

As soon as the report on public credit was printed, the Speaker of the House sent a copy to Coxe, who emphatically approved.[38] Hamilton's proposals, after all, coincided with views Coxe had supported in essays and private correspondence. In his *Enquiry into a Commercial System* of 1787 he had proposed that Congress salvage public credit by taxation and by the sale of public lands and had pointed to the desirability of a sinking fund. On the eve of the new Congress in 1789 he had urged upon Madison the necessity of prompt attention to the establishment of a sound fiscal system, recommending both the funding of the national debt and the settlement of state debts.[39] Now Coxe anxiously awaited congressional confirmation of Hamilton's program. His congressional friends soon informed him, however, that the prospects were not encouraging. That this was partly the result of the opposition of some Pennsylvanians must have been even sadder news.

The ablest and most formidable of Hamilton's congressional opponents was James Madison, whose support the secretary had expected. Madison's objections centered around a question that was as much moral as economic: Who should receive the stock to be issued by the new government in exchange for the certificates of indebtedness of the defunct Confederation government? These certificates, which were granted to individuals for goods and services provided during the Revolution, had diminished in price proportionately to waning confidence in the fiscal solidity of the Confederation government. Many original owners, whether because of need or as a hedge

38. Muhlenberg to Coxe, Jan. 21, 1790, Coxe Papers.
39. Coxe to Madison, Mar. 18, 1789, Madison Papers, Lib. of Cong.

against further depreciation, had sold them to individuals willing to gamble on a rise in their value. In Madison's view it would be a violation of public faith, justice, and credit to reward the speculators with the face value of stock purchased at a substantial discount. Instead, he recommended a compromise. "Let it be a liberal one in favor of the present holders," he said. "Let them have the highest price which has prevailed in the market; and let the residue belong to the original sufferers."[40]

Madison's proposal touched off a debate that, as John Marshall said, "seemed to unchain all those fierce passions which a high respect for the government and for those who administered it, had in a great measure restrained."[41] Hamilton and his congressional supporters argued that the discrimination urged by Madison not only would be a patent violation of national honor but would plunge the Treasury into an administrative quagmire. Coxe agreed and also believed that the cry for discrimination was actually a request to reward the slovenly financial record and irresponsible behavior of the states. "Had they sustained the debt at its just and intrinsic value, by paying only the interest, and declaring the principal inviolable," he wrote in 1792, then "the original creditor would not have had cause to complain, nor would the purchaser have had an opportunity to speculate in the property of the soldier, the widow, the orphan, and the patriotic lender in the hour of public need."[42] In 1790, however, Congress was dealing not with what should have been but with what was, and Hamilton's opponents were convinced that the secretary's plan was designed to aid greedy speculators at the expense of patriots who had come to the aid of their country in its hour of peril. The argument in favor of discrimination was stated most persuasively by Madison, who introduced his motion providing for such a policy with an address that FitzSimons described to Coxe as one that "would do honor to his Philanthropy and Ability before Any Assembly on Earth." However, the Virginian's eloquence was not enough to override the belief, as FitzSimons phrased it, "that his Plan When Examined will be found Impracticable," and his motion was defeated by a vote of 36 to 13.[43] It now appeared certain that Hamilton's proposals for funding the debt of the central government would be adopted, whether or not in modified form.

Assumption of state debts was quite another matter. The position taken by most congressmen depended not simply on their opinion of Hamil-

40. *Annals of Cong.*, II, 1194.
41. John Marshall, *The Life of George Washington* . . . , II (New York, 1930 [orig. publ. Philadelphia, 1805]), 216.
42. Coxe, "Observations on the preceding letters of 'a farmer,' addressed to the yeomanry of the united states," *American Museum*, XII (1792), 276.
43. FitzSimons to Coxe, Feb. 12, 1790, Coxe Papers; *Annals of Cong.*, II, 1298. FitzSimons told Coxe that the congressmen who supported Madison did so merely as a "Compliment to the mover." FitzSimons to Coxe, Feb. 28, 1790, Coxe Papers.

ton's effort to enhance the power of the national government but also on the extent to which their own states stood to benefit by the measure. Massachusetts and South Carolina, whose large Revolutionary debts remained virtually unpaid, strenuously supported Hamilton's proposal, as did Connecticut. Maryland, Virginia, North Carolina, and Georgia, which had paid most of their debts, just as vigorously opposed assumption. A majority of congressmen from other states—New Hampshire, New York, New Jersey, and Delaware—were uncommitted. The swing state, so its congressmen believed, was Pennsylvania. "As to our own state," George Clymer boasted to Coxe, "the measure is in itself indifferent, and nothing may be considered in it but its natural fitness and propriety."[44]

Coxe did not agree that Pennsylvanians were quite so disinterested. "All the public creditors here are against the assumption," he wrote to Hamilton in early March. Holders of the continental debt were opposed, he went on to explain, because they feared it would increase the number of creditors among whom limited federal revenues would be divided; so too were holders of the state debt opposed, as they "would rather take the chance" with Pennsylvania than with the federal government. To Coxe the underlying basis for Pennsylvania's opposition was the comparatively modest size of the state debt and the proportionately large amount of the continental debt owned by its citizens. He considered such a pursuit of self-interest at so critical a time to be myopic. "My argument with them all," he informed Hamilton, "is that the revolution of 1789, for as such I view it, was intended to settle a great number of public difficulties . . . and that it then was and is now evident that concessions of particular advantages would be necessary to enable us to surmount those difficulties."[45] But as any man with Coxe's extensive experience as a merchant must have realized, loyalty to the Union was not likely to override considerations of personal advantage.

For the moment, however, what Coxe viewed as disinterested public spiritedness won. On March 8, 1790, by a count of 31 to 26, including the votes of two ill representatives who were carried into the House, a Committee of the Whole endorsed the assumption.[46] Such a slender margin, as Hamilton's supporters well knew, was dangerously close. The representatives from North Carolina, who were known to oppose assumption, were expected momentarily, and other representatives who voted affirmatively were by no means firm allies. The fears of the bill's supporters were well founded. On April 12 the question was again taken up in a Committee of

---

44. Clymer to Coxe, Mar. 3, 1790, FitzSimons to Coxe, Feb. 28, 1790, Coxe Papers.
45. Coxe to Hamilton, Mar. 5–9, 1790, Hamilton Papers, Lib. of Cong.
46. *The Journal of William Maclay, United States Senator from Pennsylvania, 1789–1791*, with an Introduction by Charles A. Beard (New York, 1927), 204, hereafter cited as *Maclay Journal*.

the Whole, and this time rejected by a vote of 31 to 29.[47] Although optimists like FitzSimons believed that the members of the House might reconsider their vote, the failure of repeated efforts in the lower chamber to restore this controversial clause to the funding bill indicated that assumption, if not dead, would have to be revived by the Senate.[48]

Several weeks earlier, another problem came to the fore, thus affording Congress an opportunity to put aside temporarily the thorny issue of the public debt, on which, so appearances indicated, no consensus would be reached. "The proceedings of Congress on the Report of Col. Hamilton have been long interrupted by the Memorials, relating to Slavery," James Madison informed Coxe on March 28.[49] These memorials, praying for the abolition of the slave trade, were submitted by Pennsylvania and New York Quakers and by the Pennsylvania Abolition Society, of which Franklin was president and Coxe secretary. Assuming that Madison was aware of his agency in the latter petition, Coxe felt some explanation was in order. In an obviously oblique defense of his own position, he informed Madison that members of the Pennsylvania society had supported the memorial on two grounds: the conviction that its moderate tone would obviate bitter sectional debate, and the belief that since provisions for the debt would swiftly be made, it would not interrupt the vital work of Congress. He was wrong on both counts. In the end, the issue was buried, largely as a result of the ferocity with which southerners assailed even this modicum of federal power over slavery.[50]

Such setbacks were counterbalanced for Coxe by the success of his indefatigable lobbying in behalf of American manufactures.[51] His influence was most conspicuous in the draft of "An Act to promote the progress of Useful Arts," a measure he had enthusiastically championed for years. Patent

47. *Annals of Cong.*, II, 1525.

48. *Ibid.*, 1531. See also Clymer to Coxe, May 1, 1790, FitzSimons to Coxe, Apr. 27, 1790, Coxe Papers.

49. Madison to Coxe, Mar. 28, 1790, Madison Papers, Lib. of Cong.

50. Coxe to Madison, Mar. 31, 1790, Madison to Coxe, Mar. 28, 1790, *ibid*.

51. Coxe's efforts can be seen in the several articles on manufactures that he published at this time. An article published in the *Columbian Magazine* was entitled "Address to the Land-holders, and other citizens, of New Jersey, showing the practicability, and other advantages, of establishing useful manufactures in that State" and appeared in Mar. 1790 (pp. 171–174). An incomplete, undated draft was endorsed by Coxe as follows: "Part of some Essays for N. Jersey, sent to Governor Paterson for publication 1789 or 1790. N.B. some part was republished in the Columbia Magazine by W. Young, 2d and Chestnut Streets." Coxe Papers. This partial draft is also part of another article in the same series. Although that article has not been found, the whole was presumably published in a New Jersey newspaper. See also "Spanish Wool," enclosed in Coxe to Madison, Mar. 31, 1790, Madison Papers, Lib. of Cong.; "To the Editors of the American Museum," signed "Z," *American Museum*, VII (1790), 227–228. For Coxe's authorship, see Daniel W. Coxe to Coxe, May 7, 1790, Coxe Papers. A footnote to the article

and copyright legislation, prompted by a number of petitions recommending it, had been considered in the first congressional session, where a bill affording protection to both inventors and authors had been introduced. Due to "the multiplicity of other important business," action on the bill was repeatedly postponed until August 17, when it was formally held over until the next session.[52] Soon after reconvening on January 7, 1790, Congress, prodded by President Washington's State of the Union message recommending the encouragement of "new and useful inventions" and the "promotion of science and literature," again took up the question of securing patents and copyrights. This time Congress severed the two issues by considering separately the protection of literary rights and inventions. The latter was provided by a bill reported out of committee in mid-February and scheduled for consideration by a Committee of the Whole on February 24.

In the interim Thomas FitzSimons sent Coxe a copy of the proposed patent bill, so that "if any thing Occurs to you Respecting it I may benefit of your Good Advice." It was a congenial assignment. Coxe carefully studied the proposed measure, making a number of changes, stylistic and substantive, that he promptly forwarded to FitzSimons.[53] When debate on the bill

---

stated that one of the mills described, that for "roping combed wool, hemp, and flax, is possessed by Tench Coxe, esq."

In standard bibliographies and catalogs Coxe is credited with the authorship of *Observations on the Agriculture, Manufactures and Commerce of the United States*, a 102-page pamphlet published in New York in 1789. Abundant internal evidence indicates that the attribution is erroneous, as does the title page of the work in the library of Thomas Jefferson (presumably the basis for designating Coxe as the author). In Jefferson's library the pamphlet is bound in a volume on the flyleaf of which Jefferson wrote, "Tracts American viz.—Sundry papers and pamphlets by Tench Coxe." But Jefferson had obviously decided that the work was not written by Coxe; although "*by Tench Coxe* was originally written on the title by Jefferson, only the word *by* remains, the rest having been forcibly removed and now represented only by a hole in the paper. This was probably done by Jefferson himself." E. Millicent Sowerby, comp., *Catalogue of the Library of Thomas Jefferson*, III (Washington, D.C., 1953). Even a casual reading of *Observations on the Agriculture, Manufactures, and Commerce of the United States* demonstrates not only that Coxe could not have written it but also that its author was a New Englander.

52. Before 1789 all the states had granted patents and copyrights, the former ordinarily by private acts. The early history of patent and copyright can be followed in Bruce W. Bugbee, *Genesis of American Patent and Copyright Law* (Washington, D.C., 1967), 131–148. The explanation for the postponement was offered by Hartley. *Annals of Cong.*, I, 1056–1057.

53. FitzSimons to Coxe, Feb. 22, 28, 1790, Coxe Papers. Coxe also corresponded with Clymer and Madison about the proposed legislation. See Clymer to Coxe, Jan. 18, 29, Mar. 3, 7, 1790, *ibid.*; Coxe to Madison, Mar. 21, 1790, Madison Papers, Lib. of Cong. Clymer was receptive to Coxe's recommendations. On Jan. 18 the congressman informed Coxe that "having obtained a printed copy of the bill to promote the progress of the sciences, etc.," he had called on a member of the committee handling its preparation and "filled in the several parts," implying that this information had been furnished by Coxe. Coxe Papers. Again, on Mar. 3, Clymer informed his Philadelphia correspondent that he planned to submit to the committee information that Coxe had offered on the patent bill. Coxe Papers.

resumed on March 4, the Pennsylvania congressman, well armed by his unofficial adviser, took an active part in the House debate. After adoption of a number of amendments, the patent bill was approved and sent to the Senate, where it was subjected to yet additional changes. The differences between the two chambers having been ironed out, "An Act to Promote the Progress of the Useful Arts" was signed by the president on April 10, 1790. It was, along with the Judiciary Act of 1789, one of the most important acts of the First Congress. Just as the former remains the cornerstone of the American judicial system, so the patent law remains, despite alteration, the basic statute on that subject. It is, of course, impossible to determine precisely which of Coxe's recommendations were accepted, but the measure did bear the stamp of his ideas, or so one witness, who should have known the facts, averred. Observing that "many alterations in Stile and some in Substance" had been made in the bill during the course of its progress through Congress, Thomas FitzSimons informed Coxe that among them "are some Suggested in your letter to me."[54]

Although he had labored diligently on its behalf, Coxe considered the patent law as only a first step toward the encouragement of manufactures through active and large-scale government support. He was particularly disappointed that the constitutional scruples of the authors of the bill had prevented the extending of patents to cover imported machinery. Although he did not doubt that the talent and ingenuity of his fellow Americans would lead to technological innovation, he believed it essential that they also "draw upon that great fund of Skill and Knowledge, particularly of the useful Arts, which Europe possesses." To that end he proposed to Madison that Congress set aside a million of the most valuable acres in the national domain "as a fund" to be used to encourage the introduction of inventions and discoveries by both natives and foreigners.[55] It was a proposal he had made as early as 1787, and one he would continue to advocate. But Madison was not convinced by Coxe's plausible argument that such action was well within the constitutional authority of Congress. "The Latitude of authority" that the Philadelphian assumed, Madison replied, had been "strongly urged and expressly rejected" by Congress, which had "no more power to give a further encouragement out of a fund of land than a fund of money."[56] To Coxe, conversely, Congress, in the absence of express constitutional prohibitions, had the power to do what was necessary and proper to promote a balanced national economy.

54. FitzSimons to Coxe, undated, but probably written Apr. 1790, Coxe Papers.
55. Coxe to Madison, Mar. 21, 1790, Madison Papers, Lib. of Cong.
56. Madison to Coxe, Mar. 28, 1790, *ibid.*

To one as ambitious as Coxe, the self-assumed position of unofficial adviser to congressional acquaintances was frustrating, and he awaited with mounting impatience appointment to an office that might afford him open responsibility and some public recognition for policies he had hitherto recommended in private letters and anonymous essays. In the spring of 1790 the opportunity he craved was at hand. Early in April news reached him that William Duer had resigned as assistant secretary of the Treasury. Afflicted with an extraordinarily keen acquisitive urge and not overly scrupulous about how it was satisfied, Duer, had his speculations in the public debt then been known, might have served as Exhibit A for Hamilton's critics who charged that members of the Treasury were lining their own pockets by exploiting their access to inside information. Although Hamilton was oddly reluctant to admit Duer's culpability, he must have been as pleased by the opportunity to replace him as Duer was by the prospect of devoting full time to his business interests. Certainly Coxe was eager to secure the appointment, as witnessed by remarks made in the course of a conversation with Timothy Pickering, a rival contender for the post. "His present profession was never pleasing to him," Pickering reported Coxe as saying. "Having for two or three years past, *devoted* his time and attention to the great objects of the Union, to the prejudice of his private affairs, a change for a public employment is become really desirable." Nor was Coxe deterred by the paltry annual salary of $1,500 allowed the assistant secretary, since, in Pickering's words, "he has a fortune under his foot." Thus circumstanced, Coxe did not hesitate to apply directly to Hamilton, dispatching in the space of a few weeks two letters announcing his availability and eligibility for the vacant post.[57]

"There is a prospect of Tench Coxe succeeding Duer in the assistancy of the Treasury," Senator William Maclay noted on May 3. For once the senator, an indefatigable collector of official gossip, was correct. Two days earlier Hamilton had offered the post to Coxe, urging him to assume his duties as quickly as possible.[58] That Coxe should have importunely solicited so subordinate a post was due to his hope that it might prove a stepping-stone to a higher one. Hamilton's reasons for selecting him are more of a mystery. Since he had read a number of Coxe's articles, Hamilton was certainly aware of their shared wish that the Constitution be made an in-

---

57. [Pickering] and Upham, *Timothy Pickering*, II, 443–444. The letters to Hamilton dated Apr. 6 and 27 have not been found. They were acknowledged in Hamilton to Coxe, May 1, 1790, Coxe Papers. Although Hamilton referred to the letter of Apr. 27 as that in which Coxe made "an offer of service," it is a reasonable conjecture that the earlier letter was designed to lay the groundwork for the formal application.

58. *Maclay Journal*, 249. Coxe's official appointment, signed by Hamilton and dated May 10, 1790, is in the Coxe Papers.

strument for achieving national economic growth.[59] But there were other reasons for the appointment. William Maclay may have correctly analyzed the secretary's motives when he observed that "Hamilton sees that the campaign will open against him in the field of publication and he is providing himself with gladiators of the quill, not only for the defense but attack." To Maclay, Coxe, afflicted as he was with "the literary itch, the *cacoethes scribendi*," was the ideal candidate. More likely, however, the secretary of the Treasury was bowing to political pressure. Responding to the application of Timothy Pickering, Coxe's partner in land speculation, for the same post, Hamilton remarked that "had personal considerations alone influenced" him, he might have chosen Pickering. Coxe's appointment was the result, he said, not only of his "great industry and very good talents" and "extensive theoretical and practical knowledge of Trade" but also of other "reasons of a very peculiar nature."[60] Among these, presumably, was the expediency of acquiescing in the wishes of Coxe's congressional friends, whose votes on the assumption of state debts—then languishing in Congress—he wished to win. If so, Hamilton would be disappointed. As the years passed, however, he would be even more disappointed with the appointment itself.

In replacing Duer with Coxe, Hamilton had not cleared the Treasury of the charge of speculation but rather had exchanged a big-time speculator in securities for a big-time speculator in lands. In defense of Coxe's appointment it must be said that had speculators been disqualified from holding office under the new government, the civil service would have been depleted. If Hamilton had been prescient, he would have been far more disturbed by the possible dubiousness of his new assistant's personal loyalty. As one of the best-qualified economists the country could offer, Coxe was too ambitious to selflessly serve a man who was supremely confident of his superior ability and who did not so much belittle as ignore the pretensions and claims of his subordinates. Eventually, Coxe would transfer his loyalty to a man more to his liking—Hamilton's most prominent critic, Thomas Jefferson.

For the moment, however, Hamilton was satisfied, and Coxe was elated. Five days sufficed for Coxe to put his business affairs in order and to make living arrangements for his family. The former were handed over to his capable brother, Daniel W. Coxe, who presumably had been readied for just such an occasion; the family arrangements were more complicated. Rebecca Coxe was pregnant with their fourth child, expected in August, and it seemed unwise for her to undertake the closing of their large house

---

59. See Coxe to Hamilton, Nov. 30, Dec. 16, 1789, Coxe Papers; Coxe to Hamilton, Mar. 5–9, 1790, Hamilton Papers.
60. *Maclay Journal*, 252; Hamilton to Pickering, May 13, 1790, Pickering Papers.

and the setting up of another one in New York City. Instead, plans were hurriedly made for her to stay for a time with Tench's parents in Sunbury, a decision that appeared the more suitable in view of Coxe's expectation that Congress would obviate his family's residence in New York by moving the capital to Philadelphia. In the interim, he successfully solicited James Madison's help in securing lodgings for himself at Mrs. Dorothy Ellsworth's rooming house, where he had stayed while attending the Continental Congress in 1789 and where Madison now resided.[61] Having arranged for a sulky to take his family to the country and having supervised the packing of a part of his library and his refurbished wardrobe, Coxe boarded the New York stage on May 6. Buffeted along at a pace of five or six miles per hour, he had ample leisure to contemplate his new post, which he hoped would be only the first of a distinguished public career.

61. Coxe to Madison, May 4, 1790, Madison Papers, Lib. of Cong.

8 🐚

Assistant Secretary of the Treasury

On May 7, 1790, three days before his appointment as assistant secretary of the Treasury became effective, Coxe arrived in New York. No stranger to this bustling city of 29,000 people, he was not so blinded by loyalty to Philadelphia as to overlook the charm of its chief rival. Its main thoroughfare, Broadway, was a wide, paved street, bordered by brick walks and lined with buildings whose architecture was in both the English and the Dutch styles. Many of these were mercantile establishments, but there were also attractive residences surrounded by well-tended gardens. Nearby were Columbia College, where his friend John Kemp was professor of mathematics,[1] and Trinity Church, then under construction. New York's waterfront, the site of the offices of many of his business acquaintances, was even busier than the harbor with which he was so familiar. At once provincial and cosmopolitan, New York was a proper setting for the new government. To Coxe the city also afforded a movable feast. Here was the center of power, here the men with whom he had corresponded and could now converse on public affairs, here the political notables who might further his official career.

The fledgling civil service he joined was for the most part neither professional nor particularly able. Many of the tasks were of a routine nature—posting ledgers, checking accounts, conducting outgoing correspondence, and maintaining letterbooks—requiring little more than clerical competence.

---

1. John Kemp to Coxe, Nov. 17, 1790, Coxe Papers.

This was not, in Leonard White's words, "an age of experts."[2] In a bureaucracy that included so few trained and well-qualified men, Coxe was conspicuous. In him the miniature civil service gained the one official who could—in the language of a later day—be termed a professional economist.

Coxe was in yet other ways atypical of federal officials of the first two decades of the nation's history. Although he was unusually competent, he was obliged to serve in subordinate posts throughout a long career. His administration of the agencies committed to his care—the revenue service and the purveyorship, for example—was exemplary, but his accomplishments were ignored, at least by those whose recognition of them counted. Although at one time or another he was the confidant of the nation's most distinguished statesmen—Hamilton, John Adams, Jefferson, and Madison —he alienated all except Madison. To Hamilton, who at first relied on Coxe more than on any other Treasury official, he became an object of contempt. To Adams, who at the outset of his official career was on friendly terms with him, Coxe was soon seen as an officious, insubordinate civil servant and a political pariah. To Jefferson, whom the Philadelphian loyally served both as an unpaid official assistant and as a political lieutenant, Coxe eventually appeared an intemperate and importunate office seeker, a pest who deserved to be scotched by silence. Jefferson would neither recognize Coxe for his significant contributions to the sometime secretary of state nor reward him for his strenuous support of the Republican cause in 1800. Even Madison, who for three decades maintained a warm relationship with Coxe, was unwilling publicly to admit his privately acknowledged regard for his friend's creative approach to public policy. The fault lay in Coxe, not in the prominent politicians who spurned him. The problem was neither official ineptitude nor negligence but instead stemmed from Coxe's own exaggeration of what was in fact uncommon talent and from his continual demand that others regard him as he estimated himself. His father, as we have seen, had given him such recognition, and so presumably had other immediate relatives and close friends. But to expect that the nation's leading politicians should do so was a fancy that in the end frustrated his ambition. Coxe was also stymied by his occasional display of the aristocrat's hauteur, which when projected onto the political arena prompted him to scorn those he considered less competent than himself and to claim from acknowledged peers the perquisites stemming from shared superiority. The predictable result was vengefulness by fellow civil servants, like Oliver Wolcott, Jr., and

2. Leonard D. White, *The Federalists: A Study in Administrative History* (New York, 1948), 303.

repudiation by those, like Hamilton and Jefferson, who in intellectual endowment and adeptness at statecraft were in fact superior to Coxe.

Although the particular cast of Coxe's character may have created an atypical official career, he was in yet other ways the paradigmatic civil servant of his day. Like Oliver Wolcott, Jr., Timothy Pickering, Samuel Meredith, and Richard Harrison, he was what a later generation would call a professional public servant. For Coxe, as for all these men, public office was the desideratum, and he sought it as determinedly as he expertly exercised the duties of the posts he held. He personifies that brand of official who either assisted or directed the administration of government departments and whose successful accomplishments are often solely attributed to a few outstanding secretaries like Jefferson, Madison, Hamilton, and Gallatin. Coxe represents, too, those bureaucrats whose comparatively long tenure provided essential continuity in government operations as the nationally prominent department heads came and went. But, on balance, his atypicality or typicality matter less than his personal accomplishment. During his long service as assistant secretary of the Treasury, commissioner of the revenue, and purveyor of the United States, as well as in some lesser posts, he substantively contributed to the success of the first administrations in our national history. And it is worth remarking that he held one office or another for all but two years of the crucial decades between 1790 and 1810. The most important, and to Coxe the most congenial, of these posts was assistant secretary of the Treasury.

Promptly on assuming office, Coxe, pleased with the "carte blanche given me here," undertook a systematic survey of Treasury operations, including a study of the fiscal powers granted by the Constitution and of the relevant statutes, orders, and correspondence of the department. With all the enthusiasm of a novice, he made ambitious plans for collecting economic data that would make his office the New World equivalent of the Board of Trade in England or of Jacques Necker's "board of researches and informations" in France. Coxe's plan was modeled on Necker's and called for the establishment of a comprehensive file on each of the states. This file was eventually to be used as the basis for "a book of documents for the 13 states and the U.S." that would "unfold the past exertions of this country," as well as its capacities. Although Coxe never completed the project, it represented the germ of an idea that would bear fruit four years later in his only major book, *A View of the United States*.[3]

---

3. Coxe to Benjamin Rush, May 16, June 4, 1790, Rush Papers, Hist. Soc. Pa., Philadelphia. In 1790 Coxe made a modest beginning on his plan by publishing "Notes concerning the united states of America, containing facts and observations relating to that country, for the in-

Despite such energetic plans for expanding his office to include what would be called a bureau of statistics a century or more later, Coxe had ample leisure time to enjoy New York's social life. The atmosphere was rendered more agreeable by the presence of the new nation's chief officials, who, according to Coxe, received him in a manner both "genteel and kind." On his first day in the capital he called on Vice-President Adams, who had heard of Coxe through Benjamin Rush and John Brown Cutting. The vice-president not only returned Coxe's visit on the following day but subsequently often invited him to dinner "with the heads of Departments, foreign ministers, etc. contrary to the usual course of our new ceremonies." Coxe also dined with members of the Pennsylvania delegation and other congressmen; spent a good deal of time with Madison, whom he found "a charming companion," and with Jefferson, to whom he had been recommended by Benjamin Rush; visited Hamilton's family, finding Elizabeth Hamilton "a very unassuming good woman"; and occasionally met the president and the first lady.[4] He was also on friendly terms with the diplomatic corps, notably Antoine René Charles Mathurin de La Forest, the unofficial French consul general, and Barbé-Marbois, French chargé d'affaires, with whom he often conversed on European and American affairs. Coxe needed no introduction to the city's leading merchants, with whom he had been closely allied for almost two decades, and he was now afforded an opportunity to see old business and personal friends like Edward Goold, the Ludlows, the Beekmans, and the Livingstons. That some of them, like himself, had chosen the tory side in the American Revolution must have served as a reminder that his past might yet jeopardize his future.

Coxe daily expected that his appointment to the Treasury would provide antagonistic journalists with an occasion once again to call attention to his war record. He shared his anxiety with Rush. But for the only time in Coxe's career, such fears were misplaced.[5] "A few complained—more were satisfied—but the majority of our citizens were silent upon the

---

formation of emigrants," in the *American Museum*, VIII (1790), 35–42. In this article Coxe described the agriculture, commerce, and manufacturing of the country in order to demonstrate its prosperity, its attractiveness for foreigners, and its vast potential.

4. Coxe to Rush, May 16, 1790, Rush Papers; Coxe, "To the Editor," *Aurora*, Nov. 1, 1800; Coxe to Rush, June 4, Sept. 10, 1790, Rush Papers; *Maclay Journal*, 253; Rush to Thomas Jefferson, May 4, 1790, Boyd *et al.*, eds., *Jefferson Papers*, XIX, 123. That Coxe did not see Jefferson more often was owing to the Virginian's "indisposition." "He has been attacked with a head ache," Coxe reported to Rush, "that comes on and withdraws with the Sun" and for this reason "is not much, if at all in company." Coxe to Rush, May 16, 1790, Rush Papers.

5. Coxe to Rush, May 16, 1790, Rush Papers; Rush to Coxe, May 18, 1790, Coxe Papers. The only printed attack on Coxe that has been found appeared in the *Independent Gaz.*, June 12, 1790. The article, entitled "The Vision," took the form of a rather heavy-handed satire in which the writer dreams that he returns to the United States in 1800 to find a monarchy estab-

Subject of your appointment," Rush reassured him on May 18, adding that if the appointment were publicly criticized, Coxe's newspaper allies, like Andrew Brown, "stood ready with *charged* pens" to rush to his defense. With uncharacteristic modesty Coxe explained to Rush that his immunity was a result of the "unimportance deemed to belong to the appointment." He was spared the knowledge that some whom he considered his political friends—Robert Morris, James Wilson, and, strangest of all, Thomas Fitz-Simons—privately criticized "with great asperity" an appointment they publicly approved.[6]

When Coxe took office, Hamilton's plan for restoring the public credit was bogged down. The House was proceeding to draw up a bill dealing only with the funding of the national debt, foreign and domestic, as the members were convinced that the solid majority against assumption was intransigent. But the success even of this modified version of Hamilton's plan, as the Speaker of the House reported to Coxe, was doubtful. Assumption has been "the sine qua non with the Eastern States," Muhlenberg wrote, "whilst others perhaps would rather see the whole present System destroyed than consent to the same."[7] A funding bill without assumption was hotly debated during the weeks immediately following Coxe's arrival in New York and, as much to his dismay as to Hamilton's, was adopted on June 2 and sent to the Senate. Moreover, almost as if events were conspiring to render his official debut as inauspicious as possible, the removal of the capital to Philadelphia also appeared in jeopardy.[8]

During the first months of the session the residence issue had been deceptively absent from congressional debate. It was discussed, however, at caucuses of the various delegations and at unofficial gatherings of congressmen, some of whom, certainly those of Pennsylvania, New York, and Vir-

---

lished and on reading the court calendar learns that Coxe is secretary of the Treasury, Joseph Galloway is secretary of state, and Benedict Arnold is secretary of war.

6. Rush to Coxe, May 18, 1790, Coxe Papers; Coxe to Rush, June 4, 1790, Rush Papers; *Maclay Journal*, 249. See also Daniel W. Coxe to Coxe, June 8, 1790, Coxe Papers. That Robert Morris and James Wilson should have spoken of Coxe's "character" in such a way is surprising. That FitzSimons should have done so is extraordinary in view of the warm friendship the letters between himself and Coxe in 1789 and 1790 clearly attest.

7. Frederick A. Muhlenberg to Coxe, May 2, 1790, Coxe Papers.

8. For an account of assumption, the removal of the capital, and the famous compromise of 1790, see Jacob E. Cooke, "The Compromise of 1790," *William and Mary Quarterly*, 3d Ser., XXVII (1970), 523–545. My interpretation of the compromise is at odds not only with the traditional version but also with the modification of that account offered by Kenneth R. Bowling, "Politics in the First Congress, 1789–1791" (Ph.D. diss., University of Wisconsin, 1968). Bowling's objections to my argument, along with a reaffirmation of my own position, can be followed in Kenneth R. Bowling's "Dinner at Jefferson's: A Note on Jacob E. Cooke's 'The Compromise of 1790,'" with a rebuttal by Jacob E. Cooke, *WMQ*, 3d Ser., XXVIII (1971), 629–648.

ginia, still considered it the vital issue. On April 13, the day after the crucial vote on assumption, FitzSimons described to Coxe the anger of the Pennsylvania delegation on discovering "a Combination between So. Carolina and Massachusetts with New York to disappoint any expectation of the Removal of Congress." "If my apprehensions shall be Realized," he added, "We shall not be long together for the Irritation is so great that it would be Vain to hope for any Union of Sentiment on any other question."[9]

The Pennsylvanians, employing a modified form of the strategy used in the first session, decided to remove the irritant and to further congressional progress toward removing the capital to Philadelphia, ostensibly as the temporary site. In 1790, as in 1789, they still hoped the move would become permanent. Even if the effort failed, Senator Maclay confided to Coxe, "a miscarriage can place Us in no Worse situation than we now are."[10] It soon appeared that the Pennsylvanians had succeeded; though the Senate turned down Maclay and Morris's proposal that Philadelphia be made the temporary capital, the House on May 31 decisively approved a similar motion made by FitzSimons.

Advantageously situated at a rooming house filled with congressmen among whom these parliamentary maneuverings were a constant subject of conversation, Coxe anxiously followed the fall and rise of Philadelphia's chances. After passage of the House resolution in favor of his native city, he was confident of its ultimate success. "The Senate is now the place," he wrote. "A very judicious N. Carolinian assures me both their Senators will be with us, and the opinions seem much in our favor. Several things will operate for us. So large a majority of the Representatives, the fear of a proposition for the *permanent* seat in Pennsylvania, and some other considerations will affect the votes of the Southern people."[11] Perhaps Coxe's Pennsylvania congressional friends, more conscious of the Senate maneuverings that had defeated their hopes in the previous session, were less optimistic. They should have been.

Philadelphia's triumph in the House was aborted in the Senate on June 8—"a day of confusion," according to Maclay—when the House resolve was rejected.[12] To the indignation of the Philadelphia boosters, the lower house not only refused to insist on their former vote but also abandoned Philadelphia altogether and substituted Baltimore. Instead of winning either the temporary or permanent capital, it appeared probable that they would win neither.

9. Thomas FitzSimons to Coxe, Apr. 13, 1790, Coxe Papers.
10. William Maclay to Coxe, Apr. 30, 1790, *ibid.*
11. Coxe to Tench Francis, May 31, 1790, *ibid.*
12. *Maclay Journal*, 277.

To compound Coxe's disappointment, it still did not seem likely that Congress would endorse in toto Hamilton's report on the public credit, especially now that the House had readily emasculated it by cutting out assumption. Hamilton was even more dismayed. However, he did not share his assistant's engrossment in the location of the capital. Believing it of minor consequence whether his own city, Baltimore, Philadelphia, or the Potomac be selected as the site and frantically searching for some means to assure the passage of assumption, Hamilton apparently decided that the residence might be the bait with which to catch the votes necessary to rescue his program. Although he was prepared to offer what it was not within his power to sacrifice, he was not mistaken in believing that the capital site was a lure at which some congressmen would eagerly snap. Had he any doubts about the Pennsylvanians, the transparent eagerness of his assistant secretary would have dispelled them. Coxe, Hamilton concluded, would make an ideal negotiator.

On June 13, two days after the House had spurned Philadelphia, the secretary of the Treasury decided to approach that city's most ardent supporters through a fellow Pennsylvanian. Coxe was designated to meet with his friends Clymer and FitzSimons in order "to negotiate a bargain: the permanent residence in Pennsylvania for her votes on the assumption, or at least as many votes as would be needful." With the president's private secretary accompanying Coxe, his mission seemed to bear the imprimatur of the Washington administration. Its underlying purpose, as Senator Maclay perceived, was "to open the conference with Mr. Hamilton on this subject." A day or so later the secretary of the Treasury did confer with Senator Robert Morris,[13] and this, according to the traditional wisdom, was the first step toward the famous compromise of 1790.

This compromise, virtually all historians assert, took the form of a bargain on the two controversial issues then before Congress—assumption and the residence.[14] It was negotiated by Hamilton, Madison, and Jefferson at Jefferson's house in Maiden Lane on or about June 20 at one of the most famous dinner parties in American history. The arrangement agreed upon, according to the well-known account, was that certain provisions of the assumption that Virginians regarded as inequitable would be modified; that

13. *Ibid.*, 284. The only extant account of Alexander Hamilton's negotiations with Morris is that recorded by Maclay, who repeated the story as related to him by Morris. *Ibid.*, 284–285.

14. The best account is Bowling, "Politics in the First Congress," a model monograph that accepts the traditional story while revising it in important particulars. In his excellent study of public finances during the Confederation era, E. James Ferguson demonstrates that the settlement of state accounts was an essential part of the famous compromise. Ferguson, *The Power of the Purse: A History of American Public Finance, 1776–1790* (Chapel Hill, N.C., 1961), 322–325.

Madison, while not voting for it, would not oppose the amended measure; that Hamilton would round up enough votes for passage of the residence bill; and that Jefferson or Madison would then secure enactment of assumption by persuading two Virginia congressmen—Alexander White and Richard Bland Lee—to support it. The three principals to the bargain kept their promises, and within a month or so the two measures were enacted.

So the accepted historical account goes. It should, however, be modified in a number of important particulars. Although the dinner meeting at Jefferson's house did take place and the agreement as usually described was there made, the bargain could not have been consummated. For one thing, too few congressmen were involved to provide even the swing votes on either measure. More important, different coalitions assured the success of the two bills. Each was treated separately, and passage of each was due to sub rosa congressional negotiations and compromises relating only to that measure. Thus, the bargain over the residence was arranged by Pennsylvania and Virginia congressmen before the famous dinner meeting; and the crucial bargain over assumption did not involve the residence but a reallocation of the amount of state debts to be assumed and a compromise on the interest rate to be paid on the funded debt. Moreover, the dinner table bargain involved votes in the House of Representatives, whereas the crucial battle for both assumption and the residence took place in the Senate. Nor is there any evidence that either Madison or Jefferson was responsible for the success of assumption or that Hamilton rounded up even one vote for the residence.

There was, in fact, no reason why the Treasury secretary should have bothered, for the Pennsylvanians, among whom he (with Coxe's help) was supposed to secure the requisite vote, had previously committed themselves to a Potomac-Philadelphia bill. The upshot was that when the residence bill again came before Congress, it was agreed that Philadelphia should serve as the capital for a decade, at the end of which the government would remove to a permanent location on the Potomac. Having won a consolation award, which they confidently expected to turn into the grand prize, the Philadelphia boosters had every reason to be jubilant.[15]

Coxe received the happy news in the city that soon would be the nation's capital. He had returned home at the insistence of his wife. As "the time of my confinement begins to draw near," Rebecca had written on June 20, "I cannot help feeling much unhappiness to know what is to become of me at that time," adding reproachfully that her life was, after all, "of some consequence to my children." Thus importuned, Coxe left New York early

---

15. The measure became law on July 16, 1790. For an amplification of the account in this paragraph, see Cooke, "Compromise of 1790," *WMQ*, 3d Ser., XXVII (1970), 523–545.

in July and, after a stopover in Sunbury to pick up his family, was in Philadelphia by July 5.[16] Although reluctant in her last month of pregnancy to risk the day-long trip to New York and the strain of setting up a new household there, Rebecca was even more fearful of an outbreak of yellow fever in Philadelphia. And so, with all the haste her bulky figure allowed, she arranged the packing of sufficient household effects and clothing for a brief stay in the nation's short-lived capital. Coxe, also busy with arrangements for the move, was more concerned with rescuing the Treasury's fiscal program, on which he, like Hamilton, pinned his hopes for the success of the new nation.[17]

Prospects for the Treasury program were encouraging by the time Coxe returned to New York in mid-July.[18] On July 16 the House bill providing only for the funding of the national debt was amended by the Senate to incorporate the assumption of state debts. Largely because Hamilton's judicious concessions made the measure more palatable to its former opponents, the Senate bill was approved by both houses on July 26. The advocates of assumption had at last reached the end of the rough legislative road they had traveled with such determination.[19] To both Coxe and Hamilton a cornerstone had been laid on which could be built a fiscal structure that would withstand the tremors of dissension at home and the winds of conflict gathering force abroad.

For the moment, Coxe was rescued from the complexities of debt purchase, actuarial calculations, and sinking fund operations by a different and more congenial assignment—arrangement for the approaching removal of the national capital to Philadelphia. The shipment of records and funds, as well as the selection of appropriate quarters, was the responsibility of the departmental secretaries. Hamilton promptly delegated the task of overseeing the move of the Treasury to Coxe, who also unofficially assumed the role of coordinator of arrangements for other executive departments and the Congress. Even before Congress adjourned on August 12, Coxe had initiated preparations by eliciting the aid of his brother Daniel and his friend Samuel Miles, the mayor of Philadelphia. Writing "merely as a private Gentleman," he inquired of Miles on July 29 "whether any of the public buildings are intended for the use of the three departments of State, of War,

16. Rebecca Coxe to Coxe, June 20, 1790, Daniel W. Coxe to Coxe, June 28, 1790, Coxe Papers.

17. During his brief stay in Philadelphia, Coxe reported to Hamilton on the state of public opinion regarding residence, funding, and assumption. Coxe to Hamilton, July 9, 10, 1790, Hamilton Papers, Lib. of Cong.

18. Coxe to Hamilton, July 10, 1790, Hamilton Papers; Daniel W. Coxe to Coxe, July 14, 1790, Coxe Papers.

19. The law was passed on July 26. For a more detailed account of the passage of this bill, see Cooke, "Compromise of 1790," *WMQ*, 3d Ser., XXVII (1970), 523–545.

and of the Treasury" and also recommended architectural changes in the city's "new Hall" in order to make it suitable as the national capitol.[20] Over the next few weeks he not only completed requisite arrangements for the Treasury but also served as an unpaid real estate agent. He rented his own house (which he had leased from Ann Pemberton in 1787) on Chestnut and Third streets to the Treasury for an annual sum of $660; for Hamilton's personal residence he secured Rush's house; and for congressional acquaintances he also made arrangements for suitable houses.[21] The details are of greater antiquarian than historical interest, but by October—thanks in part to Coxe's assistance—plans for the official move to Philadelphia were completed.

Although he would have preferred to be in Philadelphia while arranging for the transfer of government, Tench had been obliged to remain in New York with his wife, who late in August gave birth to a son, their fourth child.[22] A month or so later the Coxes were on their way home, where a new house awaited them on Second between Walnut and Spruce streets. Freshly decorated and roomy enough for their growing family, the house, adjoined by stables, was handily located near Coxe's office and his many friends on adjoining streets.[23]

To Rebecca, weary of living for months with relatives and then in temporary quarters in New York, and to Coxe, who never felt at home in any other city, it must have been a joyous homecoming. Philadelphia encompassed within a few blocks the social circle in which they felt most at ease. But to Coxe his native city represented something more than people. Benjamin Rush spoke for them both when he described it as "the emporium of Science as well as Commerce for the United States."[24] Certainly it was to Coxe the most civilized of American cities. Where else could he find so many congenial men, companions who shared his commitment to expanding knowledge and to the virtues of republicanism? Where else could

20. Coxe to Samuel Miles, July 29, 1790, Miles to Coxe, Aug. 2, 1790, Coxe Papers. See also Daniel W. Coxe to Coxe, July 23, 24, 1790, *ibid.*

21. On arrangements for the Treasury, see Samuel Meredith to Coxe, Aug. 21, 1790, *ibid.*; Coxe to Meredith, Aug. 26, 1790, Independence Hall Coll., Philadelphia; R.G. 217, acct. nos. 1403, 1117, General Accounting Office, Miscellaneous Treasury Accounts, National Archives. Coxe also arranged for the redecoration of the Treasury's new quarters. See Daniel W. Coxe to Coxe, Sept. 24, Oct. 5, 1790, Coxe Papers. On arrangements for congressional acquaintances, see FitzSimons to Coxe, Aug. 28, 1790, Ralph Izard to Coxe, Sept. 6, Oct. 14, 26, 1790, Rush to Coxe, Sept. 7, 13, 23, 1790, Coxe Papers; Coxe to Rush, Sept. 10, 1790, Rush Papers.

22. This was Alexander Sidney Coxe. Charles Coxe to Coxe, Aug. 19, 1790, Daniel W. Coxe to Coxe, Aug. 21, 1790, William Coxe, Jr., to Coxe, Aug. 21, 1790, Coxe Papers.

23. Coxe to Rush, Sept. 10, 1790, Rush Papers; Daniel W. Coxe to Coxe, Oct. 8, 1790, Coxe Papers. The rent was £100 per year. Arrangements had been made by Daniel W. Coxe. See Daniel W. Coxe to Coxe, Sept. 8, 15, 1790, *ibid.*

24. Rush to Coxe, June 8, 1790, Coxe Papers.

he find institutions devoted to scientific study (like the American Philosophical Society) or organizations dedicated to furthering his own absorbing interest in mechanical invention and agricultural innovation (like the Pennsylvania Society for the Encouragement of Manufactures and the Useful Arts or the Philadelphia Agricultural Society)? Where else those "noble libraries" (to use John Adams's phrase) and the museums that made the nation's chief commercial metropolis its cultural center?

The country's most cosmopolitan city was even more alluring to Coxe now that it was also the federal capital. To him, as to other aristocratic Philadelphians, the presence of the nation's top officials provided a social catalyst, enhancing the enjoyment of a society otherwise too familiar to be exhilarating. However, to some backwoods republicans it was neither enjoyable nor exciting. Commenting on "the gloomy severity" of the city's prominent Quakers, Senator Maclay observed that he knew "of no such unsocial city as Philadelphia."[25] But those more disposed than Maclay to participate in what Abigail Adams once described as "one continued scene of parties upon parties" knew better.[26]

Coxe's unimpeachable family credentials, more than his official position, assured him invitations to the drawing rooms of the city's most prominent hostesses. Dressed in blue coat, black breeches, and ruffled shirt, his hair carefully powdered and perfumed, he was a familiar figure at the balls held twice monthly by the Pennsylvania Assembly, as well as the soirees of social leaders like Mrs. Robert Morris and Mrs. William Bingham. The pacesetters for Philadelphia society, however, were the first family. Arriving in the new capital late in November, the president took up quarters in Robert Morris's elegant residence on the south side of Market near Sixth Street. It was a house Coxe knew well. The residence of Sir William Howe during the British occupation, it had also been occupied for a brief time by Howe's American successor, Benedict Arnold. It was, in one sense, particularly appropriate that the new president and the royal commander should have occupied the same residence, for Washington's mode of entertainment was as courtly as that of the Howe brothers had been. Had Coxe been inclined to dwell on such matters, he might have found a degree of irony in the reflection that he had far more often been a guest of the British commander than he now was of a republican president.

But if his official rank did not assure automatic invitations to Washington's levees and dinner parties, Coxe was compensated by his social relationship with many members of Congress and with other high-ranking officials—the vice-president and Mrs. Adams, who had rented a house from

25. *Maclay Journal*, 331.
26. Quoted in Peterson, *Jefferson and the New Nation*, 420.

one of Coxe's close family friends; the secretary of the Treasury, who had moved into Rush's residence; Jefferson, who had rented a large house on Market Street; and European diplomats and visitors, whose presence made the city seem the more cosmopolitan.

To Coxe and to other promoters of Philadelphia it was only proper that the selection of the nation's finest city as the temporary capital should now be made *in perpetuo*. Surely, federal officials once having sampled the advantages of the city—its commercial activities, its centrality, its cultural life—would find them irresistible. It remained only to provide the general government with offices and other public buildings as handsome as Pennsylvania's famous capitol, Independence Hall, and particularly to improve on the city's already superior intellectual and cultural opportunities, about which Coxe shared Benjamin Rush's confidence that they would "do more to prolong the residence of a republican Congress among us than covering our federal hall with carpets or paving our streets with silver dollars."[27] Convinced that his own office, along with Congress, would permanently remain where it was, Coxe immersed himself in the myriad of administrative details his work entailed.

The Treasury Department offices at Coxe's former residence were a hive of activity. From Hamilton's office on the first floor came reports to Congress, circulars to customs collectors, and correspondence with other Treasury officials. From the adjoining office Coxe lent such assistance as was requested. The scope and duties of his office were not well defined. When the Treasury Department was established, specific responsibilities were prescribed for all its major officers, but not for the assistant secretary.[28] The adjective affixed to Coxe's position was obviously intended to be a sufficient description of his job: he was to assist the secretary, by whom he was appointed, in whatever capacity or ways that Hamilton should dictate. In brief, the power and importance of the office depended on the degree of authority the secretary was disposed to grant and the initiative and talents of its occupant.

What William Duer had made of the post during his seven-month tenure cannot be determined. In Hamilton's papers, including the official records of the Treasury, there appears only one specific reference to a task assigned Duer—a trip to Philadelphia to negotiate a loan with the Bank of North America.[29] The silence of the record certainly can be explained by the

27. Rush to Coxe, Aug. 15, 1790, Coxe Papers.

28. The act of Sept. 2, 1789, establishing the Treasury Department only stipulated that the assistant secretary was to assume responsibility for the "records, books, and papers" of the department should the office of the secretary become vacant.

29. Syrett *et al.*, eds., *Hamilton Papers*, V, 369–371, 416.

close daily association of Hamilton and Duer, which made written communication unnecessary. Coxe's responsibilities also remain a mystery—neither the voluminous papers of the Treasury nor Hamilton's own correspondence make explicit the duties of the assistant secretary.

That Hamilton, alone among the cabinet officers, had been given an assistant suggests the importance of his department. It was far and away the largest of the executive offices created under the new government and, as Hamilton remarked in 1792, "Most of the important measures of every Government are connected with the Treasury."[30] He might well have added that this was even truer for a new government, like the United States, whose chief problems were fiscal. The Articles of Confederation, whatever its other defects, had foundered on the rock of fiscal irresponsibility, and the survival of its successor hinged on the adoption of measures that would reestablish confidence at home and abroad by the restoration of public credit. More than that, a major task of the new government, at least as Hamilton and other nationalists saw it, was to enchain thirteen scattered and formerly sovereign states into one nation. The Treasury was the sole department affording the links by which this could be done. Only it, in Leonard D. White's words, "had an extensive field service located in every large town and every section of the country."[31] Only it had a truly national constituency: importing merchants, ship owners, and those concerned in the fisheries were reached by the customs service; bank managers, stockholders, speculators, and other borrowers or investors were involved in the operations of the Bank of the United States; owners of the public debt, state and national, were in contact with loan commissioners; manufacturers and contractors were tied to the Treasury's procurement agents; and many thousands of other people were affected by the extensive internal revenue service.

By the time Coxe took office, Hamilton had established a large portion of the Treasury's far-flung "field service" and efficiently arranged for its supervision. The central Treasury office in 1790 consisted of thirty-nine people (including the department's six chief officers), and even this modest staff seemed large compared with the four clerks in the State Department or the three who handled the business of the War Department.[32] In addition to his assistant, Hamilton's major subordinates in the Treasury were: the comptroller, Nicholas Eveleigh; the auditor, Oliver Wolcott, Jr.; the treasurer, Samuel Meredith; and the register, Joseph Nourse. All were well known to Coxe except Wolcott. Although the job of the comptroller may have been

30. Hamilton to Edward Carrington, May 26, 1792, *ibid.*, XI, 442.

31. White, *The Federalists*, 117.

32. *American State Papers: Documents, Legislative and Executive, of the Congress of the United States* (Washington, D.C., 1832–1861), *Finance*, I, 34, hereafter cited as *American State Papers, Finance*.

functionally more important, Coxe was generally regarded as the second highest official in the department.

Coxe was confident that his demonstrated knowledge and industry must merit Hamilton's favor, and therefore he considered the undefined scope and consequent flexibility of his office as its greatest assets. Here was the opportunity to administer and perhaps to mold the policies he had hitherto furthered only by his writings and correspondence; here was the opportunity to work in the new government's most important executive department, in close cooperation with its influential chieftain, who was regarded by some observers as the president's prime minister. Seldom one to shower praise on another, Coxe, at least during his first months in office, was impressed by Hamilton's energy and administrative skill. The Treasury secretary was an unostentatious man who possessed "many virtues and many talents," Coxe assured Rush. "He is a man of great, constant industry and immense occasional exertions—of a very firm mind with a great deal of caution and prudence."[33]

It was surely a cautious enough description of a man whom posterity would regard as a brilliant, bold, and imaginative statesman. Coxe's failure to give full faith and credit to Hamilton's ability was, however, less a result of obtuseness or a lack of prescience than of envy of the Treasury secretary's preeminent display of those very talents on which Coxe prided himself. If Hamilton was aware of his assistant's self-assessment or of his implied claim to the secretary's position, he was as unwilling to pander to the first as he was to satisfy the latter. In time this would so sour their relationship that Coxe would manage to convince himself that Hamilton's accomplishments were trifling in comparison with the reprehensible end he believed they were designed to achieve. That goal was the establishment of a monarchy. This transmogrification, however, would occur only after five years of personal frustration. In 1790 Coxe, aware that the Treasury secretary was "the administrative architect of the new government," was intent on becoming his chief draftsman.[34]

Hamilton assigned to his assistant a variety of tasks, some of substance and a great many routine. Considerable paper work was handled by Coxe's office, though in 1791 he had only eight clerks as compared to the eleven in Hamilton's office.[35] One of his assignments was to assist Hamilton in negotiating contracts for the army for rations and other supplies, a task the Treasury Department had quietly assumed without benefit of statutory authority. Another was to help in handling the mechanics of funding both

33. Coxe to Rush, Sept. 10, 1790, Rush Papers.
34. White, *The Federalists*, 127.
35. Broadus Mitchell, *Alexander Hamilton: The National Adventure, 1788–1804* (New York, 1962), II, 358.

the assumed state debts and the continental certificates. Coxe's correspondence suggests that he also played some part in the operation of the sinking fund, by which the debt might be retired or the price of securities stabilized by government purchases. Other duties more closely resembled those of a corresponding secretary than those of an adviser on policy. At Hamilton's instructions, for example, he occasionally wrote to collectors of the customs or to lighthouse keepers on housekeeping matters and was often requested to ascertain the price of needed supplies.[36] To describe in detail these and other routine duties would be more wearisome than profitable.

Simply to recount the tasks performed by Coxe would be to overlook both the essential nature and the significance of the relationship between him and Hamilton. Whatever impact Coxe had on the work of the Treasury Department lies not so much in his competent performance of tasks, many of which would have been relegated to clerks in his own countinghouse, but in the influence he was able to exercise in his day-to-day association with a superbly gifted man whose talents he complemented. However different their backgrounds, they both had a working knowledge of the mechanics of mercantile transactions and a commitment to measures designed to protect and foster American commerce. Whether or not Hamilton was—as most historians insist—the particular spokesman and ally of the merchant class, his chief assistant was inescapably conditioned by tradition, training, practice, and personal loyalties to that class's interests. On matters of public policy, moreover, they were in agreement: they shared a conviction that sound public credit was the bedrock of viable nationhood, a crusader-like zeal for the growth of manufactures as the essential prerequisite for a balanced economy, and a belief in planned economic development with governmental patronage. Hamilton was the master strategist, Coxe the able tactician; the secretary was the creative statesman, his assistant the able statistician. At his best, however, Coxe too was an innovative economist in the sense that he, like Hamilton, was able to apply the traditional wisdom to serve the needs of a new situation.

Most significant was Coxe's contribution to the numerous reports Hamilton was called upon to submit to Congress, both those major state papers—on the bank and on manufactures—on which Hamilton's fame measurably rests and the less consequential, though contemporaneously im-

36. *American State Papers, Finance,* I, 590–592. For Coxe's involvement in the sinking fund, see Coxe to William Irvine, Aug. 15, 24, 1790, Irvine Papers, Hist. Soc. Pa., Philadelphia; Coxe to Samuel Meredith, Aug. 26, 1790, Independence Hall Coll.; Jeremiah Wadsworth to Coxe, Aug. 29, 1790, Coxe Papers. For Coxe's duties as a corresponding secretary, see Benjamin Lincoln to Hamilton, Aug. 31, 1790, Syrett *et al.,* eds., *Hamilton Papers,* VI, 587–588; Jeremiah Olney to Hamilton, Sept. 2, 1790, *ibid.,* VII, 20; Coxe to unknown recipient, July 23, 1791, Coxe Papers; Coxe to James C. and Samuel W. Fisher, Nov. 16, 1790, Conorroe Papers, Hist. Soc. Pa., Philadelphia.

portant, reports on other subjects. "In the year 1790," Coxe wrote many years later to President James Monroe, "the business of *the public lands* was committed to the Secretary of the Treasury, who requested me to sketch a report and to collect and prepare all the materials, in my powers, which I did."[37] He also assisted Hamilton, at least to the extent of providing books and papers on the subject, in the preparation of the Report on the Establishment of a Mint, on which the secretary was engaged in the winter of 1790, and he furnished advice on a number of other matters such as trade with the Orient.[38] Although we will never know the exact manner or extent of his influence, it is at least certain that he helped to shape Hamilton's grand design, including his proposals for a national bank, his Report on Manufactures, and his plans for the establishment of the Society for Encouraging Useful Manufactures.

Hamilton's report on a national bank was the single most important proposal presented to the Congress that assembled in Philadelphia on December 6, 1790, the first session to be held in the temporary capital. A week after opening ceremonies in its new quarters, an appropriately and handsomely furnished plain brick building next door to the statehouse, Congress received the secretary of the Treasury's "Second Report on the Further Provision Necessary for the Establishing Public Credit" (better known as the Report on a National Bank), which the House had requested the preceding August.[39] Like his first report on the public credit, the bank report was designed not only to facilitate establishment of the nation's credit but also to strengthen its new government. In asking Congress to charter a great quasi-public corporation, Hamilton was arguing for a broad interpretation of the Constitution. He was convinced that the precedent thereby established would be of inestimable importance in affording the national government the flexibility necessary to meet its present problems and future needs. The boldness of his plan is startling even today. In an agricultural country where even the few banks in operation were viewed with suspicion, he argued that such institutions were "nurseries of national wealth" and proposed a central bank that would facilitate the fiscal operations of the government. In a country accustomed to a feeble administration of the central government, he proposed that the government charter a major institution that he predicted would, in turn, bolster and expand the entire economy.

There were, of course, precedents for the Bank of the United States. Hamilton was intimately familiar with the Bank of New York, for which he

---

37. Coxe to Monroe, Sept. 9, 1822, Coxe Papers. Hamilton's report on vacant lands was sent to Congress on July 20–22, 1790. Syrett *et al.*, eds., *Hamilton Papers*, VI, 502–506.

38. See Coxe to Hamilton, Nov. 15, Dec. 31, 1790, Aug. 1791, Hamilton Papers.

39. This request was made on Aug. 9, 1790. The report was sent to the House on Dec. 13–14, 1790, Syrett *et al.*, eds., *Hamilton Papers*, VII, 236–342.

had served as an attorney and a member of the board of directors and had perhaps drafted the constitution. He also was familiar with European precedents and theories of banking—with Adam Smith's *Wealth of Nations*, with Malachy Postlethwayt's *Universal Dictionary*, which he had studied closely during his youth, and with the history of the Bank of England, his principal foreign model. The American precedent to which he paid greatest attention was the Bank of North America, and it was here that Coxe's influence was greatest.

The disproportionate space devoted to the Bank of North America is the one part of Hamilton's report that strikes the modern reader as conspicuously archaic. Hamilton himself provided the explanation. That institution had been, like the bank he was proposing, quasi-public in nature, the country's first "national" bank. The secretary was keenly aware that supporters of the Philadelphia bank wanted to engraft upon the existing bank the characteristics Congress believed necessary for a national bank, rather than to have a new bank established.[40] This awareness was no doubt reinforced by Coxe, who had a firsthand knowledge of the views of that city's mercantile and financial leaders.

Even before Congress formally requested Hamilton on August 9, 1790, to recommend further provisions for supporting public credit, he had deputized Coxe to sound out Thomas FitzSimons on the feasibility of converting the Bank of North America into a national bank and to elicit the congressman's views on the proper constitution of any new bank. Although FitzSimons, who also consulted Robert Morris and George Clymer on the subject, supported the creation of an entirely new institution, other Philadelphians did not.[41] William Bingham, a director of the Bank of North America, had earlier proposed to Hamilton that "a more extensive Superstructure be engrafted" onto the old bank by greatly increasing its capital stock.[42] Such a plan was, however, an anathema to New Englanders, who believed that it would provide unfair advantages to an essentially local institution.

The task of resolving these differences was assigned to Coxe, who many years later affirmed that "in 1790, when the Bank of the U.S. was es-

---

40. *Ibid.*, 341.

41. "Memoranda of Mr. FitzSimon's Remarks on proposed national Bank," July and Aug. 1790, Coxe Papers. The memorandum was probably submitted to Hamilton. In his remarks FitzSimons recommended that the relationship of the new bank to the government be similar to that between the Bank of England and the British government. He explicitly rejected the notion that the Bank of North America should be so reconstituted as to serve as a national bank. He also argued against the notion that the "United States should become stockholders" in any new bank.

42. William Bingham to Hamilton, Nov. 25, 1790, Syrett *et al.*, eds., *Hamilton Papers*, V, 552.

tablished or at least planned, I was the agent between the Eastern and Pennsylvania interest." Although precisely what he did is unknown, Coxe, as a recent scholar has remarked, "no doubt made it clear to Philadelphia's bankers that Hamilton desired to coexist peaceably with all local banks and that the competition between the Bank of the United States and the Bank of North America" would be, as Hamilton later observed, "compensated by obvious advantages."[43] Despite Coxe's attempts to pacify his fellow Pennsylvanians, however, Hamilton still considered it necessary to publicly answer the arguments advanced in support of enlarging the Philadelphia institution.

Accordingly, a good part of his report on a national bank was devoted to answering negatively the question: Is there a bank "already in being . . . which supercedes the . . . necessity of another"? His approach was to discredit the only candidate, the Bank of North America. The debates and the attendant pamphlet warfare over that institution's recharter in the Pennsylvania assembly in 1785 and 1786 "provided Hamilton with the arguments that he lists and then refutes in his 1790 Report."[44] Although historians have paid considerable attention to Hamilton's familiarity with the speeches and essays of such leading supporters of the Bank of North America as Gouverneur Morris, James Wilson, and Pelatiah Webster, they have all but overlooked his reliance on the writings of Tench Coxe.

One of the ablest literary warriors against the claims of the Bank of North America, Coxe had objected to its recharter largely on the grounds that it was not sufficiently accountable to the public, whose needs, as well as those of the state, it presumptuously scorned. Here, with supporting evidence, was an argument tailor-made for Hamilton's account of the Bank of North America, which was designed to show that, far from being an acceptable public institution, it was "the mere Bank of a particular State." The indebtedness to Coxe goes further. Many of Hamilton's arguments against the Pennsylvania bank—on the "improper rule" regulating the election of directors, on "the want of precautions to guard against foreign influence insinuating itself into the Direction of the Bank," on its "want of a principle of rotation," and on the absence of any restriction confining the debts of the bank to the amount of its capital—are remarkably similar to those presented by Coxe. The likelihood that Hamilton relied on his assistant is strengthened by the closeness of their views on banking, a coincidence that surely must have been made clear in their frequent discussions at the Trea-

43. Coxe to Albert Gallatin, Jan. 23, 1813, Gallatin Papers, New-York Historical Society, New York City; Baumann, "Democratic-Republicans of Philadelphia," 303.
44. "Report on a National Bank," Syrett *et al.*, eds., *Hamilton Papers*, VII, 243, 323. Approximately one-sixth of Hamilton's report was taken up in answering this question.

sury.[45] Just as Coxe believed that a bank "wisely and justly constructed, would be a public good," Hamilton asserted that "public utility is . . . truly the object of public Banks." Just as Coxe argued that a bank should be viewed "as a branch of the political œconomy, important in its magnitude and in its operations and effects," so Hamilton wrote of a bank's utility "to the administration of the finances" and "in the general system of the political œconomy." Just as Coxe had recommended for the Bank of North America a new plan "substantially the same as that of the bank of England," so Hamilton largely based his proposal for a new national bank on the English model.[46]

To whatever extent the report incorporated Coxe's ideas, it unmistakably bore the imprint of Hamilton's particular genius. Unmarred by the prolixity that characterized some of his (and almost all of Coxe's) writings, it was the ablest of Hamilton's memorable state papers. The manner in which he skillfully marshaled facts and made clear the complexities of banking and monetary policy without oversimplification combined to create an extraordinary treatise. As William T. Franklin, describing the reception of Hamilton's report in London, wrote to Coxe: "If all Subjects were treated in this Way, Knowledge would be much more easily acquired—and Libraries might be made portable."[47]

A majority of Congress was willing to accept the knowledge Hamilton was intent they acquire. A bill chartering the Bank of the United States was passed by the Senate on January 20, 1791, was sent to the House, where debate began on February 1, and two weeks later was adopted by the decisive vote of 39 to 20. The congratulations Hamilton and Coxe must have exchanged at the Treasury were premature, however. On February 14 the bill was presented to Washington, who immediately asked the attorney general, Edmund Randolph, for his opinion on its constitutionality. Randolph pronounced against the bank, but his opinion was pedestrian and unconvincing. The president next turned to his secretary of state. Jefferson, a legal fundamentalist, favored a strict construction of the Constitution, one characterized by a rigidity and literalness that, if adopted, would have severely limited the power of the government. That two of his cabinet members should find the proposed bank unconstitutional disturbed the president,

45. *Ibid.*, 325, 328, 326, 339. Coxe had furnished Hamilton with copies of his writings on the Bank of North America before he was appointed assistant secretary. Coxe to Hamilton, Mar. 5–9, 1790, Hamilton Papers. On one subsequent occasion Coxe again submitted his ideas on paper. See Coxe's notes on "Memoranda of Mr. FitzSimons's Remarks on proposed national Bank," Coxe Papers.

46. [Coxe], *Thoughts concerning the Bank of North America . . .* , 1, 5; [Coxe], *Further thoughts concerning the Bank*, 1; Syrett *et al.*, eds., *Hamilton Papers*, VII, 325, 319.

47. William T. Franklin to Coxe, Apr. 7, 1791, Coxe Papers.

who, not yet satisfied, sent copies of their arguments to Hamilton with a request for yet another opinion.

The Treasury secretary, in turn, elicited his assistant's ideas as to the validity of the objections raised by Randolph and Jefferson. Coxe recalled many years later that though "no man had more deference for the principal Gentlemen opposed" to the Bank, he nevertheless "put my affirmative opinion of the legality or constitutionality of it, on these two grounds: First, that the grant of Charters could be made by the legislature, *touching objects within its jurisdiction*, it being so clearly incidental to the power of legislation, that it was unnecessary to specify it. . . . Secondly, that congress having power to regulate commerce *among* the states and with the Indian tribes have full jurisdiction over such trade, so as to establish a right constitution of a chartered company therefor, or a Bank."[48] Coxe's first point was also the fundamental premise on which Hamilton based his argument on the bank's constitutionality; his second point, though not used by the secretary of the Treasury, nor for many decades endorsed by the Supreme Court, was a remarkable forecast of the interpretation of the commerce clause that would prevail in the mid-twentieth century.

Although he may have welcomed Coxe's supportive arguments, Hamilton's ideas were largely fixed, and his defense of the constitutionality of the bank was—John Marshall's opinion in *McCulloch* v. *Maryland* perhaps excepted—the most persuasive argument for a broad interpretation of the Constitution in American political literature. Whether influenced by Hamilton or convinced that the will of Congress should prevail, Washington on February 25, 1791, signed into law "an Act to Incorporate the subscribers to the Bank of the United States." Although the measure was, as time would show, a politically divisive one, Coxe, in close touch with many of the nation's leading merchants, could have assured Hamilton that at least the nation's business and financial groups heartily endorsed the new bank.[49]

Coxe gave such time as he could spare from his official duties to the irksome task of terminating his own business affairs. Upon accepting the office of assistant secretary in May 1790, he had withdrawn from the partnership of Coxe and Frazier and had taken steps to divest himself of his other business interests except land speculation. The exigencies of his office

48. Coxe to Gallatin, Jan. 23, 1823, Gallatin Papers.
49. Coxe publicly defended the bank in "Reflexions relative to the stock of the bank of the United States and to the national funds," *American Museum*, X (1791), 168–171. He offered a particularly persuasive argument in favor of the establishment of branch banks. He was also delegated some responsibility for overseeing the Treasury Department's role in their creation and operation. See Buchanan & Robb to Coxe, Dec. 25, 1791, Coxe to Samuel Smith, June 29, 1792, Coxe to John T. Gilman, Jan. 10, 1793, Coxe Papers.

certainly would have forced him to do so in any event, but the commands of the law afforded no alternative. The act establishing the Treasury stipulated that no member of its staff should, directly or indirectly, take part in commerce, own, in whole or in part, any merchant vessel, purchase public lands, or trade in public securities. Having actively engaged in each of the prohibited activities, Coxe was called upon to relinquish more than perhaps any other top official in the new government's sparse civil service. But he readily did so.

Coxe's concern in Coxe and Frazier was handed over to his brother Daniel, who was to look after Coxe's interests during the protracted period necessary to wind up the firm's complicated affairs and also to handle such financial matters as otherwise would have required Coxe's personal attention.[50] Coxe's choice was well made. Daniel, a more astute merchant than his older brother and, in time, a far more successful one, competently handled the liquidation of Coxe and Frazier's tangled accounts and smoothly placated Nalbo Frazier, who was frequently irascible because of the burden of settling the affairs of one firm while simultaneously launching his own business, this time in partnership with his brother John.[51]

Although eager to shed mercantile affairs in which he patently was no longer interested, Coxe balked at disposing of his public securities at the moment when their value was rising. Instead, he transferred his holdings to his brother Daniel, to be held in trust for Coxe and the owners for whom he held them. Although his portfolio was not large in comparison with that of other prominent Philadelphia merchants or, for that matter, some of his congressional acquaintances, it represented a sizable investment. Its precise value is difficult to determine,[52] but he owned various forms and varying amounts of the state debts of New Jersey, Maryland, South Carolina, and Georgia, as well as Continental securities, which amounted, principal and

50. The *Fed. Gaz.*, June 14, 1790, printed a notice, dated May 11, 1790, stating that "the partnership of Coxe and Frazier was dissolved the 5th Instant."

51. Daniel W. Coxe to Coxe, May 7, 11, 19, 1790, Coxe Papers; Nalbro Frazier to Charles Hamer, Aug. 10, 1790, Frazier's Letterbook, New York Public Library, New York City. Frazier's labors to wind up the affairs of Coxe & Frazier can be followed in his business letterbooks at N.Y. Public Lib.

52. The difficulty of determining the size of Coxe's investment is owing to his ownership of stock registered in the names of his brothers Daniel and John Coxe; in the absence of relevant correspondence, it is impossible to distinguish between their own holdings and those they held in trust for Tench. The difficulty is compounded by Coxe's possession of securities that belonged to his former correspondents and that were subsequently conveyed to them (Coxe to John Habersham, Sept. 14, 1790, Daniel W. Coxe to John D. Coxe, July 14, 1791, Coxe Papers) and by the impossibility of determining whether Loan Office certificates that he exchanged for government stock were his own or belonged to former business correspondents. There is also no way of determining what proportion of stock funded by Coxe, Furman & Coxe belonged to Tench. See Moore Furman to Coxe, Jan. 20, 1789, Furman to William Coxe, Sr., Mar. 3, 1791, *ibid.*

interest, to at least $3,000, but perhaps as much as $15,000. His largest holding was in securities of the state of Georgia, and he unhesitatingly put pressure on subordinate Treasury officials of that state to assure their unquestioned acceptance and prompt payment.[53]

What Coxe asked of others he, in turn, willingly bestowed. To fellow officials and to friends he granted favors unstintingly and openly, even though high standards of official probity would have dictated forbearance. This was particularly true of the advice he offered correspondents who inquired about speculation in the public debt. Thus from William Irvine, himself a government official, Coxe in August 1790 received the following query: "Can you with propriety give an opinion how high you will be able to bring" the price of public stock, "and at what point of time they will probably be at the highest? . . . I do not wish to make any other use of it than as a guide to dispose of a part of my own" stock. In reply, Coxe shared his reasons for expecting a rise in price, advising Irvine that "this is not your time to sell."[54] He also counseled Joseph Whipple, collector of the customs at Portsmouth, New Hampshire, who, "not having at present any agent or Correspondent at Philadelphia for transacting private business," solicited Coxe's advice and assistance about "subscribing to the loan of the federal debt." To his friend Thomas FitzSimons, to give a final example, Coxe obligingly supplied information about the acceptability of Rhode Island certificates that had been offered the Pennsylvania congressman "in payment of a debt that has long been Withheld from me."[55]

53. See "Account" dated 1791–1793 and headed "Six p cent Domestic debt. Daniel W. Cox, of Philadelphia," Coxe Papers. His total holding in securities of the state of Georgia was $3,130.50. *Ibid.* A "Certification by Joseph Nourse" attests that on Mar. 31, 1791, accrued interest of $21.42 was paid on the principal of $1,887 registered on the books of the Treasury under the name of Daniel W. Coxe. *Ibid.* Also in the Coxe Papers is an "Abstract of Certificates of Public Debt," Sept. 22, 1790, in the name of John D. Coxe listing certificates totaling $2,513. See also Daniel W. Coxe to John D. Coxe, July 14, 1791, Coxe to Daniel W. Coxe, Sept. 13, 1790, Daniel W. Coxe to Coxe, Sept. 10, 1790, *ibid.* For Coxe's holdings of New Jersey and Maryland money, see Daniel W. Coxe to Coxe, Jan. 30, 1791, William Tilghman to Coxe, Feb. 18, 1790, *ibid.*; Coxe to Tilghman, Feb. 4, 1790, Tilghman Papers, Hist. Soc. Pa., Philadelphia. For evidence of his ownership of South Carolina and Georgia securities, see Daniel W. Coxe to Coxe, Oct. 5, 1790, Coxe Papers. Coxe also owned an undetermined amount of Continental currency, exchangeable at the ratio of one dollar certificate for every $100 of the old currency tendered (Daniel W. Coxe to Coxe, June 7, 1790, *ibid.*), and he held money of this kind belonging to Moore Furman and Isaac Hartman; he exchanged this currency for new certificates. See also Coxe to Furman, May 21, 1791, Habersham to Coxe, Nov. 3, 1790, Coxe to Habersham, Feb. 7, 1791, *ibid.*; Coxe to Habersham, Sept. 14, 1790, Society Papers, Hist. Soc. Pa., Philadelphia.

54. Irvine to Coxe, Aug. 20, 1790, Coxe Papers; Coxe to Irvine, Aug. 24, 1790, Irvine Papers. Irvine was a member of the Board of General Commissioners on the Accounts of the Several States.

55. Joseph Whipple to Coxe, Nov. 7, Dec. 2, 1791, Coxe Papers; Coxe to Whipple, Nov. 20, 1791, Houghton Library, Harvard University, Cambridge, Mass.; FitzSimons to Coxe, Aug.

Coxe was even more generous in providing counsel and assistance to prospective subscribers to stock of the Bank of the United States, and in view of the large speculative profits that ensued, his acquaintances had every reason to be grateful. Subscriptions to the new bank, authorized by Congress in February 1791, were postponed four months in order to allow sufficient time for prospective investors in remote parts of the country to learn of the $8,000,000 in stock available for public purchase. Within an hour after the subscription books were opened on July 4, however, the entire sum was greatly oversubscribed by eager investors, among whom were thirty members of Congress, states like New York and New Hampshire, and institutions like Harvard College and the Massachusetts Bank. Due to a continued heavy demand, the price of stock soared. Weeks before the subscription was opened, the more avaricious of Coxe's friends had solicited his advice and assistance,[56] and, once it was clear what a speculative bonanza bank stock afforded, additional requests flooded his office.

Perhaps the most brazen appeal came from Senator Philemon Dickinson, brother of John Dickinson, who (exemplifying what he described as a "Spirit of Speculation which exceeds everything known in this Western World") asked Coxe to share with him such inside information as he might be able to procure. Among other improper questions, Dickinson, a large stockholder in the Bank of North America, asked if Hamilton, as rumored, intended to request that Congress authorize an alteration in the law "respecting the . . . admission of the Stockholders of the *Old* Bank, into the new"? Could Coxe also tell him "what Mr. H's Ideas are of the *dividends* which will probably arise, when the Bank is organized"? Did Hamilton, finally, intend to "recommend an *increase* of *Stock*"? Although Coxe's reply to these indiscreet questions has not been found, he did manage to procure for Dickinson twenty-five of the bank's shares. What he arranged for one friend he happily did for others—among them Arthur Lee and Dr. James McClurg of Virginia, Elbridge Gerry and Fisher Ames of Massachusetts, and Nicholas Gilman of New Hampshire—and wound up running, in effect, a commission-free brokerage business.[57]

By present-day standards Coxe's willingness to serve as an invest-

---

20, 28, 1790, Coxe Papers. For other examples of Coxe's advice on stock transactions, see Coxe to Furman, May 16, 1791, to Richard Bassett, May 19, 1791, to James McClurg, Aug. 31, 1791, *ibid.*

56. Hammond, *Banks and Politics*, 123; McClurg to Coxe, June 13, 24, 26, 1791, Philemon Dickinson to Coxe, June 27, July 2, 1791, Coxe Papers.

57. Dickinson to Coxe, July 13, 1791, Coxe to Dickinson, July 18, 1791, Coxe to Elbridge Gerry, July 16, Sept. 15, 1791, Gerry to Coxe, Aug. 4, 1791, Coxe to McClurg, July 16, Aug. 31, 1791, McClurg to Coxe, July 22, Aug. 17, 19, 29, Oct. 31, 1791, Bingham to Coxe, Dec. 24, 1791, Arthur Lee to Coxe, Jan. 10, 1792, Fisher Ames to Coxe, May 31, 1791, Coxe to

ment counselor for select friends while holding a major post in the department measurably responsible for the bank's operations was manifestly an official impropriety. So, too, was his use of members of the Treasury Department field service—customs collectors, revenue supervisors, and the like—to assist in conducting his private business affairs, though he obligingly offered reciprocal services. Such also was the case when he tried to purchase land in the District of Columbia during an official visit to the Potomac area in the summer of 1791 to observe and to report on the progress made in laying out the projected capital city.[58] But as Coxe saw it, such activities were unexceptionable, and in his defense it should be emphasized that his was a time when the distinction between one's public and private business was not clearly demarcated.

There was, by contrast, no official indecorum in affording acquaintances essentially clerical or administrative favors like registering their stock or forwarding their dividends. To name all those he helped in this and other ways (by entertaining them and their visiting friends, by forwarding their pay vouchers, by collecting debts owed them in Philadelphia, and by purchasing and forwarding articles ranging from clothes to coaches) would be to list an impressive number of the prominent Americans of his day.[59] Although Coxe was not a mere vulgar opportunist, his behavior was largely dictated by irrepressible political ambition, including hopes of succeeding Hamilton as secretary of the Treasury. Had gratitude been a distinguishing trait of those to whom he extended so many favors, their support would have been assured.

Coxe did not rely on influence alone, however, but pinned his ambition to the Treasury, where he hoped to make a record of such indispensable assistance and brilliant achievement that recognition and promotion would be assured. The problem was that Hamilton neither wanted rivals nor needed to rely on an assistant for the executive ability that he possessed to a preeminent degree. Driven by "a passion for order, system, punctuality,

---

Ames, June 7, 1791, Nicholas Gilman to Coxe, June 30, 1791, Coxe Papers. Coxe was also asked to arrange for the subscription of 150 shares for the state of New Hampshire. Coxe to Gilman, July 11, 1791, to Gilman and Josiah Bartlett, July 9, 30, 1791, Gilman and Bartlett to Coxe, June 30, 1791, *ibid.*

58. In addition to illustrations of land transactions carried on in cooperation with Treasury officials given later in the text, see Coxe to Thomas Marshall, Jan. 2, 1795, to Edward Carrington, Dec. 29, 1792, Carrington to Coxe, Jan. 6, Dec. 18, 1792, June 22, 1796, John Davis to Coxe, Jan. 23, 1794, *ibid.* On Coxe's attempts to purchase land in the District of Columbia, see Daniel Brent to Coxe, Aug. 13, 1791, Samuel Hanson to Coxe, Aug. 22, Sept. 15, 1791, Benjamin Stoddert to Coxe, Sept. 28, 1791, James M. Singun to Coxe, Nov. 7, 1791, *ibid.*

59. The instances of favors are too numerous to list even partially here, but see his correspondence with James Iredell, Edmund Randolph, Aaron Burr, William Vans Murray, George Cabot, Thomas Hartley, Otho H. Williams, and Richard Henry Lee, to name but a few.

accuracy, and energy," Hamilton tended increasingly to oversee personally even the details of Treasury operations. Certainly his staff, Coxe included, would have been amused at the absurdity of John Adams's later charge that "the real business" of the Treasury Department "was done by Duer, by Wolcott, and even . . . by Tench Coxe."[60] Although he was not in principle opposed to granting considerable discretion, Hamilton in practice assumed the initiative himself and exercised the ultimate authority. It was not that he shouldered responsibility because he loved power; it was rather that he exercised power because there was no need to delegate authority. Nor did Hamilton intentionally minimize the importance of his assistant and other subordinates or calculatedly withhold from them official and public praise. The point was rather that Coxe wished to enlarge the powers of his office and craved public recognition, neither of which Hamilton was likely to sanction. Frustration was inevitable, and by March 1791, as his disappointment mounted, Coxe had decided that the assistant secretaryship was not the stepping-stone to high office that less than a year earlier he had believed it would be.

A barometer of Coxe's dissatisfaction was his willingness to surrender the assistant secretaryship, ostensibly the second most important job in the Treasury, for the office of comptroller. Its first incumbent, Nicholas Eveleigh, had performed his duties perfunctorily and by March 1791 was too ill even for that. Aware that the position would soon be vacant, either by Eveleigh's resignation or his death, Coxe carefully weighed its advantages and drawbacks. Its major attractions were the atypical degree of discretionary authority with which it was statutorily vested and the extent to which its work was unsupervised by Hamilton, under whom the comptroller became, in Leonard White's words, "the most influential officer *per officis* in matters of administration."[61] Its major disadvantage, by contrast, was that it theoretically ranked below the assistant secretaryship. Weighing concrete benefits against an intangible asset, Coxe opted for the former.

Sometime early in April 1791 he signified to Hamilton "his wish to be considered for the office of Comptroller." The secretary, though scrupulously courteous, responded that he had already firmly resolved to appoint the auditor of the Treasury, Oliver Wolcott, Jr. Even if there were not circumstances "which originated at the time of Wolcott's appointment to his present office" that prevented him "from moving in favor of any other person," Hamilton said, he was convinced that "the relation between the offices of the Comptroller and Auditor creates a kind of pretension in the

---

60. White, *The Federalists*, 126; John Adams, *Correspondence of the Late President Adams; originally published in the Boston Patriot . . .* (Boston, 1809), 54–55.
    61. White, *The Federalists*, 345.

latter to succeed the former." To soften the blow, Hamilton remarked that he could "see as many public advantages" from Coxe's own appointment as that of "any other person" and assured Coxe that he should feel free to apply to the president.[62] For Hamilton to hand out such a sop was as atypically generous as it was gratuitous. For Coxe, attuned as he usually was to the nuances of polite conversation, to grasp it so eagerly was as aberrational as it was impolitic. Perhaps his pride would not allow him to confront even the possibility that Hamilton considered Wolcott's ability and usefulness superior to his own, or the wish may have been the father of self-deception. In any event, he not only acted on what he interpreted as the secretary's recommendation that he apply to the president but also called on Hamilton's most conspicuous political enemy to forward the job application. Jefferson was happy to oblige.

"Mr. Eveleigh, the late Comptroller of the Treasury, is dead," Oliver Wolcott, Jr., wrote his father on April 16. "There will be much competition for the office; who will be successful I cannot say. I have full reason to believe, that the Secretary of the Treasury wishes that it may fall to me."[63] There were, as Wolcott surely knew, only two in the race—himself and Coxe. The latter got off to a fast start. Within hours after he learned of Eveleigh's death, Coxe dispatched to Jefferson a long letter enclosing his application for the office, explaining the grounds of Hamilton's preference for Wolcott and quoting the secretary of the Treasury's assurances "that he would by no means advise my declining to apply to the President." Would the secretary of state consult with Madison about the propriety of his application and, if the two men reacted favorably, forward it to the president?[64] Jefferson was confident of Coxe's qualifications and surely delighted at an opportunity to meddle in the affairs of the Treasury, against whose secretary his personal animosity had steadily grown over the preceding months, and he did not bother to consult with Madison. Instead, on Sunday morning, April 17, the day after receiving Coxe's letter, he promptly wrote to the president, then on a tour of the southern states. He enclosed not only Coxe's letter of application, along with a part of the latter's letter to himself, but also "a blank commission; which, when you shall be pleased to fill it up and

62. Hamilton to George Washington, Apr. 17, 1791, Syrett *et al.*, eds., *Hamilton Papers*, VIII, 293–294.

63. Oliver Wolcott, Jr., to Oliver Wolcott, Sr., n.d., George Gibbs, ed., *Memoirs of the Administrations of Washington and John Adams, Edited from the Papers of Oliver Wolcott, Secretary of the Treasury* (New York, 1846), I, 64. This letter is undated; however, since Eveleigh died on Apr. 16, 1791, it was presumably written on that day or shortly thereafter.

64. Coxe to Jefferson, Apr. 16, 1791. The first two pages of this letter were enclosed in Jefferson's letter to Washington, Apr. 17, 1791. Paul Leicester Ford, ed., *The Works of Thomas Jefferson* (New York, 1904–1905), VI, 246–247. The remaining three pages are in the Jefferson Papers, Lib. of Cong.

sign, can be returned for the seal and counter-signature."[65] It was the kind of deft and subtle political maneuver at which Jefferson excelled. By sending the president a blank commission along with Coxe's letter of application, he might manage to contrive the appointment of his own friend in the Treasury Department before Hamilton's letter recommending Wolcott could reach the South—if, that is, Hamilton cooperated by procrastinating for a few days.

The secretary of the Treasury did not cooperate. Even before the presidential party left Philadelphia on March 21, he had told Washington that should Eveleigh die, Wolcott was the man best qualified for the comptrollership, and on the same day that Jefferson wrote his letter recommending Coxe, he had dispatched a persuasive letter in support of Wolcott's appointment. Having shrewdly guessed that Coxe would enlist Jefferson's support, Hamilton skillfully parried it. "Other characters will be brought to your view by weighty advocates," he remarked, and though he inserted an intervening paragraph before mentioning Coxe, Washington could have entertained little doubt about the character to whom Hamilton referred any more than he could have questioned, once Jefferson's letter was before him, the identity of the chief "weighty advocate." Hamilton did not imply that he doubted Coxe's ability or loyalty. "On the score of qualification," as well as "on personal accounts," he said, no appointment "would be more agreeable to me." But Wolcott also was qualified, and Hamilton believed he should be preferred.[66]

Jefferson's shrewdness was, in this instance, no match for Hamilton's adroitness. By tying his own management of the Treasury Department to Wolcott's invaluable assistance, Hamilton made the president's acquiescence into a vote of confidence for his own conduct of the Treasury. Washington's response was cryptic. "Mr. Wolcott may be informed it is my intention to appoint him to the office of comptroller," he wrote to Hamilton on June 13, 1791; he passed over Jefferson's letter of recommendation with diplomatic silence.[67]

Though he may have smarted under the rebuff, Coxe too was silent. Perhaps he had convinced himself that his contribution to national economic policy would outweigh Wolcott's administrative skill, however great. It was to Coxe, after all, that Hamilton had entrusted the preparatory work for his *Report on Manufactures,* a state paper certain to be of major importance.

65. Jefferson to Washington, Apr. 17, 1791, Ford, ed., *Works of Jefferson,* VI, 246–247.
66. Hamilton to Washington, Apr. 17, 1791, Syrett *et al.,* eds., *Hamilton Papers,* VIII, 291–294.
67. Washington to Hamilton, June 13, 1791, *ibid.,* 470. Although both Jefferson's and Hamilton's letters were written on Apr. 17, the former "by some odd accident of circumstance" reached Washington only on his return to Mount Vernon, two months later. Dumas Malone, *Jefferson and His Time,* II, *Jefferson and the Rights of Man* (Boston, 1951), 353.

9

The Encouragement of Manufactures

However varied and indeterminable the origins of the sources on which Hamilton relied in preparing his Report on Manufactures, Coxe was the single individual whose influence was most decisive.[1] "A proper plan or plans" for the encouragement of manufactures had been requested by the House of Representatives on January 15, 1790, five months before Coxe's appointment to the Treasury. Knowledgeable though Hamilton was on economic subjects generally, except during his boyhood mercantile apprenticeship in the West Indies he had not had the opportunity to acquire the kind of detailed data he believed necessary for the preparation of such a report. He promptly took steps to obtain such information by sending on January 25 a circular letter to prominent promotional societies throughout the country requesting reports on the state of local manufactures. Among them was the manufacturing society in Philadelphia, whose secretary, Tench Coxe,

---

1. This assessment is at odds with the two ablest explorations of the subject, Mitchell, *Hamilton: National Adventure*, II, 151, and Syrett *et al.*, eds., *Hamilton Papers*, X, 12. Although I was in part responsible for the editorial note on the subject in the latter volume, my restudy of the subject (based on the discovery of additional pages of Coxe's draft of Hamilton's report) convinced me that Coxe's contribution was more significant than previously realized. I argued this thesis in "Tench Coxe, Alexander Hamilton, and the Encouragement of American Manufactures," *WMQ*, 3d Ser., XXXII (1975), 369–392, an essay drawn from and substantially the same as the present chapter. In this chapter, however, I have not repeated the detailed evidence in support of my argument (notably the comparison between Coxe's draft and Hamilton's report); the interested reader is referred to my published essay for the evidence, especially 372n, 374n, 372–377.

was among the nation's best-known and most active advocates of manufactures.[2]

In response to Hamilton's queries, Coxe provided a bright picture of the current state and future prospects of manufactures both in Pennsylvania and in the country at large.[3] But he also described the difficulties under which domestic manufactures labored, pointing to those the Treasury secretary would discuss at length in his report. Included among these hindrances were a shortage of labor, the related need for "machines and secrets in the Useful Arts," and the want of adequate capital. Although he generally endorsed Coxe's economic diagnosis, Hamilton emphatically did not share the Philadelphian's belief that dependence on British "goods and habits in trade" was a defect in the new nation's economy, one that must be corrected by the cultivation of France. Nevertheless, what Hamilton must have viewed as heretical views on foreign policy mattered less to him than the rightness of Coxe's domestic prescriptions. Certainly no American of that day was a more indefatigable advocate of Hamilton's brand of economic nationalism than was Coxe.

It was recognition of this that was in part responsible for Hamilton's decision to appoint Coxe assistant secretary of the Treasury in May 1790 and to assign to him, soon after the Philadelphian took office, the task of collecting additional data on American manufactures and of preparing a report on their current state and on the means whereby they might be encouraged. Coxe swiftly began to carry out the assignment. On May 11 he addressed to Treasury officials a circular letter repeating Hamilton's request of the previous January for information, and he devised an efficient filing system for this material, as well as for data on commerce, agriculture, and general economic conditions in the states and their subdivisions.[4] Although he counted on Treasury officials to supply reliable statistics, Coxe was by no means dependent upon them. As secretary of the Pennsylvania manufacturing society, he had corresponded with similar organizations in other states, and his acquaintance both with Philadelphia's leading merchants and

2. "Hamilton to The President Directors and Co. of the Society for the incouragement of Manufactures etc. [of] Philadelphia," Jan. 25, 1790, Coxe Papers. Aware of Coxe's repute, Hamilton had three months earlier submitted to the Philadelphian a number of queries concerning economic conditions in Pennsylvania (Hamilton's letter of Oct. 26, 1789, has not been found). Coxe, always ready to discuss his favorite subject, not only answered Hamilton's specific questions but also submitted a general survey of "the present state of the navigation of Pennsylvania with a comparison of the same with that of the principal Nations of Europe," as well as eight other articles. Coxe to Hamilton, Nov. 30, 1789, *ibid*. The articles submitted are listed on the endorsement of the draft of this letter.

3. See *ibid*. for a partial draft of Coxe's letter dated Feb. 1790.

4. Syrett *et al.*, eds., *Hamilton Papers*, VI, 209n. See also Coxe to Benjamin Rush, May 16, 1790, Rush Papers, Hist. Soc. Pa., Philadelphia.

with the country's best-known advocates of manufacturing provided him an extraofficial and countrywide network of well-informed correspondents. Some of them, such as Jeremiah Wadsworth and William Paterson, were members of Congress and available for informal consultation; others, like Andrew Van Bibber of Baltimore and Nathaniel Hazard (who wrote to Coxe frequently and at length), were eager to share their knowledge of local conditions; and a third group, including Thomas FitzSimons and William Barton, were longtime Philadelphia associates. It was fortunate that Coxe could command such assistance, for the available (though incomplete) evidence suggests that the Treasury officials whose aid he solicited were either uncooperative or uninformed.[5]

Unlike Hamilton, who labored over draft after draft before he was satisfied with the report he submitted to Congress on December 5, 1791, Coxe prepared only one draft, which he obviously dashed off quickly, perhaps in a day or two. This celerity was due neither to carelessness nor to indifference but rather to a mind so stocked with information on the subject that scant preparation was needed. After all, he had written article after article describing the condition of domestic manufactures and the necessity and means of their encouragement. He was also at that time sending off to the *American Museum* weekly segments of his rebuttal to Lord Sheffield's *Observations on American Commerce*. In these articles Coxe included a detailed examination of the current state of the American economy.[6] The nature of his draft—the avoidance of theoretical considerations, the generalizations drawn from his files of facts and statistics—was attributable to his strict interpretation of the congressional mandate that the secretary of the Treasury prepare a plan for "the promotion of such manufactures as will tend to render the United States independent of other nations for essential, particularly for military, supplies."[7] If interpreted literally, and Coxe did so,

5. Coxe's correspondence on manufactures may have disappeared in fires that destroyed many Treasury Department records. That he collected more information than the Treasury records indicate is suggested in a "Supplementary Note" on household manufactures that was published in his *View of the U.S.* and that he said was based on inquiries made in preparation for the Report on Manufactures. There is also an undated letter in the Coxe Papers that was sent to members of the Pennsylvania Manufacturing Society inquiring in detail about the manufacture of paper.

In March 1791 Coxe again tried to obtain aid from Treasury officials, sending out another circular that stipulated more precisely the type of information needed. Coxe to Collectors of the Customs, Mar. 10, 1791, Hamilton Papers, Lib. of Cong. Although the replies were more satisfactory, he was obliged, nevertheless, to rely primarily on his own copious collection of economic data.

6. "A brief examination of lord Sheffield's observations on the commerce of the united states of America" was first published in the *American Museum*, IX, X (1791). For bibliographical information, see chap. 10, n. 1, below.

7. *Journal of the House of Representatives of the United States*, I (Washington, D.C., 1826), 141–142.

this resolution merely called for the recommendation of measures to accomplish the goal specified, not for a defense of these manufactures, whose desirability was assumed in the resolution, much less for an analysis of the comparative advantages of agriculture and manufactures or a foray into political economy. Coxe, in sum, tailored his sententious report to congressional specifications.

Coxe's draft for Hamilton's report, probably written during January or early February 1791, was a tangle of deletions, linear insertions, marginal notations, and other alterations.[8] After an opening paragraph in which he briefly stated why the "expediency of encouraging manufactures . . . appears at this time to be generally admitted," Coxe offered a survey of practices by which European nations had traditionally sought to achieve self-sufficiency in the supply of articles indispensable to national economic vitality and military strength. To his list of familiar devices, such as protective or prohibitive duties, bounties, and premiums, he joined a discussion of their applicability to American conditions and needs, thus outlining a plan compounded of European precedent and domestic exigencies. Coxe then turned to an enumeration of those manufactures necessary for defense "or which may be deemed most essential to the Government and citizens of the United States." His description of the ones he regarded as vital (gunpowder, brass, iron, wood, sailcloth, cotton goods, and linen articles, for example) included proposals on how best to encourage them. Both the articles enumerated and the recommendations offered were essentially those the secretary of the Treasury would present in his report six months later.[9]

Hamilton probably began systematic and sustained work on Coxe's report in February 1791, shortly after it was submitted. Four months later, on June 22, the secretary directed a circular to the newly created supervisors of the revenue requesting detailed information on the past, present, and prospective state of manufactures in each revenue district; soon thereafter he may have begun his review of European writings on national economic policy. Whatever he learned from the latter, the replies to his circular letter that trickled in during the summer and fall of 1791, though a valuable guide to prevailing economic conditions, did not significantly influence his report. As its closest students have remarked, "The information which he appeared most anxious to obtain," such as the comparative costs and profits of agriculture and manufactures, "was not readily available."[10]

---

8. For a description of Coxe's draft and an explanation of why scholars have not fully recognized its importance, see Cooke, "Coxe, Hamilton, and the Encouragement of Manufactures," *WMQ*, 3d Ser., XXXII (1975), 372n.

9. Coxe's "Draft," Coxe Papers; Hamilton's "First Draft," Syrett *et al.*, eds., *Hamilton Papers*, X, 43–46.

10. Syrett *et al.*, eds., *Hamilton Papers*, X, 10.

During the torrid days of August and September, Hamilton remained in the capital, turning out no less than four drafts of his report. The foundation on which he elaborately built was Coxe's draft, most of which, though reorganized and sometimes rephrased, survived Hamilton's successive revisions. The latter were submitted to Coxe, who made comments and corrections on them.[11]

The Report on Manufactures submitted to Congress on December 5, 1791, has been widely regarded as the greatest of Hamilton's memorable triad of reports. The judgment is a curious one, however. Leaving aside the considerations that it was the only one of his major reports that Congress failed to adopt and that its subsequent influence (particularly on a protective tariff) is indeterminable, it lacks the creative boldness, the conciseness, and the readability of his Report on the Public Credit, as well as the taut organization and intellectual force of his Report on the Bank. Prolix and repetitious, the Report on Manufactures was also more derivative than inventive. As the editors of the most recent edition of Hamilton's writings observe, " It contains few, if any, specific proposals that even the most enthusiastic supporters of Hamilton could maintain were original. In this sense, the Report is as much a product of its times as the creation of its author."[12] The subject had, after all, been repeatedly explored by political economists abroad and aired time and again by American advocates of a balanced national economy, most notably by Coxe.

What Hamilton did was to add to Coxe's compendium a philosophical argument for the indispensability of American manufactures to an essentially agricultural and underdeveloped nation. Unlike Coxe and other American economic nationalists, the Treasury secretary was not content to infer the need for manufactures from their observable utility at home and abroad. He rather sought to demolish the theoretical assumptions on which European economists and philosophers—notably the Physiocrats and Adam Smith (Hamilton's principal intellectual target)—based their objections to the "artificial" encouragement of manufactures. If belief, and thus practice, flowed from theory, then the way to amend error was to assail false theory. Hamilton's unique accomplishment was to present the case for manufactures not only in practical but also in theoretical terms. The written record contains no hint that Coxe (though a close student of European political

11. For the evidence that Hamilton built on Coxe's draft, see Cooke, "Coxe, Hamilton, and the Encouragement of Manufactures," *WMQ*, 3d Ser., XXXII (1975), especially 347n. For evidence that Hamilton submitted his revisions to Coxe, see the manuscript drafts of Hamilton's Report on Manufactures in the *Hamilton Papers*, particularly the fourth draft. The material that the editors have there identified as written in an unidentified hand is in Coxe's writing. Syrett *et al.*, eds., *Hamilton Papers*, X, 124, n. 107.

12. Syrett *et al.*, eds., *Hamilton Papers*, X, 1.

economists) contributed to Hamilton's exposition of economic theory. (We cannot, of course, know what transpired in their frequent conferences at the Treasury Department.) The Philadelphian's demonstrable contribution lay elsewhere: the secretary of the Treasury's more practical discussion of the utility of manufactures (including his assistant's favorite literary technique of appealing to past accomplishment as the harbinger of yet greater success) was substantively and illustratively the same as Coxe's.

Coxe's contribution to the Report on Manufactures was confined neither to his preliminary sketch of it nor to his editorial assistance on the Treasury secretary's own drafts. Many of Hamilton's seemingly independent ideas and recommendations were precisely those that Coxe had propounded in his writings, most notably in his essays on manufactures and commerce published in 1787 and in "A brief examination" (1791) of Lord Sheffield's *Observations on American Commerce*.[13] One might, of course, argue that such similarity was merely fortuitous, but in view of Hamilton's familiarity with his assistant's writings, such a possibility must be ruled out.[14] If Hamilton needed information on American manufactures or sought arguments in support of their encouragement, it is surely reasonable to assume that he would have turned to one whose "great industry," "very good talents," and "extensive theoretical and practical knowledge of Trade" he respected and with whom he was in almost daily association.[15] His own assistant was, in sum, the nation's most influential advocate of the ideas and program set forth in the secretary of the Treasury's report.

Since Coxe's views are discussed elsewhere in this book, the claim need not be demonstrated elaborately at this point. Certainly Coxe and Hamilton held the same view of the relation between manufactures and national power and prestige. The advantages Hamilton attributed to manu-

13. In an annotated version of Hamilton's Report on Manufactures a number of references are made to parallel statements in Coxe's writings. *Ibid.*, 230–340. It would be possible to make many more.

14. Coxe had sent to Hamilton at least eight of his essays before his appointment as assistant secretary. According to an endorsement on the draft of Coxe to Hamilton, Nov. 30, 1789, Coxe Papers, the articles enclosed were:

"1. Enquiry—(Museum)
2. An address to the friends of American Manufactures—(Museum)
3. A paper on the future legislation of Commerce addressed to R. H. Lee, Esqr.—(Museum)
4. A Continuation of the address on the Subject of American Manufactures—(Museum)
5. Thoughts on the future prospects of America published in Dunlaps paper of 1788 about Septr. or Octr.
6. An account of the Navigation etc.
7. Spanish Wool
8. Succedanea for foreign liquors."

15. Hamilton to Timothy Pickering, May 13, 1790, Pickering Papers, Mass. Hist. Soc., Boston.

factures—the heart of his report—were the same as those the Philadelphian had stressed time and again: the division of labor, the utility of machines, the expansion of economic opportunity, the creation of additional modes of investment, and an enlargement of the market for agricultural produce. Their emphasis on the last of these advantages suggests a mutual desire to dispel the notion that an agricultural South and an industrial North were natural antagonists and to reiterate their conviction, to use Hamilton's words, that the sections so "succour" and "befriend" each other as to come "at length to be considered as one." To both men the indispensable consequence of such national unity would be economic progress, defined as the promotion of manufacturing at home and the acquisition of wide foreign markets. To neither of them, however, was such progress automatically guided, as Adam Smith believed, by some hidden hand. The momentum for the desirable changes required "the incitement and patronage of government."[16]

But to stress their common repudiation of Smith's laissez-faire, as well as of the Physiocratic doctrine that agriculture is "the most beneficial and productive" economic activity, is to overlook an important difference in emphasis and tone, one that rendered Coxe, in Leo Marx's words, "a subtler and more farsighted—if less candid—advocate of industrialization than Hamilton."[17] More attuned than his official superior to the susceptibilities of a predominantly agrarian nation, Coxe was more intent on demonstrating the benefits of a partnership between the farm and the factory than in proving the superiority of the machine. Hamilton, for his part, offered no equivalent of Coxe's "implication that, somehow, technology would help America reach a kind of pastoral stasis." Hamilton was a more consistent mercantilist, arguing that self-sufficiency and wealth were the sure means to secure the ultimate goal of national power and thus American supremacy. Coxe did not disagree, but, as Marx perceptively observed, he "saw the need to couch this aim in the language of the prevailing ideology." Unlike Hamilton, Coxe understood that his countrymen "preferred not to acknowledge wealth and power as their goals," and he recognized "that Americans would be more likely to endorse the Hamiltonian program with enthusiasm if permitted to conceive of it as a means of fulfilling the pastoral ideal."[18] But Coxe did enthusiastically champion Hamilton's program, particularly its insistence on the indispensability of manufactures to a balanced economy.

Their collaboration—and such it was—on the Report on Manufac-

16. Hamilton's "Report," Syrett *et al.*, eds., *Hamilton Papers*, X, 267, 293.
17. *Ibid.*, 231; Marx, *Machine in the Garden*, 168.
18. Marx, *Machine in the Garden*, 167–169.

tures was a natural result of Coxe's encyclopedic knowledge of the American economy and Hamilton's intellectual creativity, as well as their shared commitment to economic nationalism. The precise extent of the contribution of each is less important. The famous report indubitably bore the imprint of Hamilton's own ideas and program; yet Coxe's role in its preparation cannot be swept aside as merely that of a compiler of useful facts and figures. Although not the kind of state paper Coxe would have produced alone, the report clearly reflects both his industrious research and the policies that he had previously proposed and would continue to champion for more than two decades. An eclectic in economics as well as in statecraft, Hamilton doubtless relied on whatever sources were at hand, but when the lineage of the Report on Manufactures is traced, the major threads are found to lead to Tench Coxe.

Not only did Coxe collaborate with Hamilton on the Report on Manufactures, but he also played a major role in the creation of the Society for Establishing Useful Manufactures, the most ambitious industrial experiment in early American history. The S.E.U.M. was a practical demonstration of arguments that would be presented in the Report on Manufactures. Although Hamilton's support and participation were crucially important, Coxe must be credited with both the initial idea and the plans for its actualization. He had outlined proposals for the creation of a government-sponsored manufacturing town several months before Hamilton lent the prestige of his office and his enthusiasm to such a project; long before that Coxe had been among the most active and prominent members of the Pennsylvania Society for the Encouragement of Manufactures and Useful Arts, whose accomplishments Hamilton attempted to nationalize.[19] As discussed earlier, Coxe had dispatched his own agent, Andrew Mitchell, to England to clandestinely make models of textile machinery, and when this attempt at industrial espionage failed, he had arranged for the local construction of laborsaving machines, patterned on British models, that would be utilized by the proposed national society.[20]

Coxe's acquisition of this machinery was made possible by George Parkinson (subsequently an employee of the S.E.U.M.), an English emigrant who had brought with him to the United States purportedly valuable industrial secrets culled during his years as a weaver in Darlington. On January 11, 1790, Coxe and Parkinson signed a partnership agreement according to which the Englishman, averring that he "possessed . . . the Knowledge of all

---

19. I am indebted for this observation to Baumann, "Democratic-Republicans of Philadelphia," 316.

20. For the story of Mitchell and Coxe, see "Contract between Andrew Mitchell and Tench Coxe," Aug. 9, 1787, Mitchell to Coxe, Aug. 16, Oct. 3, 24, 1787, Feb. 1, Mar. 3, 7, May 4, June 4, 1788, and two undated letters, Coxe to Mitchell, Sept. 21, Oct. 21, 1787, Coxe Papers.

the Secret Movements used in Sir Richard Arkwright's Patent Machine" (which his own improvements made also applicable to the manufacture of hemp, flax, worsted, and silk), agreed to construct and deliver to Coxe a working model of an experimental mill. Ownership of the model, patent rights, and all profits made by its use were vested equally in the partners. In return, Coxe agreed to pay Parkinson £16 a month for the period required to construct the model and £400 out of the first profits earned, to furnish all requisite supplies, to procure a patent, and to arrange for the passage of Parkinson's wife and children from Liverpool to Philadelphia.[21]

Within three months the Englishman had complied with his part of the bargain, and Coxe promptly forwarded Parkinson's patent petition and model of a flax mill to his friend George Clymer, congressman from Pennsylvania, who was requested to present them to the secretary of state and the attorney general. Bureaucracies then, as now, moved slowly, but a patent was finally granted in March 1791.[22] On March 24 Parkinson announced that the American government had officially endorsed his evasion of those English laws that were intended to prevent the emigration of skilled artisans and the purveyance of industrial secrets. His patents, Parkinson's advertisement stated, consisted of "improvements upon the mill or machinery . . . in Great Britain" that were of the utmost importance to the United States and were now available to "any individual or company on terms to be agreed upon."[23] No one responded, however, until Parkinson's business partner prevailed on Hamilton to recommend the Englishman to the directors of the S.E.U.M. Whether or not Coxe benefited personally from the arrangement (and he apparently did not), he was aware of no impropriety.

To Coxe every effort in support of manufactures, whether private or official, was a form of public service; his recommendation of Parkinson was on a par with his public proposal of policies that would find fruition in the S.E.U.M.[24] And he was a tireless propagandist for his policy proposals. In

21. "Articles of Agreement," Jan. 11, 1790, *ibid*. See also George Parkinson to Coxe, Apr. 15, 1794, *ibid*. Coxe arranged for the passage of Parkinson's family through James Maury, United States consul at Liverpool. See Coxe to Maury, May 4, 1791, Maury to Coxe, July 29, 1791, *ibid*.

22. The story of the patent petition can be followed in William Coxe, Jr., to Coxe, Jan. 22, 1790, Thomas FitzSimons to Coxe, Feb. 12, 1790, George Clymer to Coxe, Apr. 22, May 1, 1790, Daniel W. Coxe to Coxe, May 15, July 23, 24, 1790, *ibid*.; Coxe to Thomas Jefferson, Mar. 14, 1791, Jefferson Papers, Lib. of Cong. See also Parkinson to Coxe, July 12, Dec. 7, 1792, Coxe Papers. Parkinson's patent is dated Mar. 17, 1791. Davis, *History of American Corporations*, I, 399.

23. *Fed. Gaz.*, Mar. 24, 1791.

24. Indeed, before his appointment to the Treasury Department, Coxe had made no secret of his personal interest in Parkinson's machinery. An article in the May 1790 issue of the *American Museum*, perhaps written by Coxe, described the Englishman's invention, adding in a footnote that the aforesaid "mill for roping combed wool, hemp, and flax, is possessed by Tench

"A brief examination," for example, he pointed to the introduction of labor-saving machines as a means of rapidly exploiting America's abundant resources and of incidentally enriching its citizens, suggesting that "the public creditors, the owners of perhaps fifteen millions of sterling money of now inactive wealth, might at this moment do much towards the introduction of the cotton mills, wool mills, flax mills, and other valuable branches of machine manufacturing." For this purpose, he recommended that a subscription of $500,000 in transferable stock, payable in public paper, be floated; that this be used as collateral for a loan of specie from a cooperative foreign nation; and that the capital so raised be employed in the purchase of an extensive area of land and the erection thereon of manufacturing establishments. If "persons of character" were to proceed "with judgment and system" in such a plan, Coxe concluded, "they would be sure of success in their manufactories; they would raise a valuable town upon their land, and would help, to support the vallue of the public debt."[25]

Coxe, then, had proposed precisely the type of model manufacturing city Hamilton would recommend; here, as the foremost authority on the S.E.U.M., Joseph E. Davis, comments, were foreshadowed "the features of the mature project."[26] Such features were also prefigured in other articles published by Coxe at this time: on the importation of skilled workers and machinery, on a lottery to raise supplementary funds, and on government sponsorship or support of manufactures. In his writings Coxe also threw out as bait for prospective investors in a manufacturing town the possibility of windfall profits from rising land values, and he persuasively presented the case for the practicability of proceeding initially with the manufacture of cotton goods. The Society for Establishing Useful Manufactures, in fine, was constructed according to Coxe's blueprint.

This assertion of Coxe's influence is rendered the more certain by the similarity of the society to his "Plan for a Manufacturing Society," prepared in April 1791. First shared with Hamilton and then submitted to Jefferson, the "Plan" was an elaboration of the proposal that Coxe had made in "A brief examination."[27] In his "Plan for a Manufacturing Society," Coxe once

---

Coxe, esq." *American Museum*, VII (1790), 288. Once he was appointed to the Treasury and became involved in the plans for the S.E.U.M., however, Coxe said nothing more publicly of his partnership with Parkinson.

25. Coxe, "A brief examination," *ibid.*, IX (1791), 179–180.

26. Davis, *History of American Corporations*, I, 351. Davis convincingly spells out the similarities between Coxe's proposal and the S.E.U.M. That Hamilton's published papers contain no evidence that he was considering such a society before the preparation of Coxe's plan in Mar. or Apr. of 1791 is suggestive.

27. Coxe to Jefferson, Apr. 15, 1791, Jefferson Papers. A draft of the "Plan" is in the Coxe Papers.

again recommended that a capital of half a million dollars be raised by subscriptions (to funded stock of the federal government, however, he now added stock of the Bank of the United States) and that this sum be used as security for a foreign loan (Holland was now designated) of the same sum in specie. Stockholders in the corporation should apply for an act of incorporation to one or more of the state legislatures, which should also be asked to authorize lotteries for funds to improve internal navigation and to encourage settlers desiring to move to the model city. The customary corporate structure was recommended: stockholders should elect a number of directors, who in turn should appoint a manager.

The first major task of the directors would be the purchase of suitable land, situated, in order to assure easy and cheap transportation, on a navigable river and containing streams with adequate power to run the machinery. The area so acquired should be laid out in lots to be sold, rented, or leased to manufacturers, tradesmen, and other interested settlers. Although Coxe believed that if it were feasible a variety of manufactures should be supported, he argued that under existing circumstances only those should be encouraged that were suitable for the introduction of laborsaving machines or for the institution of "*labor-saving processes*." What were the advantages of his plan? Coxe ticked off the familiar ones: enhanced confidence in government and bank stock "by creating a new object for them," an increment in the value of improved land, and, above all, handsome profits from the society's manufacturing operations.[28]

Coxe's "Plan for a Manufacturing Society" dovetailed precisely with Hamilton's ideas and may indeed have been prepared at the Treasury secretary's request. "The more I have considered the thing," Hamilton remarked to William Duer in a letter enclosing Coxe's proposal, "the more I feel persuaded that it will equally promote the Interest of the adventurers and of the public and will have an excellent effect on the Debt."[29] He had already discussed the plan informally with a number of prominent businessmen, Duer included, and by the summer of 1791 was ready to carry it out. Leaving Coxe in charge of other Treasury affairs, he traveled in July to New York, where he lent the prestige of his office and his personal influence among the city's leading capitalists to the launching of the project. Whether because of the contagion of his enthusiasm or the speculative bent of New York's business community, the society's capital stock of $100,000 was promptly subscribed, and on August 9 a number of its larger stockholders met at New Brunswick, New Jersey, to discuss ways of raising additional capital and to lay plans for the formal organization of the society. The

28. Coxe, "Plan for a Manufacturing Society," Coxe Papers.
29. Hamilton to William Duer, Apr. 20, 1791, Syrett *et al.*, eds., *Hamilton Papers*, VIII, 300.

secretary of the Treasury was authorized to begin negotiation for a suitable charter, to secure qualified artisans for the manufacture of cotton, and to advertise the project in the country's principal newspapers.[30]

Early in September, as the previously depressed stock market propitiously showed signs of recovery, Hamilton made public the society's "Prospectus," a carefully contrived promotional document, already privately circulated and designed to attract investors.[31] Its purpose, like the Report on Manufactures that Hamilton was then preparing, was to demonstrate that both the national and individual interests would be promoted by industrialization; unlike that report, however, the focus of the "Prospectus" was on private gain rather than the public weal. Accordingly, it emphasized the current state of domestic manufacturing, pointing to its disadvantages and advantages and presenting a plan by which the former might be obviated and the latter secured. The benefits were those to which industrial propagandists had often pointed—the abundance of raw materials and the absence of foreign competition.[32] The alleged handicaps, as Hamilton, Coxe, and many others had repeatedly insisted, could easily be overcome—the labor shortage by the introduction of machines, by the employment of women and children, and by the encouragement of immigration; the lack of capital by "a proper application of the public Debt" and by a pooling of individual and corporate resources. The "Prospectus" called for seed capital of $500,000—made up of $100 shares to be subscribed either in public stock or in specie—and proposed that whenever one-fifth of this sum had been raised, a manufacturing establishment capable of producing paper, cotton goods, and other items should be chartered by New York, Pennsylvania, or New Jersey, preferably the last. To that end the "Prospectus" included a model for the charter. Like the recommended corporate structure, this included virtually all of Coxe's favorite proposals—the incorporation of the manufacturing town, the establishment of a lottery, and the investment of company funds in the purchase of lands and the construction of the necessary buildings.

Whether Hamilton or Coxe actually drafted the "Prospectus" is neither determinable nor particularly important. More significant is the inclusion in that document, though in amplified and occasionally modified form, of Coxe's "Plan for a Manufacturing Society" drafted in April of the same year, a plan whose implementation had been made possible by Hamilton's influential advocacy.[33]

---

30. Davis, *History of American Corporations,* I, 370, 373–374.

31. See "Prospectus," Syrett *et al.,* eds., *Hamilton Papers,* IX, 144–153.

32. Coxe, "A brief examination," *American Museum,* XI (1791), 180.

33. This conclusion was also reached by Davis, *History of American Corporations,* I, 356.

Hamilton and Coxe also collaborated on the decision to locate the manufacturing town in New Jersey. The choice was made as early as April 1791, and the "reasons which strongly recommend" that state ("it is thickly populated—provisions are there abundant and cheap. . . . Its situation seems to insure a constant friendly disposition" to the advancement of manufactures) were explained in the S.E.U.M. "Prospectus." But precisely where should the town be situated? On the Passaic, the Raritan, or the Delaware River? Each location had merits, and each had the support of influential landowners eager to reap the profits accruing from enhanced land values. In an effort to arm himself with facts to counter the importunities of land speculators, Hamilton in mid-August engaged two agents to reconnoiter the more likely sites. Some weeks later they laconically reported that the falls of the Passaic River offered "one of the finest situations in the world," the Delaware "several good situations," and the Raritan none at all.[34] Since no supporting evidence was offered, this recommendation was of no practical use, and the secretary of the Treasury, having himself no special interest in such a comparatively minor matter, turned the problem over to his assistant.

Coxe was willing to find a location for the model town but was by no means disinterested. The extensive landholdings of his father-in-law, Charles Coxe, included property on the proposed Delaware River site near Trenton, as well as on the Raritan, and Charles Coxe was understabably eager that the manufacturing city be located at one place or the other. The fulfillment of his wish depended for the moment on Thomas Marshall, the agent deputized by Coxe to resurvey the various sites proposed. Charles Coxe was not backward in pressing his case. Should Marshall see fit to recommend that the model town be located on Charles Coxe's property, the Treasury agent was authorized by its owner to report to his boss that "Coxe offers every *other* Lot, free of Purchase to Col. Hamilton."[35] While politely discreet, Marshall was unobliging. Instead, he rhapsodically endorsed a site on the Second River, three miles from the center of Newark and a mile from the Passaic River, and despite William Duer's preference for the falls of the latter, Marshall stuck firmly to his recommendation.[36]

The decision lay with the yet-to-be-appointed directors of the

---

34. William Hall to Hamilton, Aug. 29, Sept. 4, 1791, Syrett *et al.*, eds., *Hamilton Papers*, IX, 121, 171.

35. Charles Coxe to Coxe, Oct. 10, 1791, Coxe Papers. For a fuller account of Thomas Marshall's inspection of eligible sites and Charles Coxe's stratagems to have his property chosen, see Cooke, "Coxe, Hamilton, and the Encouragement of Manufactures," *WMQ*, 3d Ser., XXXII (1975), 386–387.

36. Marshall to Coxe, Sept. 21, 27, Oct. 10, 1791, Hamilton Papers; Charles Coxe to Coxe, Oct. 10, 1791, Coxe Papers; Marshall to Hamilton, Oct. 2, 1791, Syrett *et al.*, eds., *Hamilton Papers*, IX, 267–269.

S.E.U.M. The appointment of directors awaited, in turn, the granting of a satisfactory charter by the New Jersey legislature. Demonstrating that its twentieth-century partiality to large corporations has a long history, that body promptly granted all that was asked, and on November 22, 1791, Governor William Paterson, whose name tactfully was chosen for the newly chartered town, signed the bill creating the Society for Establishing Useful Manufactures. Its corporate structure was roughly the same as that recommended by Coxe in his plan of the previous April and reiterated in the society's "Prospectus"—overall direction by a board of directors and management by a governor and deputy governor. More important than its formal organization and status as a New Jersey corporation was its control by a coterie of wealthy eastern businessmen, mostly New Yorkers ("I wish very much," John Kemp wrote to Coxe, "there had not been So many Speculators among them"),[37] and its establishment under federal auspices (if the quasi-official support of the secretary of the Treasury can be so construed).

At the first meeting of the board, held on December 9, 1791, Hamilton's friend Duer, the rich and influential New Yorker whose speculations covered the whole sweep of American economic activity, was elected governor.[38] The board also discussed the controversial question of a location, as well as the secretary of the Treasury's nominations for the society's top jobs (William Hall, Joseph Mort, Thomas Marshall, William Pearce, and George Parkinson). Of these, at least two were based on Coxe's recommendations. Parkinson, Coxe's "business partner," was recommended as a foreman in the cotton mill. Pearce, whom Hamilton had employed "in preparing Machines for the use of the Society," had become Coxe's protégé soon after the English inventor arrived in America in the summer of 1791. It was Coxe who (through the agency of William Seton, on whom he enjoined secrecy) submitted to President Washington descriptions and drawings of Pearce's machines and who drafted Pearce's petition to Jefferson, Knox, and Edmund Randolph for patents on a number of textile inventions, including a double loom to be operated by one person. It was also Coxe who persuaded Pearce to sell to Coxe's own partner, Parkinson, all of Pearce's "right title interest and property" in his inventions "so far as regards hemp and flax."[39]

37. John Kemp to Coxe, Dec. 25, 1791, Coxe Papers. The directors of the society consisted of seven New Yorkers and six Jerseymen. For information on their business careers, see Davis, *History of American Corporations*, I, 392–398.

38. Nathaniel Hazard presumably was alone in the conviction that Coxe would "be at the Head of that splendid Undertaking." Hazard to Coxe, Oct. 4, 1791, Coxe Papers.

39. Hamilton to Governor and Directors of the S.E.U.M., Dec. 7, 1791, Syrett *et al.*, eds., *Hamilton Papers*, X, 345; William Pearce to Jefferson, July 25, 1791, Coxe Papers. Pearce had been recommended to Coxe by Jefferson. Coxe to Jefferson, July 13, 1791, Jefferson Papers. Jefferson also backed Coxe's request to reimburse Pearce for his expenses by assuring William

Given his acquaintance with many of the artisan émigrés in Philadelphia, Coxe may also have been instrumental in selecting the other three top employees proposed by the Treasury secretary, especially since Hamilton, as his leading biographer concedes, "had no experience for this special task," in which successful execution "must spell success or failure for the best plan."[40]

Although Coxe was in a position to designate some of the employees of the S.E.U.M. and although Hamilton proposed that he should help manage the society, Coxe had no control, unfortunately for his father-in-law, over the location of the proposed town. The society's directors, beset by importunate property owners like Charles Coxe and torn by "clashing personal interests," repeatedly deferred the decision, finally selecting the falls of the Passaic River, next door to Newark.[41]

Neither of the Coxes need have been disappointed, for the decision was of no great consequence. Within months the society was in trouble; within a few years it had collapsed. No doubt the experiment was premature; perhaps to have succeeded at all the society would have to have been either public or quasi-public, subsidized by state funds (the application of federal funds at that time would have been out of the question). Whatever the larger issues, more mundane things were directly responsible for the failure of this ambitious attempt to achieve national economic planning by harnessing private capital. Adequate capital was not forthcoming. Initially, S.E.U.M. stock was snapped up with the same avidity that national bank stock had been. But when the time came to make the first quarterly payment for stock, formerly eager investors had second thoughts.[42] This was owing not only to doubts about the viability of the society but also to a financial panic in the spring of 1792 that brought a sharp fall in government securities and occasioned the bankruptcy of the governor of the corporation and several of its directors.

Only a group of myopic speculators could have entrusted the man-

---

Seton, cashier of the Bank of New York, that all charges, including the Englishman's passage to America, would be repaid. Seton to Hamilton, June 11, 1792, Syrett *et al.*, eds., *Hamilton Papers*, XI, 506. Secrecy about Pearce's machines was necessary, Coxe explained, because an attempt had "been made to induce Mr. Pearce to take away or give up his Machinery, and to return to Europe." Coxe to Seton, July 15, 1791, Coxe Papers. For the draft of Pearce's petition to Jefferson in Coxe's hand, undated, see *ibid.*

40. Mitchell, *Hamilton: National Adventure*, II, 182.

41. Coxe to Hamilton, May 20, 1792, Hamilton Papers; Davis, *History of American Corporations*, I, 402–405, 418; Mitchell, *Hamilton: National Adventure*, II, 183. Despite Hamilton's proposal, Coxe became neither a director nor a shareholder of the S.E.U.M.

42. Of the $625,000 subscribed by Dec. 1791, Davis calculates that the stockholders actually paid in somewhere between $240,000 and $300,000. Davis, *History of American Corporations*, I, 405, 475.

agement of what might have been a great experiment in economic planning to Duer, one of the great risk-takers of his day, a man unlikely to forgo personal advantage for the good of any cause. With Duer, the chief administrator, in debtors' prison, the society's directors, numbed by his and their own financial reverses, faced the futile task of trying to recover a large sum of money that had been entrusted to Duer and for which he failed to account.[43] As if the "financial visionary Duer" had not caused trouble enough, Pierre L'Enfant, a "talented engineering visionary," added to the society's woes.[44] Employed to prepare a plan for the new town, the French engineer attempted to duplicate the imaginative design he had recently completed for the new federal capital, stubbornly refusing to acknowledge that the resources of a fledgling private corporation were not those of a national government. In brief, by the time the board held its third meeting in April 1792, the funds of the society were depleted, its leadership discredited, and its affairs in confusion.

Bewildered by the hopeless disarray of the society's affairs, those directors who were still solvent called on the St. George of the Treasury Department to slay the dragons of malfeasance and inefficiency. Although Hamilton promptly came to their rescue, not even his managerial wizardry could long arrest the downhill course of this once-promising venture. By the late summer of 1792 his timely first aid, combined with a rising stock market, did superficially appear to have given the society a new lease on life, but his intervention, ironically enough, was itself a serious impediment to recovery. His political battle with Jefferson was then raging fiercely, and his intemperate newspaper attacks on his cabinet colleague did more to arouse hostility against himself than to discredit Jefferson. For the S.E.U.M., this contributed to a steady erosion of the public confidence necessary to buoy successful stock flotations. "The newspapers of 1792," in Joseph E. Davis's words, "interestingly reveal the scope and vehemence of the attacks which the new enterprise sustained, and their connection with the party warfare which was just now reaching an unprecedented height."[45] They reveal, too, the strong counterattack mounted by the society's supporters, who rushed also to the defense of Hamilton, his personal integrity as well as his policies.

The ablest of the gladiators defending Hamilton was Coxe. The occasion for his familiar entry into the journalistic arena was the publication in August and September 1791 of a series of "Letters addressed to the yeomanry of the united states" attacking the "dangerous scheme of . . . mr.

---

43. For an account of the effect of Duer's bankruptcy, see Hazard to Coxe, Mar. 17, 1792, Coxe Papers.

44. The quoted phrases are from Mitchell, *Hamilton: National Adventure*, II, 185.

45. Davis, *History of American Corporations*, I, 426.

Secretary Hamilton, to establish national manufactories."[46] The author was George Logan, the prominent Quaker doctor of Philadelphia, who as a United States senator a decade later would be one of Coxe's closest Pennsylvania political allies. To "A Farmer," as Logan pseudonymously signed himself, Hamilton's much-touted grand industrial design was controlled by "a junto of monied men, under the immediate patronage and protection of government." Led by Hamilton, this nefarious group had finagled from the New Jersey legislature "one of the most unjust and arbitrary laws . . . that ever disgraced the government of a free people." According to Logan, the legislature had sacrificed the interests of a majority of citizens by granting to "a few wealthy men" the exclusive jurisdiction of an extensive area and an unconscionable number of unconstitutional privileges. The law establishing the S.E.U.M. subverted "the principles of . . . equality, of which freemen ought to be so jealous," fostered "inequality of fortune," and strongly suggested a predisposition "to an aristocracy." But while Logan ostensibly stalked the society, he was really after bigger game: Hamilton, author of the "flimsy" Report on Manufactures. To Logan such iniquitous Federalist measures as funding, the bank, and excise laws were to "an alarming degree" undermining American liberties—stripping all power and influence from the farmer, the artisan, the merchant, the small-scale manufacturer, and the laborer and consigning them "to contempt, or, at best, to the sad privilege of murmuring without redress."[47]

Coxe was convinced that no one was better qualified than himself to prepare a point-by-point refutation of this assault on Hamilton's alleged "dangerous scheme" to encourage manufactures (of which Coxe was the author).[48] To Coxe, "A Farmer" personified the agrarian prejudice of far too many Americans and also illustrated an important historical law: "Measures intended for the public good, and really calculated to produce that desirable end, have been honestly misunderstood, or wilfully misrepresented." The illuminating light of reason, he believed, would dispel the wrongful lessons inferred from the past and would reveal the true facts of

46. George Logan's *Five Letters addressed to the yeomanry of the united states: containing some observations on the dangerous scheme of governor Duer and mr. Secretary Hamilton to establish national manufactories* was published in pamphlet form on Aug. 21, 1792, and reprinted in the *National Gazette* (Philadelphia), Aug. 29, Sept. 5, 19, 1792, and in the *American Museum*, XII (1792).

47. Logan, "Letters addressed to the yeomanry," *American Museum*, XII (1792), 213, 162–163.

48. See "Observations on the Preceding Letters" by "A Freeman" in *American Museum*, XII (1792), 167–170, 217–221, 272–278. The title of these articles was made meaningful by the consent of Mathew Carey to print his friend's articles immediately following Logan's "Letters to the yeomanry of the united states." Coxe identified himself as the author in a letter to Jacob Broom of Jan. 24, 1794. Coxe Papers.

the present. Coxe presented his rebuttal in a series of articles simply entitled "Observations on the Preceding Letters."

Coxe's first assignment was to give his antagonist a lecture on current events. Contending that the analogies Logan drew from European experience were uniformly false, he offered example after example to show that the recent history of Holland, France, and England, far from demonstrating the futility of government sponsorship of manufacturing and of supervision of the economy, actually proved their unqualified success. The author of the "Letters to the yeomanry" was also deplorably misinformed, Coxe argued, about the perquisites and purposes of the "national manufactory." It emphatically was not, as Logan implied, a federally subsidized corporation enjoying exemptions, privileges, and bounties granted by Congress. It was rather a bold effort on the part of public-spirited individuals to promote the nation's economic self-sufficiency.[49]

Just as his adversary had used the S.E.U.M. as a springboard for an attack on Hamiltonian policy generally, so Coxe turned his "Observations on the Preceding Letters" into a defense of measures that he himself had helped to formulate. To him the "Farmer's" assault on Hamilton's program was not only gratuitous but perverse. Logan's view of funding as a system by which the property and rights of the poor were handed over to "wealthy gamesters and speculators" was benighted and was superficially plausible only because it overlooked the sorry and essentially immoral record of the states, a record that had made the federal system imperative. Logan's views on banking were so confused, Coxe asserted, that one must first assume the basis for Logan's argument before proceeding to refute it. Logan's protest against the excise law was similarly based on specious premises. Most objectionable of all was "A Farmer's" assertion that if this country had as "firm and equitable" a constitution as that of France, Americans would be spared the baneful program imposed by the Federalists. Coxe retorted that even "in the midst of their revolution" the French National Assembly "had countenanced the commercial laws, funding system, bank and excise" adopted by the American Congress and alleged by Logan to be so hostile to the true principles of liberty and equality. To Coxe, Hamilton's policies and, inferentially, his own were "entitled to all the merit of being an efficient instrument of public justice, honour, and prosperity," one that "all the foreign world applaud and admire, as wise and efficient."[50]

Although so able an antagonist brought out the best in Coxe, his impassioned rebuttal was characteristically not without guile. In his capac-

49. [Coxe], "Observations on the Preceding Letters," *American Museum*, XII (1792), 167–169, 218.
50. *Ibid.*, 272, 274, 275–277.

ity as Hamilton's loyal assistant, Coxe sought to refute Logan's fervent defense of French commercial policy at a time when he was assisting Jefferson in preparing a statistical blast at British restrictions on American trade and an implied defense of a closer connection with France. And Coxe was not altogether candid in his rebuttal of his antagonist's accusation that the charter of the Society for Establishing Useful Manufactures was an instance of pernicious special-interest legislation. The society was, in fact, controlled by a small number of well-to-do investors, most of them New York speculators. In defense of his own position, Coxe denied that the New Jersey legislature had confided to a few rich men exclusive jurisdiction of the manufacturing town or conferred on them any other particular or unconstitutional privileges. To the contrary, he argued, the statute in question democratically gave to the citizens of the new town the right to reject incorporation and reserved to the state authority over the area. In yet another instance Coxe stretched the truth even beyond the broad limits of eighteenth-century polemical warfare: the society's stock, he insisted, was owned by "farmers, merchants, lawyers, physicians, women, minors, landed men, . . . citizens of various states," as well as by moneyed men.[51] But such lapses were perhaps venial sins only, at least in contrast with a number of Logan's even grosser distortions, and they do not appreciably mar the soundness of Coxe's defense of the much-maligned S.E.U.M.

But more than rhetoric and argument were needed to save that undertaking. Plagued by a host of problems, the society lingered for a few years, finally coming to an end in 1796.[52] The failure of the S.E.U.M. by no means put an end to Coxe's dream of burgeoning industrialization sponsored by a paternalistic state. Such a development was to him an indispensable ingredient of a balanced national economy, for which he continued to be one of the country's most prolific and persuasive spokesmen. And in the 1790s, as over succeeding decades, his writings entitled him to high rank among American political economists. That the quality of his writings suffers if judged by standards other than those of late eighteenth-, early nineteenth-century America is another matter.

51. *Ibid.*, 219.
52. For an able description of the reasons for the society's failure, see Mitchell, *Hamilton: National Adventure*, II, 191–192.

10 ⚛

The Economic Nationalist

To read Coxe's economic writings is to be reminded of Tocqueville's comment that the American mind is either concentrated upon the practical and parochial or else diffused in formless reverie and that in between lies a vacuum. Coxe, Philadelphia merchant qua political economist, clearly exemplifies the first of these alternatives. Both the activist temper of his mind and his functional interest in ideas led him to exalt practical knowledge. For Coxe, thought did not guide actions; actions either defined thought or made it unnecessary. His was not a carefully reasoned, much less a philosophical, position, for he was blithely unaware of the conventional dualism of theory and practice. To him what was useful was good, and what was good could best be described by incontrovertible statistical data. Avid in his collection of facts and figures, he was seldom inclined to ask and answer awkward questions about them. Their meaning was implicit and self-evident: the short history of the United States demonstrated that society could progress by conscious human effort. The political, cultural, and, above all, economic advance of the new nation was one of the most remarkable success stories in the annals of history. Even so, its actual accomplishments were only a spring seedbed bearing the signs of an approaching and luxuriant summer.

Although many of Coxe's observations may appear to a later generation as singularly platitudinous and a good many of his ideas as merely the common coin of the time, his message nevertheless was congenial to and needed by a generation supremely conscious that the development of commerce and industry was eroding the mores of an agricultural society. He also spoke on behalf of an influential group of Americans who believed that prosperity and greatness must be predicated on a balanced national economy, which would particularly include a thriving state of manufactures.

Thus far, Coxe displayed a remarkable instinct for the future. Futuristic ideas, as well as currently familiar thinking, dominated his writings; he was convinced that change was an inevitable and welcome condition of American development and that the inevitable result of change was moral as well as material progress.

These themes and ideas were expressed in his most ambitious research project of the 1790s, "A brief examination of Lord Sheffield's observations on the commerce of the United States of America," published in 1791, first serially in the *American Museum* and newspapers and then in pamphlet form.[1] Sheffield was an English landowner who over the years following the American Revolution dedicated himself to maintaining the full vigor of his nation's navigation acts—"guardian," as he described them, "of the prosperity of Britain."[2] The spokesman for many of his countrymen, he was heralded as "the tribune of the shipbuilders and shipowners" and widely hailed as England's most influential, persuasive, and intractable opponent of the American clamor for a preferred position within Britain's commercial system. In rebuttal of such a claim Sheffield argued that the citizens of the United States, "this now foreign and independent nation," could not expect to enjoy both the benefits of British subjects and the rewards of independence. "The whimsical definition of a people *sui generis*," he wrote in a passage that (perhaps because of its plausibility) especially irritated Coxe, "is either a figure of rhetoric which conveys no distinct idea, or the effort of cunning, to unite at the same time the advantages of two inconsistent characters."[3]

Coxe, convinced that such observations were largely mistaken when made in 1783 and that they had been outmoded by his country's new frame of government, gave an emphatic negative. Asserting that Sheffield's "con-

1. "A brief examination" was printed in six installments in the *American Museum* in Mar., Apr., May, June, and July 1791 (IX, 121–126, 177–183, 217–226, 233–241, 289–295, X, 9–16). The first essay also appeared in Andrew Brown's *Fed. Gaz.*, Apr. 4, 5, 1791. The second number of the series was first published in the *Fed. Gaz.*, Apr. 6, and was republished in the Apr. issue of the *American Museum*, along with Coxe's third number; they were printed in reverse order (No. 2 was on pp. 217–226; No. 3 on pp. 177–183. Mathew Carey's explanation of the reversal is on p. 177). Subsequent numbers were also published in the *Fed. Gaz.* on May 13, 14, 16, June 14, 15, 16, 17, July 14, 15, 16, Aug. 8, 9, and 10, 1791. To these six articles Coxe, "on further reflection," added "a seventh number and . . . two additional notes on American manufactures." The work thus enlarged was published in pamphlet form by Carey, Stewart & Co. in Philadelphia in Nov. 1791. An English edition edited by Capel Lofft was printed by Philips & Co. in 1792. The articles were republished in 1794 as chap. VIII of Book I of Coxe's *View of the U.S.*

2. Sheffield, *Observations on American Commerce*, 1. Although the first printing of this work was in 1783, the citations below are to the "much enlarged" edition of 1784.

3. Gerald S. Graham, *Sea Power and British North America, 1783–1820: A Study in British Colonial Policy* (Cambridge, Mass., 1941), 23; Sheffield, *Observations on American Commerce*, 2.

temptuous menaces" had encouraged among some Americans misplaced doubts about their own success and prowess and had reinforced the erroneous conviction of many Englishmen that "they have the world at their command," Coxe promised to dispel error by the light of reason. The essays that followed demonstrated that in his view the primary function of reason was not so much to discover fundamental laws as to uncover facts. To Coxe, Anglo-American differences were primarily differences of fact, and "facts, accurately ascertained and candidly stated," would shed "the light of indisputable truth," allowing nations amicably to seek mutually beneficial policies. His failure to see that what is fact to one nation may be falsehood to another reflected both his confident patriotism and the unreflective cast of his mind. What he did clearly and correctly perceive was that "wisdom in negotiating nations" consisted of a diligent "search for their common interests, as the fittest ground of treaty." If this were done, the United States and Great Britain could reach a "salutary and reasonable" accord.[4]

Although the promise of brevity made in the title of his "A brief examination" was not kept, Coxe, unfortunately for his readers, stuck faithfully to the pledge he made in his first essay that "little regard will be paid to order." The formlessness of his work was partly a result of the organization of Sheffield's book, one-half or more of which was devoted to a description of American imports from Europe. Sheffield divided these imports "into those in which Great Britain will have scarce any competition; those in which she will have competition; and those which she cannot supply to advantage."[5] In refutation, Coxe centered his attention on those goods that, according to Sheffield, Britain could send to America without danger of competition, but he also randomly discussed production in the United States of the imports listed under Sheffield's other two categories. Coxe's technique was to compare the statistics presented by Sheffield in 1783 with his own compilation of statistics for 1789 and 1790, and in this approach lay both the major strength and the greatest shortcoming of his work. The statistics he presented effectively refuted his antagonist's assertions but drowned his own readers in a sea of facts. He did not question the dubious intellectual propriety of premising one's research on certain fixed ideas and then selecting only such data as proved one's original assumption. This Coxe did when he transparently selected facts consonant with his own view of what recent American history should have been, and in this sense (though he did not recognize the affinity) he shared with the eighteenth-century philosophers the idea that the past had to be imagined if it was to be of any use.

4. Coxe, "A brief examination," *American Museum*, IX (1791), 235, 236, 126, 235.
5. *Ibid.*, 121; Sheffield, *Observations on American Commerce*, 7.

Coxe's theme was the new nation's tremendous expansion in population, wealth, and territory. As sanguine of the American future as he was proud of its past, he trained his heaviest barrage of facts on Sheffield's complacent assumption that the United States must indefinitely remain an economic vassal of Britain. Offering an armory of statistics in support of his argument, Coxe replied that the United States was increasingly importing manufactures from other countries and that as its population increased its own manufactures were growing by leaps and bounds. It remained only for his countrymen to pursue policies that would accelerate such trends. Instead of slavishly cultivating commerce with Britain, he wrote, they "would be more wise to court the capitalists, manufacturers, and artizans, of the several kingdoms of Europe, which are overcharged with private wealth and population." Instead of exchanging the products of American agriculture and extractive industries for foreign, particularly English, manufactures, the United States, producing an abundance of raw materials and possessing unlimited resources of power, should encourage its own manufactures, "protected by its own laws." Awareness of "the immense savings and the extensive advantages" thus to be derived would, Coxe predicted, "make converts of the whole nation, though gradually, yet infallibly."[6]

Among those converts, Coxe (though he discreetly refrained from saying so) presumably counted most of his fellow Federalists, to whose commercial policies "A brief examination" was an implicit challenge. Reflecting the view that prevailed among a good many thoughtful Americans during the years immediately following the Revolution and that persisted in the 1790s, Coxe believed that the wealth of nations depended on commercial freedom. Victimized by the trade restrictions and prohibitions of other nations, the United States must, in his view, achieve commercial freedom by first doing unto other nations as they did unto it. As Coxe surely knew, such beliefs could not have been further from those advanced by Hamilton. To the secretary of the Treasury the national interest demanded that the United States focus on the practical advantages of trade with Great Britain. As the source of 90 percent of the federal government's revenue, trade with the British paid the interest and principal on the national debt, thus maintaining public credit. Coxe too saw the importance of public credit, but he also advocated a program of economic nationalism that would encourage his countrymen to cut the economic ties that bound them to England.

To Coxe, in sum, the fundamental issue of Anglo-American commercial relations was subsumed under "the general question of reciprocity." If other countries granted the United States advantages denied it by England,

---

6. Coxe, "A brief examination," *American Museum*, IX (1791), 179, 237; Coxe, *View of the U.S.*, 250.

then the latter had no "claims to a participation in the commerce of the United States" equal to those of more friendly nations. Nor had Britain any just cause of complaint if the Americans adopted "*countervailing* regulations." Coxe found not the least degree of reciprocity in commercial relations between England and the United States, and to answer those who did —perhaps he had in mind his boss in the Treasury Department—he contrasted the restrictions imposed by each country by listing them in parallel columns. The inescapable conclusion to be drawn from the comparison was as clear as it was simple: "the absolute and important truth" that the commercial impediments placed by American laws on trade with Great Britain "are much less considerable" than the corresponding and gratuitously harsh restrictions and prohibitions imposed by the British on United States trade. Equally clear was the virtually inevitable outcome of such an unjust disparity. "The currents of commerce, like those of the rivers," Coxe wrote, "will certainly be turned from that side where obstructions are created." But Coxe apparently believed that nature might be assisted by man-made dams. Perhaps the time had come, he asserted, for Congress to increase the country's "moderate" import duties, currently averaging about 8 percent, to a figure ranging from 14 to 33⅓ percent and to impose an outright prohibition on the importation of certain articles. Any attempt by England to retaliate would redound to the benefit of Americans, who might thus be encouraged to transport their own goods in their own vessels and to manufacture at home or ship from other nations such articles as were normally imported from Britain.[7]

Such a prospect was all the more pleasing to Coxe because of its possible international repercussions. In a passage that would prompt Jefferson, as we shall see, to undertake a new departure in the country's foreign affairs, Coxe pointed out that American insistence on the principle of reciprocity might inspire European nations—notably France, Spain, and Portugal—also to adopt countervailing measures. An American-European concert based on commercial reciprocity would, he predicted, leave Great Britain hemmed in by restrictions similar to those imposed by her own navigation acts, touted by Sheffield as the cornerstone of English prosperity.[8] To many Americans, angered by the seeming impunity with which the British sought to restrict the commerce of their former colonies, Coxe's bold insistence on the practicality and desirability of American initiative in the adoption of a retaliatory alliance was a reassuring affirmation of the new nation's increasing strength and prestige. His position was also superficially plausible. Unfortunately, Coxe took for granted the very things that needed to be proved. Was En-

7. Coxe, *View of the U.S.*, 247, 246, 242–245, 250, 251.
8. Coxe, "A brief examination," *American Museum*, IX (1791), 235.

gland, in fact, so dependent on the American market that she would bow to commercial pressure? Conversely, was not American dependence on Britain so great as to make retaliation a form of national masochism? Was the American economy as balanced and mature as Coxe's argument assumed? If not, was national aspiration a proper basis for policies directed against a nation in contrast with which America, whatever her future, was in fact economically underdeveloped and militarily powerless?

Such questions disturbed neither Coxe nor other like-minded Americans, most notably Jefferson and Madison, who enthusiastically applauded Coxe's verbal assault on England's commercial restrictions. For Madison's part, the same indignation had underpinned the navigation act he had proposed to the First Congress, and he expressed his approbation of "A brief examination" by sending a copy to an English correspondent.[9] Jefferson was apparently even more impressed by such a forceful defense of congenial ideas from Hamilton's assistant, who was by now also assisting the secretary of state. Coxe's reply to Sheffield's *Observations on American Commerce*, Jefferson remarked in a letter to Sir John Sinclair with an enclosed copy of that work, was "written by a very judicious hand." Both Jefferson and Madison also saw to it that Coxe's views would be brought to the attention of Whitehall by presenting the first installment of "A brief examination" to Major George Beckwith, the British agent then resident in Philadelphia.[10] Coxe's position on commercial policy thus not only was shared by the chieftains of the emerging Republican party but was fast becoming sound "party" doctrine. And perhaps Coxe, as well as Jefferson and Madison, had uppermost in mind the partisan purposes to which the Philadelphian's plea for countervailing commercial measures might be put. "The Assistant Secretary of the Treasury has been employed during the recess" of Congress, a Philadelphia merchant wrote to his correspondent in Liverpool, "in publishing a series of papers . . . intended to shew that these States are not so dependent on Foreign States with respect to Commerce as has been heretofore supposed. They are wrote with much candour and moderation, and are esteemed a preparation for a [navigation] Bill intended to be brought forward for the purpose."[11]

Whatever more practical goal "A brief examination" may have been designed to secure, it at least achieved its manifest purpose. Coxe effectively

9. This is an inference drawn from the statement in Boyd *et al.*, eds., *Jefferson Papers*, XIX, 570, that Madison "sent a copy of Coxe's reply to Sheffield by 'a gentleman . . . on his way to England.' "

10. Jefferson to Sinclair, *ibid.*; Coxe, "To the Public," *Aurora*, Oct. 30, 1800. Coxe himself provided Maj. George Beckwith with copies of subsequent installments. *Ibid.*

11. Extract of a letter from James & Shoemaker of Philadelphia to Edgar Corrie, Sept. 10, 1791, enclosed in Corrie to Lord Hawkesbury, Oct. 18, 1791. Cited in Boyd *et al.*, eds., *Jefferson Papers*, XIX, 570.

demonstrated that Sheffield's *Observations on American Commerce* was more an expression of British prejudices and wishful thinking than an accurate prediction of the American future. For Sheffield's view of the United States as an agricultural nation dependent in perpetuo on others for shipping and manufactures, he substituted the picture of a vigorous, balanced national economy; for Sheffield's version of America's insuperable economic handicaps, Coxe presented a picture of a youthful nation not only possessing all the prerequisites for, but actually in the very midst of, rapid and sustained economic growth. Sheffield was intent on preserving the policies of the past by adducing the facts of the present; Coxe was intent on drawing the contours of the present by inferences from the future. Just as the Englishman chose to see America as a stable society, so Coxe saw it as a progressively changing one. Although the contrast between their views thus appears sharp, the dissimilarity of their portraits was owing primarily to the different forms dictated by their national perspectives, to the contrasting hues of British and American patriotism. But such differences aside, their ideas and approach were remarkably similar. Neither was concerned, unlike Adam Smith or other more prominent economists of the day, with discovering and applying economic laws. Both were attached to the expediential and were scornful of theories. Just as Sheffield sought to defeat measures designed to liberalize Anglo-American trade, so Coxe sought to defend policies designed to promote American economic independence. The similarity goes further. Both were ardent nationalists and both were mercantilists in the sense that their primary concern was national self-sufficiency and power. And each in his way typified salient features of his own society. Just as Coxe symbolized his countrymen's naive faith in progress, so Sheffield personified the stale conservatism that Edmund Burke effectively derided.

Coxe not only laid bare the reactionary nature of Sheffield's *Observations on American Commerce* but also convincingly demonstrated that British policy in the 1790s was still based on the assumptions that Lord Sheffield had vigorously defended in 1783. This was witnessed—if proof were needed—by the report of a committee of the Privy Council issued in 1791, news of which reached Coxe from William Temple Franklin after the first six numbers of "A brief examination" had been published.[12] This

---

12. "Report of the Committee of the Privy Council on trade between the British dominions and America" (1791), in *Collection of Interesting and Important Reports and Papers on Navigation and Trade* (London, 1807), hereafter cited as *Interesting and Important Papers*; Coxe to Tobias Lear, Nov. 15, 1791, Coxe Papers. The report came to his attention, Coxe wrote a decade later, when "I was engaged in the sixth number of my reply to Lord Sheffield. My zeal for the interest of my country, and for its harmony with England, induced me to write the seventh number, as a covert reply to some of the contents of the report." *Aurora*, Oct. 30, 1800. Actually, he added three additional numbers. See Coxe, *View of the U.S.*, 111.

highly secret report was the work of Lord Hawkesbury, like Lord Sheffield an implacable enemy to liberal treatment of American commerce. The current state of Anglo-American trade, Hawkesbury insisted, was decidedly advantageous to Britain—the balance of trade had been steadily growing in her favor, the ban on American ships from the West Indies had enhanced her naval power, trade with her other North American colonies had grown more profitable, the number of American ships employed in overseas trade had decreased, and American shipbuilding had declined.[13] Lord Hawkesbury's committee believed that affairs would remain in such a happy state as long as the United States adopted no discriminatory legislation against British commerce. Such an affirmation of the status quo (one that might appropriately have been entitled "How to Grow Rich by Losing an Empire") underscored the appositeness of Coxe's strictures against it.[14] Although naive in believing that the walls of the English commercial system would come tumbling down at his trumpet call of reason, he was not mistaken in assuming that a change in policy depended on a change in theory. Once Britain understood that a profitable relationship with her former colonies did not depend on the rigid maintenance of her mercantile system, then, as Coxe said, she would be able to "commence the formation of liberal arrangements, solidly founded in the mutual interest of the two nations." It was a sound argument, though it came twenty-five years too soon. Not until the Treaty of Ghent in 1815—"an eloquent register of historical process" that finally marked "the decay of British mercantilist concepts"—would Coxe's prediction be realized.[15]

In the meantime, Coxe's failure to influence English officials was offset by the praise heaped on his work.[16] The author of the piece, commented the English *Monthly Review*, was "an able and well-informed writer," who "with more temper and moderation than might be expected" had effectively refuted Lord Sheffield's anti-American strictures. In attributing "A brief examination" to Coxe, the *Monthly Review*'s anonymous critic also remarked: "Why *assistant* treasurer? Why are able men, if not pushed forward by *undeniable* interest, generally found in *subordinate* offices; while the nominal chief engrosses all the honour and the emolument? . . . Abilities

13. "Report on trade," in *Interesting and Important Papers*, 66–69, 77–78, 82, 85.

14. The quotation is from Peterson, *Jefferson and the New Nation*, 427.

15. Coxe, "A brief examination," *American Museum*, IX (1791), 226; George Dangerfield, *The Awakening of American Nationalism, 1815–1826* (New York, 1965), 2.

16. See Coxe's correspondence with Pierce Butler, Tobias Lear, John Beckley, John Adams, James Iredell, John Jay, George Cabot, Jonathan Dayton, William S. Johnson, Fisher Ames, Enoch Edwards, Thomas Jefferson, and Benjamin Hawkins. Among the English readers of Coxe's pamphlet was Lord Sheffield. Enoch Edwards reported to Coxe from London that "I met Lord Sheffield at Sr. John's and he was very sour about a Publication of your's—he arraigned it very severly." Edwards to Coxe, Aug. 17, 1793, Coxe Papers.

must be put, it seems, to short allowance even in America, to keep them alert!"[17]

Coxe chose to keep his abilities alert by preparing another series of articles, this time addressed "to the feelings and Judgment" of his own compatriots.[18] Published in 1792, his pamphlet *Reflexions on the State of the Union*[19] was designed to dispel doubts about the soundness of the American economy and to remind his countrymen that as "natural friends" they should "perceive the wisdom and the high duty of cultivating a spirit of mutual allowance and concession."[20] Once persuaded, all Americans, Coxe believed, would accept his prescription for national prosperity and greatness: a balanced and independent economy. As in his other writings, Coxe in these essays displayed no appreciable concern with either the orderly progression of ideas or their systematic analysis. Instead, he once again drenched his readers in statistics (lists of the exports of the United States, for example, and descriptions of virtually all its infant manufacturing establishments) and plied them with glowing accounts of America's abundant raw materials and of how they could be converted into manufactured goods.

Coxe's *Reflexions on the State of the Union* enlarged on three themes: the promotion of manufactures to achieve a healthy national economy; the purblindness of those special interest groups—notably, southern planters and northern merchants—who failed to see the essentiality of a balanced economy; and the boost given to American economic growth by Hamilton's financial policies. The benefits to be derived from manufacturing were those Coxe had emphasized time and again in previous articles: a favorable balance of trade, described by Coxe as *"the metaphysics of commerce"*; independence from costly and sometimes capricious reliance on foreign manufactured articles; an increase of foreign trade by the export of manufactured goods; the diversification of American capital investment; self-sufficiency in time of war; additional jobs for American immigrant workmen, as well as for "the wives and children of our citizens, and . . . black women, old men, and children"; and, somewhat paradoxically, the introduction of laborsaving machinery. In view of such manifest advan-

---

17. *Monthly Review* (London), IX (1792), 220–221.

18. Coxe to Lear, Feb. 11, 1793, Coxe Papers.

19. Coxe's "Reflexions on the state of the union" was published in five parts in the *American Museum* from Apr. through Aug. 1792 and republished under the same title in pamphlet form (Philadelphia, 1792). It also was printed in a Boston newspaper and in the *Pennsylvania Herald* (York). See Ames to Coxe, June 14, 1792, Thomas Hartley to Coxe, June 27, 1792, Coxe Papers. It also appeared in Coxe's *View of the U.S.* as chap. IX of Book I, 286–379.

20. Coxe, *View of the U.S.*, 286. Its "special purpose," Coxe wrote to John Jay, was to convince "those in the Southern states, who complain of the operations of the Government and who entertain fears about the balance of trade etc., that they are really mistaken." Coxe to Jay, Nov. 8, 1794, Coxe Papers.

tages, the encouragement of manufactures was "a great political duty" demanding positive and prompt action by the state and federal governments.[21]

Coxe also believed that manufactures deserved the support of those Americans who, motivated both by mistaken self-interest and misunderstanding of sound economic principles, had hitherto opposed it. Conspicuously misplaced were the fears prevalent among southerners that the promotion of manufacturing would enrich the northern and middle states at the South's expense. Such apprehensions, Coxe said, were based on a failure to recognize the economic interdependence of the agricultural and the industrialized states. The most effective way to promote agriculture was to create a stable home market for its products by introducing and nurturing manufactures. Coxe next sought to quiet the apprehensions of that "respectable proportion of our mercantile citizens" engaged in international trade. Foreign commerce, as well as the coastal trade, would be "enlivened" by manufactures, he assured merchants. Among many other inestimable advantages, manufactures would promote "in an easy, certain, safe, and cheap way, the naval capacities and strength of the United States" and would relieve American merchants of the loss sustained by the customary premium on bills of exchange remitted in paying for European manufactures.[22] To Coxe the southern planter as well as the northern capitalist, the small farmer as well as the artisan, and the international merchant as well as the domestic trader would derive incalculable benefits from the fostering of manufactures. And in his rhapsodic supportive argument he implied that economic diversification was the central purpose of American society, its raison d'être.

Coxe had only praise for Hamilton's economic program. Not even the secretary of the Treasury himself could have claimed more for it: it had restored public credit, increased the availability of capital, prompted the establishment of a sound circulating medium, and accelerated economic activity generally in agriculture, commerce, and manufacturing.[23] In this and

21. Coxe, "Reflexions on the state of the union," *American Museum*, XI (1792), 256–257, 130, 132, 254–256, 259.

22. *Ibid.*, 187, 190, 191.

23. In an article published a year earlier, Coxe had praised Hamilton's program while seeking to dispel some popular misunderstandings about it. In this essay Coxe attributed the rise in the price of both government stock and that of the Bank of the United States to enhanced public confidence in the financial integrity of the United States, which had been inspired by Hamilton's program. The rise in prices was owing also to the "quickness of action, which sudden transactions from distress and disorder to great prosperity generally produce in nations and individuals." More important, the striking and "disagreeable" fluctuations in the price of bank stock "have been occasioned," Coxe wrote, "by the want of the necessary knowledge among a very large number of the public creditors and stockholders." Despite his approval of funding and assumption, Coxe did not—any more than Hamilton—literally endorse the then current cliché that "a public debt is a public blessing." Coxe believed that "it is actually profitable to a people

in other ways as well Coxe's commitment to a program of economic nationalism was once again manifest. It was so strong that he seemed to be saying, Build here a perfect state and let the rest of the world go by. The Americans would derive "greater blessings" from a "sedulous cultivation of their interests at home," he wrote, "than from almost any arrangements which the conceptions of foreign nations will probably lead them to propose."[24]

Coxe's *Reflexions on the State of the Union* was, as Fisher Ames said, a "good physic" for "the rant of eloquent ignorance," unredeemed by "a single fact," with which American journals "were formerly stuffed." Like Hamilton's memorable state papers, Coxe's essays were inspired by the vision of "something noble and magnificent in the perspective of a great Federal Republic, closely linked in the pursuit of a common interest, tranquil at home, respectable abroad. . . ."[25] That neither Hamilton nor Coxe asked precisely how such a government would be made to serve human ends was less a reflection of callousness than an expression of faith that, once established, a strong, secure nation and a prosperous, abundant economy would provide the solution for problems yet unresolved.

To Coxe, even more than to Hamilton, the road to that bright future would be lined with factories. Foreseeing that the likely outbreak of a general war in Europe would provide an opportunity to speed up industrialization, Coxe in 1793 returned to his familiar theme, his idée fixe. In an article published in the spring of that year, he discussed the possible disruption of United States foreign trade during the course of a war among nations that ordinarily bought American raw materials and supplied its manufactures.[26] Here was a compelling reason for prompting his countrymen immediately to "infuse into their towns and cities . . . manufacturing capital, industry, and skill." Although the progress already made in this direction afforded "the most comfortable reflection," the current situation, he believed, offered a chance to take advantage of European weakness and to advance national strength. How could this be accomplished? Coxe returned to a suggestion he had made two years earlier in "A brief examination," a

---

to evince a real ability and a sincere disposition to discharge such debts, as they may have been obliged to contract." "Reflections relative to bank stock and national funds," *American Museum*, X (1791), 168–171. The article was signed "A friend to sober dealing and public credit. A.A."

24. Coxe, "Reflexions on the state of the union," *American Museum*, XI (1792), 128.

25. Ames to Coxe, June 14, 1792, Coxe Papers; Syrett *et al.*, eds., *Hamilton Papers*, III, 106.

26. The article was first published in *Dunlap's American Daily Advertiser* (Philadelphia), May 20, 1793, under the title "Reflections on the Affairs of the United States, Occasioned by the Present War in Europe, Recommended to American and Foreign Capitalists." It was later republished in *View of the U.S.*, 380–404, under the title "Some Ideas Concerning the Creation of Manufacturing Towns and Villages in the United States, Applied by Way of Example to a Position on the River Susquehannah."

suggestion that had, as we have seen, found fruition in the Society for Establishing Useful Manufactures. Now was the time, Coxe argued, to establish another model manufacturing town, this time located in Pennsylvania, contiguous to or near the Susquehanna River (where Coxe himself owned extensive tracts of land). To Coxe the very fact that the United States did not possess some of the advantages of other manufacturing countries—notably roads and canals—made the establishment of such a model city all the more important. Conceding that such a grandiose scheme was not likely to be adopted soon, he nevertheless believed it worthwhile "to exemplify what might be done with a given capital."[27] Underpinning Coxe's proposal was his familiar faith in the value of economic planning. But as the Society for Establishing Useful Manufactures would soon demonstrate, such an ambitious project had no chance of success, largely because Coxe's countrymen were unreceptive. They believed rather in the superior productivity and social benefits of agriculture and, in the spirit of Adam Smith, in the beneficient operation of invisible but automatic economic laws.

Persuaded that a policy of drift was mistaken, Coxe convinced himself that he could convert his countrymen to his own program of economic nationalism. By mid-1793 he was busily assembling material for a book he hoped would accomplish just that.[28] A *View of the United States*, published in Philadelphia in 1794 and reprinted in London the following year, was, Coxe explained in its introduction, a "collection of papers" previously published, "introduced in each instance by concise explanatory remarks, and closed by such brief observations on its particular subject as arise in the present time."[29] These introductory and concluding remarks were brief (seldom more than a page) and added little of substance to the original essays. Except for numerous statistical tables, the only other new material was a

---

27. Coxe, *View of the U.S.*, 382, 380, 401, 483. Coxe suggested that $500,000 be raised for a model city in one of three ways: by subscriptions to the capital stock of a company "to be temporarily associated for the purpose, without any exclusive privileges"; by a lottery; or by a direct appropriation from the state of Pennsylvania. The money so amassed would be used for the purchase of land and the erection of buildings. To whomsoever the profits might go, the investment would result in a 100% increase in the value of the lands in the area. Coxe proposed that $500,000 be allocated for the purchase of 2,000 acres of land on the Susquehanna River, "to be regularly laid off" as a manufacturing and trading center. Houses, as well as "useful workshops, and manufactories by water, fire or hand," were to be erected in the town, and canals and roads to facilitate transportation were to be constructed. *Ibid.*, 385–393.

28. Coxe wrote that he had been preparing his book for publication in the summer of 1793, but "the epidemic malady which occurred in Philadelphia, towards the end of that season, prevented the execution of the design at that time." *Ibid.*, 449.

29. Coxe, *A View of the United States of America, in a Series of Papers Written at Various Times between the Years 1787 and 1794 ... Interspersed with Authentic Documents ...* (Philadelphia, 1794), 1–2. The purpose of the book was described by Coxe on the title page: "The Whole Tending to Exhibit the Progress and Present State of Civil and Religious Liberty,

final section, amounting to about 12 percent of the book, that consisted of essays hurriedly written on the eve of publication.[30] Although Coxe would subsequently turn out hundreds of articles, those reprinted in *A View of the United States* announced the essential themes that his later writings would merely amplify. This was not because he was mentally ossified by the age of forty but rather because the nation's fundamental problems remained constant, and when in the last years of Coxe's life new solutions were adopted, the change, gratifyingly to him, was in the direction to which he had pointed all along.

In 1794 the policies Coxe had recommended over the previous seven years gained added force by both the juxtaposition of his many essays and the addition of repetitious but persuasive new ones. Here was a sustained plea for national self-sufficiency to be achieved by an economy carefully equilibrated so as to encourage the rapid growth of manufactures without imperiling agricultural prosperity—the leitmotiv of Coxe's economic thought. Never questioning the desirability or constitutionality of direct government intervention in the economy, Coxe, like Hamilton, called for policies designed to promote national prosperity, to furbish the nation's international repute, and to shore up its military strength.

Although Coxe's book was applauded by his contemporaries (some of whom clearly were more intent on reassurance that America could produce authors than on a critical assessment of the book's merits), the mid-twentieth-century historian must employ a different and a double standard of judgment. He must measure the work by the standards of Coxe's own day while also judging it from the perspective of the literature of political economy in Europe at that time and in this country subsequently. By whatever criteria evaluated, *A View of the United States* was not artfully done, in either design or execution. It abounded in repetitions and revealed more than a trace of fact-benumbed pedantry. Large sections of it engage the present-day reader's attention no more than would a statistical abstract or a reference work on physical and economic geography. To deserve stature as a

---

Population, Agriculture, Exports, Imports, Fisheries, Navigation, Ship-Building, Manufactures, and General Improvement." It was reprinted in London "for J. Johnson in St. Paul's Church Yard" in 1795.

30. The titles of the new articles were as follows: "Containing a Summary Statement of the Principal Facts, which Characterize the American People, and Their Country or Territory"; "Reflections upon the Best Modes of Bringing the Forest Lands of the United States into Cultivation and Use"; "Miscellaneous Facts and Observations Concerning the State of Pennsylvania, Supplementary to the Fourth Chapter of the First Book"; "Concerning the Public Debts, and Revenues of the United States"; and "Miscellaneous Reflections Upon Certain Important Facts and Considerations, which Occur, at the Present Time, in the Affairs of the United States; Intended as a Conclusion to this Collection." *Ibid.*, 427–457, 477–512.

first-rank political economist, Coxe needed to move beyond the presentation of essentially statistical observations and to transcend his parochialism. Yet gauged by the standards of his time and place, *A View of the United States* has considerable merit. It was superior to many similar contemporary works, and as a source of economic data deserves comparison with Hamilton's better-known Report on Manufactures, on which Coxe had collaborated. The value of Coxe's book lay in its presentation of otherwise inaccessible information, not in its heuristic value; his originality lay in applying already-current ideas, not in devising new theories or even in critically commenting on the rich literature of political economy then available.

Coxe was familiar with the literature of political economy, however, for he assiduously collected what for his day was an impressive library, which he read and discussed with his circle of friends. He was, for example, a close student of Adam Smith's *Wealth of Nations* and Necker's *Finances of France*; he had more than a passing knowledge of Montesquieu's *Spirit of Laws*, Hume's *Essays*, Steuart's *Political Economy*, and Blackstone's *Commentaries*; and he read and kept on his library shelves standard compendia and reference books on history, law, finance, and the commercial regulations and systems of other countries.[31] Such reference works mirrored his overriding concern with facts. Although blithely unaware of any lacunae in his knowledge, Coxe revealed in his writing no particular interest in abstract thought other than a commitment to the virtues of American "democracy" and a devotion to "liberty." In other words, Coxe reflected certain assumptions of his generation instead of reflecting upon them. But this, paradoxically enough, is largely responsible for his historical significance. He pulled things together, synthesized them, and in so doing came to personify a major development of his time. His economic nationalism was of incalculable importance for the future of American history. Merely by hammering away at the possibility of a balanced and vigorous economy, he helped to temper a subsequent generation's acceptance of laissez-nous faire. He was also a precursor of those who actively opposed the new order, the so-called American school of economists, which included men like Daniel Raymond, Henry Carey, John Rae, and Frederick List.

Coxe's collected essays have historical value for still another reason: they mirror the mercantile mind of his day. In and out of office Coxe

---

31. See especially James Wilson to Coxe, Oct. 16, 1789, William Coxe, Jr., to Coxe, Nov. 1, 1790, Coxe to William L. Smith, Dec. 13, 1791, Edward Jones to Coxe, Feb. 23, 1795, Mathew Carey to Coxe, Mar. 10, 1797, Coxe Papers. For a description of a portion of Coxe's library, see Ezekiel Forman to Coxe, Apr. 6, 1800, Coxe Papers. For listings of books Coxe ordered from British book dealers, see "Invoice" dated Feb. 2, 1792, Coxe to James Phillips, May 16, 22, 1791, William Cass to Coxe, July 23, 1791, Phillips to Coxe, July 26, 1791, *ibid.*

retained the standards and presuppositions of a Philadelphia merchant. This is one clue to both the merits and the shortcomings of his writings, for just as his essays provided a useful guide (discounting, of course, their superpatriotic bias) to the state of the country's economy, so they were often as uninspired and dull as the pages of a ledger. The cast of Coxe's mind was neatly revealed in the last paragraph of *A View of the United States*: the climax to five hundred pages of lavish praise of his country's accomplishments and prediction of its yet more glorious future was an account of the increase in the export of flour.[32]

The overarching purpose of Coxe's writings was to demonstrate the development of the United States from its "very disagreeable condition" in the 1780s to its prosperous state in 1794. To him this achievement exemplified "the progressive course of things" propelled by "incessant changes," and the result of it was the closest thing to utopia that history had hitherto witnessed. His idyllic picture of the world's most perfect state was nowhere more brightly painted than in *A View of the United States*. The Americans, he wrote, had "exploded" principles of religious intolerance, placing "upon one common and equal footing every church, sect, or society, of religious men"; they had abolished the political tyranny that had been the scourge of mankind through previous history; they had replaced the privileged and repressive societies of the Old World with a democratic society of equal opportunity, one whose sole object was "*the maintenance of peace, order, liberty, and safety.*" "America," Coxe wrote, "has not many charms for the dissipated and voluptuous parts of mankind," but for the "rational, soberminded, and discreet," as well as for "the industrious and honest poor," it afforded "great opportunities of comfort and prosperity."[33] It was, in sum, an open society in which success was the rule and failure virtually unknown.

Although the United States may have been riding the crest of the historical wave, Coxe's case for its transformation since the Revolution was grossly overstated. He did, however, symbolize the national self-glorification of an awkward age that, uncertain of its identity, exaggerated American uniqueness, and despite his heavy-handed ridicule of Lord Sheffield's snide comments on "the idea that the United States are a country, *sui generis*," Coxe emphatically believed that it was just that.[34]

The shrillness of Coxe's defense of the United States suggests a nagging uncertainty. He dispelled it, at least to his own satisfaction, by recourse to the dogma of progress. Although he professed to deduce his belief in progress from the evidence on all sides of him, it was in fact an act of faith,

32. Coxe, *View of the U.S.*, 512.
33. *Ibid.*, 3, 1, 427, 428, 444, 437, 440–443.
34. Coxe, "A brief examination," *American Museum*, IX (1791), 125.

which included confidence that such flaws as marred the American performance would "yield ere long to the powers and influences which have erradicated much greater evils of the same kind." His belief in the ability of what he once termed "the mechanical powers of the human mind" to produce illimitable progress was as great as that of a Condorcet or a Godwin. But it was not the fate of mankind but that of his own country, not the nation's past but its future that dazzled him, suggesting the astuteness of Tocqueville's observation that "democratic nations care but little for what has been, but they are haunted by visions of what will be."[35]

The great issue of Coxe's inquiry was, then, the dynamics of change, but what was conspicuously lacking was any interest in the dimensions of change. Confident that the partnership between economic growth and political freedom would continue to develop and to triumph over every obstacle, he questioned neither the fact of the union nor the diversities and conflicts that might impede or abort its progress. The absence of any countervailing moral or human goals afforded an oppressive limitation to his thought. Henry Adams's caustic comments on Jefferson's confident belief in the doctrine of "democratic progress" is also applicable to Coxe. Apropos of this dogma, Adams wrote: "What will you do for moral progress?"[36]

Although Coxe confused the means of achieving the abundant society with the end of a just society, he was preeminently the child of his age. But his blindness to the inequities and conflicts of his time was less defensible. His voluminous writings afford no hint that the operation of the American economy would result in a structured hierarchy of wealth and income and thus in a system of privilege. He willed to believe that the exploitation of the nation's remarkable resources would be the panacea for all its conceivable problems. Even if he could have divined the advice of Tocqueville, he would not have understood the aptness of the Frenchman's observation that "the Americans contemplate this extraordinary progress with exultation, but they would be wiser to consider it with sorrow and alarm."[37]

35. Coxe, "Reflexions on the state of the union," *American Museum*, XII (1792), 80; [Coxe], "The state of Pennsylvania," *American Museum*, VII (1790), 299; Alexis de Tocqueville, *Democracy in America*, ed. Phillips Bradley (New York, 1954), II, 78.
36. Henry Adams, *History of the United States of America during the Administrations of Jefferson and Madison*, I (New York, 1962 [orig. publ. New York, 1889–1891]), 179.
37. Tocqueville, *Democracy in America*, I, 420.

11 ⚡

Assistant to Jefferson

Thomas Jefferson's accomplishments as secretary of state, Coxe remarked, were "a monument of diplomatic knowledge and learning, judgment, decision, impartiality and independence," rivaled by no other American statesman of his day.[1] The two men first met in the late spring of 1790, shortly after Coxe arrived in New York to assume office as assistant secretary of the Treasury. Although surely prompted to a degree by self-serving ambitions, Coxe promptly fell under the spell of the courteous Virginian, whose uncommonly penetrating and cultivated mind was not concealed by his polite diffidence. If Senator Maclay can be credited, Jefferson's charm was indeed considerable. His "face has a sunny aspect," Maclay wrote in May 1790. "I looked for gravity, but a laxity of manner seemed shed about him. He spoke almost without ceasing. But even his discourse partook of his personal demeanor. It was loose and rambling; and yet he scattered information wherever he went, and some even brilliant sentiments sparkled from him."[2] What impressed Maclay appears to have dazzled Coxe. For his part, Jefferson, always highly susceptible to flattery, welcomed this addition to his influential coterie of admirers.

But this amiable relationship between Jefferson and Coxe, personal as well as official, was also based on certain affinities that overshadowed the natural differences between a southern Republican planter whose political creed was vigorously antistatist and an urban Federalist merchant whose political theory was consistently that of an interventionist. Both were aristocrats, sharing the manners and social standards characteristic of both the

1. *Aurora*, Sept. 27, 1800.
2. *Maclay Journal*, 265–266.

Virginia gentry and the Philadelphia elite. Although Jefferson was far more learned and sophisticated than Coxe, they had in common wide-ranging interests in science and technology, in the arts and education, and in history and politics. They also shared complementary needs: Coxe's need for the type of recognition that Hamilton was incapable of granting was matched by Jefferson's need for the kind of assistance that Coxe was well equipped to supply. During his five years abroad as American minister to France, Jefferson had kept abreast of economic developments at home, but he did not have the detailed information upon which Coxe could easily draw. For his part, Coxe, although no sycophant, relished the esteem of famous men and no doubt responded to the Virginian's tendency "to err on the side of personal compliment."[3] Perhaps more important was the two men's gradual awareness of the similarity of their views on critical aspects of American foreign policy.

Whatever the bases of their early friendship, the mutual distrust of Hamilton that would eventually bind the two politically was not initially present. In the spring of 1790 Jefferson was as willing to cooperate with the secretary of the Treasury as Coxe was eager to promote Hamilton's policies. Nor were there as yet definite boundary lines between departments. The division of responsibility was vague, jurisdictions overlapped, and precedents were yet to be established. Coxe could see no reason for restricting his loyalty to merely one department, no reason why—so long as he competently performed his duties at the Treasury Department—he should refrain from also assisting the secretary of state. Such aid seemed a display of disinterested patriotism rather than an impropriety.

Coxe's unsolicited assistance to the State Department, like his advice to the secretary of the Treasury, predated his own appointment as a federal official. In January 1790 he had written to John Jay, Jefferson's predecessor, offering advice on the preparation of a report that Congress had instructed Jay to submit on the subject of uniform weights and measures. Coxe recommended that the secretary utilize the work of Robert Leslie, a watch-and-instrument maker in Philadelphia, who had invented an apparatus that would assist in making possible "invariable standards for weights and measures, communicable and recoverable at all times and among all Nations."[4] The inventor, though Coxe did not in his letter share the fact, was also his own employee.[5] Leslie's invention of "a single Pendulum capable of being sufficiently varied in length to answer the purposes of the two" previously necessary pendulums was, Coxe wrote to Jay, a major step in the

---

3. Malone, *Jefferson: Rights of Man*, 353.
4. Coxe to John Jay, Jan. 25, 1790, Boyd *et al.*, eds., *Jefferson Papers*, XVI, 618.
5. See the contract between Coxe and George Parkinson, Jan. 1790, Coxe Papers.

progress of both general and applied science, appropriate particularly to the establishment of a uniform standard for weights and measures.

Although Jay promised to pass on the information to his successor, Coxe decided to assure this by also soliciting the services of James Madison. Coxe requested that Madison, with due regard to the requisite secrecy, make sure that Leslie's discovery was brought to the attention of the new secretary of state. Madison willingly agreed to do so, and Leslie's proposals were subsequently incorporated in the Report on Weights and Measures that Jefferson submitted to Congress in July 1790.[6] Although not adopted, the report, as Dumas Malone comments, enhanced the Virginian's "deserved fame and, if he had had the choosing, no doubt he would have preferred to be remembered by it rather than by any other paper he drafted as secretary of state."[7] Nor was Jefferson likely to forget the services of those like Coxe who had helped to make it possible.

This was only a token of what Coxe was willing to do. Gratified by the ready acceptance of his protégé's invention, Coxe offered soon after he arrived in New York in May 1790 to share with Jefferson his own expert knowledge of economic subjects. The Virginian, who some years earlier had seen Coxe's *Address to the friends of American Manufactures* and who had read and taken extensive notes on his *Enquiry into a Commercial System*, was presumably amenable,[8] but nothing immediately came of the offer, largely because Coxe was preoccupied with arrangements for the removal of the federal government to Philadelphia. Soon after the secretary of state reached the new capital in November 1790, however, Coxe repeated the offer, and Jefferson, burdened with requests from both Congress and the president for reports on a variety of subjects, readily accepted. The secretary's most pressing task was the preparation of a report on the cod and whale fisheries, a subject on which Coxe began firing off facts and figures of the kind that he would barrage the Department of State with until Jefferson's retirement three years later.

The report on the fisheries was prepared in response to a memorial of the Massachusetts legislature that had been referred to the secretary of state by the House of Representatives.[9] The subject was not a new one to Jeffer-

6. Jay to Coxe, Jan. 30, 1790, *ibid.*; Coxe to James Madison, Mar. 21, 1790, Madison to Coxe, Mar. 28, 1790, Madison Papers, Lib. of Cong.; "Report on Weights and Measures," Boyd *et al.*, eds., *Jefferson Papers*, XVI, 602–675.

7. Malone, *Jefferson: Rights of Man*, 280.

8. Thomas Jefferson had received copies of Coxe's pamphlets, published in 1787, from John Browne Cutting, among others. Boyd *et al.*, eds., *Jefferson Papers*, XIX, 123, 411. For Jefferson's notes on Coxe's *Enquiry into a Commercial System*, see *ibid.*, 132–133.

9. The representation of the Massachusetts General Court had reached Jefferson in mid-Aug. For a comprehensive survey of the background of the subject, see Boyd *et al.*, eds., *Jefferson Papers*, XIX, 140–172.

son, who as representative to France had closely examined the history and conditions of American whaling as preparation for his insistent attempts to persuade the French government to relax laws that crippled this industry. But since Jefferson wished to base his report on far more extensive and detailed information than he had readily available, he welcomed the aid of a talented statistician. Although as a "practical merchant" Coxe regarded himself merely as a "theorist upon this subject," his industrious research quickly compensated for any lack of firsthand knowledge.[10] From Hewes and Anthony, a Philadelphia firm, he successfully solicited a comparison of prices in the major New England fishing ports before the Revolution and currently, as well as a detailed description of the differences between vessels employed in the cod and the whale fisheries.[11] He interviewed, with less success, other Philadelphia merchants active in the New England trade; he pored over statistical information available in the Treasury Department files; and he carefully studied such books and articles on the subject as he could find. The result was the collection of enough material for a book. Virtually all of it was submitted to Jefferson in the form of two research reports and compilations of factual data and statistical abstracts.[12] One of the reports was an

10. Coxe to Jefferson, Nov. 23, 1790, *ibid.*, XVIII, 62.

11. Coxe to Hewes & Anthony, Nov. 18, 1790, Coxe Papers. Coxe explained his reasons for selecting this firm to Jefferson as follows: "Mr. Anthony was bred to the Sea out of Rhode Island and is a man of judgment and probity—and now a partner of one of the principal houses in Philadelphia, who do *half* the New England business of the port." Coxe sent Joseph Anthony's response to his queries (Anthony to Coxe, Nov. 27, 1790, Boyd *et al.*, eds., *Jefferson Papers*, XIX, 196–197) with its enclosures concerning the cod and whale fisheries to Jefferson. Coxe to Jefferson, Nov. 29, 1790, *ibid.*, 195–196. The enclosures were as follows: (1) "Answers to Queries on the Fisheries"; (2) "Table of Prices"; (3) "A comparison of the prices of pickled and dried Fish in New England with those of Butchers Meat of common qualities in the Philadelphia Market, and of pickled Meats for Sea Stores"; and (4) "Calculation of the Bank fishery in a Schooner of fifty Tons." For the enclosures, either printed or described, see *ibid.*, 197–198, 198–199, 195, 195–196.

12. Coxe to Jefferson, Nov. 23, 1790, Boyd *et al.*, eds., *Jefferson Papers*, XVIII, 62. In this letter Coxe enclosed not only an essay on the American fisheries (see n. 13, below) but reports on those of Holland, Labrador, Prussia, Greenland, the Davis Strait, and Hamburg, as well as "A Comparison of prices of fish and meat in New England and in Philadelphia markets." For Coxe's "Notes on the Dutch and Prussian Fisheries," see *ibid.*, XIX, 175–182. For further correspondence between Coxe and Jefferson on the subject of the fisheries, see Jefferson to Coxe, Nov. 30, 1790, Coxe to Jefferson, Jan. 27, 30, Feb. 1, 1791, *ibid.*, XVII, 102, XIX, 116–117, 118–119, 237–238. Particularly useful to Jefferson were Coxe's supplementary notes on Alexander Hamilton's "Abstract of the Tonnage of foreign Vessels entered in the Ports of the United States from October 1st 1789 to September 30th 1789." Coxe's supplementary information was sent to James Madison, who sent it on to Jefferson. For Coxe's undated letter to Madison, see *ibid.*, XIX, 234–235. According to Julian Boyd, Jefferson "evidently intended to include this document" by Coxe "in his report, for he caused one of his clerks to transcribe it from the text furnished Madison." *Ibid.*, 235. Jefferson was also obliged to Coxe for yet another amplification of the secretary of the Treasury's "Abstract of the Tonnage." That study, Coxe explained, "does not show to what ports or kingdoms the vessels are dispatched," a deficiency Coxe supplied in an undated report to the secretary of state. *Ibid.* Among other infor-

undated paper describing the expenses and the quantity of items needed for seamen and ships and the duties imposed on such as were imported. The other report was a bulky essay entitled "Miscellaneous Notes on the Fisheries" that contained "every idea (though some of them are very light)" Coxe believed might be of interest.[13]

Based on thorough and careful research, Coxe's "Miscellaneous Notes" was far more than the title purported. In addition to historical facts and comprehensive data on the present state of the fisheries, it also presented an essay on current national affairs, including a sustained argument for the revamping of commercial policy. Arguing that the American fisheries enjoyed natural advantages unrivaled by any other country, Coxe pointed to the cheapness of vessels, the superiority of seamen, and the low cost of provisions. The case for the protection of this industry, he argued, was unassailable—it was essential to a thriving carrying trade and to national defense. Convinced that measures must be taken for its relief, he recommended a long list of proposals, including an exemption from tonnage duties, a ban on the importation of fish from countries that prohibited the entry of fish from the United States, and the encouragement of home consumption. These recommendations were included in Jefferson's report, though Coxe offered a number of other proposals that were not. His essay was a more comprehensive treatment of the subject, both descriptively and analytically, than Jefferson's report. To cite only a few of several possible illustrations, Coxe presented a more exhaustive analysis of the national advantages derived from the industry, a more detailed description of British, Dutch, and French regulations as compared to those of the United States, and a fuller explanation of the grounds for optimism that markets for the cod and whale fisheries would increase.

---

mation Coxe furnished Jefferson was an "Abstract of the Produce of the Fisheries exported from the United States, from about August 20th, 1789 to September 30th, 1790." *Ibid.*, 224. According to Boyd (*ibid.*, 168), Jefferson perhaps also obtained from Coxe an undated "Tabulation showing imports of products of the fisheries by France and the French West Indies as compared to the rest of the world." This "Tabulation" is in the Jefferson Papers, Lib. of Cong.

13. Jefferson endorsed the report on expenses and duties as received on Feb. 1, 1791. Among the items discussed by Coxe were molasses, salt, tea, rum, duck, cordage, hemp, twine, woolens, and iron. He also included statements on tonnage and on the Massachusetts poll tax. As a closing statement Coxe added "A further remark relative to the abolition of the Tonnage of six cents." This information was incorporated by Jefferson in his report on the fisheries. Boyd *et al.*, eds., *Jefferson Papers*, XIX, 210–211. For Coxe's "Miscellaneous Notes on the Fisheries," comprising 40 pages and enclosed in his letter to Jefferson of Nov. 23, 1790 (see n. 12, above), see *ibid.*, 182–195. Coxe subsequently published a brief article based on his "Miscellaneous Notes." See "The importance of the fisheries considered as a part of the instruments of national defence and offence," signed "Columbus," *American Museum*, XI (1792), 176–177.

The similarities between Jefferson's report and Coxe's "Miscellaneous Notes" are far more important than the differences, however.[14] The thesis of both was the necessity of encouraging and protecting industries so vital to the prosperity and defense of the nation. Jefferson made the point, and Coxe stressed it again and again when he argued for the utility of the fisheries viewed both as a branch of domestic industry and as a market for related manufactures. Their recommendations emphasized that though the superior position of the country's fisheries made direct support unnecessary, the industry's importance and the handicaps under which it operated justified indirect aid. If upon a casual comparison of the two documents one does not immediately detect such similarities, it is because Jefferson's report was informed by a theme tucked away in the interstices of Coxe's "Miscellaneous Notes."

Few who read the secretary of state's report on the cod and whale fisheries, submitted to Congress early in February 1791, could have failed to detect its pervasive anti-British bias. The English, according to Jefferson, were as incorrigible as their policies were deplorable. As the chief competitors of the United States, they had refused to cooperate in mutually beneficial commercial policies, preferring regulations for "mounting their navigation on the ruins of ours." To Jefferson, as to Coxe, such obdurateness was an invitation to retaliatory legislation, about which the British could not justly complain. "Admitting their right of keeping their markets to themselves," the secretary of state explained, "ours cannot be denied of keeping our carrying trade to ourselves. And if there be anything unfriendly in this, it was in the first example." By way of contrast, Jefferson pointed to examples of friendliness on the part of France, whose continued cultivation, he said, was important not only because the French were "co-operators against a common rival" but because they took a sizable proportion of American exports.[15]

But the prosperity of the fisheries, particularly the whale industry, could not, as Jefferson knew, be assured merely by maintaining amicable relations with France. What should be done about England? Her excessively high duties or prohibitions and her restriction of trade to British ships rendered the export of American fish and of spermaceti oil to that country either impossible or unprofitable. Arguing that such *"ex parte* regulations

14. See "Jefferson's Notes and Outline for the Report on the Fisheries," Boyd *et al.*, eds., *Jefferson Papers*, XIX, 204–205. Here Julian Boyd, who otherwise has minimized Coxe's contribution to Jefferson's report, conceded that "Jefferson's Notes" were "based in part on the documents supplied by Tench Coxe." *Ibid.*, 205.

15. Jefferson's "Report on the subject of the cod and whale fisheries . . ." was submitted to the House on Feb. 1, 1791. See *ibid.*, 206–236, where the report is printed, along with its appendices.

can only be opposed by counter regulations on our part," Jefferson proposed an American navigation act to counter that of England. To him "reciprocity" of this kind was not only equitable but imperatively dictated by the national interest. How else could American commerce flourish and the country defend itself? The alternative Jefferson presented was a parade of horribles: useless ships, an end to shipbuilding, young men no longer answering the call of the sea, produce transported only by foreigners, and national peril in time of war.

Despite such hyperbole, Jefferson's report retains, in the words of a recent scholar, "intrinsic value and interest" and "will be illuminating even now to most laymen."[16] Particularly striking was Jefferson's manifest sympathy for the hardships of an industry that he personally was as unfamiliar with as were Yankee sailors with tobacco cultivation. Also notable, particularly in view of his agrarian preferences, was his recognition of the indispensability of the fisheries to the American economy and to national defense, an awareness doubtless enhanced by Coxe's research report. The Americans must in this instance, Jefferson asserted, copy the otherwise reprehensible policies of the English and encourage an industry that was a spur to manufactures, an important branch of the carrying trade, and a reservoir of seamen.

That Jefferson's report was substantively the same as Coxe's "Miscellaneous Notes" is as indisputable as the exact extent of Coxe's influence is conjectural only. The secretary of state, unlike his presidential chief, who on occasion found it convenient to sign state papers drafted by aides, would not have entertained even the possibility of accepting as his own a draft written by another. A superb literary craftsman, Jefferson did not need to do so. And in this fact lies an explanation of the seeming qualitative disparity between his report and Coxe's "Miscellaneous Notes." The former was characteristically adorned by a stylistic felicity that Coxe's writings rarely displayed. Jefferson was a creative thinker as well as a masterly writer. Although Coxe was an uncommonly able journalist, his superior talent lay in the straightforward presentation of assiduously collected factual material. Such observations, far from discrediting the inference that the secretary of state relied heavily on the research of his assistant, suggest instead how easily and effectively Jefferson could have incorporated another's data into an essay bearing the unmistakable imprint of his own style. And after one takes into account that on the subject of the fisheries, as on other aspects of American commercial policy, the two men held similar ideas, it still seems reasonable to insist that the secretary of state was significantly influenced by the work of his voluntary aide. Jefferson's own estimate of the

16. Malone, *Jefferson: Rights of Man*, 332.

value of Coxe's work was demonstrated by his continued reliance on Hamilton's top assistant.[17]

Coxe gladly continued to cooperate with Jefferson. While busily engaged in compiling notes on the fisheries, he signified his willingness to perform "any little service it may at any time hereafter be in my power to render" that might promote the secretary of state's "individual convenience" or lessen "the fatigues" of his office. Jefferson soon found it convenient to accept the invitation, for as early as February 1791 he was busily rounding up ammunition for a manifesto of American economic independence. His report on the fisheries, so Coxe's friend Phineas Bond, the British consul in Philadelphia, reported to Whitehall, appeared "to have been designed as the introduction of a series of proceedings calculated to promote measures very hostile to the commercial interests of Great Britain."[18] Bond was correct. Jefferson's report on the privileges and restrictions imposed by foreign nations on United States commerce would be the culmination of his concerted campaign against Britain's commercial system.

An opportunity for Jefferson to publicly present a persuasive plea for American commercial independence was provided by Congress. After pigeonholing a navigation bill that would have prohibited the importation of non-British goods in British vessels, the House of Representatives on February 23, 1791, referred the whole problem of commercial policy to the secretary of state for study and recommendations. In view of his known admiration for the French people and his alleged unfriendliness toward Britain, his critics, especially Hamilton, had no doubt of the result. If the outcome was predetermined, however, the policies of the British were as much responsible as Jefferson's own animus. If the English would "meet us fairly half way," Jefferson had written in November 1790, "I should meet them with satisfaction, because it would be for our benefit." But convinced of British "avarice of commerce," he did not consider their cooperation likely—a viewpoint shared by other influential public figures and prominent publicists (notably Madison), who, like Coxe, had examined English policy and were convinced that threatening commercial discrimination was Ameri-

17. My interpretation of the relationship between Coxe and Jefferson differs from that presented by Julian Boyd in the *Jefferson Papers*, XIX. (See especially the editorial notes on pp. 121–127, 558–579.) Boyd's viewpoint is indicated by the following sentence: "It is a mistake to suppose that Jefferson's reliance upon Coxe extended much beyond a natural desire on his part to augment and correct his own considerable body of data, which was of such range and depth that Coxe was able to make additions to it chiefly because he had access to customs records in the Treasury." *Ibid.*, 124.

18. Coxe to Jefferson, Nov. 23, 1790, *ibid.*, XVIII, 62; Phineas Bond to the duke of Leeds, Mar. 14, 1791, Jameson, ed., "Letters of Phineas Bond," II, Am. Hist. Assn., *Report for 1897*, 475.

ca's only effective means of achieving a negotiated settlement.[19]

On March 4, 1791, shortly after he learned of Congress's request to the secretary of state for a report on commercial policy, Coxe once again placed himself at Jefferson's disposal, sending as an implicit exhibit of his usefulness "some returns of tonnage" that even in an imperfect state "exhibit interesting facts."[20] Although Jefferson needed neither this nor further evidence of Coxe's energy and encyclopedic knowledge of American commerce, he received on the following day a twenty-five-page manuscript based on data that Coxe had compiled for a committee appointed by the House of Representatives to propose measures for the promotion of American trade.[21]

This paper, entitled "Thoughts on the Navigation of the United States," was an effective argument in support of certain commercial policies, most of which Jefferson already advocated or would soon champion. Starting from the premise that his countrymen were extraordinarily adept at shipbuilding and navigation, Coxe discussed the national advantages to be derived from the promotion of these and auxiliary enterprises. To this end he recommended eighteen "measures for encouraging the Navigation of the United States." Among these were the exemption of American coasting and fishing vessels from tonnage duties, the application of the surplus derived from levies on tonnage to the provision of navigational aids and naval facilities, the promotion of manufactures related to American navigation or to national defense by permitting the free importation of essential raw materials, "the encouragement of manufactures in general," and the enactment

---

19. Jefferson to Francis Kinloch, Nov. 6, 1790, Boyd *et al.*, eds., *Jefferson Papers*, XVIII, 80.

20. Coxe to Jefferson, Mar. 4, 1791, *ibid.*, XIX, 360.

21. For Coxe's "Thoughts on the Navigation of the United States, and concerning further means of encouraging it," see *ibid.*, 411–416. Coxe also enclosed "a little pamphlet of his written about four years ago on American commerce and another on American Manufactures which, tho not a part of the subject, has a near relation to it." The enclosures were *An Enquiry into a Commercial System* and *An Address to the Friends of American Manufactures*, both written in 1787. Coxe's letter to Jefferson of Mar. 5, 1791, enclosing his "Thoughts on Navigation," reads: "Mr. Coxe has the honor to enclose to Mr. Jefferson some notes upon navigation marked (A) which he prepared at the request of the Chairman of the Navigation Committee." Boyd *et al.*, eds., *Jefferson Papers*, XIX, 411–416. The committee to which Coxe referred was appointed on Dec. 15, 1790, "to bring in a bill or bills making further provision for the encouragement of the navigation of the United States." *Annals of Cong.*, II, 1804. The committee consisted of 12 members, with Elias Boudinot as chairman. *Journal of the House*, I, 14. Since Coxe had submitted at least two (and probably three) reports to that committee (Coxe to James Madison, Jan. 13, 1791, Madison Papers, Lib. of Cong.), the manuscript he transmitted to Jefferson may have been based on all of them. My interpretation of the genesis and significance of Coxe's "Thoughts on Navigation" differs from that in Boyd *et al.*, eds., *Jefferson Papers*, XIX, 449–450, where it is conjectured that "the handwriting" of the last two paragraphs of Coxe's essay "suggests they were added after the main body of the notes had been composed." *Ibid.*, 416n. My own examination of the manuscript of Coxe's "Thoughts on Navigation" (Jefferson Papers) does not bear out that conjecture.

of measures "to exempt American ships in the foreign trade from the tonnage of 6 cents" and "to confine the importation of goods to the ships of the nation making or producing them and our own."

Although the secretary of state presumably reacted somewhat chillily to an appeal for the fostering of manufactures by a paternalistic government, he fully shared Coxe's insistence on the imperativeness of commercial retaliation against Great Britain by the adoption of an American navigation act. A measure "confining importations to our ships and those of the nation making or producing the commodities," Coxe wrote in words that Jefferson could only have applauded, "must prove a very efficient measure." What if Great Britain complained? Coxe's reply was surely what Jefferson wanted to hear: That country should be told that such an act "*is taken from her own existing laws and that we are ready to repeal our clause as it regards all our dominions, if they will repeal as generally.*"

Such ideas, however forcefully put, were addressed to one who had long since been firmly convinced that they should be the essential basis of American commercial policy. More novel, and thus to Jefferson more exciting, may have been the concluding paragraphs of Coxe's "Thoughts on Navigation." Here, in Julian Boyd's words, Coxe "advanced to new and bolder ground," not only arguing that the navigation act he proposed would enhance America's share of the international carrying trade but also adding this "astonishing suggestion": "Were France, Spain and Portugal to adopt the *confining regulation* the carrying trade of the world would sustain a considerable revolution, and, consequently, considerable effects would be produced upon the balance of *naval* power." In "this brief, climactic paragraph" pointing to "a possible revolution in world trade," Coxe provided "an epitome of the instructions that within a fortnight Jefferson sent to American representatives abroad."[22]

But although Coxe's "Thoughts on Navigation" served as a spur to prompt action, it was perhaps even more important as a persuasive presentation of ideas that Jefferson would affirm in his report on American com-

---

22. Boyd *et al.*, eds., *Jefferson Papers*, XIX, 416, 256. The editor of this work has asserted that "some of Coxe's suggestions were advanced for the time" and has discussed them at length and complimentarily, but he has concluded that "the very comprehensiveness" of Coxe's "proposals robbed them of the kind of direct, concentrated thrust that characterized the efforts of Madison and Jefferson." Although Boyd has stated that "A brief examination" (*American Museum*, IX, X [1791]) was "a far more timely and useful document than the discursive 'Thoughts on the Navigation,'" he has nevertheless emphasized the significance of the last paragraph of the latter work. However, while I agree with Boyd's further observation that the influence of Coxe's "Thoughts on Navigation" on Jefferson "must remain in the realm of conjecture," I do not consider his own conjecture plausible. "It is extremely unlikely," Boyd surmised, "that Coxe, whose commercial views derived largely from his experience as a merchant, could have brought a new and unanticipated possibility to the attention of the Secretary of State, whose long years as legislator and diplomat had schooled him to think in terms of na-

merce two and a half years later. The question of who borrowed from whom is, of course, unanswerable, but Coxe's proposition "that no foreign nation can be reasonably displeased with or consider itself as improperly treated by a general regulation the tendency of which is to produce the same effect upon their navigation or commerce, which their *general* or *particular* laws produce and are avowedly intended to produce upon ours," was (the awkward phraseology excepted) that which Jefferson would present in his famous state paper.

The thesis of Jefferson's report also dovetailed with the argument presented in "A brief examination," the series of essays that Coxe published in rebuttal of Lord Sheffield's defense of Britain's navigational system. The first installment of Coxe's exposé of the fallacies underpinning Sheffield's *Observations on American Commerce* was published in the March 1791 issue of the *American Museum*, a month after Congress requested the secretary of state to report on American commerce.[23] This period, Coxe remarked, was "interesting and critical" because of the likelihood that Congress might soon determine "the policy, which the united states ought to observe, in *the legislation of commerce*." He thus pointedly alluded to the possible adoption of an American navigation act such as Madison had offered in the congressional session that just ended. It was a possibility that Jefferson, like Coxe, happily entertained, and the secretary of state was eager to use it as a weapon in his diplomatic arsenal. He could thus only have welcomed Coxe's promise to present indisputable facts that would "enable our own legislature and those of foreign nations, to discover the ground of common interest."[24]

---

tional policy. . . . On the contrary, it is probable that Coxe made the suggestion because he knew it to be an idea Jefferson already had in mind." Boyd *et al.*, eds., *Jefferson Papers*, XIX, 560–562. For my objections to the argument by which the latter statement is supported, see n. 26, below. I am indebted to Boyd for the insight into the importance of Coxe's proposal, as well as for the connection of the proposal with the instructions Jefferson sent in Apr. to American diplomats overseas.

23. *American Museum*, IX (1791), 121–126. For full bibliographical information on Coxe's "A brief examination," see chap. 10, n. 1.

24. *Ibid.*, 126. In Boyd *et al.*, eds., *Jefferson Papers*, XIX, 559, it is conjectured that "Jefferson himself had inadvertently stimulated Coxe to undertake" a rebuttal of Sheffield's *Observations on American Commerce* "when, shortly before Congress convened" in Dec. 1790, "he sought to borrow from him the latest edition of Sheffield's treatise." Such a possibility is, I think, highly unlikely in view of the explanation Coxe himself offered for his decision to publish a reply to Sheffield's *Observations on American Commerce*. See *View of the U.S.*, 111–112. The possibility is rendered the more improbable by a statement in a letter from Coxe to Jefferson enclosing the first article of "A brief examination." "I have *for some time*," Coxe wrote, "entertained an opinion that it would be an useful Service to the United States to demonstrate to every man of Candor in the British Nation the very great errors and deviations from fact, which are to be found in Ld. Sheffields pamphlet." Boyd *et al.*, eds., *Jefferson Papers*, XIX, 587–588, italics added.

Predictably, Coxe focused on Anglo-American relations, setting forth the evidence that to him conclusively demonstrated that it was to Great Britain's advantage to encourage commercial amity with the United States. The Americans were not dependent (as Sheffield had argued) on either British imports or British ships. Coxe substantiated his argument by pointing to the "improvement of our own resources and manufactures," the trade concessions from other nations, the "discovery and attainment of new internal resources," and the evident willingness of countries other than Britain "to furnish us with credits, and sometimes in more eligible shapes." There was yet another and even more compelling reason why England should initiate rather than disdain commercial concessions to her former colonies, and he had stated it to Jefferson a month earlier in the last paragraph of his "Thoughts on Navigation." "It would diminish the number of British Vessels," Coxe now repeated, "if the united states and all other maritime countries should deem it expedient to enact into a law of their respective nations, the clause of the British statute, by which the importation of all foreign goods is confined to native bottoms, and to those of the nations producing the article."[25] What Coxe thus once again proposed, and at a "critical juncture" in American foreign affairs, was, "in effect, a veiled but clearly discernible outline of Jefferson's policy."[26] This was tellingly revealed by the incorporation of Coxe's proposal in instructions that the secretary of

---

25. Coxe, "A brief examination," *American Museum*, IX (1791), 225.

26. Boyd *et al.*, eds., *Jefferson Papers*, XIX, 566. Although I have relied on Boyd's perceptive analysis of the contemporary significance and originality of Coxe's proposal of the joint adoption by the United States and friendly European powers of a program of retaliatory measures against Britain's navigational system, I do not agree with the further contention that Coxe's recommendation was inspired by Jefferson. The appearance of the first issue of Coxe's "A brief examination" in the *American Museum* in Mar. 1791 was, according to Boyd, "a fortuitous occurrence" that "enabled Jefferson to utilize the public press in advancing" his "idea of a European concert." Immediately upon reading the first article of Coxe's series, Jefferson "seized the opportunity and gave counsel to Coxe that is obvious even though unrecorded." Relying on the conjecture that since Jefferson did not acknowledge Coxe's essay in writing, the secretary of state must have done so in "a personal and private conversation," Boyd has further maintained that "it seems clear that Jefferson consulted Coxe, encouraged him to proceed, and guided him in his approach to this central question of foreign policy." The claim that "the hand that influenced" the second of Coxe's essays on Sheffield "was unmistakeably that of the Secretary of State" is based on elaborate circumstantial evidence, which would require an essay virtually as long again as Boyd's lengthy editorial note to refute. Only a simplified summary of the latter's argument with a cryptic statement of the basis of my disagreement can be given here. Among Boyd's contentions are these: Although Coxe had expressed an intention of publishing his series in the *American Museum*, he changed plans and first published his second article in Andrew Brown's *Federal Gazette*, where number one had also appeared; and the second number of Coxe's articles, "which was obviously written . . . after Jefferson had seen the first, presented a remarkable contrast" to Coxe's first number, which "had assumed no position with respect to American commercial policy." Boyd *et al.*, eds., *Jefferson Papers*, XIX, 559, 562–

state promptly dispatched to American envoys in France, Spain, and Portugal. In these instructions he recommended a "concert of retaliatory measures . . . founded in a desire for universal reciprocity." Jefferson underscored his championship of Coxe's argument by sending to these diplomats copies of the first three numbers of "A brief examination."[27]

The secretary of state may also have contrived to use Coxe's manifesto of American commercial freedom as a ploy in Anglo-American diplomacy. Jefferson himself handed a copy of the first installment of "A brief examination" to George Beckwith, Britain's unofficial American representative, who conveniently lodged at the same rooming house as James Madison. The secretary of state may also have encouraged Coxe to send subsequent essays in the series to the Englishman.[28] Whether at Jefferson's urging or not, Coxe on April 17 called on Beckwith and presented him with the second and third of his serial assault on Sheffield's *Observations on American Commerce*. The British agent promptly forwarded the articles to his Foreign Office superiors in London, cryptically commenting that they were "not considered here as a private production."[29] To Beckwith the inference to be drawn from this situation must have been pellucid: if the assistant secretary of the Treasury Department, presumably a bastion of pro-British sentiment, publicly advocated retaliatory legislation aimed at England's restrictive commercial system, then "the interests of the Empire in this country" were in a "critical condition." Coxe did his best to enhance this sense of

---

563, 567, 563. My objections, briefly stated, are as follows: First, there was nothing unusual in Coxe thus altering his publishing plans. He did so on other occasions, as in 1798 when he expanded what he initially planned as two articles on United States foreign policy into nine essays (see chap. 17, n. 14). Moreover, as a silent partner in Brown's paper, he had acknowledged an obligation to publish his work in the *Federal Gazette* and continued to do so even after the partnership with Brown was dissolved in the summer of 1790. Also, the remaining four numbers of Coxe's "A brief examination" also appeared in the *Gazette* (see issues of May 13, 14, 16, June 14, 15, 16, 17, July 14, 15, 16, Aug. 8, 9, 10, 1791), suggesting that he had all along intended simultaneous newspaper and magazine publication. Second, what Boyd finds to be the "remarkable contrast" between the first and second numbers of "A brief examination" need not have been owing to Jefferson's influence. A shift in emphasis from one essay to the next in a series is not uncommon, and Coxe did so in other instances. Finally, the opening and closing sections of Coxe's first essay did explicitly and, more tellingly, implicitly include assumptions about American commercial policy.

27. Boyd *et al.*, eds., *Jefferson Papers*, XIX, 568.

28. Coxe, "To the Public," *Aurora*, Oct. 30, 1800; Boyd *et al.*, eds., *Jefferson Papers*, XIX, 568–569, where it is concluded that Jefferson "may have prompted Coxe to hint in this indirect manner that the publication had the blessing of government. The fact that Coxe was a subordinate of the official who was the chief defender of the British interest in the United States made the revelation all the more pointed. Such a use of indirect means" was "characteristic of Jefferson's style of diplomacy." *Ibid.*, 569.

29. Boyd *et al.*, eds., *Jefferson Papers*, XIX, 568, citing Beckwith to Grenville, Apr. 17, 1791.

crisis by giving Beckwith "copies of each of the seven numbers for himself and his friends in Europe."[30]

The secretary of state's more general reliance on the wealth of data that Coxe presented in his rebuttal of Lord Sheffield is, however, not so precisely determinable. The thesis set forth by the assistant Treasury secretary must, at the least, have confirmed the Virginian's own viewpoint, while also affording evidential data for his report on American commerce. Moreover, "A brief examination" provided proof of the industriousness and ideological soundness of a talented political economist who freely, even importunately, offered his assistance.[31]

Jefferson's report on American commerce would be delayed time and again. He worked on it intermittently, initially planning to present it to the session of Congress scheduled for the fall of 1791. In the interim, however, Great Britain decided to inaugurate normal diplomatic relations with her former colonies and designated George Hammond to be the first English minister to the United States. Hammond arrived in August of that year. With delicate diplomatic negotiations under way in Philadelphia, Jefferson thought it imprudent to publicly criticize Britain and accordingly postponed the submission of his report. It was finally sent to Congress on the eve of his retirement in December 1793.[32]

In the meantime, Coxe supplied enough research material for a volume on the subject. The nature and range of the material he sent Jefferson is indicated by this chronological sampling: on March 4, 1791, returns of tonnage and a promise to send returns of imports; on April 15, 1791, a return of United States tonnage for the preceding year and a promise to send

30. *Ibid.*, 569, citing Beckwith to Grenville, June 14, 1791; Coxe, "To the Public," *Aurora*, Oct. 30, 1800. Although Beckwith did share his anxiety with Lord Grenville, he did not mention Coxe's name or official position.

31. Another example of Coxe's aid to Jefferson was his revision of the forms transmitted by the State Department to American consuls in foreign ports as guidelines for their half-yearly reports. In April 1791 Jefferson sent Coxe a sample form, asking him "for any hints for its improvement either by insertions or omissions." Apr. 20, 1791, Benjamin Franklin Collection, Sterling Memorial Library, Yale University, New Haven, Conn. He could have found no more cooperative and qualified consultant. Although aware that the consular returns were a unique source of the information on which proposals for a sound national commercial policy might be based, Jefferson lacked detailed knowledge of the exact kind of data that needed to be solicited. Coxe, relying on his experiences as an international merchant and his extensive research into the nature and conditions of American trade, was able quickly and easily to draw up a long list of substantive recommendations. These were calculated to provide the United States "the advantage of minute information" both on the precise nature of its own foreign trade and on the economic conditions prevailing among its chief customers or rivals. "Remarks on the consular return," n.d., Coxe Papers. A copy of this was enclosed in Coxe to Jefferson, Apr. 23, 1791, Jefferson Papers.

32. "Report on the privileges and restrictions on the commerce of the United States in foreign countries," Dec. 16, 1793, Andrew A. Lipscomb and Albert Ellery Bergh, eds., *The Writings of Thomas Jefferson*, III (Washington, D.C., 1903), 261–283.

out a Treasury Department circular to collectors of the customs directing them to supply additional information on exports and imports, so designed that "it may be seen in what quantities we obtain the several kinds of supplies from the several foreign nations"; on July 19, 1791, two letters giving information on the commercial regulations of the United Netherlands; on December 8, 1791, an abstract showing the quantity of manufactured goods sold in the United States by selected foreign countries, followed some weeks or months later by a promise "to send the returns of Exports the moment Mr. Hamilton is finished with it"; and on February 20, 1793, information on the Danish trade and on Holland's trade with her West Indian islands.[33]

Coxe also assisted Jefferson in the preparation of other state papers. When in March 1791 the president requested the secretary of state to submit a report on unclaimed lands in the northern and southwestern territories, Coxe readily furnished material on the subject. It took the form of a long research report, drafted in August 1791, on the disposition of western lands.[34] Two years later information on another aspect of the same subject, this time on the boundaries of lands between the Ohio River and the Great Lakes acquired from the Indians, was supplied by Coxe at Jefferson's request.[35]

Coxe did not confine himself to providing material for State Department reports; unsolicited, he aided Jefferson in yet other ways. He forwarded newspaper clippings, political rumors, and foreign intelligence in which he believed the secretary of state might be interested; he passed on requests from acquaintances; and he helped to find competent personnel for the State Department.[36] Such cooperativeness was repaid by Jefferson's confidence not only in Coxe's ability but also in his discreetness and, as time passed, in his personal loyalty and ideological soundness.

33. Coxe to Jefferson, Mar. 4, Apr. 15, July 19, 1791 (two letters), Feb. 20, 1793, Jefferson Papers. These are but a few of the many letters that Coxe wrote to Jefferson between 1791 and 1793 that contained information Coxe believed might be useful and pertinent in drawing up Jefferson's report on commerce. In the Jefferson Papers there are numerous other documents in Coxe's hand, most undated and without covering letters, that perhaps were carried by messengers in Coxe's office to the State Department. Virtually random examples include: a memorandum on ships built in Philadelphia between Mar. 1790 and Mar. 1791, n.d.; a memorandum on British commerce and prices current in London, Aug. 27, 1791; a note giving information on British and Swedish duties [1791]; a note on duties in Holland on distilled spirits, n.d.; and a report on the "Subdivisions of the carrying trade," n.d.

34. Coxe to Jefferson, Aug. 6, 1791, Coxe Papers. A request by the president for a report on this subject was made on Mar. 3, 1791. Jefferson's report to Washington is in Ford, ed., *Works of Jefferson*, VI, 321–322. The president's report to Congress, submitted on Nov. 10, 1791, is in *American State Papers, Lands*, I, 22–28.

35. Coxe to Jefferson, Mar. 7, 1793 (two letters), Jefferson Papers; Jefferson to Coxe, Mar. 8, 1793, Franklin Collection.

36. It was Coxe, for instance, who in 1791 supplied Jefferson with a "copious abstract" from the confidential report of the Committee of the Privy Council that argued in favor of the rigid maintenance of the English navigational system ("To the Public," *Aurora*, Oct. 30, 1800),

The relationship that existed between Coxe and Jefferson was not in any sense as close as the friendship between the secretary of state and James Madison. Although the views of the Philadelphia capitalist and the Virginia planter did coincide on a great many public issues, Coxe stoutly supported a brand of economic nationalism—including protectionism, funding and assumption, and central banking—that Jefferson stridently denounced, at least when advocated by Hamilton. Nor could Jefferson with any consistency have shared Coxe's enthusiasm for the encouragement of manufactures, redolent as it was to him of reprehensible mercantilist principles. In fact, the convergence of the ideas of Coxe and Jefferson ended at the Atlantic coastline. Far from sharing Jefferson's faith in laissez-faire, Coxe, like Hamilton, believed that the doctrines of mercantilism should be tailored to the needs of the new nation. And in striking contrast to the Virginian's unfavorable view of Hamilton's program, Coxe insisted that it was "consistent with the public interest" and was both "just and beneficial."[37]

Jefferson's tolerance of ideas held by the assistant secretary of the Treasury seems to have been matched by his abhorrence of them when expressed by the secretary. The paradox is greater when one reflects that the divergence between the views of Jefferson and his friend Coxe was actually greater than that between the ideas of the secretary of state and his archrival. Although Hamilton was "widely hailed in later years as the father of the American protective system" and as the nation's most notable advocate of American industrialization, Coxe was in fact a more ardent protectionist and a more zealous exponent of manufactures.[38] Nevertheless, Jefferson overlooked in Coxe what he otherwise viewed as heresy, perhaps because (Hamilton excepted) the Virginian's "political instincts were to conciliate."[39] For his part, Coxe would not have understood what students of later generations have seen as the radical and irreconcilable differences between

---

with information he had received in the same year on England's proposed new corn law (Coxe to Jefferson, Mar. 14, June 30, 1791, Jefferson Papers), and with a report from his brother Daniel on the plundering of American commerce in the West Indies (Coxe to Jefferson, Sept. 15, 1793, Jefferson to Coxe, Oct. 3, 1793, Jefferson Papers). See also Coxe to Jefferson, July 23, Aug. 27, Sept. 5, 1793, Jefferson to Coxe, Sept. 10, 1793, Jefferson Papers. An example of a request passed on from an acquaintance was when Coxe relayed "an application . . . whether it will be illegal or, in any respect improper for a Citizen of the United States to accept the business . . . of an agent" for prizes sent to Philadelphia by French warships, "public and Private." Coxe to Jefferson, May 17, 1793, Jefferson Papers. See also Coxe to Jefferson, May 16, 1793, *ibid*. On finding personnel, see, for example, Coxe to Jefferson, May 9, 10, 11, 15, 1793, *ibid*.

37. Coxe, "Reflexions on the state of the union," *American Museum*, XII (1792), 14.

38. Malone, *Jefferson and His Time*, III: *Jefferson and the Ordeal of Liberty* (Boston, 1962), 158.

39. The quotation is from Peterson, *Jefferson and the New Nation*, 397, who does not, as I do above, make Hamilton an exception.

Jefferson and Hamilton. During his first years in the Treasury Department, Coxe believed (though his fierce partisanship would in later years obliterate the memory) that the two statesmen pursued many of the same goals and in some instances the same policies.

Nor was Coxe's endorsement of Hamilton's financial and Jefferson's commercial policies as inconsistent as it superficially appears. A good number of other Federalists, notably merchants in Philadelphia and elsewhere, similarly saw no incompatibility in supporting Hamilton's fiscal program and opposing his foreign policy. To them, as to Coxe, the national, as well as their own, interest dictated commercial freedom, and this they believed could best be attained by resistance to the restrictions of British mercantilism and by expansion of trade with other countries. The proponents of economic nationalism, in sum, shared a belief in the necessity of national self-sufficiency but were divided on the means of achieving it. And this, no matter how seemingly contradictory his behavior, eventually prompted Coxe to march into Jefferson's camp flying a Hamiltonian flag.

Coxe's initial gestures of friendship toward Jefferson soon turned into behavior that was imprudent to the point of rashness. As the personal and political animosity between his superior in the Treasury Department and the secretary of state mounted, Coxe found himself committed to a course of action that in the end would besmirch his reputation and cripple his public career. No doubt he justified his behavior by reminding himself that he was half-Hamiltonian and half-Jeffersonian, and it is true, in Merrill Peterson's words, that he "worked both sides of the street . . . not only because he had an eye for the main chance politically but also because there were two distinct sides of economic nationalism."[40] But he should have realized that in a government increasingly characterized by ardent partisanship and keen departmental antagonism, he could not, so long as he was the subordinate of the head of one of the two rival departments, remain neutral by serving both sides. At least his behavior had a measure of consistency—in the political duel between Hamilton and Jefferson, as during the contest between America and Great Britain a decade and a half earlier, Coxe believed that the middle ground was tenable. In neither case would the combatants have agreed.

Perhaps Coxe was misled by the geniality with which champions of the rival secretaries greeted each other in Philadelphia drawing rooms. He himself was socially at ease whether in mixed political or strictly partisan company, which indicates that Philadelphia society was not, in fact, as politically polarized as the stereotyped account suggests. After all (to give only

40. *Ibid.*, 429.

two of many possible examples), Jefferson saw no difficulty in entertaining Hamilton's assistant, and the Treasury secretary did not hesitate to ask Coxe to join him at a dinner party honoring Joseph Priestley, English radical and friend of Jefferson.[41]

That Coxe continued to enjoy the hospitality of both Hamilton and Jefferson despite his apparently divided loyalties was in part a reflection of his impeccable social status. In the nation's capital prominent public officials and the local elite amiably mixed, but the standards of Philadelphia were still largely set by the small circle of aristocrats into which Coxe had been born. Nevertheless, Philadelphia's social leaders warmly welcomed what Rufus Griswold described as the "Republican Court," and they unhesitatingly made Washington the center around which Philadelphia society revolved. The president, a leading member of the Virginia gentry who insisted on a formal and elaborate social protocol, was typecast for the role. Other government officials, like Coxe's friend Senator Pierce Butler of South Carolina, also entertained in a lavish, though in a somewhat less stilted, manner.[42] For the city's elite there was an exciting acceleration of an already active social life—more balls and dinners, new occasions for conspicuous consumption that had previously been somewhat wasted on friends and relatives, who in Philadelphia high society tended to be the same.

Coxe's family connections were extremely complex. Whether closely or distantly, he was related to many of the city's leading families, whose members overlooked personal idiosyncrasies and political loyalties and characteristically measured status by lineage. Coxe's incontestable claim was reinforced by his official position, which, though not top-notch, he cleverly exploited to woo the nation's more influential leaders. He cultivated not only Hamilton, Jefferson, and Madison, but also Vice-President John Adams (with whom Coxe developed a cordial relationship in the early 1790s), other New Englanders such as Elbridge Gerry, George Cabot, Roger Sherman, and John Langdon, and southerners such as William Vans Murray, Richard Henry Lee, and John Dawson.[43]

"The principal families" of Philadelphia "appear to live in great

41. Hamilton to Coxe, June 27, 1794, Coxe Papers. Some years later Coxe submitted to Joseph Priestley a proposed "Constitution of the Northumberland Academy," outlining "a System of Education . . . of the most practical kind." The draft of the constitution, endorsed "Project Proposed 1794 or 5 on Dr. Priestly's taking that position," is in the Coxe Papers.

42. Rufus Wilmot Griswold, *The Republican Court; or American Society in the Days of Washington* (New York, 1854); H. E. Scudder, *Recollections of Samuel Breck, with Passages from his Note-books, 1771–1862* (Philadelphia, 1877), 188.

43. Coxe, for example, went to considerable trouble in 1791 to find Adams a suitable residence in Philadelphia. See Adams to Coxe, Aug. 20, Sept. 13, 1791, Coxe Papers. See also Coxe to Adams, June 15, 1791, *ibid.*; Adams to Coxe, June 19, Sept. 13, 1791, Coxe to Adams, June 30, Sept. 3, 13, 20, 1791, Adams Papers, Mass. Hist. Soc., Boston.

harmony," commented the vice-president's wife, Abigail Adams. "We meet at all the parties merely the same company." (Her husband might well have added some years later, after Coxe began publicizing Adams's private letters and conversations, that they had far too much of the company of Tench Coxe.) Certainly Coxe took part in the winter round of teas, dinners, card parties, and balls that prompted Mrs. Adams to remark on another occasion that the Philadelphia social whirl was unmatched by that of any European city.[44]

Coxe did at times attend the extremely lavish social occasions of Ann Willing Bingham, the niece of Coxe's first wife,[45] and of William Hamilton, a boyhood friend of Coxe's, but more to Coxe's liking was the society of other friends and relatives whose red-brick and white-marbled houses fronted the tree-lined streets of central Philadelphia, among them the Francises, McCalls, Yeateses, Powels, Shippens, and Penns. Here entertainment was less lavish, and company rather more selectively provincial, though here, too, social status was underscored by rich clothes, handsomely decorated houses, and milling servants. Fortunately for Coxe the underscoring did not determine status, for as Joshua Francis Fisher, one of the city's social arbiters, put it, "social position did not depend on wealth."[46] Manners, attendance at the proper schools, membership in the right clubs, and, above all, an aristocratic background were the crucial determinants. Not even Coxe's severest critics could deny that he had courtly manners; he was suitably educated (and by dint of hard study far more learned than most of his peers); he was a longtime member of Philadelphia's Dancing Assembly; he was a member of the vestry that jointly served the wealthy and fashionable parishes of Christ and St. Peters churches; and he came from a family that the most cynical snob would not have presumed to scorn, though his wife's may occasionally have afforded irresistible material for drawing-room gossip.[47] If Rebecca's respectability was challenged, it was fortunate that it was not brought to Coxe's attention. A mere rumor that his aunt, Elizabeth Lawrence, had intimated that one of Rebecca's musical compositions might not be original was enough to provoke a letter in which Coxe came just short of challenging Mrs. Lawrence to a duel.[48]

Such behavior was atypical of Coxe. Graceful and debonair, uncommonly charming and ingratiating, he would have been at ease in even more

44. *Letters of Mrs. Adams. The Wife of John Adams. With an Introductory Memoir by Her Grandson, Charles Francis Adams*, 4th ed. rev. (Boston, 1848), 354, 352–353, 359.
45. See, for example, William Bingham to Coxe, Nov. 20, 1792, Coxe Papers.
46. Joshua Francis Fisher, "Recollection," cited in Rasmusson, "Capital on the Delaware," 115.
47. Rasmusson, "Capital on the Delaware," 142, 164.
48. Coxe to Elizabeth Lawrence, "Saturday" 5, 1792, Coxe Papers.

cosmopolitan and sophisticated company. At Philadelphia dinner tables his knowledge and clever banter made personal converts of his most hardened political opponents, until, perhaps, they heard new rumors of Coxe's deviousness and intemperate partisanship. By the mid-nineties, forty-odd years old, Coxe remained as slender as during his youth. Of a fair complexion, with an elongated but symmetrical head, a slightly pointed nose, sandy-colored, lightly powdered, and longish hair that had begun to recede, accentuating his high forehead, Coxe was a striking figure even among the dandies of the capital's society. (He was also, so an unfriendly critic said, a man of extreme vanity.)[49] Only his narrow, tight lips betrayed the repressed restlessness, the tensions of one who aspired to act on a set grander than a Philadelphia drawing room. It was, however, a spacious enough stage for Rebecca Coxe, to whom the capital's showy and spritely society must have seemed dazzling in contrast to the placid routine of the West Jersey squirearchy. What she once described as a "recluse part of the world" was, however, a pleasant retreat, and she spent each summer and autumn at Sidney. To the Coxe children—of whom by the mid-nineties there were six—Charles Coxe's country estate was life's delight.[50] Only under parental compulsion did they return with their mother to Philadelphia, where Rebecca, like other members of the gentry, arrived in time to prepare for the winter social season, which got underway in December.

For Rebecca the social season must in one sense have been trying. Although from a family that by Jersey standards was as rich as any, she was now confronted with an ostentatious display of wealth that must have made the Coxes feel poor. They were so by contrast only, of course, and their large house on the north side of Walnut just above Fourth Street was not conspicuously less impressive than the residence of wealthier relatives who lived nearby. Rebecca's days were full—supervision of servants and children, morning visits that were de rigueur among Philadelphia society matrons, balls and suppers, and when possible piano practice and the composition of songs. One of her pieces, entitled "Arise My Fair," was extravagantly praised by Congressman William Vans Murray, who also complimented Mrs. Coxe on her pleasing "style of singing."[51] There were also arrangements to be made for the Coxes' frequent and numerous guests—politicians and publicists, visiting dignitaries and local celebrities, top-rung society and those who were still climbing.

Although family tradition and training must have left Coxe with a

49. *Independent Gaz.*, Nov. 26, 1788.
50. Rebecca Coxe to Coxe, July 29, 1792, Coxe Papers. The Coxes' six children were Ann Rebecca, b. 1783; Tench, b. 1784; Francis S., b. 1789; Alexander S., b. 1790; Charles S., b. 1791; and Sarah Redman, b. 1793.
51. William Vans Murray to Coxe, July 1, 1792, Coxe Papers.

residue of the aristocrat's traditional scorn of the arriviste, he cordially accepted newcomers, particularly those whose literary accomplishments he respected. So it was with Peter S. Du Ponceau, a native Frenchman who came to America in 1777 as secretary to Baron von Steuben, settled in Philadelphia, became one of the new nation's principal authorities on international law, wrote distinguished books on legal history and on jurisprudence, and also achieved international recognition for his research in linguistics. For almost three decades Du Ponceau was one of Coxe's closest associates, his legal adviser, one of the assignees to whom he handed over management of his property, and a constant companion. Mathew Carey, the Philadelphia publisher and political economist, was another firm friend, as was the newspaper editor Benjamin Franklin Bache, whose execration of Federalism had made him the pariah of Philadelphia polite society. Coxe was also on cordial terms with other Republicans frowned upon by the Federalist elite, among them Alexander J. Dallas, secretary of the commonwealth, Chief Justice Thomas McKean, and Congressman Peter Muhlenberg—all men with whom Coxe's partisan career would be inseparably linked. The diversity of Coxe's acquaintances calls to mind Philadelphian William Bradford's comment that in capital city society "the cream, the *new*—and much of the *skim* milk" were "all mixed together." In words that may also have applied to Coxe, Bradford added that the "cream now and then seemed to curdle with disdain."[52]

No hauteur tinctured Coxe's relationship with members of the capital's diplomatic community and with prominent foreigners who visited Philadelphia in the 1790s. Phineas Bond, Jr., a former tory and the British consul, was a close family friend. Pierre Auguste Adet, the French minister, and Antoine René Charles Mathurin de La Forest, France's consul general for the mid-Atlantic states, were acquaintances, as was the Viscount de Noailles, Lafayette's brother-in-law, with whom Coxe spent pleasant hours discussing politics and literature, particularly Coxe's own writings.[53]

But of the foreigners resident in Philadelphia, Coxe must have been most frequently in the company of England's chief ambassadorial representative, George Hammond. The first British minister to the new nation, Hammond was presented to the president early in November 1791. Since Coxe's sister's family, the Allens, were among Hammond's London acquaintances, he soon thereafter also introduced himself to Coxe. It is likely that Hammond met his future wife, Margaret, a daughter of the Allens, at the

52. William Bradford to Mrs. Bradford, May 6, 1790, Bradford Papers, Hist. Soc. Pa., Philadelphia.

53. See Pierre Auguste Adet to Coxe, June 26, 1795, Coxe to Viscount de Noailles, Aug. 7, Nov. 30, 1795, de Noailles to Coxe, Aug. 1793 and n.d. [1793], Coxe Papers.

Coxe home, where the Allen children frequently visited. Hammond and Margaret were married in May 1793, and Coxe must surely have remained on intimate terms with the daughter of his favorite sister, though, for obvious reasons, he preserved not a word on the subject. So too was Hammond discreet, and his official dispatches, filled with accounts of conversations with the secretary of the Treasury, make no reference to his familial ties to Hamilton's assistant. Perhaps he knew what other officials in the nation's capital suspected: although Coxe staunchly championed Hamilton's domestic policies, his brand of Federalism bore no trace of partiality for England. Coxe embraced, instead, the views of Hammond's skillful antagonist at the State Department, Thomas Jefferson.

12 ↝❧

Commissioner of the Revenue

For almost a year after Jefferson became secretary of state, differences between Hamilton and himself were kept under cover, but by the early spring of 1791 Jefferson was beginning to talk of "a sect" that believed the British constitution "to contain whatever is perfect in human institutions." And he began to imply to confidants that Hamilton was the ringleader. The secretary of state soon convinced himself that Hamilton was "not only a monarchist, but for a monarchy bottomed on corruption," and that measures such as assumption and the bank had been put through Congress by the Treasury secretary's sycophants—a "phalanx" of stockjobbers bent on enriching themselves.[1]

Jefferson's attribution of hidden and sinister motives to his colleague in the Treasury was matched by Hamilton's growing mistrust of the secretary of state. Hamilton considered demagoguery, as personified by Jefferson, to be the real threat to American republicanism, not monarchism. Jefferson, so Hamilton was convinced, was driven by an insatiable ambition to dominate the entire government. The enemy of sound public credit, Jefferson was intent on subverting the country's carefully contrived financial structure. He was a visionary philosopher whose ignorance of economics was matched by his idealized view of man. Consumed by a raging fever of anglophobia, he was an apostate to French principles. Above all, Hamilton was convinced that his rival was actuated by personal rancor. And perhaps he was right.

This is not to impugn Jefferson's obvious sincerity but to suggest that his dislike of Hamilton's purported principles was grounded in an intense personal antipathy. It was understandable. Opposites may repel as well as

1. Ford, ed., *Works of Jefferson*, VI, 186, I, 177–179.

attract, and the contrast between the two was striking: the New York arriviste and the Virginia aristocrat; the short, erect, dapper lawyer and the tall, stooped, indifferently attired planter; the genius whose chief guide had been experience and the philosopher whose learning was as broad as his interests were wide. One was intense, fiercely ambitious, intolerant of mediocrity, and the other relaxed, even insouciant, already world famous, amiably tolerant. At least they shared the capacity to inspire great personal loyalty, and Coxe, attracted though he may have been by some principles espoused by each, was by temperament and background conditioned to feel a greater affinity with Jefferson.

It was the departmental, as distinguished from the personal and political, rivalry between Hamilton and Jefferson that caused Coxe difficulty. Even the most fulsome of Hamilton's admiring biographers concede that his penchant for meddling in the work of other departments was incurable.[2] And Coxe could scarcely have been blind to Jefferson's resentment of the Treasury secretary's covert interference in the affairs of the State Department. Nor could Coxe have been unaware of Hamilton's angry reaction to the news that a part-time employee of the State Department, the poet Philip Freneau, was the full-time editor of the *National Gazette*, founded by Madison and Jefferson in the fall of 1791 to publicize the nefarious motives and schemes of the secretary of the Treasury. In brief, even if Coxe had trouble deciding which of the principals in this political duel was hero and which villain, he should have known that in trying to serve both he was jeopardizing his relationship with each. Neither Hamilton nor Jefferson would appreciate him once his assistance was no longer to their own immediate advantage. For Jefferson that time would not come until a decade later, hard upon Coxe's instrumental role in electing him president. Hamilton's appreciation would end much sooner, an event that Coxe may have had a premonition of during the early months of 1792.

The occasion of Coxe's momentary anxiety was the appointment on January 19 of a House committee to consider what alterations should be made in the Treasury and War departments. The members of the committee were three staunch Federalists, Smith of South Carolina, Wadsworth of Connecticut, and Benson of New York—all of whom could be expected to follow the secretary of the Treasury's advice.[3] Would Hamilton find ways of jettisoning an assistant whose aid was dispensable now that the last of the secretary's great triad of reports had been submitted to Congress? It was at least conceivable that he might. Coxe was also justifiably worried that if his own views on commercial policy were aired (though his opinions had been

2. Frederick Scott Oliver, *Alexander Hamilton: An Essay on American Union* (New York, 1907), 213; Mitchell, *Hamilton: National Adventure*, II, 297–298.
3. *Annals of Cong.*, III, 328.

published anonymously, his authorship was no secret) or if his relationship with Jefferson came to light, his demotion or even dismissal from office might be contrived by parliamentary legerdemain.

When on February 29 the House committee finally brought in a report, Coxe's apprehensions were removed only to be replaced by humiliation. Although the measure authorized the abolition of the assistant secretaryship, it substituted an office of commissioner of the revenue—a new position that Coxe, wishing a more precise delineation of his duties, had his heart set on and that Hamilton may have promised him. Yet the report included at least two provisions to which Coxe strenuously objected: the first assigned the comptroller of the Treasury responsibility for superintending, "under the head of the Department, the collection of duties on imports and tonnage," hitherto a duty statutorily conferred on the secretary himself;[4] the second designated the comptroller to be acting head of the Treasury in the absence or physical incapacity of the secretary, a responsibility that had been delegated to the assistant secretary by the act creating the Treasury Department and that Coxe had on several occasions exercised.[5] To Coxe these provisions were a personal affront, the more so because they appeared to subordinate him to Wolcott, his rival in the department and a man he previously, at least in theory, had outranked. What a select committee had done, however, the whole House could undo, and for that Coxe confidently counted on an influential number of congressional allies—Pennsylvanians like FitzSimons, Hartley, Muhlenberg, and William Findley, and friends like Madison, Gerry, Gilman, and William Vans Murray—whose support he actively solicited.

But Coxe's rescue came from an unexpected quarter. Hamilton intervened on his assistant's behalf, though why he bothered is a conundrum in view of his irritation at Coxe's efforts "to embarrass the progress of the Bill" in order to "give it a complexion favourable to his ambition" and his annoyance at Coxe's thinly veiled threat that passage of the bill as initially proposed would give "an astonishing and very unpleasing Complexion" to "a respectable part of the federal interest." In any event, an "Act Making alterations in the Treasury and War Departments," adopted on May 8, the last day of the session, was, so Hamilton later recalled, "shaped in conformity with suggestions from me to Individuals."[6] Coxe could have wished

---

4. *American State Papers, Miscellaneous*, I, 47; "An Act to establish the Treasury Department," Sept. 2, 1789, *U.S. Statutes at Large*, I, 65–67. Coxe insisted that customs should not come under the direction of the comptroller, since that officer "ought not to sit in Judgement" on collectors' accounts, as this would create a flagrant conflict of interest. Coxe to Alexander Hamilton, May 6, 1792, Hamilton Papers, Lib. of Cong.

5. *American State Papers, Miscellaneous*, I, 47.

6. Hamilton to George Washington, Feb. 2, 1795, Syrett *et al.*, eds., *Hamilton Papers*, XVIII, 252; Coxe to Hamilton, May 6, 1792, Hamilton Papers.

for nothing more. Not only was the coveted office of commissioner of the revenue created and assigned specific and congenial duties, but, more gratifying, the powers of the comptroller were not enlarged. The supervision of the collection of duties on impost and tonnage was left to the discretion of Hamilton, and the direction of the affairs of the Treasury in the absence of the secretary was left to the judgment of the president rather than confided to Wolcott.[7]

As had been prearranged, Coxe was promptly appointed commissioner of the revenue.[8] "It is a circumstance very pleasing to your Friends," commented Thomas Hartley, one of Coxe's congressional friends who had helped to make the position possible. It was also a circumstance extremely pleasing to Coxe, who labored for hours on a fulsome letter of appreciation to Washington.[9] It must have been agreeable to Hamilton, who broadly defined both the scope and discretionary authority of Coxe's new office. Nevertheless, the power and perquisites of the position hardly seem to warrant the resoluteness with which Coxe had sought it. The commissioner was statutorily charged with responsibility for the collection of all revenues except those accruing from impost and tonnage duties and was directed, as had been the assistant secretary, to perform such other duties as the department head might require.[10] Hamilton promptly delegated to the commissioner's office responsibility for lighthouses and auxiliary navigational services, a task Coxe had performed as assistant secretary.[11] The Treasury secretary continued to rely on the Pennsylvanian for assistance, both consequential and minor.

Coxe's principal task was supervision of the internal revenue service (established by a law of March 1791 for the collection of the taxes on foreign and domestic distilled spirits), over which Hamilton (in an atypical

---

7. Although Coxe was spared what he would have considered a public humiliation, his victory was temporary. On Oct. 25, 1792, in a circular to the collectors of the customs, Hamilton wrote: "I have concluded to commit the immediate superintendance of the Collection of the duties of impost and tonnage to the Comptroller of the Treasury." Syrett et al., eds., Hamilton Papers, XII, 620.

8. His commission, signed by Washington and Thomas Jefferson and dated May 9, 1792, is in the Coxe Papers.

9. Thomas Hartley to Coxe, May 29, 1792, Coxe to Washington, n.d., ibid. The importance Coxe attached to this brief letter is attested by the dozens of deletions and insertions made on the draft.

10. In accord with the act making changes in the Treasury Department, Coxe also reviewed, along with the auditor of the Treasury Department, accounts and claims that Wolcott, when auditor, had passed on. Pursuant to this responsibility, Coxe and Richard Harrison reviewed at least 10 complicated complaints during the brief period between May and Sept. 1792, including one of the Secretary of War, one of Silas Deane, and one of Robert Morris.

11. Treasury Department Circular to the Superintendents of Lighthouses, May 22, 1792, Syrett et al., eds., Hamilton Papers, XI, 417–418.

delegation of authority) gave him virtually free reign.[12] Coxe not only exercised considerable administrative discretion but also participated in the formation of policy. Theoretically, of course, he had only the power to advise; the power to consent remained with Hamilton and ultimately with the president. Nevertheless, his role in the decision-making process was influential and often decisive. This was conspicuously demonstrated in the months immediately following his appointment as commissioner by his authorship of proposals for reorganization of the revenue service. After two months of careful investigation and frequent conferences with Hamilton, Coxe completed a draft of a lengthy and detailed new plan. Approved without modification by the secretary of the Treasury, it was sent to Washington, who gave his official sanction on August 4.[13]

During succeeding months Coxe drafted additional reforms and regulations that were subsequently issued by Washington as presidential "acts," and he recommended alterations designed to correct abuses and otherwise to improve the system.[14] His most elaborate and influential report, submitted to Hamilton on December 11, 1792, described the defects of the previous excise laws, suggested remedial measures, and proposed other modifications in the revenue service. Although these proposals were not immediately acted upon, their merit, as well as their favorable reception by Hamilton and Washington, was demonstrated by the incorporation of the great majority of them in the revised revenue law adopted by Congress in June 1794.[15]

The scope and content of Coxe's bulky correspondence as commissioner attest an administrative ability that explains Hamilton's willingness to overlook what by 1793 he regarded as his subordinate's official disloyalty and political heresy. Briefly to describe Coxe's work is to offer in miniature a history of the operation of the nation's first internal revenue service: he

---

12. "An Act repealing, after the last day of June next, the duties heretofore laid upon Distilled Spirits imported from abroad, laying others in their stead; and also upon Spirits distilled within the United States, and for appropriating the same," Mar. 3, 1791, *U.S. Statutes at Large*, I, 199–214. For Coxe's explanation of the safeguards against arbitrariness see his "Observations on the letters of 'a farmer,'" *American Museum*, XII (1792), 277.

13. See Coxe to Hamilton, July 25, 1792, Letters of the Commissioner of the Revenue, 1792–1793, R.G. 58, National Archives; Hamilton to Washington, July 30, 1792, Washington to Hamilton, Aug. 5, 1792, Syrett *et al.*, eds., *Hamilton Papers*, XII, 136–137, 166–167. The "act" of the president was sent to the revenue officers by Coxe in a circular letter of Aug. 17, 1792. Letters of Commr. of Rev., 1792–1793, R.G. 58.

14. See Coxe to Hamilton, Sept. 12–18, Oct. 20, 1792, Letters of Commr. of Rev., 1792–1793, R.G. 58; Washington to Hamilton, Oct. 1, 1792, Syrett *et al.*, eds., *Hamilton Papers*, XII, 514–515.

15. "An Act making further provisions for securing and collecting the duties on foreign and domestic distilled spirits, stills, wines and teas," June 5, 1794, *U.S. Statutes at Large*, I, 378–381.

recommended changes in federal and state legal codes requisite to the effective enforcement of the revenue regulations; brought to the secretary's attention cases of incompetence or malfeasance in office; was on the alert for possible defects in the excise law, which when detected were reported to Hamilton with recommendations for their correction; investigated and reported on cases involving conflicts of interest, the most flagrant of which was the ownership or operation of stills by revenue officers; and contributed substantively to the secretary's reports to Congress dealing with the revenue service by providing necessary accounts, statistics, and statements.[16]

The most difficult task for the commissioner was the collection of the whiskey tax in the face of popular resistance, centered, to Coxe's embarrassment, in the western counties of Pennsylvania. Here in 1792 opposition erupted into violence, countered by a presidential proclamation of September 15 admonishing and exhorting all persons "to refrain and desist from all unlawful combinations and proceedings" obstructing enforcement of the laws.[17] By the year's end the situation in Pennsylvania's four western counties was comparatively calm, indicating the desire of vigilant Treasury officials and still-defiant distillers to avoid a confrontation. That the distillers considered the truce only temporary was shown by the Whiskey Insurrection of 1794. In the interim, Coxe took the middle of the road, advocating reform of the excise law, along with maintenance of the principle of obedience to the law.[18]

In addition to administering the internal revenue service, Coxe was in charge of purchasing supplies for the army. In 1792 the act that created the office of commissioner of the revenue also assigned to the Treasury Department responsibility for "all purchases and contracts for all supplies for the use of the Department of War," an enlargement of some duties the Treasury had been performing since 1790. For two years Coxe played an important, though an indeterminate, role in carrying out this task.[19]

16. On recommendations for effective enforcement of revenue regulations, see Coxe to Hamilton, Dec. 14, 1792, Letters of Commr. of Rev., 1792–1793, R.G. 58. On cases of incompetence in office, see, for example, Coxe to Hamilton, Dec. 15, 1792, in which Coxe reported the unfitness of James Collins, a subject he found "extremely painful in a public and private view." *Ibid.* On recommendations for defects in the excise law, see Coxe to Hamilton, Dec. 13, 21, 1792, Jan. 13, 1793, *ibid.* On investigations of conflicts of interest, see Hamilton to Coxe, Jan. 26, 1793, Syrett *et al.*, eds., *Hamilton Papers*, XIII, 511; Coxe to Hamilton, Jan. 29, 1793, Hamilton to Coxe, Mar. 6, 1793, Letters of Commr. of Rev., 1792–1793, R.G. 58; Coxe to Hamilton, Jan. 6, 1794, Reports of the Secretary of the Treasury, 1784–1795, Vol. IV, R.G. 233, National Archives.

17. James D. Richardson, ed., *A Compilation of the Messages and Papers of the Presidents, 1789–1902*, I (Washington, D.C., 1903), 124–125.

18. Coxe's role in the Whiskey Rebellion can be followed in Letters of Commr. of Rev., 1792–1793, R.G. 58; George Clymer Letterbook, Coxe Papers; Syrett *et al.*, eds., *Hamilton Papers*, XII.

19. Coxe to Hamilton, May 20, 1792, Hamilton Papers; Coxe to Robert Elliot and Elie Wil-

Coxe's specifically designated administrative duties constituted only a part of his Treasury Department responsibilities. Hamilton took full advantage of the statutory provision that the commissioner of the revenue should in addition to his stipulated duties perform such other services as the secretary of the Treasury might direct. In view of what has already been said of Coxe's assignments as assistant secretary (which he continued to perform as commissioner of revenue), it is unnecessary to recount them. Not only was he called on to carry out any number of chores unconnected with the commissionership, but he was also entrusted with politically delicate tasks. It was Coxe who investigated the complaints of Andrew Fraunces, a former clerk in the Treasury Department who in 1793 broadcast the slander that Hamilton had appropriated for his own private use money legally due Fraunces, though neither Coxe's cajolery nor his threats could discourage this dismissed officeholder from his path of vengeance by character assassination. It was Coxe, similarly, who was deputized to ferret out the identity of "a gentleman in the Treasury Department" who anonymously published in a New Hampshire newspaper an article, republished in Philadelphia, intimating that President Washington was pro-French. It was Coxe, again, who was called on to investigate the political orthodoxy of Treasury officials reputedly engaged in subversive activities, such as membership in democratic societies.[20] It was also Coxe's polemical skill on which Hamilton could rely in the newspaper defense of the department's program. "It is a certain fact," John Beckley, clerk of the House of Representatives, wrote in September 1792, "that the whole weight of supporting" the Treasury secretary's "own measures through the public papers, has . . . fallen upon Coxe and himself, not a single publication on that side having been sent to the press from any pen but theirs."[21] That Hamilton so heavily relied on one with whom he often disagreed and whom he personally disliked is eloquent testimony to Coxe's unusual administrative ability, an ability for which most of his contemporaries failed to give him credit.

For Coxe personally there were psychic rewards. Although his was a second-string office, it did give him a gratifying sense of power, largely from promoting the careers of others. Just as Hamilton allowed him a wide berth in administering the field services committed to his care, so the secretary

---

liams, Feb. 23, 1793, to Gabriel Christie, Mar. 7, 1793, Coxe Papers; Hamilton to Coxe, Dec. 18, 1793, Oliver Wolcott, Jr., Papers, Conn. Hist. Soc., Hartford.

20. For complaints of Andrew Fraunces, see Coxe to Hamilton, Dec. 18, 1793, Coxe Papers. On the slanderous New Hampshire newspaper article, see Coxe to Arthur Livermore, June 26, 1793, *ibid.*; this article is printed in the *Fed. Gaz.*, June 1, 1793. On Treasury officials engaged in subversive activities, see, for example, Hamilton to Coxe, June 19, 1794, Coxe Papers.

21. John Beckley to James Madison, Sept. 19, 1792, Madison Papers, New York Public Library.

also characteristically accepted Coxe's nominees for vacant or newly created positions.[22] "I remind you," Coxe acrimoniously wrote to Hamilton in January 1795, "that from the day of the Nomination of the Treasury agent for Loans in August 1790 to the present time I have been called upon by you with great frequency to furnish the Names of persons suitable for public Employment of every description and degree of importance, at home or abroad." He also made certain that his nominees had a clean bill of political health. He had consistently "objected with frankness and perseverence," Coxe insisted, "against such as were likely from dangerous weaknesses or from more culpable circumstances to injure the Government." And his recollection was right; Hamilton had confidently relied on Coxe's recommendations, largely because he knew that they were based on careful homework.[23] Indeed, Coxe's influence was such that had the revenue officers been numerous enough and himself charismatic enough, he might have enlisted a cadre of national support for his own political advancement. Unfortunately for him, neither was the case. He was, instead, saddled with a degree and variety of official duties for which he received only the paltriest recognition.

The purchase of supplies for the War Department, the administration of the federal navigational system, and the supervision of the internal revenue service—all added up to a burdensome work load at which even the most tireless administrator might have balked. Coxe perhaps would not have complained if he had been given an adequate staff. In his office, located on the corner of Third and Chestnut a few doors from Hamilton's office, he was assisted by an office manager (William Barton), three clerks, and a messenger—half the number of employees he had had as assistant secretary and a miniature operation by contrast not only to modern bureaucracy but even to the much larger clerical staffs in other divisions of the Treasury Department.[24] This situation was not the result of an invidious distinction in favor of the register, the auditor, or the comptroller; it was a consequence of their having responsibility for the bulk of the Treasury's record keeping.

22. In at least one instance, it would have been better for Coxe if Hamilton had turned down his recommendation. Following the resignation of George Clymer as supervisor of the revenue for Pennsylvania in the spring of 1794, Coxe first prevailed upon Gen. Henry Miller of York to accept the post and then persuaded Hamilton to recommend the appointment. Coxe to Miller, June 19, 21, 1794, to Hamilton, June 27, 1794, Hamilton to Coxe, June 27, 1794, Coxe Papers. Coxe also may have been instrumental in rounding up the support of Jefferson and Edmund Randolph for this appointment. Miller not only turned out to be the most careless, uncooperative—and perhaps corrupt—supervisor in the country but also the nemesis measurably responsible for Coxe's official downfall.

23. Coxe to Hamilton, Jan.(?), 1795, *ibid*. For examples of nominations made by Coxe, see his correspondence, particularly between 1790 and 1793, with Hamilton, George Gale, Henry Wynkoop, George Cabot, Robert Morris, James Jackson, Benjamin Goodhue, and William Vans Murray, *ibid*.

24. On Jan. 3, 1793, Coxe reported to Hamilton that his staff consisted of:

Coxe's office, though entailing considerable paper work, was, by comparison, of a more supervisory nature. Nevertheless, ever-mounting piles of correspondence and an expanding administrative sphere made him increasingly restive.

It was fortunate that he did not reveal his restlessness to Hamilton, who, disturbed by the discovery of what he regarded as instances of his assistant's insubordination, might have been pleased at a pretext for firing him. The secretary's initial suspicions were aroused, ironically enough, neither by Coxe's official discontent nor his friendship for Jefferson but by a dispute over patronage.

The conflict between Hamilton and Coxe began in 1792 and concerned the appointment of a revenue inspector for an additional (or third) survey in Maryland. As was his custom, Hamilton left the nomination of a suitable candidate up to Coxe, who, in turn, called on the supervisor of revenue for Maryland, George Gale, for recommendations. Gale came up with three names—William Perry, an independently wealthy state senator who had the strong support of Hamilton's longtime friend Dr. James McHenry; Samuel Chamberlaine, Jr., one of Maryland's wealthiest citizens; and William Richardson, a state official whose family was prominent in local politics. Sometime in the autumn of 1792 Coxe recommended these names to Hamilton, and the two men agreed, so Hamilton recalled six months later, that all three candidates should be submitted to the president "with a decided recommendation of *Perry*."[25] The actual appointment awaited the convening of the Third Congress in December.

During the interim Coxe, with Hamilton's approval, sought the reaction of leading Maryland politicians to the appointment and uncovered the important political fact that Senator John Henry and Representative William Vans Murray, both residents of the new survey area, were of the opinion that Perry's appointment "would not be considered as advantageous to

---

"William Barton, principal Clerk at . . . . 800 Dollars p Annum.
John Mease . . . . .Clerk at 400
Peter Footman . . . . .do. at 400
Ezekiel Forman . . . . .do. at 400
Michael Gitts, Messenger and Office keeper 200

Dollars   2200"

Letters of Commr. of Rev., 1792–1793, R.G. 58. In 1792 there were 39 clerks and 2 messengers in the office of the register and 20 clerks in the office of the auditor. *American State Papers, Miscellaneous*, I, 57–58, 60–62.

25. Hamilton to James McHenry, Apr. 5, 1793, Syrett *et al.*, eds., *Hamilton Papers*, XIV, 287–289.

the public service." Henry and Murray, along with a number of other Marylanders who had a stake in the appointment, agreed that the two best qualified men were John Eccleston, a new entry in the large field of candidates, and Richardson, though they revealed "a manifest disposition to support Mr. Eccleston." On the morning of December 14, immediately following the receipt of Coxe's report on the matter, Hamilton discussed it with the president, who decided with characteristic political acumen that "Perry is strongly objected to by some; Richardson is recommended by everybody—Ergo Richardson is the safest appointment."[26] Richardson's appointment was accordingly made on December 19, 1792, and here the story would have ended, except for two developments.

On December 20, 1792, Hamilton received a confidential letter from Supervisor George Gale, who went over Coxe's head and angrily protested the proposed appointment of Richardson. Gale attributed the appointment to the influence of the revenue commissioner's Maryland relatives, the Tilghmans, from whom Coxe had prejudicially "received a very unfavorable impression of Mr. Perry."[27] Hamilton might well have overlooked such an instance of family influence had he not been aware that James Tilghman, Coxe's first cousin, was a "devoted follower" and "disciple" of John Francis Mercer, under whose sweeping and irresponsible charges Hamilton was then angrily smarting. Hamilton was also disturbed by the knowledge that by heeding Coxe's advice he had disappointed his close friend James McHenry, who had insistently supported Perry. The more Hamilton thought about his subordinate's behavior the more it rankled. The whole episode has "lain heavy on my mind," the secretary wrote in a letter of apology sent to McHenry four months later, and "I have meditated it ever since that issue took place." More by innuendo than explicit statement, Hamilton made it clear that he considered himself the victim of Coxe's officiousness and guile. McHenry got the point. Observing that he had all along been aware of Coxe's sinister influence, he replied, "I perceive he understands his business, or rather the intrigues of a court."[28]

Of itself the incident scarcely warrants retelling, but it indicates the drift of events. Two months later Hamilton received a much more explicit warning from William Heth, a collector of the customs in Virginia, whose artless efforts to win the secretary's favor and whose flamboyant egotism

26. Coxe to Hamilton, Dec. 14, 1792, Letters of Commr. of Rev., 1792–1793, R.G. 58; Hamilton to McHenry, Apr. 5, 1793, Syrett *et al.*, eds., *Hamilton Papers*, XIV, 287–289.

27. The Tilghmans' opposition to William Perry resulted from the defeat of James Tilghman by William Hindman, Perry's brother-in-law, in Maryland's congressional election of the fall of 1792. The Tilghmans sought Coxe's aid in proscribing Hindman's supporters.

28. McHenry to Hamilton, Nov. 18, 1792, Syrett *et al.*, eds., *Hamilton Papers*, XIII, 157; Hamilton to McHenry, Apr. 5, 1793, McHenry to Hamilton, Apr. 14, 1793, *ibid.*, XIV, 287–289, 316–317.

prompted long letters couched in so florid a style and characterized by such exuberantly wild exaggeration that they enliven the otherwise dreary pages of official Treasury records. In a footnote to a sentence in which he described the unreliability of former tories, Heth remarked: "If I am not greatly mistaken my dear Sir, you have a Man near you whose pen—nothwithstanding the magnanimity of his Country, in so far forgetting his crimes, as to give him an important office . . . —has been employed in abusing the measures of government, and particularly, your Official conduct; and whose study has been to sap, and undermine *you*, in hopes of filling your place." In an obvious reference to Jefferson, Heth added that all this was being accomplished "through the Interests of   , you know who." Soon, Heth said, he might be able to tell all, but in the meantime he cautioned Hamilton to watch his assistant "narrowly." "Attend closely to the motions of his eyes, and changes of countenance when he may suppose you are placeing confidence in him, and you will not be long in discovering the *perfidious, and ungrateful* friend."[29] If a correspondent far removed from the nation's capital, where gossip swarmed like summer mosquitoes, could write in this way, one is entitled to wonder what Hamilton must have been told in conversation.

Hamilton certainly heard enough to prompt him to take a closer look at the company Coxe was keeping in the State Department and to wonder about infiltration of the Treasury by his political opponent. On a number of occasions, Coxe later recalled, the secretary brusquely interrogated him about the political reliability of employees in the commissioner's office, implying that they were enemy agents. Hamilton also did not hesitate to express, though mostly through intermediaries, his displeasure at the assistance Coxe was providing to his principal political rival.[30] Convinced that this aid had in no way interfered with his Treasury duties and stung by what he construed as gratuitous meddling and ill-founded enmity, Coxe must have felt that he would have fared better had he chosen openly to serve Jefferson full-time. And though the latter's callous ingratitude a decade or so later might suggest otherwise, at the time Coxe was right.

At the end of July 1793 Jefferson, fed up with political abuse and squabbles and eager to return to the tranquility of Monticello, announced

29. William Heth to Hamilton, June 14, 1793, *ibid.*, 544.

30. Coxe to Hamilton, Jan. 1795, marked "Letter not sent," Coxe Papers; Coxe to Jefferson, n.d. [but between Dec. 1801 and May 1802], Appointment Papers, R.G. 59, National Archives. Hamilton had all along been aware of Coxe's cordial relationship with Jefferson. A decade or so after the event, Coxe recalled that soon after Philadelphia became the national capital, he had remarked that the secretary of state should be second in line to succeed the president. On the day following his remark, Coxe said, he was "called on by Mr. J. [William Samuel Johnson] of the Senate and an earnest expostulation took place." Hamilton, Coxe continued, "considered it as a preference of a person whom he called his Enemy." *Ibid.*

his intention to retire at the year's end. At this time he proposed to Madison (perhaps with a promotion for his friend Coxe in mind) that the Treasury be reorganized by dividing it "between two equal chiefs of the Customs and Internal taxes." But, he lamented, such a meritorious plan had no chance of success so long as the Federalists retained control of the Senate.[31] Indeed, Senate approval of any sound measure, Jefferson commented to Monroe, was impossible so long as that body was dominated by a party composed of "the old tories, . . . merchants who trade of British capital, paper dealers, and the idle rich of the great commercial towns."[32] Coxe could have told him better, had it not been impolitic for an old tory, merchant, and paper dealer to do so. Jefferson, inflexibly convinced that Hamilton and his followers had managed to impose their policies on even his own department, would not have been receptive to correction. If Hamilton and his associates had not had this influence, Jefferson believed, neither his own policy nor France would have been discredited.

John Adams disagreed. The pro-French forces had been routed by no political party, however composed, but rather by an act of nature. In August 1793, Adams recalled years later, a Philadelphia mob, numbering in the thousands, had "day after day threatened to drag Washington out of his house and effect a revolution in the Government or compel it to declare War in favour of the French Revolution against England." A revolution was aborted, so Adams believed, only by the deadly plague that struck the nation's capital in late summer.[33] On August 28 the Philadelphia *General Advertiser* printed a report from the College of Physicians that "the malignant and contagious fever . . . now prevails." The disease had first been detected a week earlier in the congested area along the waterfront, but it soon spread rapidly to other sections of the city. Within days after medical confirmation panic struck, and those thousands who could afford to do so fled the hot, infested, and stench-laden air for nearby towns or, preferably, the country. Fear was as contagious as the plague appeared to be, and in the weeks ahead thousands more departed.

Coxe could count himself fortunate that he was already away. Late in July he had left the capital for "a couple of weeks of air and exercise" at his father-in-law's rural estate. It was a pleasant vacation, with long horse-

31. Jefferson to Madison, Aug. 11, 1793, Madison Papers, Lib. of Cong. John Steele of North Carolina was virtually alone in the belief that Coxe was a leading contender for Jefferson's post. Steele wrote to Coxe on Dec. 23, 1793: "It was always my expectation that you would succeed Mr. Jefferson yourself. Mr. R. may have an abundance of talents, but they are not of the proper cast for such an office." Coxe Papers.

32. Jefferson to James Monroe, June 4, 1793, Ford, ed., *Works of Jefferson*, VII, 361–362.

33. Adams to Jefferson, June 30, 1813, Lester J. Cappon, ed., *The Adams-Jefferson Letters: The Complete Correspondence between Thomas Jefferson and Abigail and John Adams*, II (Chapel Hill, N.C., 1959), 346–347.

back rides in the mornings and evenings, interspersed with "three or four hours business daily." His return to Philadelphia was delayed by a sudden attack of influenza, and by the time he felt well enough to travel, news of the plague had reached Sidney, where he remained, with occasional trips to his father's house in Sunbury, until November.[34] There was time for relaxation (though this was marred by the sad news of the death of his favorite uncle, James Tilghman), time to reflect on the political fever that in spring and summer had raged as fiercely as the plague did now.[35] "The condition of this town is . . . truly alarming," his chief clerk, William Barton, reported on September 9. "The prevalent disease . . . proves fatal in almost every instance." Barton also relayed the news that Hamilton had been stricken and, despite the constant attention of his physician, appeared unlikely to recover. This report, Coxe learned a day or so later, was exaggerated—Hamilton's recovery was remarkably rapid, and within five days he was no longer in danger.[36]

Few other patients were as lucky. Although mid-September brought reports that the fever was abating, the worst was yet to come. In the meantime, the commercial life of the usually busy metropolis slowly ebbed. "The number of Houses, shops, stores etc. that are shut up is astonishing, all business seems at a stand," one of Coxe's correspondents wrote on September 16. So, too, was the public business. Hamilton's office was "entirely deserted," Wolcott had moved his office "to Dr. Smith's house at the Falls of Schuylkill," and Coxe's office remained open only because of the intrepidity of three of his clerks—Barton, Ezekiel Forman, and John Mease—who, despite Coxe's insistence that they leave for the country, remained on duty, as did the staff of his house on Walnut Street.[37] They were atypical. As Barton said, the city continued to be "defected by thousands, and the alarm continues." By early October there were often a hundred deaths a day. "The distress . . . among all classes of people," according to Dr. Benjamin Rush, "was nearly equal to that which was produced by the great plague in London in the years 1664–65." The statistics told the macabre tale: at least four thousand and perhaps as many as six thousand people died. Before the end of the month, however, a merciful frost came, blanketing the city with the hope that the epidemic would soon be over. To Coxe, busily making plans to open the commissioner's office at his father's house, it was good news. Even better was the personal report he received a few days later: "The busy hum of industry again pervades our streets, and the lofty canvas is now as

34. Coxe to Capt. P. Dennis, July 24, 1793, William Vans Murray to Coxe, Aug. 15, Sept. 27, 1793, William Barton to Coxe, Aug. 19, 1793, Coxe Papers.

35. William Tilghman to Coxe, Aug. 30, 1793, *ibid.*

36. Barton to Coxe, Sept. 9, 11, 16, 1793, *ibid.*

37. Ezekiel Forman to Coxe, Sept. 11, 16, 1793, Barton to Coxe, Sept. 11, 16, 23, 1793, *ibid.*

usual flowing on the water," one of his clerks wrote on November 4.[38] Coxe had already joined other officials near Philadelphia and on November 10 was back at 139 Walnut Street, where he was united with his family six days later. "The weather is cool, bright and a little windy," he wrote to John Adams a day later. "The appearances are comfortable," and "the town looks beautifully clean."[39]

It also was to him still the only suitable capital city, whether prone to yellow fever or not. "Apprehensive . . . that wishes to remove the Government to the Northward may have entered into the minds of some," he took it upon himself to apprise congressmen who hesitated to return "of the actual healthiness of the city on certain authority." Especially eager that Pennsylvania's congressmen set a good example by promptly returning, he even invited them to stop over at his house "on the Skirts of the city" for reassurance.[40] He need not have worried. Congressmen and federal officials were daily arriving; by the time the first snow of the season fell on December 1, Congress was ready to convene and the civil service was functioning normally. Foreign dispatches, however, told an unhappy tale.

Determined to cut off the flourishing American trade with French Caribbean ports, British officials issued during 1793 a number of orders-in-council that cavalierly ignored the rights of neutrals and played hob with American commerce. To Jefferson, whose resignation became effective on December 31, the public mood was at last ripe for his report describing and indicting foreign (but especially British) restrictions on American commerce.

Requested by Congress in February 1791, that report had been delayed time and again, the latest deferral having taken place in February 1793. By that time Jefferson had completed a draft of his report, which he planned promptly to submit, and he had once again solicited Coxe's aid. Coxe had been asked to check the report's accuracy, to indicate the requisite corrections, and to make other recommendations. This he had done, noting in pencil suggested alterations—on "questions of fact" and "modes of expression"—on all but one of the nineteen pages. But instead of committing

38. L. H. Butterfield, ed., *Letters of Benjamin Rush*, II (Princeton, N.J., 1951), 746; John Mease to Coxe, Nov. 4, 1793, Coxe Papers.

39. Coxe to John Adams, Nov. 11, 3, 6, 1793, Adams Papers, Mass. Hist. Soc., Boston; Wolcott to Coxe, Oct. 28, 1793, Coxe Papers.

40. Coxe to Benjamin Stoddert, Nov. 19, 1793, Coxe to Pennsylvania Congressmen, Nov. 16, 1793, Coxe Papers. See also postscript, dated Nov. 20, to the copy of the latter letter sent to Daniel Herster, Coxe to John Ashe, Nov. 25, 1793, *ibid.* A rumor was circulating in Philadelphia, Coxe wrote Adams, that Congress might remove to New York. It had, he said, "produced immense agitation among the most influential of our people." Coxe to Adams, Nov. 18, 1793, Adams Papers. Coxe also sent Vice-President Adams frequent bulletins both on the health situation in Philadelphia and on the state of domestic and foreign affairs. Coxe to Adams, Nov. 3, 6, 11, 18, 1793, Adams Papers.

his substantive proposals to paper (his ideas on the "subject in general" and thoughts prompted by the "present momentous state of things"), he had suggested that he communicate them in person to Jefferson. For this purpose the two men had met early on the morning of February 6.[41]

Since neither participant kept a record of the conversation, Coxe's verbal recommendations and Jefferson's reception of them cannot be determined. All but a fraction of Coxe's penciled changes, however, were accepted and incorporated by Jefferson in the draft of his report. More important than this essentially editorial contribution was Jefferson's reliance on the information his tireless aide had supplied over the preceding two years. If fact and interpretation are inextricable, then Coxe was Jefferson's collaborator rather than merely a research assistant. In any event, the report Jefferson submitted to Congress on December 16, 1793, kindled the fire Coxe had laid in his research reports and in his essays on American commercial policy.

The "Report on the privileges and restrictions on the commerce of the United States in foreign countries" was Jefferson's carefully devised reply to Hamilton's alleged subservience to British economic rapacity, the summation of the commercial policies Jefferson had unsuccessfully tried to pursue as secretary of state—in effect, his second declaration of national independence.[42] Objectively, or perhaps deceptively, factual except for its last section, the report was an account of the burdens imposed on the United States by those countries with whom the great bulk of its foreign trade was conducted—Spain, Portugal, France, Great Britain, and the United Netherlands. It was also a morality tale, the story of a well-intentioned young nation set down among hostile powers of the Old World, of a country eager to promote commercial freedom but hemmed in by closed commercial systems. It was, more specifically, an account of the particularly sinister acts of one villain, England, among a cast of many offenders. The dismal story was relieved, however, by the entry of a character willing to aid the nation in distress. The hero was France.

To the student of Jefferson's ideas the most arresting aspect of the report is not so much its defense of commercial freedom as its advocacy of manufactures by a man characteristically labeled as the nation's most renowned exponent of agrarianism. This was a result, perhaps, of the con-

---

41. See Jefferson to Coxe, Feb. 5, 1793 (Jefferson Papers, Lib. of Cong.), acknowledging receipt of Coxe's "Notes on the Report of the Secretary of State made in consequence of the reference of the House of Representatives of the   day of   1791." There is a draft of these notes in Coxe's hand in the Coxe Papers and a clerk's copy with further insertions by Coxe in the Jefferson Papers. See also Coxe to Jefferson, Feb. 5, 1793, enclosing Jefferson's copy of the report with notes in pencil by Coxe. *Ibid.*

42. Lipscomb and Bergh, eds., *Writings of Jefferson*, III, 261–283.

tagion of the enthusiasm that animated Coxe's pleas for a balanced and national economy. Whether so or not, the point is at least worth airing, both because Jefferson read reams of Coxe's bulky notes during the preparation of his report and because of the apparent harmony of their collaboration.

Certainly the two men were in perfect agreement on the manner by which foreign restrictions on American commerce might be counteracted. Both accepted the principle of reciprocity by the adoption of countervailing measures. What would be the results? Eventually the British would be forced to modify their discriminatory navigation system, while in the interim a policy of retribution might provide the occasion for "promoting arts, manufactures and population at home."[43] Although an accurate forecast of a program President Thomas Jefferson would follow fifteen years later, it was, in 1793, as plausible as time would prove it illusory: the English, engaged in a war they regarded as a struggle for survival, were not likely to bow to American pressure.

James Madison believed otherwise, and two weeks after the submission of the secretary of state's report he introduced into the Congress a number of resolutions that incorporated Jefferson's principal recommendations. Adding specificity to Jefferson's generalities, Madison's proposals, all aimed squarely at Great Britain, asked for an increase in tonnage rates for nations with whom the United States had no treaty and a decrease for those who had signed treaties. He also recommended an unspecified hike in the duties on a number of enumerated foreign imports, countervailing measures against nations that restricted our shipping, and retaliatory penalities on goods imported from any country that seized American vessels or cargoes.[44] Ironically enough, Madison's commercial propositions were designed to achieve the very goal of Hamilton's policies—an American mercantilist system. The difference was over its proper foreign orientation, whether France or England.

Although the similarity may have been lost on the secretary of the Treasury, the difference emphatically was not, and he lost no time in preparing a rebuttal. On New Year's Day he solicited the aid of Coxe, though aware of his subordinate's contrary convictions and extradepartmental activities. "What regulations have been made by France since the commencement of the present Revolution" on such American exports as flour, tobacco, rice, and naval stores, Hamilton asked? Having already studied the subject for Jefferson, Coxe replied two days later, promising promptly to send yet additional data.[45] There was little time. In striking contrast to the leisurely

---

43. *Ibid.*, 276, 278, 279, 280, 282.

44. *Annals of Cong.*, IV, 155–158.

45. Hamilton to Coxe, Jan. 1, 1794, General Records, 1791–1803, R.G. 58, National Archives; Coxe to Hamilton, Jan. 3, 1794, Hamilton Papers. See also Coxe to Hamilton, Jan. 10, 1793, *ibid.*

pace at which Jefferson had prepared his report, Hamilton completed his rejoinder in about two weeks. Since there had been no congressional mandate for a Treasury report, his reply took the form of a speech delivered on January 13, 1794, by William Loughton Smith of South Carolina. Jefferson, who had retired to Monticello two weeks earlier leaving to Coxe's care the protection of his official reputation against predictable attacks, was not deceived. "I am at no loss to ascribe Smith's speech to its true father," he told Madison. "Every tittle of it is Hamilton's except the introduction."[46] As for Coxe, had he taken himself or public affairs less seriously, he would have been amused at having been called on to aid Hamilton in the refutation of statistics and other data that he himself had supplied the Treasury secretary's major antagonist.

46. Jefferson to Madison, Apr. 3, 1794, Ford, ed., *Works of Jefferson*, VIII, 141; Coxe to Jefferson, June 25, 1801, General Records of the State Department, R.G. 59, National Archives.

13 🦋

An Insurrection in
Western Pennsylvania and
a Battle in the Treasury

Although his views on American commercial policy were squarely Jeffersonian, Coxe held a staunchly Hamiltonian position on domestic policy. This stand was nowhere more evident than in his enthusiastic endorsement of Hamilton's insistence that federal laws, particularly the excise on whiskey, be obeyed, even at the cost of coercion. After the confrontation between the defiant distillers of western Pennsylvania and embattled revenue agents in the fall of 1792, the Washington administration had pursued a policy of pacification, spearheaded by Coxe's recommendation of measures to repeal the excise law's more unpopular features. Had the excise itself been the only irritant, these actions might have been successful, but the westerners also vociferously opposed the administration for other reasons, notably its failure to secure the opening of the Mississippi River, its inability to obtain British relinquishment of posts in the Northwest, and its alleged partiality for the former mother country. It may also be that these Pennsylvanians were "visionaries" who "inveighed against courts of justice, salaries, and in fact, were at war with all restraints of government whatever," including taxation, direct or indirect.[1]

---

1. H. M. Brackenridge, *History of the Western Insurrection in Western Pennsylvania, Commonly Called the Whiskey Insurrection, 1794* (Pittsburgh, Pa., 1859), 25. The definitive book-length study of the insurrection is Leland D. Baldwin, *Whiskey Rebels: The Story of a Frontier Uprising* (Pittsburgh, Pa., 1939). Baldwin's interpretation is challenged in Jacob E. Cooke, "The Whiskey Insurrection: A Re-Evaluation," *Pennsylvania History*, XXX (1963), 316–346.

During the first eight months of 1794 developments demonstrated that the Treasury Department's moderation was not enough to dam the tide of western discontent. Beginning in the spring, rumblings of discontent and of occasional violence reached Coxe's office. In March disaffected distillers threatened John Neville, inspector of the survey, with retaliation by the local militia if he did not resign his office. In May and June attacks were made on the property of two distillers who insisted on complying with the law. In July revenue offices in Westmoreland and Washington counties were besieged, and mail packets en route from the west to Philadelphia were seized.

At Treasury headquarters in Philadelphia such patent violations of the law were particularly disturbing because of accompanying reports that magnified even an individual offense into a riot. For information on the state of affairs in Pennsylvania's fourth survey, Coxe relied on the reports of his chief subordinates in that state, notably George Clymer, the supervisor. Clymer, in turn, based his information on that supplied by local revenue agents. Because this circuitous route to obtaining information could not be avoided, the reports on which Hamilton based his recommendations to the president were only as reliable as these Treasury officials were objective. And the revenue agents of the westernmost survey of Pennsylvania were anything but impartial. Neville and his staff were too partisan to be fair, and George Clymer tended to see a conspiracy under every still. Nor did Clymer hesitate to disagree with Treasury Department policies he believed misguided. Once, when forwarding to his subordinates "some printed observations of the Commissioner of the revenue" explaining revisions in the excise law designed to placate the westerners, Clymer described Coxe's changes as "vain endeavors . . . of reasoning the perverse into the duty of obedience."[2]

Had Coxe known of Clymer's slur on his own attempts at pacification, he might have contemplated a reform of the personnel rather than the regulations of the revenue service. The most recent regulatory modification was contained in an act of June 4, 1794, which, among other concessions, provided that all actions arising under the excise laws no longer be cognizable solely in federal courts but, as the delinquent distillers demanded, in state courts as well. Nevertheless, by midsummer 1794 it appeared to both contestants that the situation had changed for the worse. The change, as it appeared at Treasury headquarters, was from sporadic outbursts of violence by the westerners to a systematic and popularly supported campaign de-

2. George Clymer to Inspectors of the Revenue, June 15, 1794, to John Neville, June 28, 1794, Clymer Letterbook, Coxe Papers. Clymer, "impatient of trouble," resigned. Although his successor, Gen. Henry Miller, Coxe's nominee, was more objective, he had far greater failings.

signed to shut down operation of the federal revenue system in the fourth survey. The switch, as it appeared to the western dissidents, was made by the federal government from a policy of moderation and forbearance to one of repression and reprisal. By late July, Coxe and other government officials were certain that the reports of violence then pouring in on the Treasury Department indicated not, as some Republicans said, isolated instances of misconduct but the opening salvos of insurrection. Hamilton, and presumably Coxe, now believed that the time had come for a show of force.

"Sundry papers were sent to you today by Judge Wilson to get the hand writing proved. Did you get them? Has the needful been done? Have they been returned? Pray be in Town tomorrow Morning at seven o'Clock," Hamilton urgently wrote Coxe on August 1.[3] Such an importunate summons was based on developments more consequential than the completion of affidavits. Hamilton needed information from the chief of the revenue service to buttress a brief supporting military intervention as the policy best suited to handle the imminent insurrection; his argument was to be presented later that morning to the president, cabinet, and Pennsylvania's Governor Thomas Mifflin. The cabinet discussion was inconclusive, and Washington requested the conferees to submit written opinions. Again, Hamilton called for the use of troops to quell what he unhesitatingly termed treason. The attorney general agreed. "Insurgency was high treason," William Bradford said, "a capital crime, punishable by death," and must be put down by force. The secretary of war also favored intervention but cautioned that certain preparatory steps should first be taken. The new secretary of state, Edmund Randolph, and Mifflin dissented. Randolph objected to force for prudential reasons, and the governor on the grounds that military intervention was unnecessary because the situation should be handled by the state.[4]

The decision was up to the president. Aware that even as the cabinet deliberated, some five thousand dissidents, many of them armed, were assembling at Braddock's Field near Pittsburgh, Washington must have considered the nation threatened at every turn—by disunion at home, by menacing hostility abroad. His decision was prompt. The citizens of the western counties were in an open rebellion that must be suppressed. Before ordering the army to march west, however, Washington first issued a proclamation on August 7 commanding the insurgents to disperse and exhorting all inhabitants of the area to "prevent and suppress dangerous proceedings." He then

---

3. Hamilton to Coxe, Aug. 1, 1794, Coxe Papers.

4. Hamilton's opinions are in the Hamilton Papers, Lib. of Cong. The opinions of the other members of the cabinet are in the Washington Papers, Lib. of Cong. For Thomas Mifflin's opinion, see Mifflin to George Washington, Aug. 4, 1794, *American State Papers, Miscellaneous*, I, 97–99.

awaited the report of the commissioners appointed to negotiate with the insurgents.

In the meantime, hopes for a peaceful solution were dimmed by an unsolicited report Coxe received from Hugh Henry Brackenridge, a Pittsburgh lawyer and novelist. Then a candidate for Congress, Brackenridge played an equivocal role during the summer and fall of 1794 that satisfied neither the insurgents nor the advocates of law and order. In this instance he cast himself in the role of defense attorney for his western neighbors. The Washington administration should know, he informed Coxe, that resistance to the excise law was not attributable to any congenital affinity for violence or opposition to government. It was rather "the principles and operation of the Law itself" that rendered the excise tax "obnoxious," so odious, indeed, that the United States could not enforce it, even with armed force. Do not believe, Brackenridge warned Coxe, that "this insurrection can be easily suppressed." Indeed, the question was not whether federal troops would march to Pittsburgh, but whether the insurgents "will march to Philadelphia, accumulating in their course, and swelling over the Banks of the Susquehanna like a torrent, irresistable and devouring in its progress."[5]

If Brackenridge genuinely sought a rapprochement, as he presumably did, his letter spoke eloquently either to personal fears or to his naiveté. Having provisionally decided to employ force, federal officials, far from being deterred by such threats, were more likely to increase the size of the army than to disband it. And Coxe made certain not only that Hamilton and Washington read the letter but that prominent state officials also received copies.[6] Brackenridge's seeming ultimatum, Coxe thought, was actually only one more piece of evidence in a case whose outcome, if not predetermined, was daily becoming more certain. Events, no one of which was critical, were inexorably drawing the Washington administration into an armed confrontation that it deemed unavoidable and that the insurgents, perhaps prompted by disbelief, did nothing to avert.

The dispatch on August 26 of Coxe's carefully contrived reply to Brackenridge was an exercise in futility; the Pittsburgh lawyer was as unlikely to alter his views as the administration was to change its policies. Presumably aware of this, Coxe chose to write a general essay on the nature of free government and to indicate the suicidal course the insurgents were traveling. "The vital principle of our unequalled Governments," his lecture began, was that "*the public will*, when constitutionally expressed by repre-

5. Hugh Henry Brackenridge to Coxe, Aug. 8, 1794, Coxe Papers.

6. See Coxe to Mifflin, Aug. 18, 1794, to Samuel Smith, Aug. 26, 1794, to Alexander Hamilton, Aug. 28, 1794, to Henry Lee, Aug. 29, 1794, Alexander J. Dallas to Coxe, Aug. 20, 1794, Henry Lee to Coxe, Sept. 8, 1794, *ibid.*

sentatives elected without fraud or violence," creates an overriding "obligation to obedience." Forcible opposition to a law thrice sanctioned by the representatives of the people was nothing less than "sin against the political gospel." If the dissidents continued to "desert this great Commandment of freedom," righteous Americans would condone any such "strong measures" as might be necessary to punish the transgression. Turning from religious metaphors to historical analogy, Coxe suggested that his fellow Pennsylvanians badly needed to study their past. An excise had been passed in Pennsylvania as early as 1700; between that date and 1744, fifteen such laws had been enacted; after Independence the state's most illustrious patriots had supported similar measures in 1779, 1780, and 1781. "Is it unreasonable to say," Coxe rhetorically asked, "that as the excise was first established in Pennsylvania in the year 1700 that it ought not to be repealed in the ninety-fourth year of its existence by any thing but fair reasoning?" How did the vociferous opponents of the tax in western Pennsylvania account for the tax's acceptance by virtually every other part of the Union? Were the citizens of other states less acquainted "with the nature of free government than the inhabitants of our western counties"? The insurrectionists were, Coxe asserted, unhistorical and unobservant apostates from the American democratic faith.[7]

Coxe's letter, which was published in the *Pittsburgh Gazette* and republished elsewhere, might well have affected the course of events had Brackenridge been authorized to negotiate for his fellow westerners. As things were, it should at the least have been a sobering reminder that the dangerous scene staged by the Pittsburgh lawyer had failed to intimidate the president's principal advisers. Although unawed, the secretary of the Treasury, for one, was impressed by Brackenridge's confirmation of his own worst fears. Perhaps, too, the resolve of the president, to whom Hamilton promptly sent Coxe's letter, was strengthened. Certainly this was what Coxe had intended. For only in such an indirect manner could he now affect decisions concerning the federal service he ostensibly directed; once the problem had been turned over to the president and his cabinet in early August, Coxe's part in the decision-making process had become marginal. But the outcome involved him personally and officially. At stake were not only the assurance that the right ideas had prevailed but also his own record as chief administrator of

7. There are two drafts of this letter in the Coxe Papers, one dated Aug. 17 and the other Aug. 20. Both are endorsed Aug. 26. The draft dated Aug. 20 was reprinted in the *Pittsburgh Gazette*, Sept. 20, 1794, despite Coxe's request that it be considered confidential. For information on republication elsewhere, see Coxe to George Thatcher, Sept. 27, 1794, Boston Public Library. For information on other articles that Coxe wrote on the subject, see Brackenridge to Coxe, Sept. 15, 1794, Coxe Papers. There is also an undated draft of an article on the insurrection in the Coxe Papers.

the internal revenue service. Possibly he did not know that his future official career was also at stake.

By September 9 the president, despairing of an amicable settlement and disturbed that the season during which military operations were feasible was rapidly passing, approved orders for a general rendezvous of troops at Carlisle. Aware of the prestige his presence would lend the punitive expedition, Washington decided personally to assume command of the fifteen thousand militiamen from Pennsylvania and the neighboring states of Maryland, New Jersey, and Virginia. Hamilton was also determined to go along, rationalizing that since measures of his own department were the ostensible cause of the insurrection, it could not "but have good effect" for him to share in the "danger to his fellow citizens." Since Coxe believed himself to be statutorily designated as the second-highest-ranking officer in the Treasury, his heart must have leapt at Hamilton's promise to the president to leave his department "in a situation to suffer no embarrassment by my absence."[8] As it happened, Coxe was to suffer what the Treasury did not. His personal embarrassment, mingled with sharp disappointment, prompted behavior that assured the denial of what Hamilton was already inclined to keep from him—the secretaryship of the Treasury.

On September 30, 1794, the president, with characteristic terseness, recorded in his diary: "I left the City of Philadelphia about half past ten oclock this forenoon accompanied by Colo. Hamilton."[9] On the preceding day, the Treasury secretary had hurriedly cleared his desk and, as his last major task, had left instructions for the conduct of the department's affairs during his campaign in the west. The acting head of the department, and by implication Hamilton's heir apparent, would be Oliver Wolcott, Jr. "I commit to you during my absence," he informed the comptroller, whose acquiescence he had obviously secured previously, "the management of those matters which are reserved to my superintendence under the constitution and regulations of the Department." Coxe learned of the arrangement the following day when he opened the letter containing his own official instructions, delivered only after the secretary had left the capital.[10] Not only was

---

8. Hamilton to Washington, Sept. 19, 1794, Washington Papers.

9. John C. Fitzpatrick, ed., *The Diaries of George Washington, 1748–1799*, IV (Boston, 1925), 209.

10. Hamilton to Oliver Wolcott, Jr., Sept. 29, 1794, Syrett *et al.*, eds., *Hamilton Papers*, XVII, 290–291. There is a copy of this letter in the Coxe Papers. Hamilton's letter to Coxe has not been found. On Sept. 30, 1794, Coxe wrote Samuel Hodgdon: "I received this day after the departure of the Secretary of the Treasury a letter desiring me to attend to the forwarding of supplies for the militia army till the arrival of the Secretary of War. I had not the opportunity to see the Secretary before he went, or I would have requested this service to be committed to some other person. Either that, or the duties of contracts and purchases, the ordinary and extraordinary business of the Revenue, or other Duties of my office must suffer." Letters of Tench Coxe, Commissioner of the Revenue, Relating to the Procurement of Military, Naval, and In-

he to serve under someone he had previously regarded as his subordinate in rank, but his duties as the Treasury Department's procurement agent, an unwanted chore that Hamilton only a few days earlier had promised to relieve him of altogether, were greatly enlarged.[11] In the spring of 1794, when problems in collecting the whiskey excise were steadily mounting, Coxe had been given virtually sole responsibility for War Department purchases, an assignment that would not have been particularly burdensome had it been confined, as previously, to contracts for provisions and clothing.[12] But the job had been handed to Coxe precisely at a time when the responsibilities it entailed were magnified many times over. His assignment as procurement agent for the army, the navy, and the Indians, Coxe recalled eight months later, was given "to me on the 4th of April upon an hour's Notice and conference in the afternoon of that day." Now it would also be his responsibility, the secretary's instructions read, to superintend the forwarding of supplies to the militia army, an assignment the Treasury secretary himself, in the absence of the secretary of war, had assumed.[13]

Why did Hamilton choose such devious means to secure an arrangement that, if not a direct violation of the law, was certainly contrary to the spirit of the legislation regulating the conduct of his department? Two years earlier, as he surely remembered, Congress in the course of debate over changes to be made in the Treasury had deleted the part of a proposed bill that designated the comptroller as acting head of the department in the event of the absence or physical incapacity of the secretary, and instead had vested in the president the requisite authority to name an acting secretary. Coxe, whose lobbying activities had been in large part responsible for the change, assumed that as commissioner of the revenue he remained, as he had been as assistant secretary, the second-highest officer in the department. It was a plausible enough assumption, and one that Hamilton shared until his growing distrust of Coxe prompted him during the year preceding September 1794 to change his mind.[14]

---

dian Supplies, R.G. 75, National Archives. Since Hamilton's decision to assign Coxe those duties had been made by Sept. 28, 1794 (see Hamilton to George Gale, Sept. 28, 1794, Syrett *et al.*, eds., *Hamilton Papers*, XVII, 285), and probably earlier, he obviously could have informed Coxe of it personally had he not wished to avoid doing so.

11. See Coxe to Hamilton, Dec. 4, 1794, Letters of Commr. of Rev., 1794–1795, R.G. 58; Coxe to Hamilton, Dec. 28, 1794, Coxe Papers.

12. Coxe to Henry Knox, Apr. 14, 1794, Letters of Commr. of Rev., Relating to the Procurement of Military, Naval, and Indian Supplies, R.G. 75; "Report of Tench Coxe to the Secretary of the Treasury," Dec. 22, 1794, *American State Papers, Naval Affairs*, I, 9.

13. Coxe to Hamilton, Dec. 28, 1794, Coxe Papers. Knox had left Philadelphia for Maine in Aug. because of adverse news regarding his financial affairs and landholding in Maine. In taking over his office, Hamilton assumed responsibility for making arrangements not only for financing but also for recruiting, equipping, and supplying the western expedition.

14. As assistant secretary, Coxe had been left in charge of the department during Hamilton's

Whether Hamilton chose the revenue commissioner (as Congress presumably had intended he should) or the comptroller as acting department head, the proper legal procedure (particularly in view of the long absence he expected) would have been to secure the president's formal authorization. His negligence to do so, Hamilton explained some months later, was the result, among other considerations, of "the hurry of the period." Saddled with "the weight both of the Treasury and War Departments, under circumstances that required great exertions in both," he said, he overlooked "a measure which motives of caution . . . recommended."[15] Although Washington surely would have endorsed whomever the secretary of the Treasury selected to act in his stead, Hamilton's explanation of his remissness (as well as other aspects of the incident) appears contrived. In fact, the manner in which he acted clearly suggests his wish to avoid what he later termed an "official collision" with Coxe. Disenchanted with his once highly prized assistant, he obviously took advantage of a convenient opportunity indirectly to reveal what otherwise he must forthrightly have said.

To Coxe the decision was humiliating. Certain for so long that his service to the Treasury Department merited his appointment as its secretary, he now found himself bypassed for one whose abilities he scorned. Having for years carried out major assignments, some involving policy decisions of substance, he was now relegated to a comparatively subordinate position. Thus correctly perceiving that Hamilton had ignored his claims and snubbed his ambition, Coxe made no effort to conceal his anger. On October 1, at the close of a letter to Hamilton describing what he had done to assure the forwarding of militia supplies, he wrote: "This business for the War Department does no service to the business of the Revenues and Light houses. It obstructs me from them in a degree that is not satisfactory to my self."[16] It was strong language in an age when such dissatisfaction customarily was expressed with courteous obliqueness, and Hamilton could scarcely have misinterpreted its meaning.

---

infrequent absences. See for example, Hamilton to Coxe, May 9, 1791, Coxe to James McClurg, July 16, 1791, Coxe Papers. After Coxe's appointment as commissioner of the revenue, Hamilton continued the same practice. Thus when the Treasury secretary went to Newark to attend a meeting of the Society for the Establishment of Useful Manufactures—a week after Coxe's appointment as commissioner—he left the supervision of the department's affairs in Coxe's hands. See Coxe to Hamilton, May 20, 1792, Hamilton Papers.

15. Hamilton to Washington, Feb. 2, 1795, Syrett *et al.*, eds., *Hamilton Papers*, XVIII, 251. In a letter of complaint written some years later Coxe remarked that "Mr. Wolcott, on a personal enquiry made of him, informed me, *that he had no authority whatever from the President.* I apprized him on the spot that I could acknowledge *no* other." Coxe to Pennsylvania members of the House and Senate, Jan. 25, 1798, Coxe Papers.

16. Coxe to Hamilton, Oct. 1, 1794, Letters of Commr. of Rev., Relating to the Procurement of Military, Naval, and Indian Supplies, R.G. 75.

Despite his smoldering resentment, Coxe carried out the assignment conscientiously. Laggard War Department officials responsible for purchases of military stores were constantly prodded; the dispatch of supplies to various places in the west was coordinated; requests from special agents in nearby states charged with supplying their militia were promptly honored or sent to Hamilton for approval; recommendations were made for the appointment of a commissary for army supplies in the west; and arrangements were made for the more efficient supply of army provisions in the future. Although the secretary of war returned to Philadelphia in early October, Coxe's duties were not appreciably lightened. Henry Knox, portly and amiable but a lackadaisical administrator, occasionally issued directions, but for the most part arrangements for procuring supplies continued to be Coxe's responsibility.[17]

Coxe's task was itself trying enough, but it was rendered the more irksome because of the lack of specific information or instructions from Hamilton. In the past Coxe had carried out similarly burdensome chores without complaint or open criticism of Hamilton. Now, all had changed. In a representative letter to Knox he remarked apropos of an application from an army contractor: "I have no information from the Secretary of the Treasury of his having employed this Gentleman" or others, "and, of course, I am entirely unacquainted with the extent or nature of their Agencies or his authorities to them."[18] To Hamilton he was even more blunt: commenting on certain irregularities in requisitions for the pay of the Maryland militia, Coxe remonstratively observed that since his own responsibilities had been "interfered with by some operations of other agents not made known to me" (presumably Hamilton's), "I am without the necessary knowledge of what has been done in order to determine now what ought to be done. I wish to be immediately informed of any thing wh[ich] it may be useful or necessary for me to do." In sum, Coxe made it abundantly clear that since Hamilton considered him unqualified to direct the department, he would demonstrate his unwillingness to exercise the requisite talents.[19] In view of Hamilton's defense of policies for which Coxe himself shared responsibility,

17. Coxe to Hamilton, Oct. 1, 4, Nov. 27, 1794, to Samuel Hodgdon, Sept. 30, Oct. 4, 1794, to Nicholas Fish, Sept. 24, 29, 1794, to George Gale, Oct. 4, 1794, *ibid.* Coxe also continued to bear responsibility for procuring both Indian and naval armament supplies.

18. Coxe to Henry Knox, Oct. 16, 1794, *ibid.* Coxe had valid reasons for complaining. Since Hamilton insisted on approving all army contracts, his inaccessibility made it difficult to complete negotiations for rations and other army supplies for 1795. As acting secretary of war, moreover, Hamilton before his departure had personally overseen the procurement of material for the militia army, and, when he delegated the task to Coxe, he had failed to inform his commissioner of the revenue of the details of arrangements still pending.

19. Coxe to Hamilton, Oct. 18, 1794, *ibid.* See also Coxe to Hamilton, Oct. 4, 8, 10, 13, 15, 21, 24, 1794, *ibid.*

such Byzantine acedia was a revealing gauge of Coxe's chagrin at Hamilton's interim arrangement for the Treasury.

Nevertheless, Coxe did continue steadfastly to support the western policy. The news "that the insurgency . . . is crushed" gave him "the utmost pleasure," he assured John Jay on November 8. His fellow citizens in western Pennsylvania would "never trifle again with this Government." Although the military operation had been expensive, he was convinced that "the incidental and immediate advantages of it fully compensate us."[20] Whatever else may be said of Coxe's behavior, it was at least to his credit that he was able to perceive the advantages to the public of an expedition that had resulted, so he thought, in such severe personal disadvantages.

Indeed, his quotidian discontent might have abated, had the Treasury secretary promptly resumed personal direction of the department. Instead, Hamilton (unlike the president, who returned to the capital in mid-October) decided to accompany the army on its four-week march to Washington, Pennsylvania, the cradle of the insurrection, and then to Pittsburgh. For his part, Coxe blunderingly misjudged the state of his boss's mind. Hamilton was then at his most imperious. As de facto commander of the western expedition, the president's chief of staff, and, in all but name, prime minister, he wielded power hitherto beyond his reach. He was too busy ferreting out evidence of treason, interrogating suspects, and making plans for their indictment to be disturbed by the sniping of a member of his staff in Philadelphia. To Coxe such cavalier indifference was even more galling than his demotion, and by early November he was "meditating a retreat" from what was becoming more and more an intolerable situation. "I shall endeavor," he wrote to an acquaintance in Virginia, "to reach the calm of private Life."[21] Ardent in his wish to succeed Hamilton and not yet prepared to admit that his ambition had outrun the limits of the possible, he soon changed his mind, electing instead to continue his self-defeating course of passive cooperation punctuated by constant complaints.

By the time Hamilton returned to Philadelphia late in November, it was much too late for Coxe to resume amicable relations with the secretary, much less to win a nomination for promotion. On December 1, three days after his arrival in the capital, Hamilton informed the president and the Speaker of the House of his intention to resign on January 31, 1795. That Coxe would not even be considered as a successor was clear to most knowledgeable observers, but not yet to Coxe himself. Tenaciously unwilling to

---

20. Coxe to John Jay, Nov. 8, 1794, Coxe Papers.
21. Coxe to Francis Corbin, Nov. 8, 1794, *ibid*. See also Corbin to Coxe, Nov. 19, 1794, *ibid*.

abandon hope and encouraged by acquaintances like William S. Smith, who wrote from New York that "your friends here expect" the vacancy "will fall to your lott," Coxe sounded out Thomas Hartley and probably other congressional allies on the possibility of securing their support for the coveted appointment.[22] But by mid-December he could no longer evade the fact that the Yankee rival he had so long contrived to outdistance was at the finish line.

For Coxe the knowledge of opportunities lost and of ambition shattered was almost too painful to be silently endured. Equally distressing was the awareness that he was powerless to influence Hamilton or in any way to alter the course of events. He relieved his frustration by making Hamilton's remaining weeks in office as uncomfortable as possible. That this surly obstinacy would, in actuality, damage himself more than it would disturb Hamilton was an insight Coxe did not have.

Coxe did see to it that he was not ignored. He scarcely allowed Hamilton time to settle into his office before sending off a letter reminding him of his promise, made the previous September, to relieve Coxe of the burden of military procurement. Such duties were, as they always had been, "actually incompatible with the due execution of the proper and other business of the Commissioner of the Revenue."[23] Hamilton not only both remembered and agreed but had foreseen Coxe's reminder. Two days previously he had written the president asking that Congress be requested to authorize a new Treasury Department official charged solely with responsibility for procuring military supplies. That assignment, he said, could not be conducted by the head of the department or by any of its other officers "without being less well executed than it ought to be." Unwilling to await congressional action, Coxe demanded immediate relief, and by December 10 Hamilton verbally agreed that Tench Francis, Coxe's uncle, might be authorized to administer "the Military business of the Treasury" in all the states except Pennsylvania. This was still not enough, Coxe wrote to Hamilton a day or so later: it would only "diminish" the impediments to "my proper Office business," not remove them.[24] Immediate and total relief from this Sisyphean task was the only acceptable solution.

22. William S. Smith to Coxe, Dec. 9, 1794, Thomas Hartley to Coxe, Dec. 9, 1794, *ibid*. To Coxe's inquiry about the feasibility of his appointment to the Senate should he not be nominated Treasury secretary, Hartley replied: "That any Appointment will be attended with immense Difficulty—Whether any of the Gentlemen mentioned before you will give way is uncertain—and if you all stand together my Calculation can give me no Conclusion." *Ibid*.

23. Coxe to Hamilton, Dec. 4, 1794, Letters of Commr. of Rev., 1794–1795, R.G. 58.

24. Hamilton to Washington, Dec. 2, 1794, Syrett *et al.*, eds., *Hamilton Papers*, XVII, 416; Coxe to Hamilton, Dec. 10, 1794, Letters of Commr. of Rev., Relating to the Procurement of Military, Naval, and Indian Supplies, R.G. 75. Tench Francis was Coxe's mother's brother.

Hamilton by now had doubts that the revenue commissioner had satisfactorily conducted even his proper office business. The time for a readjustment of the compensation allowed officers of the revenue service was long overdue, he curtly informed Coxe on December 9. "I take it for granted," he added in an obvious reproof, that the necessary information has been collected and "that everything is now mature for the completion of the arrangement." That it had not been completed, Coxe tartly replied, was Hamilton's fault, not his own. The requisite arrangements would have been made six months earlier had not Hamilton decided that the president, already overworked, should not be burdened. Since that time Coxe had remained ready and prepared to conclude the matter, but "the attention of the President and of yourself to the urgent Business of the Insurrection with the absences incidental thereto have left no opportunity for this object." Anyway, Hamilton's memory must be slipping, for Coxe had already submitted the necessary information to him, along with a request that he come to a decision about the principles upon which the new compensation arrangements should be based.[25] Instead of displaying forbearance, Hamilton retaliated, manifestly hoping to goad his assistant into retiring. Day after long December day brought ever more pointed reminders from the secretary's office that Coxe had been remiss in his duties; day after day the latter's anger at such reproaches mounted.

This was only the beginning, and as Hamilton ordered report after report, Coxe's resentment at being bypassed for the secretaryship turned into a conviction that he was being persecuted for fictitious offenses.[26] On December 20 he received a letter from Hamilton forwarding a congressional resolution calling for information on progress made in building the ships authorized the previous March and instructing Coxe to report to him on the subject. It was a reasonable enough request, and three months earlier Coxe would have so considered it. Now it was interpreted as a slur on his management of the naval armament, and his reply, a staccato recital of more facts than strictly were necessary, was transparently designed as much to vindicate himself as to inform the secretary.[27]

Hamilton's reaction no longer bothered Coxe. The Philadelphian dropped even the pretense of civility when he replied on December 27 to a note in which the secretary brusquely reminded him that although an appli-

25. Hamilton to Coxe, Dec. 9, 1794, General Records, 1791–1803, R.G. 58, National Archives; Coxe to Hamilton, Dec. 13, 1794, Letters of Commr. of Rev., 1794–1795, R.G. 58.

26. Coxe was particularly incensed, for example, by Hamilton's instructions that in the future all Treasury communications to the War Department should be communicated by the secretary of the Treasury, not by Coxe's office. Coxe to Knox, Dec. 18, 1794, Letters of Commr. of Rev., Relating to the Procurement of Military, Naval, and Indian Supplies, R.G. 75.

27. Hamilton's letter of Dec. 20, 1794, has not been found. See Coxe to Hamilton, Dec. 22, 1794, *ibid.*

cation he had forwarded to the secretary's office requesting a sizable advance of money should have been accompanied by appropriate supporting statements, it nevertheless would "be regular that the Commissioner of the Revenue express his opinion" of the applicant. For a number of tersely stated reasons—all to the point that Hamilton had undermined the essential duties of his office—Coxe curtly and petulantly refused to carry out Hamilton's directive. He would give no opinion on such applications and henceforth would do nothing more than "transmit them to your Office."[28] In subsequent letters he was even more blunt.

Although he would have preferred to ignore Coxe's gibes, Hamilton decided that he must "avoid the appearance of admitting by silence what may be hereafter liable to misconstruction." It had never been his intention, he wrote to Coxe on December 29, "to impute to you blame for any delays or deficiencies . . . in the execution of these portions of the business of the Department which are confided to you." While unwilling to concede that these were so heavy as to preclude the "practicability" of their satisfactory discharge, Hamilton admitted that they were of a "magnitude and difficulty sufficient to render partial defects and omissions probable" and excusable. For this reason, he had conscientiously forborne censure of Coxe's conduct, but, at the same time, he was not willing "to acquiesce in a transfer of the responsibility for any delays or deficiencies that may have occurred from you to me." Reverting again and again to Coxe's implicit criticism of his long absences from the capital (the charge that obviously most irritated him), Hamilton hit back where he knew Coxe was most vulnerable: "You were informed" that "Mr. Wolcott was to act in my stead," and "with a representative of me on the spot, with no particular restrictions on the freedom of your conduct," the absences ought not to have occasioned any "material interruptions of the business in your charge." Nevertheless, in view of the short time left to him as secretary, it was "more than ordinarily" his wish "to avoid anything like official collision."[29]

All in all, it was as cooperative and charitable a letter as Coxe could have expected. Obsessed by his crumbling career expectations, however, he was unable even to recognize conciliatory overtures. "I am really not sensible of any delays or deficiencies in the execution of my duties beyond the other officers of government and the course of human nature," he retorted. Far from ever having purposely censured Hamilton, Coxe claimed that what "created pain" in his mind was the conviction that the secretary's correspondence was calculated "to leave ground of future censure" of his own

---

28. Coxe to Hamilton, Dec. 26, 27, 1794, *ibid.*; Hamilton to Coxe, endorsement on letter of Tench Francis of Dec. 26, 1794, General Records, 1791–1803, R.G. 58.

29. Hamilton to Coxe, Dec. 29, 1794, Wolcott Papers, Conn. Hist. Soc., Hartford.

conduct. Obviously unappeasable and unapologetic, he ended his letter with the terse comment that he would refrain from "any further explanatory remarks or observations."[30]

Coxe's carefully nurtured vengeance would come once Hamilton was safely out of office, and during the intervening weeks he silently forbore. It was not easy, as was witnessed by a bitterly recriminatory letter that he labored over for long hours, only then to decide that it should not be sent. Nothing he had previously written revealed so clearly the shape his angry disappointment was taking, or the form it soon would assume. The distorted picture he sketched of the Treasury was one Jefferson and his Republican followers would have admired: Hamilton the ruthless commissar, Hamilton the enemy of free government.

The suppressed letter was prompted by the secretary of the Treasury's request that Coxe submit a list of nominees for vacant positions in the revenue service. He would make no recommendations on his own, Coxe replied, but only relay the names of candidates proposed by others. Why should he do more? Despite "all the pains" he had endured and the time-consuming "enquiring and reflection I have applied to accomodate you and serve the United States," Hamilton had repeatedly admonished him that it would be "fruitless" for him to nominate "persons unfriendly to the Government." Since Coxe and Hamilton both believed that only such candidates as were free "from Enmity to the constitution" should be nominated for public office, what prompted such gratuitous admonitions? To Coxe the answer lay "in the difference of our opinions upon the Theory of Government." What was the bearing of these differences on appointments to office? Coxe, unswervingly "holding the cardinal principle of the constitution to be that of representation," could not in good conscience countenance "the introduction of any provision by which hereditary organs of the people at large could enact or execute the national laws." Although obliquely stated, the meaning of this curt comment was clear: Hamilton, himself an advocate of a hereditary government, had given his sanction to the appointment of candidates who shared his preference.

The consciousness of his own "great attachment to our Government" and the remembrance of his "sufferings in mind and fortune" on its behalf at last compelled Coxe to protest Hamilton's criticism. "This is the third Occasion and the third form in which Ideas of this Nature have been intimated by you," Coxe wrote, proceeding also to argue that on each occasion Hamilton had been emphatically wrong.[31] It was a sad finale to a relation-

30. Coxe to Hamilton, Jan. 2, 1795, Letters of Commr. of Rev., Relating to the Procurement of Military, Naval, and Indian Supplies, R.G. 75.
31. Coxe to Hamilton, Jan. 1795, Coxe Papers. There are two drafts of this letter, one of

ship that Coxe himself had first assiduously sought and then carefully nourished. It was also ironic if one recalls that it was a former tory who now lambasted as a secret monarchist a man who had served in war and peace alike as Washington's most trusted aide. In Coxe's defense, however, it should be noted that his conviction, shared by so many of his contemporaries, would in time be sanctioned by a good many, perhaps most, American scholars.

In any event, on January 31, 1795, the last day of Hamilton's tenure in office, Coxe dropped the mask of patience he had worn over the preceding month. "A very painful sense of duty has impelled me," he wrote to Washington, to report a serious violation of the law on the part of the retiring secretary of the Treasury and his designated successor. Enclosing a copy of Hamilton's letter of September 29, 1794, authorizing Wolcott to serve as acting head of the Treasury Department, Coxe alleged that it was in contravention of both the law establishing the department and the amending act of May 1792. Apropos of the former statute Hamilton's instructions constituted "a suspension of the Check" explicitly imposed upon him: the Treasury secretary had transferred to the comptroller authority that only the president could legally delegate.[32]

Technically Coxe had a strong case, particularly with regard to the act of 1792 making alterations in the Treasury and War departments. But it was not justiciable, and the president, before whom it had to be argued, had obviously prejudged it. This being the situation, precisely what did Coxe believe his letter would accomplish? Was he merely attempting to set the record straight? If so, neither Washington nor Wolcott was likely to cooperate or even to care. Could Coxe possibly have been so unaware of the relationship between Washington and Hamilton as to believe that the former would heed his complaint without first consulting the cabinet member on whom he had most confidently relied? If so, he committed a blunder of some magnitude. What he in fact did was to provide Hamilton with an opportunity to discredit him with the president.

Not that Hamilton needed an excuse. Five days before leaving the Treasury, he had taken steps to assure that Coxe would receive no presidential favors. Replying to Washington's request that he comment on the qualifications of Joseph Habersham of Georgia for Wolcott's replacement as comptroller, Hamilton seized the occasion to undermine Coxe's chances for that post. Having expressed doubts that Habersham "would be an eligible

---

which is complete. Although employing somewhat variant diction, both letters express the same ideas.

32. Coxe to Washington, Jan. 31, 1795, Miscellaneous Letters, 1790–1799, R.G. 59, National Archives.

appointment," the outgoing secretary also implicitly expressed reservations about the commissioner of the revenue by strongly recommending one of his subordinates, Edward Carrington, revenue supervisor for Virginia, for the job. Although the appointment of a Virginian to the office, as Hamilton himself had pointed out, would violate the administration's "distributive geographic rule," Washington offered the position to Carrington, who declined it.[33] The president then again turned to Hamilton for advice. Would not Coxe be a suitable appointment?

Now was the time for Hamilton to say explicitly what he had implied two weeks earlier, and he performed the hatchet job deftly and swiftly. If it were not for *"very peculiar personal circumstances,"* he would agree that "the fittest arrangement, upon the whole, would be to consign the *temporary* execution of the Comptroller's office to The Commissioner of the Revenue." But it was peculiarly unfitting both because it would "be unpleasant to Mr. Wolcott" and because there was "real danger that Mr. Coxe would first perplex and embarrass, and afterwards misrepresent and calumniate." Hamilton's presumptuousness in speaking for Wolcott aside, his remark perfectly mirrored the view he took of his own long association with Coxe. His alternative nomination similarly reflected the extent to which his grudge against Coxe had warped his judgment: all things considered, he said, the most eligible candidate in the department was the auditor, Richard Harrison, who, Hamilton did not add, had all along been prized for his skill at bookkeeping, not his ability or potential as a top administrator. Washington, a far more shrewd judge of Hamilton than the latter was of his own former assistants, ignored the New Yorker's recommendation and chose instead to steer clear of interdepartmental rivalry by appointing an outsider.[34]

Hamilton's opinion of Coxe was already well known to Washington. On February 1 the president had turned over to Hamilton, without comment of his own, Coxe's letter of January 31 describing the secretary of the Treasury's misdeeds and indicting Wolcott as an accessory.[35] Hamilton's prompt reply on February 2 was an expert legal brief and a devastating assault on Coxe. The revenue commissioner had all along had "more business confided to him than his talents for execution were equal to," Hamilton wrote, conveniently overlooking his own three-year reliance on Coxe. "I considered him as an inferior officer in the department to Mr. Wolcott and after the disposition he had shewn I should have regarded it as treating Mr. Wolcott ill to have invested him even with a temporary superiority. In the

33. Hamilton to Washington, Jan. 26, 1795, Edward Carrington to Washington, Feb. 7, 1795, Syrett *et al.*, eds., *Hamilton Papers*, XVIII, 194–195.
34. Hamilton to Washington, Feb. 12, 1795, *ibid.*, 259–261. The appointment eventually went to John Steele of North Carolina.
35. Washington to Hamilton, Feb. 1, 1795, *ibid.*, 242.

last place, I had much greater confidence in the proper and efficient execution of the business by Mr. Wolcott than by him."[36] Skilled in adversary proceedings, Hamilton was able to make his indictment of Coxe and the defense of his own conduct superficially plausible, but they would not have convinced an impartial judge or a judge willing even to listen to the other party involved. Since Washington was neither of these, the New York attorney's clever marshaling of carefully selected facts determined the case.

The personal relationship between Coxe and Hamilton ended with the reproaches they hurled at each other in the winter of 1795. Time did not heal, nor did charity soften, the bitter distrust that supplanted what had been an extraordinarily productive and creative official collaboration. Instead, Hamilton would soon convince himself, if he was not already certain, that what he once said of Pennsylvania was personified by Coxe: that state's "political putrefaction," he wrote in October 1794, "is greater than I had any idea of."[37] By the same token, Coxe would soon be certain that Hamilton symbolized the monarchical conspirators who stymied both his country's progress and his own career. That career was for the moment in the hands of his victorious rival, Oliver Wolcott, who on February 3, 1795, officially succeeded Hamilton as secretary of the Treasury.

If, as Hamilton implied, Wolcott found his official association with Coxe "unpleasant," it is curious that once he assumed the secretaryship he did not, whether by means open or covert, seek the Pennsylvanian's resignation. It is also puzzling that Coxe did not quit the Treasury, since, as Hamilton correctly perceived, Coxe had been for four years engaged in an "incessant struggle for preeminence" over Wolcott. That neither of these things happened was presumably because Wolcott appreciated Coxe's experience and ability and because the latter was reluctant to surrender public office, however disdainful he might be of his boss. It may also be that Wolcott, a more flexible man than the stereotype would allow, was willing to overlook what Hamilton alleged to be the "intrigues" of one with whom the new secretary had worked closely and for whom he perhaps felt a certain affinity. Certainly the two men had much in common. Like Coxe, Wolcott was a member of his state's elite. His grandfather had been a colonial governor of Connecticut, his father a signer of the Declaration of Independence and governor of Connecticut, his uncle a Speaker of the House of Representatives and a supreme court judge in Connecticut. Like Coxe, Wolcott was a dedicated and able public servant, serving successively as auditor,

---

36. Hamilton to Washington, Feb. 2, 1795, *ibid.*, 248–253.
37. Hamilton to Rufus King, Oct. 30, 1794, Charles R. King, ed., *The Life and Correspondence of Rufus King, Comprising His Letters, Private and Official, His Public Documents and His Speeches*, I (New York, 1894), 575.

comptroller, secretary of the Treasury, United States Supreme Court justice, and finally as governor of Connecticut. But there the similarity ends. Wolcott was not a distinguished journalist or economist; neither was he driven by boundless political ambition or dreams of personal grandeur based on the possession of vast estates. A more secure and self-possessed man than the Philadelphia grandee, the Connecticut aristocrat had "strong practical good sense and native shrewdness" but "no desire to obtain a shining reputation, and little ambition, other than to fill honorably an honorable station."[38] That he also had a strong streak of self-righteousness and was capable of mean-spirited vindictiveness were lessons Coxe, to his misfortune, would learn in 1797.

Although Coxe was indignantly certain (as a journalistic critic would observe years later) that "the office he possesses is not competent to his own notions of his own merits," he nevertheless continued over the next two years to perform his Treasury Department duties conscientiously, though somewhat perfunctorily.[39] Now freed of the onerous War Department purveyorship, he could competently administer the revenue and coast guard services and have time not only for the family and social life he enjoyed but, more important, for the land speculation in which he was becoming more and more deeply involved. There was time, too, to indulge his journalistic bent, now the more gratifying because it allowed him to exercise on public opinion the influence he no longer exercised on Treasury Department policy. Jay's Treaty soon provided him a splendid opportunity.

38. Gibbs, ed., *Memoirs of Administrations of Washington and Adams*, I, 173–174.
39. *Aurora*, Aug. 18, 1804.

14 🐝

An Apostate Federalist

Coxe, like most other Americans, had high expectations for the treaty John Jay was negotiating with the British. In the spring and summer of 1794 Coxe had furnished Jay with statistics on American trade, as well as unasked-for advice on the conduct of the American envoy's diplomatic mission. To Coxe the data he had supplied conclusively demonstrated that the United States, Britain's best customer and natural commercial ally, was in a strong bargaining position; the copy of his recently published *A View of the United States* that he sent to Jay in November 1794 provided, so he believed, yet more powerful ammunition.[1] On November 19, weeks before Coxe's book reached him, Jay had signed the document that would bear his name—the best-known peacetime treaty in our history. It was a conciliatory measure, Jay wrote to Coxe on December 18, one that revealed on the part of England "the best Disposition towards us." Since to Jay the Philadelphian was identified primarily as Hamilton's assistant and thus as a faithful Federalist, he could not have known that what he considered a promising demonstration of England's "good will . . . friendship and cordiality with us" would appear to Coxe a demonstration of ineradicable enmity that promised only further aggravation.[2] A large number of Coxe's countrymen emphatically agreed with him. As Chief Justice Jay to his surprise would discover, his treaty was poorly calculated to convert those who were convinced that friendship with France, rather than impartial neutrality, should be the cornerstone of American foreign policy.

Painfully aware that he had been forced to negotiate from a position

1. Coxe to John Jay, May 3, 4, 7, 8 (2 letters), 25, Nov. 8, 1794, Coxe Papers. See also Jay to Coxe, July 18, 1794, *ibid.*
2. Jay to Coxe, Dec. 18, 1794, *ibid.*

of weakness, Jay believed it incontestable that he had secured all that was then possible from the British foreign secretary, Lord Grenville. Unaware that many of his countrymen believed that his reach should have been much greater, he counted himself fortunate to have secured any concessions at all. In fact, Britain had promised to give up the northwestern posts by June 1796, to pay for the spoliations upon American commerce, and to sign a commercial treaty granting the United States certain limited trading privileges with India and with the British West Indies. In return, Jay had renounced maritime principles that the United States had hitherto considered inviolable (in effect, the familiar insistence of neutral nations on freedom of the seas) and had instead accepted Great Britain's interpretation of international law. Specifically, he had acquiesced to Britain's definition of contraband of war, her contention that provisions could not under all circumstances be carried to enemy ports in neutral ships, her insistence that trade with enemy colonies prohibited in time of peace was also illegal in time of war, and her demand that America not open its ports to the ships and privateers of England's enemies.

Although the more extreme chauvinists in both England and America might view their country's concessions as a surrender of national honor, Jay and Grenville had, in fact, worked out a quid pro quo based on a realistic assessment of the prevailing power situation. They were convinced, moreover, that the treaty was as important for the machinery it established for settling further disputes as for what it formally stipulated. Joint commissions were to be set up for arbitrating the amount of compensation for spoliations, satisfying the claims of British creditors against American citizens, and fixing the northwest boundary between the United States and Canada. As events would quickly show, however, a good many Americans considered such amicable arrangements inconsequential when compared with what they regarded as other lamentable features of the treaty. The aspects that aroused the greatest furor were the absence of any offer of compensation for slaves freed by the British in 1783, the silence on impressment of bona fide United States sailors by the English navy, the failure to secure for Americans the unrestricted privilege of trading with the British West Indies, and the stipulation that American ships would not carry molasses, sugar, coffee, cocoa, or cotton to any part of the world except the United States. Given the military and naval disparity between the two nations, Jay believed that such restrictions, however harsh, were the inevitable price of any treaty at all.

Soon after the treaty was delivered to the secretary of state on March 7, 1795, President Washington called an emergency meeting of the Senate. Once it convened on June 8, the president submitted Jay's handiwork without any opinion of his own. After two weeks of debate conducted in secret session, the Senate by a vote of 20 to 10 (precisely equal to the constitutionally necessary two-thirds majority) advised him to ratify the treaty, on the condition that the clause restricting American trade with the British West Indies be suspended pending further negotiations. Although it was left unclear whether Washington should reopen negotiations before signing the treaty or ratify it and negotiate subsequently, he opted for the latter course, finally signing the document on August 18.

Weeks before Washington approved the treaty, its provisions were leaked by opponents to Philadelphia newspaper editors, who, as one of Coxe's congressional correspondents remarked, "have not spared to expose it . . . for the purpose of finding fault."[3] This was an understatement. Sparked by the exposures of the press, a popular furor erupted that had not been matched since the violent days of tory witch-hunts during the Revolution. A boisterous crowd surrounded the house of the British minister in Philadelphia; Jay was assailed as a traitor; and Hamilton was stoned by an angry mob in New York. These were not the only demonstrations; protest meetings were held in Boston, in Charleston, in Portsmouth, New Hampshire, and elsewhere—all similar to the outbursts in western Pennsylvania that a large majority of Americans had denounced only a year earlier. To many people it seemed "that civilization was at a cross-roads" and that they must "choose between two opposite types of government, of life, of ideals," between anarchy and order.[4]

However thick the ideological gloss with which it was covered, the issue was fundamentally partisan, with Federalists stoutly defending the treaty against the shrill attacks of Republicans. The confrontation was an important milestone in American political history. Not only did the debate signify the maturity of the country's first political parties, it also occasioned fundamental shifts in political loyalties. An influential number of prominent public figures who had steadfastly supported the Washington administration—men like John Dickinson, John Langdon of New Hampshire, and Charles Pinckney—now openly embraced the Republican opposition. In Philadelphia the issue widened the political division among the city's merchants. To those already disenchanted with Federalist policy, the treaty "confirmed their worst fears that decisions at the highest level of government would continue to be heavily weighed in favor of British trading interests"; to those not yet fully or openly committed to the opposition, it was an effective political catalyst. Coxe was representative of the latter point of view. Publicly demonstrating how he had edged to the Republican

3. George Thatcher to Coxe, May 24, 1795, *ibid.*
4. Bernard Faÿ, "Early Party Machinery in the United States," *PMHB*, LX (1936), 380–381.

camp, he hurriedly prepared four lengthy articles scoring the treaty.[5]

The first of Coxe's essays appeared in the form of a public letter to the president in the *Philadelphia Gazette* on July 31, 1795, two weeks before Washington made up his mind to sign the controversial treaty. In accordance with the polemical canons of the time, the essays were published pseudonymously, but Coxe's identity as the author, "Juriscola," was well known, at least to the small and tightly knit circle of government officials and their correspondents. According to Coxe, Secretary of State Edmund Randolph, himself soon to be accused of political apostasy and worse, "informed Mr. Wolcott that I was the writer of Juriscola, censured me, and manifested a clear wish that I might go on and injure myself by the publications." Wolcott promptly tattled to Hamilton. The New Yorker was not surprised: "I do not wonder at what you tell me of the author of a certain piece," he replied. "That man is too cunning to be wise. I have been so much in the habit of seeing him mistaken that I hold his opinion cheap." Coxe himself made no secret of his authorship of the "Juriscola" articles, particularly to like-minded (or at least, in his view, open-minded) acquaintances like William Vans Murray, who complimented Coxe that "the manner and style differ . . . to advantage from your other pieces. There is more ease and ardour."[6] If by "ease" Murray meant stylistic grace, his literary sense was blunted, but he was an expert in the detection of mood. Coxe's ardor, unmistakable to friend and enemy alike, was so great that it characteristically spilled over into prolixity. But he was one of a large company. Dozens of American scribblers scathingly denounced Jay's Treaty in tediously long articles that lend credence to the observation of a defender of the document "that it had more critics than readers."[7]

The purpose of Coxe's "Examination of the Pending Treaty" was to present to the president "such considerations, as appear to recommend . . . suspension" of ratification in order "to procure *all such meliorations of the treaty, as candid and reasonable investigation shall point out.*" Only the

---

5. Roland M. Baumann, "John Swanwick: Spokesman for 'Merchant-Republicanism' in Philadelphia, 1790–1798," *PMHB*, XCVII (1973), 156; "An examination of the pending Treaty with Great Britain, To the President of The United States," *Philadelphia Gaz.*, July 31, Aug. 4, 8, 12, 1795. A draft of the fourth article is in the Coxe Papers. In a letter to Jefferson of Oct. 30, 1795, Coxe wrote, "Just after the publication of No. 4 I found it certain that he [Washington] had given his approbation to it. Tho a few more papers relative to the question of War Debts, were prepared, I determined to stop, because I thought it might be supposed I wished to censure the Executive of which I was a part." Jefferson Papers, Lib. of Cong. Coxe must have prepared at least three more essays in this series. In the Coxe Papers there are a number of fragmented essays dealing with British war debts, one of which is numbered "VII."

6. "To the Editor," *Aurora*, Nov. 1, 1800; Hamilton to Oliver Wolcott, Jr., Aug. 5, 1795, Syrett *et al.*, eds., *Hamilton Papers*, XIX, 97; William Vans Murray to Coxe, Aug. 13, 1795, Coxe Papers.

7. Marcus Cunliffe, *The Nation Takes Shape, 1789–1837* (Chicago, 1959), 47.

most cursory investigation on his part was needed to show, as the Senate already had pointed out, that the restrictions imposed by Article XII on American trade with the British West Indies cried out for amelioration. To Coxe, as to virtually every other critic of the treaty, this article was a deprivation rather than a concession. It was particularly objectionable because it was a "great and unnecessary deviation" from the principle of reciprocity, which Coxe believed should be fundamental to international commercial relations. England had grossly violated that principle by denying privileges equivalent to those generously accorded to that country in United States ports. Such a "plain discrimination against us" was to Coxe the more damaging because, "as our productions are yearly more and more converted into . . . manufactures, our privilege will be constantly narrowed."[8]

As a former international merchant, Coxe was understandably concerned about the West Indian trade. But his preoccupation with Britain's failure to grant compensation for slaves carried off by the departing British army in 1783 was puzzling. As a longtime member of the Pennsylvania abolition society, Coxe might have shared Jay's repugnance at the assumption that human beings were merely a species of property. To the contrary, however, his treatment of the subject—taking up approximately three-fourths of his treatise—would have done justice to the South's most ardent defender of slavery. The argument that "there is strictly speaking no property in men" was rendered invalid, Coxe believed, by laws of both nations countenancing slavery—a fact attested, if proof were needed, by British law and practices in the West Indies and by the first United States census. Coxe buttressed his attack on what he regarded as England's unconscionable denial of justice to American slaveowners by adverting not only to Anglo-American practice but to current international and ancient Roman law and to history.[9]

Why did a Philadelphian, a leading exponent of commercial expansion and reciprocity as essential props of the national interest, choose to deemphasize the treaty's restrictions on American trade, to ignore its cavalier disregard of his country's maritime rights, and to focus instead on its failure to compensate Americans for the seizure of black men whose enslavement he otherwise deplored? A clue to Coxe's preoccupation was his linking of the slave issue and the article in Jay's Treaty providing for the appointment of commissioners to determine the payment of prewar debts owed by Americans (mostly southerners) to British subjects. It was well known, he wrote, that in 1782 the American peace commissioners "had

---

8. "An examination of the pending Treaty," *Philadelphia Gaz.*, July 31, 1795.
9. *Ibid.*, Aug. 4, 1795. Even if one were to argue that the larger part of the Negroes carried away had gone "voluntarily into the British lines," Coxe wrote, this scarcely exculpated the British. "They were '*Runaways.' The master's right was not impaired.*" *Ibid.*

represented the parts of this country which owed money to Great Britain, as in some degree incapacitated from paying their debts by the loss of the negroes."[10] What had been true in 1782 was still true in 1795. Coxe's emphasis on the connection between the refusal of southerners to pay the debts they owed in England and the British seizure of blacks suggests that he was mirroring the South's chagrin at Jay's alleged betrayal of its interests. As he gingerly approached commitment to a party whose top leadership consisted of Virginians, was he obliquely revealing his lapse from Federalism and his loyalty to them? If so, it was not only a declaration of political defection but also a denial of his commitment to the antislavery cause. His views were now those to which his friend Jefferson could readily have subscribed, though perhaps with more painful twinges of conscience. The battle over Jay's Treaty was Coxe's political Rubicon. Having crossed to the Republican shore, he remained publicly mute until the autumn of 1796, when it appeared that his pen might assist the perfect paragon of Republicanism, Thomas Jefferson, to drive the Federalists, Oliver Wolcott not the least among them, from office.

The presidential contest between John Adams and Thomas Jefferson in 1796 presented Coxe with a cruel choice—whether by silence to show token loyalty to the administration of which he was a part and thus secure his office for a time at least, or by support of Jefferson to declare his political apostasy and thus court Federalist retaliation. If fidelity to beliefs that over the preceding two years had gradually hardened into articles of faith was to be the criterion, his choice was certain.

His growing commitment to Jefferson was in direct proportion to his mounting distrust of a number of highly placed Federalist associates, notably Hamilton and John Adams. By 1796 his vague suspicion that a conspiracy was afoot to undermine American republicanism had developed into a conviction. As early as April 1794, months before his break with Hamilton, he had been shocked by gossip, confidentially relayed to him by Senators John Langdon and John Taylor, that Vice-President Adams had openly expressed to a number of his Senate colleagues a decided preference for monarchy. Although the news was not so traumatic as he later alleged,[11] it was convenient additional proof of a conclusion to which he was moving with seeming inexorableness. Another milestone had been the debate over Jay's Treaty, which had transmogrified an issue involving the proper orientation of the nation's commercial and foreign policy into a stark ideological

10. *Ibid.*
11. See, for example, *Aurora*, Oct. 30, 1800.

polarity: republicanism versus monarchy. Coxe, like so many of his countrymen, became the willing prisoner of this abstraction.

By the summer of 1796 Coxe's political creed had assumed the appearance it would bear for the remainder of his long life. This ideology was expressed in a letter to a fellow Republican in New Hampshire. He began with the cliché that the preservation of free government was the sine qua non of the American political system. Since the people might often "be deceived or mistaken in their choice," however, how could this be secured? "Montesquieu spoke not more than half the truth when he affirmed virtue to be *the cardinal principle* of Republics," Coxe replied. "*Intelligence* in the Body of the people is quite as important." This attribute, his somewhat circular argument went, was safeguarded by such constitutional guarantees as "the perfection of the Judiciary" as "*independent Censors*," by the "exclusion of ecclesiastical influence from our government," and by the "diminution of feudal prejudices." With the equal rights of Americans thus placed upon such solid ground, the country's electorate would resist the blandishments and arguments "of friends of hereditary power."

Coxe's ideas on foreign policy were also now formed into permanent shape—a shape determined by anglophobia. The victory of the reactionary powers intent on crushing France would, he sincerely believed, mean the subversion of republican governments, the destruction of "churches which are not orthodox," and the restoration of "great feudal estates." Conversely, a French victory would "terminate in a more extended knowledge of the errors of unjust Government, in church and state, and in the diffusion of some improvable notions of liberty in countries, which are now strangers to its name."[12] Here was a pro-French foreign policy, cut to the pattern of Republican ideology, to which Coxe would be inflexibly committed.

To attribute Coxe's shift in political loyalty exclusively to ratiocinative principles, however, would be contrary to the pattern of his career. Certainly his contemporaries did not do so. William Duane, a shrewd though prejudiced judge, rhetorically queried years later whether "Tench's principles, if he has any, do not partake of the nature of the willow." Another critic would remind Coxe that it was in 1796 "you began to worship the rising sun."[13] Yet such remarks ad hominem suggest a partial rather than a whole truth; though ambition may have quickened Coxe's pulse, it did not necessarily warp his critical judgment. He would have been atypically obtuse had he not known on which side his political bread was buttered. How could he, after all, reasonably aspire to high office in a party dominated by

12. Coxe to Nathaniel Gilman, July 23, 1796, Coxe Papers. For Coxe's pro-French sentiment in 1793, see Coxe to John Ashe, Nov. 25, 1793, *ibid*.; Coxe to William Irvine, Nov. 16, 1793, Irvine Papers, Hist. Soc. Pa., Philadelphia.

13. *Aurora*, Aug. 22, 1804; *Gaz. of U.S.*, Nov. 4, 1800.

an enemy like Hamilton, whose friends were certain to monopolize most of the available space? Now that Washington's glow was fading away, he may have believed that the popularity of the Federalist party would also diminish. Perhaps, again, he perceived the drift of history. One can only say with certainty that as his discontent increased his well of idealism rose.

Coxe's switch from the Federalist to the Republican camp was neither sudden nor atypical. It was the result not only of long-smoldering personal resentment against Hamilton but also of impersonal developments that prompted other men with professional backgrounds and ideas similar to Coxe's to march under Jefferson's standard. Had Federalism, consistent with the stereotype, been the sole political faith of most merchants, capitalists, and large speculators in securities and lands, Coxe's defection would be too capriciously personal to warrant more than passing attention. But the Federalist party was no more homogeneous than the Republican: both were, in the mid-twentieth-century cliché, large umbrellas. Coxe was representative of the speculative-entreprenurial wing of the Republican party, a group that in Philadelphia included rich merchants, brokers, and speculators such as Blair McClenachan, Stephen Girard, Matthew McConnell, Charles Biddle, Charles Pettit, and John Swanwick. Swanwick's views were typical. He was opposed to the pro-British commercial and revenue policies of the Washington administration, advocating instead a balanced and independent national economy, high tariffs calculated to secure reciprocity, and navigation acts to protect American shipping.[14]

In siding with the Republican party, Coxe was not embracing the agrarian views of its southern wing, but, along with many other "merchant Republicans," was endorsing the fiscal features of the Hamiltonian program while repudiating the foreign policies on which Hamilton believed it must be premised. Whether or not Coxe and like-minded economic nationalists were correct in assuming that the two were separable (the contrary case, in any event, would be hard to prove), they were, in one respect, carrying Hamiltonianism to its logical conclusion. Such proponents of economic nationalism were more committed than Hamilton himself to the growth of manufactures and to their encouragement by federal bounties and protective tariffs. They were also more flexible than the Treasury secretary, as indicated by their willingness to risk severing traditional ties in order to enhance the steady expansion of American commerce.

There was, nevertheless, a certain element of paradox in Coxe's sup-

---

14. For the information on Swanwick, I am indebted to Roland M. Baumann's excellent article "John Swanwick," *PMHB*, XCVII (1973), 131–182. For Coxe's denial of the charge that he had promised that Swanwick's race in 1793 for a seat in the state legislature against William Lewis "would be supported by the Treasury Department," see Coxe to Thomas Morris, n.d. [but presumably Oct. 1793], Coxe Papers.

port of Jefferson's presidential candidacy. Here was a staunch defender of Hamilton's financial policies actively supporting that program's inveterate foe; an exponent of national manufactures and leading proponent of the Society for Establishing Useful Manufactures enlisting under the ensign of the country's best-known agrarian; a former city merchant endorsing a man who distrusted both cities and capitalists; a former tory allying himself with the author of the Declaration of Independence; an officer of the Pennsylvania abolition society joining forces with a slaveholder. What, then, committed Coxe to Jefferson's candidacy? They shared not only an assurance of position and order, but also a belief in the uniqueness of American civilization and a messianic vision of the American republic. They both feared that the vitality of that Republic was being sapped by secret monarchists. Yet with Coxe, as with Jefferson, a genuine social revolution was something not even considered. Although they did not erect rigid barriers between themselves and the common man (as a later generation, drenched in new riches, would), neither could have imagined a world without servants. They shared, above all, a conviction that the country must loosen its ties to England, ties that the Jay Treaty had temporarily tightened.

The great issue in the campaign of 1796 was American foreign policy —whether to elect Jefferson and thus affirm the French alliance and court war with Britain or to vote for Adams and endorse an Anglo-American rapprochement and risk a war with France. Phrased another way, the election was, to some extent, a national referendum on the Jay Treaty, which Congress had approved by only a razor-thin vote and to which a large number, perhaps a majority, of Americans objected. It was an issue tailor-made for Republicans, and Pierre Auguste Adet, the meddlesome French minister, helped them keep it in the foreground. On October 27 Adet informed Secretary of State Timothy Pickering of an arrêt issued four months earlier by the French Directory stating that France "will treat the flag of neutrals in the same manner as they shall suffer it to be treated by the English."[15] In his abrasive explanatory letter the French minister minced no words—the action of his government was in retaliation for American favoritism toward England, exemplified in the Jay Treaty. That the purpose of his flagrant disregard of diplomatic protocol was not so much to intimidate Pickering as to impress American voters was suggested by the publication of his letter in the Philadelphia *Aurora* four days before the voters of Pennsylvania were to select presidential electors.

Pennsylvania was a key state in the election of 1796. The capital city was the storm center of American politics, and its vote, as Jefferson had

---

15. *American State Papers, Foreign Relations*, I, 576–577.

observed in 1792, "can generally turn the balance."[16] Because of its diversified economy, ethnic mix, and religious variety, Pennsylvania also represented in microcosm the pluralistic nature of American society. There, too, party lines were more rigid, and statewide political organizations were more efficient than elsewhere.[17] This was the political milieu in which Coxe would operate, effectively though controversially, over succeeding decades; here was the scene of important partisan developments that he in significant ways typified.

The Republican campaign in Pennsylvania was masterminded by John Beckley, clerk of the House of Representatives and the general campaign manager for his fellow Virginian, Thomas Jefferson. Coxe, an intimate associate of the prominent Virginians in the capital city, had been acquainted with Beckley for several years, but the two became firm political allies only after Coxe became receptive to the gossip of Hamilton's traducers. No critic was more indefatigable or irresponsible than Beckley, who from his advantageous position in the House poured out a stream of rumors about the New Yorker's iniquities, particularly his allegedly corrupt influence on Federalist congressmen and his leadership of a cabal of secret monarchists. Jefferson believed most of these stories, and so too, from January 1795 on, did Coxe.[18] But the real significance of Coxe and Beck-

---

16. Faÿ, "Early Party Machinery," *PMHB*, LX (1936), 381; Jefferson to Thomas Mann Randolph, Nov. 16, 1792, Ford, ed., *Works of Jefferson*, VII, 179.

17. Raymond Walters, Jr., "The Origins of the Jeffersonian Party in Pennsylvania," *PMHB*, LXVI (1942), 440.

18. On occasion Beckley supplied Coxe with documentary verification of political gossip. The most conspicuous instance occurred on Oct. 10, 1796, when Beckley wrote to Coxe the following cryptic note: "Enclosed are Hamilton's precious confessions. Be pleased to preserve every scrap; they are *truly* original and authenticated by himself." Coxe Papers. The enclosure was obviously the documents relating to the notorious Reynolds affair. These papers had been handed over in Dec. 1792 to Beckley for copying by the clerks in his office. This is not the place to relate the involved story of Hamilton's adulterous relationship with Maria Reynolds, an account of which Hamilton himself presented in Aug. 1797 to the public in order to clear himself of the imputation of malfeasance in office made by James Reynolds, Maria's husband. But by revealing the hitherto unknown fact that the documents relating to the Reynolds affair were in Coxe's possession, Beckley's note throws new light on this frequently recounted and still unsolved mystery story. It is generally agreed that these documents were turned over by Beckley to James Callender, who in July 1797 published them in his *The History of the United States for 1796 . . .* , charging that the former Treasury secretary was guilty of illegal speculative ventures with James Reynolds, an accusation originally made by Reynolds himself. The documentary evidence on which the accusation was based—consisting largely of allegedly relevant depositions and copies of letters from Hamilton to Reynolds—had earlier found its way to Rep. Frederick A. Muhlenberg, who shared it with two Virginians, Sen. James Monroe and Rep. Abraham Venable. On Dec. 14, 1792, the three men called on Hamilton and stated that having "become possessed of some documents of a suspicious complexion," they wished "to afford" the Treasury secretary "an opportunity of explanation." To clear himself of this charge, Hamilton confessed to these unofficial congressional interrogators that, in his words, "my real crime" was not "improper pecuniary speculation" with Reynolds, but "an amorous

ley's close association resided in their tireless, and in time successful, labors to elect Jefferson president of the United States. Although Beckley "has gone down in history as a mysterious person who carried tales and worked behind the scenes," he actually "merits attention less as a political informant than as one of the leading party-organizers of the 1790's," according to Noble E. Cunningham, a close student of Beckley's career.[19] The same, at least for the latter half of the decade, might be said of Coxe. Their collaboration in political management began in the election of 1796.

Beckley emerged in Pennsylvania as "an early prototype of a now familiar figure—the party manager."[20] In an unprecedented publicity campaign he saw to it that the state was blanketed with political propaganda and, to prevent mistakes by careless or illiterate voters, passed around sample tickets. Some "30,000 tickets were gone thro' the State, by Express, into every county," he informed Madison in mid-October. And thanks to Beckley and other Republican leaders, the debate in Pennsylvania, as elsewhere, over the proper goals of foreign policy and the best manner to implement them was subtly turned into the more general and popularly effective issue of the survival of American republicanism. The trick was as

---

connection with his wife, for a considerable time with his privity and connivance . . . with the design to extort money from me." The congressmen appeared to be persuaded and agreed to reveal neither the charges against Hamilton nor his confession of adultery. But the door to public exposure was left ajar when the three investigators called on John Beckley to make copies of the incriminating documents in their possession. It was these papers that Beckley sent to Coxe, some months before Callender's initial publication of them. In the preface to his *History of the U.S.*, Callender called attention to a rumor "that Mr. John Beckley is the author of this volume" and emphatically denied it, asserting that Beckley "is unacquainted with my handwriting, and I could not be sure to distinguish his." Syrett *et al.*, eds., *Hamilton Papers*, XXI, 130–131, 122, 133. Although there was, of course, no need to say so, Callender was familiar with the handwriting of Coxe, with whom he occasionally corresponded. (Two letters that Callender wrote to Coxe dated only "1794," in the Coxe Papers, suggest that the two men saw each other with some frequency; a warm relationship can also be inferred from the letter from Callender to Coxe, Dec. 1, 1796, *ibid.*, which was in answer to an unfound letter Coxe had written to Callender.) This fact obviously does not prove that Coxe supplied Callender with the copies of the Reynolds documents, but when combined both with Callender's denial of Beckley's agency and with other circumstantial evidence, it makes such a conclusion appear plausible. Relevant evidence can readily be inferred from what has been written thus far in this biography of Coxe and need only be summarized here in the briefest possible form: (1) By 1796 Coxe had switched his allegiance to Jefferson and believed that top Federalists were dangerous monarchists who should be publicly discredited; (2) the chief culprit was Hamilton, who had snubbed Coxe's ambition and who, the Philadelphian believed, was public enemy number one (Coxe would have considered the exposure of the former Treasury secretary's misdeeds a public service); and (3) as his subsequent career revealed, Coxe's characteristic mode of attacking his political enemies was to publish documentary evidence in his possession that purportedly proved them guilty of nefarious deeds or dangerous ideas.

19. Noble E. Cunningham, Jr., "John Beckley: An Early American Party Manager," *WMQ*, 3d Ser., XIII (1956), 44.

20. *Ibid.*, 52.

simple as the logic was misleading: since the Federalists supported the treaty and hence close ties with Great Britain, they must also, like the English, favor aristocracy and monarchy. The Federalists, of course, merely reversed the equation: since the Republicans opposed the treaty, they must be Frenchified democrats and Jacobins.

Whether the imputation of monarchism or of Jacobinism was the more effective issue, Pennsylvania's voters were captured by the Republicans' superior organizational campaign. In swamping the state with promotional literature, sample ballots, and stump speakers, Beckley had able assistance. Philadelphian John Smith, a close associate of Coxe's, later recalled that in 1796 he undertook a three-week journey of six hundred miles during which "there was not one day I was not on horseback before the Sun Rose nor put up at Night till after it Set." He distributed "7,000 Tickets and 9,000 Handbills," organized public meetings, and addressed any crowds he could find.[21] Obviously, the voters were receptive listeners. Unbothered by considerations of class, profession, or wealth, they voted the party ticket. For Congress, for example, they spurned the Federalist candidacy of Edward Tilghman, a former tory and now a well-to-do lawyer, and reelected John Swanwick. On November 4, to the jubilation of Republicans, they also repudiated the claims of John Adams, Washington's heir presumptive, giving him one vote to Thomas Jefferson's fourteen. As Coxe's Virginia friend John Dawson predicted, it was "an important day" that "will terminate fabulously to republican government."[22]

The news of such a triumph in a state widely regarded as a bellwether brightened the hopes of Jeffersonians everywhere. These hopes grew almost daily with the news and rumors of ever-deepening dissension among the Federalists. Party discord was damaging enough to Adams's prospects, but the division was even more serious because of the electoral college system then prevailing. The Constitution provided that each elector cast two ballots of equal value and that the candidate winning a plurality be elevated to the presidency, with the second highest becoming vice-president. This awkward arrangement held no particular terror for the Republicans, who were agreed that Jefferson and not his running mate, Aaron Burr, should be president. It was otherwise with the Federalists, some of whom were determined to employ this constitutional loophole to elevate Thomas Pinckney of South Carolina, the second-spot candidate, over Adams. The opportunity was provided by Pinckney's greater popularity in the South and West and seemingly equal strength with Adams north of the Potomac River. The Republicans gleefully publicized these Federalist intrigues, while inwardly glowing at the knowl-

21. John Smith to Coxe, Dec. 14, 1800, Coxe Papers.
22. John Dawson to Coxe, Nov. 4, 1796, *ibid.*

edge that if enough Federalist electors threw away their second votes to assure the success of their favorite, they would instead insure the election of Thomas Jefferson.

Emboldened by the Virginian's smashing success in Pennsylvania and the enticing prospect of the Federalists handing Jefferson victory by default, Coxe decided that it was time for him to come to Jefferson's assistance. His aid took the form of a series of ten articles addressed "to the Electors of the President of the United States." The first number appeared on November 9, 1796, with others following at regular intervals throughout that month. The essays appeared in the *Gazette of the United States*, in other newspapers, local and distant, and, after the publication of the eighth number, also in pamphlet form.[23] Coxe's selection of the pseudonym "A Federalist" clearly indicated the bipartisan purpose of his partisan tract. The quondam Federalist's point of departure was a campaign philippic by a loyal Hamiltonian, William L. Smith, congressman from South Carolina. Writing under the signature "Phocion," Smith examined "The Pretensions of Thomas Jefferson to the Presidency" and defended Adams's proper claims in the most ambitious and well-publicized Federalist tract of the campaign.[24] Its scathing attack on Jefferson's deficiencies and its comparative neglect of Adams's merits provided Coxe with an opportunity to reverse the formula and by discrediting Adams to defend Jefferson. That he eagerly grasped such a task at the eleventh hour suggests that this service to Jefferson was also a form of self-service. Or perhaps it was self-deception, for though Coxe most certainly was a knowledgeable man, he most conspicuously lacked self-knowledge. He easily jumbled his distrust of the political beliefs of Hamilton and Adams, his commitment to republicanism and his undoubted patriotism, his frustrated ambition, and his admiration for Jefferson into a self-righteous profession of indignation at alleged attempts to subvert the American republic.

Nevertheless, Coxe's defamation of Adams was the single most important Republican partisan tract of the campaign, though it presumably failed to influence very many Federalists. Its significance, moreover, did not lie in any intrinsic merits, stylistic or substantive, but rather in Coxe's

23. "To the Electors of the President of the United States," signed "A Federalist," appeared in the *Gaz. of U.S.* on Nov. 9, 11, 14, 15, 16, 17, 18, 21, 24, 25, 29, and 30, 1796. The essays were reprinted in other newspapers and in pamphlet form. The pamphlet was entitled *The Federalist: Containing Some Strictures upon a Pamphlet, Entitled, "The Pretensions of Thomas Jefferson to the Presidency, examined, and the Charges against John Adams, refuted." Which Pamphlet Was First Published in the Gazette of the United States, in a Series of Essays, under the Signature of "Phocion"* (Philadelphia, 1796). It contained the first seven essays and half of the eighth. Coxe must have planned to enlarge the series and print them in a second pamphlet, for he concluded the first pamphlet by stating "end of first part."

24. The "Phocion" essays appeared in Oct. 1796 in the *Gaz. of U.S.* These essays also appeared in pamphlet form in Oct. and Nov. 1796.

success in defining for the Republicans the fundamental issue of the campaign. As was de rigueur, Coxe began with a tribute to Washington, for whom the friends of representative government could cherish the "comfortable truth" that at a time when the combined powers of Europe were intent on stifling republican government in France, Washington had stood fast as "an indisputable enemy" to every attempt at "hereditary domination." Coxe bestowed such praise in order to emphasize his central point: the danger of confiding the presidential authority to John Adams, a man "who has no faith, no confidence in representative or elective government, who believes, *with the jealous enemies of our constitution abroad,* that a monarchical constitution is . . . better than our federal constitution."[25] Since the charge against Adams had been made many times before by dozens of zealous Republicans, what more was there to do than repeat the slur? Coxe's answer was to microscopically examine Adams's ponderously scholarly disquisitions on political theory, his three-volume *Defence of the American Constitutions* and his more recent "Discourses on Davila." Starting with the assumption that these were royalist tracts and then focusing only on what seemed to prove his point, Coxe made his task easy.

Had not Adams said that "it is no fault in the English constitution to have *an hereditary king*—no fault to have *an hereditary nobility*"? If he found nothing wrong with such institutions in England, Coxe implied, surely he would find no fault with their introduction in the United States. Had Adams not baldly stated that the Europeans "would defeat themselves" if they aimed at popular control of more than one of the branches of government? The clear purport of this remark, "A Federalist" explained, was Adams's implicit repudiation of "the excellent federal plan" provided by the Constitution and his wish to abolish "our present representative government." Had not Washington's heir presumptive expressly affirmed that "a limited monarchy, especially when limited by . . . an aristocratical and democratical power in the constitution, may with *strict propriety* be called . . . a republic"? To Coxe it logically followed that Adams would view any future attempt to impose hereditary governments on the American states as consonant with the provision in the Constitution guaranteeing to every state a republican form of government. Had not the vice-president held up England (as Coxe paraphrased his remarks) "as the great exemplar for America and mankind," her government " 'the most stupendous fabric of human invention' . . . , the political *magnum bonum*, matured by time upon the tree of knowledge"? Such beliefs, according to Coxe's sophistic rejoinder, amounted to an explicit declaration by Adams that the Constitution and government of the United States would inevitably have "the most *deteriorating* influ-

25. [Coxe], *The Federalist*, 6–7.

ence" upon all Americans "unless we hasten to make our president and senate *hereditary*."[26]

Like many of his fellow partisans, Coxe was too much the victim of the political phobias of the day to be capable of reading Adams's works objectively or even intelligently. Believing that the American government was riddled with monarchists, he could not perceive that Adams distrusted democracy no more than any other form of government and that what Adams in fact feared was absolute power, no matter what the form of government. Also Coxe was engaged in semantic difficulties of the most baffling kind. He nowhere made it clear what he meant by "aristocracy," "democracy," or, particularly, a "republic," precisely because their meanings were to him self-evident. He lacked, ironically enough, the perception that once prompted John Adams to observe that a republic might mean "any thing, every thing, or nothing."[27]

Coxe exempted Thomas Pinckney from the conspiratorial charges leveled against the Federalist presidential candidate. The South Carolinian, he confidently asserted, "gives rise to *no alarms* . . . because he is universally admitted to be *attached to representative or elective government*."[28] Presumably unaware that Hamilton, in Coxe's view Adams's monarchical co-adjutor, strongly preferred Pinckney for the presidency, Coxe doubtless was subtly attempting to persuade those who felt obliged to support a Federalist to vote only for Pinckney, thus enhancing the chances of Jefferson's election.

Jefferson's own qualifications for the presidency, however, filled only a few pages of Coxe's wordy philippic. "Phocion" had censured the Virginian, Coxe believed, because that critic was "*unconsciously* steeped in the acidulated gall of *self-deceiving* prejudice." In reply to the charge that a philosopher, if one admitted Jefferson's pretensions to that title, "of all beings . . . makes the worst politician," Coxe pointed to numerous exceptions, most notably to Philadelphia's most prominent philosopher, Benjamin Franklin. But Coxe reserved his most withering scorn for what he viewed as Smith's gratuitous and disgraceful exploitation of the race issue. This was, he believed, a transparently inconsistent ruse, calculated to persuade northerners that the Republican candidate was a racist and, at the same time, to condemn him before southerners as an abolitionist. To counter Smith's effort "to excite against Mr. Jefferson the displeasure of the blacks in the city of Philadelphia" by charging that he had repeatedly averred that blacks were inferior to whites, Coxe offered a résumé of the Virginian's civil rights

26. *Ibid.*, 18, 22, 23, 29, 31, 38–39.
27. James Madison to J. H. Tiffany, Apr. 30, 1819, Charles Francis Adams, ed., *The Works of John Adams, Second President of the United States . . .* , X (Boston, 1856), 378.
28. [Coxe], *The Federalist*, 6.

record—his unsuccessful proposal that the Declaration of Independence include an article censuring George III's support of the slave trade, his sponsorship of a bill in the Virginia legislature to outlaw that nefarious traffic, and, most important, his "magnanimous" proposal that the descendants of slaves be offered "the elevating condition of political liberty, at a *future day*." In flat contradiction to this proposal, Smith had sought to alarm southern slaveowners by charging that Jefferson "had once formed the extravagant project of *emancipating all the slaves* in Virginia" by shipping them "off to some *other* country . . . *like a herd of black cattle*, God knows where."[29] Coxe's defense of Jefferson's middle-of-the-road position (or so it was at that time) was persuasive. Since Jefferson's stand so perfectly coincided with his own, it should have been.

There was no similar correlation in Coxe's endorsement of Hamilton's financial policies as "*wise*, necessary, and *inevitable*." It was a measure of both his conviction and his integrity that he refused to pass over the subject in silence, however expedient the omission might have been. The establishment of the bank was, he said, not only a statesmanlike act but one that "neither this nor any other civilized nation can avoid." The funding of the public debt was a "matter of simple justice" and of "prudence." It was his own support of these cornerstones of Federalism, he argued, that entitled him rather than Adams to be styled a true Federalist. Obviously basing his charges on conversations with his erstwhile friend, Coxe affirmed, "without fear of contradiction," that the vice-president "greatly disapproves of the funding and banking systems" and does not hesitate to describe them as measures that had and would "produce extreme and extensive ills."[30] Whether Coxe credited his readers with only marginal intelligence or with mind-benumbing partisanship, he obviously believed they would not raise the obvious and awkward question to which his argument logically led: If Adams's opposition to Federalist fiscal policy disqualified him for the presidency, why did not Jefferson's better-known and far more extreme opposition render him even more ineligible?

Undisturbed by this apparent illogic, Coxe forwarded copies of his "Address to the Electors of the President" to Republican friends in other states for publication in local newspapers and, in pamphlet form, circulated it among voters and presidential electors.[31] Nor was he bothered by the possible personal repercussions of thus publicizing his authorship. His thinly

---

29. *Ibid.*, 7–8, 10, 11, 13–14.

30. "To the Electors," *Gaz. of U.S.*, Nov. 30, 1796; and [Coxe], *The Federalist*, 44.

31. Manning J. Dauer, *The Adams Federalists* (Baltimore, Md., 1953), 103. See also John Livingston to Coxe, Nov. 27, 1796, Moore Furman to Coxe, Nov. 28, 1796, Samuel Law to Coxe, Dec. 12, 1796, John Dawson to Coxe, Dec. 11, 1796, Isaac Bloomfield to Coxe, Nov. 30, 1796, Coxe Papers.

290 | Tench Coxe

veiled anonymity would not, in any event, have deceived any of the country's political cognoscenti. By liberally sprinkling his articles with personal allusions and by identifying himself as a Treasury Department official who, though a Jeffersonian, supported Hamiltonian finance, he had openly proclaimed himself the pseudonymous "Federalist." Having done so, he affirmed his commitment to Jefferson by publishing additional newspaper articles attacking his former associates who believed themselves to be the defenders of true Federalism.[32] Among other services to the Virginian's campaign, he sought to persuade Senator John Langdon of New Hampshire to publish an account of Adams's 1794 alleged confession of a preference for monarchy, and he attempted to convince Philip Freneau to expose those who "insidiously introduced into the National Gazette" articles designed "to deceive" its editors and all good Republicans.[33] In both cases Coxe was unsuccessful.

By advertising his authorship of the "Federalist" articles and by supporting Jefferson in other ways, Coxe invited the personal attacks that promptly followed. In one respect they were justified. His insistence on the monarchical designs of Adams and other of his former Federalist associates did appear mere gasconade in light of his delay in unmasking the plot until it was politically expedient. One contemporary critic thus plausibly asserted that the writer of the verbose defamation of Adams then appearing in the *Gazette of the United States* "is a disguised *Anti*, muffled in a *Federal* cloak," who is "a certain *officer of the federal government*, known to be dissatisfied with the present administration because some ridiculous pretensions have been overlooked. He expects under a new one, to rise more rapidly." Nor did his enemies allow him to dissociate his loyalist record and his republican present. The author who signed himself "A Federalist," a representative critic charged, was in fact a former tory who would soon learn, should his candidate win the election, that Jefferson had no more sympathy for traitors than did Adams. The scattered applause with which Republicans greeted Coxe's "Address to the Electors" was, in brief, drowned out by a Federalist chorus of abuse. To his critics he was a political Proteus, a viewpoint succinctly expressed years later by a poetaster who wrote in the *Aurora*:

32. Under the signature of "Greene," for example, Coxe scathingly denounced one "Pelham," who in an article published in the *Connecticut Courant* (Hartford) had argued that the time was fast approaching when the New England states might have to separate from the Union. See the *New World* (Philadelphia), Nov. 30, 1796. "Pelham" was printed in the *New World* on the same date.

33. John Langdon to Coxe, Nov. 4, 1796, Philip Freneau to Coxe, Nov. 22, 1796, Coxe Papers.

> This Man
> All things by turn
> And nothing long.[34]

To Coxe the angry reaction of his former Federalist allies was inexplicable. His only offense had been "from knowledge and from reflection" to express with "decorum" and "respect" a "very decided, but I trust, a liberal opposition" to Adams's "predilection for monarchy." His own motives, moreover, were as honorable as his articles were meritorious. Search "the whole field of election publications," he said, and one could find no "more decent and respectful set of papers." They did "equal honor to free elections and to the decency of free and principled discussion," he proudly affirmed a few years later.[35] Crediting, as one surely must, the sincerity of his belief that Adams was the chief conspirator in a monarchical plot, he had every reason to be proud. But sincerity is not all. The true test is not the attribute itself but the nature and quality of its purpose and its fidelity if not to truth at least to reality. Coxe's underlying purpose was the American rejection of European conservatism, which to him enshrined an otiose set of principles. Although during the Revolution he had been a timid traditionalist, he now emerged as a root-and-branch reformer, advocating the eradication of the European past by exposing and convicting American monarchists. It was as if his determination to atone for his loyalty to the crown by becoming "a good American" had led him, once he achieved that status, to label his own American antagonists as tories all. Nevertheless, in his haste to expose and damn American monarchists, he overlooked the essential facts that Adams and an overwhelming majority of Federalists also believed the aristocratic and monarchical institutions of the Old World had no place in the new Republic and that the conspiracy he dreaded was a figment of his imagination. The dragon this partisan Saint George fought lived three thousand miles away.

At home the outcome of the strenuous battle waged by the Jeffersonians in defense of republicanism remained in suspense as the returns of the election trickled in. During the bitingly cold days of that December, Coxe confidently awaited popular confirmation of his own political acuity. By Christmas, however, he was obliged to confront the dismal certainty that John Adams would be the country's second president. But whether Adams's own successor as vice-president would be Pinckney or Jefferson was far from certain. When news of the electoral count reached the capital city during the early days of the new year, doubt was dispelled: the final tally gave Adams

---

34. "A Hint," *Gaz. of U.S.*, Nov. 18, 1796; "Philo-Adams," *ibid.*, Dec. 1, 1796; *Aurora*, Aug. 18, 1804.
35. *Aurora*, Nov. 1, 1800.

71 votes, Jefferson 68, and Pinckney 59. The next vice-president would thus be Thomas Jefferson, a prospect that dismayed a good many stalwart Federalists, for whom Fisher Ames spoke when he described the outcome as a "formidable evil." "Two Presidents, like two suns in the meridian," he predicted, "would meet and jostle for four years, and then Vice would be first."[36]

Such a possibility was as enticing to Coxe as his own immediate prospects were discouraging. Would Adams continue in office a man who had labeled him the nation's number one public enemy, in politics a myrmidon of English monarchy and in economic philosophy a recreant Federalist? Would Wolcott tolerate in the Treasury Department a man whose name had become an eponym for political inconstancy and fickleness? Although both questions, oddly enough, would be answered affirmatively, Coxe's support of Jefferson's candidacy in 1796, like his loyalty to George III in 1776, had a decisive effect on his subsequent career. Just as the earlier decision had rendered his patriotism thereafter suspect, so the later choice stamped him as a political turncoat, not to be fully trusted even by those to whom he gave unstinted loyalty. Why he should have been so labeled is another matter, for in neither instance was he atypical, and in the mid-1790s, having outgrown his tory past, he was actually in conformity with the epoch's current. The answer lies not so much in his apostasy as in his insistence on publicizing his conversion to the Republican cause. Similarly circumstanced, most people would have remained discreetly silent. But Coxe, unable to shed the egocentricity of youth and still caught up in the conviction that his official bosses would display the forbearance of his doting father, was impelled publicly to proclaim his abjuration of Federalism and allegiance to the Jeffersonian ideals. So it was that his very virtues of open-mindedness and political flexibility became the source of mistrust. Nevertheless, the shrillness of his insistence on the rectitude of his political principles left a nagging uncertainty about his disinterestedness. In any event, the advice given Coxe in the midst of the presidential campaign by his father was sound. "Refrain from political vexations," William Coxe admonished, "and confine your attention to your office or official duties and your private fortune and affairs."[37] Although the latter were almost beyond retrieval, Coxe now intended to avoid "political vexations."

---

36. Ames, ed., *Works of Ames*, I, 211, 213.
37. William Coxe, Sr., to Coxe, Nov. 16, 1796, Coxe Papers.

15 🕊

Federalist Vengeance

There were, in Coxe's view, solid grounds for believing that his able administration of the internal revenue service would guarantee his job. His belief no doubt was strengthened by what he believed to be the virtual autonomy enjoyed by the commissioner of the revenue. This independence was symbolized by the location of the commissioner's office several blocks away from that of the secretary of the Treasury.

Coxe's primary responsibilities after the election were essentially the same as they had been in Hamilton's day. The most important phase of his work, in terms of the number of agents required and the amount of revenue received, continued to be the collection of taxes on distilled spirits. Other taxes that had come under the jurisdiction of his office as a result of the nation's preparedness program of 1794 included those on property sold by auctioneers, on snuff and refined sugar, on carriages, and on licenses issued to retailers of foreign spirits and wines.[1] The collection of these taxes, however, was not as easy as one might assume. A good many supervisors and inspectors were incapable of filling out even the elementary forms that the commissioner prescribed; they often ignored clearly labeled columns, lumped together receipts from all taxes, or, more irritating, did not even bother to submit the requisite returns. Also, the several revenue statutes often failed to make clear the precise nature of the item to be taxed and the exact role or authority of revenue agents.

Most troublesome of all was the carriage tax. Although extreme, the difficulties in the way of its collection may in a general way be taken as representative. The problems were not only procedural but semantic. By

1. Oliver Wolcott, Jr., to Coxe, Dec. 8, 1794, Wolcott Papers, Conn. Hist. Soc., Hartford. For a description of these taxes, see White, *The Federalists*, 451–452.

what criteria were revenue agents to differentiate among a dozen or so different types of carriages, chariots, chaises, post chaises, curricles, coaches, and chairs? Perplexed congressmen had evaded the problem by providing that where doubt existed a carriage should be considered as belonging to the general group it most closely resembled.[2] But since revenue agents were more often than not unwilling to exercise discretion, the problem was turned over to Coxe. So too was the devising of plans for a lawsuit to test the constitutionality of the act.[3]

At issue was whether the carriage tax was one of the "direct" taxes that, though not explicitly defined in the Constitution, must be apportioned among the states according to their populations. To resolve the question, Wolcott decided to institute proceedings leading to a decision by the federal courts. The necessary arrangements were made by Coxe, who directed Edward Carrington, supervisor of Virginia, to initiate a test case. Since the Judiciary Act of 1789 provided that federal circuit courts could take cognizance of only those suits involving at least $2,000 and since the carriage tax was small, it was necessary to arrange amicable litigation based on a statement of fictitious facts. For this purpose Carrington rounded up a Virginian named Hylton, who agreed to act as plaintiff in a suit alleging that the imposition of an excise on his fictitious 125 private chariots (the number he would have had to own to pay a tax of $2,000) was unconstitutional. When the circuit court divided on the constitutional question, it was decided to appeal the case to the Supreme Court.[4] Again Coxe made the arrangements. Since Hylton was tired of legal charades, it was necessary for the government to employ attorneys to argue both sides of the question (Hamilton appeared as special counsel for the government, though surely not at Coxe's request). Finally, in March 1796 the Supreme Court ruled that a tax on carriages was not direct and thus was valid without apportionment among the states.[5] More than anyone else, Coxe deserved credit for the successful issue of the government's case.

Eighteen months later Coxe was instrumental in initiating another case that had significance in the history of American law. It concerned a bribe offered to Coxe by Robert Worrall, an Englishman then resident in Philadelphia. Late in September 1797 Worrall, who was eager to win a con-

---

2. "An Act laying duties upon Carriages for the conveyance of Persons," June 5, 1794, *U.S. Statutes at Large*, I, 373–376.

3. Coxe to Alexander Hamilton, Jan. 14, 1795, to Edward Carrington, Jan. 14, 1795, Letters of Commr. of Rev., 1795–1797, R.G. 58, National Archives.

4. In the circuit court "Judge Wilson . . . was in favor of its constitutionality and Judge Griffin, the district judge of Virginia, against it." Coxe to William Polk, Aug. 10, 1795, *ibid.*

5. 3 Dallas (U.S.) 171–184 (1796). Coxe's role in the case can be followed in Letters of Commr. of Rev., 1795–1797, R.G. 58.

tract for construction of a lighthouse on Cape Hatteras and a lighted beacon on Shell Island (present-day Ocracoke Island), North Carolina, wrote to Coxe offering him half (or about $1,866) of his estimated profit of £1,400 for the award of the contract. Coxe promptly reported the offer to the president and to Wolcott and then busied himself in securing corroboratory evidence. This was submitted to Supreme Court Justice William Paterson, who, after consultation with other officials, advised that though there was no statute covering the offense, federal courts had power under common law to punish activities within the reach of constitutional power.[6]

The case was adjudged in April 1798, five months after Coxe was dismissed from office; it was heard by the circuit court for the Pennsylvania area, Supreme Court Justice Samuel Chase and District Court Judge Richard Peters presiding. Since the two judges disagreed on the essential question of whether or not "the common law is the law of the *United States*, in cases that arise under their authority," the case might have been dismissed, but, instead, a brief prison term and a light fine were imposed on the defendant.[7]

United States v. *Worrall*, though not itself a viable precedent, dealt with a knotty and contentious legal issue, one finally settled in 1812 when the Supreme Court ruled that federal courts did not possess common law jurisdiction.[8] As Coxe recognized, the constitutional question at issue in the Worrall decision was more important than the specific facts or people involved, and he could take justifiable credit for casting the form in which the case was adjudicated, just as he could also take pride in having arranged the more consequential carriage tax case.[9]

Devising plans for important litigation was child's play compared to Coxe's difficulties with uncooperative or inept revenue supervisors. Daniel Stevens of South Carolina was both, and no technique Coxe employed, whether cajolery, reprimand, or threat, significantly altered the situation. Although Coxe repeatedly implored his careless subordinate to pay closer attention to official records, Stevens continued to submit accounts that were "erroneous and imperfect." The least Stevens could do, Coxe wrote in exasperation, was to look over the various forms and ascertain what particular certificates and account sheets should be used for what purpose.[10] Neverthe-

---

6. Coxe to Jonathan Roberts, Jan. 30, 1821, to Wolcott, Sept. 28, 1797, William Paterson to Coxe, Oct. 16, 1797, Coxe Papers. For Coxe's deposition of Oct. 1797, see *ibid.*

7. *U.S.* v. *Worrall*, 2 Dallas (U.S.) 384–396 (1798).

8. *U.S.* v. *Hudson and Goodwin*, 7 Cranch (U.S.) 32 (1812). Some legal scholars believe that the court ruled wrongly in this case. They argue that the Judiciary Act of 1789 did confer such power on the federal courts. See Charles Warren, "New Light on the History of the Federal Judiciary Act of 1789," *Harvard Law Review*, XXXVII (1923), 73.

9. See Coxe to William Rawle, Apr. 20, 1798, Coxe Papers.

10. Coxe to Daniel Stevens, Mar. 25, Apr. 9, 1795, Letters of Commr. of Rev., 1795–1797, R.G. 58.

less, Coxe stopped short of recommending that the incompetent South Carolinian be fired. The reason is not hard to find: Stevens, like other supervisors, was doubling as Coxe's land agent. It was fortunate that this never came to Wolcott's attention.

No such conflict of interest complicated Coxe's relationship with an even more inept subordinate, Henry Miller. Precisely why Coxe and Hamilton insistently urged Miller to accept the supervisorship of Pennsylvania is as much a mystery as Coxe's patience in silently bearing with Miller's ineffectualness for two and a half years. A Revolutionary War veteran and a native of York, Pennsylvania, Miller had no discernible qualifications except the support of his fellow townsman Congressman Thomas Hartley and of the United States senator from western Pennsylvania, James Ross.[11] As early as February 1795 Coxe had begun to upbraid Miller for remissness in submitting required reports, and he continued to do so during the remaining years of his tenure as revenue commissioner. In January 1798 Coxe commented that he could "exhibit 54 letters in 15 Months to the Supervisor" of Pennsylvania, "several of which call him to an account in the most solemn and cogent terms." These letters proved futile. Miller made no effort to keep adequate records, neglected to submit required accounts, and, despite Coxe's understated warning that such "things will produce a very disagreeable impression," refused even to offer excuses for his delinquency.[12] Allowing him to remain in office was a mistake of some magnitude, though Coxe could not know that this miscreant would be transformed into his own official nemesis.

Wolcott, the man who would accomplish this legerdemain, could not justly blame Coxe for Miller's ineptness, for it was Coxe who kept him informed of the unsatisfactory state of Pennsylvania's revenue, though Wolcott ignored this information. Nor could the secretary in any other respect fairly fault Coxe's administration of the commissioner's office. Lighthouse affairs were handled with dispatch, congressional requests for reports were promptly and efficiently met, voluntary recommendations for improvement of the revenue service were from time to time submitted, and official instructions were carefully carried out. It was for these reasons that the Treasury secretary tolerated as the second-highest-ranking official in his department a man he increasingly suspected, both personally and politically. But forbearance was not Wolcott's strong suit, and in the summer of 1796, by then aware of his subordinate's political apostasy, he decided that Coxe needed to be shown who the Treasury boss really was. That, like Hamilton under

11. See Coxe to Henry Miller, June 17, 21, 1794, to Hamilton, June 27, 1794, Hamilton to Coxe, June 27, 1794, Coxe Papers.

12. Coxe to Miller, Feb. 20, 1795, Letters of Commr. of Rev., 1795–1797, R.G. 58; Coxe to John Taylor, Jan. 10, 1798, Coxe to Miller, Dec. 30, 1795, Coxe Papers.

similar circumstances, he chose to accomplish his object obliquely suggests either that Coxe was a formidable antagonist or that Coxe's political support appeared stronger than the written record reveals.

In early July, Wolcott notified Coxe that responsibility for preparing reports on the nation's exports was being shifted from the commissioner's office, to which Hamilton had assigned it, to the register's.[13] Though seemingly a trivial administrative change, it was to Coxe an underhanded and deliberate attempt to whittle down his own and his office's importance and to deprive him of raw material he considered indispensable for his writings on economics. He did not accept the decision tamely. Since "the statements of Exports" had been "uniformly rendered by this office from the first establishment of it to the latest period," Coxe complained to Wolcott, the discontinuance of the responsibility would "carry an appearance to the Legislature and Executive Departments and indeed to the community in general of a disinclination or incapacity to perform my duties as usual" and would be a serious "wound to my reputation as an Officer." Perhaps Wolcott did wish to inflict such a wound, though he based his refusal to reconsider the decision on the grounds that the task was merely clerical and that Coxe should be happy to be relieved of it.[14]

From this grew the spreading distrust that soon enveloped the Treasury Department's top officials. The secretary believed that Coxe could do no right; the commissioner of the revenue thought Wolcott was a myopic provincial intent on undermining the national interest by persecuting one of its leading proponents. That neither man would yield seemed certain, yet Wolcott hesitated to dislodge the Philadelphian, largely because the tradition of party loyalty and party patronage was hardly begun.

In the meantime, Coxe cultivated those he viewed as "true federalists," a vague and elastic term covering inveterate foes of what was generally regarded as Federalism—men like Jefferson, Edward Livingston of New York, and his old friend John Dickinson of Delaware, like himself a neo-Republican, as well as regular Federalists like Robert G. Harper and Timothy Pickering.[15] With Pickering, who was appointed secretary of war in January 1795 and secretary of state seven months later, Coxe sought to establish the same type of relationship he had enjoyed with Jefferson. In

13. Previously, customs officials had submitted to Coxe statistics on only the amount of exports from their districts; all other returns were submitted to the office of the comptroller. The communication by which Wolcott informed Coxe of this change in policy has not been found, but see Coxe to Wolcott, July 13, 1796, Coxe to Collectors of the Revenue of Impost and Tonnage, July 19, 1796, Letters of Commr. of Rev., 1795–1797, R.G. 58.

14. Coxe to Wolcott, July 13, 1796, *ibid.*; Wolcott to Coxe, July 15, 1796, Wolcott Papers.

15. See Thomas Jefferson to Coxe, June 1, 1795, July 10, 1796, Jefferson Papers, Lib. of Cong.; Edward Livingston to Coxe, May 18, 31, 1797, John Dickinson to Coxe, May 4, 1797, Coxe to Robert G. Harper, Apr. 23, 1796, Coxe Papers.

view of his and Pickering's long personal association and partnership in land speculation, he had good reason to believe that he would succeed. Coxe later recalled that he had often endeavored to moderate the New Englander's political "ardor" and had "placed a great dependence" on Pickering's "intercourse with, and friendship and confidence in me." Convinced that this native Yankee was outside the circle of New England monarchists who, Coxe believed, sought to control the administration, Coxe relayed to him reports from his own correspondents on affairs in Britain, France, the West Indies, and Louisiana. Of these informants the most observant was Coxe's brother Daniel, who during the course of a long business trip to New Orleans in the spring of 1797 sent Tench reports on Spanish-American affairs, some of which the latter confidentially transmitted to Pickering.[16] The secretary of state was appreciative, but if for that reason Coxe believed Pickering would protect him against reprisals by other New England Federalists, he was grievously mistaken.

Following Coxe's slashing attacks on John Adams during the presidential contest, no loyal Federalist, much less a prominent member of the administration, was likely to intercede on the commissioner's behalf. This was apparent to everyone except Coxe, who even believed that once the campaign was over, Adams would forgive all and resume friendly relations with him. Whatever the early sources of his behavior (and one is entitled to speculate that it had to do with exceptional parental indulgence), Coxe acted as if any offense he had commited would be charitably forgiven without even a token show of contrition. Presumably he also believed that to call attention to his talent was to obviate the need for remorse. In any event, he was persuaded that the way to reingratiate himself with Adams was to display his public-spiritedness and mastery of national and international affairs by submitting to the new president, as he once had to Washington's secretary of state, essay-like letters. This he did a month after Adams's

---

16. *Aurora*, Nov. 1, 1800. In Aug. and Sept. 1795 Coxe submitted his ideas on Spanish-American relations to Timothy Pickering, recommending various ways by which the United States might secure concessions from Spain and increased trading privileges with the Spanish West Indies. Coxe to Pickering, Aug. 31, Sept. 1, 1795, Coxe Papers. In 1797 Coxe transmitted to the secretary information received from Daniel W. Coxe on Spanish activities in New Orleans. Coxe to Pickering, Oct. 4, 24, 27, 1797, Pickering Papers, Mass. Hist. Soc., Boston. In the spring of 1796 Coxe sent to Pickering and President Washington a letter he had received from "General Rochambeau the younger." He had known Rochambeau, Coxe explained, "during his late residence in Philadelphia," where the Frenchman "often manifested to me a concern for the preservation of harmony between the two countries." Coxe to George Washington, June 14, 1796, Coxe Papers. In two letters written from Paris in Feb. and Mar. 1796 (one dated Feb. 18 and one undated), Rochambeau had described to Coxe the unfavorable reaction of the French public to Jay's Treaty. The treaty, Rochambeau said, would wreck Franco-American commercial relations, causing France "to consider America as a British possession." *Ibid.* Pickering gratefully acknowledged Rochambeau's letters, of which, with Coxe's permission, he kept copies. Pickering to Coxe, June 16, Oct. 18, 1796, *ibid.*

inauguration, enclosing in a private letter a long article on Franco-American affairs. The article was cast in the form of seven questions "concerning the possible grounds of dissatisfaction on the part of France against the United States."[17] The implicit and self-evident answers added up to a spirited defense of French policy and a recommendation that the president preserve peace by dispatching a personal envoy to iron out difficulties with America's Revolutionary War ally. Although he intended to do just that, Adams must have been startled at this unsolicited advice from a man who had only recently lambasted him as the chief of a pro-British monarchical faction. Whether surprised or not, he passed over the letter in silence, perhaps unwilling to dignify Coxe's presumption by an answer.

Naively expecting a type of charity Adams was incapable of exercising, Coxe was disappointed not only by this rebuff but also by his exclusion from presidential social functions. After his election, Adams never once, Coxe complained a few years later, "asked me even in the routine of official entertainment to his table though he had asked me when I supported his election with the most distinguished people in our country, both native and foreign."[18] Perhaps for once an indirect signal came through clearly. For Coxe, thus ostracized from official society, it was a cruel spring.

Coxe decided, though only momentarily, to give up his highly prized office and even drafted a letter of resignation. Although it had been his intention to "return to private life" for some time, his polite, even deferential, letter to Adams stated, personal affairs forced him to do so sooner than expected.[19] Studiously avoiding any allusion to political differences between himself and the president, Coxe specifically attributed his decision to the crisis in his financial affairs occasioned by Thomas Ruston's unconscionable and illegal behavior. "Duty and Respect to the Government and people of the United States impel me," he concluded, to resign "before I shall sustain the harsh measure which is to be dispensed to me."[20] The letter was no sooner written than Coxe changed his mind, perhaps because he decided that he might not go bankrupt after all, perhaps because he could not bring himself to abandon public office. The decision not to resign was unfortunate. In view of the events of the next six months, he would have been

17. Coxe to John Adams, Apr. 5, 1797, McHenry Papers, Lib. of Cong. Coxe's expectation of forgiveness was the more unrealistic in view of his continued attacks on Adams, attacks that the president was surely aware of. Shortly after Adams's election, to give one example, Coxe sent to the members of the Pennsylvania legislature an account of Adams's alleged support of Connecticut claimants to the lands in dispute between the settlers of that state and of Pennsylvania. "To the Editor," *Aurora*, Nov. 1, 1800.

18. "To the Editor," *Aurora*, Nov. 1, 1800.

19. He had considered resigning as early as Jan. 1797. See James Swan to Coxe, Jan. 21, 1797, Coxe Papers.

20. Coxe to John Adams, n.d., endorsed "not sent," *ibid.*

spared personal and public humiliation by voluntarily relinquishing a post from which Wolcott was determined to drive him.

The Treasury secretary's resolve was clearly the consequence of his resentment of the Pennsylvanian's declaration of political allegiance to Thomas Jefferson. Aware that his department could operate efficiently only as long as the relationship of the secretary with the commissioner was based on mutual respect and trust, Wolcott became far more conscious following the election of 1796 that Coxe lacked precisely these traits. Had the secretary been somewhat less staunchly self-righteous, he might have recognized that it was not so much Coxe's official conduct as his political views that were insufferable to him. But even this would not have palliated the crudely underhanded manner by which he sought to coerce the Philadelphian into resigning. Lacking craftiness, Wolcott revealed himself to be merely peevish.

By the early spring of 1797 Wolcott was at last ready to trap this Pennsylvania fox. In the course of a routine conference on lighthouse affairs, as Coxe was calmly and politely replying to a seemingly routine question, Wolcott, according to Coxe, "broke out into the most unexpected declarations that my light House communications were crude and undigested." When Coxe, "greatly surprized," requested some specific examples, the secretary instead of replying angrily retorted that he would make a representation to the president.[21] This was only the beginning. Having decided to rid himself of Coxe, Wolcott had no difficulty in uncovering what he construed as instances of arrogance, deviousness, calculated rudeness, political disloyalty, and official incompetence. In all but the last, his suspicions may have contained the proverbial grain of truth, but he conveniently overlooked the possibility that if Coxe was guilty as charged, his own retention of him in office for more than two years made him an accessory after the fact.

Wolcott pursued Coxe with a ferocity that made Hamilton's tactics of the winter of 1794/1795 appear tame. Every letter or report from Coxe's office was microscopically examined for evidence of misconduct and insubordination; the slightest rumor of Coxe's misdeeds passed on by fellow Federalists (particularly if from Connecticut) was taken as conclusive proof of wrongdoing. Coxe, angered by the secretary's sudden assault, fought back, sometimes defending himself, sometimes counterattacking. "It is true,"

21. Coxe to Wolcott, Nov. 3, 1797, *ibid.*; *Aurora*, Nov. 1, 1800. Coxe later recalled that "but a few months after Mr. Adams'" election, "I calmly challenged the representation," observing that throughout his Treasury career he "had made a long and diversified series of reports and applications, upon the business in question, to or through President Washington and secretary Hamilton, President Adams and Wolcott, every one of which had been confirmed by the President of the time, with few or no alterations, and with a very few slight observations." Wolcott, Coxe said, "was driven from the ground without a word, but I saw in his representations at the President's, my ideal faults were all to be remembered." *Aurora*, Nov. 1, 1800.

he understatedly confessed some months later, "that to his indecency and insults I have not replied with an absolute tameness." He might as well have, for his defense, whether mild or impassioned, was futile.[22] Wolcott held all the trumps, while Coxe's own hand (which he mistakenly believed to be strengthened by strong congressional support) was defenseless. That he refused to believe this was a result of his conviction that as long as he continued properly to perform his public duty, he was invulnerable.[23]

Wolcott knew better, and by the time he left the capital in mid-July 1797 for a Connecticut vacation, he had convinced himself that Coxe's misdeeds were not to be viewed as isolated instances of official indiscretion but as parts of an elaborately contrived plan to defy his authority and publicly to discredit his administration of the Treasury Department.[24] This would be the theme of a fifty-page bill of complaint in which he described the figures Coxe had woven into a carpet of intrigue and deceit.

In the meantime, Coxe, still deep in self-deception, resolved to remind vacationing officials like the Treasury secretary of his superior dedication to duty by remaining at his desk. But the almost insufferably hot and humid weather of Philadelphia in late summer soon caused him to regret the decision, the more so since it appeared likely to make him a martyr, literally as well as figuratively. During the sultry days of early August there were frightening accounts of cases of the dreaded yellow fever; by the middle of the month these had reached epidemic proportions, and, as during the plagues of 1793, 1795, and 1796, thousands of people boarded their doors and joined the familiar exodus. By official proclamation streets where the pestilence raged were barricaded, houses inhabited by fever victims displayed yellow flags, adjoining residences were vacated, and the stricken were, when possible, transported out of the city.

"The Solemn stillness is truly affecting," wrote one of few remaining residents. "The Hearse is become a principal object in our Streets, a dreadful note of preparation."[25] Soon the capital was a ghost town—the War Office had moved to the falls of the Schuylkill, the State Department to Trenton, and the Treasury, except for the commissioner's office, to Gray's Ferry. Still Coxe remained, ignoring the pleas of his family that he immediately leave for the country. William Coxe, Sr., ever the sternly blunt patri-

22. Coxe to John Taylor, Jan. 10, 1798, Coxe Papers. The futility of Coxe's defense was attested (had Coxe been willing to credit the evidence) by a rumor that Timothy Pickering in the course of a conversation held during the summer of 1797 had commented that the members of the Adams administration "did not like" Coxe's "politics," that they "wished to get rid" of him, and that they then "did not know how but that they were determined to get rid" of him. *Aurora*, Nov. 1, 1800.

23. *Aurora*, Nov. 1, 1800.

24. Wolcott to Coxe, July 13, 1797, Wolcott Papers.

25. John Mease to Coxe, Sept. 3, 1797, Coxe Papers.

arch, had no sympathy with such stubbornness. "When thousands have left the City, when your own offices have left it a week, . . . when a Wife and eight helpless Children must be left to an unfeeling World, when aged Parents . . . think you acting the madman," he wrote to his son on August 30 from his new home in Burlington, New Jersey, "you obstinately reject all means for your personal safety." "Mortify me with no more Letters from the City, but remove instantly." Coxe promptly obeyed and removed his office for a little over two weeks to join the Treasury Department at Gray's Ferry.[26]

On September 3 Wolcott returned from Connecticut to Gray's Ferry. Having brooded over the subject for a month, he chose as his first order of business to bring his contumacious revenue commissioner to heel. Day after day Coxe was summoned to a conference in the cramped quarters of the secretary's office; here Wolcott presented, piece by piece, the evidence he had accumulated of Coxe's refractory behavior: Coxe had misinterpreted the excise law, he had repeatedly bypassed Wolcott by issuing unauthorized instructions, he had misrepresented the affairs of the internal revenue service, he had gratuitously badgered the secretary about affairs that were not his concern, and he had obstinately refused to carry out orders. Since the bulk of Coxe's records were still in Philadelphia, he could not promptly produce the records demanded or be expected to remember the precise contents of his many circular and other letters.[27] Wolcott surely knew this. But the inaccessibility of Coxe's papers did not matter. During the humid days of September and on into the following month, Wolcott gave what time he could spare from all but the most pressing Treasury business to the preparation of a damning recital of Coxe's misconduct. His desk cluttered with the records he had painstakingly amassed, he drafted page after page, his anger mounting as he wrote. By the time the secretary left Gray's Ferry for Philadelphia, his pamphlet-length arraignment was completed and turned over to a clerk for copying.

"I find myself compelled by considerations of duty and self respect," Wolcott began his letter of October 14, to express "my entire disapprobation" of the "general scope and complexion" of Coxe's conduct. Although conceding that any one incident "separately considered would appear of slight importance," he was convinced that "on a collective view . . . the evidence of premeditation" on Coxe's part would "justify my animadver-

---

26. William Coxe, Sr., to Coxe, Aug. 22, 30, 1797, Wolcott to Coxe, Oct. 14, 1797, *ibid.*

27. Coxe remained in Philadelphia until Aug. 29. Mease to Coxe, Aug. 30, 1797, *ibid.* He left Gray's Ferry for Burlington on Sept. 10. Wolcott to Coxe, Nov. 6, 1797, *ibid.* William Coxe, Jr., made arrangements in Burlington for his brother's office by renting quarters from the trustees of the local academy. William Coxe, Jr., to Coxe, Sept. 7, 1797, *ibid.* See also Coxe to unknown recipient, Sept. 6, 1797, *ibid.*

sions." Since he had obviously decided in advance what his investigation of Coxe's record would reveal, he had no difficulty selecting incidents that were germane to his case and then so interpreting them as to prove the preconceived guilt. He made in all six specific charges, describing each in great detail and exhibiting, where possible, copious and carefully chosen extracts from Coxe's letters.[28]

The first accusation involved the delinquency of an inspector of the revenue in Massachusetts. Wolcott, without consulting his commissioner of the revenue, had taken steps to correct the situation, and Coxe, indignant at being officially bypassed, had demanded that he be given copies of all the secretary's correspondence on the subject. Wolcott considered his second charge to be more serious. Although too technical to allow an intelligible précis, it involved presidential "acts" or plans governing the organization and regulation of the internal revenue service and alleged that there was "no colour of authority" for Coxe's queries to subordinates about the legality of supervisors of the revenue doubling as inspectors. Item three was manifestly dictated by Wolcott's pique at the commissioner's supposedly persistent efforts to flout his superior's authority. This petty accusation was that Coxe had presumed to send to his subordinates copies of a bill still pending in Congress, along with comments on the measure's provisions. Wolcott's fourth complaint was related to Coxe's administration of the nation's lighthouses; he charged that the revenue commissioner had been remiss and then arrogant when replying to the secretary's questions about machinery purchased abroad. The fifth allegation, like the second, centered on what was essentially an administrative technicality. At issue was Wolcott's interpretation of a section of an act of March 1797 that had made changes in the rules governing the collection of the license fees and taxes on distilled spirits, an interpretation that Coxe disputed. The last and the flimsiest in Wolcott's perfervidly exaggerated catalog of charges was that Coxe had attempted to gloss over the "deplorable want of system and energy in the Office of the Supervisor and Inspectors" for Pennsylvania and thus shielded the flagrant misconduct of Supervisor Henry Miller.

The conclusion of Wolcott's star-chamber proceeding was an impassioned defense of his discharge of the heavy burdens of the secretaryship and a slashing attack on Coxe's obstructionist conduct. Question followed question, though to each Wolcott would accept from Coxe only a negative answer. "I ask, has your Office been conducted upon proper and reasonable

---

28. Wolcott to Coxe, Oct. 14, 1797, *ibid.* The letters that Coxe wrote Wolcott have not been found and probably never will be, since the commissioner of revenue's letterbook for the period between Mar. 29, 1797, and Dec. 1797 is missing. However, Wolcott's long letter of Oct. 14, 1797, summarizes and makes references to nine of Coxe's letters. *Ibid.*

principles? Is it right that you should avail yourself of the peculiar nature of your duties . . . to cast burdens upon me? Is it fair, that instead of diminishing my cares . . . you should perplex me by a conduct so unconciliating, metaphysical, and incongruous as I have described?" As he answered each question for himself his indignation intensified. "Sir! things must not be so," he angrily exclaimed. Although Coxe could scarcely have missed the point, Wolcott made it pellucid: "I now announce to you a determination which is immutable; your official deportment must essentially change; while I retain my present Office, I will be in fact as well as in name Secretary of the Treasury; you shall not direct my conduct; on the contrary I will direct yours. . . . I will receive no bifaced, indigested communications; the records of your Office must exhibit nothing disrespectful or tending to criminate my Conduct."

It was an ultimatum the most insensitive reader should have understood, and the only sensible response was resignation. But as Coxe, sitting in a rented schoolroom in Burlington, where he had temporarily established his office, read it, his almost insupportable anger was replaced by obstinacy. Stunned by the savageness of the assault, he lost the capacity to exercise sound judgment and chose instead to contest the inevitable. Should a conscientious and competent public servant like himself, he asked, silently accept the accusation that his conduct had bordered on the criminal? He thought not. Allowing his pique to dictate to his judgment, Coxe promptly began drafting a detailed defense against each of Wolcott's charges. The first installment was written in Burlington, but it was necessary, he decided, to be on the spot in Philadelphia, especially since his official records were there.

Learning from one of his clerks on October 24 that "the yellow fever was abating" and that "this days rain and cold will be a further inducement for returning," Coxe hurriedly oversaw the packing of his files. By October 27 he was on his way to the capital city, having arranged for his children to attend school in Germantown and reluctantly leaving his wife, who was slowly recovering from a long illness.[29] Once Coxe was back at his desk in Philadelphia, his characteristic sanguineness, bolstered by confidence in the persuasiveness of his pen, allowed him conveniently to overlook the fact that Wolcott's accusations—based on personal animosity and filled with casuistry—were unanswerable on any rational grounds. This strategic blunder was followed by a tactical one: instead of a single, carefully considered rebuttal, he hurriedly dashed off letter after letter, randomly replying to one or another of the accusations, each letter providing Wolcott with yet another pretext for firing him.

29. Mease to Coxe, Oct. 24, 1797, *ibid.*; Coxe to Pickering, Oct. 27, 1797, Pickering Papers; Rebecca Coxe to Coxe, Nov. 5, 1797, Coxe Papers.

There were "expressions in your letter," Coxe explained in his letter of October 18, "which are at least liable to be construed into imputations of intended breaches of public duty and morality" and "cannot remain unexplained and unanswered upon the files of the Treasury Department" (thus repeating to Wolcott what Hamilton three years previously had said to Coxe). In this first installment of his defense Coxe centered on the accusation that he had willfully misinterpreted the excise law, the fifth of Wolcott's charges. The burden of his defense was an account of conversations between himself and Wolcott that the latter had overlooked in his letter of October 14 and an assertion that he had never questioned the authority of the secretary of the Treasury to make the final decision on all legal issues, no matter what his own views.[30]

The second installment followed three days later and was a lengthy rebuttal to Wolcott's second charge that his instructions respecting the conjoined duties of supervisor and inspector had been unauthorized and mistaken. The conciliatory tone of Coxe's first letter was now replaced by an air of injured innocence. What had been done was "perfectly at my discretion," Coxe affirmed. Had he failed to take cognizance of a defect in the rules governing the revenue service, it was his "calm and sincere" conviction that he "should have been to blame for any ill consequences." Anyway, by what right did Wolcott presume to censure him for conforming to precedents "well-known" and "higher" than the secretary's opinion? Why did Wolcott never mention the subject to Coxe prior to his letter of October 14? The secretary's "insinuations" that he had been misled by Coxe were, in sum, "entirely unfounded."[31]

And so it went. In a letter of November 3 Coxe responded to the allegation that he had flouted Wolcott's authority when he had unilaterally made arrangements for the country's lighthouses. The revenue commissioner claimed that in this sphere he exercised administrative discretion authorized by statute and legally conferred by Hamilton.[32] Such indeed were the facts. But nothing that Coxe could say in explanation of his conduct (which revealed at its worst nothing more serious than occasional official carelessness and personal arrogance) was of any use. And it was for this reason that his defense was lackluster and halfhearted. Even so, his counterattack was tailor-made for Wolcott's purposes.

As if enough could not be said of Coxe's misdeeds, Wolcott submitted

---

30. Coxe to Wolcott, Oct. 18, 1797, Coxe Papers.

31. Coxe to Wolcott, Oct. 21, 1797, *ibid.*

32. Coxe to Wolcott, Nov. 3, 1797, *ibid.* By the end of the first week in Nov., Coxe interrupted his defense in order to prepare a report on internal revenues requested earlier by the House of Representatives. Coxe to Wolcott, Nov. 10, 1797, *ibid.*

detailed rejoinders to each of the rebuttals. They added little substance to his case against Coxe but rather confirmed the unalterable judgment he had rendered on October 14: Coxe was a Philadelphia Jesuit whose every statement was "hypercritical" and devious, whose sole purpose was to discredit him by bald misrepresentation or insidious innuendo. Wolcott was undisturbed by his own exemplification of the very traits he attributed to Coxe, and his tortuous logic and prolix recital of the facts of a case he had already judged suggest that he was more intent on convincing himself than Coxe.

It did not take him long. A twelve-page letter of November 6 was designed to prove Coxe was "evasive and disrespectful"; on November 9 eighteen pages were required to reach the anticlimactic declaration that "with whatever levity or sophistry you think fit to treat my remarks, I will convince you that I am serious, and in earnest. On the return of the President, I shall therefore make our late correspondence the basis of a representation against you, *for deliberate misconduct in Office.*"[33] Neither the Treasury secretary nor the revenue commissioner could have had many hours to spare for official business. Indeed, if the efficient operation of the Treasury demanded much time from its principal officers, the national interest was the innocent victim of this official war. Nevertheless, Coxe continued battling Wolcott, who gladly stayed in the ring.

Although Coxe was too dazed to realize it, the secretary had already dealt a knockout blow. The exchange of correspondence, which Wolcott had promptly transmitted to Adams on his return to Philadelphia on November 25, was, in turn, submitted to a review board composed of Wolcott's cabinet colleagues, Timothy Pickering, James McHenry, and Charles Lee—all of whom were virtually certain to back up a fellow cabinet member and to give the president the opinion he surely wished.[34] They were even more partisan than was necessary. Ignoring Coxe's defense, they merely summarized the case for the prosecution and thus easily reached the decision that Wolcott "has just cause of complaint . . . occasioned by the improper conduct of the Commissioner of the Revenue." They concluded that "there is sufficient reason for Mr. Coxe's dismission from office; and we

33. Wolcott to Coxe, Nov. 6, 9, 1797, *ibid.* Coxe replied to this letter on Nov. 10: "The notice you have given me of your intention to charge me before the President with deliberate misconduct in Office gives me none of those agitations which the consciousness of real misconduct would excite." *Ibid.*

34. On Nov. 29 Wolcott wrote to Coxe that their exchange of correspondence "relative to your Official conduct" had "been by me laid before the President" and that if Coxe had any further comments to make, he should forward them immediately for transmission to Adams. Wolcott to Coxe, Nov. 29, 1797, *ibid.* Coxe immediately applied to Wolcott for a copy of the charges. "I learned with astonishment," he later recalled, that the charges "had been made orally and that copies of my unfinished defensive course of letters were delivered as evidence." *Aurora*, Nov. 1, 1800.

think the public good requires it."[35] Despite the ex parte proceedings, they were perhaps sincerely convinced of their verdict. Nevertheless, at least one of them, Timothy Pickering, Coxe's longtime friend and business partner, may well have had a momentary sense of misgiving. One would hope so, for otherwise not even the saving grace of charity relieves the stereotyped picture of this stern, insensitive, and self-righteous Yankee.

John Adams had no misgivings. He promptly authorized the resolution of an issue that had never really been in doubt. "The President of the United States has directed me to inform you that having determined to make a new appointment to the Office of Commissioner of the Revenue your services are no longer required," Wolcott gloatingly wrote to Coxe on December 23.[36] Although he could scarcely have been surprised, Coxe's reaction was predictable: rather than silently suffer a humiliating public defeat, he would take arms against his opponent and with the help of highly placed public officials slay him.

Incredibly, Coxe first turned to Adams, even though the president had been, in Coxe's words, "as silent as the grave" to a previous appeal. Overlooking the manifest evidence that Adams was only slightly less antagonistic than Wolcott, Coxe convinced himself that the man he had recently accused of monarchism would exercise his kingly prerogative and assure him a fair hearing. He was certain, so he later explained, "that Mr. Adams was duped into my removal by several persons operating upon his feelings, in regard to my opposition to his election."[37] Since few people then or since have credited John Adams with selflessness, it was an extraordinary compliment. More remarkable yet were the means by which Coxe hoped to enlighten this would-be king. "It will be of public Utility that you should see a letter of the late Secretary of the Treasury to the present Secretary of the Treasury of 1794 under which the latter undertook to act contrary to the

35. Timothy Pickering, James McHenry, and Charles Lee to John Adams, Dec. 18, 1797, Adams Papers, Mass. Hist. Soc., Boston. On the same day Coxe submitted a final installment of his defense, this one dealing with the revenue service in Pennsylvania. Wolcott replied to this letter on Dec. 19, 1797, stating that it had been forwarded to the president. Coxe Papers. Also on Dec. 18 Coxe began to draft another letter on the same subject. Since the draft (Coxe Papers) is incomplete and since no finished copy is in the Wolcott or Adams Papers, it must not have been submitted. Instead he sent to Wolcott an unfound letter requesting permission to inspect all of the papers he had submitted as revenue commissioner to the secretary's office. Wolcott curtly turned down the request. Wolcott to Coxe, Dec. 19, 1797, Coxe Papers. Yet another letter was begun on Dec. 19 and handed over to a clerk for copying on Dec. 21. The copy is unfinished, presumably because Coxe, having learned that he had already been fired, saw no need to transmit it. *Ibid.*

36. Wolcott to Coxe, Dec. 19, 1797, *ibid.*

37. *Aurora*, Nov. 1, 1800. Coxe had written to Adams on Dec. 2, requesting a copy of Wolcott's "representation" against him and information on the letters the Treasury secretary had submitted to the president. Coxe to Adams, Dec. 2, 1797, Coxe Papers.

expressed intentions of the legislature," Coxe wrote to Adams a few hours after receiving his letter of dismissal.[38] The president should also know that in August 1797 Wolcott had acted with similar illegality by designating the comptroller to serve as temporary head of the Treasury. If Coxe was implicitly appealing to Adams to bury the past, he was asking that another do what he himself was singularly incapable of. Here was a replay of the Hamilton-Washington scenario of January 1795; here an assumption that Adams might heed what Washington had ignored; here an instance of skewed judgment that might have startled even those who were already unmitigatedly hostile to Coxe.

Most staunch Federalists greeted Coxe's dismissal with satisfaction. George Cabot spoke for them when he congratulated Wolcott on finally having expelled "a traitor from the treasury, who never deserved to have been trusted." To have tolerated "such a fellow in office after his duplicity was known," the former Massachusetts senator admonished, had been a demonstration of appalling "weakness in the government." To Coxe's fellow Republicans, however, his expulsion was clearly an act of political retaliation, though they did not necessarily agree with the former revenue commissioner that it was an unalloyed blunder. Jefferson expressed the Republican viewpoint when he remarked to James Monroe that "the dismission of Tench Coxe from office without any reason assigned is considered one of the bold acts of the President. Tant mieux."[39] To Coxe, who craved personal vindication, such a lofty attitude was impossible. Once he realized that Adams would in no way help him, he decided to wield some of the influence he believed he had stored up in Congress over the preceding years. Coxe was convinced that the many congressmen for whom he had done favors would not sit idly by and allow a man like Wolcott, manifestly less talented and less politically important than himself, to treat him so shabbily. But they did just that, despite Coxe's petitions praying a scrutiny of his official conduct, despite his efforts to undermine the credibility of his accusers by offering public proof of their own alleged illegal official behavior, and despite his charge that he "had been offered up as the first sacrifice" to the "designs of the monarchists," particularly their ringleader, John Adams.[40]

38. Coxe to Adams, Dec. 23, 1797, Coxe Papers.

39. George Cabot to Wolcott, Jan. 19, 1798, Gibbs, ed., *Memoirs of Administrations of Washington and Adams*, II, 9; Jefferson to James Monroe, Dec. 27, 1797, Ford, ed., *Works of Jefferson*, VIII, 351–352. See also Jefferson to James Madison, Jan. 3, 1798, Ford, ed., *Works of Jefferson*, VIII, 356. A number of Coxe's Federalist friends did express indignation at the treatment accorded him. See, for example, John Neville to Coxe, Jan. 8, 1798, Moore Furman to Coxe, Jan. 17, 1798, Francis Corbin to Coxe, Feb. 20, 1798, Coxe Papers.

40. *Freeman's Jour.*, June 12, 1804. Coxe voiced his charges against his accusers in a letter to the House of Representatives, Dec. 26, 1797, *Annals of Cong.*, VII, 775. The charges were printed in Claypoole's *American Daily Advertiser* (Philadelphia), Dec. 28, 1797, and reprinted

Far from investigating such charges, Coxe's supposed congressional allies would doubtless have endorsed Jefferson's cryptic response to his friend's dismissal: "Tant mieux." His father-in-law was more explicit. Commenting on a letter Coxe had written to Pennsylvania's congressmen, Charles Coxe wrote: "I don't See what end it can answer. . . . According to the vulgar Sailer House it may be truely said you have no more chance than a Cat in Hell without claws."[41]

Coxe's pen was indeed blunted. By mid-February even a man with his self-assurance could no longer sustain the belief he expressed a month earlier that his "standing with the republican part of the federal interest throughout the union" enabled him to represent "all important truths and arguments" to the "hearts and understandings of his political allies."[42] Instead, the fog of his complacency, all along flecked with anxiety, now lifted and was completely blown away by yet another public humiliation. This was the selection of a virtually unknown fellow Pennsylvanian to succeed him as commissioner.[43] It was consoling, however, that this final affront prodded a number of his congressional allies into action. Jonathan Williams, Coxe's longtime business ally and friend, introduced a resolution calling for the abolition of the office of commissioner of the revenue, defending this proposal in debate by consulting notes supplied by Coxe.[44] Supported by most of the Pennsylvania delegation, the move, though unsuccessful, was, as Adams's congressional partisans perceived, an oblique attempt to vindicate Coxe.

Coxe was now cheered by any show of support at all, for instead of the congressional and public sympathy he had confidently expected, he had been drenched in newspaper abuse. The lead was taken by *Porcupine's Gazette*. Here the familiar story of his youthful toryism was gleefully retold and his demand for an investigation repeatedly mocked. "It is reported Citizen Coxe is preparing a very heavy octavo . . . in defense of his official conduct," the editor, William Cobbett, commented on January 17. "We shall, no doubt, see a curious specimen of the sophistical reasoning of this plausible casuist." The members of Congress, recognizing that they "have no more to do with his dismissal than the chiefs of the Cherokee nation,"

---

in other newspapers. See also Jonathan Dayton to Coxe, Dec. 27, 1797, Coxe to Dayton, Dec. 27, 1797, Coxe to John Taylor, Jan. 10, 1798, Taylor to Coxe, Feb. 1, 1798, Coxe to Pennsylvania members of Congress, Jan. 24, 1798, Coxe Papers. At Coxe's request, his letter to the House of Representatives was published in the *Philadelphia Gaz.*, Jan. 26, 1798.

41. Charles Coxe to Coxe, Feb. 9, 1798, Coxe Papers.

42. Coxe to John Taylor, Jan. 10, 1798, *ibid.*

43. William Miller was appointed commissioner on Feb. 1, 1798, and served to Dec. 31, 1803.

44. *Annals of Cong.*, VII, 784, 801, 841–842. A draft of Coxe's notes is in the Coxe Papers.

have "left him to his fate," the editor chortled two weeks later, recommending that Coxe use his newly gained leisure time "to write us an elegant and minute description of General Howe's triumphant entry into Philadelphia." Such attacks were the more galling because of the refusal of Cobbett and of the *Gazette of the United States*, where Coxe had once been a favorite columnist, to print the articles he wrote in his defense.[45]

But as he had repeatedly demonstrated, Coxe was remarkably resilient. Personal attacks sharpened his belief that his assailants were motivated by both relentless hostility to the virtuous ideas he personified and jealousy of his indisputable talent. "Was not the road open before him to the highest honours of the state?" he asked some years later. "His talents as a financier, and his knowledge" of the American economy had been acknowledged even by his enemies. "If he had studied self-interest and private ambition; or preferred his own aggrandizement to the glory and honor of his country, he had only . . . to bend the knee at the shrine of John Adams, and the highest honours awaited him."[46] Although the latter claim was patently false, Coxe's pride in the possession of talents and knowledge that Adams and Wolcott refused to credit was not far off the mark, as they soon would learn. In ridding themselves of a personally objectionable official, they had unwittingly created a full-time Republican party organizer and an effective partisan publicist who would measurably contribute to the defeat of the Federalist party. In the meantime, Coxe was preoccupied by measures to forestall the loss of the hundreds of thousands of acres of land he had purchased during his years as a federal official.

45. *Porcupine's Gazette* (Philadelphia), Jan. 17, Feb. 1, 1798. See drafts of articles addressed to the "Gazette of the United States," n.d. and Mar. 1798, Coxe Papers.
46. *Aurora*, Nov. 19, 1800.

16 🪢

Land Entrepreneur and Litigant

Coxe's big plunge into land speculation came during the relatively short period from 1792 to 1796, although earlier he had made extensive land purchases in Pennsylvania and elsewhere.[1] He was not alone. Thousands of other investors, large and small, were caught up in the land boom that commenced in the early 1790s and that over the next few years became an orgy of speculation, nowhere wilder than in Pennsylvania. The frenzy was not confined to that commonwealth, but the stakes for which the gamesters of Pennsylvania played—millions and millions of acres of land —were extraordinarily high, and the subsequent bankruptcies were precipitate and numerous.

Coxe could not, of course, foresee the result of events, impersonal and personal, that would soon shove him to the brink of bankruptcy. But even during the years of the great land boom, a more prudent man might have perceived that to gamble so extravagantly on so slender a bank account was sheer madness. But blinded by the bright dream of well-peopled, prosperous farms where once had been unsettled backlands, he mortgaged the present for the future and continued his reckless speculations. His obsession with this fantasy was nowhere better revealed than in the figures he jotted down on hundreds of letters on as many subjects. Although the precise transactions to which they referred are indeterminable, the thou-

1. Coxe's correspondence involving his numerous land deals is so voluminous that to provide full annotation would require as many pages of notes as of text. The details of the various speculations that are briefly summarized in this chapter can be followed in the bulky land correspondence and documents in the Coxe Papers. Important supplementary material is in the Ephraim Kirby Papers, Duke University, Durham, N.C.

sands of doodles clearly related to acres acquired or dreamed of, to projected profits, and to money owed.

Pennsylvania's land boom was launched by a single piece of legislation, a law passed in April 1792. This act, later to bedevil Coxe as secretary of the state Land Office from 1799 to 1801, opened to sale for twenty cents per acre five million acres of state lands in what were then Allegheny and Northumberland counties. Although ostensibly designed to protect actual settlers, the bill included loopholes big enough for even giant speculators to walk through. This mischievous measure merely whetted speculative appetites, which were further sharpened by a number of related developments. Credit was easy; stocks were rising; steady population growth was predicted; the dreaded Indian threat in the state was all but erased; internal improvements were making possible the transportation of tides of settlers to the backcountry; the war then raging in Europe seemed to promise an expanding agricultural prosperity; and, as more and more land was brought under cultivation, the extension of the area of settlement seemed virtually limitless. All these things led to the conviction that the demand for lands would rapidly accelerate, bringing a sharp rise in their value.[2] Irresistibly lured by such an enticing reward, land speculators swarmed like bees around a honeycomb to the Pennsylvania Land Office.

None was more dazzled by the prospect of quick riches and the magic of steadily rising land prices than Coxe. A week or so after passage of the law of April 3, 1792, he wrote to William S. Smith, John Adams's son-in-law and himself an incurable big-time speculator, that the time was ripe for launching ambitious projects. "If your friends in Europe have a mind to go into this thing," he proposed, "I will proceed with them upon this plan—I will be interested in the general concern as far as 20,000 acres . . . provided they will furnish the money for the whole." Coxe was to be designated agent and take a 5 percent commission payable in lands. That he was in an advantageous position to serve potential investors was suggested by his timely comment that he had already "engaged several of the authorized Surveyors to make examinations of their Districts for me and to make me Statements of the situation, quality etc. of large bodies of choice lands as promptly as possible."[3] This potentially lucrative deal did not materialize, but Coxe had not confined his interest to northwestern Pennsylvania. Within a few months he had rounded up warrants to 30,000 acres in the counties of Northampton and Luzerne and duly presented them to the Land Office,

2. Between the passage of the new land law in Apr. 1792 and Feb. 1794, applications for almost 10,000,000 acres of land were received by the state, though, revealingly enough, only something over 700,000 acres had been paid for by the later date. Norman B. Wilkinson, "Land Policy and Speculation in Pennsylvania, 1779–1800" (Ph.D. diss., University of Pennsylvania, 1958), 168.

3. Coxe to William S. Smith, Apr. 12, 1792, Coxe Papers.

along with claims to much smaller acreage elsewhere in the state.

Coxe's great speculative splurge in Pennsylvania lands came in the spring of 1793. But because of his rapidly dwindling capital, a part of which he wished to reserve to support a large family that could scarcely be fed and housed on his slender official salary, he found himself obliged either to curb his growing land hunger or to find a rich partner. The search for the latter was swift and easy. Alexander Hamilton, then Coxe's boss at the Treasury Department, recommended John B. Church, the husband of Elizabeth Hamilton's sister. Having amassed a tidy sum from contracts negotiated with the French army serving in America during the Revolution and from subsequent successful speculation in French funds, Church was then leading the life of a well-to-do English gentleman. In March 1793 he came through with a loan of $5,000 and a $5,000 investment of his own, the whole to be expended in the purchase of lands jointly for himself and Coxe. In expectation of such a proposal, the Philadelphian had arranged earlier in the same month to buy about 16,000 acres of land, mostly in Northampton County, from two speculators, Blackwell W. Ball and Dr. Francis J. Smith, neither of whom was to be trusted, as Coxe would learn. But Coxe's business acumen was by now so blunted by acquisitiveness that he looked closely neither at this partnership nor at other purveyors of allegedly valuable lands. Within a month he had acquired an additional 31,000 acres from other speculators, bringing his springtime purchases for Church and himself to 47,000 acres. A few thousand of these Coxe shared with his close congressional friend William Vans Murray, who was so eager to buy them that he hazarded a trip to Philadelphia at a time when that city was in the grips of a yellow fever epidemic.[4]

The involutions of the subsequent history of the Church-Coxe partnership were complex enough to provide employment for a good number of Philadelphia lawyers. The story in oversimplified outline was this: the lands sold to Coxe by Ball and Smith were encumbered with a debt the two speculators owed to one Thomas Billington, and to snarl matters further, rival claimants disputed the right of Ball and Smith to convey the land to either Coxe or Billington. At Coxe's instigation the issue was brought before the State Board of Property in January 1794 and was decided in favor of Coxe eighteen months later. During the interim Billington had sold the lands in question to a group of speculators headed by William Bingham. The contestants agreed to submit this and other subsequent complications to arbitration. In December 1796 an award was made to Coxe. Even so, the requisite warrants, withheld for so long, were not forthcoming, and the exact location of the land was protractedly disputed. In 1808, after years of hearings and court trials, litigation was still pending in the case of *Ball* v.

4. William Vans Murray to Coxe, Sept. 1, 1793, *ibid.*

Coxe, but the dispute was soon thereafter settled. Coxe himself wrote the last word on a legal tangle that would have taxed the ingenuity of even the most expert authority on the law of real property. On August 14, 1819, he remarked in a memorandum presumably intended for his heirs: "This case finally settled in favor of T. Coxe and Co and Lands sold, settled for etc. long since."

The course of Coxe's relations with Church did not run much more smoothly. For one thing, a contract in 1794 for the sale of a part of their lands to Whelan, Miller, and Company of Philadelphia was objected to by the secretary of the Treasury, Church's attorney, and Coxe was obliged to secure a reconveyance of the bulk of the acreage thus sold. For another, Hamilton, who devoted considerable time to Church's affairs after he resigned from the Treasury in January 1795, paid particularly careful attention to a controversy involving his former assistant, whose integrity he distrusted as much as he did his politics. And as Coxe had every reason to know, Hamilton was not only a resourceful antagonist but also a singularly expert and alert lawyer. In Coxe's case Hamilton's skill was necessary, for year followed year and the money borrowed from Church remained unpaid, largely because Coxe lacked the funds and would not part with his lands. An expensive and drawn-out lawsuit was required to force him to pay the debt, which was finally settled in 1809, sixteen years after it was incurred.

Whatever Coxe may have learned from the imbroglio with Ball and Smith, the lesson was neither prudence nor caution. There may have been honest land brokers in Pennsylvania, but he was singularly unable to find them. Thus, in 1793 he contracted on his own account for extensive tracts distributed throughout the commonwealth. His most important buy was from Edward and Henry McHenry for about seventeen hundred acres in what was then Northumberland County. In view of Edward McHenry's position as official surveyor and his consequent ability to stake out claims to superior lands, the arrangement appeared to Coxe as advantageous as it was collusive. The McHenry brothers turned out to be as untrustworthy as Ball and Smith. Title to the lands they conveyed to Coxe was promptly contested by Mathias Hollenback, a big-time land jobber and an old hand in the corrupt practices and the legal trickery so essential to speculative success at the time, and by Supreme Court Justice James Wilson, a prince among Pennsylvania's lordly speculators, and others for whom most of the land had previously been surveyed and warranted. In March 1796 Coxe finally secured a hearing before the Board of Property, whose members invalidated his rivals' claim, although allowing six months for an appeal of the decision to a state court. But the ejectment proceedings that Coxe promptly instituted dragged on year after year, in one court after another, and were still pending in 1806, when he sold his title to the lands to Edward

Tilghman, himself both a claimant to the tracts in question and attorney for Coxe's adversaries in the case. The price was twenty-five cents an acre, exactly what Coxe had paid thirteen years earlier, and a poor enough bargain, surely, to dampen the enthusiasm of all but the most dauntless speculator.

Dauntless Coxe indisputably was. Although by the end of 1793 he owned, held warrants, or had contracted for about 292,000 acres, he was hungry for more. Since his funds were all but depleted, it was now time to test his confident assumption that by selling a part of what he owned at an enhanced price he could buy additional and more cheaply priced lands. The proof was not forthcoming. Neither Enoch Edwards, his London agent, nor the salesmen he had commissioned at home were able to dispose of more than a few thousand acres, and these at no impressive markup.

As befitted a student of economics, Coxe tailored his speculations to the pattern of this discouraging market and during 1794 bought only a few scattered tracts of land. It was a sound decision that was consistent with the plan he had somewhat earlier described to one of his agents: "I wish to be able to retire from business when I chuse" and "wish to have a competent income provided for my wife and a large and increasing family."[5] That he would succeed appeared likely in view of both his share of Coxe family lands in New York state and the money handed over to him at this time by his father. By the spring of 1795, however, the forbearance he had exercised for a year was ended by promising economic indicators pointing to an upsurge in land values. Foreign developments and fortuitous events at home "have . . . produced considerable Effects," he wrote to Albert Gallatin on April 10. "The consequences upon new lands is very considerable. I have ascertained to a certainty purchases in Virginia, Penns. and New York to the amount of 1,100,000 Acres in the present and last Week."[6] Presumably afraid that the supply would run out or that the price would climb out of reach before he acquired his coveted share, Coxe resumed his purchases, particularly in Virginia and New York.

In New York he centered his attention on the Minisink Patent, where he agreed to share in a purchase made by James and Benjamin Barton of 25,000 acres, which initially they had offered to Robert Morris, who wisely turned down the offer. The ensuing complexities made even the involved Ball and Smith entanglement seem child's play. Because of New Jersey's claim to some of the lands, the vagueness of the boundaries, the conflicting titles of other speculators, and the legal incapacity of the original conveyor

5. Coxe to Kirby, Jan. 7, 1794, Kirby Papers.

6. Coxe to Albert Gallatin, Apr. 10, 1794, Gallatin Papers, New-York Historical Society, New York.

to dispose of the land, Coxe was aware for once that he had been mulcted and prudently refrained from paying any but a fraction of the purchase money. Finally in 1797, confronted by legal proceedings in New York courts, he managed to round up sufficient funds to satisfy his exasperated creditors and to secure title to a fraction of the land, though exactly how much or on what terms was doubtful until 1817, when by an unspecified arrangement he finally settled the problem.

His purchase of lands in Virginia (where he had acquired extensive acreage in the 1780s) resulted in less of an impenetrable legal thicket but was also a matter of dispute for at least two decades. The 24,000 acres in question, for which Coxe began negotiations in 1795, were located in Lee County, the most western and southern county of the state. The purchase was made in August 1796 from James McCalley, who like most of Coxe's real estate agents was as remiss in granting a sound title as he was resourceful in litigation. But though Coxe was unable to detect moral deficiencies in his business partners, he was tenacious in holding onto even the slipperiest title. As of 1795 the Virginia lands seemed a mere bagatelle, and Coxe, demonstrating the adage that human desires grow with the means of their gratification, was at last ready to emulate his forebear Dr. Daniel Coxe, who had owned a good chunk of the North American continent. Tench decided to acquire a sizable part of an American state that lay within what had once been Carolana.

The opportunity to purchase these southern lands was provided by the presence in Philadelphia of Andrew Baird and Lewis Beard, two agents for the Rutherford Land Company, which laid claim to half a million acres of land in western North Carolina. Sometime in the spring of 1795 Baird approached Coxe with an enticing offer: the trustees of his company were willing to offer a part or the whole of their extensive holdings east of the Blue Ridge mountains in Rutherford County for nine cents an acre.[7] Eager to speculate in the southern lands that were sharpening the greed and depleting the funds of speculators from Maine to Georgia, Coxe was receptive. Here was a sparsely settled area of incalculable potential value, here the possibility of an estate that might rival Dr. Daniel Coxe's ownership of West Jersey!

Very little salesmanship was necessary to persuade Coxe to purchase 100,000 acres. According to a contract signed on June 27, 1795, one year

7. William W. Erwin and Andrew Baird to Coxe, Sept. 17, 1795, Coxe Papers. The Rutherford Land Company, consisting of 18 members, apparently had acquired its extensive holdings in North Carolina from James Greenlee, "a man of large Fortune" in Burke County. The land offered to Coxe included the present-day county of Rutherford, as well as Henderson, Polk, Cleveland, and Buncombe counties. Baird was a former New Jersey ironmaster and was acquainted with members of the Coxe family.

would be allowed for the payment in specie of the requisite $9,000, a staggering sum for a government official whose annual salary was $1,200 a year.[8] It was made possible in part by the sizable sum he had realized in his partnership with Frazier—a good portion of which he had already expended on Pennsylvania lands—but mainly by the largess of his father, who "for and in consideration of . . . one dollar and the love I bear him" assigned "unto my son Tench Coxe" in the autumn of 1795 a negotiable bond for $5,610, bearing interest at 7 percent.[9] The elder Coxe was aware of his son's incurable land mania and had insisted that the money be used for the purchase of a house in Philadelphia or in other ways that might render the financial situation of Tench's family more secure. His son, preoccupied with the acquisition of additional lands, had no interest in such, to him, comparatively unimportant things.

In the fall of 1795 Baird, who was now the sole representative of the Rutherford associates, dangled before the Philadelphian the rich fare still available, certain that a mere 100,000 acres had only whetted his appetite. Convinced that he had found the bargain of the decade, Coxe was easily tempted. In November 1795 the two men reached a verbal agreement that Coxe would buy an additional 80,000 acres, again for the price of nine cents an acre. When a formal contract was signed on January 1, 1796, the Pennsylvanian was the proud owner of 180,000 acres, or one-third of the land to which the Rutherford Land Company claimed title.[10]

Confident that land would steadily rise in value, Coxe was eager to buy still more. Since his own capital was rapidly being depleted, he, like countless other land speculators of the time, decided that he should sell a part of his holdings for at least double what he paid for them and use the proceeds to snap up yet additional lands. He selected as his principal sales agents two Connecticut speculators, Ephraim Kirby and Samuel A. Law, already brokers for his Pennsylvania lands. Although he offered them a partnership in his North Carolina purchase, they cautiously opted for a 5 percent commission on all sales, preferring to let Coxe take the risks.[11] Conveniently overlooking the fact that unimproved backlands were already glutting the market, Coxe not only chose to take the risks but was also contagiously optimistic about doing so. "I am willing to sell, at twenty cents, one hundred thousand acres of land in *North Carolina*," he wrote to a prospective agent shortly before his second contract for lands in that state

---

8. Early in July 1795 Coxe made a down payment of $6,000. The remaining debt of $3,000 was paid in Aug. 1796. *Ibid.*

9. For William Coxe's assignment, dated Oct. 21, 1795, see *ibid.*

10. Coxe to Kirby and Samuel Law, Dec. 6, 1795, Kirby Papers; Baird to Erwin and Lewis Beard, Jan. 2, 1796, Coxe Papers.

11. Coxe to Kirby and Law, Dec. 6, 1795, Jan. 16, 1796, Kirby Papers.

had been concluded. They were located "in a county . . . in which is now a court house, iron works, four or five great roads," plentiful livestock, abundant timber, rich soil, and in the future perhaps a navigable canal to Charleston.[12]

Coxe thus solicited Nathaniel Gorham, supervisor of the revenue for Massachusetts, to be his principal land agent. To thus use his own subordinates in the revenue service to promote his private fortune appears from today's perspective to be a flagrant abuse of public office. Although he did not comment on the matter, Coxe presumably saw no conflict of interest. It was merely a convenient way of promoting the interests of his acquaintances while enriching himself. Nor did Gorham, who was one of the biggest speculators of the day, see anything amiss with the proposal. That he refused was owing instead to his preoccupation with western rather than southern lands. Other federal officials, less deeply enmeshed in speculation than Gorham, accepted with alacrity similar offers by Coxe. Such was the case with his own subordinates in the Treasury Department like John Kilty, supervisor of Maryland, John S. Dexter, supervisor of Rhode Island, Daniel Stevens, the incompetent top revenue official in South Carolina, and William Polk, supervisor of North Carolina, who both sold lands to Coxe and peddled them for him. Coxe also secured the assistance of federal officials not connected with his own department—men like John Davis of Massachusetts, who was both a United States district attorney and Coxe's land agent, and John Kittera of Lancaster, who represented Pennsylvania in the House of Representatives and Coxe's business interests during congressional recesses.[13] Other civil servants, though not his agents, provided valuable information and advice. John Steele, North Carolina congressman and from 1796 to 1802 comptroller of the Treasury, obligingly offered counsel about the reliability of speculators and the quality of land in his native state. Timothy Pickering, himself a speculator in North Carolina lands and Coxe's partner in Pennsylvania land purchases, also gave advice. From Jefferson, Madison, and James Monroe, Coxe recalled decades later, he "obtained . . . information constantly."[14] In sum, although Coxe was perhaps unique in using fellow federal officials to further his own business interests, his and their involvement in land speculation was so typical as to preclude comment, much less judgment.

---

12. Coxe to Nathaniel Gorham, Nov. 7, 1795, Coxe Papers.

13. For Coxe's use of his subordinates as land agents, see, for example, John Kilty to Coxe, Feb. 16, 1797, Coxe to John S. Dexter, May 5, 1796, Dexter to Coxe, July 9, 1796, Apr. 8, 1797, Daniel Stevens to Coxe, Jan. 13, 1797, Coxe to Stevens, Mar. 21, 1797, Richard Lewis to Stevens, May 12, 1797, *ibid*. For the assistance Coxe secured from other federal officials, see Coxe to John Davis, July 3, Aug. 27, Dec. 17, 1796, Mar. 3, 1797, Davis to Coxe, Aug. 22, 1796, John Kittera to Coxe, Mar. 13, 1797, Coxe to Kittera, Mar. 16, 1797, *ibid*.

14. John Steele to Coxe, Oct. 3, Dec. 17, 1796, Coxe to W. Hawley, Sept. 22, 1820, *ibid*.

George Washington, for example, was one of the biggest and most successful speculators of his day. Henry Knox was more interested in his Maine lands, purchased in partnership with the prince of American speculators, William Duer, than in the affairs of the War Department. Had the members of the House and Senate who were involved in land speculation absented themselves, neither house would have had a quorum.

Aware of the excellent company he kept and (perhaps for that reason) undisturbed by doubts about any conflict of interest, Coxe pursued land purchases with an engrossment and energy matched only by his quest for high office. "I am not discouraged about any thing I have bought, if we keep in peace and harmony abroad and at home," he informed his North Carolina venders.[15] Other northern speculators were similarly bullish. William Constable of New York, having heard of Coxe's North Carolina purchase and placing "a firm reliance" on his business acumen, expressed a wish to share what he viewed as the Philadelphian's speculative bonanza. In January 1796 Constable inquired if Coxe would like to buy the remainder of the Rutherford Company's lands on joint account. Had the esteem of fellow businessmen pleased him a fraction as much as did that of statesmen and philosophers, Coxe would have been highly flattered by such an offer from one of the biggest speculators of his day. He was at least reassured by this confirmation of his own judgment, and two days later he made a counterproposal designed to give himself and the New Yorker possession of the entire 540,000 acres to which the Rutherford Land Company had staked out a claim. Although precise terms of the arrangement are not known, Constable and Coxe reached a tentative partnership agreement and decided to send one Joseph Burr to western North Carolina to inspect the lands.[16] In the late winter of 1796 Burr duly arrived there, but not as the representative of Coxe and Constable; he went, instead, as the agent of Tench Coxe.

Believing that what was good for a partnership must be doubly good for himself, the Philadelphian had decided to act alone. On February 6, 1796, he informed the trustees of the Rutherford Land Company that he "ventured . . . to make an offer for the whole remainder, vizt 360,000 Acres on a credit of two years from this time without interest at ten Cents per acre or I would give nine cents and interest from the purchase." In view of his lament only three weeks earlier that the want of funds precluded further land purchases, such a rash proposal was an indication of what he would

15. Coxe to Erwin and Beard, Dec. 24, 1795, *ibid.*
16. William Constable to Coxe, Jan. 17, 1796, *ibid.* Coxe offered to sell Constable a part of his 180,000 acres in return for part of Constable's purchase of two-thirds of the company's remaining land. Coxe to Constable, Jan. 19, 1796, *ibid.* For the partnership agreement, see Constable to Coxe, Jan. 28, 1796, *ibid.*

have liked rather than of what he could have.[17] Fortunately he quickly realized this, and instead of buying out the company, he purchased on February 9, 1796, a comparatively modest tract of 90,000 acres. Far from dropping his plans for buying the remaining 270,000 acres, however, he followed the signing of this contract with a letter to the company's trustees requesting a "description of the several large tracts" and "draughts of the whole 540,000 acres."[18] His acquisition of the half of that area he did not own depended on the success of his agents in finding purchasers willing to pay his inflated prices for the land he did own. Seeing no reason why they should not, he spurred them on with glowing accounts of the superior quality of his lands.

Coxe's salesmen did not share the enthusiasm. Was Coxe unaware that other speculators as shrewd as he were also peddling western North Carolina lands, Samuel Law asked? In what ways were Coxe's tracts superior to theirs? "They and you, in purchases, are upon a par," Law wrote. "But if *they* will take up with 10-15-20 or 25 per cent advance, and *you* ask 100, it is probable that you must wait for a while, unless ignorance, ardent and presumptuous, should fall in your way." Coxe's own ardor, stoked by cupidity, blinded him to such unaccommodating facts. He preferred to contemplate the financial promise implicit in the favorable report submitted from Rutherford County by his surveyor, Joseph Burr, to whom western Carolina was the New World Canaan, a land of milk and honey. Convinced that his sales agents, unlike Burr, were unnecessarily pessimistic and short-sighted, Coxe shared his visions of riches with them. "I do think that a grand Stroke might be made if some Monied men were to enable me to purchase the rest of those lands and then we were to proceed with friends, Judgment, and industry to settle towns, build Mills, improve iron banks etc. etc." "Think well and early of this," he admonished them.[19]

By this time Coxe was absorbed in yet more grandiose plans. Just as he had proposed some years earlier the creation of a model manufacturing town on the banks of the Susquehanna, so he now drew up a blueprint for a model city in Rutherford County. To this end he proposed to establish a land company based on four hundred shares of stock. As chief promoter he would subscribe to two hundred shares and invite two other individuals to subscribe to one hundred shares each. The three proprietors would themselves improve or sell one-half of the company's lands to actual settlers, while retaining the other half "for rise in value." The company would be responsible not only for improving inland navigation but also for designing

17. Coxe to Erwin, Greenlee, and Beard, Feb. 6, 1796, Coxe to Constable, Jan. 17, 1796, *ibid*.

18. Coxe to Erwin, Greenlee, and Beard, Feb. 9, 1796, *ibid*.

19. Law to Coxe, Feb. 22, 1796, *ibid*.; Coxe to Kirby and Law, Apr. 27, 1796, Kirby Papers. See also Joseph Burr to Coxe, Apr. 15, 1796, Coxe Papers.

and building a town that included a church, a school, and a library, as well as facilities for local industries like sawmills and gristmills. Such a plan would lead to a virtual economic miracle: the settlement and improvement of one part of the land would precipitate a sharp and steady increase in the worth of the reserved part; the wilderness would be turned into a garden, and the promoters enriched beyond the dreams of even Carolana's original proprietors. What Dr. Daniel Coxe had failed to do, in short, his great-grandson might accomplish. In any event, Coxe's "Plan of a valuable and profitable Settlement in the County of Rutherford, in North Carolina," along with his "Minutes concerning the State of North Carolina," was printed in broadside form and during the spring and summer of 1796 was circulated by his agents throughout the country.[20]

As if nothing short of possession of the entire western part of the state would slake his thirst for North Carolina lands, Coxe now reopened negotiations with the Rutherford Land Company. In August 1796 he bought 122,240 acres more, edging his total holdings in that state to the half-million mark.[21] His bullishness on this occasion came not only from his characteristic speculative mania but also from the expectation of resigning his official post in order to assume the far more profitable position of American agent for the vast Penn estates. The job had been proposed to him by Gouverneur Morris, then resident in Paris as the representative of a number of rich American landowners and speculators. In a letter of April 13, 1796, Morris assured Coxe that "no Man is fitter to execute the Business now opened to you." Whether so or not, no man was more eager to acquire such an agency. Coxe, explaining that he had "no views to a different situation in our government" and did not intend to leave Philadelphia when the capital moved to the Potomac, replied that a firm offer like Morris's "would confirm my disposition to retire into private life." His terms were a guarantee of 600 guineas for each of three years, plus all requisite expenses and certain fringe benefits.[22]

Although the contract with Morris fell through, Coxe was not discouraged. By midsummer he had devised a grandiose plan by which his retirement might be accompanied by even greater profits. "There are yet to be made in this country great and valueable purchases of land in Bodies from 1,000 to . . . 300,000 Acres," he wrote to Morris on July 21, describing lands available from owners "not aware of their value," from those

---

20. See, for example, Coxe to Dexter, May 5, 1796, to Davis, July 3, 1796, Coxe Papers.

21. The purchase was made on Aug. 22, 1796. "Memo of a deed," Feb. 15, 1797, *ibid.* Having sold their Rutherford lands, the company a few weeks later offered Coxe a sizable slice of Burke County, which he wisely turned down for lack of funds. Coxe to Erwin, Baird, Beard, and Greenlee, Sept. 7, 1796, *ibid.*

22. Gouverneur Morris to Coxe, Apr. 13, 1796, Coxe to Morris, June 21, 1796, *ibid.*

"tired of holding them," and from speculators who had "overshot their Capitals." To exploit such an unparalleled opportunity for quick riches, Coxe suggested that if Morris and his friends "have a mind to embark . . . upon a scale which would yield me 3,000 Guineas, I would hasten my purpose of with-drawing from my present engagement." Convinced that foreign capitalists might be persuaded to invest at least $500,000, Coxe expressed his willingness "to be concerned one-tenth" in every purchase of American lands by a company such as he proposed; "one half of that shall be repaid by me in a year. . . . The other half shall remain to me as a commission for my trouble" in acting as the company's agent. How could such a scheme fail in a country so abundantly endowed, so astonishingly prosperous, as the United States? "*Certainty and profit* are *no where else* so combined," Coxe wrote. "No where else have a *people* been transferred to a *wilderness* of great productive capacity and most favorably situated. But if such has been our progress from *Nought*, what must it be in future, when men, arts, and capital are derived to us . . . from . . . every other country where birth or commerce has occasioned civilized men to be found."[23] As a prognosis Coxe's eloquent statement was sound; as a description of what was possible for his generation it was unrealistic. That Coxe had only a vague perception of economic realities in the mid-1790s was demonstrated by his insistence on buying up a good part of North Carolina.

Within a month following his land purchase in August 1796, reservations that might all along have curbed his enthusiasm began to crowd in and continued to do so increasingly. Month after month brought additional evidence that the Rutherford associates had treated him shabbily. The full faith and credit he gave to the representations of Baird, Beard, Erwin, Greenlee, and other trustees of the company was, though characteristic, startlingly naive; it presumably did not occur to him to question their eagerness to sell to him such allegedly valuable lands at such a low price, or to question the fidelity with which they would honor their contracts. Among the problems Coxe would encounter were these: the refusal of the company to fulfill a promise to survey the lands in 640-acre tracts; their misrepresentation of the number of acres in the tracts as surveyed; their seemingly calculated delay in submitting descriptions of his lands and the inaccuracy of those they did supply; their remissness in searching out titles, forcing upon Coxe the necessity of long and tedious disputes over conflicting claims; their culpability in passing on to him improperly executed titles; and their failure

23. Coxe to Morris, July 21, 1796, *ibid.* Writing nine months later, Morris turned down Coxe's proposal. "The Dearth of Money and the consequent Embarrassments public and private force Men to limit their Views and Operations to a narrow Compass," he wrote, adding that "from the various Tricks which have been plaid they are led to doubt the Utility of Land Speculations in America." Morris to Coxe, May 20, 1797, *ibid.*

to explain or to send drafts for the 540,000 acres they claimed to hold. Coxe's monotonous letters of complaint to the company elicited friendly and evasive replies, including repeated promises to right every wrong.

In the meantime, Coxe, convinced that a speculative windfall was in the offing, energetically continued to promote the sale of his Carolina lands at inflated prices. As if believing that his own confidence might do the trick, he assured his many agents that profitable sales awaited only renewed efforts and greater diligence on their part. There was no reason that sales of his North Carolina lands should not be made at a dollar an acre, he lectured them in December; sales of one-half of his estate at that reasonable price "would make the remainder worth four Dollars or more."[24] Although he was daydreaming, he was also faithfully reflecting the irrepressible optimism of the land speculators of his day. For some only debtors' prison could squash it, among them his acquaintance Robert Morris and his own partner Dr. Thomas Ruston. Coxe's enthusiasm was dampened by the blunt reports of a number of his salesmen. John Davis wrote from Boston that the land bubble had been pricked, producing "an almost invincible reluctance . . . to any *Land Contracts*." Coxe's expectations were misguided, John Dexter wrote from Providence; widespread economic reversals "have intirely destroyed all enterprize and for ought I see will produce almost total bankruptcy."[25]

Although Coxe did reluctantly accept these incontrovertible facts, he believed them to be reversible. There has been "a damp to many objects of Business, and to nothing more than to new lands," he wrote to the Rutherford Land Company on May 16, but "when pursued with care and judgment and paid for they appear to me in several views a valuable property."[26]

Thus persuaded, Coxe embarked on yet another speculative venture. Late in May 1796 there arrived a private letter from the Treasury Department supervisor for North Carolina, William Polk, who, like the revenue commissioner, owned a sizable part of that state's western lands. Would Coxe be interested in purchasing a valuable tract of land in Mecklenberg County? He was, and within a month a tentative agreement had been reached between the two revenue officials for the transfer of 40,000 acres at nine cents an acre; Coxe was to pay by October 12, 1798.[27] By that time Coxe

24. Coxe to Davis and Dexter, Dec. 17, 1796, *ibid.*
25. Davis to Coxe, Mar. 3, 1797, Dexter to Coxe, Apr. 8, 1797, *ibid.*
26. Coxe to Erwin, Greenlee, and Beard, May 16, 1797, *ibid.*
27. William Polk to Coxe, May 26, 1796, *ibid.* The notice of agreement between Coxe and Polk, n.d., reads: "Purchased by Tench Coxe of Wm. Polk by proposal of July 3d. 1796: acceptance of 19th Sept. 1796: contract made and entered into on the 19th. Decemr. 1796. ratified and executed on or before 23d Jan. 1797." *Ibid.* The initial agreement was for the purchase of 20,445 acres; the extra land was added to the agreement at an unspecified time. Coxe to Polk, July 3, 1796, to Waightstile Avery, Dec. 4, 1799, *ibid.*

faced the dismaying prospect of losing not only his Mecklenberg purchase but also a large part of the estate bought from the Rutherford associates, the jewel in his would-be baronial crown.

Land speculation was inherently a dangerous game, one that could only be won if the vacant lands already purchased were quickly sold and settled to provide the money to pay the debts incurred in their purchase. In Coxe's case, however, neither the rate of population growth nor the influx of immigrants was sufficient to provide the requisite settlers, an essential fact that he, though a close student of demography, refused to recognize. Nor did he, in common with many others, perceive that a great extension of business enterprise founded upon borrowing and credit was hazardous at a time when constant war threatened to paralyze Europe, to which the American economy was still closely tied. In fact, the land craze of the 1790s, like the stockmarket frenzy of the 1920s, was bound to end in a crash. The panic that rocked the country, especially its commercial centers like Philadelphia, in 1796 and on into 1797 compelled Coxe, as well as other land buccaneers, to confront economic reality. However, he would likely have faced retrenchment and hardship in any event, for his financial troubles were, as Coxe admitted, less the product of a downswing in the business cycle than of "the unexpected dishonesty of a rich man."[28] The culprit was Dr. Thomas Ruston.

Ruston is one of the "mystery men" of the early national period. The friend of some of America's most distinguished physicians, among them Benjamin Rush and Hugh Williamson, as well as of the most prominent entrepreneurs of the day, Robert Morris, John Nicholson and others, Ruston, a native of Chester County, Pennsylvania, studied medicine in Edinburgh and practiced in London during the Revolution. Returning to America in 1785, he, like so many other American physicians of the time, preferred public life to his professional business. He was an unsuccessful candidate in a contested election for a seat on the Supreme Executive Council, a director of the Bank of Pennsylvania, and, succeeding Coxe, chairman of the Board of Managers of the Pennsylvania Manufacturing Society's cotton factory in Philadelphia. Like Coxe, he was also a prolific essayist who persuasively presented the case for a balanced national economy, most particularly for the encouragement of manufactures.[29] But for Ruston, even more than for Coxe, such activities, however public-spirited and personally gratifying,

28. Coxe to John D. Coxe, Feb. 10, 1797, *ibid.*

29. Constable, Rucker & Co. to Tench Tilghman & Co., Sept. 15, 1785, *ibid.*; Thomas Ruston to Thomas Mifflin, Oct. 26, 1789, *Pa. Archives*, 1st Ser., XI, 632–633; Coxe to the president and directors of the Bank of Pennsylvania, n.d., Coxe Papers. See also petition of Ruston

paled by contrast to an overarching preoccupation with the enticing potential rewards of land speculation. And Ruston was able to indulge his taste. Having inherited through his wife rich estates in Ireland, Ruston not only could maintain a "valuable and elegant double BRICK HOUSE" in Philadelphia, "having a marble-paved Hall . . . two parlors . . . an elegant drawing room," and an adjoining carriage house and stables, but without practicing his profession could, at least to all deceptive appearances, afford extensive estates elsewhere.[30]

Coxe's disastrous business association with Ruston began in the spring of 1793, when the two men jointly purchased 62,000 acres of land in three Pennsylvania counties (Northumberland, Luzerne, and Northampton) from a consortium of land speculators. The partnership appeared to be profitable, and Coxe, perhaps too dazzled by that to look closely at the doctor's perilous overextension of credit, did not question the business acumen or integrity of a man at whose speculative wizardry other Philadelphians also marveled. So it was that without hesitation and without guarantees or collateral Coxe made his own financial security measurably dependent on the caprice of another by endorsing for the Philadelphia physician four notes totaling $7,000.[31]

Although Coxe must earlier have heard rumors of Ruston's financial difficulties, it was not until the spring of 1795 that he became aware of their implications for him. On April 10 he was informed that notes drawn by Ruston and endorsed by him were "laying over protested" at the Bank of Pennsylvania; two months later the cashier of that institution curtly informed Coxe that if the notes were not promptly "paid or removed . . . they will positively be put into the Hands of the Attorney General to be sued for."[32] Either Ruston came through with acceptable collateral or Coxe was given a stay of execution, for nothing was heard of the matter for a year and a half. Whatever arrangements were made, Coxe's faith both in the physician's solvency and in his willingness faithfully to discharge his financial obligations was unshaken, or else not even he would so recklessly have plunged into North Carolina land purchases between June 1795 and September 1796. By the latter date he realized how colossally misplaced his

---

as "Chairman of the board of Managers" of the Pennsylvania Manufacturing Society to the House of Representatives [1789], and drafts of articles on encouragement of manufactures, *ibid.*; *American Museum*, XII (1792), 91–92, 94–95.

30. For Ruston's inheritance, see Coxe to George Barclay & Co., Jan. 4, 1802, Coxe Papers. Ruston's house was described in the *Philadelphia Gaz.*, Aug. 13, 1802.

31. The purchase of Coxe and Ruston is described in William Harrison to Coxe, Jan. 24, 1797, Coxe Papers. For Coxe's endorsement of Ruston's notes, see the *Aurora*, Aug. 4, 1802; Jonathan Mifflin to Coxe, June 22, 1795, Coxe Papers.

32. Jonathan Mifflin to Coxe, Apr. 10, June 22, 1795, Coxe Papers.

confidence had been. Not only was his once-trusted partner close to bankruptcy, but he was also under an indictment for fraud. The story was one that Coxe would repeat to sympathetic friends, to less sympathetic creditors, and, through the pages of the Philadelphia press, to a presumably interested public for the next decade and longer.

In June 1795 Ruston, hounded by importunate creditors, hit on a way to safeguard his property.[33] On June 27 he drew up a deed assigning his estate to undesignated trustees who were to hold it in trust for his wife and three children, and in this form the document was "signed, sealed, and pretended to be delivered." On July 2, five days later, the blank spaces left for the trustees were filled in with the names of Charles Heatly, Ruston's lawyer, and John Hunt, a Philadelphia clergyman. The completed instrument was not recorded until September 1796, on the eve of Ruston's imprisonment for debts totaling more than $100,000.[34] When news of the transaction reached Coxe and the doctor's other creditors, they were incensed and shrilly complained that the deed of June 27 could not legally transfer title because it was incomplete, and that, given the delay in recording the deed and the suits that had been pending against Ruston, it was patently designed to defraud Ruston's creditors.[35]

And so it was. In September 1796 the Philadelphia Court of Common Pleas found the Philadelphia speculator guilty of suspicion of fraud and sentenced him to a year's imprisonment. Justice may have been done, but what of the thirty-six judgments outstanding against Ruston? Coxe, whose attorneys could give him little encouragement, was distraught.[36] Having just contracted for another slice of western North Carolina that would require every penny of his capital, he would likely now be called on to pay more than $7,000 to discharge Ruston's protested notes. Throughout the fall his anxiety grew, relieved only by his involvement in the presidential campaign and by the preparation of articles designed to combat domestic

33. Among Ruston's creditors were the Bank of North America, the Bank of Pennsylvania, Andrew Allen, and a score of Philadelphia merchants.

34. See "To the Public," Aug. 13, 1802, *Poulson's American Daily Advertiser*, Aug. 14, 1802. According to Coxe, the total was $120,000, exclusive of interest. Coxe to George Barclay & Co., Mar. 1, 1803, Coxe Papers.

35. The tangled web of Ruston's financial empire involved many of Philadelphia's most prominent businessmen—Edward Tilghman, Moses Levy, John Nicholson, John Maybil, Samuel Coates, and Robert Morris. His crash threatened to ruin them, as well as himself. See, for example, Morris to Ruston, May 13, Nov. 6, Dec. 11, 1797, Coxe Papers. For a list in Ruston's handwriting of 98 creditors, see *ibid.*

36. "To the Public," Aug. 13, 1802, *Poulson's Daily Adver.*, Aug. 14, 1802. Coxe also had legal difficulties with William Harrison, Ruston's son-in-law, to whom Coxe had loaned money. Upon his bankruptcy in Sept. 1798, Harrison had assigned a part of his property to Coxe, who, so far as can be determined, never acquired it. See "William Harrison's Assignment," Nov. 21, 1798, "William Harrison's Return of Property," Dec. 1, 1798, Coxe Papers.

monarchism, written from his sickbed, where he lay immobilized by an unspecified illness from late October to early December. In December the dreaded blow came: he must promptly take up his notes, the Bank of Pennsylvania informed him, or take up occupancy of a cell next to Ruston's.[37]

Christmas was a cheerless day in the Coxe household. Tench spent a good part of it writing a letter to Samuel Fox, president of the Bank of Pennsylvania, explaining in elaborate detail why the security he had offered for his debt was sufficient. There was no need as he saw it to defend his proposed paper security—the bond for almost $6,000 from his father and a note from his brother Daniel for $1,600. His explanation was instead made necessary, he said, by doubts expressed by the bank's directors that the approximately 12,000 acres he had proposed to hand over as collateral might not be acceptable.[38] Although Ruston's conduct was "cruel and criminal," and he himself was only "an innocent sufferer," Coxe was willing to do all within his power. Would the bank directors look favorably on a security of 20,000 acres? To his relief the directors (a roster that included a number of his friends) tentatively accepted.[39] Coxe was made happier yet by the possibility of aid from an unexpected quarter.

"Believe me, sir," he wrote to Ruston on December 26, "your note gives me great relief of mind in my present painful situation." The doctor, still the ostensible owner of extensive tracts scattered throughout the Union, had offered to assign a large tract of his Georgia lands to his beleaguered former partner.[40] Coxe's gullibility was presumably a result of his desperation; otherwise he would have known that Ruston, having already fraudulently sought to safeguard his property against the demands of his many creditors, was unlikely to single him out as a particularly worthy case by assigning him valuable lands, even if his ownership of them had been certain. The possibility was the more remote in view of Ruston's belief that he had already been charitable. In an atypical gesture of business integrity, he had signed over to Coxe sometime earlier (probably during the summer of 1796)

37. Coxe to Jared Ingersoll, Dec. 23, 1796, Boston Public Library.

38. Coxe to Samuel Fox, Dec. 25, 1796, Gratz Collection, Hist. Soc. Pa., Philadelphia; Coxe to George Plumsted, Dec. 27, 1796, Coxe Papers.

39. For Coxe's appeals to the bank directors, see Coxe to Ingersoll, Dec. 23, 1796, Boston Pub. Lib.; Coxe to Fox, Dec. 25, 1796, Gratz Collection; Coxe to John D. Coxe, Feb. 10, 1797, Coxe Papers. The arrangement had been worked out by Coxe's brother John D. Coxe, who described it as follows: "A proposition occurs to me with which the Bank must be satisfied. Your Estate is large and your lands early taken up. Offer a Conveyance of so much as shall be perfectly sufficient to them in trust to sell and pay at the Expiration of   months if your notes are not redeemed before with a power for you to sell in the mean time for the use of the trust. They cannot hold up their faces if they refuse it." John D. Coxe to Coxe, n.d. (but Dec. 1796), *ibid.* For the bank's acceptance of the arrangement, see Fox to Coxe, Dec. 23, 1796, Coxe Papers.

40. Coxe to Ruston, Dec. 26, 1796, Coxe Papers.

notes of Robert Morris and John Nicholson worth about $11,000. Coxe might have tempered the approaching disaster by promptly presenting them for payment, but believing that these titans among a generation of giant land speculators were preeminently trustworthy, he chose instead quietly to harbor them until all his other resources, his lands excepted, were exhausted. These notes were still in his strongbox in 1798 when Morris's bankruptcy made them worthless.[41]

As Coxe, foolishly expecting first aid from Ruston,[42] congratulated himself that bankruptcy had been averted, the directors of the Bank of Pennsylvania took a closer look at the security he had proposed. They discovered that his legal title to the lands in question was by no means clear. On January 16, having by then allowed Coxe almost a month to arrange reliable security, and exasperated by his procrastination, the bank's directors informed him that "if the securities offered . . . be not completed on or before . . . the 24th Instant the . . . stay of execution" would "be then rescinded."[43] Although experienced in banking and finance, Coxe had for some unknown reason apparently expected one of the nation's most reputable banks to overlook the documentary deficiency of his title to lands he offered as collateral. Frantically he sought the necessary papers, finally obtaining them from William Harrison, Ruston's son-in-law, who found them in the doctor's desk. It was a photo finish; Coxe delivered the papers to the bank after its closing time on January 24.[44]

41. Coxe wrote to Fox on Jan. 11, 1797, that the notes were delivered to him "some time ago." *Ibid.* According to a memorandum by Coxe dated July 30, 1796 (*ibid.*), he deposited them with William Tilghman, presumably a short time after he had received them from Ruston. The notes, Coxe said, were "forced" upon him by Ruston as "a kind of footing of securing me when they were not worth near half the Money." Coxe to Nicholson, Feb. 12, 1797, Gratz Collection. On Jan. 11, 1797, Coxe had made a tentative offer of the notes to the Bank of Pennsylvania. Apparently the directors passed over the proposal in silence, thereby suggesting their distrust of the solidity of Morris and Nicholson. Coxe could not legally have assigned the notes to the bank, since Ruston's assignment to him expressly stipulated that he was to return them to Ruston upon the latter's discharge of the notes Coxe had endorsed. Coxe to Fox, Jan. 11, 1797, Coxe Papers; Coxe to the president and directors of the Bank of Pennsylvania, Feb. 1, 1797, Gratz Collection. The notes were the subject of a long and acrimonious controversy between Coxe and Ruston. See, for example, *Philadelphia Gaz.*, Aug. 11, 1802.

42. As Coxe admitted a few weeks later, Ruston after being "amused for eight or ten days . . . finally refused to do any thing, and treated me besides very improperly." Coxe to the president and directors of the Bank of Pennsylvania, Feb. 2, 1797, University Archives, University of Pennsylvania, Philadelphia.

43. Enclosure in Fox to Coxe, Jan. 17, 1797, Coxe Papers. On Jan. 9, 1797, Fox had written to Coxe that the bank "has not received from you all the title papers to the Lands offered to be conveyed in trust as security for the debts due. . . . As the Lands are not patented, which the Directors thought was the case when they agreed to accept them, the papers necessary to ascertain your title appear to be a Copy of the Application to the Land Office duly certified." *Ibid.*

44. For Coxe's search for the papers, see Morris to Coxe, Jan. 19, 21, 24, 1797, Morris to William Harrison, Jan. 24, 1797, Coxe to Morris, Jan. 24, 1797, Coxe to Harrison, Jan. 24, 1797, *ibid.* For Coxe's delivery of the papers, see Coxe to Harrison, Jan. 24, 1797, *ibid.*

Had he acted more promptly and forthrightly, the bank might have accepted the proffered security, and his financial trial would have ended as he desired. As it was, the directors were by now skeptical of any landed security he might offer and, reexamining his case, decided that no collateral other than safely negotiable notes would be satisfactory. Wishing to save himself the embarrassment of calling on his family for help, Coxe adopted stratagem after stratagem. His lengthy letters of protest, explanation, and justification to the directors of the bank having been unsuccessful, he pled in vain with John Nicholson and Robert Morris for an advance on money they owed him.[45] Finally in what was surely a measure of his despair, he turned to Ruston. "For Godsake consider the unhappy situation to which I am brought by my trust and confidence in you . . . ," he wrote on February 10, 1797. "Let me intreat and pray you be mindful of the ruin of an innocent man—his wife—eight children. . . . I sleep none—I have constant and extreme disorders in my stomach—For godsake do something to relieve me."[46] Himself already behind bars, the doctor felt no sympathy.

At last Coxe confronted the inevitable and turned to his brothers, who, foreseeing his request, had already arranged to help him. John D. Coxe, who all along had been offering legal counsel, and William Coxe, Jr., probably at the behest of his father, loaned him $8,000, accepting in return promissory notes that were secured by Tench's own notes and bonds and by designated lands.[47]

Although Coxe had weathered a major financial storm, he would confront another and then another over the succeeding quarter of a century. At least now he was able to sustain the comforting belief that his financial

45. See Coxe to the president and directors of the Bank of Pennsylvania, Feb. 1, 3, 1797, Gratz Collection; Coxe to the president and directors of the Bank of Pennsylvania, Feb. 2, 1797, University Archives, Univ. of Pa.; Coxe to the president and directors of the Bank of Pennsylvania, n.d., Coxe Papers; Coxe to John Nicholson, Feb. 12, 1797, Gratz Collection; Morris to Coxe, Feb. 15, 1797, Robert Morris Papers, Lib. of Cong.; Coxe to Morris and Nicholson, Feb. 23, 1797, Dreer Collection, Hist. Soc. Pa., Philadelphia; Nicholson to Coxe, Feb. 27, 1797, Coxe Papers; Coxe to Nicholson, Mar. 3, 1797, John Nicholson Papers, Pennsylvania Historical and Museum Commission, Harrisburg.

46. Coxe to Ruston, Feb. 10, 1797, Coxe Papers.

47. Coxe gave seven notes for a total of $8,242. Of this, $3,000 was borrowed from John D. Coxe, and $5,242 in notes were endorsed jointly by John Coxe and William Coxe, Jr. *Ibid.* Coxe's trials were still not at an end. The bank was willing to accept John D. Coxe as an endorser but refused to accept the endorsement of William Coxe, Jr., and demanded a counter-signature. Fox to Coxe, Feb. 15, 1797, *ibid.* Coxe frantically rounded up his friend Thomas Hartley and Samuel Jackson, a Philadelphia business acquaintance, as guarantors of William's endorsement, but the bank found them unacceptable. Finally his cousin William Tilghman and his friend Samuel Howell offered Coxe their endorsements, and the bank found their signatures satisfactory. See Coxe's endorsement on "Assignment," Feb. 15, 1797, Coxe to the president and directors of the Bank of Pennsylvania, Feb. 21, 1797, Coxe to John D. Coxe, Mar. 4, 1797, *ibid.*

woes were not of his own making but were rather the fault of Thomas Ruston. An all-sufficient panacea was to recoup his losses by seizing a part of the doctor's estate. But his protracted efforts were to no avail. Although Ruston served another prison sentence and then finally declared himself bankrupt, his conduct, as Coxe said in 1802, "so concealed, and embarrassed, and impeded me, that I have been unable to proceed with effect, in his affairs." Nor was he able to do so during succeeding years.[48] After almost two decades of incessant effort, protracted litigation, and unseemly public controversy, Coxe wound up with nothing more than a manuscript collection. Pursuant to an attachment issued by the Pennsylvania courts, he seized not only Ruston's financial but also his personal papers; these documents are today still in the enormous Coxe manuscript collection that found its way into the scholarly domain. Certainly Coxe considered these papers of little worth, and thus he continued to cling to the conviction, as demonstrated by the thousands of words he wrote on the subject, that the Philadelphia physician was the author of his financial woes, thus bearing prolix witness to his seemingly inexhaustible power of self-deception.

Coxe was involved in other costly suits to recover money owed to him and to discharge debts to others. Goaded by Hamilton, he was under constant pressure to pay the money due John B. Church or to face legal proceedings, and this at a time when he was in the midst of a legal battle to secure title to the lands that the money had been expended for. He was faced, too, with a suit instituted against him by Peter Fischer for the delivery of certain deeds and papers relating to contested Virginia lands. Also, he was obliged to initiate proceedings for the recovery of the money due him from Robert Morris and John Nicholson. To add to his problems, the Bank of the United States unexpectedly sued him as the endorser of a protested note of Thomas Hartley, former Pennsylvania congressman and Coxe's longtime friend. Most distressing of all, Coxe was party to legal proceedings instituted by William Polk (from whom the Philadelphian had bought lands in North Carolina) for nonpayment of debt; in these proceedings Polk sought to attach a portion of Coxe's Rutherford lands. To forestall such a possibility Coxe assigned those lands in trust to William Tilghman, Abraham Kintzing, and Richard Coxe (his wife's brother) and then proceeded to fight a protracted but unsuccessful legal battle in North Carolina courts.[49]

---

48. "To the Public," Aug. 13, 1802, *Poulson's Daily Adver.*, Aug. 14, 1802.

49. Coxe to James Hall, June 10, 1799, Coxe Papers. Coxe's papers contain piles of documents on the lawsuits described in this paragraph. The suits can best be reconstructed from the legal pleadings preserved in the Coxe Papers and from his correspondence for this period with William and Edward Tilghman.

The difficulty with Polk arose over the 40,000 acres Coxe had bought in Mecklenberg

Ever hopeful, Coxe was confident that he would emerge from courtroom after courtroom waving favorable verdicts. With the timely aid of his brother Daniel, and by stretching his own credit to the limit, he managed to retain his Carolina estate, iron-clad in the prison of his fantasy, and continued to hold onto it for another two decades.[50] Neither personal sacrifice, family privation, nor imminent bankruptcy could stay him from his self-appointed course to follow in his great-grandfather's steps. It was, however, necessary to pay his legal expense (though his cousin and warmest personal friend, William Tilghman, was his lawyer), to meet the annual taxes on his lands, and to discharge at least the interest on his debts. These added up to a staggering amount. According to a scribbled statement that Coxe entitled "Sums to be paid 1798 and after," he owed in that year $65,700, a sum that was offset by a comparatively trifling income.[51]

Coxe's debts were more than balanced, at least on paper, by his evaluation of his still-sizable landed property, which included something less than 350,000 acres in Pennsylvania (of which his title to about 200,000 acres was contested) and between 400,000 and 500,000 acres in North Carolina. If he could sell only a part of these at a profit, Coxe reasoned, he could pay off his pressing debts and still remain a potentially rich man. To accomplish this he drew up in May 1798 "Proposals for a Land Company." The company was to be based on a capital stock of 900,000 acres of land divided into one hundred shares available to "all who shall deliver either good merchandize cash, public and bank stock of the United States or any American state, good bills . . . etc. into the Hands of Tench Coxe and Company at Philadelphia on or before the 1st day of January next." The com-

County from his former subordinate in the Treasury Department, William Polk. Soon after the agreement with Polk was concluded (a "conditional" one, Coxe said, in the sense that at the outset he reserved "a right to reject" unacceptable lands), Coxe sent his wife's brother to inspect the property. Richard Coxe reported that it was of an inferior quality, implying also that the North Carolina supervisor-speculator had misrepresented it. According to Tench, he thus bowed out of the contract in Dec. 1798; according to Polk, Coxe's effort to do so was a breach of contract. The dispute, on which there are scores of documents and letters in the Coxe Papers, is summarized in Coxe to Polk, Dec. 4, 1799, *ibid*. Coxe's problem with Polk was the greater because he did not know precisely where the writ of attachment would be returned. Polk's residence, as Coxe put it, "is unfixed between Charlotte and Raleigh." This meant that Coxe had to alert attorneys in various North Carolina towns. Coxe to Absalom Tatem, Dec. 12, 1799, *ibid*. On the advice of counsel Coxe also attempted to have the case removed to a federal court. He was unsuccessful, and the case, postponed again and again, was finally decided in 1804 in a trial that was unfairly, if not collusively, controlled by Polk, a man of local prominence.

50. "Receipt," dated Dec. 30, 1797, and signed by Erwin for a note of Coxe's for $8,956 and one of his brother's for $5,828, *ibid*. Coxe had paid a total of $35,060.85 for almost 400,000 acres of land. *Ibid*.

51. "Sums to be paid 1798 and after," n.d., *ibid*.

pany thus organized would sell lots to actual settlers both from Europe and in America, thus deriving "the great benefits which always arise from an increase of population." Prospective investors, more aware than Coxe of current economic realities, were not forthcoming, and he was obliged to temporarily drop his pet project and to try to dispose of some of his lands by direct sale. But this, too, once again proved disappointing. He sold some tracts, but the favorable market that he obstinately insisted on seeing did not exist. Although a slow learner on this subject, Coxe was reluctantly obliged to concede that "lands are become dull here beyond all former experience."[52]

Where, then, could he turn for assistance? The answer, as usual, was to his father, who though he already had given a large part of his estate to his children—and a disproportionately large share to Tench—still had ample capital left. But William Coxe, increasingly enfeebled and angrily disappointed by his son's political capers and reckless land speculation, was in no mood even to proffer sympathy, much less financial aid. Instead, on May 17, 1798, he dispatched to Tench a cryptic order to come immediately to Burlington "without children or companions as I wish to confer seriously with you on my Will, relating to you."[53] What he had to say left his once-favorite son shattered: since Tench had shown himself incompetent to manage his own financial affairs, his share of William Coxe's estate would be assigned to trustees after the sizable sum he owed to his father and the bond for about $6,000 that (so Tench assumed) William Coxe had turned over as a gift were deducted. These trustees would be given the responsibility of discharging Tench's debts, paying him only such part of his legacy as might remain. Obviously enough, little would be left, and Coxe was not only shocked but indignant. "The impass to which your mind has been brought towards me . . . has oppressed me for many weeks," he wrote to his father on September 2. "I cannot face you while such degrading Sentiments of me occupy your mind. My large family will receive, through the act of my father, the deepest wound in reputation and interest."[54]

Viewing his son's behavior as a repudiation of his own way of life, William Coxe rather believed that it was Tench who had wounded his wife and children by political intemperateness and financial irresponsibility. "My Gray hairs," he exasperatedly informed Tench in September 1798, "are Compleatly brought with sorrow to the grave by your mean Teasing Letters for 3 Months past to Sacrifice *my Childrens* fortunes to enrich *yours*, Contest my Will, and Derange my affairs. Hence forward . . . you shall not

52. "Proposals for a Land Company," May 7, 1798, Coxe to Erwin, July 10, 1798, *ibid.*
53. William Coxe, Sr., to Coxe, May 17, 1798, William Coxe, Jr., to Coxe, June 6, July 29, 1789, *ibid.*
54. Coxe to William Coxe, Sr., Sept. 2, 1798, *ibid.*

interfere or meddle with my Estate in any manner whatever" nor "direct me or Tirannise over me to the Last minute of my Life."[55] Such uncharacteristic intemperateness was, of course, a manifestation of parental disappointment. Tench's financial entrapment was certainly owing to his own covetousness, though in this he was by no means singular. His business career attests to the aptness of Richard Hofstadter's perceptive remark that ours has been "a democracy in cupidity."[56]

55. William Coxe, Sr., to Coxe, Sept. 6, 1798, *ibid.*
56. Richard Hofstadter, *The American Political Tradition and the Men Who Made It* (New York, 1948), viii.

17 ❧

Republican Journalist

"I have just taken Israel Pemberton's Estate opposite the Bank," Coxe wrote to William Tilghman in February 1798, six weeks after he was dismissed as commissioner of the revenue, "and expect by June at farthest to be there with my family, business etc." The business was his proposed resumption of the mercantile career he had abandoned eight years earlier to accept a post as assistant secretary of the Treasury; during this interim his interest in trade had been overshadowed by his absorption in land speculation. He did, as planned, make an attempt to reestablish his own countinghouse, but, short of both capital and business correspondents and lacking, too, the will to start anew, he instead wound up as Philadelphia agent (and sometimes partner) of his brother Daniel, by now a peripatetic international merchant.[1]

In 1791 Daniel Coxe, after serving his business apprenticeship as Tench's representative in the liquidation of Coxe and Frazier's tangled affairs, had launched his own career, one that over the next decades made him one of Philadelphia's most prominent merchants and also, largely because he eschewed excessive land speculation, one of its richest. His first major ventures were undertaken in partnership with Reed and Forde, a well-established Philadelphia firm whose trade activities extended to virtually every major port in the world. In January 1791 he joined a business association consisting of Joseph Ball, a well-to-do capitalist willing to put up the group's capi-

1. Coxe to William Tilghman, Feb. 8, 1798, Tilghman Papers, Hist. Soc. Pa., Philadelphia. For his attempt to establish a countinghouse, see, for example, Coxe to Mr. Galline, May 8, 1798, in which Coxe described the type of business he hoped to "procure for my house." Coxe Papers. See also John H. Baines to Coxe, May 31, 1798, Abraham Kintzing, Jr., to Coxe, Apr. 22, 1798, Coxe to William Erwin, July 10, 1798, *ibid*. For Coxe's position as agent for his brother, see "Power of Attorney," Daniel W. Coxe to Coxe, Mar. 20, 1798, *ibid*.

tal, and Reed and Forde, who had long experience in the Louisiana trade. Their expectation was to exploit, by way of the Ohio Valley and by sea, the opportunities afforded by trade with New Orleans, then the most important Spanish port in the New World.[2] Such commerce was prohibited by Spanish regulations, but these were so feebly enforced that enterprising American merchants easily evaded them, primarily by funneling goods through the French West Indian ports, which were open to both United States and Spanish ships. As the representative of the consortium, Daniel Coxe sailed from New York early in February 1791 and, having touched first at a number of West Indian islands, reached Cap-Français in August. He then proceeded (presumably under French colors) to New Orleans,[3] where he established useful connections for future business ventures and profitably exchanged his cargo for local articles in demand in Philadelphia.

Having thus proved his business acuity and preferring the ship deck to a desk in Philadelphia, Daniel Coxe next made a voyage to France, a large-scale enterprise undertaken in partnership only with Reed and Forde. On May 2, 1794, soon after his arrival, he reported to Tench that "the state of things . . . is so precarious that I know not how to flatter myself with the prospect of a speedy return to America." Thus circumstanced, he could all the more heartily congratulate himself on loading rich cargoes of brandy, wine, and dry goods, valued at 300,000 livres, onto three ships. After an uneasy crossing, requiring an ever-alert lookout for British marauders, the small fleet, with Daniel Coxe aboard, finally came within sight of the Delaware Capes, then only to be captured by a British privateer and taken to Bermuda, where the ships were seized and their cargoes condemned as contraband.[4] "Thus has a voyage been frustrated," Coxe lamented to his partners, "that would have netted us at least 40,000 dollars."[5]

Over the next three years, as Tench continued to pile up hundreds of thousands of acres of land and compiled a political record that would catapult him from what he mistakenly viewed as his safe berth in the Treasury, Daniel Coxe continued his business travels, and with more success than in 1794. In May 1795 he was off again to France, which, he reported to Tench, "affords a great field for speculation." This time he stayed for nearly a year, purchasing "two large french built ships" on which he shipped to England "the largest Cargo of Grain ever imported into Liverpool." By the

---

2. Arthur P. Whitaker, "Reed and Forde, Merchant Adventurers of Philadelphia: Their Trade with Spanish New Orleans," *PMHB*, LXI (1937), 247–248.

3. Daniel Coxe to Coxe, Jan. 30, Aug. 13, 1791, Coxe Papers.

4. Daniel Coxe to Coxe, May 2, 1794, *ibid.*; Whitaker, "Reed and Forde," *PMHB*, LXI (1937), 254. For Daniel Coxe's account of the capture, see his letter to Coxe of Sept. 16, 1794, Coxe Papers.

5. Daniel Coxe to Reed & Forde, Aug. 27, 1794, Reed & Forde Business Correspondence, 1763–1823, Hist. Soc. Pa., Philadelphia.

spring of 1796 he was in London, where he remained (with occasional side trips to Lisbon) until late December 1796, dispatching cargoes to New Orleans.[6] In the early summer of 1797, after a brief stopover in Philadelphia, he took the Ohio Valley-Mississippi route to Louisiana, where he had "important Interests at stake . . . , more I believe than all the other Americans in that Country united."[7]

Soon after Wolcott and Adams had obliged Tench Coxe to exchange the title of "commissioner" for "esquire" in December 1797, Daniel returned to Philadelphia, promptly laying plans for yet more ambitious trading ventures. By now a well-to-do man, he could afford to help out his favorite brother, though his generosity stopped short of discharging Tench's enormous debts.[8] Although correspondence between them does not reveal the exact nature of their business arrangements, Tench did become his younger brother's Philadelphia agent. His tasks, while not taxing, were important and varied. He negotiated the purchase of ships required for Daniel's voyages, took out insurance on the vessels and their cargoes, and made arrangements for the dispatch of large quantities of cotton and pelts purchased for Daniel's account by the latter's Louisiana partner, Daniel Clarke, Jr., a prominent merchant and United States consular agent at New Orleans.[9] Coxe's duties also included keeping close tabs on local market fluctuations, disposing of goods in Daniel's Philadelphia warehouse as advantageously as possible, receiving and dispatching to England for sale consignments of furs from his brother's agents, purchasing and shipping to New Orleans machinery for the manufacture of cotton, along with a pirated model of Whitney's cotton gin, corresponding with Daniel's far-flung foreign as well as domestic factors, and managing his brother's financial affairs, including the purchase of bank stock and lands.[10]

To Daniel Coxe it was an agreeable arrangement, but to Tench it was much less so. Court dockets in Pennsylvania and elsewhere were crowded with cases to which he was a party, either as plaintiff or defendant, and he was increasingly absorbed in partisan politics, both as a publicist and a

6. Daniel Coxe to Coxe, June 19, 1795, Nov. 23, 1796, Coxe Papers.

7. Daniel Coxe to Timothy Pickering, Oct. 27, 1797, Pickering Papers, Mass. Hist. Soc., Boston. For an account of Daniel's trip to Louisiana, see Daniel Coxe to Coxe, June 30, 1797, Coxe Papers.

8. In addition to the return from his Louisiana business, Daniel Coxe realized a profit of about $10,000 on a venture to Havana in the fall of 1797. William Coxe, Sr., to Coxe, Nov. 5, 1797, Coxe Papers. According to William Coxe, Jr., another business adventure in the same year netted Daniel $40,000. William Coxe, Jr., to Coxe, July 18, 1798, ibid.

9. Daniel Clarke, Jr., was apparently appointed United States consul for New Orleans on the recommendation of Daniel W. Coxe. See Daniel W. Coxe to Coxe, Sept. 9, 1796, ibid.

10. Coxe's activities as his brother's business agent can be followed in his 1798 correspondence with Isaac Todd, Daniel Clarke, Jr., Theodore Bache, Willing & Francis, Hugh P. Magee, Daniel W. Coxe, William Coxe, Jr., Wharton & Lewis, and William Erwin, ibid.

party worker. At the same time (and though he was far too fond of his younger brother to begrudge his success), the conduct of large-scale mercantile transactions entailing such handsome profits was too painful a reminder of his own slender purse.

But Tench Coxe's family was not, as he liked to pretend, on the road to the poor farm. His father, though insistent that Tench's share of his estate be handled by trustees, continued obligingly to provide for his grandchildren during the many months they annually spent in New Jersey. To do so, however, William Coxe had to compete with the Coxe children's maternal grandfather, Charles Coxe. For a third of each year, and often much longer when the recurrent yellow fever plagues struck Philadelphia, Coxe was thus freed from the necessity of supporting a family that by 1798 consisted of eight children. But though a part-time father, he was a solicitous one, overseeing with especial care their formal education and their extracurricular reading, particularly in the case of Tench, Jr.[11]

Such family arrangements were agreeable to Rebecca Coxe, who still considered Philadelphia a home away from her true home at her father's Sidney estate. She, nevertheless, enjoyed the winter social season in the nation's capital, where, despite a limited budget, she and Tench continued to entertain the city's elite. Rebecca was also diverted by her continuing absorption in music, both as a composer and a performer, her pleasure in the latter having been enhanced by the arrival in 1794 of a handsome pianoforte sent to her from France by Daniel Coxe.[12] Although deeply devoted to Tench, she was largely immune from (though surely not unsympathetic to) his precarious and litigious business affairs. She may have been far less tolerant of his political activities, but on this the record is silent.

Nor does the record reveal Coxe's reaction to Philadelphia's spritely social life. It presumably afforded him relaxing relief from the depressing sight of the growing deficits on the pages of his ledgers, and though he liked to believe that his politics had barred him from Philadelphia's more select drawing rooms, his family's aristocratic status precluded such proscription. Even if he had been proscribed, his social calendar would still have been crowded. He spent evenings in the company of amiable political allies; he attended meetings of the American Philosophical Society, to which he had been elected in 1796; and he participated in the activities of other associations, as well as the Philadelphia assemblies.

---

11. Tench Coxe, Jr., to Coxe, Oct. 2, 1798, Aug. 14, 1799, William Coxe, Sr., to Coxe, July 22, 1796, Benjamin Tucker to Coxe, Apr. 1, 1796, *ibid.* For a long list of books Coxe ordered from London for his children, see Coxe to J. Robinson, Mar. 18, 1799, *ibid.*

12. Daniel Coxe to Coxe, Sept. 16, 1794, *ibid.*

That Coxe was able to enjoy life in the face of his mounting debts was only because he was counting on very substantial legacies from both his Aunt Rebecca, then eighty-two, and his father, then seventy-six. The bequest of the former, it seemed certain, would be a tidy sum; that of the latter, though tied up, would presumably be enough to pay his large debts. He continued to hope, moreover, that his father would forgo his decision to assign Tench's share of his estate to trustees. But William Coxe, increasingly convinced of his son's "total contempt of all Contracts made with me," was not open to persuasion.[13]

Tench had gone beyond the bounds of what even a permissive parent would tolerate. Having for years been pampered by his father, Tench had convinced himself that parental indulgence was limitless. Now obliged at middle age to confront the fact that he was no longer the preferred, or even potentially the prodigal, son, he was desolated. But this was only temporary, for his growing absorption in partisan politics overshadowed such personal problems, perhaps intentionally so. Although an individual's public involvement cannot always be fairly attributed to his personal problems, Coxe's immersion in partisanship did serve to drown his awareness of a rebuff too painful to contemplate.

Coxe launched his career as a party polemicist in February 1798, immediately after Wolcott dismissed him from the Treasury Department. His first major contribution was the publication of an attack on Federalist foreign policy, a part of which he had written during the preceding year as a letter to President John Adams, but for prudential reasons had then refrained from publishing. Now free to attack the policies of his former Federalist associates and encouraged by "the advice of several very eminent republicans and old revolutionaries," he expanded his original brief work into nine lengthy articles published under the signature "An American Merchant."[14] Announcing a theme that he, along with other Republican party

13. William Coxe, Sr., to Coxe, Sept. 6, 1798, *ibid.*

14. Coxe to John Adams, Apr. 5, 1797, McHenry Papers, Lib. of Cong. What Coxe sent to Adams in the spring of 1797 was the second in his series of articles signed "An American Merchant." This was entitled "Questions concerning the possible grounds of dissatisfaction on the part of France against the United States."

The quotation in the text is from a fragment of a draft of an article in the Coxe Papers. Coxe's "Neutral Spoliations," signed "An American Merchant," appeared first in the *Philadelphia Gaz.*, where five numbers were published on Feb. 3, 5, 16, Mar. 8, and 12, 1798, respectively. The whole series of nine articles was published in the *Aurora* on Feb. 6, 7, Mar. 7, 8, 9, 10, 25, 27, and 28, 1798. A number of the articles were also republished in Mathew Carey's *United States Recorder* (Philadelphia), as follows: No. 1 on Mar. 8, 1798, No. 3 on Mar. 10, 1798, and No. 9 on Apr. 3, 1798. In his *American Museum for 1798* (pp. 226–260) Mathew Carey reprinted the series, though inadvertently omitting the second article.

Coxe said he originally intended to publish only the first two essays in the series, but after an

leaders, would belabor for the next two years, Coxe argued that the United States must avoid at all costs a war with France and an alliance with England, "the first and greatest aggressor against" neutrals.[15]

Coxe's virtually book-length series was, however, not so much a defense of France (though thousands of words were devoted to that subject) as a slashing attack on British spoliations of American commerce. "If the French Republic, rendered wild and outrageous by such monstrous plans of oppression and destruction has been led by self-defense, party rage, and foreign and domestic intrigue to corresponding excesses, she is no more to blame than the governments," especially Great Britain, "which bro't her into her present condition and temper."[16] By such strained arguments Coxe was able to conclude that because one nation had begun the system of lawless aggression upon America's neutral rights, another nation was now justified in similarly violating them. But he could afford to overlook such illogicalities, for he was, after all, intent not on converting his opponents but rather on reinforcing the faith of like-minded partisans. To these Republican supporters Great Britain was still the enemy, and the tameness of the Adams administration in submitting to that country's aggression was the true cause of the treatment accorded America by the rulers of France. How did Coxe, along with other critics of Adams's foreign policy, get around the fact that France, whatever its motivation, was in fact grossly violating their own country's neutral rights? "The measure of violating the commercial rights of America," he disingenuously explained, was merely "a part of the great system of measures, violating the rights of pacific and neutral nations, adopted by the combined powers to annoy the French in their revolutionary struggle."

But for the most part Coxe ignored French spoliations by centering his attention on the misdeeds and atrocities of England between 1792 and 1797. Rather than viewing the past through the lens of the present, he chose to interpret the present in light of a one-sided account of the past. His major preoccupation, moreover, was with what from the standpoint of practicality was an irrelevant question: Who *first* violated American rights?[17] "*It is really time,*" he explained, "*for all good, prudent, and candid men to ac-*

"attack upon the motives of the writer by an essay in the *Philadelphia Gazette* . . . the paper on spoliations and headed No. 3 and those which followed were forced from the writer." "An American Merchant," *Aurora,* Mar. 27, 1798.

15. [Coxe], "An American Merchant," *Aurora,* Feb. 6, 1798.

16. *Ibid.,* Mar. 27, 1798. The British, Coxe had written in a preceding article, "never permitted the irritability of the French to be abated, nor the wounds of neutral rights to be cured. If the French became inflamed at the sight of their own wrongs, and at the vast expenses, injuries, and dangers, which they produced, Britain was the cause." *Ibid.,* Mar. 8, 1798.

17. *Ibid.,* Mar. 7, 1798.

knowledge and admit the extravagance and unwarrantableness of the various orders of the British commanders," a premise that when coupled with his cavalier disregard of the then-current English-American rapprochement and the Franco-American imbroglio, enabled him to conclude triumphantly that such an acknowledgment "is the first *plain* and *honest* step out of our present *distracting* situation." Like Madison and Jefferson, Coxe was chagrined and humiliated at his country's commercial dependence on Britain; like them, he was convinced that American commerce could be employed to wring concessions from European powers. But, unlike the Virginians, he also believed that American commerce should be used as an instrument by which American manufactures might be promoted.[18] In his emphasis on the latter, if not in political ideology, Coxe was consistent.

But the implicit purpose of Coxe's articles was not the encouragement of either political or economic freedom. It was rather the promotion of anti-British sentiment, already the country's most entrenched prejudice. An innocent and republican France was contrasted to "an *hereditary* . . . power, an *hereditary* and *luxurious* nobility, and an *unrepresented* people." This contrast, thus deceptively described, was, Coxe believed, of immense concern to Americans, or at least to as many of them as "do not wish to banish from the world truth, honour, brotherly love, humanity, and *the right of nations to govern themselves*, in exclusion of hereditary sovereigns, and of foreign influence and interference."[19]

Whatever heat Coxe may have added to partisan controversy, his articles added little to his stature as a historian or essayist. William Cobbett, that master of partisan vitriol and gross distortion, for once spoke accurately when he remarked that "Mr. Coxe . . . is a man of learning, ability, and information; but he is too prolix and too voluminous."[20] By joining the legion of publicists who tirelessly played the familiar theme of British hostility to republicanism, Coxe also once again unlatched the door to his tory past that he had resolved to keep locked.

Even before Coxe's articles were in print, *Porcupine's Gazette* had trotted out the frayed charges of toryism. They were soon taken up by Samuel Sitgreaves, a Federalist congressman from Pennsylvania, who, writing as "Milo," asserted that the style of "An Am. Merchant" "designates the author as plainly as though he had proclaimed his name." In a scathing attack on Coxe's record of fickle loyalties, Sitgreaves caustically wrote: "Always desirous to undermine the independence of his country, he is careless in whose service he becomes the pioneer. At one time the servile minion

18. *Ibid.*, Mar. 9, 1798.
19. *Ibid.*, Mar. 27, 28, 1798.
20. *Porcupine's Gaz.*, Jan. 29, 1798.

of Great-Britain; at another the baser adulator of France." Harping on the episode that Coxe's opponents seemingly never tired of, "Milo" reminded the public that Tench had escorted the British into Philadelphia in 1777. Once having guided "an enemy to devastation and plunder," he observed, Coxe "may now be seen in the no less honourable office of attempting by his writings to increase the disunion of a people, whose great . . . misfortune is their want of unanimity." Nor did Sitgreaves neglect Coxe's second-most vulnerable spot: his seven-year tenure of office under the Federalists, whose official papers he now employed to discredit them. "Had I ever held an office," Sitgreaves said, "I should not have been base and treacherous enough to prostitute the information I received from it, to the purpose of destroying that government, by whose patronage I had been supported."[21]

Coxe may have been offended by such accusations, but he was not silenced. As if nine essays on British iniquities were not already too many, he pursued the subject in yet other articles, the best of which, published in April 1798 under the signature "Columbus," was entitled a "Short View of the Question, whether it is advisable for the United States to enter into a War with France."[22] Here he pointed with telling effectiveness to the major contradiction in Federalist policy: How could those who had argued during the debate on Jay's Treaty that the nation must at all costs avoid war until it had reached maturity now consistently assert that the country's honor must be protected even at the cost of war? "By what miracle," Coxe asked, had it "happened that our infancy has in that short period been succeeded by a nervous manhood?" Coxe's attempted refutation of the reasons advanced by those advocating war with France was a creditable piece of partisan journalism.

While continuing to embroider his account of perfidious Albion and peace-loving France, Coxe struck back at his critics by counterattacks, both under his own signature and anonymously. In an indignant, though signed, letter to the *Gazette of the United States*, he protested both Sitgreaves's misrepresentation of his "laborious" research and the Federalists' display of such "implacable enmity" against a "faithful *vidette* of the constitution of laws."[23] Coxe's anonymously published defense was accomplished chiefly through Benjamin Franklin Bache of the *Aurora*, who printed, for example, a spirited defense entitled "Tench Coxe," which only the subject could have written. Admitting a brief flirtation with toryism, Coxe pled as a defense his

---

21. "Milo," *Gaz. of U.S.*, Mar. 13, 20, 1798; *Porcupine's Gaz.*, Feb. 1, 1798. For Samuel Sitgreaves's authorship, see *Aurora*, Sept. 30, 1799.

22. "Short View of the Question" was published first in the *Aurora*, Apr. 4, 1798, and republished in the *American Museum for 1798*, 203–212.

23. Coxe to John Fenno, n.d., Coxe Papers.

youth and his failure to appreciate fully the misdeeds of the mother country, insisting that once he understood the issues at stake in the quarrel, he became a firm and unswerving advocate of American independence. What did Coxe believe prompted the charges against him? The answer, he insisted, was the resentment of former tories, now Federalists, who had never changed their opinion and were "only angry because Mr. Coxe hath changed his," and their anger that he had "dissented from some of the infallible opinions of Alexander Hamilton."[24]

Coxe's biting attacks on Federalist foreign policy, as well as the vitriolic attacks on him, were characteristic of political warfare in 1798. It was a year when partisan anger and bitterness intensified, making it appear to contemporaries a virtually unparalleled time of crisis, a period when the very survival of the nation was at stake. Whatever underlying forces may have operated, foreign affairs were ostensibly responsible. The nation had weathered the tempest of Anglo-American relations of the years 1794 to 1796 (though not in a manner satisfactory to the Republicans) only to find itself locked in conflict with France. Claiming that by Jay's Treaty the United States had allied itself with Great Britain and reneged on its treaty obligations to its Revolutionary ally, the French began in 1796 a systematic policy of maritime harassment and diplomatic coercion designed to bring the ungrateful and unruly new nation into line. Not only did France, consistent with decrees of July 2, 1796, and March 2, 1797, step up its attacks on American commerce, but, intent on drawing a "cordon about the United States that would check its expansion, threaten its western territory, and make it as much a tributary to French policy as Belgium or Holland," it sent agents into the West "to stir up sedition against the United States, and to start filibustering expeditions against Spanish and British America."[25] And the Directory, persuaded that the new nation was powerless to retaliate, did not hesitate to dismiss Charles Cotesworth Pinckney, the American minister appointed in 1796 to replace the ardent Francophile James Monroe. Nevertheless, in the spring of 1797, four months after Pinckney was ordered to leave Paris on penalty of arrest, President John Adams, after consulting with his cabinet, decided to try to reach an amicable settlement of the dispute and

---

24. *Aurora*, Apr. 6, 1798.

25. Samuel Eliot Morison, *The Life and Letters of Harrison Gray Otis, Federalist, 1765–1848*, I (Boston, 1913), 60. The decree of July 2, 1796, announced that France would treat neutral nations as they allowed Great Britain to treat them. This was expanded by the decree of Mar. 2, 1797, which declared as good prize any neutral vessel loaded in whole or in part with enemy goods. *American State Papers, Foreign Relations*, II, 30–31. For an account of French assaults on United States commerce, see Secretary of State Timothy Pickering's report, dated June 21, 1797, *ibid.*, 28–63.

at the same time to prepare for hostilities by recommending to Congress proposals for strengthening the country's defenses.[26]

The treatment of Pinckney, John Marshall, and Elbridge Gerry, the American envoys appointed to negotiate with the French, is well known. Talleyrand, the French foreign minister, as if intent on pushing the United States into the war, deputized his agents—the famous X, Y, and Z—to demand of the American envoys apologies for Adams's criticism of France in his address to Congress on May 16, 1797, a "douceur for the Pocket" of twelve million livres, and a large loan. Unauthorized to accede to any such demands and convinced that France was not so much disposed to negotiate as to dictate to the United States, Marshall and Pinckney demanded their passports. Gerry, assuming that single-handedly and without official authorization he might avoid a Franco-American war, remained in Paris until Talleyrand's gibes and insults forced him also to leave four months later.

When the XYZ dispatches arrived in the United States, Adams, his advisors, most congressmen, and an overwhelming majority of all Americans were incensed by what they viewed as a calculated insult to the nation's independence and dignity. Indeed, not since the first years of Washington's administration had the Federalists been so popular. In April, May, and June 1798 messages of support rained on the president, drenching him in the popularity so long denied and so wistfully sought. Congress, encouraged by the enthusiastic backing of the country, pushed through a preparedness program that included an increase in the navy and the creation of a navy department, as well as authorization for the president to raise a provisional army and to augment the regular army. It also pushed the country to the brink of war by authorizing American merchant vessels to defend themselves against French depredations, by suspending commercial intercourse between the United States and France and its dependencies, and by declaring the Franco-American treaties void. By the time Congress adjourned on July 16, 1798, it had taken all steps short of a formal declaration of war. As has been done in subsequent crises of the twentieth century, the government also adopted measures to safeguard the country against subversion and to punish disloyalty—the notorious Alien and Sedition laws.

---

26. See Adams's message to Congress of May 16, 1797, Richardson, ed., *Messages and Papers of the Presidents*, I, 223–229. Years later Coxe wrote to Madison that he "had some reason to believe that" the essay on Franco-American relations that he had submitted to Adams in 1797 "contributed to alter a governmental determination not to send another Mission to France, after Mr. C. C. Pinckney's first expedition, alone. I naturally gave credit then, and now give credit to the President for being influenced by a number of prudential considerations, which appeared to me irresistibly to persuade to another trial." Coxe to Madison, June 18, 1805, Madison Papers, Lib. of Cong.

The crisis-spawned popularity of the Federalists was a bitter setback for those Jeffersonians who, like Coxe, confidently regarded their near-victory of 1796 as a curtain raiser for 1800. Their despair was deepened by the sight of America, the world's best hope for freedom, in league with repressive and monarchical governments against a fellow republican nation. To the Jeffersonians, French assaults on American commerce and territorial integrity were due more to Britain's actions than to those of the sorely provoked Directory, more to the Francophobia of the Federalists than to the Republicans' opposition to national defense.

Republicans like Coxe questioned neither their devotion to France nor the desirability of the close union between that country and their own. They were confronted, however, by a practical political dilemma: Since retaliation for French insults to the American flag was obviously endorsed by a large majority of the country's citizens, would not party oblivion be the consequence of partisan opposition to this? Convinced of the inequities of Federalist policy, the Jeffersonians chose to run the risk, and the manner in which they undermined the seemingly firm popular support of their rivals is one of the great success stories in American political history.

There were, as Republican leaders quickly perceived, chinks in the Federalists' superficially impregnable armor. One was the notorious Sedition Act, particularly as enforced by overzealous federal officials; another was related legislation pertaining to aliens. As Edward Livingston correctly foresaw during congressional debate, the effects of these measures were "disaffection among the States, and opposition among the people" to the Adams administration, accompanied by "tumults, violations, and a recurrence to first revolutionary principles."[27] Even more damaging to the Federalists were the taxes they were obliged to levy for the support of their program of military defense, especially provisions for a standing army, that hobgoblin of eighteenth-century Republicans. Such taxes, as Jefferson perceived, would soon cool the ardor for war.

Unpopular as these acts potentially were, a successful effort to discredit their authors required an energetic publicity campaign. As Coxe realized, this depended on the effectiveness of the Republican party press, which by a sustained and repetitious appeal to American affinity with France and antipathy to monarchical England would awaken latent national prejudices. A first step was to shore up the sagging finances of the Philadelphia *Aurora*, the country's most important Republican newspaper. Its editor, Benjamin Franklin Bache, was not only Coxe's close political ally but also a family friend. The grandson of Benjamin Franklin, Bache was a skillful political propagandist and second only to William Cobbett as a master of maledic-

27. *Annals of Cong.*, VIII, 2014.

tion. Since among newspaper editors of the time similarity apparently bred abuse, it was a tribute to Bache's skill in scurrility that Cobbett singled him out for attack. "The most infamous of the Jacobins is BACHE . . . the greatest of fools, and the most stubborn sans-culotte in the United States," *Porcupine's Gazette* announced. He "has outraged every principale of decency, of morality, of religion, and of nature," Cobbett declared on another occasion, and should be treated "as we should a TURK, A JEW, A JACOBIN, OR A DOG."[28] To Coxe, also the victim of Cobbett's vitriolic pen, such abuse must have been proof of Bache's personal rectitude and political virtue. In any event, by mid-1798 the quondam Federalist officeholder and the knight-errant of Republican journalism joined forces, and Coxe became the fiscal manager of Bache's campaign against the alleged Federalist bastion of militarism and monarchism.

Bache needed help. Not only was he under indictment for seditious libel, an indictment based on his publication of a secret state paper, but also the *Aurora* urgently required financial first aid. And Coxe was prepared to come to its assistance. A first step was to assure solvency "by a contribution of a number of Republicans living in Philadelphia," a fund-raising drive presumably headed by Coxe.[29] A second step was to provide political advice and to prepare articles for the *Aurora*. Writing some years later when he was locked in political battle with Bache's successor, Coxe claimed that beginning in 1797 and continuing over the next seven years he was responsible for a large share "of the publications of the *Aurora* upon subjects of democratic principle and democratic policy, national industry, political economy, and defense against foreign influence."[30]

Whatever the precise nature of the partnership between Coxe and Bache, it was short-lived. July was a hot and sultry month; by midmorning it was usually 90 degrees, by noon 100. The citizens of Philadelphia irritably endured the humid, sticky weather but dreaded above all else another plague of yellow fever. Late in July it struck and within a few weeks had become an epidemic, the worst since 1793. Terrified by the mounting death rate, the people fled—most of the well-to-do to their country homes and many of the poor to temporary tents and sheds hastily put up on the east bank of the Schuylkill River. Although the Coxe children had long since been shipped off to their grandparents in Burlington and Sidney, Rebecca, momentarily expecting another baby and afraid to travel, had remained in the city. It was

28. Quoted in Bernard Faÿ, *The Two Franklins: Fathers of American Democracy* (Boston, 1933), 338; *Porcupine's Gaz.*, Mar. 17, 1798.

29. *Aurora*, Aug. 11, 1802. Benjamin Franklin Bache's successor, William Duane, reported that by Sept. 1798 Bache had expended $20,000 to maintain the solvency of the *Aurora*, the returns from which were not even sufficient to pay the living expenses of his family. *Ibid.*

30. *Freeman's Jour.*, June 18, 1804.

a grisly summer for Tench, who, numbed by the sight of the dead and the dying, tried to carry on business as usual. Rebecca's baby, a boy, arrived in mid-August, and as soon as she could travel the family set out for Germantown, where Coxe had rented Jared Ingersoll's "apartments," not especially "elegant but situated in the higher part of the Town."[31]

Bache should also have left. By September most other Philadelphia journalists had suspended publication, but the two great gladiators of the city's press, Bache and Cobbett, remained behind. On September 6 Bache contracted the fever; four days later he was dead. In his last moments he dictated a "confidential memorandum" to Coxe, imploring him to preserve the *Aurora* for the benefit of Bache's "family, his country and mankind."[32]

News of his friend's death was sent to Coxe by John Smith, a close political associate, who lamented the possibly "irreparable Injury" thus dealt "the Republican Interest of this Country" and urged Coxe immediately to take steps to assure the continuation of the *Aurora*. Mrs. Bache should "continue the business . . . in her own name," Smith counseled, with the management of the newspaper handed over to an assistant Bache had employed earlier in the year, William Duane, "a Person of Considerable Talents and . . . of Prudent Conduct." Coxe, having received a letter from Duane with the memorandum Bache had dictated just before his death, readily agreed. The next day, September 13, Coxe wrote to Margaret Bache offering his condolences and describing her husband's last wishes. "All I say to you is confidential," he wrote, *"No other person* is to know it for reasons I will explain. But keep up your spirits. Something must and can be done with the paper for your advantage. . . . Rather than see Philadelphia without a free daily paper, I would engage with you or alone, or in some way or another participate in and support the paper." Although neither the source of the money nor the precise terms of the financial agreement reached with Mrs. Bache are known, Coxe almost certainly managed to procure the requisite funds.[33]

When the *Aurora* reappeared on November 1, 1798, the name of Margaret Bache replaced that of her husband on the masthead, and Duane

31. Jared Ingersoll to Coxe, Aug. 12, 24, 1798, William Coxe, Jr., to Coxe, Aug. 20, 1798, Coxe Papers.

32. Coxe to Margaret Bache, Sept. 13, 1798, *ibid*.

33. John Smith to Coxe, Sept. 12, 1798, Coxe to Margaret Bache, Sept. 13, 1798, *ibid*. Coxe's arrangements with Mrs. Bache were conducted through Duane. For the latter's report on the *Aurora*'s state of affairs, see Duane to Coxe, Oct. 5, 1798, in Peter J. Parker, "The Revival of the *Aurora*: A Letter to Tench Coxe," *PMHB*, XCVI (1972), 524–525. See also the introduction to this letter for an account of Coxe's role in the resumption of the newspaper's publication. *Ibid*., 521–523. Probably Coxe obtained the needed funds from concerned Republicans like Joseph Clay, an executor of Bache's estate, and Thomas Leiper, an ardent partisan who was also a well-to-do merchant.

was editor.[34] Although the person to whom the late editor had made the request was not identified, an editorial described Bache's confidential memorandum to Coxe when it stated that Bache's last wish had been that the *Aurora* be continued "with inflexible fidelity to the principles upon which it was founded and reared up." Coxe's generous assistance was both remembered and rewarded. Margaret Bache soon married her editor, and William Duane promptly became not only Coxe's chief publisher but also for a time his steadfast defender.[35] Since the contumacious editor is not known on any other occasions to have been susceptible to either loyalty or gratitude, it appears a safe conjecture that the two had formed a de facto partnership. In any event, by the fall of 1800 the pages of the *Aurora* were virtually given over to Coxe's defense against Federalist attacks upon him and to his own partisan philippics.

In the meantime, Coxe kept in close contact with Republican congressmen like John Dawson of Virginia and Albert Gallatin, with Pennsylvania Republican party leaders such as John Beckley, and with political lieutenants like John Smith, his most faithful supporter. It was from the latter that Coxe learned of his adopted party's reward for his contribution to the Democratic-Republican cause. At a meeting of Philadelphia Republicans on September 7 Coxe was nominated for the state assembly. Doubtless aware that his name could only damage the Republican ticket, he withdrew, aspiring for the moment to the less public but more influential role of party leader. The results of the congressional election, held some weeks later, must have been a welcome harbinger of how important this role would be. From western Pennsylvania, Albert Gallatin and John Smilie were returned to Congress; elsewhere six Republicans were elected, thus giving their party a majority of four in the state's congressional election.[36] To Coxe the victory was reassuring, but it was even more gratifying for the triumph it presaged in the approaching gubernatorial race. To achieve this victory, he now subordinated all else, even the lure of speculation in lands and the prudent management of those he tenuously held.

34. This arrangement lasted only two weeks. Beginning with the issue of Nov. 14, 1798, the *Aurora*'s masthead stated that it was published "for the heirs of Benjamin Franklin Bache."

35. *Aurora*, Nov. 1, 1798. Many years later Coxe wrote: "Duane who had arrived the year before, I believe, in the United States . . . sought to be introduced to me, a stranger to him at my own house." Coxe said he saw Duane only once again (at the printing office of Andrew Brown, Jr., where he "understood" Duane was employed) until Sept. 1798. Fragment of article on Duane [1817], Coxe Papers.

36. John Smith to Coxe, Sept. 8, 1798, Coxe Papers. For an account of the election results, see Smith to Coxe, Oct. 6, 1798, *ibid.*

18 🕸

Would-Be Governor-Maker and Land Office Secretary

Coxe is the forgotten man of the Democratic-Republican party in Pennsylvania. Historians, depending on their focus or preference, have highlighted the party contributions of William Duane, Alexander J. Dallas, or John Beckley, among others, but none has pointed to Coxe's key position. His importance is attested, first of all, by his close connection with the *Aurora*, a newspaper with influence that was, as Thomas McKean once conceded, "more powerful than could rationally have been supposed."[1] Coxe's primary role is further revealed by his membership on the committee that organized the Republican campaign, his correspondence with party leaders throughout the state, and his authorship of broadsides and circulars with which the Jeffersonians drenched the state. That contemporaries were aware of his influential behind-the-scenes role is shown by the nature and frequency of Federalist verbal assaults upon the activities and character of what one newspaper called "this would-be Governor-Maker."[2]

Coxe's prominence in party circles was demonstrated by his authorship of the first campaign document of the Pennsylvania Republicans. That document was the Republicans' "Dissent" from an "Address" to President Adams that was pushed through the state assembly by its Federalist majority. Responding adversely to Governor Thomas Mifflin's annual message reproving Adams's partisans for displaying a "spirit of party, intolerant, and

1. Cited in James Hedley Peeling, "Governor McKean and the Pennsylvania Jacobins (1799–1808)," *PMHB*, LIV (1930), 337.
2. *Porcupine's Gaz.*, May 20, 1799.

348

vindictive," the Federalists had adopted a special message approving the president's stout opposition to the vile "arts of political seduction . . . triumphantly employed" by France and her American supporters.[3] On December 20, 1798, the "Address" handily passed the assembly, though some twenty-three Republicans voted against it. Two weeks later these Republicans presented a written explanation of their opposition and requested that their "Dissent" be incorporated in the *Journal* of the house; the Federalist majority refused, largely on the grounds that the rebuttal included "indecorous" criticism of the president.

Why Coxe was asked to draft the "Dissent" is not clear, but that he was testifies to his emergence as the penman, and perhaps the strategist, of the Pennsylvania Republicans. In that document Coxe argued that "flattering addresses" do not "comport with the simple and dignified principles of Republican Government." On behalf of the minority of the Pennsylvania legislature he assailed the Federalists' "high and unqualified approbation" of the president's conduct. Adams should rather be indicted, Coxe asserted, for his numerous offenses: the enhancement of partisan conflict, the proscription of freedom of opinion, the monopoly of high public office by New Englanders and the concomitant neglect of Pennsylvanians, as well as hostility toward republican France, animus toward republicanism itself, and tacit approval of the Alien and Sedition laws. Adams's conduct had been neither "disinterested" nor "marked with a paternal solicitude for the *public good*."[4]

The Republican campaign was formally launched in February 1799 when a handful of Republican leaders held a succession of meetings in Philadelphia to decide on a popular candidate for governor. Although there were several aspirants and some acrimonious infighting by their loyal supporters, the caucus selected Thomas McKean, the state's chief justice and, in the words of one of his campaign managers, "a Violent party man . . . but . . . an upright, and impartial Judge." To promote his election a "Corresponding Committee" of seven was chosen—Coxe, General William Irvine, Colonel Samuel Miles, Alexander J. Dallas, General Peter Muhlenberg, Dr. Michael Leib, and William Penrose.[5] "I endeavored openly to get my name

---

3. Harry Marlin Tinkcom, *The Republicans and Federalists in Pennsylvania, 1790–1801: A Study in National Stimulus and Local Response* (Harrisburg, Pa., 1950), 207.

4. The "Dissent" was republished in the *Freeman's Jour.*, July 16, 1804. For Coxe's authorship, see *Aurora*, July 18, 1804.

5. Samuel Miles to Coxe, Feb. 11, 1799, Coxe Papers. Thomas McKean's chief rival was Gen. Peter Muhlenberg. His candidacy was pushed by leaders like Michael Leib and William Duane to whom the sincerity of Chief Justice McKean's advocacy of democracy was suspect. John Smith of Philadelphia, Coxe's loyal political lieutenant, claimed that he alerted Coxe, Samuel Miles, and Alexander J. Dallas to the machinations of Muhlenberg's supporters and thus thwarted the general's nomination. Smith to Coxe, Dec. 15, 1800, *ibid.* The committee to

struck out, but in vain," Coxe wrote some months later. "Others of our committee did the same . . . also in vain, for we all remained on the committee," except Irvine, who "was suddenly called home" and did not again participate in the committee's work.[6]

Considering that the campaign was to be conducted in the name of the common man, the composition of the campaign committee (Leib, physician turned politician, perhaps excepted) is arresting. Coxe was a merchant, a land speculator, a former Federalist, and a Philadelphia aristocrat; Muhlenberg was a former Federalist congressman and descendant of two of the outstanding German families in the state; Dallas was secretary of the commonwealth and a distinguished lawyer who "was much in the Philadelphia social whirl"; Miles, like Coxe, was a Federalist during Washington's administration and "one of the richer men in the State"; and William Penrose was a wealthy Philadelphia merchant.[7] These were the men now joined together to wage a war against aristocracy and privilege. At least there was consistency. Thomas McKean, whose name was emblazoned on the campaign banner under which the committee marched, was also a member of the establishment, if the state had one, and previously a conservative by any criterion then known in America. His outspoken reservations about democracy, however, weighed less than his political availability. "The Chief Justice," as one Republican leader expressed it, "would command more votes . . ." than any of "the other gentlemen—being more generally known among the people."[8] A cynic might have added that, prima facie, the committee was rather less intent on making Pennsylvania safe for democracy than on guaranteeing its own political ascendancy.

Motivation aside, the central committee (composed exclusively of Philadelphians after Irvine dropped out) conducted a masterly campaign. Its purpose, in the words of one of Coxe's Lancaster correspondents, was to set "the Mind of the uninformed and the misguided man . . . right, by stating to him plain and important Truths and by removing dangerous Prejudices" to the end that he might be stimulated "to the necessary exertions for effecting a change of Men, in order to obtain a change of measures." Its strategy called for the distribution of hundreds of copies of circular letters

---

promote McKean's election was appointed on Mar. 1, 1799, and was instructed "to be particularly attentive to the election of honest and independent men for Inspectors and Judges" and to that end to choose reliable men "to attend at each place of election to ensure fair play" in casting and returning ballots. These poll watchers were to "report to the Committee of Correspondence any irregularities which shall occur." *Aurora*, Apr. 16, 1799.

6. "To the Citizens of the State of Pennsylvania," Sept. 19, 1799, *ibid.*, Sept. 30, 1799.

7. Tinkcom, *Republicans and Federalists in Pennsylvania*, 220, 224.

8. William Barton to Coxe, Feb. 13, 1799, Coxe Papers.

among "the most proper persons" in every county; the designation of "a Committee of three or five in each township in the State"; and the circulation of information about the state's election law and about the "appointment of some persons in each Election district in the State whose business it shall be particularly to attend to its execution."[9] Such an elaborate campaign plan required careful supervision.

This the Philadelphia committee delegated to Coxe, who (if his correspondence is a reliable gauge) served both as corresponding secretary and as campaign coordinator. His role did not go unnoticed by the opposition. "Of the six persons who have stepped forward as the *canvassers* for McKean," William Cobbett commented in *Porcupine's Gazette*, "*Dallas* and *Tench Coxe* are the only ones worth attention; the other four are mere puppets to them." Of the two, Cobbett believed that only "Coxe has abilities," while Dallas must "supply the want of them by flattery and intrigue."[10] Whether such an assessment was valid or not, Coxe was indisputably the most energetic member of the committee.

The principal cogs in the Republican state machine were local officials in virtually every county from Allegheny to Chester. Working in close cooperation with Coxe and the Philadelphia committee, these chieftains developed the art of persuasion to an extent that politicians of a later era, beneficiaries of a long tradition in the practice of democratic politics, might well have envied. To the participants in this statewide network of political correspondents Coxe sent letters of advice or encouragement; he approved or vetoed local candidates; he supplied campaign fodder to those who, their partisan fervor having outrun their accuracy, were under attack by the opposition press; he traveled around the state to confer with party leaders and to speak at local rallies; and he pressed his cohorts on by urging not only victory but "a large and impressive one."[11] But, above all, he was, next to William Duane, the major penman of the Republican campaign, as wordy as he was persuasive.

Contemporaries were well aware of Coxe's role in the campaign, and at times it might have appeared that his demerits rather than McKean's qualifications were the major issue of the contest. Coxe's Federalist opponents quickly perceived that he was the ideal whipping boy—a former tory who traduced the Federalists as tories all; a former Federalist officeholder,

9. Barton to Coxe, Feb. 13, 1799, Albert Gallatin to Coxe, Apr. 4, 1799, *ibid.* For Coxe's correspondence with Gallatin concerning the campaign, see Coxe to Gallatin, Apr. 12, 26, May 11, Aug. 2, 1799, Gallatin Papers, N.-Y. Hist. Soc., New York.

10. *Porcupine's Gaz.*, Apr. 19, 1799.

11. See, for example, Coxe to "The Citizens of Pennsylvania," n.d., to Alexander Patterson, June 18, 1799, Samuel Townsend to Coxe, Aug. 28, 1799, Barton to Coxe, Aug. 29, 1799, Charles Hartley to Coxe, Sept. 10, 1799, Coxe Papers.

intimately associated with the policies of Hamilton, who now lambasted Federalist policies; a member of the nation's elite who flailed away at aristocrats. Dubbed by one newspaper as "Mr. Facing Bothways," Coxe was condemned for "the malignity of his nature" and described as the "old Tory and Traitor." The partisan value of his numerous articles could be discounted, his critics claimed, on the grounds that "the character of the author" was "sufficient security that no serious effect will be produced."[12]

No critic was more persistent or more merciless than William Cobbett. Again and again he gloated over "trimming Tench's" tory past, pointing to the inconsistency of Coxe's praise of McKean's Revolutionary War record and of his efforts to smear the Federalist candidate as a tory. Cobbett also tirelessly lashed out at the newspapers that opened their pages to Coxe's articles—the *Aurora* was termed "Mother Bache's filthy dishclout"; the editors of the *True American* were "the lickspittle tools of Tench Coxe." Although Coxe professed outrage, he could scarcely have been surprised at counterattacks in a newspaper war that was largely of his own making.[13]

Persuaded that there could not be too much of a good thing, Coxe decided sometime during the first weeks of 1799 that another Democratic newspaper should be launched in Philadelphia. Jefferson enthusiastically agreed, even offering personally to secure the backing of other Republican leaders.[14] This he attempted, but little else was done until just before his scheduled departure for Virginia on March 1. Coxe was anxious that concrete measures be taken before the vice-president left, and early in the evening of February 28 he discussed the matter with Jefferson. Immediately after this conversation Jefferson hurried to the lodgings of Congressman Abraham Venable of Virginia, where the two decided to elicit the aid of Edward Livingston, a New York congressman, who, they were disappointed to learn, was attending the theater. Returning to Jefferson's quarters, they were joined by a third Virginian, Congressman John Nicholas. It was agreed that Venable should draw up proposals for the newspaper and submit them to Coxe. Among other things, the plan called for subscriptions of $500 each by a number of patrons, including Jefferson and Coxe. Jefferson persuaded a few of his close Virginia partisans to become subscribers, and Coxe and his Philadelphia party associates apparently rounded up some support, but

12. *Gaz. of U.S.*, Sept. 4, Oct. 2, 3, 1799; *Claypoole's Daily Adver.*, Oct. 4, 1799. For other attacks, see *Gaz. of U.S.*, Aug. 1, 6, 7, 17, 20, 1799; *Porcupine's Gaz.*, Apr. 19, 22, 24, 29, May 3, 7, 13, 15, 25, June 29, Aug. 20, Sept. 6, 1799.

13. *Porcupine's Gaz.*, Apr. 19, June 29, May 25, Apr. 23, May 13, 1799.

14. The proposed newspaper may have been the subject Thomas Jefferson wished to discuss when on Feb. 14, 1799, he wrote Coxe a note requesting "the favor of an interview with him this evening. He would call on Mr. Coxe but thinks the chance of being alone and unobserved would be better if Mr. Coxe would make it convenient to come to his lodgings between 8 and 9 this evening." Jefferson Papers, Lib. of Cong.

the project failed because few Republican leaders were willing to invest such a sum, no matter how desirable the goal.[15]

Coxe allayed his disappointment by energetically pursuing other means of circulating the partisan addresses and articles that he had hoped to publish in the projected newspaper. The first circular letter of the committee of correspondence, dated April 9, had already been distributed throughout the state, and the correct attribution of its authorship to Coxe had embroiled him in an acrimonious and seemingly interminable newspaper controversy. Baited by Cobbett of *Porcupine's Gazette*, among others, Coxe used the pages of the *Aurora* for self-righteous defenses of his conduct and for slashing counterattacks at the opposition.[16] Another newspaper might, as Jefferson and Coxe had believed, have promoted the Republican cause, but it could scarcely have done more to disseminate Coxe's own views than the *Aurora* did.

Coxe's major target was the Federalist gubernatorial candidate, James Ross. A native of York County, Ross had served a legal apprenticeship in Philadelphia before going west, first to Washington County and then to Pittsburgh. His successful career in local politics was capped in 1794 by election to the United States Senate, where he loyally supported Federalist measures. "Smooth, polished, and even-tempered," he was an effective campaigner, popular not only in western Pennsylvania but also among Federalists throughout the state.[17] He also had behind him a well-organized party machine, no less efficient than that of the opposition.

Had Ross's own qualifications or party organization and campaign practices been the sole criteria of success, the Federalists would have been in a strong position. Like their Republican rivals, they organized a statewide network of committees of correspondence directed by a central committee in Philadelphia. They too swamped the state with campaign literature, in their case designed to expose what one partisan writer called "the cabalistic cant of Jacobinism." They too courted the German vote, even asserting that James Ross "almost leaves the impression of being an upright and strong

---

15. The crucial role that I ascribe to Coxe differs from other accounts of this subject. See, for example, Noble E. Cunningham, Jr., *The Jeffersonian Republicans: The Formation of Party Organization, 1798–1801* (Chapel Hill, N.C., 1957), 131–133, and Donald H. Stewart, *The Opposition Press of the Federalist Period* (Albany, N.Y., 1969), 11. My interpretation is largely based on inferences from the exchange of letters between Coxe and Jefferson on the subject. See Coxe to Jefferson, Apr. 29, June 21, 1799, Jefferson to Coxe, May 21, 1799, Jefferson Papers. For Jefferson's attempts to raise money, see Cunningham, *Jeffersonian Republicans, 1789–1801*, 131. For Coxe's efforts, see Miles to Coxe, July 5, 1799, Coxe Papers.

16. For Coxe's authorship of the circular letter, see *Porcupine's Gaz.*, Apr. 19, May 13, 1799. The letter was printed in the *Aurora*, Apr. 16, 1799. For the newspaper attacks, see, for example, *Porcupine's Gaz.*, Apr. 19, 22, 24, 29, May 3, 7, 1799; *Aurora*, Apr. 18, 24, 26, 1799.

17. Tinkcom, *Republicans and Federalists in Pennsylvania*, 228.

German." Like their opponents, they cried foul when the opposition hit upon an innovative political gambit.[18] Each party, moreover, characterized the attacks of the other as "calumny" or "scurrility," while describing their own partisan invective as a defense of "morality" or "decency." And each invoked their partisan patron saints—the Republicans chanted the names of Franklin and Jefferson, while the Federalists (in this instance rather better supplied) sang hymns in praise of Washington.[19] The Federalists, like the Republicans, charged their opponents with harboring tories, and, of course, Coxe lent credence to the accusation. The advantage the Republicans enjoyed, then, was not to be found in party organization, much less in their greater faith in the people, but rather in the greater popularity of some of the issues they raised. The Federalists found themselves forced to defend unpopular measures, right or wrong, for which their party was responsible.

However, on the single most important issue of the campaign there was little difference between Federalists and Republicans. If the amount of ink spilled on the subject is a reliable guide, both parties viewed the election as a character contest to decide whether McKean or Ross had the shadier past or had committed the more heinous offenses against the people. Coxe contributed to the calumnious campaign of 1799 by charging that five years earlier Ross had encouraged and supported Pennsylvania's "whiskey rebels." Relying once again on information acquired as a federal officeholder, he asserted that the Federalist candidate had attended mass meetings in protest against the whiskey excise, had advised distillers to institute suits against federal revenue officers, and, more serious, had excited them "to fatal violence against the officers."[20] It was, of course, gross misrepresentation of Ross's conduct. It was also an example of inconsistency run riot: Coxe,

18. *Claypoole's Daily Adver.*, Oct. 4, 1799; *Ein Ernstlicher Ruf an die Deutschen in Pennsylvanien . . .* (Lancaster, Pa. [1799]), hereafter cited as *A Serious Appeal*. The Republicans complained, for example, when the Federalist committee of correspondence for the city of Philadelphia, meeting at Dunwoody's Tavern late in Aug., drew up an address to the voters for circulation on the eve of the election, seven weeks away. When the rumors of this tactic were confirmed, Republican leaders were enraged, perhaps because they had not thought of the stratagem themselves. "When we find their motley composition printed *without a date, on the evening subsequent to the departure of the Western mail*," the Republican committee indignantly asked, "is there an impartial freeman, who will hesitate to pronounce, that the object of delay has been to prevent detection on the spot? Is there an honest Elector . . . who will hesitate to condemn *such* means for attaining it?" This article, which appeared in *Claypoole's Daily Adver.*, Oct. 2, 1799, was signed by the members of the Republican committee.

19. Representative was the remark of the pamphleteer who, in an address to the Pennsylvania Germans, referred to "our good old general Washington," who saved "you from the hands of the king of England when you were poor and insignificant," and asked if any good American could "still listen to those who have called our dear old Washington, the father of our country, a murderer and a traitor?" *A Serious Appeal*.

20. Coxe's remarks were first publicized in the *Gaz. of U.S.*, Sept. 16, 1799. His reply to James Ross's defense, dated Sept. 19, appeared in the *Aurora*, Sept. 30, 1799. Debate on Coxe's allegation continued for some weeks longer. See the attack of "Manilius" on Coxe, *Claypoole's Daily*

whose own Republican cohorts were accused of fomenting disobedience to the excise law in 1794, was berating the Federalist candidate for precisely the same offense. But it was typical of the campaign, one characterized by such misrepresentation and scurrility as to cast doubt on the familiar observation that the presidential elections of 1828 and 1840 reached new low points in American politics.

More significant historically are the occasional hints that the emphasis on personalities in the Pennsylvania gubernatorial race may have veiled the extent to which the Republican campaign was designed to protect the property rights of a number of its leaders. At issue were land claims in the Wyoming Valley, an area in which a bitter controversy had raged for decades between Connecticut and Pennsylvania claimants. It is sufficient here to note that by an act of 1799 the Pennsylvania legislature attempted to solve the long-standing problem by validating the claims of Connecticut settlers acquired before the December 1782 decree of Trenton, which had awarded the lands in question to Pennsylvania. For some speculators the law was a hard blow. For one thing, lands surrendered by Pennsylvania claimants were to be graded and paid for according to a quasi-judicial determination of their value; for another, the act provided no guarantees for lands claimed by titles secured after December 30, 1782, especially their protection against Connecticut claimants.[21] The issue was put before the voters by Francis J. Smith, with whom Coxe had engaged in large-scale land deals, in a campaign pamphlet sent to Coxe for approval. "We behold a federal majority assuming the right of deciding peremptorily claims existing in dispute betwixt individuals to lands in Wyoming," contrary to the state constitution, Smith wrote. "I must mention here also," he continued, "the aggravated hardships to which they have doomed the holders of unsatisfyd warrants, who trusting to the justice of Government, advanced Large Sums of monney." Only a Republican victory, he said, would correct such injustices. "The election of the Chief Justice," as Coxe explained in a letter to Alexander Patterson, another prominent land speculator, "is best, both for the rights of the citizens, and for the particular rights of property."[22]

Coxe and other Republican leaders were battling those whom Smith described as "the federalists known also by the name of Aristocrats"—battling not only for abstractions like republicanism but also for more concrete

Adver., Oct. 4, 1799, and Coxe's reply, *ibid.*, Oct. 8, 1799. Some of the campaign fodder Coxe directed at Ross came from Gallatin. See Gallatin to Coxe, Apr. 4, 1799, Coxe Papers.

21. *Pa. Archives*, 2d Ser., XVIII, 715–720.

22. Francis J. Smith, "Address to the Electors of . . . Northampton County," June 22, 1799, Coxe to Patterson, June 18, 1799, Coxe Papers.

and somewhat less elevating goals.[23] It all suggests how easily the acquisitive impulse could be equated with democracy. It suggests also that some Republican bosses were intent on making the best of things for themselves. Although a man may play an important role in a movement without necessarily typifying it, Coxe, combining as he did lofty ideals with the pursuit of personal advantage, does appear to have personified the Pennsylvania Democrat of that time. The point was not lost on contemporaries. "What could have tempted Samuel Miles and Tench Coxe to set their names to a paper that said anything about pecuniary speculations?" asked a writer in the *Gazette of the United States*. "Perhaps the word 'pecuniary' is used to distinguish them from 'Land' speculations. . . . 'Those who live in houses of glass,' etc.—you understand me."[24]

Although some Republican leaders may have pursued their own economic interest by smearing rival land jobbers who happened also to be their political opponents, national issues were at stake in the campaign and redounded to the benefit of the Republicans. Coxe summed up the more important issues in a circular letter he drafted for the Republican committee: "An encrease of public debt and expenditures; a continuing augmentation of federal taxes and imposts; the dangers of a foreign war; an extensive establishment of land and naval forces; a marked disregard of the national militia; and the introduction of impolitic and irritating laws."[25] As this summation indicated, the Republicans were well aware, as one local leader put it, that the voters "will be more readily convinced of the ruinous and unnecessary prodigality of the present Administration *by the applications of the Tax gatherer* than by the soundest Logic or the best political Arithmetic. There is, as Mr. Gallatin has observed, '*Great Sensibility in the Breeches pocket.*'"[26] But an even more effective issue for the Republicans—one under which ruinous taxes could be subsumed—was peace, peace that would bring an end to collaboration with the ancient enemy, the British monarchy, and begin a rapprochement with the country's Revolutionary ally, France. Granted the popularity of a campaign for peace, however, how could it be made germane to a contest for the governorship of Pennsylvania? The difficulty was all the greater in view of John Adams's well-publicized efforts to negotiate a settlement of the quasi-war with France.

On February 18, 1799, Adams, without previously consulting his cabinet, members of Congress, or Federalist leaders, had cryptically an-

23. "Address to the Electors of . . . Northampton County," June 22, 1799, *ibid*.
24. *Gaz. of U.S.*, Aug. 6, 1799.
25. "To the Republicans of Pennsylvania," Apr. 9, 1799, *Aurora*, Apr. 16, 1799. Among the "impolitic and irritating laws" Coxe would have included the Alien and Sedition acts. He discussed the Alien law in an incomplete draft of an article. Coxe Papers.
26. Barton to Coxe, Feb. 13, 1799, Coxe Papers.

nounced the nomination of "William Vans Murray, our minister resident at the Hague, to be minister plenipotentiary of the United States to the French Republic" to negotiate a diplomatic settlement. But under pressure from Federalist congressmen, Adams agreed a few days later to name a three-man commission instead of a single envoy.[27]

With the president having apparently snatched the issue of peace from them, how then could the Pennsylvania Republicans continue to exploit it? One way was to deny Adams's sincerity and to continue to brand him a warmonger.[28] Coxe found an even more effective way: ignore Adams's quest for peace and concentrate instead on his and his party's attachment to Great Britain and to monarchy. This was the means by which the Republicans turned what was superficially a disadvantage into an emotionally charged, tellingly effective issue. The logic underpinning the position—however sincere its proponents may have been—was as simple as it was faulty. The Republicans argued that the foreign policy of the Adams administration was pro-British and that the British were monarchists hostile to republicanism everywhere; therefore, Adams and his Federalist supporters were monarchists secretly intent on subverting the American government.

To Coxe, whose views were archetypal of Pennsylvania Republicans, it was only necessary to find proof of the president's monarchism. And since Coxe believed that the writings and rumored conversations of John Adams offered evidence aplenty, he proceeded without qualms to publish accounts of confidential conversations and gossip that he had kept a careful record of during his years as a Federalist officeholder. This was done in the course of one of his many defenses against the personal attacks leveled against him by the opposition press. In commenting on his own great exertions to prevent the reestablishment of monarchy in the United States, Coxe remarked that his comments were particularly appropriate at the time, as "two members of the Senate have made to him the following statement, viz: that the candidate [Adams] declared to them *that he hoped or expected to see the time when it would be believed that the people of the United States could not be happy without an hereditary chief executive and a senate that should be hereditary or for life*." The two senators to whom Coxe referred were John Langdon of New Hampshire and John Taylor of Virginia. Although they had repeated Adams's indiscreet comment in confidence and had previously

---

27. Richardson, ed., *Messages and Papers of the Presidents*, I, 272.

28. Those Republicans who wrote detailed article after long-winded article (like Coxe's "Columbus" in 1795 and "Honestus" in 1799) elaborating the reasons why the United States should refrain from declaring war on France displayed considerable disingenuousness. Although some Federalists did favor such a war, it was not the official position of either the administration or Congress, both of whom eschewed a formal declaration of war in favor of a program of preparedness.

refused to authorize its publication, Coxe, convinced that since "British influence bestrode the land like a Colossus," the "public safety requirest" extreme measures, decided that now was the time to forgo gentlemanly scruples and to reveal evidence so damning that it would convince all but the most purblind of the president's guilt.[29]

On the same day, April 26, 1799, that he published "proof" of Adams's monarchism, Coxe also printed additional evidence on which he had impatiently been sitting since the president had acquiesced in his dismissal from the Treasury Department. This was a letter from Adams to Coxe of May 1792 in which the then vice-president, criticizing the appointment of Thomas Pinckney as United States minister to England, had confided to Coxe that "suspecting much British influence in the appointment, were I in any executive department, I would take the liberty to keep a vigilant eye upon them [Britain's myrmidons like Hamilton]."[30] Before publishing this in the *Aurora*, Coxe must have shown the original to the editor. Even Duane, reckless as he characteristically was, would not have been so imprudent as to print it without authentication. But once persuaded, he was as eager as Coxe to take all possible advantage of such seemingly damaging evidence. Goaded by the taunts of the Federalist press that the letter was a forgery, Duane published the full text in the *Aurora* on July 24, accompanying it by further documentary evidence of a monarchical conspiracy in the United States.

Secretary of State Timothy Pickering promptly sent the president a copy of the July 24 issue of the *Aurora*, reminding him that this was yet one more example of the "uninterrupted stream of slander" directed by Duane against the administration. Pickering suggested that the government should retaliate with legal proceedings calculated to punish the contumacious editor. These the outraged secretary put in train by submitting a copy of Duane's article to William Rawle, United States attorney in Philadelphia, and directing him to commence a prosecution for seditious libel "if the slander on the American government" justified it.[31] Duane was promptly arrested and duly arraigned. His trial was scheduled for the October term of the United States circuit court. In the interim Rawle, acting on Pickering's advice, scrutinized the *Aurora* for additional libelous material, easily finding what he sought.

Coxe was in a ticklish position. Should he come forward and offer an attested copy of Adams's letter, as well as other material, as proof of the

29. *Aurora*, Apr. 26, Aug. 30, 1799.

30. *Ibid.*, Apr. 26, 1799.

31. Timothy Pickering to John Adams, July 24, 1799, to William Rawle, July 24, 1799, Pickering Papers, Mass. Hist. Soc., Boston. Pickering, assuming that William Duane was actually a British subject, also suggested that the editor be banished from the country as an unfriendly alien.

truth of the alleged libel, or should he wait until he was subpoenaed, as Duane, despite their friendship, was certain to demand that he be? Doubtless Coxe hoped to procrastinate, but on August 6 he received a curt letter from Alexander J. Dallas, Duane's attorney and a fellow Republican campaign manager, asking that he transmit the original papers or certified copies of them for use at Duane's trial. Although Coxe stalled, alleging that Duane had promised not to publish Adams's letter (a tepid defense, considering he had shown Adams's letter to any number of people from whom he had exacted no promise of secrecy), he was finally obliged to acquiesce. If he had not complied, it is likely that he would have been revealed publicly as the person responsible for the libel on the president, though no knowledgeable Philadelphia newspaper doubted that he was.[32]

So far as Duane and Dallas were concerned, the letter was necessary to win a dismissal of the case. On October 15, 1799, the circuit court, with Justice Bushrod Washington of the Supreme Court and Judge Richard Peters of the federal district court presiding, convened in Norristown, having been forced to vacate Philadelphia because of a yellow fever epidemic. As the defendant's representative, Dallas immediately took the offensive by asserting that Duane had in his possession an authenticated copy of the letter in which Adams had implied suspicion of "much British influence" in the United States. When the court obligingly played into Dallas's hands by voicing doubt that any such document existed, Dallas triumphantly asserted that his client would happily produce it. "The Court and the District Attorney, were, for a moment, struck with astonishment," Duane later gloated, "and a large concourse of people assembled to see the Editor of the Aurora hauled over the coals of the sedition ordeal expressed their feelings by a sudden but impressive emotion of surprise and conviction." Among those who displayed surprise, though not conviction, was Justice Washington, who querulously and lengthily discussed the letter's admissibility as legal evidence, finally declaring that "it might possibly be admitted."[33] In view of the provision in the Sedition Act of 1798 making truth a defense against an alleged libel, the court's decision rendered Duane's vindication likely. Encouraged by Washington's ruling and confident that Coxe and other political cohorts would soon document yet other libels charged against the

---

32. Dallas to Coxe, Aug. 6, 1799, Coxe Papers. For other correspondence between Dallas and Coxe, see Coxe to Dallas, July 13, 1800, *ibid.* For Coxe's account of the episode, see *Aurora*, Oct. 6, 1800. Coxe's cooperation was presumably won at the price of an agreement that he would not appear as a witness in Duane's defense. This at least appears a plausible inference, as Coxe was in Philadelphia when Duane's trial took place two weeks later and would have been in no position to refuse Duane's request, had the latter been insistent.

33. *Aurora*, Nov. 1, 1800. Justice Washington is quoted in James Morton Smith, *Freedom's Fetters: The Alien and Sedition Laws and American Civil Liberties* (Ithaca, N.Y., 1956), 286.

Aurora's editor, Dallas asked that the trial be postponed. Although "some confusion was manifested, and some legal pantomine was played off," the court acceded, scheduling the resumption of the case for June 1800. Duane was freed on $3,000 bail. Unintimidated, he continued during that interval to ring the charges of British influence, with, as it turned out, immunity. Embarrassed by the publicity given Adams's indiscreet letter, Federalist authorities dropped the case. According to Duane, the president himself made the decision not to proceed.[34]

Coxe's cooperativeness, though he may have had no choice, had rescued Duane from a prosecution for which Coxe himself was largely responsible. Nevertheless, the two men had together succeeded in distilling the national questions at stake in the Pennsylvania gubernatorial campaign to one potent issue: John Adams's preference for monarchy, shared, so it was implied, by his party. Expressed another way, the fundamental alternatives now became monarchy or republicanism, and for this legerdemain the Federalists could find no political talisman.

Coxe and his partisans were not troubled by doubts over the means by which to discredit their opponents. As they saw it, their object was to curry votes, not to win a debating contest, and during the final weeks before the election on October 8 success seemed certain. Far from relaxing, however, the Republicans stepped up their activities. All the members of the central committee assembled frequently at the Rising Sun Tavern, near Germantown. Coxe and Michael Leib met three times a week, and individual committee members conferred with McKean. These party leaders spurred on county and township campaign captains, did favors for local politicians, and promised political plums to those who cooperated. The state's German and Irish populations were assiduously cultivated, voters were carefully instructed on the proper method of casting their ballots, and the state was deluged with copies of the *Aurora*, as well as broadsides and "addresses" in both German and English.[35] In its final important salvo of the campaign the committee (conveniently overlooking the records of Republican newspapers like the *Aurora*) lashed out at the "licentiousness" of an opposition press "controlled and corrupted by the example and audacity of an alien monarchist." In yet another instance of the pot calling the kettle black, the committee considered it degrading that its rival, the Federalist central cam-

34. *Aurora*, Oct. 3, 1800. For a verbose account of Duane's indictment and trial, see his article, *ibid.*, Nov. 1, 1800. See also *ibid.*, Oct. 3, 30, 1800.

35. Barton to Coxe, Feb. 13, 1799, Samuel Bryan to Coxe, Sept. 20, 27, 1799, Dallas to Coxe, Oct. 6, 1799, P. Denham to Coxe, Sept. 25, 1799, James Gibson to Coxe, Sept. 4, 1799, Israel Israel to Coxe, Sept. 27, 1799, Michael Leib to Coxe, Sept. 24, 1799, Frederick A. Muhlenberg to Coxe, Oct. 2, 1799, John Thompson to Coxe, Sept. 20, 26, Oct. 1, 1799, Townsend to Coxe, Aug. 28, 1799, Coxe Papers; *Gaz. of U.S.*, Sept. 14, 1799; *Aurora*, Sept. 30, 1799.

paign committee, had had the audacity to sign their defamatory and scurrilous circular letters. Anonymous abuse was preferable to acknowledged assault. Writing in the *Gazette of the United States*, one Federalist "Detector" was happy to provide the former. The authors of the "Address to the Republicans of Pennsylvania," he said, were guilty of "every grade of vice," having drunk "the last dregs of corruption." They were "beings whose breath is *contagion*, whose presence is leprosy, and whose company is *death*, to the good name of every man."[36]

A majority of Pennsylvania's voters who went to the polls early in October did not seem to be offended by the Republican tactics. "Letters from every quarter are highly favorable," Alexander J. Dallas informed Coxe on October 6. The official returns confirmed his optimism: of the 70,679 ballots cast (twice as many as in the previous gubernatorial race), McKean won by a majority of about 5,000, almost precisely the number the Republican committee had predicted. The election may have been, as one of Coxe's correspondents put it, "a Glorious Triumph" for republicanism; it assuredly was the personal triumph of political leaders like Coxe who now confidently awaited the suitable reward that Governor Thomas McKean had the power to bestow.[37]

"I am just offered by the Governor of this State the office of the Secretary of the General Land office," Coxe wrote to William Erwin on December 22, 1799. Having assumed that in recognition of his leadership of McKean's campaign he would be appointed secretary of the commonwealth, the most powerful nonelective office in the state, Coxe was less than flattered. But with characteristic aplomb he adopted his father's advice that "you must try to stand well with the House and Governor and [eventually] get something better."[38] Precisely why the governor should have chosen a major political chieftain for a minor post or a large land speculator to oversee the Land Office is undeterminable. Perhaps there was no other position available, and perhaps the possibility of a conflict of interest did not occur

36. "To the Republicans of Pennsylvania," Sept. 27, 1799, *Claypoole's Daily Adver.*, Oct. 5, 1799; *Gaz. of U.S.*, Oct. 8, 1799.

37. Dallas to Coxe, Oct. 6, 1799, Gibson to Coxe, Oct. 17, 1799, Coxe Papers. The Republican committee had forecast that their candidate would receive a majority of 5,700. McKean secured 38,036 votes to Ross's 32,643. The Republicans also won control of the Pennsylvania assembly by electing 41 of its 76 members, while the Federalist majority in the senate was reduced to 2. The election, however, was not as one-sided as this might suggest. Ross may have lost the election, but he carried 13 counties and the city of Philadelphia, while McKean carried only 12 counties.

38. Gibson to Coxe, Oct. 17, 1799, William Coxe, Sr., to Coxe, Dec. 26, 1799, *ibid.* Coxe's expectation that he would be appointed secretary of the commonwealth was shared by others. See, for example, Patterson to Coxe, May 12, 1800, *ibid.*

to him. It would, after all, have been virtually impossible to have found an eligible candidate who was not also a speculator, and in appointing one, McKean was in line with the general practice of the day, not only in Pennsylvania but also nationally. And the governor did not necessarily consider the office an inferior one. At a time when the commonwealth's principal revenue was derived from the sale of lands, the agency was of primary importance, and McKean was determined that it be efficiently and honestly administered.

The Land Office was in urgent need of reform. Reopened in April 1781 as successor to the long-existent provincial land office, it had operated without the close supervision of the governor or the assembly for almost two decades, during which time its officials had been guilty of the most flagrant malpractices. The agency consisted of three principal officers: a secretary, its principal administrative officer, who received applications, issued warrants, prepared patents, and "attended the Governor and the Committees of the Legislature";[39] a receiver general, its comptroller and accountant; and a surveyor general, overseer of the survey and of the validation of land grants. Of these officials, the surveyor general was far and away the most important; under his jurisdiction were the many deputy surveyors authorized to survey and return claims. It was a system that permitted not only arbitrary surveys and decisions but also, for those officials open to corruption, profitable collusion with big-time speculators. And the great majority of the surveyors, as Norman Wilkinson's definitive study of Pennsylvania land policy has demonstrated, were indisputably receptive.[40]

None was more corrupt than General Daniel Brodhead, surveyor general from 1789 until his dismissal in 1800. Brodhead amassed a fortune through his close collaboration with some of the biggest speculators of the day, notably John Nicholson, the state's comptroller general, and Nicholson's partner, Robert Morris. The general's cleverness in complicity was matched by his extraordinary, though perhaps calculated, ineptness as an administrator; the records of his office and those of the secretary's office were in such a confused condition that even the most skilled auditor would have had trouble understanding or unraveling them. For this state of affairs Brodhead shared culpability with the clerks in the secretary's office who were too busy profitably serving the interests of major speculators to be bothered by routine duties. The sorry condition of the Land Office was the

---

39. Coxe to James Monroe, Sept. 9, 1822, *ibid.*

40. Wilkinson, "Land Policy and Speculation in Pennsylvania," 95. For an explanation of speculation by deputy surveyors, some of whom were legislators, see Wilkinson's description of the activities of John Adlum, *ibid.*, 129, 155.

more striking because the stakes in the corrupt game its officials played were so high—millions of acres of Pennsylvania's public domain.[41]

It was Coxe's awareness of these stakes that was largely responsible for his acceptance of a post that, as his father reminded him, paid too low a salary and demanded responsibilities disproportionately great. The position required too that he sacrifice the amenities of Philadelphia for residence in the small, provincial town of Lancaster, the state capital since 1799. To such hardships Coxe cheerfully resigned himself, and on the morning of January 6 he boarded the stage for a long journey along the recently improved turnpike from Philadelphia to Lancaster.[42] Conferences with state officials were held, living quarters were found, and by February he was able to return to Philadelphia in order to arrange to rent his house, to auction off most of his furniture, and to accompany the members of his family on their trip to Lancaster. The family presumably needed a reassuring and cheerful companion, for to them the change from what Joel Barlow once called "the first and most liberal of our cities" to a rustic town was a cultural shock. The capital's population of 5,000 consisted largely of petty officials, provincial lawyers, and backcountry legislators—people with whom the Coxes were not in the habit of associating. The children were enrolled in Patrick Farrelly's newly established private school, where their misbehavior suggests some difficulty in adjustment. Rebecca could at least look forward to a summer's respite in Sidney, and Coxe relieved his exile by organizing a "Social Club" that was actually a Republican party caucus.[43] In any event, his captaincy of Jefferson's Pennsylvania presidential campaign and the burdens of his office assured that he was too busy to be bored.

The superintendence of the Land Office had never been more taxing, largely because of the inept and corrupt administration of Coxe's predecessors. Governor McKean, determined to make a clean sweep of the agency, fired its principals (most conspicuously its master of malfeasance, Surveyor General Brodhead) and deputized Coxe to make wholesale removals of

41. *Ibid.*, 175–236. A knowledgeable correspondent informed Coxe that the widespread corruption among deputy surveyors "was first introduced at the head and from thence spread." Samuel Maclay to Coxe, Apr. 1, 1800, Coxe Papers.

42. William Coxe, Sr., to Coxe, Dec. 26, 1799, John Beckley to Coxe, Jan. 7, 1800, Coxe Papers. Coxe had difficulties finding sureties for the bond that he had to post before leaving Philadelphia for Lancaster. See William Coxe, Sr., to Coxe, Jan. 1, 1800, *ibid.* The £10,000 bond was finally signed by Daniel W. Coxe and Edward Burd. "Deed for Penn. Land Office Bond," Jan. 3, 1800, *ibid.*

43. Joel Barlow to Coxe, Sept. 25, 1809, Coxe Papers. For details of the move, see Tench Coxe, Jr., to Coxe, Jan. 10, 20, 1800, Sampson Levy to Coxe, Feb. 8, 1800, John Connelly to Coxe, Mar. 3, 11, 1800, Patrick Farrelly to Coxe, Apr. 24, July 22, 1800, Coxe to Farrelly, July 25, 1800, "Organization of the 'Social Club,'" n.d., *ibid.*; Coxe to Gallatin, Feb. 21, 1800, Gallatin Papers.

lesser officials, including all clerks. Warmed by the power that the appointment of their successors conveyed, Coxe found this a congenial assignment.[44] Another task, not so pleasant, was the organization of the Land Office's papers. But with the aid of a chief clerk and four assistants (one of them his son Tench, Jr., whose clerkship his father described as "imperfect"), he made rapid strides in cataloging and recording records that for decades had been carelessly, even criminally, neglected.[45] They had been strewn loosely in piles or in unidentified bundles on the floors and shelves in a cramped office that was itself a fire hazard.

Coxe not only straightened out official records, but, aware that many poorer settlers were ignorant of the laws and procedures governing land purchases, also drew up a "carefully digested" guide to official procedures. This he circulated through the state and had printed in many newspapers. Concerned, too, that the west be rapidly settled, both to enhance the state's prosperity and to strengthen its defense against marauding Indians, he took "pains to bring into public Notice especially in our Seaports and foreign Countries the Law of this state enabling Aliens to acquire, hold, and dispose of Lands." More important yet, Coxe, as he boasted in 1801, saw to it that "dispatch without dispatch money" was "introduced into the Land Office."[46] Because of his sweeping dismissal of dishonest officials, Pennsylvanians were at last assured fair and equal treatment by an important agency "whose jurisdiction," as he reminded McKean, "extends to the right of soil, public and private, of the whole State."[47]

44. Brodhead was dismissed on Apr. 15, 1800, and was succeeded by Samuel Cochran. Concerning this and other changes, Samuel Maclay wrote to Coxe on May 13, 1800, that "the New appointments will in my opinion render your Situation much more comfortable than you could have been with the former colleagues, as I am told on Good authority there was a Settled Design to render you as uncomfortable as Possible in order to force you in to a Resignation." Coxe Papers. For Coxe's power of removal, see Maclay to Coxe, Apr. 1, 1800, *ibid.* Coxe received many letters of application during the months succeeding his appointment. See, for example, Edward Mott, Jr., to John M. Taylor, Dec. 20, 1799, George Worrall to Coxe, Dec. 30, 1799, John Weaver to Coxe, Jan. 15, 1800, Mrs. John Hall to Coxe, Jan. 20, 1800, James Gibson to Coxe, Jan. 23, 1800, Richard Adams to Coxe, Feb. 23, 1800, Samuel Bryan to Coxe, Apr. 28, 1800, Vincent Gray to Coxe, June 5, 1800, John Henry Baker to Coxe, July 19, 1800, Mathew Irwin to Coxe, July 22, 1800, *ibid.*

45. Coxe to Mrs. John Hall, Jan. 21, 1800, *ibid.* Coxe's chief clerk was George Worrall. See Worrall to Coxe, Jan. 15, 1800, *ibid.* For information on his other clerks and their arrangements, see Coxe to Thomas McKean, Apr. 9, 1800, *ibid.*

46. Coxe to McKean, May 14, 1800, Coxe Papers; *Intel. & Weekly Adver.*, Aug. 26, 1801. See also "Report of the Secretary of the Land Office of Pennsylvania to the Governor, in obedience to his direction of the 24th of October, 1800," Nov. 1, 1800, *Pa. Archives*, 2d Ser., XVIII, 741–748; Coxe to McKean, May 14, 1800, Coxe Papers.

47. See Coxe's report to Gov. McKean, Nov. 1, 1800, *Pa. Archives*, 2d Ser., XVIII, 741–748. For Coxe's recommendations for further reform of the Land Office, see his report to the Pennsylvania assembly, Dec. 17, 1800, Coxe to N. B. Boileau, Jan. 16, 1801, Coxe Papers. See also Coxe's undated draft of a petition for the holders of unsatisfied warrants and of a bill for their relief, *ibid.*

Not the least of Coxe's achievements after eleven months in office was his contribution to the permanent resolution of the thorny problem of land titles in the Wyoming Valley, a controversy that had plagued Pennsylvania for half a century. This often-told tale can be repeated here only in the most cursory way.[48] In the 1750s the colony of Connecticut, claiming ownership of an extensive tract of land on the eastern bank of the Susquehanna River, known as the Valley of the Wyoming, chartered the Susquehanna Company, under whose auspices Connecticut pioneers moved into the area. Pennsylvania officials stoutly resisted such claims to lands they firmly insisted were well within William Penn's proprietary charter. The result was recurrent civil war as Pennamites and Yankees, each supported by their own government, struggled for control of this scenic valley. Pennsylvania held virtually all the trump cards, and it played them unhesitatingly and not always fairly. Finally, following the Republican triumph in the 1799 gubernatorial election, the Yankees were at last afforded a measure of overdue justice when the Pennsylvania assembly adopted on April 4, 1799, a so-called "Compromise Act" granting compensation to commonwealth claimants and title confirmation to Connecticut settlers.[49]

As secretary of the Land Office, Coxe arrogated to himself the task of supervising implementation of the act. Assuming a policy-making role that was legally vested in the attorney general and the governor, he proceeded to issue instructions to the commissioners appointed to oversee the compromise settlement. He also gave unsolicited advice to Governor Thomas McKean, Attorney General Joseph McKean, and the members of the assembly.[50] Coxe also prepared broadsides, articles, and pamphlets for circulation

48. The Wyoming controversy can be followed in Robert J. Taylor, ed., *The Susquehannah Company Papers*, X, XI (Ithaca, N.Y., 1971).

49. "An act for offering compensation to the Pennsylvania claimants of certain lands within the seventeen townships in the county of Luzerne and for other purposes therein mentioned," Apr. 4, 1799, *Pa. Archives*, 2d Ser., XVIII, 715–720.

50. For Coxe's implementation of the "Compromise Act," see "Report of the Secretary of the Land Office," Feb. 13, 1800, *ibid.*, 726–728; Coxe to the Pennsylvania assembly, Feb. 13, 1800, Jan. 1801, Coxe Papers. For Coxe's correspondence with the commissioners, see Coxe to the commissioners, July 30, Aug. 12, 14, 23, Sept. 11, 22, 25, 1800, Coxe Papers; *Pa. Archives*, 2d Ser., XVIII, 389–421. There were several changes in the membership of the commission. Those initially appointed pursuant to the act of 1799 were Isaac Whelen, William Irvine, and Thomas Boude. Soon after they began work in Feb. 1800, Whelen was replaced by Andrew Porter. In 1801 the entire slate of commissioners was replaced by Thomas Cooper, John Steele, and William Wilson. See Coxe to William Boude, Apr. 15, 1801, Coxe Papers. Coxe's greatest affinity was with Cooper, whose letters encouraged the former's officiousness. See, for example, Cooper to Coxe, June 10, 1801, *ibid.*

To both Gov. Thomas McKean and Atty. Gen. Joseph McKean, Coxe pointed out defects and loopholes in the 1799 law, recommending administrative and legislative changes. See Coxe to Thomas McKean, Jan. 31, Oct. 3, Dec. 8, 1800, *Pa. Archives*, 2d Ser., XVIII, 721–724, 740–741, 749; Coxe to Thomas McKean, Feb. 10, 28, Apr. 16, May 14, Aug. 17, 1800, Coxe Papers;

in the Wyoming townships. The most ambitious of these was a pamphlet, published in the spring of 1801, that presented a persuasive plea for acquiescence in the execution of the Compromise Act, which had already been accepted by all the Connecticut settlers except an insignificant number of malcontents.[51] Coxe was rightly persuaded that he had measurably contributed to the termination of a half-century of conflict.[52] "What member of the legislature, what Officer of the Government, what interested or disinter-

---

Coxe to Joseph McKean, Feb. 6, 1800, *Pa. Archives*, 2d Ser., XVIII, 724–725; Coxe to Joseph McKean, July 30, 1800, Coxe Papers. Joseph McKean was neither receptive nor cooperative. See Joseph McKean to Coxe, Aug. 13, 1800, *ibid.*

51. Coxe's activities as a publicist can be followed in his correspondence with the Luzerne commissioners in the *Pa. Archives*, 2d Ser., XVIII, 389–421. See also *Aurora*, Mar. 8, 1800. As an example of Coxe's writings, see a broadside entitled "Connecticut Claim. Part I. Jurisdiction and State's Right of Soil," n.d., Coxe Papers. Part II has not been found. This broadside is reprinted in the *Pa. Archives* without attribution of authorship under a headnote that states: "The following article from a newspaper in Lancaster was printed in Broadside for distribution among the settlers in Wyoming." 2d Ser., XVIII, 736–767. On Coxe's pamphlet pleading for acquiescence, see Coxe to the Luzerne commissioners, July 16, 1801, *Pa. Archives*, 2d Ser., XVIII, 404. Coxe's pamphlet was entitled *An Important Statement of Facts, Relative to the Invalidity of the Pretensions formerly made upon the Pennsylvania Lands, by the unincorporated Companies of Connecticut Claimants, and by those who claimed under those Companies; in a Letter from the Secretary of the Land-office, to the Pennsylvania Commissioners, intended to evince the Liberality of the Government and Land-holders of Pennsylvania, in the Act of the 4th of April, 1799, and the Releases of 120 to 180,000 Acres under the same* (Lancaster, Pa., 1801). Coxe reported to Gov. McKean on Dec. 10, 1800, that its real purpose was "to prevent persons of property, character, and information" in Luzerne and in New England "from engaging in the Connecticut intrusion in future." Coxe Papers. It was for this reason that he "covered Copies of the Statement to a great number of Considerable men in all the States north of us. The Governors, Senators and Representatives, Judges, Members of the State legislatures, Lawyers, Landed men, etc., the Attorney general of the United States, and every other public Man from N. England, from Washington to Massachusetts are served with Copies. . . . I think it unnecessary to justify the State in the ground she may be compelled to take, that all America should know this Affair; I have therefore sent some copies to Washington, Delaware, Maryland, N. Jersey, and have a promise from Duane to publish the paper in 3 or 4 Aurora's which go through Virginia, the Carolinas, Georgia, Kentucky and Tennessee." Coxe to Thomas Cooper, June 26, 1801, *Pa. Archives*, 2d Ser., XVIII, 396.

52. Entertaining "Convictions, not Suspicions" of the "Characters" of many of the Connecticut claimants, Coxe pursued them as zealously as he had tracked monarchists during McKean's gubernatorial campaign. This he did through correspondence with the commissioners, who readily acknowledged Coxe's "Assiduity, industry and talent" and his assistance in unraveling the tangled land titles of the area, but by the time Coxe resigned as secretary they were weary of his officiousness. See the commissioners to Coxe, July 13, 1801, *Pa. Archives*, 2d Ser., XVIII, 447–458.

Coxe unhesitatingly exerted pressure on cases in which he had a personal interest or in contests concerning the claims of friends. See Coxe to the commissioners, Aug. 29, 1801, *ibid.*, 421. See also the following correspondence with Pennsylvania claimants, Coxe to William Bingham, Aug. 1, 1800, Coxe to Richard and John Penn, Feb. 12, July 31, 1800, George Palmer to Coxe, Nov. 15, 1800, William Tilghman to Coxe, Aug. 19, 1800, Coxe Papers. This behavior lent some credence to the later comment of a hostile journalist that "if Mr. Coxe were governor we'd have no trouble from the Connecticut intruders; his interest in that quarter is amazing." *Aurora*, Sept. 3, 1804.

ested Citizen," he appropriately asked, had "done more" to secure "a liberal and valid execution" of the Compromise Act?[53]

Coxe was also entitled to a major share of credit for equitably settling a bitterly fought battle between speculators and homesteaders for control of the state's vast western domain. The looseness of Pennsylvania's land laws (whether by design or not) had resulted in millions of acres being acquired during the 1780s and 1790s by rich speculators like Samuel Wallis, James Wilson, William Bingham, John Nicholson, Robert Morris, and many less affluent (or perhaps less resourceful) citizens. Among this group of smaller speculators were Coxe's friends Thomas FitzSimons, Miers Fisher, Bishop William White, Thomas Willing, Benjamin Rush, Samuel Fox, and, of course, Coxe himself.

Leading to this situation was the most controversial land law of the period, that of 1792, which opened to public sale five million acres of state lands northwest of the Allegheny and Ohio rivers. Although touted as a democratization of the previous system, it was, in fact, one of the most "evil pieces of land legislation" ever enacted.[54] The measure did lower the price of land to twenty cents an acre, and, in theory, erected safeguards against monopolization by speculators. The latter provision was accomplished by restrictive clauses stipulating that grantees must settle their lands within two years after the issuance of warrants, must maintain continuous residence for five years after initial settlement, and must during that time make specified improvements in the absence of which the state could vacate the warrants.

---

53. Coxe to the commissioners, July 24, 1801, *Pa. Archives*, 2d Ser., XVIII, 408. Coxe also helped to shape legislation by which the state of Connecticut acquiesced in Pennsylvania's control of the area. This was done consonant with an act of Congress of Apr. 28, 1800, by which Connecticut ceded jurisdiction of the Western Reserve (a 3,000,000-acre tract of land on the southern shore of Lake Erie), accepted the Trenton Decree of 1782 as the definitive settlement of the Wyoming controversy, and agreed to eschew any impairment of the rights then awarded Pennsylvania. *Annals of Cong.*, X, 661–662, 1495–1496. Actually, the latter stipulation was made at the behest of Coxe, who, having been instructed by Gov. McKean to ensure the interests of Pennsylvania, served as backstairs adviser to the commonwealth's congressmen. From them he received copies of the original bill, to which he recommended a number of changes (including the proviso described above). These were then sent to Gallatin, who moved their adoption by the House. Many years later Coxe explained the part he played as follows: "I was . . . authorized by Governor McKean to adjust with the Pennsylvania and Connecticut members of Congress the cession of the Connecticut western reserve, upon principles compatible with the just rights and interests of this state, in which I succeeded so as to obtain a deed of quit claim of the Connecticut pretensions to all the land within our boundaries, under the sanction of Congress." Coxe to James Monroe, Sept. 9, 1822, Coxe Papers. Coxe's role can be followed in Coxe to Gallatin, Feb. 21, Mar. 2, 25, Apr. 2, 1800, Gallatin Papers; Coxe to Robert Waln, Mar. 3, 1800, to Henry Drinker, Mar. 17, Apr. 9, May 10, 1800, to Thomas McKean, Apr. 16, 1800, Drinker to Coxe, Apr. 9–10, 1800, Leib to Coxe, Apr. 25, 1800, Coxe Papers.

54. Paul Demund Evans, *The Holland Land Company* (Buffalo, N.Y., 1924), 107. See also Elizabeth K. Henderson, "The Northwestern Lands of Pennsylvania, 1790–1812," *PMHB*, LX (1936), 133–139.

(An exception was made for those who already occupied the land by a proviso that such actual settlers, after arranging and paying the fee for a survey, might apply for a warrant, paying the purchase money within ten years.) Had this been all, the act would have spelled ruin for big-time speculators, who could not conceivably comply with such conditions. But, not surprisingly in view of the number of land jobbers who sat in the assembly and the lobbying activities of their fellow speculators, the measure included one all-important escape clause. Section 9 stated that the settlement and improvement provisions could be waived if any settler or grantee attempted to comply with them but was prevented from doing so "by force of arms of the enemies of the United States," an unmistakable reference to Indians. As there was chronic warfare in the west, this superficially innocuous section proved a bonanza to speculators, who promptly proceeded to take out warrants "sufficient to cover nearly *eight* counties," without bothering to erect a cabin or a fence.[55]

The mischievous proviso included in the land law of 1792, in sum, left open to interpretation certain substantive questions. What, precisely, constituted "prevention" from settlement and improvement? Would the five-year settlement requirement be insisted on when prevention ceased, or would the warrantees be excused therefrom upon showing they had tried to settle? What would be the legal status of prior actual settlers on lands that land companies or other speculators now held warrants to? Following the signing of the Treaty of Fort Greenville that restored peace to the area in 1795, these questions had to be answered by officials of the Land Office, the Board of Property, and the courts, and influential land speculators confidently counted on these authorities for favorable answers. The confidence of the speculators seemed to have been well placed when in December 1797 the Board of Property, on the advice of Attorney General Jared Ingersoll, ruled that patents might be issued to warrantees for unsettled lands upon presentation of "prevention" certificates signed by a deputy surveyor and attested by two justices of the peace. This ruling, in effect, endorsed the contention of large-scale speculators that if once a grantee was prevented from beginning a settlement by Indian warfare, he was automatically exempted from any further effort. The speculators' triumph was, however, short-lived; two years later the state supreme court, on appeal, reversed the Board of Property and ruled instead that a warrantee must show proof of actual settlement within two years following the cessation of the Indian war, as specified by the land law of 1792.[56]

---

55. *Democratic Press* (Philadelphia), Oct. 26, 1809.
56. The case was *Morris v. Neighman*, 4 Yeats (Pa.) 450. See Henderson, "Northwestern Lands of Pennsylvania," *PMHB*, LX (1936), 143–144.

Most Pennsylvanians, particularly actual settlers and squatters, hailed the case as a victory for the common man. But big-time speculators, whose title to hundreds of thousands of acres was thus jeopardized, were determined, by whatever legal stratagem, to secure a reversal of the decision (especially large enterprises like the Holland Land Company and the Pennsylvania Population Company, which commanded the resources for drawn-out litigation). This was the situation when Coxe took over as secretary of the Land Office, and he contributed significantly to the final settlement of a legal wrangle that determined the control of ownership of the northwestern part of Pennsylvania.

The administration of the 1792 act, though subject to judicial process, was left largely to the Land Office, which before Coxe's appointment as secretary had paid scant attention to the claims of actual settlers. Although one might have predicted that a land buccaneer like Coxe would favor speculators and the giant land companies, he proved instead to be impartial. He was the exponent of the faithful execution of land laws that had ostensibly been designed to provide opportunities for needy settlers but instead had been outrageously exploited by rich investors. "The transallegheny business, and the innumerable deceptive modern entries and warrants to cover old rights," he wrote to Gallatin in 1801, "require firmness, intelligence and vigilance in a degree never before necessary in this department. It is easier to sell millions of acres to Messrs. Morris, Nicholson, Wilson, and Holl[and] and Population Companies, Bingham, Drucker, Wallis etc. than to settle the mass of incomplete titles, which now remain and which include every variety of which real property admits." Coxe's position came as a rude jolt to his fellow speculators. But, undeterred by their disappointment, he unswervingly upheld what he viewed as the public rather than private interest. Persuaded that many of the warrants held by the Holland Land Company had been secured in collusion with corrupt deputy surveyors, he was largely responsible for the rejection of its claims. And when this decision was appealed to the state supreme court, he prepared the commonwealth's case. *Holland Land Company* v. *Tench Coxe* was heard before supreme court justices Shippen, Smith, and Yeates, who in a two-to-one decision handed down in September 1801 rejected the company's petition for a mandamus.[57]

57. Coxe to Gallatin, July 3, 1801, Gallatin Papers. Although this case is listed as the *Commonwealth* v. *Tench Coxe Esq.*, the case was referred to by the three justices as the *Holland Land Company* v. *Tench Coxe* or *Wilhelm Willink et al.* v. *Tench Coxe*. The full record of the case as reported by Dallas can be found in 4 Dallas (Pa.) 170. In 1803 the Holland Land Company anonymously published a pamphlet entitled *Report of the Case of the Commonwealth vs. Tench Coxe, Esq. on a motion for a Mandamus, in the Supreme Court of Pennsylvania: Taken from the Manuscript of the Fourth Volume of Mr. Dallas's Reports, Published with his Consent* (Philadelphia, 1803). This 137-page pamphlet included not only the opinions of the three justices but also a long introductory discussion of the background of the case that was heavily weighted on the

To Coxe, who sat in the courtroom in Philadelphia as the opinion was read, the ruling was, as one of his correspondents complimentarily wrote, the gratifying conclusion to his own "indefatigable exertions in favor of the actual settlers," by which "order and fidelity in our harassed society over the Allegheny River" had been restored. And despite Chief Justice John Marshall's subsequent decision on behalf of the United States Supreme Court in favor of the Holland Land Company's claim, the Pennsylvania case, owing to its previous implementation by the legislature, did indeed restore "order and fidelity" to the disputed area.[58]

---

side of the Holland Land Company. Its author was James Gibson, a large land speculator and attorney for the land company. Also included were documents corroborating Gibson's case and various memorials and reports of legislative proceedings involving the Holland Land Company that had taken place between Mar. 1801 and Apr. 1803.

For examples of Coxe's search for material requisite to the case, see Coxe to Joseph McKean, July 24, 1801, Presley Nevill to Coxe, July 30, 1801, Andrew Ellicott to Coxe, Sept. 5, 1801, Coxe Papers.

58. John Greer to Coxe, Dec. 1801, Coxe Papers. For Coxe's opinion on the Supreme Court case of 1805, see Coxe to William McArthur, Mar. 20, 1806, *ibid*. For Coxe's assessment of his overall accomplishments as secretary of the Land Office, see his "A Short Defense," *Intel. & Weekly Adver.*, Aug. 26, 1801.

19 ᨠ
Coxe and the Making
of a President

     In the presidential election of 1800, as in the state gubernatorial race of the previous year, Coxe was one of Pennsylvania's key strategists. Though he was merely one of Jefferson's many political lieutenants, his role was vitally important in the development of early American democratic politics. His prominence in the politics of a state that was the hub of an interstate Republican network and that developed the pattern for future party organization and campaign tactics, as well as the historical importance of the election of 1800, points to a previously unrecognized but uncommon political significance.

     Jefferson's most tireless and powerful party managers in Pennsylvania were Coxe, Duane, and Beckley, who, in close cooperation with Gallatin, Dallas, and McKean, created the institutional structure and raised the issues that made party victory possible. During the first eight months of 1800 the Republican campaign in Pennsylvania was similar to that of the previous year in terms of organization and issues. One difference was the comparatively minor role played by the Philadelphia committee. Instead, the political organization was centered in Lancaster, now the capital, where Coxe played the major role. Here he corresponded with party leaders throughout the state, conferred regularly with others, relayed political news and rumors to Governor McKean, and kept abreast of political developments elsewhere by correspondence and conferences with prominent Republican leaders.[1]

---

1. See Coxe's correspondence for 1800 with William Beale, John Beckley, Joseph Brandon, Aaron Burr, John Dawson, Mahlon Dickerson, Albert Gallatin, David Gelston, William Irvine, Michael Leib, and John Smith, Coxe Papers.

Two of the most effective of the Republican publicists in Pennsylvania were Coxe and Duane. And if it is correct to attribute to the *Aurora* measurable responsibility for Jefferson's election, then Coxe, Duane's de facto partner on the *Aurora*, must also be given a share of the credit. All in all, there was considerable justification for the assertion of one Federalist editor that the Republicans were "led and directed" by Coxe. Observing that "Tench has filled five columns of this morning's *Aurora* with a patchwork of lies," a critic asked, "How stands the business of the land office?"[2] But Governor McKean expressed no dissatisfaction with Coxe, perhaps because he, like many politicians after him, valued party service as much as administrative diligence. If so, Coxe was the ideal public servant, rivaled only by his friend John Beckley, who had been dismissed in May 1797 from his clerkship of the House of Representatives because of his partisan activities on Jefferson's behalf and who was now able to work full-time for the Republican cause.

Although Beckley had openly enlisted under the Virginian's banner sooner than Coxe, the official careers of the two men were remarkably similar. Both worked for the Republicans while holding office under a Federalist administration, both were fired for their partisan activities, both wished for restitution and revenge, and both were skillful journalists (though Coxe was the more prolific). The similarity goes further. Just as Coxe had no scruples about dredging up and publishing every scrap of confidential information that he had acquired during seven years in government service, so Beckley energetically circulated the evidence—most of it hearsay—that he had sedulously collected about the misdeeds of notable Federalists, especially Hamilton. Finally, both Coxe and Beckley interpreted official documents so as to provide evidence for whatever they wished to find, and then they adduced the documents as proof of their unshakable belief that the Federalist decade was largely the history of a grand conspiracy to undermine American freedom.[3]

The organizers of Jefferson's Pennsylvania campaign knew that the

---

2. *Philadelphia Gaz.*, Nov. 8, Sept. 27, 1800.

3. Beckley's major contribution to the 1800 campaign was his *Address to the People of the United States*, which included a brief biography of Jefferson—"the first of him," Merrill Peterson remarks, "and the first of all campaign lives." Some 5,000 copies of Beckley's pamphlet were printed and distributed widely. Peterson, *Jefferson and the New Nation*, 640. Beckley struck out at Hamilton even before the campaign of 1800 was well underway: "I am now busily engaged in pursuit of a full collection of facts to establish on the part of the federal Government the creation of the prescriptive principle of disqualification to offices and the application of it in each state, connected with Mr. Hamilton's original scheme of Espionage," Beckley wrote to Coxe in Jan. 1800. "It strikes my recollection that sometime ago I lent you [to copy] Mr. Hamiltons original proposition to the late president for an Organized System of Espionage thro' the medium of Revenue Officers, with Mr. Jeffersons objections thereto. . . . You will *feel* how critical it is for me *now* to be possessed with it." Beckley to Coxe, Jan. 24, 1800, Coxe Papers.

outcome of the election depended not only on winning a majority of the Pennsylvania vote on election day in October, but also on securing control of both houses of the state legislature. The legislature was of such importance because it was debating the vital question of how the commonwealth should choose its presidential electors. The Jeffersonians, confident of victory, were intent on maintaining the practice of choosing electors by a general ticket. Their opponents, who had lost the previous election, were bent on securing election by districts. Having won control of the lower house of the assembly, the Republicans in December 1799 easily pushed through that body a measure stipulating that the voters of the whole state be presented with a general ticket. The Federalists, enjoying secure control of the senate, countered with a bill providing that the state be divided into districts that were to be arranged to constitute, in effect, a gerrymander. Since the political stakes were high, neither party was willing to compromise, and the campaign of 1800, much to the dismay of its Republican leaders, was fought to secure a popular victory that the legislature might foil.[4]

But in the late spring of 1800 it did not seem likely that Pennsylvania, however its vote might be cast, could prevent Jefferson's election. Republicans were at that time irrepressibly optimistic that victory was within their reach. Enthusiastically united behind a popular chieftain, who remained isolated but not incommunicado on his Virginia mountaintop, they viewed with satisfaction the acrimonious squabble between John Adams and other Federalist leaders, including members of his own cabinet. As Theodore Roosevelt once observed, Adams's party included "many men nearly equal in strong will and great intellectual power," whose "ambitions and theories clashed; . . . while in the other party there was a single leader, Jefferson, supported by a host of sharp political workers." But Adams, incapable of serving as the "arbiter of contending factions," was himself measurably responsible for the plight of his party.[5] Having for years endured subordinates he believed to be disloyal, he chose to dismiss them at the height of the

---

4. The Pennsylvania election law had expired, and a new measure was required for the approaching election of 1800. Although Gov. Thomas McKean had toyed with the idea of calling a special session of the legislature, he decided, as influential party leaders advised, to postpone a meeting until after the fall elections. See Gallatin to Coxe, May 14, 1800, *ibid*. Coxe was among those leaders. "The only Probable way" for Pennsylvanians to "get their voice in the Election for president and Vice President," he believed, was for "the Governor to convene the Legislature . . . immediately after the Annual Election—then make a Law for a Joint vote of Both houses . . . to Elect the Electors." Beale to Coxe, Sept. 6, 1800, Coxe Papers, paraphrasing remarks made by Coxe in conversation.

5. Theodore Roosevelt, *Gouverneur Morris* (Boston, 1888), 279–280; Oliver Wolcott, Jr., to Fisher Ames, Dec. 29, 1799, Gibbs, ed., *Memoirs of Administrations of Washington and Adams*, II, 315.

campaign. The first to go was Secretary of War James McHenry, guilty more of incompetence than, as the president believed, unswerving loyalty to Adams's bête noire, Alexander Hamilton. Four days later, on May 10, the president, in the midst of an unseemly temper tantrum, requested the resignation of his secretary of state, and when Pickering refused, Adams curtly informed him that he was "hereby discharged."[6] The president's timing was singular. Why, only a few months before the election, did he dismiss these prominent cabinet officers for offenses that, so he said, they had been guilty of from the beginning of his administration? Perhaps, as Hamilton, Pickering, and other Federalists charged, the results of the election in New York had convinced him that he no longer had to appease the Federalists of that state, much less their acknowledged leader, Hamilton; now he hoped that by sacrificing unpopular members of his cabinet he could gain support elsewhere.

"The New York Election," one of Coxe's correspondents announced on May 8, has resulted "in the complete triumph of the republican Interest. . . . Consider by this Measure, that Mr. Jefferson's election for President is Secured."[7] Jefferson and his party lieutenants agreed. The New York election had been for state officials, but the state legislature would then choose the presidential electors. With so much at stake Aaron Burr had put together a galaxy of Revolutionary War heroes and concentrated his attention on the Federalist stronghold of New York City. His shrewd political tactics were successful. The whole Republican ticket for the assembly was elected, heralding Jefferson's capture of New York's twelve electoral votes and Burr's own selection as Republican candidate for vice-president.

Although Republican confidence that the days of the Federalists were numbered was buoyed, party leaders were correct in concluding that they could not afford to relax. The Federalist party, far from being moribund, appeared capable of overcoming the disadvantages that hamstrung it in the late spring of 1800. It was still a national organization, particularly strong in New England, which was virtually certain to remain in the Federalist column. Therefore, if Adams could carry South Carolina, as seemed possible, and pick up some votes in Pennsylvania, as he was almost certain to do, he could win reelection even in the face of his defeat in New York. Nor did the rift within Federalist ranks necessarily have to jeopardize his chances, for it was clear even then that, as Woodrow Wilson would later remark, "if

---

6. John Adams to Timothy Pickering, May 12, 1800, [Pickering] and Upham, *Timothy Pickering*, III, 488. Coxe claimed that Pickering was removed from office because he "was himself endeavouring by the Election of General Pinckney to prevent the election of Mr. Adams." Coxe, *To the Republican Citizens of the State of Pennsylvania* (Lancaster, Pa., 1800). The pamphlet was also printed in the *Aurora*, Sept. 27, 1800.

7. John Smith to Coxe, May 8, 1800, Coxe Papers.

the President leads the way, his party can hardly resist him." But Adams's problems were compounded when the Federalist caucus decided to support Adams and his running mate, Charles Cotesworth Pinckney of South Carolina, equally, and when a group of disgruntled party leaders, including Hamilton, determined to focus on the vice-presidential candidate as their "single object."[8] In view of the masterly campaign tactics and strategy of the Republicans, such machinations were more likely to prove fatal to both Federalist candidates than to assure Pinckney's election.

Although occupied with state politics, Coxe was a conspicuous member of his party's efficient national organization. He circulated campaign literature published in other states and sent to him by political allies. He gave campaign speeches on behalf of Jefferson; following one of these a Federalist antagonist "punished" what he considered Coxe's "ungentlemanly vulgarity, by severely wringing the nose of the offender." Coxe distributed pamphlets and other material manufactured in Pennsylvania to out-of-state politicians. One such Republican, John Dawson, anxious about the German vote in Virginia, requested that Coxe send "some newspapers in that language" to Fredericksburg, where "they may do good."[9] Coxe also entertained visiting Republicans who stopped over in Lancaster for party meetings. Wade Hampton, leader of the common man's party in South Carolina and reputedly the wealthiest planter in the United States, conferred with Coxe during a visit to the Pennsylvania capital in June; Abraham Bishop of Connecticut was there in October and November to discuss "certain public measures," as were Pierce Butler of South Carolina and Albert Gallatin. Coxe regularly corresponded about party prospects with Republicans elsewhere and often received copies of letters they wrote to other Pennsylvania party chieftains. His most reliable and loyal correspondent, however, continued to be John Beckley, who, aware of every shifting political wind in the Union, spent more time in calculating possible election returns than in keeping the records of the two courts to which McKean had appointed him clerk.[10] In brief, Beckley was the interstate coordinator of the campaign, and Coxe was an important strategist.

8. Alexander Hamilton to Theodore Sedgwick, May 4, 1800, Hamilton Papers, Lib. of Cong. See also Gallatin to Coxe, May 14, 1800, Coxe Papers.

9. *Philadelphia Gaz.*, Nov. 1, 1800; John Dawson to Coxe, Sept. 28, 1800, Coxe Papers. See also Leib to Coxe, Apr. 18, 1800, William Barton to Coxe, July 31, 1800, *ibid.*

10. Wade Hampton to Coxe, June 29, 1800, Coxe Papers. See also David Gelston, John Swartout, James Nicholson, and Matthew L. Davis to Coxe, Oct. 24, 1800, Burr to Coxe, Oct. 25, 1800, William Duane to Coxe, Oct. 2, 1800, Beckley to Coxe, Nov. 3, 1800, Andrew Eppe to Coxe, July 8, 1800, Dawson to Coxe, Sept. 28, Oct. 13, 1800, Samuel Smith to Coxe, Oct. 9, 1800, John Smith to Coxe, Aug. 25, 1800, *ibid.* In a letter of Oct. 25, 1800, Burr referred to the communications that Coxe had sent him "in the course of the summer" as "always replete with amusement and instruction." *Ibid.* Coxe attended political rallies in and around Lancaster (George Thomas to Coxe, July 1800, *ibid.*), distributed campaign literature to local leaders

Coxe's most conspicuous contribution was as a party polemicist, refining by constant repetition the issues he had so often defined during the gubernatorial race the previous year. His technique was evident in the first major pamphlet he contributed to the campaign, *Strictures upon the Letter imputed to Mr. Jefferson, addressed to Mr. Mazzei*, published under the nom de guerre of "Greene." The letter in question was written by Jefferson in 1796 to his longtime friend, Philip Mazzei, a Florentine, who during the early years of the American Revolution had been Jefferson's neighbor in Virginia. Although concerned for the most part with his friend's personal affairs, Jefferson's letter also described "an Anglican, monarchial and aristocratical party" that had sprung up in the United States. In an obvious allusion to Washington, Jefferson referred to "men who were Samsons in the field and Solomons in the council," who "have had their heads shorn by the harlot England." The letter was political dynamite, and when published in American newspapers in May 1797, the Federalists pounced upon it as a means of exploding the political career of Thomas Jefferson. While the latter maintained a discreet silence, Coxe, presumably after consultation with the vice-president, decided that the best tactic was a counterattack.[11]

The purpose of Coxe's *Strictures upon the Letter* was to prove that Jefferson's criticism of the country's pro-British policies not only was justified but was too mild and dispassionate a description of a fiendish monarchical conspiracy that threatened the very existence of American republicanism.

(Beale to Coxe, Sept. 6, 1800, *ibid.*), and circulated copies of the *Aurora*, bundles of which Duane regularly sent him (Duane to Coxe, Nov. 3, 1800, Coxe Papers). He also received importunate demands for jobs and heard the complaints of political correspondents about the distribution of patronage; representative is Alexander Patterson to Coxe, Aug. 4, 1800, *ibid.* Nor did Coxe neglect Republican prospects in strategic cities like Philadelphia (John Smith to Coxe, May 8, June 16, 24, July 25, Aug., 1800, *ibid.*) and others outside Pennsylvania (Gallatin to Coxe, May 14, 1800, *ibid.*). For his relationship with Beckley, see Beckley to Coxe, Sept. 29, Oct. 5, 27, 30, Nov. 3, 1800, *ibid.*

11. [Coxe], *Strictures upon the Letter imputed to Mr. Jefferson, addressed to Mr. Mazzei* (n.p., 1800); Thomas Jefferson to Philip Mazzei, Apr. 24, 1796, Ford, ed., *Works of Jefferson*, VIII, 235–241. Coxe's defense of Jefferson appears to have been based in part on conversations held in 1797 between the two men. Charging that Jefferson's letter had "undergone one cunning *alteration* by his Enemies" (*Strictures upon the Letter*, 3), Coxe pointed to the use of the word "form" for "forms" in Jefferson's remark that an object of the English monarchical party in America was "to draw over us the substance, as they have already done the forms of the British government." By "forms," Coxe said, Jefferson had meant that the president's birthday was celebrated like the king's birthday, that "the King's Levee had been imitated by the President's Levee." *Ibid.*, 4. Since this was the charge Jefferson himself regarded as the most serious one and since Coxe presumably would not otherwise have emphasized it, it is reasonable to assume that the two had discussed the matter. Moreover, according to Jefferson's biographer, "the best if not the only explanation of the letter Jefferson ever gave in writing" was in a letter to Madison of Aug. 3, 1797. Ford, ed., *Works of Jefferson*, VIII, 331–334. That this explanation is roughly the same as that offered by Coxe in his *Strictures upon the Letter* strengthens the supposition that the two men c‹

"People out of the way of Politics, have little notion of the lengths to which Persons have gone, on the subject of Monarchy in this Country," he explained. Once again Coxe lashed out at President John Adams. He was, charged Coxe, the leader of a pro-British conspiracy, an avowed monarchist intent on subverting American liberty.[12] By misunderstanding and distorting the president's own published writings, Coxe turned his defense of Jefferson into an attack on Adams. Indeed, the deftness with which Coxe plucked hints of monarchism from Adams's ponderous writings was astonishing. But he did not confine himself to these alone. As was his wont, he also relied on documents, conversations, and rumors that he had carefully kept records of during his years in the Treasury Department. By thus choosing once more to conduct a mudslinging campaign, Coxe set out on a course that eight months later would prompt an unfriendly newspaper to remark: "It is a proverb now, 'At a table where there is *Tench*, no honest man eats.' "[13]

Coxe's *Strictures upon the Letter* was not only a prelude to months of attack on Adams but also an indication of the nature and substance of the Republican campaign. Again and again the charge would be made that Adams was a monarchist; again and again the evidence adduced would be from Coxe's grab bag of documents and rumors.

Adams was the object of another major campaign document of the Pennsylvania campaign—an "Address" of the Lancaster Republican Committee. Written by Coxe, this lengthy pamphlet was distributed throughout the state and republished in Republican newspapers elsewhere.[14] It was written, Coxe said, so that "the real enemies of Representative Government may be thoroughly known." Who were they? Adams, of course. And the president's writings and purported conversations were once again brought forward to demonstrate his "monarchical and aristocratical views." But this time Coxe enlarged his lasso in order to entrap other avowed monarchists, among them Alexander Hamilton, to whose political heresies he had previously made only veiled allusions. This "eminent and influential person," who "beyond any other citizen" had traduced Jefferson, had once "declared that though he favoured the first movements of the French Revolution, he dropt them . . . when the Republic was established." Coxe brought forth even more damning evidence: this commander of an army of "hired regulars,

12. [Coxe], *Strictures upon the Letter*, 10–11. Coxe was so blinded by the image of John Adams as a dedicated and ruthless monarchist—an image largely of his own making—that he assumed it was Adams, not George Washington, that Jefferson had in mind when he spoke of "Solomons in the council."

13. *Gaz. of U.S.*, Nov. 8, 1800.

14. Coxe, *To the Republican Citizens*. The pamphlet was forwarded to New Jersey, Maryland, and Delaware by Beckley. Beckley to Coxe, Sept. 29, 1800, Coxe Papers. It was also published in the *Aurora*, Sept. 27, 1800. The Lancaster Republican committee consisted of Coxe, Timothy Matlack, Frederick A. Muhlenberg, Jacob Carpenter, and Samuel Bryan.

and party, and monarchic volunteers" had recommended "the abolition of all the state constitutions," as well as the establishment of a monarchical government. Having proved to his own satisfaction that Adams and Hamilton harbored "monarchistic, aristocratic, and unconstitutional views," Coxe boldly marched to the conclusion that their allies must be similarly tainted. That "the principal Northern and eastern Federalists in power are in favor of a monarchy" was, he said, an established fact about which "there should be no more reserve, no evasion, no deception, no timidity."[15]

This central theme of Coxe's "Address" was embroidered by other emotive issues. Jay's Treaty was trotted out to show "the monstrous claims upon us" by the British; the Alien law was denounced; and the familiar alarm was rung on the then-axiomatic dangers of a "standing army." The familiar bread and butter issue of taxes was not overlooked either. "In the beginning of the present Federal Government," Coxe wrote, "it was the great attracting charm of our Country, that we had no Land or House tax, a trivial Salt tax, no stamp duty, moderate custom house duties, and proportionate Public Expences." What serpent had destroyed this tax-free Garden of Eden? The perfidious British, of course, whose influence had "corrupted" not only officials of the Adams administration but "the Federalists generally." It was a significant and shrewd concatenation: high taxes and British influence, relief from taxation and friendship with France. Nevertheless, Coxe tediously returned time and again to the issue under which he symbolically subsumed all others: monarchism, represented abroad by Great Britain and personified at home in John Adams.

In 1800, as in 1799, a major item in the indictment of the president was the letter Adams had written to Coxe in 1792 charging that British influence had been instrumental in the appointment of Thomas Pinckney as American minister to England. The publication of this letter had earlier led to a charge of seditious libel against Duane, but, this having been withdrawn, it was republished on August 28, 1800, in the *Aurora*, where it reappeared with monotonous regularity over the succeeding two months.

If Philadelphia newspapers can be used as a reliable indicator, Adams's letter to Coxe was the hottest issue of the last weeks of the campaign, more important than Hamilton's better-known diatribe against the president. The republication forced Coxe to defend himself against charges of betrayal of a former friend by denying responsibility for the publication of the

15. Coxe, *To the Republican Citizens*. The reference to the recommendation was, of course, an allusion to Hamilton's well-known speech of June 18, 1787, before the Constitutional Convention in which he called for a high-toned government modeled on the English. At this time the speech was known only to those who had attended the secret session of the convention and to the few others to whom some members had repeated its substance. Coxe's information came from Adams's secretary of state, Timothy Pickering. See the *Aurora*, Oct. 9, 1800.

letter and placing the blame on Duane. No doubt he believed what he said, but his defense was disingenuous.[16] Nevertheless, Coxe, chief prosecutor in the case of the state versus Adams, was now placed in an even more central role. As much in question as the guilt of the defendant were the ethics of the prosecutor, and it is a reasonable surmise that on the latter issue the Republicans were unlikely to pick up many votes.

The denouement of the affair was a veritable opéra bouffe. Stung by Thomas Pinckney's "unwarrantable suggestion" that the Adams letter was "*a forgery* calculated for electioneering purposes," Coxe determined to prove its genuineness by "his own positive Deposition," along with those of Frederick A. Muhlenberg and William Barton, and by the "exhibition" of Adams's letter to Pierce Butler, senator from South Carolina. The depositions attesting that the letter in Coxe's possession was in the handwriting of John Adams were duly published in the *Aurora* and redundantly elaborated on by Coxe, who obviously assumed truth to be a defense against his libel. That in this case the libel was not so much the publication of the letter as the unwarranted implications Coxe and Duane persistently drew from it was conveniently overlooked.[17]

Nevertheless, perhaps a half-conscious awareness of his unfairness accounts for Coxe's zeal in uncovering further evidence of Adams's monarchism. Coxe found this new evidence for the *Aurora* in the remarks of Andrew Steele, a South Carolina clergyman then in Lancaster. In the course of an evening's conversation with Coxe and two other Republican leaders, Reverend Steele observed that charges made by Coxe in a recent attack on Adams could be verified.[18] Indeed, he "knew circumstances in support of the facts therein mentioned which he would state in writing." The following morning Coxe received the promised letter and, though Steele had requested that it be kept out of the newspapers, promptly forwarded it to William Duane. Published without its author's signature but with Coxe designated the recipient, the letter read:

It was currently reported at New Haven, after president Adams had passed through that place, about 30th of June last, that in conversation with several gentlemen there, he had delivered sentiments to the following effect: "That there is a strong party in our government devoted to the interests of Britain, and wishing to establish Monarchy here. That he had long been opposing that party—that he believed the

16. His defense was an article, "To the Public," signed "Tench Coxe," which appeared in the *Aurora*, Oct. 6, 1800.

17. *Ibid.*, Oct. 21, 1800. The original depositions are in the Coxe Papers. Pinckney's charge had been made in a Charleston newspaper, a copy of which Duane sent to Coxe on Oct. 2, 1800. Coxe Papers. Dated Sept. 15, 1800, Pinckney's letter was published in the *Aurora*, Oct. 3, 1800.

18. The Republican leaders at the Lancaster conference were William Barton, prothonotary of Lancaster, and William Dickson, a Lancaster newspaper editor.

Federalists would now be the first to oppose the Laws of their Country; for that since the appointment of the Envoys to France, they have been the most seditious men in the Union—and that we shall never have liberty or happiness in this country, until our First Magistrate is Hereditary."

The president's remarks, so the letter stated, were made to Pierpoint Edwards, Gideon Grainger, and Reverend James Dana, father of Congressman Samuel W. Dana.[19]

That there was some impropriety in publishing such hearsay and considerable inconsistency in demonstrating that the man who was supposedly the symbol of British influence and monarchy himself opposed and distrusted a pro-British faction harboring monarchical designs disturbed neither Coxe nor Duane. Instead, Coxe accompanied the publication of the anonymous letter with a lengthy article in which he spelled out the implications of the conversation. Who are the men of whom Adams spoke, Coxe asked? "Why did he not remove them?" If Adams really "opposed the anglo-monarchic men in our government," why did he appoint to important government posts men such as Hamilton, Charles C. Pinckney, Rufus King, William L. Smith, and Uriah Tracy? All of whom, Coxe said, the president must have known to be monarchists. Although Coxe's own critics were too busy harping on his tory background to do so, they might well have rejoined: Why did Coxe, knowing his Federalist associates to be monarchists, remain in office for seven years? With a splendid disregard of such questions, Coxe proceeded to secure affidavits from those who had also heard Reverend Steele's charge. As with the depositions concerning Adams's letter, these were published in the *Aurora* on October 2.

For the remainder of October, Coxe's efforts to prove by documentary evidence that Adams was the ubiquitous enemy of American democracy dominated not only the *Aurora* (described by the opposition as "Coxe's paper") but the Philadelphia press generally.[20] His opponents were no less persistent and no more scrupulous than he. Instead of pointing out the fallacies in Coxe's strenuous efforts to indict Adams by distorted documentary proof, they replied with slanderous personal attacks on Coxe. The whole episode—it scarcely can be dignified by the word *debate*—appears superficially to have been designed to titillate the public by indulging its appetite

---

19. Andrew Steele to Coxe, Sept. 23, 1800, in the *Aurora*, Oct. 2, 1800. Although goaded by the opposition press to do so, Coxe consistently refused to publish the name of his informant. Instead he sent Steele's name to William Rawle, chairman of the Philadelphia Federalist Committee, who was urged to show it to any skeptical person "from Georgia to Maine." Coxe, "To the Philadelphia Gazette," Sept. 30, 1800, *Philadelphia Gaz.*, Oct. 4, 1800. Copies were also sent to Gen. Samuel Smith of Baltimore and Tobias Lear in Washington. *Aurora*, Oct. 6, 1800.

20. *Philadelphia Gaz.*, Nov. 1, 1800.

for slander. In any event, scarcely a day passed without one or another Federalist newspaper, notably the *Philadelphia Gazette*, lashing out at Coxe with gross sarcasm, ridicule, or abuse. As had been the case previously in his career, this was owing to his personal vulnerability as well as to his political prominence. Along with other familiar indictments, critics charged that Coxe had served as a member of the Board of Refugees established by the British for the trial of Americans who fell into their hands, that he had "been concerned in the death of Captain or Mr. Huddy," that he had "imposed himself" upon the Republican party, and that he was "ready at all times to let out his pen and his conscience to the highest bidder." One writer asserted that "was monarchy to be established here, and Tench could get promotion under it," Coxe "would be the first man in America" to come to its support. The attacks were summed up in the following verse.

> First I set to Washington
> Then crossing o'er to Howe, Sir,
> I figured in with Hamilton,
> And with your Honor now, Sir.[21]

As Federalist newspapers attempted to repel their opponents' smear campaign by smearing Coxe, and as the *Aurora* increasingly gave over its pages to defenses of Coxe's conduct, it soon seemed that Coxe, rather than Adams's or Jefferson's qualifications or offenses, was the central issue of the campaign in Pennsylvania. "That William Duane fills the office of Secretary of the Land-office, and Tench Coxe that of Editor of the Aurora," commented the *Philadelphia Gazette*, "is merely the effect of personal accommodation, and has not, we believe, yet received the sanction of his Excellency the Governor." "Sore and restive" under the attacks of the opposition, "Tench Coxe is continually snivelling in the Aurora," commented another critic. By December the *Philadelphia Gazette* was content merely to announce in large type "TENCH COXE IS INSANE."[22]

Such personal attack only sharpened for Coxe the hideous features of the demon that stood so squarely in the way of democratic (or perhaps personal) fulfillment. If he could unmask other chief culprits, as well as President Adams, the nefarious plot of the Federalists would stand starkly exposed. Alexander Hamilton, of all people, came to his aid. Enraged by reports that Adams had shrilly denounced him as the leader of a "damned

---

21. *Aurora*, Oct. 8, 1800; *Philadelphia Gaz.*, Nov. 8, 1800; *Gaz. of U.S.*, Nov. 4, 1800; *Philadelphia Gaz.*, Oct. 9, 1800. For Coxe's attempts to exonerate himself from the charge that he had been a member of the Board of Refugees, see Samuel Smith to Coxe, Oct. 9, 17, 19, 1800, Coxe Papers. See also the *Aurora*, Oct. 8, 9, 23, 1800. For other articles denouncing Coxe, see *Philadelphia Gaz.*, Sept. 26, Oct. 8, 9, 14, 30, Nov. 1, 18, Dec. 9, 1800.

22. *Philadelphia Gaz.*, Nov. 19, Oct. 9, Dec. 10, 1800. For examples of the defenses of Coxe, see the *Aurora*, Oct. 6, 8, 9, 30, Nov. 1, 4, 7, 19, 1800.

faction" of "British partisans," Hamilton demanded that the president avow or disclaim the alleged remark. Angered even more by Adams's refusal to reply, the New Yorker rashly determined to expose the shortcomings of his own party's president. In October he sent prominent Federalists a verbose letter depicting Adams as a neurotic personality, a man obsessed by a "vanity without bounds, and a jealousy capable of discoloring every object," one possessed with "disgusting egotism" and an "ungovernable indiscretion of . . . temper." Although Hamilton's diatribe was ostensibly written for only a chosen few of his party, he was not displeased when the letter was reprinted and circulated throughout the country. What he actually did was to create a situation calculated to make the most mindless partisan blink. Here was the president of the United States, himself accused by Coxe and other Republicans of being the head of a pro-British conspiracy, charging the most prominent member of his own party with being the leader of a faction of British partisans. Hamilton, "the 'Colossus of Federalism,'" was now attacking the president, in Dumas Malone's words, "with a violence entirely comparable to that of the Republican journalists and pamphleteers whom the party in power had sought to silence as dangerous enemies of the government."[23] Coxe, like other Republicans, ignored such bizarre contradictions, choosing to believe that the intramural squabbles of the Federalists were mere bluster, thinly disguising a mutual commitment to monarchy. "I affirm that Alexander Hamilton, esq did declare to me, at a meeting on official business that he was a monarchist," Coxe announced shortly before the publication of Hamilton's letter.[24] And he saw no reason to recant. But as even Coxe must have been aware, such charges against Hamilton were already standard partisan fare, too familiar to be particularly effective. And, in any event, Adams, not Hamilton, was the presidential candidate—the dragon to be slain. Since it never occurred to Coxe that there might be differences in danger and vulnerability even among dragons, he frantically cast about for additional evidence of the president's guilt.

Coxe selected Benjamin Rush as his next witness against Adams. To drag the distinguished physician into the fray without first consulting him, while certainly knowing that Rush wished to remain aloof from the name-calling, was a gratuitous affront to a friend of twenty-five years' standing. Nevertheless, in the course of one of his many defenses, Coxe wrote: "Let me draw from under the cover in which they have been too long wrapt, the

---

23. [Alexander Hamilton], *Letter from Alexander Hamilton, Concerning the Public Conduct and Character of John Adams, Esq. President of the United States* (New York, 1800); Malone, *Jefferson: Ordeal of Liberty*, 488.

24. *Aurora*, Oct. 9, 1800. Coxe went on to say that "I stated the fact in 1795, from a sense of duty, to Timothy Pickering, esq then secretary of state and war. . . . I risk this statement without fear of contradiction by Mr. Hamilton or Mr. Pickering." *Ibid.*

useful talents of Benjamin Rush. If he adds not to the proofs of monarchism of Mr. Adams, and of many of the supporters of that gentleman's election and of general Pinckney's, then will I endure in silence all the criminations which party hatred and animosity can invent or desire."[25]

Upon reading the article, Rush promptly sent Coxe a personal letter that registered sadness rather than anger. Expressing his regret at having been "drawn by your publication of this morning from the retirement I have sought, and the ignorance I have studied of the public affairs of our country, for nearly twelve years past," Rush emphatically denied that he had any knowledge of Adams's alleged monarchism. Nor did the doctor agree with Coxe's sweeping charges against the Federalists, most of whom, as he recollected having said to Tench, were loyal republicans. "I expect you will correct the statement you have published," Rush concluded, "and thereby do justice to your old friend." Too partisan to be just, Coxe refused, insisting instead that the doctor join the witch-hunt. Rush, though he found such exchanges "extremely disagreeable," published a dignified but firm reply that affirmed he had never heard Adams "express a wish for a monarchy in the United States" but rather had "uniformly heard him say, what he has published in his works, that our present government was best calculated for our country."[26] A man less driven by passionate partisanship would have passed over Rush's public letter in silence, thus ending an unsavory episode even at the cost of some slight personal embarrassment.

Coxe could easily have retired from the fray after the Republican victory in Pennsylvania on October 14, the very day Rush's letter appeared in print. In the lower house of the Pennsylvania legislature the party captured fifty-five out of seventy-eight seats; of the seven state senators chosen, the Republicans elected six; in the congressional contest they seized ten of the thirteen seats.[27] However, the jubilation of the Republicans was curbed by their failure to win a majority in the state senate, where the Federalists retained control by a razor-thin margin that might be enough to allow them to thwart the expressed preference of three-fifths of Pennsylvania's voters for Jefferson and Burr. This failure may partly explain why Coxe, disappointed but still lashed by ambition, maintained the party vigil and, fighting his better instincts, furiously renewed his public feud with Rush. It was nothing more than *"honest obedience to a clear and indispensable duty"* that forced him to bring Rush "forward as a *witness* for the people's information," he explained in a lengthy public answer to Rush's letter. Commissar-

25. *Ibid.*
26. Benjamin Rush to Coxe, Oct. 9, 15, 1800, Coxe Papers. Rush's reply was dated Oct. 11, 1800. See the *Philadelphia Gaz.*, Oct. 14, 1800. Rush's Oct. 9th letter to Coxe was published in the *Aurora*, Oct. 18, 1800.
27. For detailed election returns, see the *Aurora*, Oct. 17, 1800.

like, he asked for an interrogation of his old friend. "What, I ask, would not a former member of Congress and *Convention*, a patriot of 1776 and 1789, so under duress, prove to the electors when properly examined?" Even John Beckley was aghast. Imploring Coxe to call a halt to the feud, Beckley wrote: "The Doctor's age and situation, his past services and sacrifices, his friendship and sympathy with you in scenes of public and private feeling, urge you powerfully in conjunction with your own Sensibilities, to spare the pain which a further pursuit of him may inflict."[28]

Rush, though he had tried to be forbearing, considered Coxe's recommendation of star-chamber proceedings against him as more than even the strong foundation of a twenty-five-year intimate relationship could bear. "In a Will in which I had appointed you one of my Executors," Rush wrote to Coxe on October 20, "my friendship for you was placed upon record with a hand that was rendered feeble (as I then thought) by the near approach of death. . . . I never read, nor heard a Word to your disadvantage, without feeling the most sensible pain. You were associated in my mind with the beginning of all my domestic happiness." Now, Coxe's reckless charges had terminated such long-standing trust and affection, and Rush was left with only the wish that the whole episode might "be buried forever with all the letters and communications that have passed between us in the grave of our former friendship."[29]

Coxe's unseemly performance starkly revealed his temporary loss of any sense of propriety, his unwillingness even to entertain the possibility that self-knowledge begins where fierce partisanship and political mythology end. He rationalized his behavior with the belief that the vital issue of Adams's monarchism overrode mere personal decorum, and one could have as easily leveled a mountain as to have shaken this conviction. Although he sincerely believed that secret monarchists, disguised as Federalists, lurked in the corridors of power, the ferocity with which he stalked them suggests that something more than a zealous commitment to republicanism was at issue for him. The battle, that is, may well have been as much intrapsychic as interparty. Was he perhaps consumed by rage because his youthful toryism had barred him from high public offices held by men, like Adams, Hamilton, and, above all, Wolcott, who had luckily made the right decision in 1776, but who otherwise were no better qualified than himself? In the process of repudiating his own monarchism had he imperceptibly and unknowingly come to believe that others harbored similar sentiments but lacked the candor to acknowledge or the courage to renounce them? Was

28. "To the Public," *ibid.*, Oct. 18, 1800; Beckley to Coxe, Oct. 30, 1800, Coxe Papers.
29. Rush to Coxe, Oct. 20, 1800, Coxe Papers. See also Rush to Coxe, Oct. 9, 15, 17, 18, 1800, *ibid.*; *Aurora*, Oct. 17, 18, 1800.

monarchism thus to him a secular form of original sin, overcome only by public confession and private contrition? Was his own guilt, in sum, assuaged by attributing to others the will to do what he had once done? One can only say that the fury with which Coxe assailed alleged monarchists and the groundlessness of his charges must be explained in terms of private rather than public pathology.

Complacently unaware of such distinctions and propelled by unresolved conflicts that he perceived as partisan imperatives, Coxe continued to pour into the pages of the *Aurora* the sworn testimony of Adams's accusers. His memory appeared to be a kind of magical samovar from which he could draw proof after proof, and when empty he could make it flow again and yet again. Thus it was that he reintroduced evidence he had already repeatedly publicized in the *Aurora* in 1799—the 1794 Senate chamber conversation in which Adams allegedly had commended a hereditary chief executive and senate. This time, however, Coxe decided that his witnesses, Senators Langdon and Taylor, must be persuaded to take the stand and attest the accuracy of his charge. John Beckley revealed better judgment than Coxe. To the latter's request for cooperation, Beckley was unreceptive. Even if Langdon and Taylor "could be immediately induced to come forward," he cautioned, it still might prove "impossible that your views can be accomplished within time to produce any effect." This consideration aside, he added, "I do not now think with you that so much depends on extraneous matters." The critical question in Pennsylvania was the method of appointment of electors, and it "must be decided *principally* under the influence of local and domestic considerations."[30] Such advice from a man who shared with Coxe top billing as the Republican party's most indefatigable and successful seeker of hidden motives and plots must have been startling. But Coxe was not persuaded, and it took only a gentle prod to topple Beckley from his objective stance.

Senator Langdon "is now here and will be in Lancaster on Monday next," Beckley wrote in a letter to Coxe on October 30 from Philadelphia. "I have conversed with him, respecting his testimony of Mr. Adams's Monarchism, and he is fully disposed to give it to you without *abatement*." Beckley not only obliged Coxe in this particular instance but also gladly joined him in the hunt for additional affidavits to prove Adams's guilt. Beckley's letter was taken to Lancaster by Abraham Bishop, Republican stalwart of Connecticut, who, Beckley wrote, "will corroborate *incidentally* and *collaterally* every thing respecting Mr. Adams's Monarchic declaration to Mr. Dana and Mr. pierpoint Edwards at New Haven. Other interesting communications Mr. Bishop will make to you, and you will find in him a

30. Beckley to Coxe, Oct. 27, 1800, Coxe Papers.

powerful Auxiliary to aid all our united views and wishes at Lancaster."[31] Certainly Beckley's initial but short-lived disapproval of his friend's excessive zeal had not been based on any fundamental divergence of views. Both were inflexibly convinced of a Federalist monarchical conspiracy; they only disagreed on which manifestation of the plot their attention should be centered. Just as Coxe believed that it was of first importance to convict the Federalist ringleaders by sworn testimony, so Beckley was convinced that priority should be given to thwarting British efforts to bribe the Pennsylvania legislature.

"There is One thing more important than any you have suggested, to be guarded against," Beckley admonished his partisan ally, "and that is *British* gold. . . ." It was "sufficient to hint" that the British minister, Robert Liston, was in Philadelphia and had "his Eyes fixed upon the business at Lancaster. Every individual upon whom Seduction can be practiced, should be doubly watched." Lest Coxe should believe that these fears arose merely "out of vague suspicion," Beckley supplied what he believed were incontrovertible facts. Liston had just drawn $68,000 out of the bank, following which "two private dinners were given him at old Willing's," attended by a former state senator whose plans to travel to Lancaster were widely known. To rescue the commonwealth, Beckley recommended the organization of Rousseau-like committees of inspection: twenty of Coxe's most trusted "and secret friends" should be chosen "1st: to notice and report all Strangers coming to and remaining at Lancaster, during the Sessions. 2d: to mark their persons, abodes, apparent business and intercourse. 3d: to observe the Senatorial *boarding houses*, their comings, goings etc. . . . 4th: To observe equally our *friend* and our *enemy* Senators, since the War may be carried into our own Country." Beckley presumably had battle plans ready. Four days later he sent a courier to Lancaster with "one or two ideas . . . which I did not think advisable to commit to paper."[32]

Beckley's exaggerated fears and drastic proposals were surely a reaction to the political nightmare he and other Pennsylvania Republicans were experiencing. Having labored by means fair and foul to assure Jefferson's triumph in Pennsylvania, they were now in danger of having their glittering prize snatched away. The slender majority of two by which the Federalists controlled the state senate afforded them the alluring possibility of turning

---

31. Beckley to Coxe, Oct. 30, 1800, *ibid*. John Langdon promptly supplied the testimony. In a statement dated in Lancaster, Nov. 3, 1800, and endorsed "in presence of Tench Coxe," he described at length Adams's conversation in the Senate, even adding a statement about which Coxe had not previously known: Adams had said "with some warmth, laying his hand on the Table 'I tell you, sir, that elective Government will not do.'" *Ibid*.

32. Beckley to Coxe, Oct. 27, 30, Nov. 3, 1800, *ibid*.

defeat into victory. And now, even had the Republicans been able to perform political miracles, the approach of election day (December 3 was the day prescribed for the electors in each state to cast their votes) precluded the adoption of an act providing for the selection of electors by popular vote. The choice devolved upon the legislature, which the governor called into special session to convene on November 5. The political problem confronting the legislators was as simple as it was difficult to solve: whether to choose the electors by joint or concurrent ballot of both houses. If a joint ballot were selected, all or at least a large majority of Republican electors would be chosen; if a concurrent ballot, there might ensue a deadlock that would deprive Pennsylvania of her votes in the electoral college. If the letters of John Beckley are to be credited, Coxe, on the spot in Lancaster, took the lead in the Republican struggle.

"You must be prepared with a *Resolve* . . . that an appointment of Electors of a president and V. P. . . . *Shall* be made by joint ballot of the two houses of Assembly," Beckley advised Coxe a week or so before the assembly convened. "You should have every thing *cut and dry* . . . and be ready . . . to seize the *first precious moment of action* before *delay, pause,* or *procrastination* can work its business of seduction." Coxe, erasing from his mind impending suits for debts, other personal concerns, and his Land Office duties, was prepared to do whatever lobbying or writing could accomplish.[33]

But the combined efforts of Coxe, Beckley, Duane, Dallas, and other Republican leaders were no match for the obstinacy of the senate Federalists. On November 10 the lower house voted by an overwhelming majority for a bill mandating a joint vote. The senate responded by providing for concurrent selection. The resulting deadlock, continuing week after week, imperiled Pennsylvania's chance of casting any electoral votes. In the end, the Republicans, acting on the advice of the governor and other party leaders, gave in and accepted a compromise providing for eight Republican and seven Federalist electors. The stratagem of the Federalists, more clever than decent, was successful; the overwhelming Republican victory at the polls had been thwarted.[34]

Why had it happened? Was Federalist obstinacy motivated, as the traditional wisdom has it, by a belief in elitist government and a distrust of democracy? According to Governor McKean, who should have known, it was prompted rather by a scramble for the spoils of office. The "catastro-

---

33. Beckley to Coxe, Oct. 30, 1800, *ibid.*
34. According to Coxe, the Federalists were not satisfied with this flagrant disregard of the popular will, and they attempted to deprive Pennsylvania of its vote altogether. This was done, so it was alleged, through covert maneuvers to prevent the counting of the state's vote by contriving that the ballots be lost on the way to Washington, D.C. See the *Aurora*, Dec. 9, 1800.

phe," he informed Jefferson, was owing to the "ambitions and schemes" of three Federalist senators: John Woods, Samuel Postlethwaite, and Dennis Whelen. Woods, the brother-in-law of James Ross, hoped that he and Ross would be appointed to major federal offices; Postlethwaite, brother-in-law of Henry Miller (whose appointment as supervisor of the revenue in Pennsylvania, ironically enough, Coxe had been responsible for), was intent on assuring that Miller retained his office; Whelen, also a nepotist, feared that his brother, Israel, might lose his post as purveyor of public supplies. These three men, ably assisted by Federalist officeholders present in the state capital, "governed their colleagues." It may also well be, as one knowledgeable scholar has remarked, that McKean himself was "forehandedly sharpening a large axe" for clearing out the Federalist officeholders in Pennsylvania.[35] In any event, the incentives he attributed to the Federalists also strongly motivated the leaders of his own party. The feverish activity of Coxe, Beckley, and a host of other Republican party workers was symptomatic of a disease common to both Federalists and Republicans—the itch for public office. It was because their rivals' symptoms were so transparent that Federalist senators gambled on the Republicans' willingness to compromise rather than risk Jefferson's election and the spoils they expected.

In the meantime, returns trickled in from other states. Coxe's national network of political allies kept him abreast of the results. John Beckley, who had gone to Washington to be at Jefferson's side when, Beckley hoped, his patron became president-elect, sent frequent and detailed reports. John Dawson, Coxe's longtime friend from Virginia, also wrote from Washington, where he spent his time compiling voting statistics and rumors while awaiting the opening of Congress.[36] These letters to Coxe were filled with news from South Carolina, which was considered the pivotal state. The Republican campaign there was under the capable direction of Charles Pinckney, United States senator and cousin of General Charles C. Pinckney, the Federalist candidate. The political arena in which the senator operated, however, was a confused one, owing largely to the available options proposed by one or another of the state's political leaders. Some favored the elevation of General Pinckney over Adams; others proposed an all-southern ticket joining Jefferson and Pinckney; Charles, the political renegade of the Pinckney family, was certain that he could carry the state for Jefferson and Burr. Charles's confidence was based on his awareness of a shift in power from the seacoast planters and merchants (who had kept South Carolina in

35. Tinkcom, *Republicans and Federalists in Pennsylvania*, 253–254.
36. Beckley to Coxe, Nov. 20, 21, 22, 24, 1800, John Dawson to Coxe, Nov. 26, 27, Dec. 12, 1800, Coxe Papers. Dawson's letters indicate that he heard from Coxe frequently. The letters from Coxe have not been found, however.

the Federalist column throughout the 1790s) to the planters and farmers of the Piedmont and westward.[37] And this confidence was not misplaced. The inland counties furnished a Republican legislative majority that chose eight electors pledged to Jefferson and Burr. The Jeffersonians were thus assured of seventy-three electoral votes; the Federalists could count on only sixty-five. A Republican triumph "is now certain," John Dawson wrote to Coxe on December 12, "on which event I congratulate you and my country."[38]

Coxe, as other close political associates also recognized, deserved congratulations. These would not, however, be forthcoming from the paladin of the Republican crusade, Thomas Jefferson, who, for the moment, was not even certain that he, rather than his running mate, would receive the presidential prize.

37. For Pinckney's confidence, see, for example, his letters to Duane and Beckley, quoted, respectively, in Beckley to Coxe, Nov. 3, 1800, and Duane to Coxe, Nov. 3, 1800, *ibid*. For the shift in power in South Carolina, see Ulrich B. Phillips, ed., "South Carolina Federalists," *American Historical Review*, XIV (1909), 529–543, 731–743.
38. Dawson to Coxe, Dec. 12, 1800, Coxe Papers.

20 ❧

Disappointed Office Seeker

"All the Electoral returns are in," John Beckley informed Coxe on December 31, 1800, "and result in an Even vote for Jefferson and Burr, 73 each."[1] Once it was certain the decision would devolve upon the House of Representatives, the question for Coxe and other stalwart Jeffersonians became what, if any, advantage the Federalists would take of their control of the lame-duck Congress. Would they abide by their often-stated principle that though the voice of the people might sometimes be the voice of Satan, it must nevertheless prevail, or would they be unable to resist the opportunity to deprive the Virginian—to them the personification of atheism and radicalism —of the highest office in the land? Jefferson thought he knew. The Federalists, he wrote, "propose to prevent an election in Congress, and to transfer the government by an act to the C[hief] J[ustice] or Secretary of State or to let it devolve on the Pres. pro tem. of the Senate till next December, which gives them another year's predominance, and the chances of future success." The Republicans, he was certain, would do all in their power to secure a legislative decision, but if they failed, the "dissolution of the government and danger of anarchy" might be prevented by what he described without specificity as "a concert between the two highest candidates."[2]

Coxe, discounting the more cheerful views of Washington correspondents like John Dawson who assured him that no effort would be made to block the Virginian's election, shared Jefferson's pessimistic prediction. He sought to obviate it, however, by means of an address to Congress published on January 12, 1801, in the *National Intelligencer*. Asserting that the failure

1. John Beckley to Coxe, Dec. 31, 1800, Coxe Papers.
2. Thomas Jefferson to Coxe, Dec. 31, 1800, Jefferson Papers, Lib. of Cong.

of the House to sanction the voters' obvious choice would be "deeply injurious to tranquility, order and property," he submitted to the nation's congressmen "the apparent reasons for chusing Mr. Jefferson"; included among these were Jefferson's long and distinguished career as a public official and the electorate's obvious intention that he fill the post.[3] This appeal to conscience was circulated in Congress by Coxe's friends. Senator John Brown of Kentucky reported that the address was considered "by our party" as "judicious and well adapted," but, as reports from other acquaintances in the capital city soon confirmed, it had no detectable influence on either Jefferson's political opponents or his running mate.[4]

By early January it was widely and plausibly rumored in Washington that Burr had no intention of surrendering his constitutional right to try for the presidency, and the House became the scene of unseemly stratagems by despondent Federalists, encouraged by Burr's ambiguous position, to overrule the popular will. Gossip, both well founded and wild, circulated in the corridors of the Capitol and in congressional boardinghouses. One rumor was that the Federalists intended to postpone any decision until after March 4, when in the absence of a duly elected president the office would go to the Speaker of the House. Another report (repeated to Coxe by Senator Brown) was that Jefferson's opponents had "it in contemplation to defeat the election altogether, and under authority of the sweeping Clause 'to provide for the general welfare' " to pass an act designating an ad interim president. Fearful that his own appointment to high office was thus jeopardized, Coxe wrote anxious letters to congressional correspondents like Peter Muhlenberg, who replied that "we are . . . not so much in the horrors here . . . as our friends in Philadelphia seem to be." Such complacency was not shared by Jefferson, who wrote to Coxe on the morning of February 11, as balloting commenced in the House, that whether himself or Burr "will be elected and whether either I deem perfectly problematical: and my mind has long been equally made up for either of the three events."[5] Such resignation doubtless stood him in good stead during succeeding days as roll call after roll call produced no decision. Finally, on the sixth day and the thirty-sixth ballot, his opponents bowed to public opinion and elected him the nation's third and its first Republican president. Whatever Jefferson's gratification, it

---

3. John Dawson to Coxe, Jan. 2, 1801, Coxe Papers; "To the House of Representatives of the United States of America," signed "An American," *National Intelligencer and Washington Advertiser* (Washington, D.C.), Jan. 12, 1801. For Coxe's authorship of this article, see John Brown to Coxe, Jan. 14, 1801, Coxe Papers.

4. Brown to Coxe, Jan. 14, 1801, Coxe Papers. For the other reports on the effect of the address, see, for example, Peter Muhlenberg to Coxe, Jan. 16, 19, Feb. 5, 1801, Dawson to Coxe, Dec. 28, 1800, Jan. 2, 1801, Brown to Coxe, Jan. 14, 1801, *ibid.*

5. Brown to Coxe, Jan. 14, 1801, Peter Muhlenberg to Coxe, Jan. 16, 1801, *ibid.*; Jefferson to Coxe, Feb. 11, 1801, Jefferson Papers.

scarcely could have exceeded that of eager would-be officeholders like John Beckley and Tench Coxe, who impatiently awaited their chief's inauguration and their own expected rewards.[6]

At noon on March 4, 1801, the fifty-seven-year-old statesman, surrounded by well-wishers, walked the short distance from his lodging at Conrad's boardinghouse to the unfinished Capitol, where the oath of office was administered by Chief Justice John Marshall, Jefferson's cousin and future antagonist. The man who stood before Marshall was, in Henry Adams's description, "very tall . . .; sandy-complexioned; shy in manner, seemingly cold; awkward in attitude, and with little in his bearing that suggested command."[7] His inaugural address was delivered in a low mumble, audible only to those immediately around him; but what they did hear was characterized by that remarkable grace and felicity of style that makes Jefferson's state papers among the most memorable in our history. Abounding in aphorisms, it was an artful statement of the principles that Jefferson believed "should be the creed of our political faith—the text of our civil instruction." It was also a call for the restoration of harmony and mutual respect and for what we now call bipartisanship. "We have called by different names brethren of the same principle," Jefferson said in one of his most captivating sentences. "We are all Republicans; we are all Federalists."[8]

Tench Coxe, a former Federalist and now an ardent Republican, must have disagreed. That all Americans should be good Jeffersonians was to him axiomatic, but he did not believe that all Federalists, most particularly those of monarchical proclivities, were good Republicans. Nor did he agree with Jefferson's avowal of laissez-faire—his call for "a wise and frugal Government, which shall restrain men from injuring one another" and "shall leave them otherwise free to regulate their own pursuits of industry and improvement." "Wise and frugal," yes, Coxe would have replied, but also one that would promote economic growth by the enactment of supportive legislation. Coxe wanted a government that would encourage manufactures, as well as agriculture and commerce, which Jefferson did propose. But Coxe could take comfort in the awareness that Jefferson's profession of agrarianism was open to modification in practice, just as his stance as the statesman above parties had not in the past excluded ardent partisanship.

Convinced that Jefferson's partisanship would include a full measure of gratitude to political lieutenants, Coxe was sanguinely expectant. During the Pennsylvania campaign it had been openly rumored that he was a candidate for the secretaryship of the Treasury and, as one hostile newspaper put

6. See, for example, John Smith to Coxe, Feb. 12, 13, 18, 1801, Beckley to Coxe, Feb. 13, 1801, Coxe Papers.

7. Adams, *History of the U.S.*, I, 185.

8. Richardson, ed., *Messages and Papers of the Presidents*, I, 309–312.

it, that he had kept himself "busy in forging letters and certificates" to promote his "pretensions to the office." Despite his defenders' heated denials of the latter charge, as well as of the attribution of motivation, Coxe's closest political allies believed that he was in the running for that post; the most influential of them, William Duane, recommended him to the president-elect as the most eligible candidate.[9] Although Jefferson did not agree with this appraisal, he was certainly aware of the Philadelphian's major contribution to the Republican campaign (if only because Coxe and his boosters did not let him forget it), and during the winter and early spring of 1801 he openly acknowledged Coxe's importance. For his part, Coxe was serenely certain that March 4, 1801, marked the beginning of a new era in American history, the progressive unfolding of new policies and national trends that he, an important architect of the Republican victory, would help to direct.

Determined to leave as little as possible to chance, Coxe solicited the aid of congressional allies like Peter Muhlenberg, personal supporters like John Beckley, and longtime friends like John Dawson of Virginia. He also, like many other hungry office seekers, set forth his own claims.[10] On January 25, 1801, in the first of the epistolary fusillades with which he would bombard Jefferson over the succeeding months, he wrote that if it were recalled that he had "suffered deeply from principle," and if it were admitted that he had made strenuous efforts to restore good government, then he was entitled, on the grounds of "public prudence and virtue," to "a proportionate remembrance." To this Jefferson gave a Delphic reply: wait until arrangements can quietly be made.[11]

Coxe was unable to entertain the notion that one of the richest plums of the patronage tree would not be plucked for himself, and he mistook Jefferson's evasiveness for reassurance. Accordingly, in mid-April the Philadelphian, adopting more the tone of a king-maker than a supplicant, informed Jefferson of the offices for which he was available. If John Adams had not cut short his career in the Treasury Department, he would have had "high claims" to its secretaryship; his "habits in naval matters" and "attention to our public affairs" qualified him for the Navy Department. If such important positions were unavailable, he was willing to agree to an appointment as supervisor for Pennsylvania, "one of the sixteen which as Commissioner of the Revenue I superintended"; or he would, if the presi-

9. *Philadelphia Gaz.*, Oct. 11, 1800; *Demo. Press*, Jan. 18, 1812.

10. See, for example, Coxe to Muhlenberg, Jan. 16, Feb. 28, 1801, Beckley to Coxe, Feb. 18, 1801, Dawson to Coxe, Mar. 21, 1801, Coxe Papers. Coxe also had his own agent on the spot, his former clerk Ezekiel Forman, who while seeking a job for himself also made repeated inquiries about Coxe's prospects. Forman to Coxe, May 7, Sept. 11, Oct. 1, 1801, *ibid.*

11. Coxe to Jefferson, Jan. 25, 1801, General Records of the State Department, R.G. 59, National Archives; Jefferson to Coxe, Feb. 11, 1800, Jefferson Papers.

dent insisted, serve as collector of the customs for the port of Philadelphia, largely because of its high pecuniary rewards. If all else failed, he would accept the lowly office of naval officer of the port of Philadelphia, primarily because he wished to remain in his native city, though he would "reluctantly" accept a call to the nation's capital, an oblique reference to the commissionership of the revenue, from which the Federalists had dismissed him.[12]

Although Coxe remained confident that he would in some way be officially rewarded, he was disappointed at not being included in the first Republican cabinet. With most of Jefferson's choices, he had no quarrel. He regarded Madison as preeminently qualified for the State Department and if the Treasury Department had to go to another, he considered Gallatin as competent to direct it.[13] The appointments of Henry Dearborn of Maine and Levi Lincoln of Massachusetts as secretary of war and attorney general respectively were to him unexceptionable if, as appeared obvious, Jefferson insisted on thus using the patronage to convert New England to Republicanism. Coxe was, on the other hand, disgruntled at not being awarded the secretaryship of the navy, a post the new president offered in quick succession to four other Republicans, only to be refused by men Coxe considered less politically prominent and less qualified than himself. Nevertheless, he remained imperturbably certain that he would be suitably rewarded, his confidence buoyed by reassurances of fellow Republicans among whom, as one of them reminded him, "the opinion generally prevails that you will be appointed to some . . . important office under the General Government."[14]

It was one of Jefferson's first important patronage appointments that undermined Coxe's composure, forcing upon him the unaccommodating awareness that his expectations had been built upon sand, that Jefferson's gracious acceptance of service was not tinctured by any feeling of reciprocal obligation. The appointment, which occurred soon after Jefferson's inauguration, was that of Peter Muhlenberg, congressman and senator-elect from Pennsylvania and Coxe's close political associate in the campaign of 1800. Muhlenberg was to be supervisor of the revenue for the state of Pennsylvania, an office that Coxe had confidently counted on if passed over for more important ones. The president had based his choice on the recommendations of Thomas McKean, who wished to rid himself of a popular rival for the governorship, and of Gallatin, who relied on the recommendations of Pennsylvania Republicans like William Findley. Coxe, numbed by

---

12. Coxe to Jefferson, Mar. 10, 23, 1801, Gen. Rec. of State Dept. R.G. 59.

13. "I do not complain," Coxe wrote to James Madison, that "Mr. Gallatin was preferred to the Treasury Department, tho I think there should have been some negociation in that subject." Coxe to Madison, June 11, 1801, Madison Papers, Lib. of Cong.

14. John Miller to Coxe, Feb. 27, 1801, Coxe Papers.

the shock, apparently did not ask himself why the appointment had been made, but instead redoubled his efforts to secure at least a well-paying position.[15] He also promptly informed Jefferson, who must have been both shocked and annoyed at the tone of the letter, that in view of his own superior qualifications and just political deserts the appointment was personally objectionable. Muhlenberg should be offered another post to make way for his own appointment. If the president remained adamant, and by implication unreasonable, on this, Coxe expected a suitable consolation prize—if not an office in Philadelphia then the secretaryship of the navy, for which, as he put it, "*on cautious reflection* I do not feel myself incompetent."[16]

Jefferson, like all newly inaugurated presidents for a century and a half to come, was smothered in letters of application for office, most deferential, many fawning, a few forthright, but none as imperiously demanding as those from Coxe. It was true, as Coxe was aware, that the president was neither unmindful of the rewards due his more stalwart supporters nor unwilling to remove officeholders to make room for deserving Republicans. But neither of these presidential characteristics worked in favor of Coxe. For this double standard Coxe's imperiously importunate letters were largely responsible.[17] As late as March 26, 1801, Jefferson had described to Governor McKean "in warm and feeling terms" his "esteem and friendship" for Coxe and the high estimate in which his "merits, services and sufferings" were held. The president also promised McKean that "as soon as the administration get together" and "full and permanent arrangements are taken," Coxe would be "immediately and particularly noticed."[18] As Coxe's letters rained in on Jefferson, however, the Virginian perhaps remembered instead the observation that he had made to Coxe two years earlier: "Once a man has cast a longing eye on" appointive office, "a rottenness begins in his

15. Coxe to Jefferson, Mar. 10, 23, 1801, Gen. Rec. of State Dept., R.G. 59. William Findley admitted Coxe's claims to the position of supervisor of the revenue but insisted that the man purportedly responsible for swinging the state's German vote to Jefferson had a superior one. Findley to Albert Gallatin, July 8, 1801, Gallatin Papers, N.-Y. Hist. Soc., New York City.

16. Coxe to Jefferson, Apr. 19, 1801, Gen. Rec. of State Dept., R.G. 59. Jefferson's first appointee as secretary of the navy, Benjamin Stoddert, had resigned Apr. 1, 1801. Henry Dearborn served ad interim until July 15, 1801, when Robert Smith was appointed.

17. Coxe himself believed, so he told Madison, that the "ingenious and covert unfriendliness" of his political rivals was responsible for Jefferson's failure to appoint him to a high office. Although he did not identify his enemies, he presumably was referring chiefly to Alexander J. Dallas. Coxe to Madison, June 11, 1801, Madison Papers, Lib. of Cong.

18. The quotations are from Beckley's description of Jefferson's letter of Mar. 26, 1801, to Gov. Thomas McKean, a letter that was shown to Beckley by the governor. Beckley to Coxe, Mar. 31, 1801, Coxe Papers. Jefferson's letter has not been found. His letter of Mar. 25, 1801, to McKean is in the McKean Papers, Hist. Soc. Pa., Philadelphia, but its contents do not square with Beckley's summary.

conduct." In any event, Jefferson's opinion of Coxe had changed, his own promises were forgotten, and he ceased even to mention Coxe, much less to praise him. The president was, whether he liked it or not, reminded of him by Gallatin, who felt obliged to relay the belief of Pennsylvania politicians that Coxe should be rewarded, and perhaps by Madison, on whom Coxe repeatedly pressed his claims and who considered these claims well founded.[19]

If Jefferson had had an open mind on the subject or had been intent on fair play, he would have agreed, but by the late spring of 1801 he appears rather to have been primarily interested in how best to get rid of a leading and prominent supporter, who though loyal had become a pest. The method he chose was cruel, perhaps intentionally so. He offered Coxe two jobs in the internal revenue service, an inspectorship of a survey and a collectorship (both subordinate positions not requiring Senate confirmation), for which Coxe as revenue commissioner had himself nominated candidates. In any event, considering Jefferson's known opposition to excise taxes, both jobs were likely to be abolished soon. The president's offer was no less devastatingly insulting to Coxe because of the superficially polite and appreciative letter in which it was conveyed. It was indeed true, Jefferson said, that the Federalists had "unjustly removed" Coxe from his office in 1797 and that his subsequent efforts to assure the triumph of true republican principles were commendable; he was thus entitled to a suitable political reward. This had not been forthcoming, because Coxe had expressed a disinclination to leave Philadelphia and because, unfortunately, the Senate would have been more antagonistic to him "than against some common characters."[20]

Whatever Jefferson's motivation, his offer was as demeaning as his explanation of it was disingenuous.[21] How had he for almost a decade so graciously acknowledged with apparent sincerity the services of a man he so deeply distrusted? Had he, unwittingly or not, adopted the belief of Coxe's

19. Jefferson to Coxe, May 21, 1799, Jefferson Papers. For Coxe's pressure on Madison, see, for example, Coxe to Madison, Apr. 3, June 11, 1801, Madison Papers.

20. Although Jefferson's letter of June 17, 1801, offering Coxe these jobs has not been found, and Coxe did not specifically designate which jobs were offered, Coxe's prolix protests make it clear that the posts were those stated in the text. See especially Coxe to Jefferson, Nov. 8, 1801, Gen. Rec. of State Dept., R.G. 59. This is also borne out by a report from Beckley written from Philadelphia on June 24. Beckley informed Coxe that from what Jefferson, Madison, and Gallatin had recently told him, he conjectured that "the Inspectorship of this survey, with the addition of a collectorship" would be offered to Coxe. Beckley to Coxe, June 24, 1801, Coxe Papers.

21. Perhaps Jefferson included Coxe among those "revolutionary tories" who "have a right to tolerance, but neither to confidence nor power." Jefferson to John Dickinson, July 23, 1801, Ford, ed., *Works of Jefferson*, IX, 281. Never charitable toward loyalists, Jefferson had removed the supervisor of New Hampshire largely because "he was a Revolutionary Tory," and thus Jefferson may have balked at the contradiction of appointing a well-known tory to high office. See Jefferson to Gallatin, Nov. 12, 1801, Henry Adams, ed., *The Writings of Albert Gallatin*, I (New York, 1960 [orig. publ. 1879]), 60.

Federalist opponents that Coxe was a political trimmer, a man whose seem-ing political fervor only cloaked his patent opportunism? Did Jefferson, shrewd politician that he indisputably was, act on the assumption (doubtless correct) that Coxe was a political liability? Was the president's behavior merely another demonstration that when stung by criticism he could be incredibly petty? Whatever the answers, there was considerable justification for the observation Mathew Carey made to Joel Barlow a decade later: "If Mr. Jefferson had never committed a political sin but his base ingratitude" to Coxe, that would be reason enough for censure.[22] Although Coxe was unwilling publicly to criticize the president, he found Jefferson's offer hu-miliating, and his predictable reaction was angry defiance, which sealed his official fate.

"You will be pleased to consider me as not disposed to accept the appointment you mention," he wrote to Jefferson on June 24, dictatorially adding that if it was known that the president had "meditated the offer," Jefferson should promptly announce "that on reflexion you did not think it proper to make it." The proposed appointment, he continued, was not only personally degrading but would elicit "very unpleasant remarks in reference to yourself and your arrangements." As Coxe wrote, his bitterness mounted; in page after page he repetitiously spun out his superior claims and Jeffer-son's unconscionable refusal to credit them, the evil deeds of Federalists who yet remained in office, and the president's culpability in doing nothing to remove them. Too angry to know that he had already written a thousand words too many, Coxe persisted, sending another, even longer letter in the same vein on June 25.[23]

To Jefferson it was a startling performance: a political leader, one of several from Pennsylvania, presuming to lecture the president on his derelic-tion of duty and to demand immediate appointment to a designated office! None of Jefferson's most trusted and influential advisers, neither Gallatin, nor Madison, nor any other, would have been so presumptuous, though it is also worth noting that Jefferson would not have treated them so shabbily.

For his part, Coxe's self-defeating behavior was prompted by his un-mitigable despair as he saw his carefully and laboriously contrived political career demolished by a few strokes of Jefferson's pen, as well as by his out-rage at what he regarded as a public and devastating personal affront. A professional desert lay ahead—no offices, high or medium. In following Jefferson he had believed he was marching to a new Canaan, but instead the Virginian had led him into the Wilderness and left him there. It did not occur to him to ask whether he had all along deceived himself; instead his

22. Mathew Carey to Joel Barlow, Apr. 25, 1810, Coxe Papers.
23. Coxe to Jefferson, June 24, 25, 1801, Gen. Rec. of State Dept., R.G. 59.

agony, sparked by perplexity and unrelieved by reflection, drove him to the edge.[24]

A month passed, and no answer came from the president; another month passed, during which he endured his hot and cramped quarters in Lancaster in solitary despair instead of joining his family in rural New Jersey, and still Jefferson maintained an Olympian silence. By early September, stung by "the malicious taunts of illiberal enemies," Coxe could stand it no longer, and, ignoring the sage advice of his wife not "to say or do any thing more in this business as it may do you harm," he once again wrote to the president.[25] The words were harsher and his demands more importunate than they had been in June. That Jefferson had withheld a suitable appointment even "after repeated requests, after your avowing the principle of restoration, after filling so many other offices," was "an afflicting disgrace, . . . and is considered as such by the wise and good of both parties." "Any man of spirit, or who has a due sense of character," must strenuously protest this affront. If Jefferson persevered in his inexplicable refusal to provide a respectable office in Washington "or something decent at Philadelphia," it would, Coxe said, "be kind to have me informed."[26] Lacking prescience, Coxe, of course, could not know that the man at whom he railed belonged, in Henry Adams's words, "to the controlling influences of history."

A wiser man would have perceived that thus to address the politically preeminent leader of his day was to invite political excommunication. But in this, as in so many other instances, Coxe was unaware of the inner springs

24. Not only was Coxe snubbed by the administration, but his critics, unaware of his weakened political position, continued to assail him. In Aug. 1801, for example, the familiar accusation that he had received a million livres in French secret service money was republicized. The charge was a canard, for, as Coxe explained, the situation was actually this: "Joseph Anthony and Co., and some others made an adventure some years ago to the Isle of France. Their cargo of Provisions was sold to the Colonial Administration. The final balance was paid in 1,000,000 livres colonial *paper*, which they Vested in bills at six months on the Paymaster General of the Marine and Colonies at Paris. These bills were . . . expressly declared to be for provisions sold out of the Cargo of the American Ship the Hannah. They are payable to '*Joseph Anthony and Son Merchants at Philadelphia for value rec'd. of them.*' They have been passed thro the hands of Anthony to another person of the concern, from whom they came to me to collect or negociate in the end of 1798 and beginning of 1799, when I was in trade, or endeavouring to return to it. Finding last winter that I could not collect the money, I returned the bills to the owner by assignment, and added a power of Att'y. which was openly recorded here." Coxe to Gallatin, Aug. 10, 1801, Gallatin Papers. Coxe offered essentially the same facts in his public rebuttal of the charges. See *Lancaster Journal* (Pa.), Aug. 1, 8, 15, 29, Sept. 5, 12, 19, 1801.

25. Rebecca Coxe to Coxe, Aug. 21, 1801, Coxe Papers. During his months in Lancaster, Coxe had occupied himself in preparing a public defense of Jefferson's removal policy. See his article signed "A Pennsylvanian" in the *Aurora*, Aug. 22, 1801 (republished in *Lancaster Jour.*, Sept. 2, 1801). For Coxe's authorship of this article, see Coxe to William Hamilton, Aug. 18, 1801, Coxe Papers. Coxe also published at this time a defense of the McKean administration in the *Intel. & Weekly Adver.*, Aug. 26, 1801.

26. Coxe to Jefferson, Sept. 4, 1801, Gen. Rec. of State Dept., R.G. 59.

of his behavior and its likely results. He was, it is plausible to assume, acting out in the political arena a scene he had long ago and gratifyingly played in his father's household. Just as he had once been the preferred son of an indulgent parent, so he now expected to be the prodigal son of his political mentor and idol. And the denial of his claim predictably elicited not modification of the claim but rage. It was in one sense pathetic, for he was impelled to act in a manner that could only be self-defeating. Viewed in another way, his behavior was ironic, for had he perceived that his actions were prompted by irrational personal demands rather than based on an unassailable position of political strength, his pretensions might have abated or even dissolved. And had they dissolved, he would have been free to utilize more fully his indisputable talents as a political publicist and economist. As things were, he persisted in fancifully believing that Jefferson would recognize anew the talents of a gifted economist and statistician on whom he once had relied and would bestow on him the high office to which he believed himself suited. Jefferson was uncooperative, and although he did not politically anathematize Coxe, he did invoke a ban of silence. For the next six years Jefferson wrote not a word to Coxe.

Meanwhile, having tilted with the president and been defeated, Coxe had had his long-cherished hopes for a distinguished career in national politics smashed and his position as a party leader in Pennsylvania gravely damaged. Like his desertion of the patriot cause in 1776 and his desertion of the Federalists in 1796, it was an event that inexorably and decisively influenced his subsequent career. His disappointment was the keener because of his certain knowledge that he was competent to exercise any of the high offices he coveted. And he was more than ordinarily qualified when his talents and training are compared to those of many cabinet officers who served under Washington, Adams, and Jefferson. Now he was forty-six years of age, unemployed, and too old to start again in trade; his capital was invested in lands that he could barely afford to pay taxes on; he was staggering under the burden of debts he could not discharge and had ten children dependent on him for support. Since he had rashly resigned the secretaryship of the Land Office and no other employment seemed to be available, he must now, no matter at what cost to his pride, accept whatever crumbs fell from the rather skimpy federal table.

Peter Muhlenberg, who had resigned a seat in the United States Senate to accept an appointment Coxe believed should have gone to himself, came to his rescue. He renewed Jefferson's offer of the post of revenue collector for the Philadelphia area, the lowest office in the internal revenue system, one that Coxe so recently had disdained. But compared to other minor posts the position paid well, and since Coxe was financially hard pressed, he braced himself for the additional jeers of his political opponents and accepted. He assumed office early in October.[27] William Duane, Coxe's close political ally during the presidential campaign, recalled a few years later (by which time he had turned into an implacable antagonist) that to Coxe acceptance of the post was such an unmitigable humiliation that "he suddenly took a new turn—and after whining and snivelling about it every night for three months—he declared he had resolved to abandon politics; and indicated that all parties were alike."[28]

Jefferson would in fact go far toward demonstrating that administrations, if not parties, were alike; but if Coxe perceived this, his insight was short-lived. His deep commitment both to the Jeffersonian cause and to the demonization of Federalism was the anchor of concrete mooring him to the Republican party. Although personally spurned by its leader, Coxe considered the party's destiny to be of supreme importance. Both his own future and the fate of republicanism in America and the world seemed to hang on its success. Thus bound to the Republican party, he continued not only to publish numerous articles (chiefly in the *Aurora* and the *National Intelligencer*) in support of an administration that had seemingly repudiated him, but also to offer advice, largely unsolicited, to its leaders. Among the recipients of his suggestions were the president, Madison, Gallatin, and Republican congressmen. He wrote mostly to Pennsylvanians like his by-now close friend Senator George Logan, but also to longtime acquaintances like Senator Pierce Butler of South Carolina.[29]

The policies Coxe recommended covered virtually the whole sweep of problems confronting the Jeffersonians—patronage, the census, fiscal policy, the judiciary, the military establishment, western policy, economic

27. The collectorship for the city and county of Philadelphia was the best-paying job, that of supervisor excepted, in the internal revenue service in Pennsylvania. In 1801 James Ash, collector, received $1,882, while his overseer, the inspector of the revenue, received just over $500. *American State Papers, Miscellaneous*, I, 282. Coxe succeeded James Ash. His appointment, signed by Peter Muhlenberg, was dated Oct. 1, 1801. Coxe Papers. The requisite bond for £3,000 was signed jointly by Coxe and his brother Daniel. Coxe to John D. Coxe, Oct. 1, 1801, *ibid*. Coxe was charged with the specific responsibility of collecting "the spirit and still taxes, carriage, auction, sugar, license, and stamp taxes for the City and County of Philadelphia." Coxe to Madison, July 16, 1813, Madison Papers, Lib. of Cong. On Mar. 15, 1802, Peter Muhlenberg renewed Coxe's appointment as "collector of such taxes as shall be assessed on the first collection district of the State of Pennsylvania." Coxe Papers. Coxe endorsed this certificate of appointment: "declined accepting and giving bond and taking oath of office, and never acted in any one respect."

28. *Aurora*, Aug. 29, 1804.

29. For Coxe's articles in the *Nat. Intelligencer*, see his correspondence with Samuel Smith, 1801–1805, Coxe Papers. For his advice to the Republican leaders, see his correspondence with Pierce Butler, Joseph Clay, James Holland, William Jones, George Logan, Joseph Nicholson, Caesar Rodney, and John Smilie, 1801–1805, *ibid*.

policy, commercial expansion, and foreign affairs.[30] He thus cast himself in the same role in the first Republican administration that he had played during the First Congress a decade or so earlier—that of gray eminence. Jefferson must have viewed the casting as singularly presumptuous. On Coxe's part, it reflected both an astonishing misunderstanding of the nature of his relationship with the president and a startlingly mistaken assessment of his own importance in the councils of the Republican party.

The most cogent and persuasive advice he tendered to the administration concerned measures that should be taken to promote economic prosperity and growth. Refusing to acknowledge Jefferson's call for laissez-faire, Coxe confidently called for a positive state whose solicitous guidance of the economy "would inspire confidence, conciliate local interests . . . and

---

30. As early as Jan. 10, 1801, a month before Jefferson's election by the House, Coxe offered advice on the rules that should govern appointments to office. See Coxe to Jefferson, Jan. 10, 1801, Gen. Rec. of State Dept., R.G. 59. See also Coxe to Jefferson, Jan. 25, 1801, *ibid*. Additional advice was submitted in a letter written six weeks after Jefferson's inauguration. See Coxe to Jefferson, Apr. 23, 1801, *ibid*. See also Coxe to Madison, Letter I, 1801, Madison Papers, Lib. of Cong. (Coxe wrote four long letters to Madison dated only "1801," but numbered in Roman numerals, by which they are differentiated in the notes below.) Coxe's prescriptions for a Republican foreign policy were predictable: just as the Federalists had manifested a readiness to remedy every ill of which the British complained and a concomitant "disposition to make heat, embarrassment, and impatience" of every justified grievance of the French, so the Republicans must reverse such slavish "devotion to the Monarchical states" and animosity to republican states by "a return to . . . justice and the general interest of free government." Coxe to Jefferson, Jan. 10, 1801, Gen. Rec. of State Dept., R.G. 59. See also Coxe to Madison, Apr. 28, May 1, June 11, 12, 1801, Letters II and III, 1801, Madison Papers, Lib. of Cong.; Coxe to Gallatin, Apr. 27, 1801, Gallatin Papers; Coxe to Jefferson, Feb. 11, Mar. 15, 1801, Gen. Rec. of State Dept., R.G. 59. On the subject of military preparedness Coxe was, as on most other matters, a doctrinally sound Republican, insisting that America dispense with a large regular army and an expensive naval establishment and rely instead on an ever-ready militia. See Coxe to Gallatin, Apr. 27, 1801, Gallatin Papers; Coxe to Jefferson, Jan. 10, 1801, Gen. Rec. of State Dept., R.G. 59. Coxe's views on Jeffersonian finance are described in Coxe to Gallatin, Dec. 11, 1801, Gallatin Papers, and at greater length in a series of articles, under various titles and signed "Franklin," which were published in the *Aurora*, July 10, 12, 13, 1802. As representative of Coxe's advice on commercial policy, see Coxe to Gallatin, Apr. 27, 1801, Gallatin Papers. For Coxe's opinion on western policy, see Coxe to Madison, Letter I, 1801, Madison Papers, Lib. of Cong. For his support of the Louisiana purchase, see the articles signed "Columbus" in the *Tree of Liberty* (Pittsburgh, Pa.), Aug. 13, 20, 27, Sept. 3, 10, 17, Oct. 1, 1803. See also "Notes Illustrative of the boundaries and extent of Louisiana" that Coxe enclosed to Madison in a letter of Nov. 6, 1803, Madison Papers, Lib. of Cong. For a summary expression of Coxe's approval of Jeffersonian policies and confidence in the Republican as the best of all possible parties, see "The Constitutionalist," signed "Greene," in the *Aurora*, Dec. 21, 28, 1802. For Coxe's authorship, see Samuel Maclay to Coxe, Dec. 25, 1802, Coxe Papers. These articles also reflected Coxe's abiding belief that the leaders of the Federalist party—especially Adams and Hamilton—were archmonarchists who wished to destroy American republicanism. That this obsession had not diminished was attested by the 5,000-odd words he wrote on the issue. In June 1803 he returned to the subject, this time in four articles signed "Curtius," which appeared in the *Nat. Intelligencer*, June 1, 17, 24, July 1, 1803. For Coxe's authorship, see Samuel H. Smith to Coxe, June 1, 1803, Coxe Papers.

unite all in a common cause."[31] The specific proposals he made were those he had consistently advocated for a decade and a half, but they were not less adventuresome because they were not fresh.

Among the many policies and programs Coxe recommended were these: internal improvements (including the construction at federal expense of a road from the capital city to the Mississippi territory and another to Lake Erie); a "legislative library"; a board of agriculture; the appointment of an official to compile and disseminate detailed information on American commerce; "a government-sponsored study of American resources and potentialities"; and the "preparation of a system of free government for the federal territory." Additional measures that Coxe proposed included policies to accelerate economic advance in the "interior" section of the country; a commercial system based on the principle of reciprocity, a recommendation dear to Jefferson and Madison; the promotion of the cultivation, exportation, and manufacture of cotton "as a branch of our affairs, before other countries shall take it up"; and the encouragement of American manufactures generally. Manufactures "merit the fostering hand of the Government," he remarked to Gallatin, on this matter the most sympathetic member of the administration, "and I am sure it will not be withheld."[32] To Madison, who was rather less sympathetic, he wrote proposing a detailed "investigation of the present state of the arts and manufactures." Coxe was certain that this investigation would prove that "manufactures support agriculture *as much as foreign commerce*" by revealing the "magnitude or extent" of the progress and practicability of manufactures, as well as showing the wisdom of encouraging them. Coxe did credit Americans with wisely eschewing the oppressive and corrupt practices of the Old World, but, he warned, they must not at the same time reject viable European policies, such as restrictive commercial systems. By avoiding the errors and emulating the accomplishments of European practice, Coxe believed his countrymen could assure a roseate future. His optimism, as contagious as it was deceptive, was expressed in a series of articles he published in November and December 1801.[33] His

31. Coxe to Madison, May 11, 1801, Madison Papers, Lib. of Cong.

32. "The Cotton Wool of the US or the Golden Fleece," *Intel. & Weekly Adver.*, Apr. 19, 1803 (for Coxe's authorship, see George Worrall to Coxe, Apr. 7, 1803, Coxe Papers); Coxe to Gallatin, Apr. 27, 1801, Gallatin Papers. For Coxe's encouragement of manufactures generally, see Coxe to Jefferson, Jan. 10, 1801, Feb. 3, 22, Mar. 1, 10, 20, 1802, Gen. Rec. of State Dept., R.G. 59; Coxe to Madison, Letter IV, 1801, Madison Papers, Lib. of Cong. Coxe also recommended to Gallatin measures that the Treasury Department should adopt. See Coxe to Gallatin, Dec. 6, 11, 1801, Apr. 18, 1802, Gallatin Papers. See also Coxe's "Notes on the Internal Revenue Act" enclosed in Jefferson to Gallatin, Sept. 11, 1801, *ibid.*

33. Coxe to Madison, May 11, 1801, Madison Papers, Lib. of Cong.; "Reflections on the Recent Peace," signed "A Friend to Trade," *Aurora*, Nov. 30, Dec. 5, 7, 14, 17, 1801. For Coxe's authorship of this article, see William Duane to Coxe, Dec. 15, 1801, Coxe Papers. See also Coxe to Madison, Jan. 4, 1802, Madison Papers, Lib. of Cong. As part of his "investigation," Coxe

enthusiasm was based on several convictions about the future: the peace settlement recently reached in Europe would allow his countrymen to turn their attention to the development of their rich national domain; American capital, no longer drained abroad, would be invested in domestic manufactures, thus as if by magic accelerating capital accumulation and obviating dependence on Europe; and abundant opportunities awaited only the exercise of the Americans' incontestable enterprise and initiative, most particularly in the field of cotton cultivation and manufacture. All this could be accomplished without fear of foreign interference, for any attempt by unfriendly nations to stunt this robust growth would have precisely the opposite effect: in retaliation the Americans would more and more manufacture for themselves, not only achieving ever greater prosperity but in time becoming the rivals of their would-be oppressors. To Coxe, in sum, every prospect was pleasing, if only the Jefferson administration unswervingly followed the right course. And convinced that he knew what that course was, he had nothing less than a civic duty to share his knowledge with the president and his advisers.

Coxe was indeed public-spirited and patently sincere, but what he construed as duty was mixed with a sizable dose of self-interest. He never ceased to dream that he would arise as a powerful phoenix from the ashes of his defeat, and he hoped that his writings would bring on this revival. On reading his perceptive assessment and sound advice on affairs of state, would not Madison or Gallatin, or perhaps even the president, decide that his talents must be commandeered for the public service? Such a consummation, so ardently desired, was too remote to await, and although Coxe was aware that he had pressed the subject of appointment to office too far, he continued during the months following his acceptance of the post of collector to seek another appointment.[34]

Obviously incapable of fully acknowledging the administration's pretermission of what he believed to be his partisan due, he wrote to Jefferson on November 8, 1801, reviewing the sad history of his unrequited quest for office. "Tho I sacrificed my standing in public life, and in society," he explained, "and much of my utility in that *great and certain struggle* to which Republicanism is *yet destined* in America" (meaning, presumably, despite the neglect of himself), he had been obliged because of his financial plight to accept the demeaning job offered him by Muhlenberg. Jefferson's already-full cup of annoyance must have overflowed at this outburst and at

---

proposed "an exhibition of the occupation of every person in the census" and a comprehensive survey of every manufacturing establishment in the Union. Coxe to Madison, May 11, 1801, *ibid.*

34. Coxe to Madison, May 11, 1801, Madison Papers, Lib. of Cong.

Coxe's angry reaction to reports that the nature and number of his importunate applications were public knowledge in Washington and elsewhere. Coxe sharply reprimanded the president for this last indiscretion, admonishing him henceforth to keep his letters confidential. Nor did Coxe in a subsequent letter hesitate to accuse Jefferson of doing "all in your power to consummate my depression and disgrace." Despite such effrontery, Jefferson, after a delay of six months, relented (presumably because of the intervention of Coxe's congressional supporters and other friends) and in July 1802 offered Coxe an appointment as supervisor of the revenue for Pennsylvania. It was more a sop than a reward, however, since the office had already been scheduled for demolition. The new incumbent was merely called on to conduct a mopping-up operation for a commensurately paltry reward.[35]

The post of supervisor was, in any event, less degrading than an ignoble collectorship. Thus Coxe, assured by Senator George Logan that the job was an interim appointment until "something else may be provided for you," accepted.[36] The fall from a confident aspirant to the secretaryship of the Treasury to a supervisor of a comatose revenue system might well have incapacitated the heartiest political climber, but Coxe, as his Revolutionary War experience had attested, was uncommonly resilient.

During the year or so following his appointment as supervisor, Coxe continued to press his claims to something better than a virtually defunct office. Persistence, like virtue, sometimes has its rewards, and upon the resignation of the purveyor of public supplies, Israel Whelen, in 1803, Coxe was finally awarded that post, a second-string office, but one that at least served to soothe, though surely not to still, his relentless ambition.[37] He was buoyed by this long-delayed proffer of a suitable public office, one that

35. Coxe to Jefferson, Nov. 8, 1801, Apr. 1802, Gen. Rec. of State Dept., R.G. 59. See also Coxe to Jefferson, Feb. 17, 1802, *ibid.*; Coxe to [Madison?], Feb. 28, 1802, Gallatin Papers. For the intervention of Coxe's congressional supporters, see, for example, Butler to Coxe, Nov. 12, 1802, Logan to Coxe, Dec. 19, 1801, Mar. 25, Apr. 28, 1802, Beckley to Coxe, Mar. 25, Apr. 11, 15, May 21, June 16, 1802, Dawson to Coxe, Apr. 14, 1802, Coxe Papers. Coxe's interim appointment, signed by Jefferson, was dated July 28, 1802. *Ibid.* On Jan. 11, 1803, a month after Congress convened, his nomination was formally submitted and two weeks later approved by the Senate. *Journal of the Executive Proceedings of the Senate . . .* , I (Washington, D.C., 1828), 432, 440, hereafter cited as *Senate Executive Journal.* Coxe had told Jefferson in the winter of 1802 that if no other job were to be offered him, he would accept the supervisorship. See Coxe to Jefferson, n.d., Gen. Rec. of State Dept., R.G. 59. The scheduled abolition of Coxe's new job was provided for by "An Act to repeal the internal taxes," Apr. 6, 1802, passed pursuant to a recommendation conveyed in the president's first annual message. That act also leveled the entire internal revenue service.

36. Logan to Coxe, Mar. 25, 1802. Coxe received similar assurances from Beckley and Butler. See Beckley to Coxe, Mar. 28, Apr. 11, 1802, Butler to Coxe, Nov. 12, 1802, Coxe Papers.

37. The administration's decision to offer Coxe the purveyorship was made in June 1803. See Gallatin to Jefferson, June 16, 1803, Adams, ed., *Writings of Gallatin*, I, 123.

afforded at least faint hope that he might be able to assist in guiding the nation to greatness.

That Jefferson was willing to tender the appointment was not owing to any revived cordiality toward Coxe but rather to the insistence of Albert Gallatin. Having for two years listened chiefly to men who belittled Coxe's political importance, the Treasury secretary finally heeded the voice of other state leaders who had all along contended that Coxe's past party services and the continued unity of Pennsylvania Republicans required that he be appropriately rewarded. "Personal predilection for him I have not," Gallatin wrote to Jefferson on June 21, 1803. Nevertheless, "justice seemed to require" an "expression of my *opinion* in his favor."[38] It also required, Gallatin said, that Coxe be awarded something other than a booby prize. Convinced that the Philadelphian's talents should not be wasted and that he was preeminently qualified for the purveyorship (an office, paltry though its salary might be, that was far more "respectable, important, and responsible" than any other that might soon be available), Gallatin urged Coxe's appointment. Jefferson presumably thought the purveyorship a cheap price for removing a partisan nuisance.

To Coxe a higher-paying and far less taxing position would have been more desirable, especially in view of the possibility that the proffered office might be moved from Philadelphia to the embryonic capital on the Potomac, a small town surrounded by swamps and forest and unsoftened by the amenities of civilization. But, urgently in need of funds "to well educate and comfortably maintain a large and growing family" and aware that neither Gallatin nor the president was likely to propose anything more agreeable, Coxe considered the purveyorship, with all its limitations, to be better than a moribund supervisorship and accepted the offer, assuming office on August 1.[39]

Coxe was certainly correct in insisting that it was difficult to support his wife and children on his salary, but he tended to exaggerate his situation.[40] For one thing, Charles Coxe, a doting grandfather and ever-solicitous father, saw to it that his son-in-law's household was well supplied with essentials such as food (sent from Sidney to Philadelphia) and, through gifts to his daughter, with at least pocket money. For another, Rebecca and the

---

38. Gallatin to Jefferson, June 21, 1803, *ibid.*, 123–124.

39. Coxe to Gallatin, June 16, 24, 1803, Gallatin Papers. Coxe did secure from Gallatin assurances that the purveyor's office would not be immediately moved to Washington. Since Congress was not in session, Coxe was on Aug. 1 given an interim appointment and after his confirmation by the Senate (*Senate Executive Journal*, I, 455) received another commission, dated Nov. 18, 1803. Both commissions are in the Coxe Papers.

40. Coxe to Jefferson, Feb. 17, 1802, Gen. Rec. of State Dept., R.G. 59.

children still spent a good part of each year at her father's estate. Nor was the Coxe cupboard so bare as to preclude occasional guests, or the wardrobe so threadbare as to obviate acceptance of invitations from both friends and relatives.

Although Coxe continued self-pityingly to picture himself as having been socially ostracized because of his unappreciated and unrewarded contributions to the Republican party, the portrait was grossly distorted. Philadelphia social leaders were indeed, as he lamented, predominantly Federalists, and a few probably did blacklist other aristocrats who they saw as having betrayed their class by joining the democratic rabble. But, for the most part, Philadelphia society was remarkably tolerant of political dissent, if only because so many of their own numbers had gone over to the Republicans. In any event, at the city's select Dancing Assembly, in fashionable drawing rooms, and at dinner tables of the socially prominent, Coxe was much in evidence, tall and still slender, his sandy hair belying middle age, his courteous, even courtly, manner obscuring the coarse invective of which he was capable in the political arena.[41] Genial, well informed, contagiously involved in current affairs, he was—when he chose to be—a charming guest. So, too, was Rebecca Coxe, now perhaps less elegantly gowned and certainly (in view of the onset of tuberculosis) less robust than when she had joined Coxe at the soirees of prominent officials a decade earlier. In her own right a member of the elite, Rebecca was also regarded as an adornment to select salons and dinner parties because of her musicianship, which continued to be widely praised.

If Rebecca's role as Mrs. Tench Coxe was on occasion difficult, it was at least relieved by the long summer months spent in the Jersey country-side. For her these annual vacations were a welcomed contrast to managing the large house on South Third Street.[42] When all were present at Sidney the family circle was remarkably cosmopolitan. Rebecca's sister Grace was married to a Frenchman, Jacques Donatien Le Ray de Chaumont, a well-to-do manufacturer who had enthusiastically supported the Americans during the Revolution by shipping them gunpowder and by serving as host to Benjamin Franklin during his stay in Paris as American minister. Another sister, Maria, was married to an Englishman, Andrew Allen, Jr., the son of Tench's sister Sarah. Young Allen probably became acquainted with Maria on one of his

41. On Philadelphia's tolerance of dissent, see Rasmusson, "Capital on the Delaware," 111, 112, 115. For Coxe's membership in the Dancing Assembly, see *ibid.*, 164. Coxe's membership began in the 1780s.

42. Coxe to unknown recipient, Apr. 5, 1802, Coxe Papers. In 1804 the Coxes moved a few blocks to 413 Locust St., where the family stayed until 1808. After the deaths of his mother in 1800 and his father in 1801, Coxe's vacations to New Jersey became less and less frequent.

visits either to his grandparents in Burlington (only a few miles from Sidney), to his sister Margaret Allen Hammond, wife of the British minister to the United States, or to his uncle Tench in Philadelphia. Yet another sister, Mrs. Lucius W. Stockton, had, like Rebecca, married a member of the local gentry. She lived in Flemington, only a short distance from her family.[43] Nearby, too, were Tench's relatives in Burlington, his brother William, his spinster sister, and others.

Although the social life of the upper class in rural New Jersey may have been more leisurely and rather more provincial (the Coxe international set excepted) than in Philadelphia, it was nevertheless crowded and, in one sense, remarkably similar to Philadelphia. In both places it was based on tightly knit family relationships. But for Rebecca Coxe, Sidney must have afforded relief from the tensions of marriage to a man who spurned her repeated entreaties to abstain from politics, who by ever more active involvement rendered himself the object of public abuse and scorn, and whose thwarted career ambitions and frustrating business transactions must have made even his closest personal relationship something less than relaxed and comfortable.[44] Her long absences perhaps renewed the fortitude necessary to unfailingly offer solace to a husband whose needs (if the barbs of constant misfortune are the measure) were bottomless.

For the Coxe children, as for Rebecca, Sidney was as much home as Philadelphia, and Charles Coxe more attentive than their father. Charles impatiently awaited their arrival in early summer; he invented excuses to keep them with him during the autumn; and, when they did return to the city, he wrote letter after anxious letter about their well-being. By 1800 there were ten children to be concerned about: Ann, now seventeen; two younger daughters, Sarah and Mary; Tench, Jr., who at sixteen was a student at the University of Pennsylvania; and six other sons, Francis, Alexander, Charles, Henry, Edmund, and James (all bearing, appropriately enough, the middle name "Sidney").[45] As was characteristic of men of the time, Tench Coxe made only perfunctory references to his children in his correspondence, but he was, one supposes, a devoted father. It may have been for their future that he tenaciously clung to lands that, however much they appreciated in value, could make him only well-off but could make them rich.

---

43. In contrast to these well-married and thus (by the standards of the time) successful daughters, Charles Coxe's sons, Richard and Charles D., appear to have accomplished little except to have lived on their patrimony, though Charles was for a time United States consul in Tunis.

44. Coxe to John Vaughan, Aug. 1, 1806, Coxe Papers.

45. An eleventh child, a son, was born in Dec. 1802, but died six months later. Logan to Coxe, Dec. 27, 1802, *ibid.*; Coxe to Gallatin, June 16, 1803, Gallatin Papers.

Coxe's business affairs were in the early years of the new century so snarled that even his battery of lawyers had difficulty unraveling them. The essential problem, as simple as its details were complicated, remained the same, however. He was land poor. Although he did have to borrow money to pay the requisite taxes (thus increasing his already unmanageable debts), he retained most of his holdings, which, though small by contrast to the great speculators of his day, like Robert Morris or William Bingham, were nevertheless impressive. He still owned between 400,000 and 500,000 acres in western North Carolina. He claimed several hundred thousand acres in Pennsylvania, though his title to some of his holdings there was cloudy. His property in Virginia amounted to 24,000 acres and in Kentucky to 6,000; his estates in New York consisted of 5,000 valuable acres; and, in addition, he owned lots in Baltimore and considerable land in Philadelphia.[46]

Coxe's liabilities, however, were considerably greater than his assets. There were sizable claims against him from the still unliquidated accounts of Coxe and Frazier, notably debts to Prager and Company of London and to Robert Wigram, his overseas banker during the Revolution. Some of the notes he had given in payment of his North Carolina lands remained unpaid, and he was heavily indebted to John B. Church for lands purchased on their joint account in Pennsylvania. Moreover, a large obligation incurred in the purchase of Philadelphia lots remained to be settled with Mrs. Sarah Lea; he was indebted for a large sum to his brother-in-law by marriage, Chaumont; and his promissory notes for sizable sums of money advanced to him were held by his father and his Aunt Rebecca. The latter, however annoyed, could, so he hoped, be counted on to do nothing more than reprimand him. But former partners like Church and the host of other creditors whose suits against him crowded the calendars of Pennsylvania courts were not so indulgent.[47] Perhaps the most notable suit was that instigated by the Ruther-

---

46. Coxe to William Irvine, June 5, 1802, to William Coxe, Sr., Apr. 9, 1801, and an undated note on landholdings, Coxe Papers.

47. For information on the debt to Prager & Co., see Jasper Moylan to Coxe, May 16, June 26, Oct. 15, 1800, Prager & Co. to Moylan, May 14, 1800, William Coxe, Jr., to Coxe, Jan. 4, 1802, "Assignment" in Coxe to George Latimer *et al.*, assignees of Prager & Co., Nov. 24, 1800, *ibid.* For the debt to Robert Wigram, see Coxe to Edward Goold, Dec. 4, 1803, *ibid.* The amount of the debt to John B. Church in 1802 was $6,805, for which Church had obtained judgment. "Debts in 1803," *ibid.* For information on the legal proceedings instituted by Church, see William Tilghman to Coxe, Apr. 22, 1800, June 4, 1803, Edward Tilghman to Coxe, Apr. 6, 1801, Coxe to Sarah Lea, Jan. 1, 1802, William Coxe, Jr., to Coxe, Jan. 4, 1802, Coxe to Church, Apr. 7, 1802, *ibid.* On the debt owed Sarah Lea, see "Assignment" in Coxe to Sarah Lea, Feb. 1, 1798, *ibid.* For information on other cases pending against Coxe, see John Weston to Coxe, Jan. 20, 1800, Jared Ingersoll to Coxe, Jan. 24, 30, 1800, Daniel Smith to Coxe, Sept. 5, 1800, William Tilghman to Coxe, Aug. 19, Sept. 16, 1800, John Young to Coxe, Apr. 2, Sept. 18, 1800, Coxe to William Coxe, Jr., Apr. 20, 1802, Coxe Papers; Coxe to E. S. Burd, Sept. 17, 1801, Society MS, Hist. Soc. Pa., Philadelphia.

ford associates, from whom Coxe had bought the bulk of his North Carolina lands.

At issue in the litigation was Coxe's bond for about $9,000, the final payment, which had fallen due on January 1, 1800.[48] Although the sum was for lands he averred had never been delivered, he would have paid it if possible on the assumption that the Rutherford associates would come through with an assignment. The problem was that he could not hand over what he did not have. "People here have failed to pay me to the amount of $40,000.," he wrote with perhaps pardonable exaggeration to the North Carolinians on May 18, 1802, "and I have been forced to take lands in payment, which deprives me of monies I depended on." Presumably aware that they had rooked the Philadelphian, the associates were patient. They had, however, a strong legal position, and their forbearance had limits. In May 1803 Coxe's bond was put in the hands of their attorney for recovery, by a court decree if necessary. The case of *Erwin, Greenlee, and Beard* v. *Tench Coxe* was brought before the United States Circuit Court at Philadelphia, and judgment was entered for the plaintiffs.[49]

The behavior of the Rutherford associates was, Coxe believed, as unconscionable as their legal standing was shaky, and in November 1804 his attorneys accordingly drew up a counterplea, praying that execution of the judgment be enjoined. Admitting that the North Carolinians held his overdue bond for $8,965, Coxe argued that they were not entitled to recover, because they had shortchanged him by about 150,000 acres. And that was not all. After conveying to him a quantity less than contractually stipulated, they had illegally taken up lands of the best quality within the limits of his own purchase and, widening their breach of contract, had conveyed to him lands inferior to those described in their original agreement. Erwin and his associates countered by rejecting each of Coxe's complaints, asserting, for example, that they had contracted to deliver, not a specific number of acres, but rather the number that upon survey the designated area might contain. The circuit court did not agree and awarded Coxe the injunction requested, subsequently overruling the Rutherford Land Company's motion that it be dissolved.[50] Finally, after a decade of controversy and years of litigation Coxe was exempted from paying for lands that had not been delivered, and

---

48. William Erwin to Coxe, Oct. 15, 1799, Coxe Papers.

49. Coxe to Erwin *et al.*, May 18, 1802, John Hallowell to Coxe, May 16, July 12, 1803, *ibid*. The circuit court proceedings can be followed in "Erwin et al., v. Tench Coxe, Oct. 1803–Apr. 1807," n.d., *ibid*.

50. Coxe entered his plea on Nov. 24, 1804. For the many documents involved in this case, see *ibid*. See also counterplea of Erwin *et al*. of Dec. 4, 1805, *ibid*. For the court's decision, see John Hallowell to Peter S. Du Ponceau, Jan. 3, 1806, Du Ponceau to Hallowell, Jan. 15, 1806, *ibid*.

he retained possession of the 400,000 acres that eventually would, he remained confident, justify his speculative ventures.

To protect his other lands against attachment for debt, Coxe in 1800 had seized upon the expedient of a general assignment of his property (he had previously made a similar arrangement for his North Carolina property), ostensibly for the benefit of his creditors but actually to safeguard his lands. The assignees this time were his cousin William Tilghman, Abraham Kintzing, a Philadelphia merchant and longtime acquaintance, Peter S. Du Ponceau, a Philadelphia lawyer and a close friend, and George Worrall, a political associate.[51] The use of such legal loopholes provided a much-needed respite, but Coxe's financial position remained perilous, confronting him with the nightmarish possibility that he might have to part with a large chunk of his lands to ward off bankruptcy. Short of a miracle, Coxe's only hope appeared to be his expected large inheritance.

Coxe's father had remained a wealthy man despite his retirement from business twenty-five years previously. Although Tench's share of the estate had been put into the hands of trustees, it would significantly lighten his burden of debt and stave off financial disaster. His part of the estate of his spinster aunt Rebecca Coxe, who possessed sizable landed and personal property, would, on the other hand, be unencumbered. In both cases, the question was not what but when he would inherit, and, as he surely knew, his solvency hinged on the answer. Fate came to his rescue; the death of his father in October 1801 was followed by that of his aunt in March 1802.[52]

By the terms of a will dated December 27, 1800, William Coxe left his property equally to his children, with one important exception: before any division took place, John D., Daniel W., and William Coxe, Jr., were to receive certain specified lands, whereas Tench's share of the remaining estate was to be reduced by a sum (roughly $6,000) equal to that which his father had advanced to him in 1795. During the months following the signing of the original will, the elder Coxe, increasingly outraged by Tench's land buccaneering and spiraling debts, appended codicil after codicil, each imposing further restrictions. Taken together, they stipulated that his son's part of his estate should be assigned to trustees (Daniel W. Coxe, William Coxe, Jr., and William Tilghman) who were instructed to appropriate it to the payment of Tench's debts (including those due the devisor's estate). Fortunately for his creditor-beset son, William Coxe, Sr., left what for that day was a

---

51. William Tilghman to William Avery *et al.*, Apr. 25, 1800, Coxe to J. A. Pearson, Jan. 20, Feb. 11, 1800, Coxe to George Worrall, Mar. 31, 1800, Coxe to William Rawle, June 24, 1802, *ibid.*

52. William Coxe, Sr., died on Oct. 11. An obituary notice appeared in Relf's *Philadelphia Gaz.*, Oct. 14, 1801. Rebecca Coxe died on Mar. 19 or 20, 1802. Coxe to George Hammond, Mar. 28, 1802, Coxe Papers.

handsome legacy. Owing to prudent management of the tidy fortune he had inherited and enlarged before the Revolution, he bequeathed to his heirs a personal estate of well over $50,000 and real property valued at between $75,000 and $100,000. Tench's share came to at least $25,000, a sum sufficient to discharge both the debts to his father's estate and a number of other pressing obligations, particularly his share of debts remaining on the books of Coxe and Frazier.[53]

Nevertheless, the bequest was enough only to temporarily prop up a still crumbling financial situation. A sturdier brace was provided by his legacy from Rebecca Coxe, who left the large estate that she had inherited many decades earlier virtually intact except for unsecured loans that were in effect gifts to Tench. Tench thus received not only his share of that part of her property left to the children of William Coxe, Sr., but as he somewhat callously put it: "The monies I owed her are . . . paid by an act of providence." Coxe and his brothers were not satisfied with the portions they received of their aunt's estate, however. Since she had died intestate, the laws of New Jersey, where she had lived for many decades, controlled the disposition of her personal property—five-sevenths to the children of her brother William and the remaining two-sevenths in equal parts to her brother Daniel's heirs, Daniel Coxe and Grace Kempe, both former tories who had become British subjects. The distribution of her considerable real property, worth as much as $150,000, was more complicated, depending on yet-to-be determined rules governing the right of alleged aliens to inherit such property. The question, in other words, was whether the heirs of her siblings should inherit equally or whether all should go to her American legatees. It was in the context of the times an important legal question and, owing to the perseverance of Coxe and his brothers, it finally reached the Supreme Court of the United States. To their disappointment the Court ruled that since Daniel Coxe, although a loyalist and longtime resident of Great Britain, was not an alien (this was the narrow question before the Court), his heirs were entitled to inherit property in New Jersey.[54]

53. A copy of William Coxe's will of Dec. 1800, along with its many codicils, is in the Coxe Papers. For Coxe's discharge of debts, see William Coxe, Jr., to Coxe, Jan. 4, June 6, 1802, Coxe to William Rawle, June 24, 1802, *ibid*. The figures given for the estate of William Coxe, Sr., are estimates based on his son William's calculations. See William Coxe, Jr., to Coxe, Jan. 4, 1802, *ibid*. Tench Coxe estimated that after the debts to his father and other pressing obligations were paid he would receive about $8,000. Coxe to Sarah Lea, Jan. 1, 1802, *ibid*. But he presumably was overly optimistic, for according to a "note of monies paid or engaged to be paid by Wm. and Danl. Coxe out of the property intended for Tench Coxe by Wm Coxe his father," the trustees of Tench's share discharged debts of his totaling about $25,000. N.d., *ibid*.

54. Coxe to unknown recipient, Mar. 1802, *ibid*. Rebecca Coxe had loaned Tench the sum of $1,000 on two different occasions and had "advanced to a sum of $2,500 to pay off part of Church's Judgment." *Ibid*. Coxe estimated the value of property received from both his father and aunt at between $40,000 and $50,000. Coxe to William Irvine, June 5, 1802, *ibid*. Rebecca

In the meantime, Coxe could command funds (he estimated them at from $11,000 to $26,000) to pay off his major debts, leaving other debts to be settled by the alchemy of a steady rise in the value of his lands.[55] As he dreamed of the wealth his lands would bring, he doodled. On scraps of paper, on the margins and envelopes of letters, Coxe constantly jotted down figures—sometimes his debts but more often yet his landholdings. He also often drew up more formal accounts listing his current assets and liabilities. One such statement, drawn up soon after his aunt's death in 1802, is particularly revealing: his debts were estimated at approximately $58,500, his property holdings (including the expectation of a bequest from his father-in-law) at about $281,500, making his net worth $223,000.[56] Although the estimates of the value of some of his lands were mere wishful thinking, he was on paper a wealthy man, and he was fiercely determined to actualize what his ledgers seemed to promise. Yet, while refusing to sell any of his hundreds of thousands of acres of land, he was grasping frenetically, sometimes humiliatingly, for the emoluments of public office in order to provide for a large family. It all suggests, at the least, some derangement of his order of priorities.

Coxe's personal property amounted to about $50,000, largely public stock and bank funds. Coxe to Hammond, Mar. 28, 1802, *ibid.* The case concerning this personal property (*M'Ilvaine v. Coxe's Lessee*) was argued at the Feb. 1804 term of the court. A decision was handed down in Feb. 1808. 2 Cranch (U.S.) 280–337 (1804), and 4 Cranch (U.S.) 207–215 (1808).

55. Coxe to Rawle, June 24, 1802, Coxe Papers. By the end of 1802 Coxe had paid to his creditors approximately $22,000 out of his share of these estates. There remained, however, debts totaling about $10,000, plus the possible liabilities that might result from litigation still pending in the courts. "Notes of Sums Paid out of William and Rebecca Coxe's estate," n.d., *ibid.*

56. For this account, dated 1802, see *ibid.*

21 ❦

Purveyor of the United States

Coxe was preeminently qualified to exercise the office of purveyor of the United States. As purchasing agent for the War Department from April 1794 to January 1795, he had served as de facto purveyor, and his refusal to continue to discharge that duty was responsible for the formal establishment of the post of purveyor by a congressional act of February 23, 1795. Following a well-established practice, that statute assigned to the secretary of the Treasury the responsibility for overseeing the operations of the purveyor. The man appointed purveyor was authorized "to conduct the procuring and providing of all arms, military and naval stores, provisions, clothing, Indian Goods, and generally all articles of supply requisite for the service of the United States."

By making the Treasury accountable for an agency designed to facilitate the work of the War Department, Congress had created administrative confusion that was compounded by the incompetence of the first purveyor, Tench Francis, Coxe's uncle. In 1798 Congress came to its senses and, acceding to the report of a committee stating that the Treasury Department's supervision of the purveyorship resulted in a "divided, and, consequently, an imperfect responsibility, and an incomplete interfering agency," transferred responsibility for procuring military and naval supplies to the secretaries of war and navy, who were authorized to submit orders to the purveyor. The accounts, however, remained subject to the approval and audit of the Treasury secretary.[1] By this legislation the office of the purveyor was made accountable to the War, Navy, and Treasury departments.

---

1. *American States Papers, Finance*, I, 591; "An Act to alter and amend the several acts for the establishment and regulation of the Treasury, War, and Navy Departments," July 16, 1798, *U.S. Statutes at Large*, I, 610.

Although much needed, the reform was not radical enough. The purveyor was overburdened with work, particularly in view of the demands on his office resulting from the undeclared war with the French. The separation of the procurement of supplies from their storage, inspection, and transportation created official collision, rivalry, and inefficiency that would have hamstrung the operations of even a more competent purveyor than Tench Francis. No one was more aware of the problem than Alexander Hamilton, who, as inspector general from 1798 to 1800 and the most talented and energetic top-ranking officer of the army, found the supply system to be deplorably lax and mismanaged. Supervision of supply agents, he wrote to Secretary of War James McHenry (whose inept handling of the War Department, Hamilton constantly tried to improve), was "ridiculously bad. Besides the extreme delay, which attends every operation, articles go forward in the most incomplete manner. Coats without a corresponding number of vests. Cartouche boxes without belts, etc., nothing entire—nothing systematic." As for Tench Francis, Hamilton said, he was not only an inefficient administrator but also so much a Philadelphia-firster that he was unwilling to seek out supplies elsewhere, incapable, in sum, of coordinating a national procurement system. Perhaps demonstrating that one inept administrator is unlikely to flush out another, McHenry did nothing to correct the situation. Francis remained in office, as did his assistants and agents, with the result that the supply service proceeded, in Hamilton's words, "heavily without order or punctuality," "disjointed and piece-meal," and "ill-adapted to economy" and the "contentment of the Army."[2]

Francis's death in 1800 coincided with the resolution of the Franco-American dispute and seemingly opened the way for a more efficient conduct of the diminished business of the purveyorship. But President Adams's appointment of Israel Whelen, a Philadelphia merchant who had acquired some experience as an army contractor, did little to promote this happy prospect. Although honest and conscientious, Whelen had little zest for a job so taxing and ill compensated, and after two years of this thankless task he informed the administration of his intention to resign on July 31, 1803.[3]

2. Alexander Hamilton to James McHenry, June 14, Aug. 19, 1799, in Bernard C. Steiner, *The Life and Correspondence of James McHenry: Secretary of War under Washington and Adams* (Cleveland, Oh., 1907), 390–391, 403–410. The extent of Francis's and McHenry's bunglings can never be fully known, for in Nov. 1800 the building occupied by the War Department was burned, and most of its records destroyed. Writing from Philadelphia in 1807, Coxe commented that "there is nothing here relative to Mr. Francis's transactions but a pile of unimportant papers which would fill three sheets of papers." Coxe to Gabriel Duval, Mar. 19, 1807, Records of the Quartermaster General's Office, Purveyors Letterbooks, 1800–1812, R.G. 92, National Archives, hereafter cited as Purveyors Letterbooks, R.G. 92.

3. Israel Whelen had been appointed on May 26, 1800. For his resignation, see Coxe to Albert Gallatin, June 16, 1803, Gallatin Papers, N.-Y. Hist. Soc., New York City.

When Coxe assumed the office a few days after Whelen's resignation, it was scarcely better ordered than the "disjointed and piecemeal" operation Hamilton had described four years earlier. Its lack of efficiency was, however, less consequential now, if only because the comparatively large army recruited by Hamilton had shriveled away with the Franco-American rapprochement, and the Jeffersonians, spurred on by the president, were determined that it would wither yet more.

When Jefferson had assumed office, the army consisted of only approximately 4,000 out of the authorized 5,400 officers and men. Nevertheless, the Republican-controlled Congress proceeded in March 1802 to safeguard the country against militarism by reducing the army further. By eliminating the cavalry and drastically curtailing the number of engineers, the army was cut by nearly one-half. For naval protection Jefferson persuaded Congress to provide for small and inexpensive craft that could rest on the beach in peacetime and be launched in time of war—the famous "gunboats" that historians with considerable justification have so often lampooned.[4]

The same act that authorized a diminutive peacetime army also moved in the direction of enhanced civilian control. It authorized the appointment of three agents (and as many assistants as the president might consider necessary) to whom were assigned not only the duties previously exercised by a quartermaster general but also additional ones. More specifically, the new agents were entrusted, as had been the quartermaster, with receiving and forwarding all military supplies and were empowered to make such purchases as the secretary of war might direct.[5] Since the purveyor remained the War Department's principal purchasing agent, the act obviously created the possibility of a dual and overlapping procurement system that was potentially troublesome and costly.

On paper, however, the arrangement was simple, and if well administered, it could have provided at least an adequate system of army supply. Acting on orders from the secretary of war, the purveyor purchased on the best terms possible all army supplies—uniforms, blankets, arms, hospital stores, and equipment—and goods and gifts for the Indians. (Although the purveyor was officially charged with responsibility for the procurement of

4. Report of Secretary of War, Dec. 24, 1801, *American State Papers, Military Affairs,* I, 154–156; "An act fixing the military peace establishment of the United States," Mar. 16, 1802, *U.S. Statutes at Large,* II, 132–137.

5. John Wilkins, Jr., the quartermaster general during the years immediately following the establishment of the office of purveyor (1796–1802), had previously been primarily responsible for the transportation, though not the purchase, of supplies. See James Ripley Jacobs, *The Beginning of the U.S. Army, 1783–1812* (Princeton, N.J., 1947), 192–193. In addition to the duties of the former quartermaster, the new agents were assigned the duty of transporting Indian supplies and annuities and, when so directed by the secretary of war, also purchasing them.

naval supplies, the Navy Department elected to employ its own purchasing agents, to whom a commission was allowed.)[6] Once the purveyor had contracted for or actually purchased goods, his responsibility for them was at an end. All articles acquired in the Philadelphia area were delivered into the hands of the superintendent of military stores, whose headquarters were at the United States arsenal on the Schuylkill. Items purchased elsewhere were handed over to the military agents of the area for distribution. The efficient operation of the system depended both on the secretary of war's skill in coordinating the activities of his many assistants and on the cooperativeness of essentially separate and scattered officials. These things were not forthcoming, and to Coxe's dismay and the country's detriment the supply system remained, as Hamilton had described it in 1799, "without order or punctuality."

Despite such handicaps, Coxe's conduct of the purveyorship from 1803 to 1812 was more than ordinarily competent. His achievement was especially remarkable because of the formidable obstacles he confronted in conducting the "business of military purchases." One of the greatest problems in "this new-born and peaceful country" was, as Coxe saw it, procuring "instruments, utensils, patterns, and standards really good" and finding officials "with the proper education and experience" to carry out the assignment so as to promote "the interest of the United States" and to do "justice to the merchants" and manufacturers. Few were better equipped than Coxe for such a task. To his experience as a merchant and as an important federal official was joined extensive knowledge of the state and potential of the American economy. To these advantages Coxe added his preoccupation with the acceleration of the nation's economic growth and, scarcely less important, his belief that this grand goal rendered manufacturers and merchants the particular objects of the government's solicitude. Although he had not for many years actively participated in trade, he wrote in 1809, "I always feel the 'esprit de corps' which attaches me to the mercantile body." To the purveyorship, finally, he brought "steady and vigilant attention and exertion," which, as he once remarked, was essential "to effectuate . . . beneficial changes" in that office.[7]

In return for his accomplishments, Coxe deserved the plaudits of the

6. Gallatin to Thomas Jefferson, June 26, 1803, Adams, ed., *Writings of Gallatin*, I, 124. See also Robert Smith to Coxe, Aug. 23, 1804, Coxe Papers. Coxe did apparently make occasional purchases for the navy, such as saltpeter and sulfur. See Coxe to George Inglis, Sept. 1, 1803, Purveyors Letterbooks, R.G. 92.

7. Coxe, *Respectful Observations on the subject of the bill in relation to "the establishment of a quartermaster's department," in lieu of the existing military agencies, so far as it may affect the office of the Purveyor of Public Supplies* (n.p. [1811]), 8; Coxe to William Davy, July 11, 1805, to Peter Getts, Sept. 24, 1803, Purveyors Letterbooks, R.G. 92; Coxe to Vincent Gray, June 24, 1809, Coxe Papers; Coxe, *Respectful Observations*, 7.

officials—the president, the cabinet, and the Congress—who were responsible for the cumbersome arrangements and hampering parsimony under which he operated. He received instead only censure. In the end, the abolition of the purveyorship in 1812 was designed as much to insult him as to reform the shaky supply system that he had diligently tried to shore up for nine years.

During his first years in office Coxe was confident that his energetic exercise of the purveyorship could set things right. "It is an office," he wrote, "which may be rendered very instrumental to the public economy and to prevent improper conduct in all subordinate and scattered agents of purchase."[8] It was also an office, he believed, that might be used to promote trade, encourage manufactures, and soothe the country's troubled relations with the Indians. Had Congress been less stingy and the secretary of war more energetic, decisive, and imaginative, Coxe might have succeeded.

Henry Dearborn, Jefferson's secretary of war for eight years, owed his appointment to his military service during the Revolution, and, more important, to Jefferson's desire to recognize New England Republicans in his cabinet appointments. A resident of the district of Maine who had proved a steadfast partisan during a short and undistinguished stint in Congress, Dearborn appeared a politically eligible candidate to head a comparatively weak department that Jefferson had no intention of strengthening. And, in view of his proclaimed antagonism to a large military establishment, Dearborn was unlikely to object to Jefferson's stand. A man of imposing military appearance and unusual geniality, Dearborn obviously satisfied the president and apparently impressed many of his Washington colleagues; but his inveterate procrastination and indecisiveness were the despair of assistants, who depended on the secretary's dispatch and firmness for the effective conduct of their offices.

Coxe's most time-consuming responsibility and the one for which he most needed the cooperation of an efficient secretary of war was the supply of army clothing, a duty that required the effective teamwork of Dearborn, the purveyor, inspectors, storekeepers, and military agents. The paltry annual allowance (for example, each soldier annually received only one coat, four shirts, and two pairs of socks) was stipulated by Congress and designed according to patterns prescribed by the War Department. The resplendent attire that Hamilton had designed for the army (plumed cocked hats and bright blue embroidered coats for high-ranking officers, epaulettes for noncommissioned officers, and cockades and brightly decorative coats for all enlisted men) did not comport with Dearborn's notion of Republican simplicity, and during his administration of the War Department the army was

8. Coxe to Joseph Clay, Mar. 1806, Coxe Papers.

clothed more drably (but by modern standards still colorfully). Although the uniform differed for each branch of the service, the troops were generally furnished with knee-length dark blue coats with scarlet lapels, standing collars, white vests, dark blue pantaloons (white in summer), and round hats. Officers' uniforms were distinguished by gold or silver epaulettes, breast plates, white boots, and *chapeaux bras* adorned with cockade, eagle, and plume.[9]

The patterns for uniforms were selected by the secretary of war from among those transmitted by the superintendent of military stores and by Coxe, who also made numerous recommendations for altering their design either to improve their appearance or to reduce costs. The procurement of the requisite articles (hats, cockades, plumes, shoes, stockings, belts, and blankets) and materials (woolen, linen, cotton cloth, leather, and braid, among other things) was Coxe's responsibility, as was the employment of tailors and needlewomen to make the uniforms.[10] The finished products, along with related items such as garrison flags, silver medals, jackscrews, and musical instruments, were delivered into the hands of the military store-keeper, George Ingels, at the federal arsenal. Here William Irvine, superintendent of military stores, inspected them before shipping those that met specifications to the nation's scattered military stations.

A related activity was Coxe's purchase of "hospital stores," medicines, and surgical instruments, which he procured in Philadelphia for consignment to military agents who, in turn, supplied the various army posts and forts. For this aspect of his work he relied heavily on the advice of prominent Philadelphia physicians knowledgeable both about the possible medicinal needs of troops in different parts of the country and about the reliability of local manufacturers and wholesalers. That the hospital supplies were deplorably insufficient for the requirements of even a miniscule peacetime army was a result of the miserly appropriations requested by Dearborn and begrudgingly granted by Congress, rather than of any lack of diligence

9. See "An Act fixing the military peace establishment of the United States," Mar. 16, 1802, *U.S. Statutes at Large*, II, 132–137; Jacobs, *Beginning of U.S. Army*, 233; Asa Bird Gardner, "The Uniform of the American Army," *Magazine of American History*, I (1877), 486.

10. For Coxe's recommendations on uniform design, see Henry Dearborn to Coxe, Jan. 21, 1804, Secretary of War Letterbook, R.G. 107, National Archives; Dearborn to Coxe, Jan. 30, 1806, Feinstone Collection, American Philosophical Society, Philadelphia; Coxe to Dearborn, Aug. 22, Sept. 19, Nov. 14, 1803, Purveyors Letterbooks, R.G. 92. For the manufacture of clothing in 1806, to give only one example, Coxe purchased "Blue Cloth, scarlet cloth, white cloth, scarlet Rattinet, Blue Rattinet" to the value of $10,488, and "half stockings, hats, shoes, buttons, stock clasps, epaulets, plumes, cockades and eagles, black stocks, and red and blue cord," to the amount of $21,500. Purveyors Letterbooks, R.G. 92. Coxe was also responsible for disposing—by sale or otherwise—of clothing unfit for army use. Dearborn to Coxe, Mar. 19, 1805, Sec. of War Letterbook, R.G. 107.

or scrupulous attention to quality by Coxe and his advisers.[11] As a leading authority on the early history of the army has remarked: "Not even the best hospital supplies and medical treatment of that time could have saved all the sick, but at least a much larger number of them should have escaped a four-dollar coffin and a burying hole on a neighboring hill."[12] The pathos turns to irony when it is recalled that three successive secretaries of war, plus its longtime highest-ranking officer—James McHenry, Dearborn, William Eustis, and General James Wilkinson—were all doctors.

Even poorly doctored troops needed weapons, especially at a time when the possibility of war was ever present. From the beginning of his tenure as purveyor, Coxe was called on to procure ordnance supplies, gunpowder, and arms. To compensate for its sharp reduction of the regular army, Congress had in March 1803 appropriated $1,500,000 to arm and equip eighty thousand militiamen so that they might be held "in readiness to march at a moment's notice." To this end, the secretary of war apparently requested the aid of the purveyor, but the paucity of skilled workmen and of reliable contractors made it impossible for Coxe to procure even a small fraction of the arms needed. However, the difficulties encountered were largely offset, Coxe believed, by the possible long-term rewards of his endeavor: "Constant purchases for a few years," he wrote to Dearborn, "will put our manufactories of small arms upon an established footing, which is necessary to the consumate independence of our country."[13] But when first called upon in 1807 and 1808 to make extensive arms purchases, Coxe was dismayed to discover that scarcely any progress had been made.

In addition to army procurement Coxe purchased supplies for the Indian trade and the annuity goods due the various tribes, a task he had previously performed as commissioner of the revenue, at a time when such

---

11. For Coxe's consultation with physicians, see, for example, Dearborn to Coxe, Mar. 22, 1808, Sec. of War Letterbook, R.G. 107; Coxe to Benjamin Rush, Mar. 24, 1808, Rush Papers, Hist. Soc. Pa., Philadelphia; Coxe to James Mease, Mar. 3, 1810, Coxe Papers. For a description of the quantities of medical supplies provided, see Jacobs, *Beginning of U.S. Army*, 257–259. Owing to the enhanced work of Coxe's office between 1808 and 1809, the war secretary appointed Philadelphia physicians to assist the purveyor in the selection of medical supplies. William Eustis to Coxe, Jan. 24, Feb. 2, 1810, Sec. of War Letterbook, R.G. 107. There was no inspector of medicines or other hospital supplies, however, until 1810, when the secretary of war finally made such an appointment. See "To the Public," Jan. 4, 1812, broadside, Coxe Papers; Eustis to Coxe, Jan. 3, 1810, Sec. of War Letterbook, R.G. 107. In 1812 responsibility for their acquisition was taken from the purveyor and assigned to Dr. Francis Le Barron. See Eustis to Coxe, Feb. 12, 1812, *ibid.*

12. Jacobs, *Beginning of U.S. Army*, 232–233.

13. "An Act directing a detachment from the Militia of the United States and for erecting certain Arsenals," Mar. 3, 1803, *U.S. Statutes at Large*, II, 241; Coxe to Dearborn, Jan. 22, 1806, Purveyors Letterbooks, R.G. 92. For Coxe's attempts to equip the militia, see Coxe to Peter Gonter, Sept. 16, 1803, to Getts, Sept. 24, 1803, to Dearborn, July 10, 1805, *ibid.*

purchases were controlled by the Treasury Department rather than the War Department. The Indian trade was conducted through the agency of government-operated factories or trading posts established by Congress in 1796 to supply goods and provisions (spiritous liquors excepted) at slightly more than cost. Designed to obviate both the influence of foreign traders and the sharp practices of unscrupulous American merchants, the strategically situated factories, managed by Indian agents who were subsidized by a government appropriation of $150,000, proved superior to the previous private enterprise system. Within a few years they even showed a slight profit on capital invested. The Jefferson administration acknowledged the utility of such factories by increasing their number.[14]

During the first years of Coxe's tenure as purveyor, the principal agency for Indian supplies was in the hands of the superintendent of military stores and his assistants, who were in Philadelphia, while Coxe was delegated primary responsibility for the purchase of such supplies.[15] It was an extraordinarily cumbersome administrative arrangement that resulted in overlapping operations, complicated bookkeeping, uncoordinated purchasing arrangements, transportation snarls, and, most unfortunate of all, insufficient, inferior, or damaged supplies for the factories. As Coxe remarked in an undated draft of an article presumably intended for newspaper publication, "The difficult nature of this Business and the disconnected operations of two or three officers for the factories" in Philadelphia "rendered it extremely uncomfortable to persons employed in them, for the System had been so arranged . . . that much information *necessary* to one officer lay with another," thus resulting in a situation "unfavorable to the public Indian trade."[16]

Coxe's own efforts to prod Dearborn into "a thorough revision and reform of the business of the Indian Department" were unrelenting but futile. Recommendation after recommendation was dispatched to the secretary: among them were the desirability of having a supply of articles on hand in order to reap the benefits of large purchases at propitious times and to prevent delays in supply; the necessity of eliciting "from the Indian

14. Annuity goods, Coxe explained, "are little subsidies to *half foreign* tribes which may retain their peace with us. They are payments for lands." Coxe to Dearborn, Nov. 27, 1805, Purveyors Letterbooks, R.G. 92. For the administration of the Indian trade, see Edgar B. Wesley, "The Government Factory System among the Indians, 1795–1822," *Journal of Economic and Business History,* IV (1931–1932), 487–511; "An Act for establishing trading houses with the Indian Tribes," Apr. 18, 1796, *U.S. Statutes at Large,* I, 452; *American State Papers, Indian Affairs,* I, 654; George Dewey Harmon, *Sixty Years of Indian Affairs, Political, Economic, and Diplomatic, 1789–1850* (Chapel Hill, N.C., 1941), 116.

15. See Dearborn to Coxe, Jan. 30, 1804, Sec. of War Letterbook, R.G. 107; Coxe to Joseph Clay, Mar. 1806, Coxe Papers.

16. "Communication: The principal agency for the Indian Factories, at Philadelphia," n.d., Coxe Papers.

agents on the frontier the most minute information of the goods which please and displease, or would be acceptable to the Indians," information they had hitherto neglected to supply to the Indian agent in Philadelphia; and the designation of some knowledgeable official in Dearborn's office to check the schedule of annuity goods in order to assure the selection of those most conducive to encouraging "*half foreign* tribes" to "retain their peace with us." Coxe also emphasized the imperativeness of measures to prevent the delivery of "unsuitable and damaged goods" and the desirability of ending the prevailing Hobson's choice of a selection of the limited goods (or no goods at all) available on the shelves of the factories. The latter was to be done by providing a wide assortment of attractive goods whose sale should be conducted "without haste, ingenuously and fairly." While insisting on justice, fair play, and generosity to the Indians, Coxe, as paternalistic as most white Americans of his day, did not believe in self-determination. Commenting, for example, on one of the omissions in the supply list for 1806, he reminded Dearborn that while the government must of course try to pacify and satisfy the Indians, "*clothing for Women is important to civilization.*"[17]

Although the procurement of Indian and all other supplies was carried out pursuant to general guidelines established by the secretary of war, Coxe—in part because of Dearborn's laxity but also partly because of his penchant for seizing the initiative—established for himself the specific rules and standards governing his purchases. The rules were necessarily flexible, while the standards were uniformly high; yet both were guided by his determination to secure the most advantageous terms possible, "to procure sound and sightly goods for the proper uses," and "not to let anything occasion favor to an article unfit to pass." Coxe's purchases were also governed by a desire not "to injure the sellers to the public by an unreasonable exaction of a quality beyond justice." No one knew better than he that such a pragmatic approach was necessary in a country in which the manufactures, despite the unflagging promotional activities of himself and other apostles of industrialization, were still in their infancy. Consequently, articles of uniformly high quality were difficult and sometimes impossible to procure. Neverthe-

17. Coxe to Dearborn, Nov. 27, 1805, Sept. 9, 1803, Nov. 27, 1805, Feb. 28, Mar. 31, Oct. 30, 1806, Purveyors Letterbooks, R.G. 92. In 1806 Congress reformed the Indian supply system by the formal creation of the office (already established de facto by Jefferson) of superintendent of Indian trade. It was the duty of the superintendent "to purchase and take charge of all goods intended for trade with the Indian nations." For doing this—and perhaps this was the rub for Coxe—the superintendent was to receive an annual salary of $2,000. See "An Act for establishing trading houses with the Indian Tribes," Apr. 21, 1806, *U.S. Statutes at Large*, II, 402–404. Whatever its merit, the new statute did not, however, end divided responsibility for purchasing, since Coxe continued to buy some Indian goods. See Coxe to Dearborn, May 23, 1806, Oct. 14, 1808, to Thomas Tucker, Feb. 16, 1811, Purveyors Letterbooks, R.G. 92.

less, Coxe would not resign himself to accepting shoddy goods, despite the secretary of war's insistence on the most rigid economy.[18] Intent on protecting the public interest and also aware that the supply of imperfect goods would "bring censure on this Office," he repeatedly cautioned manufacturers that they must meet the specifications of their contracts. To this end, he made a number of changes in the supply system, including the negotiation of contracts with manufacturers themselves rather than through intermediary merchants or dealers, the selection of one manufacturer in an area as his principal source of supply, leaving it up to that party to make arrangements, if necessary, with neighboring manufacturers, and the employment of open bidding on supplies needed.[19]

Favorable economic conditions rendered the conduct of the purveyorship far less burdensome during the first half of Coxe's nine-year tenure in office than it would be during the crisis-ridden half-decade that preceded the outbreak of war in 1812. Until the last fifteen months of Jefferson's administration the purveyor was able to purchase advantageously in a well-stocked market. Thanks to the expansion of the country's carrying trade occasioned by the war that engulfed Europe, the economy was growing, even booming. Although the principal belligerents in the war, England and France, paid scant regard to the neutral rights of a militarily insignificant nation thousands of miles away, a precarious peace prevailed, and the Americans, ignoring for the most part the perilous chasm over which they teetered, prospered. Then in December 1807 Jefferson inaugurated his grand design of preserving peace with economic weapons. He guided a compliant Congress into the imposition of the famous embargo, a measure prohibiting the clearance of any American vessel bound to a foreign port. Although there soon was mounting evidence that this strategy was depressing the American economy more than impressing the nations of Europe, the embargo remained in effect until the end of Jefferson's presidency in March 1809, only to be replaced under Madison by a program of commercial nonintercourse that entailed a similarly severe curtailment of trade.

18. Coxe to William Irvine, Jan. 4, 1804, Coxe Papers. To the secretary of war's implied criticism that he was purchasing goods of too high a quality, Coxe remonstrated that his object was only to buy goods that were "reputable, comfortable and equal to the legislative purpose or intention of *a years Service.*" Coxe to Dearborn, Nov. 14, 1805, Purveyors Letterbooks, R.G. 92. Dearborn expected more than that: do not buy army caps annually, he wrote to Coxe on Jan. 7, 1809, going on to argue that they should last at least two years, Sec. of War Letterbook, R.G. 107.

19. Coxe to Gonter, Sept. 16, 1803, Purveyors Letterbooks, R.G. 92. Coxe's admonitions to manufacturers appear so frequently in Coxe's letterbooks as to preclude meaningful citations. See especially Purveyors Letterbooks, CCL, R.G. 92. For the changes Coxe made in the supply system, see Coxe to William Pennington, Sept. 1, 1803, to Solomon Myers, Dec. 15, 1803, Purveyors Letterbooks, R.G. 92.

Coxe's purveyorship was certainly influenced by the extent to which the "business of supply" was, in his words, "most seriously embarrassed and affected by foreign spoliations and restrictions, by the measures of non-importation, embargo and non-intercourse," and "by the consequent short-ness of foreign supplies and their unsorted condition."[20] Yet from Coxe's point of view the embargo did have one inestimably valuable side effect: the acceleration of the nation's industrialization. His enthusiasm would have been virtually boundless had it not been for the inferior articles often turned out by American manufacturers.

Early in Coxe's tenure as purveyor his choice of contractors, both the manufacturers and the middle men, appears to have followed the lead of the first purveyor, Tench Francis, of whom Hamilton had remarked that his "microscopic eye . . . can see nothing beyond Philadelphia." Coxe did somewhat expand his vision to encompass surrounding areas in both Penn-sylvania and adjacent states, and the contractors he selected were numerous and varied. A random sample demonstrates the diversity: stockings by the thousands were procured from Robert Whittle and Jacob Fink of Philadel-phia; shoes from New Jersey manufacturers (William Pennington of New-ark, Henry Bellington of Trenton, and "the penetentiary house of the state of New Jersey");[21] hats from John Lotz and Peter Auraudt of Reading; rifles from manufacturers in Lancaster and York; and drums from Henry Fraley of Germantown. Material for army clothing came from a much wider market —New York and Connecticut, for example—but uniforms were customarily manufactured in Philadelphia by master tailors according to the terms of contracts negotiated by Coxe. He also (though usually on orders from the secretary of war) made frequent purchases abroad, which included linens and other goods from Germany and manufactured articles, chiefly woolens, from Great Britain and Ireland.

The market in which Coxe shopped was by no means wide enough to satisfy either Dearborn or his successor, William Eustis, who believed that the Philadelphian was by far too attached to his hometown and the surrounding area. He may have been, but there was some truth in his exaggerated claim that "it is my practice to opperate in all the states" whenever "I may do better than . . . here."[22] Nevertheless, as Coxe's pur-veyor letterbooks reveal, he did tend to favor the manufacturers of Pennsyl-vania and to a lesser extent those of adjacent states. In view of his greater familiarity with that area and the comparatively advanced state of its manu-factures, he could scarcely have been expected to do otherwise.

20. Coxe, *Respectful Observations*, 2.
21. Coxe to Callender Irvine, Sept. 5, 1805, Purveyors Letterbooks, R.G. 92.
22. Coxe to John Milledge, Feb. 24, 1808, Coxe Papers.

Dearborn's and Eustis's charges of favoritism, moreover, must be qualified by the secretaries' own transparent loyalty to New England, whose manufacturers they insistently demanded that Coxe favor. Dearborn was particularly importunate. "If you have been impeded in the completion of clothing for the want of such cloths as those offered from Portland," Maine, Dearborn admonished in a typical letter, Coxe had only himself to blame. In another obvious reference to his native state, Dearborn went on to caution Coxe that "it should in future be recollected that there are mercantile towns in the United States besides Philadelphia," adding, in blatant contradiction of his characteristic emphasis on penny-pinching, that the purveyor should in the future allow neither "unreasonable economy nor any local feelings" to hamper the supply service. And so it went: Coxe should buy "duck and woolen goods" from manufacturers recommended by Dearborn, "suitable cloth" for military clothing was available from Portland merchants, stockings should be purchased from Cape Cod manufacturers.[23] Secretary of War Eustis also objected to Coxe's preference for Pennsylvania products, but, himself somewhat less provincial than either his predecessor or the purveyor, demanded that "the purchase and manufacture" of goods for the United States should not only benefit his native New England but also "be distributed among the several states." Coxe was annoyed by such repeated charges of favoritism both because he recognized the great advantage in buying from one manufacturer and because he believed himself to be a sincere advocate of manufactures in every part of the Union.[24]

There may have been a hiatus between Coxe's theory and practice, but he did emphatically support the spread of manufacturing. Not only was he intent on the promotion of domestic manufactures by eschewing the European for the American market whenever the price differential was not excessive (a wish the more easily fulfilled after 1807 because of the embargo and subsequent nonimportation measures), but Coxe was also always on the alert for evidences of the development of innovative techniques in manufacturing, especially laborsaving machinery. Public contracts were awarded to those who introduced such improvements when it was consistent with the War Department's insistence on economy and when the sanction of its secretary (far more readily granted by Eustis than by Dearborn) could be secured. Although interested in the gamut of American manufactures, Coxe's major concern, as always, was the cotton industry. He consistently sought to encourage that industry by urging on the war secretary the feasibility of substituting cotton or a mixture of cotton and wool (different samples of

23. Dearborn to Coxe, Nov. 5, 1808, Sec. of War Letterbook, R.G. 107. See also Dearborn to Coxe, Nov. 28, 1804, Feb. 26, May 27, 30, Oct. 22, Dec. 21, 1808, *ibid*.
24. Eustis to Coxe, Jan. 18, *ibid*. See also Eustis to Coxe, Jan. 15, Feb. 4, 1812, *ibid*. For Coxe's annoyance at these charges of favoritism, see Coxe to Milledge, Feb. 24, 1808, Coxe Papers.

which he frequently transmitted) for the army's traditional woolen cloth. He was convinced that cotton could be successfully used for the manufacture of stockings, blankets, tents, and knapsacks, as well as other things.[25] It was measurably due to his persistence and persuasiveness that on the eve of war in 1812 the country, as he boasted, was capable within "three months notice or less" of producing sufficient manufactures of cotton goods "for the whole present authorized army, navy, and marines." The savings, when the cost of these goods was compared to the corresponding prices of European articles (even if available), Coxe estimated at "about nine times the whole annual expenses of the purveyor's office."[26]

Although such claims must be weighed against his wish to magnify his own accomplishments, Coxe deserves recognition as one of the few Americans of his day who sought to resolve by means of a government-sponsored and systematic national program of industrial growth the paradox of a militarily weak, underdeveloped nation recklessly courting war with a strong and economically more mature adversary. Sharing with many of his countrymen the view that time would bring the requisite balanced economy, he, unlike most, was also aware that preparation for an imminent war could not await the inevitable progress of events. Convinced that the nation must take positive action to utilize its abundant resources and that the government, borrowing on foreign experience, must take the lead in this venture, Coxe pressed upon the administration policies he had long advocated. Why not establish in America boards or agencies equivalent to those that some European nations had established for compiling data on trade and manufactures and for considering proposals to encourage these industries, he asked Albert Gallatin in December 1809. Manufactures in particular "appear to require a constant, vigilant attention and gradual fostering," and America's "total destitution of public official attention to so great an object is without precedent in any civilized country." Why not, he asked, take advantage of the number of artisans arriving almost daily from Europe by establishing an agency to elicit from them information on European machines and manufacturing that could not otherwise be legally secured? Did not "these disjointed times in regard to external commerce, when all is despotism," require that these immigrants should be "rallied, guided and aided by the Government of the United States"? "If we are to be reluctantly forced into war," Coxe argued, the adoption of such policies would assure that the

25. Samuel Carswell to Coxe, Mar. 27, 1806, David Humphreys to Coxe, Feb. 18, 1809, Coxe Papers; Dearborn to Coxe, Jan. 6, June 24, Dec. 3, 1808, Eustis to Coxe, Feb. 13, 1810, Sec. of War Letterbook, R.G. 107. A major stumbling block to the purchase of domestic cotton manufactures, as Coxe said, was the cheaper price of imports from India. Coxe to James Burnham, Oct. 4, 1803, Purveyors Letterbooks, R.G. 92.
26. Coxe, *Respectful Observations*, 6.

country's economy might be effectively bent for the war's prosecution.[27]

Coxe was nevertheless aware that no such expansion in the area of government action was remotely possible; so he attempted to promote the public interest by insisting that government contracts be scrupulously and honestly executed. Although most students of the subject agree with Leonard White that contractors of that time were often guilty of carelessness and irregularities, Coxe's voluminous papers from his years as purveyor suggest that under his administration this was no more the situation than previously or since, and perhaps less so. Attempts were occasionally made to defraud the government, but the guilty parties were either subject to contract cancellation and nonpayment or, whenever the federal district attorney was convinced that a suit could be conveniently or successfully instituted, were prosecuted for fraud. The corruption that tarnished the reputations of so many contractors, moreover, occurred most frequently in the supply of army provisions, a business handled by regional contractors, with whom the War Department, rather than the purveyor, negotiated individual contracts for the supply of particular areas.[28]

The absence of collusion or large-scale corruption in the extensive operations of the purveyor's office was a result not only of Coxe's personal probity but also of the system of inspection prescribed for the goods he purchased. The chief inspectors during Coxe's purveyorship were William and Callender Irvine, who served successively as superintendents of military stores and who received at their headquarters at the Philadelphia arsenal the bulk of the goods purchased by Coxe. Inspection was for the most part conducted in such a way as to curb the acquisitiveness of contractors and to protect the purveyor against dishonest manufacturers whose operations he could not personally oversee but whose proper performance he was responsible for.

A substantial part of the federal budget was at Coxe's disposal, and on his careful and prudential purchases depended the state of the nation's military preparedness. The nature of the budget allocated to the department responsible for preparations for a war, as well as the importance of Coxe's agency, is revealed by a statement of his expenditures. In 1803 the funds expended amounted to $198,000 (or one-fourth of the War Department's budget); in 1804 they rose to $237,500, while constituting the same percentage of the department's budget; in 1805 they came to $271,000, about one-third of the department's expenses; in 1806 they amounted to $279,500,

27. Coxe to Gallatin, Dec. 21, 23, 1809, Coxe Papers.
28. Leonard D. White, *The Jeffersonians: A Study in Administrative History, 1801–1829* (New York, 1951), 215. See also Coxe to Peter Hunt, June 14, 1808, Purveyors Letterbooks, R.G. 92. For a discussion of the deficiencies of the system, see Jacobs, *Beginning of U.S. Army*, 349–350.

but the percentage dropped to one-fifth; and in 1807 they increased only slightly, though they constituted a somewhat higher proportion of the War Department's funds. Then in 1808, thanks to preparedness measures adopted by Congress, the sums expended by the purveyor's office quintupled.[29]

This whopping increase was the result of congressional approval on April 12, 1808, of an addition of eight regiments to the regular army, the first such increase during Jefferson's presidency. Detailed arrangements for raising and equipping the six thousand new troops were left to Dearborn, who, though proceeding with characteristic slowness, turned over the duty of purchasing the requisite supplies to the purveyor's office. By the early summer of 1808 the office was, according to Coxe, conducting an amount of business "treble the usual course."[30] For every bolt of cloth or pair of shoes, every flint, rifle, or barrel of powder he had previously purchased, he must now buy several. The difficulty of obtaining supplies of suitable quantity, quality, and workmanship, the small size of the staff at his disposal, plus the familiar problems of inspection, delays in transportation, and tardy congressional appropriations, made what would normally have been a time-consuming task into one of virtually insuperable difficulty.

For an officer accountable and responsible for the procurement of supplies vital to a new nation threatened by the bellicosity of two of the world's mighty powers, Coxe had an office staff and quarters as inadequate as his own recompense was paltry. In 1806, for example, the total granted for all the expenses of his office was $4,600. This appropriation covered supplies, contingent expenses, and office rent, as well as his salary and pay for two clerks and for a messenger who doubled as janitor (a staff so small that Coxe was obliged to call on his sons for occasional assistance). Even at a time when federal civil servants were expected to work under conditions that comported with standards of Republican simplicity, such a miniscule staff and cramped quarters for such a responsible office seemed unacceptable. The only desk other than his own in the purveyor's quarters at Eleven Pine Street, Coxe complained in 1807, "is broken and incapable of repair"; nor was there any place for keeping "confidential and valuable papers and things." Even such a shabby and bare office seemed an extravagance to

29. This information was compiled from *American State Papers, Military Affairs; Annals of Cong.*, I; Purveyors Letterbooks, R.G. 92; and Sec. of War Letterbook, R.G. 107.

30. Coxe to unknown recipient, May 25, 1808, Purveyors Letterbooks, R.G. 92. Provision was made for five additional regiments of artillery, one regiment of riflemen, one regiment of light artillery, and one regiment of light dragoons to serve for five years. "An act to raise for a limited time an additional military force," Apr. 12, 1808, *U.S. Statutes at Large*, II, 481–483. For support of the additional military force authorized on Apr. 12, Congress passed another act on Apr. 25, 1808, "An act making appropriations for the support of an additional military force," *U.S. Statutes at Large*, II, 497–498.

budget-conscious officials like the auditor of the War Department, who ordered the purveyor to cut his excessive expenses. Coxe curtly retorted that "it is impossible to do without two writing rooms and a room for accumulating books, papers and other articles connected with my public business."[31]

Unsatisfactory though his working conditions may have been, they were far more tolerable than his annual pay of $2,000, which, whether compared to that of other government offices or of similar positions in private business, was lamentably low. As Coxe correctly observed, the purveyor was asked to exercise financial and other responsibilities "in a degree unknown in the similar office of every other [nation] on Earth" for a salary that "a clerk to Hopes, Cromelins or Baring's House in Amsterdam or London" would find unequal even "to his accustomed allowance." It was the more unacceptable, he frequently lamented, because of the statutorily imposed "abstinence from other Means of profit."[32] But neither his superiors in Washington nor a penny-conscious Congress heeded his repeated petitions for increased compensation. The only solution as he saw it was to provide for himself what others refused to grant, and this he determined to do by applying "large portions of my nights and times of relaxation, which I used to apply in promoting the course of public liberty and the general prosperity of the Country," to private business. Loosely defining the business activities from which he was barred, he proposed to engage in "*an agency for the Sale of unimproved lands* and other real estate." The legality of this enterprise was uncertain, but he nevertheless undertook it.[33]

Low pay was not Coxe's only complaint about the purveyorship, for the burdens of the job were increased by the uncooperativeness and remissness of the war secretary. It was Dearborn's responsibility "to devise and invent the best patterns, models and standards; to procure inspectors of temper, fidelity and judgment," and to specify articles needed for the public service. The first was not done consistently, the second not at all, and the third seldom. Time and again Coxe was forced to request instructions on such urgent matters as the quantity and type of goods to be procured for the army or the Indian service.[34] The burden of prying instructions out of an

---

31. Coxe to Richard Harrison, Dec. 19–21, 1807, to William Simmons, Oct. 19, 1805, Purveyors Letterbooks, R.G. 92. For Coxe's inadequate staff, see Coxe to Gallatin, Oct. 18, 1806, *ibid*.

32. Coxe to Harrison, Dec. 19–21, 1807, *ibid*.; Coxe to Clay, Mar. 1806, Coxe Papers; Coxe to Gallatin, Oct. 29, 1803, Purveyors Letterbooks, R.G. 92.

33. Coxe to Levi Lincoln, Dec. 8, 1803, Purveyors Letterbooks, R.G. 92. In a printed circular dated Jan. 2, 1804, Coxe announced that he had established an office in Philadelphia for the sale of unimproved lands and lots in all parts of the United States. Coxe Papers.

34. Coxe, *Respectful Observations*, 4. For one of many possible illustrations of Coxe's requests for instructions, see Coxe to Dearborn, Feb. 8, 1806, in which Coxe posed these among other questions: Would the secretary please ask "one of the Gentlemen of the N. York Indian

inefficient boss would have been unnecessary had Dearborn been willing to delegate greater authority. As it was, he vacillated between stern insistence that no purchases, however small, be made without his prior approval and curt demands that the purveyor cease bothering him with trivia and exercise discretion both in negotiating contracts and in making other than large payments.[35] Bewildered by such erratic directions, Coxe eventually adopted the prudent course of acting only on the basis of specific instructions.

But Coxe's problems were not confined to Dearborn's remissness and capricious exercise of enjoined duties. The purveyor's office was also handicapped by the perverse obstructionism of officials charged with storing and inspecting army supplies. As chief offender Coxe would have nominated Callender Irvine, who succeeded his father as superintendent of military stores in the fall of 1804. Over the next eight years merely the official records of the incessant squabbles between Callender Irvine and Coxe would fill an oversized volume, and this would not include their protracted battle that followed Coxe's departure from office in May 1812. Irvine fought by means fair and foul (but mostly foul) to destroy his bureaucratic enemy by impugning his official integrity. It is unnecessary to relate here the tedious details of their long dispute, for though it may have had a marginal effect on public policy, the retelling would engage the modern reader only somewhat more than would a transcript of a bygone hassle between rival and disagreeable shopkeepers.[36] The decade-long charges and countercharges

Agency . . . to furnish a revised List of the Supplies for the six nations"? Would he send "instructions as to the Indian Annuities—that is to say whether purchases as last year are to be made in any instances, whether there are to be any alterations and what as to the old stipends"? Would it be possible for Coxe to be informed about appropriations for the ordnance department and for army clothing? Purveyors Letterbooks, R.G. 92. See also Coxe to Dearborn, Oct. 17, Nov. 6, 1806, Jan. 16, 1807; Coxe to Callender Irvine, Nov. 10, 1806, *ibid.*

35. To confine citations about Dearborn's changing instructions to one year, see, for example, Dearborn to Coxe, Feb. 22, Apr. 16, May 14, 26, Dec. 31, 1808, Sec. of War Letterbook, R.G. 107.

36. Callender Irvine was appointed superintendent on Oct. 24, three months after the death of William Irvine on July 29 (*Aurora*, July 31, 1804), and was allowed the same compensation and commissions as his predecessor. Dearborn to Callender Irvine, Nov. 9, 1804, Sec. of War Letterbook, R.G. 107. For almost a decade Coxe and Irvine sparred over such issues as whether it was admissible for Irvine to refuse goods purchased by Coxe according to patterns prescribed and directions issued by the secretary of war, the fairness and propriety of the complaints each made to the secretary about the other, the necessity of their complying with any instructions or requisitions issued by the other except for those explicitly authorized by Dearborn, and the charge of each that the business procedures and bookkeeping methods of the other were careless. In sum, to Coxe, Irvine was officious, incompetent, and guilty of negligence that bordered on the criminal; to Irvine, Coxe was arrogant, meddlesome, and unfit to fill more than a clerkship. Among the scores of possible examples are Coxe to Callender Irvine, Sept. 17, 1805, Jan. 17, June 2, Oct. 8, Nov. 1, 1806, Coxe to Dearborn, Oct. 4, 18, 1806, Jan. 16, 1807, Purveyors Letterbooks, R.G. 92.

hurled at each other by these raucous rivals is, moreover, historically less significant than the secretary of war's refusal either to serve as referee or to dismiss one of the contestants.[37] He elected rather to tolerate a feud that had the visible effect of an army more poorly clad than it need have been.

More consequential than Coxe's entanglement with Irvine over the inspection of clothing was the problem of arms—their procurement, manufacture, and inspection. The small supply of imperfectly made and carelessly inspected muskets and pistols was not only an impediment to the effectiveness of the army when war finally came in 1812 but also a national disgrace. Historians have often commented critically on this situation, but none has adequately dealt with Coxe's agency in arms procurement. To contemporaries the issue became something of a cause célèbre when one of the nation's most influential newspapers repeatedly charged that Coxe was guilty of supplying weapons more likely to kill the Americans who held them than the enemy. The accusation was false, but that it should have been aired at all suggests the centrality of Coxe's role.

But even with all the frustrations that Coxe experienced as purveyor, the job was not especially taxing until after the passage in 1807 and 1808 of legislation designed to shore up the country's defenses. Because of the inability of federal armories at Springfield, Massachusetts, and Harpers Ferry, Virginia, to manufacture arms, the purveyor was given responsibility for their purchase from private suppliers, a task that at times seemed to Coxe rather like an order to grow orchids in a Philadelphia garden.[38] A half-decade of energetic efforts to carry out an assignment that was always hampered by the shoddy products turned out by often-shady manufacturers, by incompetent inspectors, and by uncooperative superiors now resulted merely

37. See, for example, Dearborn to Callender Irvine, Feb. 10, Apr. 19, May 24, 1806, June 4, 1808, Dearborn to Coxe, Apr. 9, 1805, May 24, Oct. 17, 1806, Sec. of War Letterbook, R.G. 107.

38. See "An Act authorizing the President of the United States to accept the service of a number of volunteer companies not exceeding thirty thousand men," Feb. 24, 1807, U.S. Statutes at Large, II, 419–420. An important feature of this preparedness program was the procurement of additional arms. This increase in arms was attributable to the belief of the president and Congress that the foundation of national defense should be a well-equipped militia (a well-trained one presumably was of less consequence) ready to respond instantly to the president's call. Although the most diligent investigator could have found little evidence that the act of 1803 appropriating $1,500,000 to arm and equip 80,000 militiamen had resulted in an adequately armed, ever-ready, citizen army, Congress tried again in Feb. 1807 by an act authorizing the president to accept a volunteer corps not to exceed 30,000 men. These soldiers were to be armed and equipped at the expense of the United States. To assure an adequate supply of rifles and powder for these, as well as regular troops, a statute was enacted on Mar. 11, 1808, appropriating $300,000 for the procurement of additional arms. This was followed a month later by a measure authorizing an annual sum of $200,000 for "providing arms and military equipment for the whole body of the militia of the United States, either by purchase or manufacture." "An Act making provision for arming and equipping the whole body of the Militia of the United States," Apr. 23, 1808, U.S.

in frustration. Coxe summed up the situation on the eve of the War of 1812: in the absence of supplies from abroad, he had "necessarily recurred to" domestic "manufactures of arms, little used but in the revolutionary war, or at one short intermediate period." "Workmen, apprentices, standards, patterns, manufactories, and especially inspections, all things in short were to be created anew." Although by 1812 a beginning had been made, "there was of course much imperfection at first, much room and need of improvement."[39] That the work proceeded so slowly—though Coxe did not say so —was owing not to the purveyor but to penny-pinching national leaders and congressmen. These money-saving efforts produced the paradox of a country that without adequate arms boldly declared war on the world's mightiest power. Except for fortuity, the result might well have been military defeat.

Statutes at Large, II, 490–491. For Coxe's views on this subject, see "Opinion on Arming the Militia for Defense," enclosed in Coxe to Jefferson, Jan. 24, 1807, Jefferson Papers, Lib. of Cong. Coxe was instructed to purchase 2,000 rifles, 1,000 pair of pistols, and 1,000 swords. Dearborn's arrangements can be followed in his letters to Coxe of Oct. 22, Nov. 3, 9, 18, 1807, Sec. of War Letterbook, R.G. 107. For Coxe's account of his difficulties in carrying out the order, see *Demo. Press*, Jan. 19, 1811.

39. Coxe, *Respectful Observations*, 3–4. Despite such impediments, Coxe could boast to Jefferson in 1807 that "the Cost of rifles, when I came into office was $13. I have gradually reduced them to $9.50 and 10 for which they cannot be imported." Coxe to Jefferson, Apr. 6, 1807, Jefferson Papers.

22

Bid for Party Supremacy

The twin burdens of the purveyorship and snarled business affairs might have prompted a man less incurably ambitious than Coxe to forgo active participation in politics, especially as it should have been clear that neither Jefferson, nor Gallatin, the president's closest adviser on patronage distribution, nor Madison, the presumed heir apparent, intended to grant him an important government post. That this was by no means clear to Coxe largely explains his reemergence in 1804 as a contestant for Republican leadership in Pennsylvania. If successful, he told himself, the powerful triumvirate in Washington would be obliged to award him the type of prize he coveted.

Following the election of 1800 Coxe had not played a conspicuously prominent role in state politics. There appeared no compelling reason to do so. Had not the monarchical Federalists been crushed, his candidate placed in the governor's chair, and his own influence in party councils been firmly established? His affirmative answer to the latter question was mistaken, however. Although he was indeed both a confidant of McKean, clearly the single most influential political figure in the state, and a close political associate of William Duane, still the most important Republican editor in Pennsylvania, his own position was not only subject to their whim but was also imperiled by the aspirations of rival party leaders.

The demoralization of the Federalists and their consequent virtual disappearance as a viable opposition party undermined Republican unity, an effect characteristic of one-party rule. As Albert Gallatin, an astute observer of Pennsylvania politics, remarked, "Whilst the Republicans opposed the Federalists the necessity of union induced a general sacrifice of private views and personal objects; . . . complete success has awakened all those passions which only slumbered." With no Federalist villains to overcome, the Republican protagonists of the successful campaigns of 1799 and 1800 began to joust for party supremacy. Despite the occasional fusion of rival politicians to oppose or support the bid of a particular candidate, this intramural contest assumed no meaningful pattern until 1804. Instead, the confused political scene, as William N. Chambers has said in a different context, was one of "faction politics of hybrid combinations and perishable alliances," revolving around those leaders who for almost a decade had directed the party's affairs but who now had "daggers drawn, . . . each of them in one way or another" considering "his neighbor a rival."[1]

The relationships among Pennsylvania Republicans in 1802 were described in tabular form by William Duane:

1. Mr. Dallas—Offended with 2, unreservedly opposed to 4, cold to 3 and 5.
2. Dr. [George] Logan—violently hostile to 1; unreservedly opposed to 3 and 5; good understanding with 4.
3. Dr. [Michael] Leib—Hostile to 2; familiar with 1 and 4; common cause with 5.
4. Mr. Coxe—Estranged but willing to be friends with 1; friends with 2; familiar and friendly with 3 and 5.
5. Mr. [Peter] Muhlenberg—Friendly with all—but displeased with 2; and rather distant than familiar with 4.

According to Duane, "these five may be said to hold the principal weight" in Pennsylvania,[2] an observation that would have been accurate if Duane included himself (commenting also that his two closest associates were Coxe and Leib), Governor McKean (who seems to have fully trusted only Dallas), and Albert Gallatin. A number of other prominent politicians were contenders for the shaky crowns of these political heavyweights: Joseph Hiester, whose chief political asset was popularity among German voters; regional leaders like the Maclay brothers, William and Samuel; and William Findley and John Smilie, political potentates of the western counties.

The rivalries among this long list of aspirants for political supremacy would have been no more divisive than such intraparty contests usually are had it not been for the disruptive impact of three men—McKean, Duane, and Michael Leib. McKean was unswervingly intent on rewarding only his unquestionably loyal supporters and was self-righteously determined to tolerate no deviation from his own political principles; Duane was supremely confident that he alone was the true apostle of the democratic faith and was ar-

1. Albert Gallatin to Jean Badollet, Oct. 25, 1805, quoted in Henry Adams, *The Life of Albert Gallatin* (Philadelphia, 1880), 330–331; William Nisbet Chambers, *Political Parties in a New Nation: The American Experience, 1776–1809* (New York, 1963), 3.

2. William Duane to Thomas Jefferson, Oct. 18, 1802, quoted in Noble E. Cunningham, Jr., *The Jeffersonian Republicans in Power: Party Operations, 1801–1809* (Chapel Hill, N.C., 1963), 214–215.

rogantly certain that opposition to him must be owing to base corruption or a diseased mind; and Leib, Duane's loyal ally, was so "ambitious, avaricious, and envious" that, as Gallatin remarked, he was willing to blow up the flame of party discord in order "to make *his* cause a general one."[3] The political conflagration caused by the clash of these human combustibles did not occur until 1805, but in the meantime personal discord smoldered inside the apparently strong and united house of Pennsylvania Republicanism.

The election of 1801 illustrated the hidden dangers of overwhelming victory. One of Coxe's fellow partisans reported "that the reign of terror is no more" and that the Federalists had become "as mute as you please."[4] Having won a smashing victory in all but five of the state's thirty-six counties, the Republicans were now free to advance virtually without opposition the "democracy" for which they had fought. But what shape should progress take in a state that was already the most democratic in the world's most democratic nation? Perhaps the problem was, in Henry Adams's trenchant phrase, that "their democracy was so deep an instinct that they knew not what to do with political power when they gained it; as though political power were aristocratic in its nature, and democratic power a contradiction in terms."[5] In any event, issues were subordinated to an incessant contest for the spoils of office.

This question of how to distribute political plums appears to have underpinned the one seemingly substantive issue that divided Pennsylvania Republicans and agitated the legislature for the next several years—the call for judicial reform. Certainly it could be argued that the demand was based on principle, for a fundamental tenet of Pennsylvania democracy was that no institutions or public servants should be exempt from the direct control of the people. And certainly the judicial system, which was manned by traditionalists, had proved less amenable to change than any other branch of government and thus stood in need of reform. Even McKean, on this issue a conservative, agreed, though the changes he proposed were minor compared to those advocated by a majority of his fellow Republicans. Nevertheless, it was not merely inadvertent that the reforms demanded by the latter were for the most part calculated to remove judges or at least to whittle down their power, while also establishing additional judicial offices for Republicans. The reason for these reforms was expressed in one Republican "address" (tantamount to a party platform): the whole judicial machinery of the state was controlled by Federalists—"every minister of justice . . . the

3. Gallatin to Badollet, Oct. 25, 1805, quoted in Adams, *Life of Gallatin*, 331.
4. Solomon Myers to Coxe, Nov. 22, 1801, Coxe Papers.
5. Adams, *History of the U.S.*, I, 116.

officer who prosecuted, the judge who presided, the marshal who summoned the jury."[6]

The issue came to the fore in the legislative session that convened in December 1801, when the assembly adopted a number of acts calculated to pave the way for the removal of Federalist officials (especially judges) and to expand the opportunities for ravenous Republican jobseekers. The most important of these measures were vetoed by McKean, whose unwillingness to bend a millimeter to satisfy the wishes of the most prominent members of his own party clearly portended a serious constitutional and party impasse should the Republican majority prove similarly intractable.[7]

"The refusal of the Governor to sign" the "Incompatible Act," one of Coxe's political correspondents observed in February 1802, "has excited much feeling among the members of the legislature and others, and a considerable number of republicans seem disposed to take up another character at the next Election." Coxe was probably among that number. Goaded two years later by William Duane's charge that he was "extremely anxious to have governor McKean superseded" and that he had "exerted himself . . . to have *another person* taken up," Coxe admitted that he "did in writing and conversation candidly inform Mr. McKean . . . of certain things which . . . would endanger the governor's re-election, if he should not take measures to remedy or prevent them."[8] Although he prudently did not specify those things, Coxe may well have alluded to the renomination of Congressman Michael Leib, by this time Coxe's self-designated, though publicly unavowed, political enemy number one.[9]

6. *Aurora*, Sept. 27, 1802.

7. McKean had vetoed the "Hundred Dollar Act," which would have extended the jurisdiction of justices of the peace to cases not exceeding that sum, and he also vetoed the "Incompatibility Act," which was designed to spread public offices more equally by prohibiting the simultaneous occupancy of a federal and a state office. The latter bill, however, was promptly reenacted over McKean's veto. See *Pa. Archives*, 4th Ser., IV, 484–486, 496–500.

8. Ezekiel Forman to Coxe, Feb. 12, 1802, Coxe Papers; *Aurora*, Aug. 22, 1804; *Freeman's Jour.*, Aug. 27, 1804. The alternative candidate to whom Duane obviously referred was Peter Muhlenberg. Coxe's secret motive, the *Aurora* charged, "was to obtain the collectorship." *Aurora*, Aug. 29, 1804.

9. The inference plausibly can be drawn from replies that Dr. George Logan wrote to Coxe's unfound letters. See Logan to Coxe, Apr. 28, Dec. 27, 1802, Coxe Papers. Had it not been for the handicap of his tory record, Coxe himself might have challenged Leib's congressional seat. Writing at a time when his enmity against Coxe was at white heat, Duane explained in a public letter to Coxe that "you were at one time taken up in general ward committee as candidate for a seat in the congress of the U. States, in consequence of your incessant complaints of the enmity of Mr. Gallatin, and of your being neglected by government—you made so many appeals to the passions and feelings of many, of whom I was one, that for your own and family's benefit it was deemed correct to take you up as a candidate for congress, '*in order to make an impression at Washington.*' You had a majority of votes of the delegates, and on this vote you declined, hoping the nomination would have the desired effect." *Aurora*, Aug. 31, 1804. Coxe himself placed his reasons

In 1802 Leib became the center of a controversy that widened the division in the Republican party highlighted by the fight over judicial reforms. Previously, Leib's career had been unexceptionable. A Philadelphian by birth, he studied medicine under Benjamin Rush and served as a surgeon in the state militia for a brief time during the Revolution, following which he became one of the city's more prominent medical men. Like so many others of his profession, he preferred the practice of politics, and by the mid-1790s he was recognized as an influential leader of the recently organized Republican party. After serving in the state assembly during 1797 and 1798, he was elected to Congress. In the Pennsylvania gubernatorial contest of 1799 and the presidential election of the following year, he, along with Coxe, Duane, and Dallas, was a member of the inner circle that engineered the Republican victories. Reelected in 1800, Leib had a congressional record that was barren except for efforts to prove that he was a stauncher antimilitarist than the president himself. To demonstrate this, he demanded such measures as the virtual abolition of the navy and marine corps. Yet it was not his program but his personality that rendered him unpopular with congressional colleagues and suspect to a good number of Pennsylvania Republicans. Contemporary critics described him as a man of "violence and avarice," "cruelty and vindictiveness," one who did not scruple to resort to "dirty intrigues."[10]

Opposition to Leib surfaced in September 1802, two months after he had been duly renominated by conferees from his congressional district, which consisted of the city of Philadelphia and Delaware County. On September 15 a conclave of his Republican opponents met at the Rising Sun, a popular tavern at the fork of the Germantown and York roads. Here they drew up a public address deploring the rift in the party "arising from the improper character nominated to represent this county in the Congress of the U S" and calling for a general party meeting on September 21 to take remedial action. William Duane rushed to Leib's defense, savagely attacking his opponents and urging all stout-hearted Republicans to attend the meeting and block any changes in the congressional ticket. Duane's success tellingly demonstrated the undiminished influence of the *Aurora*: at the

---

for declining the nomination on the grounds that the post would "require an abstraction from private concerns and a devotion to public duties, in a degree, which my situation forbids." Coxe to Peter Muhlenberg, July 22, 1802, Coxe Papers. See also Coxe to Jefferson, Oct. 2, 1807, *ibid*. More probably, Coxe well realized, as Duane wrote, "that it was an absurdity" for him to run for public office, since "upon the single point of his desertion to the British, it was impossible that he ever could obtain the voice of this state." *Aurora*, Aug. 30, 1804.

10. Sanford W. Higginbotham, *The Keystone in the Democratic Arch: Pennsylvania Politics, 1800–1816* (Harrisburg, Pa., 1952), 18; "Memoirs of a Senator from Pennsylvania, Jonathan Roberts, 1771–1854," *PMHB*, LXII (1938), 213.

Rising Sun meeting no strong-arm tactics were necessary, for the already intimidated dissidents promptly knuckled under and passed a resolution affirming their support of the regular ticket.[11] Coxe, who had turned down the repeated and urgent requests of the Rising Sun men to join them, considered the decision a prudent one and, so he later averred, unhesitatingly gave Leib his own vote and *"persuaded others to do the same."*[12]

Since the Federalists were able to offer no more than token resistance, the Republican nomination guaranteed success at the polls. Leib thus shared in the landslide that swept McKean into the governorship for a second term. Pennsylvania was fast becoming a one-party state: in the short span of three years the Republican majority had leapt from less than 5,000 to well over 30,000 votes. Such impressive statistics were incontrovertible evidence, Coxe gloated in an article published shortly after the election, that the wise policies pursued by Jefferson had converted all Federalists except an unredeemable remnant of monarchists. Even these might be routed, Coxe wrote with himself manifestly in mind, once the president realized that Pennsylvania "with the first white population in the union . . . must not be gradually worked out of her share of the principal executive, judicial and diplomatic offices."[13] But the prospects for taking advantage of this new-found power were not bright, owing appreciably to the determination of Duane and Leib to control a party that included a number of unsubduable rivals: Coxe, Logan, Dallas, and, most indomitable of all, Thomas McKean.

Although in some respects the ties binding Coxe to Duane were increasingly restrictive, he continued for a time to side with the editor. On the patronage issue, Coxe, himself a cruelly disappointed but ever-hopeful office seeker, agreed with Duane that the governor had not properly distributed offices.[14] And despite his swelling dislike of Leib, Coxe was unwilling

11. *Aurora*, Sept. 17, 22, 23, 24, 1802.

12. *Freeman's Jour.*, June 18, 1804. Although he did not publicly oppose Leib, Coxe covertly expressed his disapproval of him by drafting for "the general assembly of the Committees of Superintendence" of Philadelphia a eulogistic address that made William Jones appear to have a monopoly on political virtue among Pennsylvania congressmen. N.d., Coxe Papers.

13. *Aurora*, Nov. 1, 1802, reprinted from the *Nat. Intelligencer*. For Coxe's authorship, see George Worrall to Coxe, Nov. 25, 1802, Coxe Papers.

14. Coxe agreed with Duane and Leib, who insisted that all Federalist officials, particularly in the Philadelphia customs service, be dismissed to make way for loyal Republicans. So it was that Coxe readily joined the *Aurora* editor in engineering a public protest to reports that a number of Pennsylvania congressmen, led by William Jones, had in February 1803 drawn up a letter reassuring Jefferson that Pennsylvania Republicans (except *"a Small minority and they too of interested persons"*) endorsed his patronage policy. In order to demonstrate that not all of the state's Republicans felt this way, Duane and his allies arranged for the convening of ward meetings at which committeemen were selected to prepare a memorial in rebuttal, but the hasty decision of Jones and his colleagues not to send their report to the president rendered any formal protest unnecessary. The quotation is from Coxe's paraphrase of Jones's letter. See Coxe to Worrall, Apr. 14, 1803, Coxe Papers.

to court Duane's wrath by publicly joining the Rising Sun group that in the summer and fall of 1803 once again sought to destroy the doctor's (and Duane's) purported dictatorial control of the Republican party.[15]

So it was that Coxe continued to write for the *Aurora*, joining Duane in slashing attacks on "Third Party men," whom he sought to equate with Aaron Burr's alleged schismatic efforts to undermine Republican unity. It was Coxe (ironically enough in view of his assumption of leadership of the Pennsylvania Quids only a year later) who during the campaign of 1803 coined the phrase "Tertium Quid," which would soon come into general usage in both national and state politics. Referring to a putative coalition of Rising Sun men and Federalists who preached moderation in partisan affairs, Coxe wrote that "moderation in the sense used by certain men is . . . *a half-way house* between virtue and vice, between truth and falsehood, where souls devoid of energy, and minds twisted with corruption may repose. . . . What an hermaphrodite thing, partaking of two characters, and yet having neither! A tertium quid . . . [is] of the *mule kind*, incapable of propagating itself!"[16] Such atypically extravagant and crude language may have disguised Coxe's covert sympathy with Leib's opponents, but it served also to maintain his increasingly fragile political alliance with Duane. The latter, having once again turned back a challenge to his and Leib's political supremacy, was in no mood to brook disagreement or opposition even from the influential Treasury secretary or the governor of Pennsylvania, much less from the purveyor of public supplies.

Despite the dangers involved, Coxe had determined by the spring of 1804 to contest Duane and Leib's control of the Philadelphia democracy. His decision was somewhat less consequential than his choice of the British side during the Revolution, his switch from the Federalist to the Republican party in the mid-1790s, or his unseemly tilt with Jefferson in 1801 and 1802, but it was a decisive turning point in his career. Coxe could not himself have explained such a critical decision except by suggesting that he considered Michael Leib unfit to sit in Congress, much less to control Pennsylvania politics. The heat engendered by ambition is, after all, sometimes directed as hot indignation toward another political climber. Nevertheless, Coxe's knowledge of Duane should have permitted an accurate forecast of the personal consequences of this political decision.

It all started innocently enough. On the morning of May 14, 1804,

---

15. Unless Coxe was playing one side against the other, the clear inference from letters written to him by Logan is that he was willing to ally himself covertly with Logan and other opponents of Leib's. See, for example, Logan to Coxe, Feb. 14, 1803, *ibid.*

16. *Aurora*, June 22, 1803. For identification of Coxe as the author, see *ibid.*, Aug. 17, 1804. That Coxe originated the term was attested by Duane, who wrote that "the *tertium quid* ought

two political acquaintances called on Coxe and invited him to attend a meeting scheduled for the Harp and Eagle Tavern on the same day. Since they candidly admitted that the purpose of the gathering was to discuss "the expediency of re-electing Dr. Leib," Coxe's acceptance indicated his willingness now to join the Rising Sun Republicans. Perhaps in recognition of his conversion, Coxe was called upon to serve as chairman of the meeting, which predictably agreed that the doctor was not an eligible candidate. It was resolved to support the election of delegates (to both ward and county nominating committees) who could be counted on to oppose Leib.[17] No effort was made to keep the meeting a secret, and as its participants doubtless anticipated, William Duane's reaction was swift and shrill.

Duane's response was intensified by his growing suspicion that Coxe had been largely responsible for the launching three months earlier of the *Philadelphia Evening Post* under the editorship of William McCorkel. The journal was obviously designed to defend the McKean administration and to provide both a mouthpiece for the Rising Sun faction and a means for mounting a counterattack against Leib and Duane. Duane's anger at such a challenge turned into fury when he thought he detected in the columns of the *Evening Post* the unmistakable style of the *Aurora*'s former star columnist, Tench Coxe. Any doubts he may have had were removed by news of Coxe's participation in the Harp and Eagle conference and the subsequent defense of the meeting in the *Evening Post*. "A writer who has been laboring for years, by day and night to make the Editor of the Aurora a dupe, and the slave to his private enmities and ambition without effect," Duane wrote on June 12, "has at length betrayed his real character." His "wretched behavior" as author "of the present political agitations in this city" was, moreover, such "as to forbid all intercourse or confidence in him or his professions." That such ostracism did not preclude an additional verbal onslaught was abundantly revealed in subsequent issues of the *Aurora*: "Janus" (one of Duane's pet names for Coxe) had placed himself at the head of the "Tertium Quids," and "his character exhibits the horrid features of this conspiracy in that light in which we predicted the third party views would at length unfold themselves." He was "a traitor to his country, who entertains an unquenchable enmity against every republican character who has stood in his way or contributed to *what he conceives to be his fall*."[18]

---

not to be uninformed that this title was that given them by the present head, Mr. Tench Coxe."
Ibid.

17. The description of the meeting is based on Coxe's account, printed in the *Freeman's Jour.*, June 19, 1804.

18. *Aurora*, June 12, 15, 1804. The *Aurora* began systematically to employ the term "Tertium Quids" on May 19, 1804, and continued to do so for the next five months.

Although surely aware that this was only the beginning, Coxe was neither intimidated nor silenced (perhaps recalling that though he had been subject to similar abuse in 1800 his cause had triumphed). "As a citizen and a deputy of a ward, he has a *right* to his opinions and will defend them," Coxe replied on June 15 in the *Freeman's Journal and Philadelphia Daily Advertiser* (the new name assumed by the *Evening Post* three days earlier). Among these defensible opinions was the unalterable conviction that "there would be great danger in running Dr. Leib for Congress," a danger that, though undefined, was to Coxe grave enough to force him into battle with the most formidable journalist of his day.[19] Duane, Coxe charged in the *Freeman's Journal* on June 18, was "arrogant, rancorous, and overbearing"; the "vulgarity of his language, and the virulence of his manner" were sufficient demonstration that he was "fitter for a bedlam than to edit a newspaper." Incapable of truth or fidelity, Duane was guilty of unhesitatingly "publishing untruths without number" and of "using the vilest epithets to those who were once his patrons and friends."[20] But to repay Duane in his own journalistic coin was, as Coxe realized, of subordinate importance. Vital to his own success was the capture of the party machinery that Duane and Leib so effectively controlled.

Because of the number of levers by which the party machinery might be operated, it can be described only at the cost of bewilderingly tedious detail. Stripped to its essentials, the system as it operated in 1804 was simple in design. Candidates for the three congressional seats accorded Pennsylvania's first district were cooperatively chosen by party members in each of its three major divisions: the city of Philadelphia recommended one man, chosen by a general ward committee that consisted of delegates from each of the city's wards; the counties of Philadelphia and Delaware each selected one candidate at general meetings that were made up of deputies from the districts into which each county was divided; and conferees from the three units then met, ironed out differences, and drew up the party ticket. Since the system was extralegal and thus based on consent, it operated smoothly only as long as there was party consensus. When, as in 1804, there was disagreement, the system could be abused by strong-arm tactics, or it could be circumvented by the holding of general meetings of all interested voters, who might there propose their own slate of rival candidates. In 1804 both these strategies were employed. In the county of Philadelphia an assembly of district delegates, controlled by Coxe and his allies, substituted William Penrose for Leib. Friends of the latter called for a general meeting at which the doctor was nominated. A similar battle with similar results went on in

19. *Freeman's Jour.*, June 15, 1804.
20. *Ibid.*, June 18, 1804.

the city, while Delaware County Republicans, surveying the partisan carnage, deferred any final decision until the last minute.[21] The upshot of all this was that the voters of the district were presented with two tickets, both including the names of Joseph Clay and Jacob Richards, the Republicans' opponents, but one containing the name of Michael Leib and the other that of William Penrose. The first was appropriately dubbed the Leib slate, and the second was interchangeably called the Quid or "Coxeite" ticket.

"*Mr. Coxe* may be emphatically called the *head* of the third party in this state," William Duane asserted, for once without exaggeration. Coxe's followers, an anonymous scribbler wrote with considerable exaggeration, "are only the *limbs* and the *tail*, the *muscles* and the *fibres*, innocent and complying as *lambs*."[22] Although the position of leadership may initially have been thrust upon him by Duane, Coxe did firmly grab the reins, and from early July until October he directed what he called the anti-Leib campaign and the *Aurora* termed the Quid campaign. William Penrose, a former Federalist with no discernible qualification for political office, displayed on occasion "courtly manners," but otherwise he left the campaign to Coxe; this situation allowed the *Aurora* to plausibly suggest that "if a capacity in a citizen to *sign his name* to a production of Mr. Coxe can entitle a man to legislative trust and public confidence, no one can have a higher claim than Mr. Penrose."[23] Certainly Coxe wrote enough for himself, Penrose, and their followers as well. As all politically active Philadelphians (and a good many Republicans elsewhere) knew, Coxe was in fact the editor of the *Freeman's Journal*, which devoted every inch of space left over from the necessary advertisements to diatribes against Leib and defenses of himself.

What prompted such an energetic campaign against such great odds? Although Coxe's own party prestige was at stake and his own political ambition patent, he and his followers avowed time and again that their overriding concern was the defeat of a man whose sole contribution to the Republican party had been to lower its moral tone. This man, they reiterated, was not only dangerously ambitious but demonstrably corrupt. The basis of the latter charge was Leib's alleged fraud in depriving the heirs of one Jonathan Penrose of their lawful inheritance, an accusation that had led to prolonged litigation and that had hounded the doctor for almost a decade. Although the case was settled out of court in 1801, Leib's critics remained certain of his guilt. In 1804 they published purported proof of his culpability in column after column of the *Freeman's Journal*.

---

21. At a meeting on Aug. 4, 1804, the Delaware County Republicans nominated Jacob Richards as their candidate (*ibid.*, Aug. 22, 1804), but they avoided endorsing any of the other contenders until election eve.
22. *Aurora*, Aug. 24, 31, 1804.
23. *Ibid.*, Aug. 18, 1804.

Coxe, still as inveterate a compiler of incriminating documents as he had been four years earlier, was the anonymous chief prosecutor. He was responsible too for a revival of the polarities he had popularized in 1800—liberty and power, monarchism and republicanism, corruption and innocence, aristocracy and the people—going so far as to republish some of the stale documents with which he had smeared the Federalists in 1800.[24] But his efforts to refurbish what once had been effective campaign propaganda were unsuccessful; Leib and Duane, both professed radical democrats, could not be cast in the role played by John Adams, nor could their Republican followers be converted into neo-Federalists. Instead, Coxe himself became the focus of the campaign, at least to the extent that Duane could make him so.

From mid-August until election day in early October the *Aurora* subordinated every other facet of the campaign, as well as all news, foreign and domestic, to the issue of Coxe's credibility. This emphasis led one New York newspaper to observe that Coxe's name had appeared in one issue of the *Aurora* "no less than seventy-five times!!!" and to comment that "Tench Coxe's name, makes almost as much noise as that of General Hamilton," whose fatal duel on July 11 with Aaron Burr was the leading news story of the summer of 1804. Bent on "making a public cause a personal controversy," Duane depicted Coxe's career as a tissue of lies and deceit.[25] Having betrayed his country in 1776, his own party in 1796, and John Adams in 1797, Coxe was in 1804 intent on betraying his adopted party and his president. Limitlessly ambitious and ruthless, Coxe would destroy all who attempted to block his stealthy drive for high office and political preeminence; boundlessly egotistical, he thirsted for revenge against those who refused to accept his own vaulted estimate of his talents. Duane's charge was not far off the mark, if, that is, one discounts his overstated style. The editor was a master of hyperbole: Coxe was "the disciple of Ignatius," "the Talleyrand of our people," "Loyola," a man so slippery that

> Detect his trick, his sophistry—in vain
> The creature's at his dirty work again.

Nor did Duane fail to plow up and then daily to harrow Coxe's toryism. He described Coxe as "a traitor who guided the murderers of his countrymen into this city" and repeatedly referred to him as "Lord Howe's guide," "Lord Cornwallis' pilot," or (in an allusion to Coxe's alleged march into

---

24. Not only did he dredge up the familiar documentary evidence of Adams's monarchism, but on July 12, 1804, Coxe reprinted in the *Freeman's Jour.*, the whole pamphlet-length *Strictures upon the Letter*, signed "Greene," that was first published in June 1800.

25. The phrase was used by John Vaughan in a letter to Coxe, Sept. 17, 1804, Coxe Papers.

Philadelphia with laurel in his hat) "the Laureled Leader of the third party."[26]

Since this was by no means the first time that the Philadelphia press had made sport of his tory record, Coxe may not have been particularly bothered by the *Aurora*'s revival of it. It was otherwise with Duane's pitiless revelation of facts he had gleaned from his own close and confidential relationship with Coxe, particularly about the latter's frustrated quest for federal office. "Truly, the office he possesses is not competent to his own notions of his merits," Duane observed on August 18. He amplified that remark on subsequent days by revealing the details of Coxe's unrequited demands for a more important job and his dissatisfaction with the one he had finally been awarded. "I tell you what," read one of the obviously planted pseudonymous articles in the *Aurora*, "Mr. Jefferson should have ... made Mr. Coxe secretary of the treasury or some other secretary (with a high salary)," thus obviating "all dread of the frowns" of this frustrated office seeker.[27] Although Coxe must have been stung by such recognizably accurate observations, there was little point in replying. To emphasize such charges would have detracted from the issue of Leib's deficiencies, which Coxe had sought to make the central issue of the campaign. Nor could Coxe effectively parry the charge, made dozens of times by the *Aurora* and supported by only the flimsiest evidence, that he was using his official influence as purveyor of public supplies to influence the election.[28]

Coxe's handicap was greater than that imposed by the usual difficulty of convincingly refuting slander, for, though himself an experienced and talented journalist, he had elected to take on a penman who was more than his match. Duane's disregard of fair play, clever juggling of words, and hints of even more delicious scandals yet to come were titillating and often amusing. Coxe's comparative restraint, his effort to persuade by reason rather than by billingsgate, and his belief that facts tediously repeated would prevail rendered his indignant and labored rejoinders dull by contrast. In brief, Duane often evoked a smile or chuckle; Coxe more often than not prompted a yawn. It was not that Coxe was unskilled in debate, for on occasion he did score telling points. Commenting that his own principles remained unchanged, he asked what "actuated the editor of the *Aurora*" from 1799 to 1804 "when he praised Mr. Coxe for liberally contributing to the contents of that paper, in supporting the principles of our government"? Did Duane not then know the "horrid features" of the "crimes" of which he

26. *Aurora*, Aug. 18, 20, 21, 22, 23, 24, 26, Sept. 1, 3, 1804.
27. *Ibid.*, Sept. 3, 1804.
28. This accusation was made in virtually every issue of the *Aurora* from mid-Aug. to early Oct. 1804.

charged Coxe in 1804, or did the "integrity and worth of a man only depend upon the whim and pleasure of Duane"?[29] However valid this or any other question, the point remained that Coxe's defenses were promptly swamped by the *Aurora*'s waves of additional slander.

Although Duane thus succeeded in making the campaign a referendum on Coxe, the larger historical question is what, if any, genuine issues he thereby obscured. Perhaps the most expert political haruspex could not have said what they were. Certainly judicial reform was not among them, though it was ostensibly still the touchstone of radical democracy in Pennsylvania. Nor was McKean's conduct as governor at issue, though it had been challenged and soon would be the most burning issue in state politics. Nor the record of Congress, which, though seldom mentioned, was praised by all; nor the leadership of Jefferson, who was claimed as the sole property of each faction. The campaign was, in fact, essentially a struggle between Leib and Coxe for control of the state's Republican party. Although much ado was made about other matters, notably the Penrose case, the *Freeman's Journal* harped incessantly on Leib's political ambition, repeatedly charging that the Republican "dictator" of Philadelphia was intent on playing the same role on a larger scale. Although Coxe was tediously portrayed as a wily traitor, Duane repeatedly cut through such partisan cant to charge that he and his followers were essentially disappointed office seekers, intent on seizing control of the *"power and patronage and official influence"* of the Republican party to assuage their ravenous appetites.[30]

The goal of this intraparty battle, then, was nothing more edifying than the spoils of office. The fundamental motive that had largely inspired the unity and remarkable energy with which the Pennsylvania Republicans fought the Federalists in 1799 and 1800 now divided the victors. Such a spectacle took place in a political atmosphere that was both rancorous and stale; it was as if innocence and freshness had disappeared within fifteen years after the launching of what Pennsylvanians, along with other Americans, viewed as history's most noble experiment in republicanism. There was, at the same time, no necessary contradiction involved, for, as George Dangerfield remarked of the New York scene at the same time, "this was the politics of opportunity in all its surreptitious glory."[31]

Having misjudged his opportunity, Coxe was obliged to leave such glory as accrued from what one historian has called "one of the most slanderous and malignant campaigns Philadelphia had ever known" to his archrivals. Coxe's defeat was heralded by two events of the last week of Septem-

29. *Freeman's Jour.*, Aug. 23, 1804.

30. *Aurora*, Aug. 23, 1804. See also *ibid.*, Aug. 20, 22, 23, 24, 30, 1804.

31. George Dangerfield, *Chancellor Robert R. Livingston of New York, 1746–1813* (New York, 1960), 306.

ber: the balloting for electoral inspectors and assessors that gave a clear victory to the Duane-Leib faction, and the decision of the conferees from Delaware County (on whose choice the outcome largely hinged) to support Leib rather than Penrose.[32] Fighting as if his rather than Penrose's political future was at stake (as, indeed, it was), Coxe continued to wage a campaign that was summed up in a lengthy address drafted by him for the signatures of his associates and published in his party's paper on election eve. The essential issue, Coxe insisted, was "the inordinate ambition of one man," Michael Leib, whose "inveterate itch to take the lead" endangered the future of democracy not only in Pennsylvania but nationally. Such Republicans as had had the fortitude to read William Duane's tens of thousands of words upon the subject may well have believed that Coxe was painting a self-portrait. In any event, on election day, October 10, the voters sent Leib to Congress and Coxe on the road to political oblivion.[33]

He was by now a willing traveler. Though accustomed to personal abuse, he was left reeling by Duane's daily onslaught. The attack, the most sustained and vicious of the editor's almost unrelieved career of character assassination, would have forced the most hardened combatant to run for shelter. But more important than the election's effect on Coxe's career or its interest as a case study of Duane's almost psychotic reaction to personal or political disloyalty was its effect on the future of the Republican party. During the course of the campaign Duane had thrown out broad hints that Coxe was merely the tool of far more influential Republicans, and as time progressed the editor began to call names: McKean was by nuance implicated, as was Dallas, but the chief villain was Albert Gallatin.[34] Although he adduced no evidence for such allegations, Duane allowed his suspicions to harden into certainty. As his opposition to Gallatin grew, so too did his belief that McKean was playing an instrumental behind-the-scenes role in the campaign to discredit both himself and Leib. This conviction would lead him and like-minded Republicans to cast around for another gubernatorial candidate in 1805.

The consequences of these developments were not confined to Pennsylvania, for that state, as John Vaughan reminded Coxe, "is so populous

---

32. Higginbotham, *Keystone in the Democratic Arch*, 68; *Aurora*, Oct. 4, 1804.

33. For Coxe's address, see "Address to the Democratic Republican Citizens of the District . . . ," Oct. 6, 1804, *Freeman's Jour.*, Oct. 8, 1804. For Coxe's authorship, see *Aurora*, Oct. 9, 1804. Leib won the election only by a narrow majority, however. Although in Philadelphia County (where the "Coxeites" had started their campaign and where they assumed they would carry) Leib won by 722 votes, his margin in the city was only 18 votes. In the district as a whole, the result was 3,992 for Leib and 3,685 for Penrose. For the results of the election, see the *Aurora*, Oct. 11, Nov. 2, 1804.

34. See, for example, *Aurora*, Sept. 4, Oct. 8, 9, 1804; *Gaz. of U.S.*, July 6, 1804; *Freeman's Jour.*, Aug. 18, 1804.

and central and consequently so influential a state, that her politics are always important to the union."[35] The same was true of New York, where in the rancorous gubernatorial race of 1804 Aaron Burr (by then on the outs with the Jefferson administration) unsuccessfully challenged Morgan Lewis, candidate of the regular Republican party organization. For the moment the spread of such intraparty rivalry was no more than a wisp of a cloud in the sunny outlook for the party's future, but more thoughtful party leaders, including the president, were not complacent. Although Jefferson awaited proof that the "rudiments" of a national third party had been formed in New York and Pennsylvania, he nevertheless believed that "it possibly may happen that we shall divide among ourselves whenever federalism is completely erradicated."[36]

If the death of Federalism meant Republican division, the presidential contest of 1804 hastened the day. With Jefferson's popularity at an all-time high, the Federalists, by now unmistakably a minority party in search of an issue, appeared to patiently await the inevitable. Their candidates, Charles Cotesworth Pinckney and Rufus King, were virtually invisible.[37] Since only Delaware and Connecticut gave their votes to the Federalists, the nationwide victory of Jefferson and his running mate, George Clinton, was an impressive affirmation of Republican policies and a seemingly decisive repudiation of Federalism, of whatever stripe.[38]

Nowhere was this repudiation more apparent than in Pennsylvania, where rival Republican leaders, so recently locked in political combat, outdid one another in professions of loyalty to Jefferson and urged the voters to close ranks before the hideous evil of resurgent Federalism. Coxe, signing himself "Benjamin Franklin Bache" (a choice that must have made Duane squirm), urged his fellow partisans to act with unanimity, lest "the enemies of the constitution . . . foolishly suppose we are divided by contests for men, or for places, so as to allow them to take the President's and Vice-President's chairs from our friends by surprise. . . . Let nothing make us backward, inactive, cold, or divided in this all important case. The Tree of Liberty will take deep root, grow high, spread wide, and be well matured under Jefferson and Clinton."[39] The landslide victory demonstrated that Pennsylvania Republicans agreed. It emphatically did not mean, however, that they were

35. John Vaughan to Coxe, Apr. 25, 1805, Coxe Papers.
36. Jefferson to Joseph Scott, May 9, 1804, Ford, ed., *Works of Jefferson*, X, 83.
37. Peterson, *Jefferson and the New Nation*, 799.
38. Two Maryland electors also supported the Pinckney-King ticket. The final tally was 162 electoral votes for the Republicans against 14 for the Federalists.
39. [Coxe], *To the Democratic Republicans of the State of Pennsylvania* (n.p., n.d.). A copy is in the Coxe Papers.

prepared to cease those intramural "contests for men, or for places" that Coxe had urged them to forgo.

Certainly William Duane was in a combative mood. Having successfully blocked Coxe's bid for party supremacy, Duane was more determined than ever, as Alexander J. Dallas observed, "to destroy the republican standing and usefulness of every man who does not bend to his will."[40] The most unbending of all, the editor of the *Aurora* decided, was Governor McKean, who dauntlessly pursued a patronage policy unfavorable to Duane, Leib, and their followers. By 1805 they had resolved to get rid of their stubborn antagonist, who was once again up for reelection. At a party caucus held in Lancaster, they nominated as their rival candidate Simon Snyder, a self-educated Northumberland County storekeeper who had acquired during his long service in the state legislature a reputation as tribune of the people. His campaign, as was de rigueur in Pennsylvania politics, was depicted as a crusade against aristocrats and despots.

Although himself the quondam head of a splinter party, Coxe deplored the schism in Republican ranks, arguing that no questions of substance divided the rival Republican factions, least of all those like judicial reform on which they professed to disagree.[41] Experience was, for once, a good teacher. The real battle between the contestants, as it had been between Coxe and Duane a year previously, was for political power and its perquisites. Predictably and understandably, Duane did not see it that way. Instead, he skillfully transmuted his personal feud with the governor into an issue of principle: it was a battle, he insisted, between equal rights and aristocratic privilege, freedom and tyranny, the virtuous people and a putative monarch. To Coxe, unalterably convinced that American party history should be told by a moralist, such a viewpoint was irresistibly attractive, despite the tainted source from which it came.

It was perhaps partly for this reason that Coxe suppressed his distaste for the company he was forced to keep and finally "openly voted against Governor McKean." How could he in good conscience support fellow Republicans, who, like McKean's supporters, welcomed a coalition with Federalists, the still-dreaded enemy? After all, Coxe's political apostasy and subsequent career as a partisan proselytizer had been based on Federalist-baiting. Following his own party line, he continued "to oppose every deposit

40. Dallas to Gallatin, Oct. 16, 1804, quoted in Cunningham, *Jeffersonian Republicans in Power*, 216–217.

41. Coxe, *An Exposition of Some Facts Relative to the Personal Conduct, and Business of the Office of Tench Coxe, Purveyor of Public Supplies* (Philadelphia, 1805), 8, 11. The constitution Coxe drafted for his proposed "Political Society of the City of Philadelphia" suggests that its purpose was to reunite his fellow partisans by prohibiting Federalist participation in Republican politics. Although the society was proposed for Philadelphia, he hoped that it would become a statewide organization.

of power in the hands of such persons, in the federal party, as are attached to monarchical, aristocratical, or hierarchal principles," or "those who even unwarily" followed them. The willingness of such persons to fuse with Republicans, Coxe observed shortly after McKean's reelection, only proved "how quickly those persons can completely rally, who failed in the Governor's and President's election of 1799 and 1800."[42]

Although Coxe was indisputably sincere, his explanation both revealed and obscured the truth. He would have been superhuman if he had not resented the ascendancy of others in a party largely of his making, men who had only covertly supported him when he had faced the full blast of the *Aurora*'s pitiless assault alone and who now shunted him aside. It was not that he sought center stage, for he did not wish again to expose himself to popular boos and to Duane's pelts; it was rather that he did not want to be consigned to the gallery. But the campaign of 1804 had persuaded most party leaders, even those who approved of his crusade, that Coxe was political poison. So deadly, indeed, that he was not included in the truce that three years later restored party harmony. Duane and Leib, whose hostility toward Coxe was implacable, saw to that. Although himself no passively innocent victim, Coxe never understood the source of such enmity, perhaps because it could not be rationally explained. In any event, the situation presents the tantalizing oddity of the stymied career of a talented man in a society presumably open to talent.

42. *Ibid.*, 4, 9.

23 🕊

Adviser on Affairs of State

"Every man who sets a just value upon private peace, should withdraw himself from the turmoil of politics," Dr. John Vaughan counseled Coxe in August 1805. The Philadelphian agreed and, although his decision was not altogether voluntary, resolved "never again" to "tread the political ground as heretofore."[1] But, persuaded also that Pennsylvania's loss might prove to be the nation's gain, he continued to remind influential Republicans of his eligibility for an office more important than the purveyorship. Their refusal to acknowledge his claim no longer drove him to despair, however. Instead, he resigned himself to his fate with the imperturbability of a politician who has known and accepted the shifting sands of power. The wounds that Duane had inflicted in 1804 were to an extent responsible for this change, as perhaps was advancing age, but personal adversity also played a large part.

As early as 1801 Rebecca Coxe had begun to show symptoms that Coxe, remembering the fatal illness of his first wife twenty years earlier, must have recognized as the first stages of tuberculosis. As the illness progressed she was more and more confined to the house and by the early summer of 1804 was unable to muster the energy even to undertake the annual sojourn to Sidney.[2] Instead, she heeded the advice of her family physician, Dr. Adam Kuhn, and accompanied by Andrew and Maria Allen set out early in August for Saratoga Springs. Here, Dr. Kuhn believed, the spas and the climate might prove curative. According to Allen, the change worked a virtual miracle: "I assure you that Mrs. Coxe has not felt an

1. John Vaughan to Coxe, Aug. 20, 1805, Coxe to Vaughan, Aug. 1, 1806, Coxe Papers.
2. William Coxe, Sr., to Coxe, Jan. 26, 1801, Charles Coxe to Coxe, July 1804, *ibid*.

hour's indisposition; . . . I have never heard what the most anxious and timid could denominate a cough."[3]

Upon Rebecca's return to Philadelphia in September, she appeared so greatly improved that Coxe unhesitatingly acquiesced in her wish to leave promptly for Sidney, where the children had stayed for the preceding three months and were now enrolled in school.[4] Once she was there, Charles Coxe, less certain than her husband that her health was restored, insisted she remain with him and implored Tench to be less importunate about her coming home. "Your impatience makes her so," he wrote, "and I am using all my influence and persuasion to detain her that she may secure such a State of health as will carry her through the winter without . . . a relapse." She eventually returned to Philadelphia and did manage to get through the winter in good health, but soon after she returned to Jersey in June 1805, she suffered a major setback. "I was attacked about four weeks ago," she wrote to Tench on August 3, "with my alarming complaint of spitting of blood for which I was bled. . . . I do not recollect ever to have seen my blood more inflamed than it was." Although her father reported to Coxe that "she follows Doctor Kuhn's directions so Strictly that there is no beating her out of it," her condition did not improve, and Tench, increasingly apprehensive, joined her in the country during the latter part of August.[5]

He was not reassured. Not only had the illness progressed, but she was so unrelievedly depressed that a number of her relatives, including Tench, Jr., insisted that her "disorder . . . is mental and nervous" and that she had only "to fortify her mind." While Rebecca reacted "favorably" to this diagnosis, resolution and courage were, of course, futile, and by late September she confided to Tench that "I am sometimes frightened about myself. I try to keep up my spirits as well as I can, but there is nothing here to raise them, but much to depress them." She was, however, reluctant to return home: "If I was to go down I should be obliged to keep up stairs and shut myself in my chamber—for I could not think of being in the parlor as it would be very disagreeable to me to expose this miserable emaciated frame of mine to the curiosity of strangers that might happen to come in."[6]

Nevertheless, at Coxe's insistence Rebecca was by late autumn back in Philadelphia. Aware that nothing could be done to arrest the fatal course of her illness, her husband vicariously endured the last agonizing months of

3. Andrew Allen, Jr., to Coxe, Aug. 26, 1804, *ibid.* For Rebecca's decision to go to Saratoga Springs, see Coxe to Vaughan, Aug. 8, 1804, *ibid.*
4. Charles Coxe to Coxe, Sept. 15, 29, 1804, *ibid.*
5. Charles Coxe to Coxe, Oct. 12, 1804, Rebecca Coxe to Coxe, Aug. 3, 1805, Charles Coxe to Coxe, July 13, 1805, Coxe to William Coxe, Jr., Aug. 17, 1805, *ibid.*
6. Charles Coxe to Coxe, Oct. 1, 1805, Rebecca Coxe to Coxe, Sept. 21, 1805, and n.d. [but autumn of 1805], *ibid.*

the woman with whom he had for so long enjoyed "a perfect union of heart and mind." She died on February 10, 1806.[7] With her was buried a part of Coxe, something of his vitality, his fortitude in the face of public abuse, his buoyancy, his confidence that the future would bestow what the past had denied.

"I have been brought by . . . this fatal Season," he wrote to his friend John Vaughan shortly after Rebecca's death, "to reflect much upon my situation and prospects in life, and an insuperable melancholy . . . hangs about my heart." He mused that perhaps he "deserved the share of pain" that had been dispensed to him. For comfort, and because he had "little to attach me to this world but the welfare of my offspring," he turned his thoughts to another world that to him afforded "the true and only solace for such a privation as mine." Although he had been a lifelong Episcopalian, a vestryman, and a participant in both diocesan and national church affairs, his religious commitment appears previously to have been rather more pro forma than fervid. Indeed, he had sometimes seemed to equate his own suffering with that of Him whom he professed to worship and, as troubled men are tempted to do, had seen himself as crucified. Following Rebecca's death, however, he entered a new religious phase. As if having himself experienced a fall, he now recognized sin. He turned to the assiduous cultivation of "religious sentiments and feelings," a preoccupation he shared in frequent letters to Dr. Vaughan and expressed by both intensive study and the preparation of articles.[8]

Although Coxe revealed a more than ordinary competence in hermeneutics, his writings on the subject are more important as indications of a personal change than as contributions to the religious thought and practice of his time. Just as his essays on secular subjects revealed scant interest in philosophy, so those on religion reflected only a minimal acquaintance with theology. He was concerned with what he termed "the instrumental" impact of organized religion: the connection between faith and the development of a more equitable and harmonious society, between the "right ideas of our Almighty creator" and our "duties towards his animated creatures of every name." Nor was he, despite his nominal Episcopalianism, a committed sectarian. The sacraments of baptism and the eucharist he referred to as "adornments," mere "rites and ceremonies" not essential to a rich spiritual life. The church of his choice was "a mere sect of Christianity, as much as any other." Had he followed the logical consequences of his pietistic creed, he would have embraced the Quaker rather than the Episcopal sect, es-

---

7. Coxe to Vaughan, Mar. 10, 1806, *ibid.*

8. Coxe to Vaughan, n.d., *ibid.* See also Vaughan to Coxe, June 7, 1806, John Dickinson to Coxe, July 31, 1806, *ibid.*

pecially as the cardinal tenet of his personal faith was a conviction that since "the conscience of men is within the exclusive empire of God," every attempt "of human governments to bind conscience" was "neither more nor less than . . . sacrilege."[9]

Although for a year Coxe's correspondence with close friends was thus infused with concern over questions of Christian faith, he slowly resumed his more characteristic absorption in secular matters, notably economic problems but also diplomatic developments. These subjects once again dominated his increasingly numerous articles and his bulky correspondence. He exchanged letters not only with those whom he hoped would translate his recommendations into policy—congressmen, cabinet officers, and the president—but now also with personal friends.[10]

Next to Dr. Vaughan, his chief correspondent was another Wilmington resident, John Dickinson, Coxe's longtime acquaintance and his newfound idol. When their correspondence commenced in 1804 Dickinson at seventy-two was at the close of his career (he died four years later); Coxe at forty-nine still hoped the best was yet to be. That their friendship so quickly flourished and deepened was largely owing to mutual respect grounded on a common involvement in public affairs and shared political convictions, but it was also attributable to Coxe's manifest admiration, expressed not only in letters and by occasional visits to Wilmington but also by the business advice and assistance he freely gave.[11]

As his affection for the author of *Letters from a Farmer in Pennsylvania* attests, Coxe's most valued and sustained friendships were with fellow authors rather than associates in business and land speculation. Many of his other correspondents were journalists: Samuel Smith and Joseph Gales, Jr., successively editors of the *National Intelligencer*; the elder Gales, editor of the *Raleigh Register*; John Binns, who launched the Philadelphia *Democratic Press* in 1807; Dr. Vaughan, who found time from his medical practice to edit the Wilmington *Delaware Gazette*;[12] and Mathew Carey, former editor of the *American Museum*.

9. Coxe to Vaughan, June 28, 1806, *ibid*. This long letter contains an excellent summary of Coxe's religious beliefs.

10. Over the decade following the death of his wife, Coxe, as in the past, had corresponded with Pennsylvania congressmen on a variety of subjects. To Daniel Montgomery, for example, he proffered advice on foreign and economic policy; to Benjamin Say he offered suggestions on the mode of taking the third census; to Andrew Gregg he proposed measures for encouraging manufactures; and to Jonathan Roberts, his closest congressional friend, he offered advice on a range of pending legislation. For additional information on Coxe's advice on pending legislation and public policy, see his correspondence with these men between 1806 and 1809, *ibid*.

11. See Coxe's correspondence with Dickinson between 1804 and 1807 in the Coxe Papers and Society MS, Hist. Soc. Pa., Philadelphia. See also Coxe to Vaughan, Aug. 8, 1804, Mar. 6, 9, 1807, Coxe to Philadelphia Chamber of Commerce, Dec. 1805, Mar. 7, 1806, Joseph Bringhurst to Coxe, Feb. 17, 1808, Coxe Papers.

12. See John A. Munroe, *Federalist Delaware, 1775–1815* (New Brunswick, N.J., 1954), 184.

Another literary correspondent was the poet Joel Barlow, an acquaintance since 1779, now back in the United States after seventeen years abroad.[13] A New Englander, Barlow chose upon his return home in 1805 to settle in Philadelphia. Regarding it as the "most liberal of our cities," Barlow believed that Philadelphia's leading citizens would enthusiastically welcome "the only man in America who devotes his life entirely to literature and the most disinterested labors for the advancement of public happiness." Instead, the "noblesse of that city," or so he complained to Coxe, "stigmatized" him "as a disorganizing Jacobin, an atheist, . . . as a sort of monster against whom they must shut their doors." By one member of the "noblesse," however, Barlow was accorded precisely the welcome he had expected. "From yourself," he wrote to Coxe several years later, "I received the kindest hospitality and every mark of goodness." But this was scarcely enough to salve his hurt pride, and in 1807, having overseen the publication of his epic poem *The Columbiad*, Barlow left Philadelphia and retired to Washington, where he sought "a residence among a people who have no *pretensions* to literature or science."[14]

Distance did not abate Barlow's friendship with Coxe, and they regularly corresponded on personal matters and, above all, on public affairs. Although the two do not always mix, the ideas of the poet and of the economist blended almost perfectly. Barlow, like Coxe, was a dedicated proponent of the idea of progress; for both, America was a land of limitless possibilities, all to be realized in a golden future; to both, the motivating forces behind that inevitable march were advances in science and technology, the certain products of human reason; to both, it was America's peculiar destiny to hasten the millennium. Barlow spoke for them both when he remarked that "the future situation of America fills the mind with a peculiar dignity and opens an unbounded field of thought."[15]

This same self-fulfilling prophecy of American destiny that sustained Coxe seems to have guided Republican leaders in their formulation of diplomatic policy. Thanks to the Peace of Amiens, which in 1801 brought a pause in the European war, Jefferson had been able during the initial years of his presidency to concentrate on realizing the "wise and frugal government" he had envisioned in his first inaugural address. Before his second term began, however, war had been renewed, with consequences that unprecedentedly imperiled American neutrality. Not only was the president confronted by two belligerents, but he was also caught between the conflicting demands of

13. Joel Barlow to Coxe, Sept. 3, 1779, Coxe Papers.
14. Barlow to Coxe, Sept. 25, 1809, *ibid.*, italics added.
15. Quoted in Russel B. Nye, *The Cultural Life of the New Nation, 1776–1830* (New York, 1960), 51.

one world power that controlled the continent of Europe and another that ruled the seas. European neutrals trembled in the shadow of Napoleon's mighty armies, while those beyond the seas were virtually helpless in the face of Britain's powerful navy. With the subsequent imposition of English maritime and French continental blockades, vessels of the United States could not trade anywhere in the world without rendering themselves liable to capture by one belligerent or another.

Because of America's vulnerability at sea, however, English violations of the new nation's neutrality were more obvious and more serious. Particularly objectionable was the impressment of seamen from United States vessels on the high seas. It was a grievance against which the American government had complained for more than a decade, always encountering the inflexible determination of England to continue a practice that ensured the full manning of its ships and thus also, or so that country believed, its national survival. So too did British officials defend the search and seizure of United States merchantmen, which according to England's unilateral interpretation of international law were engaged in illegal trade with her enemies. To Coxe, who in this instance as in many others faithfully parroted the Republican party line, both practices were reprehensible, but impressment, because it violated the rights of men rather than property, was "a peculiar and monstrous class of English wrongs to the United States." This was the implicit theme of the opinions he submitted to Madison on foreign affairs in the trying years of 1805 and 1806 in letters that the secretary of state found to be "all of importance."[16]

In the spring of 1806 Jefferson appointed William Pinkney to join James Monroe, American minister to England, in an attempt to secure an abandonment of impressment, as well as to iron out other Anglo-American differences. When Pinkney embarked in May, he carried with him Madison's detailed instructions on virtually every subject in controversy between the two countries, some of them discretionary but two inflexible: there could be no concessions on impressment and there must be a relaxation of British rules governing American reexport trade in French colonial goods. That Jefferson and Madison felt free to impose such demands was owing to a conviction that the nonimportation act adopted by Congress in April 1806 (but postponed to allow time for negotiations) would persuade England to make concessions.[17] To Coxe the statute had other merits as well. Its exclusion of

---

16. Coxe, "An Estimate of the Times," *Demo. Press*, Feb. 13, 1809; James Madison to Coxe, June 11, 1805, Coxe to Madison, June 7, 18, 1805, June 8, 12, 20, Nov. 4, 1806, Madison Papers, Lib. of Cong.

17. "An act to prohibit the importation of certain goods, wares, and merchandise," Apr. 18, 1806, *U.S. Statutes at Large*, II, 379–381. The act was postponed several times and was finally put into effect in Dec. 1807, coeval with the enactment of the famous embargo of that month.

a long list of British manufactures from the United States represented the triumph of a policy he had long advocated. Unlike the president and Madison, Coxe viewed such policy not so much as a trump card in the Monroe-Pinkney negotiations as a long-term guarantee of British respect for the new nation's neutral rights and a desirable spur to its economic growth.

On the negotiations themselves Coxe pinned little hope, believing that without more concrete evidence of American willingness to retaliate, Great Britain would continue its reckless plunder of neutral commerce. This was the subject of a long essay that he submitted to Jefferson in May 1806. Prompted by "this most awful and unprecedented crisis" in American foreign policy, the paper was subsequently published under the title *Thoughts on the Subject of Naval Power in the United States*.[18] Coxe's ostensible purpose in writing it was to persuade his countrymen "that the whole circle of our commercial rights and interests . . . can be more cheaply, more safely, and more effectually defended by wholesome statutes than by a dangerous and costly establishment of naval power."[19]

The title and alleged thesis of Coxe's essay were, however, deceptive; his strictures on naval power were designed primarily as a popular platform from which to launch his program for American progress and prosperity. His argument was that America should confine its carrying trade to imports of raw materials that might be employed "to promote and establish internal trade, of which manufactures are a most valuable part," a policy that if energetically pursued would "silently" operate "as a *fine* or *penalty* upon the foreign invaders of our maritime rights." This substitution of economic for traditional diplomatic policy could easily be achieved, he believed, by the adoption of "well devised acts of Congress" that would retaliate against the restrictiveness of British mercantilism by making possible a program of American mercantilism (though he did not, of course, use that term). "We may *now* adopt many of the regulations of the British navigation act," he wrote, going on to describe in detail its provisions.

Although the inspiration for Coxe's repetitious argument may have been the exigencies of foreign affairs in 1806, it was consistent both with

---

18. Coxe to Jefferson, May 22, 1806, Jefferson Papers; [Coxe], *Thoughts on the Subject of Naval Power in the United States of America; and on Certain Means of Encouraging and Protecting Their Commerce and Manufactures* (Philadelphia, 1806). The essay also appeared in serial form in the *Nat. Intelligencer*, Sept. 1806 (Joseph Nicholson to Coxe, Sept. 19, 1806, Coxe Papers) and in newspapers in Massachusetts (Jacob Crowninshield to Coxe, Aug. 31, 1806, *ibid.*). It was reprinted in the *Demo. Press*, May 27, 29, June 1, 3, 5, 8, 1807. Since the 1807 republication was a revised and enlarged edition, my citations are to this version. In Sept. 1807 Coxe once again republished his essay in pamphlet form, but this time only an expanded version of the essay numbered "III" in the *Demo. Press* was included. A copy of this was sent to Thomas Jefferson in a letter dated Sept. 25, 1807, Jefferson Papers, Lib. of Cong.

19. Coxe, "Thoughts on Naval Power," *Demo. Press*, June 3, 1807.

what he had advocated for almost two decades and with Jefferson's commercial policy. The argument was also saturated with his accustomed anti-British animus. The countermeasures proposed were justified by the history of English assaults on American rights, "neither few nor small." He happily provided a redundant account of these transgressions—"perversions" of the principles of search and of blockade, illegal impressment of seamen, "legalized extortions in the admirality business," and other gross violations of international law that combined had "laid a foreign axe to the root of the tree of our prosperity."[20]

That France was also wielding a sharp axe could scarcely be ignored, but to Coxe it was blunted by having been forged on the anvil of British precedent. To render plausible this fallacious argument, Coxe bludgeoned his readers with evidence of England's criminal conduct during the years preceding the Jay Treaty, no doubt hoping that by centering attention on England's past misdeeds, he might brush away the seemingly incontrovertible argument that France's ruthless disregard of American rights ought to oblige the new nation to proceed pari passu against both.

But persuaded that England was ineradicably hostile toward her former colonies, Coxe, in effect, damned in advance the document Monroe and Pinkney signed in London on New Year's Eve 1806. The American envoys, like John Jay in 1794, had been obliged to surrender their major demands in order to win a number of other concessions, though these were not inconsequential if viewed in the light of political realities. The treaty dealt with the thorny problems of neutral rights and Anglo-American trade by reaffirming the expired commercial articles of Jay's Treaty, a solution the British nationalists considered a capitulation for which the Americans should yield an equivalent. The pact also included other conciliatory articles, among them a British promise not to stop unarmed vessels within five miles of the American coast, an agreement that Anglo-American trade should be placed on a most-favored-nation basis, and a modification of restrictions on the United States reexport trade. But the price exacted for these concessions was high. Monroe and Pinkney were obliged to accept slightly tighter restrictions on American ships trading with India, a proviso that for ten years the United States would forgo discrimination against British commerce, and a postscript requiring American resistance to Napoleon's Berlin Decree. The fatal flaw of the treaty, however, was its silence on the subject of impressment—to Jefferson the central issue of the negotiations.

Coxe also found the treaty unacceptable and in a series of articles entitled "A Defence of the conduct of the President" denounced Britain's behavior as "odious and contemptible," "immoral," and "even a cause of

20. *Ibid.*, June 8, 5, 1807.

war."[21] Although for the latter phrase Jefferson would have substituted "cause of commercial warfare," he otherwise agreed. The president rejected the treaty soon after it reached his desk early in March 1807. He did not even bother to allow the Senate, though in session, to look at it.

Madison could not be quite so cavalier. As secretary of state it was his responsibility to explain the rejection of the treaty and to send it back to England with instructions that the American commissioners renew negotiations. For assistance (presumably with Jefferson's concurrence) he turned to Coxe, whose voluntary advice on the subject had engulfed the State Department over the preceding months. Since it was "highly advisable to avail" the administration of Coxe's "intelligence and experience" on subjects "relating to commerce and navigation," the secretary of state wrote on March 27, would the Philadelphian forward his opinion on a number of stated questions? The queries were so broad as actually to encompass the whole treaty. Perhaps Madison had not read the Philadelphian's voluminous letters and articles, or maybe he was seeking confirmation of his own critical view of the document; either way, had he merely weighed Coxe's papers, he would have known that to ask their author's advice on affairs of state was to invite not a report but a dissertation.

"I thought it best to lose no time," the Philadelphian promptly replied, "and therefore devoted all of yesterday . . . to reperusals and reflexion, with my pen in hand." The result was nineteen pages in small script of "*Preliminary* reflexions," discursive and turgid enough to tax the patience even of one accustomed to long-winded diplomatic dispatches. This was followed on the next day, April 2, by two additional essays, a week or so later by yet another, then on May 5 by three more.[22] They all boiled down to the argument that the treaty was irreparably defective.

Coxe continued his exercise in vicarious statesmanship even after Madison, as confident as his unofficial adviser that England would agree "to a tabula rasa for a new adjustment," forwarded new instructions to the American envoys in May 1807. Through the late spring, the summer, and on into the fall, the cascade of advice from the Philadelphia office of the purveyor continued, offering merely an elaboration of the foreign policy he

21. Coxe, "A Defence of the conduct of the President of the United States, upon the subject of the impressment of persons from American ships," signed "Juriscola," *Demo. Press*, Mar. 27, Apr. 3, 29, 1807. The quotations in the text are from Mar. 27. For Coxe's authorship, see John Langdon to Coxe, Oct. 20, 1807, Coxe Papers. Coxe also wrote an anonymous pamphlet on the subject entitled *All Impressments Unlawful and Inadmissible* (Philadelphia [1806 or 1807]). It consisted of a long introductory paragraph and an "extract of a letter from the Secretary of State to James Monroe, Esq., dated 5th January, 1804." Nine of the ten pages of the pamphlet consisted of this excerpt.

22. Coxe to Madison, Apr. 1, 2, Apr., May 5 (enclosing three articles numbered "3, 4, and 5"), May 20, 22, 29, 1807, Madison Papers, Lib. of Cong., italics added.

had advocated time and again.[23] Coxe's wordiness was in this instance not merely an expression of an ingrained habit, however; it was rather his manner of indulging an appetite so long deprived. Not only had the secretary of state solicited the type of advice Coxe had previously offered without being asked, but the Philadelphian was for the first time in six years once again conducting a cordial correspondence with the president.

Jefferson had broken his long-imposed ban of silence with Coxe in March 1807, when he acknowledged Coxe's unsigned "Opinion on Arming the Militia for Defence." Complimenting Coxe on this essay, his continued assiduous attention to the public interest, and his frequent communication of ideas "which have often been useful," the president expressed his willingness to "expunge from my mind the umbrage which had been taken" years earlier and to renew their correspondence. Coxe's pleasure was presumably tempered by the realization that the close relationship they had once enjoyed could not be restored. Nevertheless, he found it flattering to serve once again as Jefferson's aide, even though the advice he tendered was necessarily redundant. "I have ever wished that all nations would adopt a navigation law against those who have one," Jefferson confirmed in September 1807, thus assuring Coxe that their ideological affinity was unimpaired, however flawed their personal relationship.[24]

Coxe's renewal of his correspondence with Jefferson enlarged an output of letters and articles on affairs of state that would already have done credit to a practicing journalist. His writings were unusually voluminous in 1806 and 1807, largely on account of the successive shocks that rocked a nation not yet inured to diplomatic crises. The year 1806 brought

23. Madison to Jefferson, Apr. 24, 1807, in Bradford Perkins, *Prologue to War: England and the United States, 1805–1812* (Berkeley, Calif., 1961), 187–188. For Coxe's continuing advice, see Coxe to Madison, June 14, 28, 30, 1807, July 1, 2, 4, 6, 14, 21, Oct. 9, Nov., 1807, Madison Papers, Lib. of Cong.

24. Jefferson to Coxe, Mar. 27, Sept. 21, 1807, Jefferson Papers. Coxe saw to it that the relationship with Jefferson remained strained. He took advantage of Jefferson's cordial overtures to apply immediately for a position more congenial than the purveyorship. Hearing that Peter Muhlenberg, collector of the customs for Philadelphia, was about to retire, Coxe wrote Jefferson on Sept. 28, 1807, applying for the position. Coxe Papers. Within hours of hearing of the death of Muhlenberg on Oct. 1, 1807, Coxe reapplied to Jefferson for the position. See Coxe to Jefferson, Oct. [1], 1807, to Albert Gallatin, Oct. [1], 1807, Barlow to Coxe, Dec. 16, 1807, Dickinson to Coxe, Sept. 30, 1807, Dickinson to Jefferson, Sept. 30, 1807, *ibid.* Coxe wrote two more letters to Jefferson on Oct. 2, 1807, *ibid.* Jefferson, probably angered at Coxe's presumption, appointed John Shee, a Pennsylvania flour inspector. Shee was appointed during the recess of the Senate. His nomination was submitted to that body on Nov. 9 and approved on Nov. 12, 1807. *Senate Executive Journal*, II, 56, 59. When Shee died in Aug. 1808, Coxe renewed his application for the collectorship (Coxe to Gallatin, Aug. [5], 1808, to Jefferson, Aug. 5, 1808, Appointment Papers, R.G. 59, National Archives; Coxe to Madison, Aug. 5, 1808, Madison Papers, Lib. of Cong.), but again unsuccessfully. This time Jefferson awarded the appointment to John Steele, who was recommended by a number of prominent Pennsylvania Republicans.

an alarming acceleration of British seizures of American men and vessels, as well as the Burr conspiracy. To Coxe the Burr incident was an instance of "treason," "seduction of the people," "corruption of men of power," and collusion with foreign governments—all these taken together threatened "to destroy our republican institutions."[25] The year 1807 saw not only the failure of the effort to reach a rapprochement with England and renewed assaults on neutral commerce by both belligerents, but also the *Chesapeake-Leopard* affair, which in June 1807 came close to pushing an enraged nation into war with Great Britain.

That war did not come was largely owing to President Jefferson, who successfully soft-pedaled the episode. Jefferson hoped to use it and the attendant public bellicosity as fulcrums for a diplomatic settlement with England that would include reparations for the British attack on the *Chesapeake* and an end to impressment. As the futility of this policy was borne in on Jefferson during the late summer and fall, however, he became increasingly convinced that war was the alternative. But by this time, in the words of a recent historian, "the popular spirit had evaporated, the orators had fallen silent. In July, Jefferson could have had war but did not want it; now he probably wanted it but could not hope to get it."[26]

Coxe thought otherwise. In a lengthy *Examination of the Conduct of Great Britain*, published in November 1807, he submitted to "the whole world . . . the high charge that Great Britain was the first beginner of the illegitimate measures pursued to embarrass and spoliate the neutral commerce of the United States since 1791—that she has pursued it . . . so constantly, in a degree so extreme" that neutral nations were entitled to adopt retaliatory measures. England herself was "deprived of every pretence . . . to a right of retaliation" against enemies who, taking a leaf from her book, also plundered neutral commerce.[27] It was a thesis Coxe had argued dozens

---

25. Coxe to Madison, Nov. 4, 1806, Madison Papers, Lib. of Cong. Believing that "deeper matters than have yet met the public ear" were connected with the Burr conspiracy (Coxe to Jefferson, Apr. 6, 1807, Jefferson Papers), Coxe wrote thousands of words on the subject, mostly to Madison. His letters included much groundless hearsay and gratuitous advice but provided little concrete information that the administration was not already aware of. See Coxe to Madison, Jan. 11, 13, Jan., Feb. 10, Mar. 1, 2, 1807, Madison to Coxe, Feb. 1, 1807, Madison Papers, Lib. of Cong. Jefferson, whose susceptibility to rumors about Burr was as great as Coxe's, was apparently more receptive than Madison. Replying to a letter passed on to him by Joel Barlow, the president wrote: "Th. Jefferson returns his thanks to mr. Barlow for the communication of mr. Coxe's letter. . . . The fact stated as to Burr was certainly unknown to us, and therefore the further particulars which mr. Coxe says he will be willing to give, will be acceptable, and may be useful." Enclosed in Barlow to Coxe, Oct. 27, 1808, Coxe Papers.

26. Perkins, *Prologue to War*, 149.

27. [Coxe], *An Examination of the Conduct of Great Britain Respecting Neutrals* (Philadelphia, 1807). A second edition with minor corrections was published in Boston in 1808. On the last page of his copy of the pamphlet Coxe wrote: "This subject was further examined in twelve other papers, Jurisicola No. 1 to 12, in relation to the war of 1803 to 1809, in the American

of times before, but this time with a superabundance of carefully selected detail, all designed, he wrote, to assist his countrymen in choosing the wisest possible policy. If repetition spawns belief, his readers could have had no doubt that the proper conduct was to convict Britain of high crimes and to exonerate France from all guilt on the grounds of self-defense.

For Coxe, England's guilt was clear, and all that remained was to pronounce a sentence; he needed neither research nor even a second thought to find one. The United States should enact against the British retaliatory legislation banning "all their ships, both public and private," all their produce and manufactures, and all trade with all English subjects wheresoever. What if the adoption of such policies prompted England to declare war? In that event, his countrymen "ought undauntedly to meet the conflict," reminding themselves that they had little to fear. "All the neutral states—all the impartial world must be against England," he observed. In blithe disregard of England's influence as the world's mightiest naval power, Coxe concluded that "her whole injury to us will be some plunder and suspension of our trade."[28]

Coxe, however, did not believe that war was necessarily the price of retaliation. Convinced that Great Britain would protest but acquiesce, he repetitiously affirmed a program that Jefferson, agreeing with Coxe's analysis, would implement a month later with an embargo act. "We may occupy the whole field of painful interdiction," Coxe said, and "unjustly wounded in our external commerce, we may recur with wisdom and energy to the invulnerable objects of home manufactures."[29] The interdiction, as things turned out, was more painful for the United States than for England, but it did prompt the Americans to turn to manufactures.

The embargo act proposed by the president and adopted by Congress in December 1807 was commercial restriction carried to an extreme.[30] It was consistent with Jefferson's conviction, steadfastly maintained for almost two decades, that American commerce was the weapon by which the United States could secure justice from European nations. Coxe, subordinating his

---

Newspapers." For information on the publication and reception of Coxe's work, see J. D. Blanchard to Thomas Blanchard, Nov. 7, 1807, Coxe to Caesar A. Rodney, Nov. 8, 1807, Dickinson to Coxe, Nov. 18, 1807, Levi Lincoln to Coxe, Apr. 30, 1808, R. B. Livingston to Coxe, May 24, 1808, James Watson to Coxe, June 1, 1808, Coxe Papers.

28. [Coxe], *Examination of the Conduct of Britain*, 42.

29. *Ibid.*, 71.

30. "An Act laying an embargo on all ships and vessels in the ports and harbours of the United States," Dec. 22, 1807, *U.S. Statutes at Large*, II, 451–453. The ban on the importation of specified articles of British manufacture was not actually a part of the embargo act but rather of the nonimportation act of Apr. 1806, which was postponed several times and went into effect when the embargo was adopted.

concern over the efficient discharge of the purveyorship to his commitment to principle, agreed. The embargo, he wrote some months later, was "intended to save us from insufferable accumulation of plunder and insult of which the British king and Parliament, have set the world numerous and atrocious examples." His endorsement was, however, modified by a number of reservations not shared by Jefferson or Madison. These were expressed in a letter to Barlow, his Washington confidant, in which he described his fears that the inevitable tendency of such a measure would be to create discontent among Republicans (both "the sufferers by non employment" and the "mighty body of manufacturers" of articles for export) and stagnation of navigation and trade. Obviously expecting Barlow to relay his observations to Jefferson, Coxe suggested that, in view of such dismal prospects, the time had come for making public those "secret matters which have affected the decision of the government." Should not the administration reverse the policy of domestic drift, so strangely at odds with its firm foreign policy, by promptly recommending "measures to employ our produce at home, and even foreign produce"? Some months later in a letter to Madison he noted that business to the amount of $261,000,000 might soon be destroyed by the embargo and argued that the government should do everything possible "to employ men, ships, industry and capital by new plans of business," notably "*improvements* and *manufactures*."[31]

Coxe's recommendations were sound, and if they were passed on as intended, the president would have been well advised to have heeded them. But Jefferson had embarked on what he believed to be a noble experiment, and he was not susceptible to advice that smacked of criticism. Not only did he refuse to explain to the American people the grounds on which he had proposed an embargo (notably his foreknowledge of a British order-in-council of November 11, 1807, that gravely hobbled neutral trade), but he also failed to share candidly with the public the objectives he hoped to achieve by such a program of economic self-immolation. Nor did he subscribe to Coxe's call for affirmative government action, even though it might have been reasonable to reject laissez-faire on the grounds that if his administration had the power to destroy foreign commerce, it also possessed the power to repair the consequent domestic damages by a program of national economic planning.

As 1808 wore on, it became increasingly evident that the embargo, despite the draconian enforcement acts on which the president insisted, was

---

31. Coxe, "Hints to Both Parties," *Demo. Press*, Nov. 16, 1808 (for Coxe's authorship, see John Binns to Coxe, Nov. 15, 1808, Coxe Papers); Coxe to Barlow, Jan. 7, 1808, Coxe Papers; Coxe to Madison, Mar. 24, 1808, Madison Papers, Lib. of Cong. For other advice that Coxe tendered Madison on foreign affairs in 1808, see his letters of Oct. 4, and n.d., 1808, *ibid.*

unlikely to have any effect on Great Britain. The reaction of the British ministry was tellingly expressed in George Canning's sarcastic remark to the United States minister that His Majesty would gladly facilitate the repeal of the embargo as "a measure of inconvenient restriction upon the American people."[32] As Coxe surveyed what to him were the lamentable results of a once-promising policy, he turned more and more to the consideration of an alternative. He did not ponder long, and his predictable choice was consonant both with his recommendations as purveyor of public supplies and with his writings of the previous two decades. "We propose to the national government," he wrote in the *Democratic Press* on December 3, 1808, "the immediate consideration of *a system of legislative provisions for the permanent maintenance and advancement of foreign commerce*, or in common language *a well provisioned navigation act*: also the consideration of *a system of legislative provisions for the further introduction and permanent encouragement of American manufactures*."[33] His familiar proposals had no discernible effect on the administration, but Coxe, not easily deterred, awaited only a more propitious time to renew them. He did so in a lengthy pamphlet published in June 1809, three months after the inauguration of James Madison opened the possibility that a new administration might be more receptive to untried ideas.

As Jefferson's handpicked successor, Madison was assured of nomination and election. Despite a flurry of support for Vice-President George Clinton by New Yorkers and for James Monroe by a coterie of Virginians, Madison was easily the choice of the congressional caucus that met in January 1808 and, in view of the overwhelming national majority enjoyed by regular Republicans, was clearly an overmatch for the Federalist candidate, Charles Cotesworth Pinckney. Nevertheless, many Republican leaders, centering their attention on increasing factionalism in their own party and the reviviscence of Federalism, believed otherwise. Coxe, Madison's enthusiastic champion, was among those who were not so certain of the election's outcome, largely because his vision was distorted by Pennsylvania politics. He shared his "uncomfortable anticipations" with Joel Barlow, to whom he wrote in January 1808 that "such is the effect of political alliances and hostilities, that I will not answer for the conduct of Pennsylvania upon the subject of President."[34]

32. George Canning to William Pinkney, Sept. 13, 1808, *American State Papers, Foreign Affairs*, III, 231.
33. [Coxe], "Foreign Commerce and Domestic Manufactures," *Demo. Press*, Dec. 3, 1808. Attributed to Coxe in Samuel Montgomery to Coxe, Dec. 20, 1808, Coxe Papers.
34. Coxe to Barlow, Jan. 7, 1808, Coxe Papers. See also Barlow to Coxe, Mar. 20, May 15, July 3, 1808, *ibid.*

Coxe was, however, willing to do all he could to assure what he regarded as his state's proper conduct on the subject. Ending his three-year moratorium on partisan activity, he vigorously championed the candidacy of both Madison and Simon Snyder, the Republican gubernatorial candidate in Pennsylvania. Thus it was that he served as secretary of the Republican committee of his ward in Philadelphia, drawing up a public statement hailing Snyder as "honest and enlightened," lauding Madison, and praising the embargo as a "just and wise" way both of avoiding war (which he did not really believe) and of establishing manufactures (which he desired by whatever means).[35] He also turned again to his familiar tactic of smothering the opposition by thousands of words of partisan abuse. His chief target was James Ross, again as in 1799 the Federalist candidate for governor. Ross was the subject of a widely distributed pamphlet in which Coxe provided a catalog of grievous offenses as long as Ross's public career. By grossly exaggerating the Federalist's influence in the Senate and by using manifestly absurd reasoning, Coxe held Ross responsible for the crisis in Anglo-American relations, as well as for virtually every instance of alleged congressional misbehavior—the abolition of district judgeships in Kentucky and Tennessee, "perpetual taxes," excessive public expenses, "indecent hostility" to the western country, the sanction of *"Connecticut pretensions"* to Pennsylvania soil, and a host of other misdeeds. It all added up to a sorry performance.[36]

Coxe found an outlet for his verbal assaults in the *Democratic Press*, a newly established Philadelphia newspaper. John Binns, the editor, not only was receptive to Coxe's views but was willing to allow him as many columns as he wished. A refugee from English political persecution, Binns had come to Pennsylvania in 1801, settling in Northumberland County. There he established the *Republican Argus*, which became one of the state's most popular newspapers. Fortunately for his future career, he also developed a warm relationship with Simon Snyder. It was largely to further Snyder's gubernatorial candidacy that the editor moved to Philadelphia and with William Duane's blessings began publication of the *Democratic Press* on March 27, 1807. But as the new journal increasingly weaned away large numbers of the *Aurora*'s previous subscribers and as Binns emerged as a weighty contender for power in Republican politics, Duane withdrew his support and, following a slashing attack in the *Democratic Press* on Michael Leib, launched a crusade to discredit his journalistic rival. For once Duane had

35. *Demo. Press*, July 18, 1808. Additional resolutions were drawn up at subsequent meetings of the Republican committee and published on Sept. 21, Oct. 22, 1808, *ibid.*

36. [Coxe], *An Address to the Citizens of Pennsylvania, on the Situation of our Country: connected with the Public Conduct of James Ross, a Candidate for the Governmental Chair of Pennsylvania. By a Pennsylvanian* (Philadelphia, 1808). For Coxe's authorship, see Barlow to Coxe, May 15, July 3, 1808, Coxe Papers.

met his match (in shrewd political management, though not in scurrility), and Binns's political power was cemented in 1808 by the landslide victory of his friend Snyder, who like his predecessor would serve three successive terms as governor and to whom the *Aurora* had given only lukewarm support. Such a development was doubly pleasing to Coxe—not only had the assassin of his own character been successfully challenged, but the newspaper that had bested Duane was open to his own writings. And there is every reason to believe that during the campaign of 1808 he contributed frequently, just as he continued over succeeding years to fill its pages with articles on diplomacy and the American economy.[37]

Not that in 1808 the Republicans were in great need of journalistic supporters. Although there were problems aplenty, the party's solid majority appeared disinclined to hold the Jeffersonian administration accountable, and what they would not do, their opponents could not do. Nevertheless, had the Federalists been able to mount more than just a token opposition, the election might well have been a solemn referendum on Jeffersonian diplomacy, especially since the embargo seemed to be bringing the nation's once-booming economy to a standstill as the campaign progressed. However, excepting the fierce and strident opposition in New England and New York, the nation appeared, as in 1796 and 1800, to be preoccupied instead with uncloaking and publicly exposing covert sympathy for England or for France. Coxe, more adept than most at such detections and firmly believing in Federalist recidivism, was convinced that a resurgent opposition party, made up of English partisans, would crown its likely victory at the polls by a union with England.

A Federalist victory was, in fact, as unlikely as reunion with England was phantasmal, and on election day Madison and Clinton won handily, securing 122 electoral votes to 47 for Pinckney and Rufus King. The Republicans also continued in control of Congress, though their majority in the House was reduced. The vote marked a decline in the strength of the Republican party but certainly no threat to its national ascendancy. As long as the administration's experiment in economic self-sacrifice did not become, as Jefferson appeared to hope it might, the permanent basis of American foreign policy, Republican control seemed assured.

Already it was manifest that instead of wringing concessions from

---

37. John Binns, *Recollections of the Life of John Binns; . . . Written by Himself . . .* (Philadelphia, 1854). In his *Recollections*, Binns not only failed to credit Coxe's contributions to the *Demo. Press* but virtually ignored their longtime relationship. Instead, the editor chose to picture himself as among the first and most prominent proponents of manufactures, thus overlooking Coxe's pioneering advocacy and the scores of articles he wrote on the subject for the *Demo. Press*. For allusions to Coxe's writings during the campaign of 1808, see David Jackson to Coxe, Aug. 12, 1807, Thomas Leiper to Coxe, Aug. 1808, Coxe Papers; Coxe to "Editor of *Gazette of the U.S.*," *Demo. Press*, Dec. 29, 1808.

England the embargo had wrought massive unrest at home. In New England the threat of secession was ominous; elsewhere in the nation many of the administration's most loyal supporters were, in the face of Jefferson's approaching retirement, on the brink of revolt. Bowing to popular demand, Congress on March 1, 1809, repealed the embargo, substituting a nonintercourse act that legalized American commerce with all parts of the world except those under British and French control. It also mischievously stipulated that whenever either of the belligerents showed proper respect for neutral rights, trade with that nation would be renewed. The nation was still committed to economic coercion, but, as Marshall Smelser has remarked, "Jefferson's search for a bloodless substitute for war had ended in an auctioneer's cry by the Congress, which asked Britain and France to bid against each other for American favor."[38]

Coxe thoroughly opposed the new measure. Writing in the *Democratic Press*, he attacked the expedient of nonintercourse in a series of seven articles published shortly before Congress adopted it.[39] But persuaded that firm presidential leadership could turn Congress from its mistaken course, he pinned his hopes on the possibility that the new president would now endorse policies to salvage the national honor that patently had been sacrificed for profits by the nonintercourse act.

Instead, Madison opted for a policy of drift. His inaugural address of March 4, 1809, was so vague it could have given comfort to all except committed war hawks. Delivered in a low and nervously hesitant voice that made its words virtually inaudible, the address affirmed the familiar tenets of Jeffersonian diplomacy—"peace and friendly intercourse with all nations having corresponding dispositions" and a preference for "amicable discussion and reasonable accommodation of differences," not for war. Since not even Coxe, an expert exegete of presidential pronouncements, could infer much from such platitudes, he was rather more buoyed by Madison's conditional promise "to promote by all authorized means improvements friendly to . . . manufactures"—a promise the president personally pledged by wearing clothing manufactured in America from domestic wool.[40]

Convinced that Madison shared his own favorite economic panacea, Coxe was also hopeful that the new president might be persuaded to adopt the necessary policies. It was to further this happy prospect that he prepared in June 1809 *A Memoir on the Subject of a Navigation Act*. The indispensable condition for a revival of American commerce, Coxe asserted, was a

38. Marshall Smelser, *The Democratic Republic, 1801–1815* (New York, 1968), 179.

39. [Coxe], "An Estimate of the Times," *Demo. Press*, Feb. 9, 10, 11, 13, 14, 15, 16, 1809. For Coxe's authorship, see Binns to Coxe, Feb. 9, 1809, Coxe Papers.

40. Richardson, ed., *Messages and Papers of the Presidents*, I, 467. For the manner of Madison's address, see *Nat. Intelligencer*, Mar. 6, 1809.

flourishing merchant marine, "necessary to agriculture and defence" but "beneficial, and indeed requisite, to manufactures." In the best of all possible worlds the United States, protected by the beneficial operation of automatic laws, might endorse "the universal freedom of trade." Unfortunately the new nation was confronted by one of the worst possible commercial worlds, one in which foreign nations were "jealous and intelligent rivals," "unfeeling monopolizers" intent on finding ways to "lull, deceive, or coerce their improvident neighbours." For this state of things there was only one solution: "The wisdom and goodness of a parental government" that "shall save us from . . . evils," present and future. To Coxe there were no legal impediments to such paternalism; he believed the Constitution to be "predicated on the propriety, utility and necessity of a system of trade laws, founded on correct and fixed principles."[41]

Beset by hostile nations abroad and a laggard economy at home, America must, Coxe said, fulfill its own destiny, separating itself from foreign evils by using economic weapons forged in Europe. It "has really become absolutely necessary," he insisted, to adopt "*a wise system of laws,* . . . digested in the form of '*a Navigation Act*'" for the support of American trade, commerce, and manufactures. To this end he sketched out the specific provisions such an act should include, recommendations similar to those he had made to both Hamilton and Jefferson in the early 1790s and had repeated many times since.[42]

It was a sensible, even a statesmanlike, solution to an international crisis that most of his fellow citizens viewed as susceptible to resolution only by the extreme alternatives of abject surrender or a declaration of war. Perhaps the result of Coxe's prescription would in any event have been a war, but the decision would at least have been up to England. And had she chosen to fight, the Americans, aware of their own resolutely peaceable defense of their rights, might well have then enthusiastically rallied to the aid of their country. Since Coxe's policy was not tried, one cannot know; it is only certain that, rudderless, the nation drifted toward a war it finally felt obliged to declare and halfheartedly to fight.

41. [Coxe], *A Memoir on the Subject of a Navigation Act, Including the Encouragement of the Manufactory of Boats and Sea Vessels, and the Protection of Mariners* (Philadelphia, 1809), 5, 7, 8.
42. *Ibid.*, 9.

24

The Embattled Purveyor

Madison's inauguration on March 4, 1809, heralded no significant changes either in domestic policy or in foreign affairs. It rather represented the replacement of a philosopher-statesman who had proved himself a consummate politician by a fellow Virginian who was to prove himself unsuited to the exacting demands of party and presidential leadership. A longtime acquaintance of both, Coxe anticipated no shifts in policy, but he may well have hoped that the new secretary, who was appointed on March 9, would reform the War Department. At least as far as the purveyor's office was concerned, he was not disappointed.

William Eustis was, like his predecessor, a New England physician with Revolutionary War service and congressional experience. His appointment as secretary of war was primarily owing to the president's desire to acquire a geographically balanced cabinet, but, unlike Henry Dearborn, Eustis brought to the secretaryship an administrative energy and skill that belie the stereotype perpetuated by generations of historians. The traditional viewpoint was expressed in the comment by James R. Jacobs, who wrote of Eustis that he "had only a second-rate mind that dwelt on petty things; most of the time he thought in terms of schemes rather than principles. . . . As secretary of war, he was a piddling incompetent."[1] Perhaps in some matters he was, but not in his supervision of the purveyorship.

Whenever possible Eustis promptly advanced money requested by Coxe, even if some scrambling of appropriations was necessary. He did not, like Dearborn, await the purveyor's requests for directions but in cases of importance foresaw them. He thoughtfully pondered and replied to Coxe's

1. Jacobs, *Beginning of U.S. Army*, 383.

various proposals for the reform of the supply service, and himself paid careful attention to comparative prices (especially between domestic and foreign articles) and to the quality of goods supplied. He attempted, though unsuccessfully, to provide an adequate clerical staff for the purveyor's office. He uniformly cooperated not only in assuring the proper inspection of arms but also in providing suitable models to be followed by inspectors. Most significant of all, he consistently granted the purveyor a wide degree of discretion —in the negotiation of contracts, in the rejection of proposals Coxe found unacceptable, in the selection of patterns and materials for army clothing and equipment, in the imposition of uniform standards, in the decision (so long as budgetarily possible) on the quantity of articles to be supplied, and in the cancellation of contracts or in the initiation of suits for their fulfillment.[2]

For Coxe such cooperativeness was a happy change from the policy of drift that had prevailed under Dearborn, but even more gratifying was Eustis's decisive intervention on his behalf in his running battle with Callender Irvine. This came in the summer of 1810 as the result of a conference between Eustis and Coxe in Philadelphia, where the secretary usually stopped over on his annual trip to New England. Whatever the purveyor said about his archrival must have been persuasive, for a month or so later Coxe opened the most satisfying official letter he had received in years: "You will be pleased to proceed in purchasing, causing to be made up, and *inspected*, and delivered over . . . for issuing the residue of Clothing for the present year," Eustis wrote in a directive that obliquely gave Coxe authority to instruct Irvine.[3] It was, in the event, a Pyrrhic victory, for Irvine, deeply resentful, would take his revenge two years later, and it would be for Coxe a cruel one. But for the moment, Coxe was at liberty to exercise the expanding duties of his office free of personal impediment and harassment.

Such a cordial and trustful relationship with Eustis may have been bound to deteriorate, if only because Coxe himself was not altogether innocent of the obstructionism and uncooperativeness he so consistently deplored when displayed by his official colleagues. Nor was he capable, as the

2. William Eustis to Coxe, Apr. 12, 24, May 22, 29, June 3, 28, Oct. 23, Dec. 19, 1809, Jan. 9, Feb. 1, 15, Mar. 20, Apr. 9, 23, June 12, 13, Dec. 5, 18, 24, 1810, Feb. 6, 23, Mar. 9, 13, Sept. 10, Oct. 15, 1811, Sec. of War Letterbook, R.G. 107.

3. Eustis to Coxe, Aug. 26, 1810, *ibid.*, italics added. See also Eustis to Coxe, Nov. 1, 1809, July 19, Dec. 11, 1810, Feb. 12, 1811, Eustis to Callender Irvine, Jan. 2, 1811, *ibid.* Even before the summer of 1810 Eustis had issued stern orders to Irvine to cooperate with the purveyor. On May 3, 1810, for example, he wrote the superintendent that "the Purveyor . . . must exercise a discretionary power in making his purchases. When he makes the best selection that the markets permit, although they are not entirely such as could have been wished, he is considered as having performed his duty. It is presumed that the inspector will make such allowances as circumstances, the public economy and the public service require." Eustis to Callender Irvine and Coxe, May 3, 1810, *ibid.* See also Eustis to Coxe, May 8, 1810, to Callender Irvine, June 5, 1810, *ibid.*

history of his relationships with Hamilton, Wolcott, and Dearborn attests, of long acknowledging the authority of a superior. The incapacity was partially the result of his irrepressible wish to be recognized as a uniquely talented and meritorious civil servant and also the result of his related and apparently incurable practice of writing a thousand words when a hundred might have done. To Eustis, who had expressed his confidence in Coxe's judgment by granting him wide discretion, the latter trait became increasingly irritating. Acknowledging no less than twelve letters from Coxe over a brief span of time, the secretary, on January 23, 1811, curtly informed his purveyor that this was about a dozen too many. "The correspondence of this Office at this time is so voluminous and the calls for information from Congress so frequent," he complained, "that it is found impossible to travel through and answer the details embraced in your communications." The efficient conduct of business, he sagely remarked, demanded that only "principal and essential points . . . requisite to the due execution of your duties . . . should be brought under the notice of this office." Perhaps six years of Dearborn's lackadaisical secretaryship had instilled in Coxe habits he was unable to break. In any event, as letters from the purveyor's office continued to pour into Eustis's office, he replied in letters that were increasingly querulous and critical of Coxe.[4] The latter, in turn, reacted by blaming the secretary for not solving problems that were, in fact, beyond his power to control, notably Congress's dilatory handling of money bills and the unpredictability of the size of appropriations.

From the beginning, the uncertainty of congressional appropriations had occasioned inconveniences for the purveyor, who was thereby precluded from making advance contracts or from taking advantage of the Philadelphia market when it was well supplied. Nor could he, in view of the enactment of appropriation bills toward the end of the session (usually in February or March but sometimes as late as May), procure army supplies scheduled for delivery in late spring or early summer of the same year. As it was, large quantities of clothing had to be so speedily procured that careful inspection was virtually impossible: lightweight uniforms reached the troops in time for autumn chills, advantageous purchases were lost because of the inability to command ready money, and the delivery of urgently needed hospital supplies was delayed.[5]

An obvious solution was proposed by Coxe: the allocation of funds appropriated in one year for the purchase and manufacture of clothing

---

4. Eustis to Coxe, Jan. 23, 1811, *ibid.* See also Eustis to Coxe, Aug. 4, 1810, Apr. 16, June 24, Sept. 12, Nov. 15, 29, 1811, *ibid.*

5. Coxe to Henry Dearborn, Nov. 6, 1806, Purveyors Letterbooks, R.G. 92; Coxe to Eustis, Jan. 2, Mar. 6, 1810, Coxe Papers. Complaining in Oct. 1806 that the appropriation had not reached his office until Apr., Coxe advised the secretary of war that "it would be well if congress

requisite for the succeeding year. Bowing to the purveyor's persistence, Eustis submitted such a recommendation to Congress in February 1810, convincingly arguing that its adoption would allow the purveyor "to publish proposals and make his contracts" in a way calculated to promote "a spirit of competition," to assure the offer of "ample supplies . . . on terms equally advantageous with . . . imported cloths," and thus also to encourage domestic manufactures. Apparently viewing annual appropriations in somewhat the same manner as the preceding generation had viewed annual elections, Republican congressmen were unwilling to endorse this sensible solution, leaving Eustis and Coxe to solve the puzzle of how to make timely and advantageous purchases while holding an empty money bag.[6]

Coxe found such restrictions exasperating. Although willing to grant all due "submission to superior authority," he was nevertheless shocked and deeply annoyed at this refusal to adopt a mild reform expressly designed to make possible the efficient supply of "sound and fit clothing for ten thousand men," to him a "moderate provision" in a country as rich in resources as America. As things were, he wrote in June 1810, a few months after Congress had turned down the proposed administrative reform, "the appropriations of Money to purchase so late as March, the delay of patterns," and the necessity of hurriedly inspecting "240,000 pieces of goods or garments . . . and other circumstances" occasioned a tardy, inadequate supply of clothing.[7]

Although there was nothing more Eustis could do to correct the timing of appropriations, he was at least intent on remodeling the civilian supply service established in 1802. He pointed out to Congress the need for such an arrangement in a communication of May 31, 1809, and submitted specific proposals on January 1 of the following year. Observing that he had hitherto been "obliged to perform the duties of Quartermaster General," a laborious and time-consuming assignment, Eustis proposed that a quartermaster department be established to replace the system of military agents. A committee of the Senate, impressed by the secretary's accompanying argu-

---

would give in December, whatever they have no doubt about. Indeed this falls importations are important to good purchases," though many articles "are now much exhausted by private purchases. Late appropriations," he concluded, "always occasion delay and loss of advantage in purchases." Coxe to Dearborn, Oct. 30, 1806, *ibid.*

6. Eustis to William B. Giles, Feb. 4, 1810, *American State Papers, Military Affairs*, I, 258. For Congress to have approved such a measure would not have been unprecedented, however. As Eustis wrote to Giles, "On contracts for provisions made . . . by this Department, and on other contracts requiring a large capital, it has been customary to make advances of money . . . to enable the contractors to fulfil their engagements." Feb. 4, 1810, *ibid.*

7. Coxe to Eustis, May 14, 1810, to John Boyd, June 5, 1810, Coxe Papers.

ment that "to meet a war without such a department . . . justly denominated the right hand of any army, would be to disregard the practice and experience of our own and every other nation," brought in on March 12, 1810, a bill tailored to the secretary of war's specifications.[8] However, since it was not designed to punish Tench Coxe, it was not cut to the pattern desired by Senator Michael Leib. As a result of Leib's insistence and parliamentary maneuvers, the measure was referred to a select committee, consisting of himself, Timothy Pickering (another Coxe opponent), and Joseph Anderson, a former Pennsylvanian and now senator from Tennessee. Thus stacked, the committee on April 7 brought in an amended bill calling for the abolition of the purveyorship; this was adopted on April 16, 1810, and sent to the House, where on the following day it was read twice and committed.[9]

Coxe, who had followed the progress of the measure through the Senate with mounting disbelief, was flabbergasted at this unforeseen development and at the unsuspected influence wielded by a coterie of his implacable enemies. Confirmation of the scheming came from his longtime friend Senator Nicholas Gilman of New Hampshire, who wrote that his own hopes that the section of the bill abolishing the purveyorship would be deleted had been disappointed by "several members with whom that appeared to be an important point." The success of Coxe's opponents in a body consisting of thirty-four senators was to Coxe incredible enough, but more astonishing yet was the seeming acquiescence of the secretary of war, whose firm support the purveyor had been confident of. Was he mistaken, he asked in a confidential letter addressed to Eustis in mid-April? Eustis replied that his respect for Coxe was undiminished. He had not known of the proposal to abolish the purveyorship until it had been incorporated in the quartermaster bill and upon learning of it had opposed it. Unlike Coxe's congressional informants, however, Eustis did not attribute its adoption to Leib and the purveyor's other personal enemies but rather "to the sentiment common to the army and government that justice has not been done in the cloathing department." Although Eustis's almost impenetrable syntax leaves the modern reader in doubt, he appears to have shared the sentiment. It is impossible, however, to say whether he blamed himself, Coxe, or other officials. In any case, Eustis did not intend to intercede on Coxe's behalf. As far as he was concerned, congressional measures, whether he liked them or not, were "pursued according to the will and wisdom of those to whom the constitution has confided them."[10]

8. *American State Papers, Military Affairs*, I, 244, 256–257.

9. *Annals of Cong.*, XX, 657. The Senate measure provided that responsibility for purchasing be assigned to the newly authorized quartermaster general. For details of the Senate bill, see Mathew Carey to Coxe, Apr. 24, 1810, Coxe Papers.

10. Nicholas Gilman to Coxe, Apr. 23, 1810, Eustis to Coxe, Apr. 27, 1810, Coxe Papers.

Coxe emphatically did not think that the decision was wise, nor did he believe that the will of the legislature was beyond control. Convinced that others could do what Eustis would not, he hastily rounded up a group of influential lobbyists—his brother Daniel W. Coxe, who was in Washington to testify before a congressional committee, his friend Mathew Carey, who was conveniently there on business, and Joel Barlow, whom Coxe hoped would intercede on his behalf with the president. Barlow presumably did not consult with Madison, but Carey did.[11] The president, however, curtly refused to come to the aid of the embattled purveyor, perhaps because he was weary of Tench Coxe, both as a symbol of divisiveness in the Republican party and as an importunately insistent office seeker. Many congressmen were also undoubtedly tired of Coxe's energetic campaign to save a comparatively minor post, but they were given no opportunity to express their dissatisfaction. The quartermaster bill never reached the floor of the House, and with Congress's adjournment on May 1 it was buried.

Coxe had been granted a reprieve, but the purveyorship was in jeopardy as long as Leib remained in Congress. On December 27, 1810, soon after the convening of the final session of the Eleventh Congress, the doctor rose in the Senate and "gave notice that tomorrow he should ask leave to bring in a bill for the establishment of a quartermaster's department."[12] That it, like the measure he had sponsored the previous April, would include a provision abolishing the purveyorship was rendered certain when on December 31 it was referred to a select committee chaired by himself and once again including Timothy Pickering, along with a senatorial lightweight, Jesse Franklin of North Carolina.

To Coxe the attack was purgatory revisited, and it was problematical whether his allies in Washington could save him this time. At Coxe's behest Senator Gilman conferred with Eustis, reporting that "his interposition in favor of your Office will probably be withheld from an apprehension of loosing a favorite Bill." If so, the New Hampshire man wrote to Coxe on January 7, "there is too much reason to fear" that the measure, including the proviso calling for the abolition of the purveyor's office, would be adopted.[13] Other congressional supporters were equally pessimistic, and Coxe, lacking his on-the-scene lobbyists of the previous spring, attempted

---

Coxe's letter of inquiry to Eustis has not been found. Its contents can be inferred from Eustis's reply of Apr. 27, 1810, *ibid.*

11. See Joel Barlow to James Madison, Apr. 25, 1810, Barlow to Coxe, Apr. 28, 1810, Carey to Coxe, Apr. 24, 25, 26, 29, 1810, Daniel W. Coxe to Coxe, Apr. 26, 30, May 1, 1810, *ibid.*

12. *Annals of Cong.*, XXII, 36.

13. Gilman to Coxe, Jan. 7, 1811, Coxe Papers. On other congressional reactions, see, for example, William Findley to Coxe, Jan. 15, 1811, *ibid.*

to come to his own rescue by addressing to Congress a pamphlet-length defense of the purveyorship. But before there was time to have it printed and distributed, he was obliged to defend himself against an attack from another, though not unexpected, quarter.

This new offensive came from William Duane, Leib's political partner and stoutest journalistic supporter, who had awaited only a propitious moment to lend the congressional crusade against Coxe the powerful support of the *Aurora*. By mid-January, as his ally's quartermaster bill neared a decisive debate in a Committee of the Whole, Duane decided that moment had arrived. When Coxe picked up the *Aurora* on Monday morning, January 14, 1811, and began reading an article entitled "The Military Establishment," he must have been first indignant and then increasingly angry. For six years, Duane wrote, he had "meditated to take up this subject" but had delayed the project while he "digested the technical knowledge . . . which those who have had experience only can be competent to appreciate." The purpose of his assiduous research was obviously to discredit Coxe, and in this first installment of a promised series, the editor made it clear that he would persist until his object was obtained, even if the pages of the *Aurora* forwent the publication of all else. His grand theme, he announced, would be *"arms and the man,"* subjects that were "really the keys of military information." He proposed to center on the topic of "the *fitness* of arms for the use of man in war." No one who read these introductory paragraphs could have doubted what he really intended to do: on Coxe would be pinned the responsibility for the sad state of American armaments; to Coxe would be assigned the blame for every flaw in the military establishment Duane could discover or invent.

The accusation concerning arms was potentially devastating. Duane had seen and examined weapons *"which had been manufactured for the* MONEY (*for we cannot say the use*) *of the United States"* that *"were better equipped to kill American soldiers into whose hands they should be put, than an enemy."*[14] Who was responsible? Those among the *Aurora*'s readers who were well informed about the procedures for supplying the army would surely have replied "the secretary of war and the inspectors of arms." But Duane, jumping beyond logic or plausibility, promised to prove that it was rather the purveyor of public supplies who was guilty of criminal misconduct. Just how he would pull off this trick the wily editor did not immediately say. Employing the journalistic techniques of which he was a master, he approached his goal circuitously—by first proving that the arms were in fact faulty and then showing that the secretary and the inspectors were innocent, Duane would clearly indict the purveyor as the real culprit.

14. *Aurora*, Jan. 14, 1811.

Although a decade earlier Coxe had tutored Duane, the pupil had long since outstripped his former partner and patron in the art of character assassination. Coxe's initial reply, designed "to prevent misconceptions and to remove errors," was dispassionate, objective, and convincing. Although conceding that the nation afforded far too few qualified inspectors and that, regrettably, a few of them may have made mistakes, Coxe emphatically insisted that no uninspected arms had ever been shipped to the army, that the inspectors of arms were "as independent of the controul of the purveyor as the chief justice of the United States" and that he had never in any way interfered in the carrying out of their assignment.[15] Coxe believed it to be his duty to defend himself against the *Aurora*'s slanderous accusations, but no matter how persuasive his rebuttal, it was certain to afford Duane a pretext for publishing thousands and thousands of additional words. True to form, the editor announced two days after Coxe's reply was printed that in view of the purveyor's remarks he felt obliged to enlarge the scope of his own inquiry and "to take up the subject" of the supply service "generally." He planned to point out "some gross and fatal errors in the very inception of the military system," errors that "tend to render the progress of the United States *a progress backward*." Charging that such retrogression was primarily the fault of Coxe, whose conduct as purveyor "had been employed not to the use but to the great *discredit of the government*," Duane pledged himself to devote the pages of the *Aurora* to adducing unassailable proof of the accusation.[16]

Duane's real objective was to continue the assault on Coxe as long as there was a possibility that he might promote the success of Senator Leib's bill providing for the abolition of the purveyorship. That measure was taken up by a Committee of the Whole on January 16, 1811, and, to the glee of its sponsor and Duane, the body voted to have the bill engrossed and read a third time. A few days later, however, Coxe learned from a friendly Pennsylvania congressman that the bill had been postponed until June of the same year, which was another way of "virtually rejecting it" and was "a great disappointment to your *friend* Leib."[17] What had reversed the seemingly irreversible tide in favor of the doctor's cherished proposal? Perhaps Leib himself did not know, but certainly he would not have credited the published defense of the purveyorship that Coxe had arranged to have placed

15. *Ibid*. Coxe's reply appeared on the same day as the first installment of William Duane's articles on "The Military Establishment" because a few days earlier Duane had alluded in the *Aurora* to his intention to publish such a series. Finding Coxe's article evasive and thus an easy target, Duane elected to publish it simultaneously with the first of his own attacks. He did not again, however, publish any of Coxe's replies.

16. *Ibid*., Jan. 16, 1811. The issue is misdated Jan. 15, 1811.

17. *Annals of Cong*., XXII, 98; John Porter to Coxe, Jan. 19, 1811, Coxe Papers. See also Nicholas Gilman to Coxe, Jan. 18, 1811, *ibid*.

on the desk of every member of Congress.[18] Given the intangible effect of such things, perhaps he was right. In any event, Leib had lost a skirmish rather than the war. A revised battle plan was ready when the next Congress assembled.

The electorate sent many new faces to the Congress that convened on November 11, 1811, among them a group of ultranationalists familiarly, though somewhat inaccurately, known to historians as war hawks. Representing for the most part the West and the lower South—new states or frontier regions of the old ones—they were (or so historical tradition has it) ready to salvage the national honor by war, if need be. Despite their minority status and comparative youth, the militants succeeded in electing Henry Clay of Kentucky as Speaker of the House. By packing all important committees with fellow hawks, Clay promptly launched a program of national preparedness.

Military preparedness was long overdue. Madison, like Jefferson, had risked war by a policy of commercial retaliation while undermining its successful prosecution by insisting on a peacetime military establishment, thus maundering toward a rendezvous the nation perhaps did not want and was certainly unprepared to keep. In August 1809 the administration had been obliged to restore nonintercourse with Great Britain after Foreign Secretary George Canning disavowed a treaty negotiated by his own envoy in Washington. In the spring of the following year, on the eve of the expiration of the nonintercourse act, Congress passed an impetuous and mischievous substitute known as Macon's Bill Number Two. Reopening trade with both Britain and France, this measure provided that whenever either nation agreed to revoke its restrictions, the United States would then cease to trade with the other.

For the succeeding ten months American shipping, operating largely

---

18. Coxe, *Respectful Observations on the subject of the bill in relation to "the establishment of a quartermaster's department" in lieu of the existing military agencies, so far as it may affect the office of the Purveyor of Public Supplies* (n.p., n.d.). That it was published in Jan. 1811 is established by William Findley's letter to Coxe, Feb. 5, 1811, Coxe Papers. Conceding at the outset that there were compelling reasons for a change in the system, Coxe attempted to demonstrate the impracticability of handing over responsibility for the procurement of supplies to the proposed quartermaster department. So to enlarge its traditional and proper duties of storage, transportation, and distribution, he wrote, would "ensure the continuance and the extension of those embarrassments and evils which are supposed to have occasioned a desire for a wise and effectual reform of the system" and render public supplies "dearer, more irregular, more uncertain and less proper." More than that. Since such a combination of duties had "never been attempted or effected in any country," even in one "where a great variety of established manufactures and a certain and uninterrupted commerce facilitate supplies," how much less desirable would it be "in a very extensive . . . and remarkably diversified" nation like the United States. Coxe also answered Duane's attacks on the office of the purveyor and on himself in a series of five newspaper articles that appeared in the *Demo. Press*, Jan. 15, 19, 22, 31, Feb. 2, 1811.

under British licenses, once again flourished. Napoleon, dismayed, managed with transparent guile to persuade Madison that France was prepared to repeal her decrees. Although the offer was hedged about with conditions that rendered it meaningless, the president walked into the trap, carrying Congress with him. On November 2, 1810, he announced that unless Britain rescinded her obnoxious orders-in-council within three months, nonintercourse would be resumed. When the stipulated deadline came and went with no favorable response, Madison, despite abundant evidence of French spoliations of American commerce, proclaimed on March 2, 1811, a ban on further intercourse with England. This time the island kingdom was hard hit, and within a year commercial retaliation achieved what the embargo had failed to accomplish. But before news of the repeal of the orders-in-council reached Washington, the United States had already declared war.

Anticipating war, the Congress that sat from November 1811 to July 1812 had belatedly adopted a program of national defense. Although Coxe applauded the adoption of measures to improve and enlarge the country's military establishment, the big question to him was what steps would be taken to alter the system of military supply. His anxiety may have been shared by Eustis, who directed Coxe early in December 1811 "to repair to the seat of government," ostensibly to consult on measures for "making an immediate provision to procure additional supplies."[19] Certainly they conferred, but the major part of Coxe's stay in Washington was taken up with lobbying and preparing handbills and articles supporting the retention of his office.

Coxe knew before he left Philadelphia that he would need every stratagem he could devise to counter the apparent determination of the Senate to include the demolition of the purveyorship in its program for remodeling the supply service. Enemy number one was still Dr. Leib, who this time did not himself have to introduce the requisite legislation but only to promote the passage of a bill. The quartermaster bill was again introduced early in December by a committee headed by Senator Giles of Virginia. Coxe's hopes that this measure, like its twin of the preceding session, would be defeated were deflated by Jonathan Roberts, his most steadfast congressional supporter. Roberts reminded him that though Leib's influence might not appear so formidable, he was, in fact, capable of achieving "by management" what he was incapable of obtaining "from weight of character." The man against whom the doctor directed his enmity, Roberts admonished, should, if "prudent," be ever "on the watch."[20] Alertness was

---

19. Eustis to Coxe, Dec. 10, 1811, Sec. of War Letterbook, R.G. 107.
20. Jonathan Roberts to Coxe, Dec. 17, 1811, Coxe Papers.

the more imperative, as Coxe well knew, in view of the powerful journalistic support that Leib would receive.

When news reached the offices of the Philadelphia *Aurora* that the quartermaster bill introduced by Giles had passed its second reading and was scheduled for debate on December 19, William Duane did not need to be reminded by Leib that the time was right for again trotting out the weapons against Coxe. From December 20, 1811, until February of the new year the *Aurora*'s subscribers read of little but the purveyor's criminal conduct.[21] The initial numbers of Duane's exercise in billingsgate reached Coxe in Washington just before Christmas 1811. Although he would have preferred to ignore the attack, Coxe feared that the *Aurora*'s assault might undermine his strenuous efforts to persuade Congress to retain the purveyorship, and he felt obliged to acknowledge the article. His reply took the form of a broadside, dated Washington, January 4, 1812, and was intended primarily for distribution among congressmen. He strove to set the record straight by answering Duane's more flagrant charges, concluding with indisputable accuracy that "to allow men to see charges, to confront witnesses, and to examine testimony does not accord with William Duane's ideas of liberty, justice, law or humanity."[22]

Hopeful that his anti-Coxe campaign would have the desired effect on Congress, Duane was unbothered by legal niceties. His confidence had been buoyed by Senate passage on December 31 of the quartermaster bill, but there remained the more difficult assignment of assuring its adoption by the House, where a year and a half earlier a similar measure had been consigned to the table. Among Coxe's friends in the House was the chairman of the select committee to which the Senate measure was referred, David R. Williams, a South Carolina newspaper editor, planter, and cotton manufacturer. Either the committee's other members were also Coxe sympathizers or Williams was persuasive, for the Senate bill underwent a number of modifications. The major one was explained by Williams on January 16 in a speech introducing the handiwork of his committee to the House and explaining the amendments proposed. The Senate bill, he said, "was predicated on the destruction of the office of the Purveyor of Public Supplies . . . and contemplates the establishment in its place not only of a Quartermaster General of the United States, but a commissary general in the same person." In an argument that was virtually the same as Coxe had presented in his published defense of the purveyorship a year earlier, Williams went on to say that the duties of a quartermaster and a commissary general were "per-

---

21. For a sampling of these attacks, see *Aurora*, Dec. 20, 1811, Jan. 20, 21, 1812.
22. "To the Public," Jan. 4, 1812, Coxe Papers.

fectly distinct" and never were "blended in any country in the world." The quartermaster should be a military man, and the commissary general, "a man well acquainted with mercantile concerns." Williams must have told the House what it was predisposed to believe, for after a brief debate during which only two representatives objected, a bill salvaging Coxe's office was adopted in mid-January and returned to the Senate.[23]

William Duane still hoped that the Senate, shrewdly managed by Leib and influenced by the *Aurora*'s propaganda, might be persuaded to undo what Coxe's friends had contrived, even though the House increasingly appeared determined to retain the purveyorship. Duane accordingly expanded his anti-Coxe crusade, tiresomely devoting almost every issue of the *Aurora* to it. But neither this nor Coxe's lengthy rejoinders had any measurable effect on the fate of his office, which was instead abolished by congressional legerdemain. The magician, of course, was Michael Leib.[24]

When the House of Representatives' version of the quartermaster bill providing for the retention of the purveyorship was sent to the Senate on January 17, 1811, it was debated for several days and then referred to a select committee consisting of Smith of Maryland, Giles, and Leib. The committee predictably insisted on the abolition of Coxe's post, but, presumably wishing to avoid a collision with the House that might result in no bill at all, they accomplished their goal by the shrewdest parliamentary trick of the session. On February 6 Smith moved that the quartermaster bill (as amended by the House) be postponed until the following December and, scarcely pausing for breath, "reported as a substitute for the bill last mentioned" a new quartermaster bill euphemistically entitled an act "in addition to the Military Establishment of the United States." The disingenuous substitute was designed to counter House objections to the Senate's previous quartermaster bills. Instead of confiding responsibility for supply of the army to one official, it provided for two—a quartermaster general and a commissary general. By assigning the latter responsibility for purchasing, the office of purveyor became redundant and was accordingly abolished. After the adoption of minor amendments, the bill was passed on February 24 and sent to the House, whose members were presumably aware of having been outfoxed. But they could scarcely refuse to vote for the very arrangement on which, the abolition of the purveyorship excepted, they had insisted.[25]

"The Senate seem determined to legislate you out of office," Jonathan Roberts astutely observed to Coxe, "for if they can make you pass

23. *Annals of Cong.*, XXIII, 795–796, 801–803. See also David R. Williams to Coxe, Nov. 30, Dec. 6, 1816, Coxe Papers.

24. Coxe defended himself in a series of long articles entitled "To the Public" in the *Demo. Press*, Jan. 21, 22, 24, 25, 28, Feb. 1, 1812.

25. *Annals of Cong.*, XXIII, 114, 116, 120, 121, 126–127.

their ordeal they think they can dispose of you." Roberts, along with other of Coxe's more steadfast friends, fought a determined rearguard action in the House. Arguing with convincing logic "that no good purpose could be answered by the proposed change" from a purveyor to a commissary general, they resorted to one parliamentary stratagem after another, but it was all to no avail. With the nation hovering on the precipice of war, most congressmen were unwilling to forgo reform of the military supply system merely to save the job of one man, and the bill smoothly sailed through both houses, becoming law on March 28.[26]

The establishment of a quartermaster department accomplished little except to remove Coxe from office. William Duane, although gleeful over the bill's passage, did perceive the basic flaw of the new legislation. It would, he said some months before its passage, make "confusion more confounded; . . . every step taken short of a total reorganization of the military system . . . will be like groping in the dark, or walking backward." Although perhaps not fairly open to the charge of retrogression, Congress pretended to march under a banner labeled reform, while it actually stood still. To replace the purveyorship, which was abolished effective May 31, 1812, the same office was established under another name—a commissary general of purchases. To replace the essentially civilian supply system (consisting of military agents and their assistants), Congress created a quartermaster department headed by a brigadier general and assisted by deputy and assistant deputy quartermasters, who might be either civilians or army officers. Except for these changes, the new system differed from the old only in its potential for greater confusion.[27] Fearful that it might give too much power to the military, Congress, in effect, "created a dual, overlapping and competing system of supply which was an administrative impossibility on its face." Could Coxe's hurt pride have been soothed, he would have been consoled by the reflection that with the establishment of a commissary of ordnance Congress had paid him the unintended compliment of replacing him with no less than three generals.[28]

Coxe was in no mood to seek either compliments or consolation

26. Roberts to Coxe, Feb. 12, 1812, Coxe Papers; *Annals of Cong.*, XXIV, 1212–1214; "An Act to establish the Quartermaster's Department," Mar. 28, 1812, *U.S. Statutes at Large*, II, 696–699.

27. *Aurora*, Jan. 21, 1812. The new system proved so unworkable that Congress a year later was obliged to pass a law authorizing the secretary of war to prescribe the supplies to be furnished by each official. See "An Act the better to provide for the supplies of the army of the United States, and for the accountability of persons entrusted with the same," Mar. 3, 1813, *U.S. Statutes at Large*, II, 816–818.

28. White, *The Jeffersonians*, 215; "An Act for the better regulation of the ordnance," May 14, 1812, *U.S. Statutes at Large*, II, 732–734.

prizes. In a gratuitous letter to Madison written while the quartermaster bill was still pending, he refused to accept the office of commissary general, a post that Madison had no intention of awarding a man toward whom Congress had repeatedly revealed itself implacably hostile. The president's first choice was Coxe's longtime friend, William Jones, best known as the notoriously inept president of the Second Bank of the United States from 1816 to 1819. Jones declined, and Madison's second nomination, Reuben Etting, was rejected by the Senate.[29] Having been twice rebuffed, Madison deferred another appointment by allowing temporary arrangements to be made by the secretary of war, who designated a minor civil servant as purchasing agent ad interim. Although there had still been dregs left in Coxe's cup of official humiliation, it was now drained: the deputy commissary who would temporarily take over the purveyor's duties was Coxe's own former chief clerk, Benjamin Mifflin.

Coxe's chagrin was even greater because of his successful exercise of the enormously increased duties that had been imposed upon the purveyor's office during his last six months in office. The increase had been due to the resolve of the militant Republican leadership of the Congress to prepare belatedly for war. During this seven-month period no less than thirty laws to strengthen the country's military establishment were enacted, among them a provision for the increase of the regular army by the addition of ten new regiments and a corps of artificers.[30] Numerous measures were enacted to make the armed services more attractive, including larger bounties, bonuses, and pensions, liberalized pay and travel stipend regulations, and more generous clothing allowances. The burden of supplying this enlarged army had fallen on Coxe, whose minuscule staff was scarcely adequate for furnishing the token force previously authorized by Congress. "My business was quadrupled and greatly diversified," Coxe wrote a year or so later. He had been obliged to work at night and on Sundays and to call on his sons for unpaid assistance. It had also been necessary to establish "permanent auxiliary agents in the Eastern, Northern, Middle and Southern states" for the purchase of various and numerous supplies. Also, in view of "the extreme press of business," there had not been time to instruct fully or to oversee carefully the operations of this expanded field service. Nevertheless, the requisite supplies had been procured, though, as Coxe said, at the expense of "an exertion in business of which before I did not think myself capable." Despite his pardonable resentment at having been so shabbily treated after a decade of striving to overcome almost insuperable handicaps, Coxe had

29. Coxe to Madison, Feb. 24, 1814, Coxe Papers.
30. Smelser, *Democratic Republic*, 226.

continued to exercise the duties of purveyor "with the utmost energy in my power . . . till 11 oClock at Night on the 31st. of May."[31]

As the end of Coxe's term had approached, however, the affairs of his office were thrown into a state of confusion and uncertainty. Should he continue purchases until the last day, thus assuming additional obligations that another official would have to discharge? What arrangements were to be made for winding up the business of the purveyorship? To whom was he to turn over the records of his office? To what extent would he be expected to assist his successor when appointed? To these and many other important questions he had received no satisfactory answers. Toward the end of May, so he recalled two years later, "I became extremely uneasy, lest the surrender of my office . . . should not be made before the 1st of June." Anticipating censure not only of himself but also of the Madison administration, he had written "a letter of the most earnest urgency" requesting explicit instructions. Instead, Eustis had elected to send a purposely evasive letter assuring Coxe "that every official act affecting your feelings and interests which the obligations of public duty impose on me is never unacquainted with proper sensations and reflections."[32]

So things stood when on the afternoon of Friday, May 29, an emissary from the War Department, one John McKinney, appeared at the purveyor's quarters and requested that Coxe turn over his official books and papers. This, to his later regret, he unhesitatingly agreed to do, and on the following day, news of Mifflin's appointment having reached him, he reluctantly surrendered his records to his former clerk, who "peremptorily required their being sent to his own House." Whatever misgivings Coxe had about this procedure were allayed by McKinney's assurance that he "should have from Washington orders for the full use of the Books and papers for settlement."[33] As he was soon to learn, Mifflin was not amenable to orders, at least if designed to assist Coxe.

Only the most intransigent antagonist or obtuse federal official could have assumed that the extensive and complicated business affairs of the purveyor's office could be ended at the stroke of midnight on a particular day. As Coxe explained, "the extreme and increasing urgency of supplies" in the spring of 1812 rendered it impossible for his small staff properly to post his ledgers and other account books. These needed to be brought up to date and carefully checked, and Coxe required free access to them for the

---

31. Coxe to Richard Harrison, Oct. 16, 1813, "Circular to Purchasing Agents," June 1812, Coxe to Madison, Dec. 16, 1812, Coxe Papers.

32. Coxe to Madison, Feb. 24, 1814, Eustis to Coxe, May 24, 1812, *ibid.*

33. Coxe to Madison, Feb. 24, 1814, *ibid.* See also Coxe to Eustis, June 1, 1812, "Circular to Purchasing Agents," June 1812, *ibid.*

settlement of outstanding accounts totaling well over a million dollars.[34] There were other questions that urgently required answers: Was he to answer the many letters concerning his purveyorship that daily arrived? Were the military agents and his own scattered purchasing assistants to receive new instructions, now that the purveyor was no longer the officer to whom they were responsible? From what officers would they receive their instructions? Or were the military agents, as the law intended, to be replaced by deputy quartermasters? If so, what orders were to be given with regard to the cash, clothing, and property in their hands? What arrangements were to be made for hiring the clerks Coxe urgently needed to help him wind up his affairs? Eustis remained silent on these questions for weeks.[35] Meanwhile, Congress, responding to the national clamor for war, daily moved the nation closer to armed conflict with Britain. On June 1 Madison asked Congress to declare war. The bill was passed by the House a day later, by the Senate on June 17, and was signed by the president on the next day.

In view of America's geographical advantages and England's preoccupation with affairs on the continent, the administration, reflecting the opinion of the public generally, was perhaps justified in believing that the odds were greatly in its favor.[36] Even so, it is difficult to discover any justification for the administration's apparent indifference to the floundering system of military supply. Indeed, the astonishing casualness with which Madison and Eustis handled the problem was reflected in their cavalier disregard of Coxe and their inattention to the work of the officials who succeeded him. Although Congress was responsible for abolishing the purveyorship and adopting a new system that was bound to create confusion and delays, the administration was responsible for making the transition as smooth as possible. Coxe, as he repeatedly affirmed, was eager to put his nine-year experience as purveyor at the president's disposal, for, as he reminded Madison some months after the war was declared, there were, of course, "great and intrinsic difficulties in the business of our supplies," but there were also many that "might have been and might yet be prevented avoided, or diminished." Far from being requested to aid in accomplishing this, Coxe was not given directions or assistance in concluding his own public business. The secretary of war did at least commend Coxe for his past services and dilatorily got around to directing Mifflin to allow him to have free access to all of the purveyor's records. It was to no avail. Although Coxe wrote to his former clerk "often and with urgency" demanding that the secretary's orders be obeyed, Mifflin "was silent or inattentive." So, too, was

34. Coxe to Madison, Dec. 16, 1812, Coxe to John Armstrong, Jan. 18, 1814, *ibid.*
35. "Circular to Purchasing Agents," June 1812, Coxe to Eustis, June 17, 22, 1812, *ibid.*
36. *Niles' Weekly Register*, Apr. 4, 1812, II, 86.

Eustis, who apparently was not bothered by the commissary's insubordination or by the injustice of Coxe's forced, uncompensated service to the public.[37]

Neither divine intervention nor human charity lightened Coxe's burden. Mifflin's unexpected death in the latter part of August removed one uncooperative official from the scene,[38] but the Madison administration had already selected Coxe's bête noire of the supply service, Callender Irvine, as the first commissary general. Had Madison and Eustis carefully concocted the poison Coxe would find most deadly, they could have done no better.

Irvine's acceptance of the commissary generalship marked a renewal of the quarrel between himself and Coxe that would drag on for almost a decade. The issue, precisely the same as that which had previously bedeviled Coxe's official relationship with Mifflin, concerned granting Coxe permission to consult the records of his former office so that he could settle his accounts as purveyor. By any objective criterion, this should have presented no difficulties at all. Thanks to Irvine's obstructionism and the failure of his Washington superiors to guide or to reprimand him, however, Coxe was confronted by the bizarre situation of having to wind up the affairs of the purveyor's office without an account book in sight. The episode has significance beyond the merely biographical. The present-day student who plods through the thousands of pages of the purveyor's letterbooks, record books, and account books is forcibly struck by the ineptitude of the federal civil service, as well as by the powerlessness of top-ranking officials of the Madison administration to cajole or enjoin subordinates into complying with uncongenial instructions. Madison might well have pondered the possible ramifications of what he had once said of the defects of the Confederation government. The use of sanctions, he had observed, is essential to the idea of law. So also was it essential to the efficient operation of the federal bureaucracy.

Even the feeblest administration, if capable of being stirred by an elementary sense of fair play, might have arranged for a still active, though untitled and unpaid, public servant to consult his own official records. Yet this was not done. Coxe's letters to Eustis and to his successors as secretary of war went unanswered, and his appeals first to the president and then to Congress were to no avail. He was unable even to secure reimbursement for the salaries he had paid to part-time clerks authorized in the summer of

---

37. Coxe to Madison, Dec. 31, 1812, Feb. 24, 1814, to Richard Rush, Mar. 6, 1813, to Eustis, July 23, 1812, Coxe Papers. Coxe later charged that Benjamin Mifflin refused to turn over the purveyor's account books because Mifflin "appears on the books a debtor in $444." Coxe to Madison, Mar. 10, 1814, Madison Papers, Lib. of Cong.

38. Coxe to Madison, Aug. 31, 1812, Madison Papers, Lib. of Cong.

1812 by the secretary of war, much less compensation for his own time. Worse than star chamber proceedings were no proceedings at all, and though Coxe's belief that he was the innocent victim of official persecution may have been ill-founded, he was in fact the hapless casualty of official neglect.[39]

Confronted by Irvine's dogged and successful obstructionist tactics, Coxe at last concluded that he must give up the unequal contest. With the help of his sons, he "made out and rendered the remainder of the accounts in the best manner I could." By the autumn of 1813 he had succeeded in paring down the million-odd dollars that had been outstanding on his books when he left the purveyorship to the comparatively trivial sum of $2,229, which, though certain that it was not his liability, he could not account for without access to his official papers, and this Irvine refused to permit. And so the script of what was by now a farce continued to be played out, year after year.[40]

Despite the callousness with which the Madison administration repaid his competent conduct of the purveyorship and his partisan loyalty, Coxe remained one of its stoutest defenders, even though its management of the war effort might have rather merited censure. But Coxe was not only a committed Republican but a consistent one. Having for years urged his countrymen to fight rather than to acquiesce in British aggression, he viewed the War of 1812 as a means to vindicate the nation's honor and to prove its military prowess. That an ardent patriot should thus have rejoiced at just retribution for intolerable grievances is understandable; that America's most knowledgeable authority on its military establishment should have believed that the nation was prepared to contest the might of Britain was surely wishful thinking. But the War of 1812 was a rare historical illustration of the familiar saying that wishes do come true.

Having been denied the opportunity to administer the nation's supply system, Coxe characteristically sought to further the war effort by his pen. One way to do so and at the same time to procure a much-needed

39. Coxe to Madison, Dec. 16, 23, 31, 1812, Feb. 24, 1814, to Armstrong, Feb. 6, 1813, Coxe Papers.

40. Coxe to Harrison, Oct. 16, 1813, to Armstrong, Jan. 18, 1814, to Irvine, Jan. 18, 1814, to Madison, Feb. 24, 1814, *ibid*. There was such a large amount of work necessary to settle his accounts that Coxe was forced to employ "one son, about eighteen months out of college, and engaged the aid of two others drawn from their law offices," as well as his eldest son, who thus was "drawn from his commercial pursuits." Coxe to Madison, Feb. 24, 1814, *ibid*. Although on his books there was still money outstanding, Coxe insisted that the United States was actually indebted by a small sum to him. Coxe to Madison, Feb. 24, 1814, *ibid*. Coxe's account with the United States was finally settled by the comptroller of the Treasury in 1820. See William Coxe, Jr., to Coxe, Mar. 1820, *ibid*.

income was to establish his own newspaper, a plan that he, in concert with Jefferson, had unsuccessfully proposed fourteen years earlier. Coxe's "Proposals" for "The Gazette of the Union and Journal of the States," a paper to be published daily in Philadelphia and three times weekly for distribution elsewhere, was published in May 1813. Dedicating his new journal to "THE FREEDOM OF THE PEOPLE and to THE PROSPERITY and THE INDEPENDENCE of our Country," Coxe "proposed to pay the utmost attention to the collection and publication of useful information, concerning every branch of the national industry." Who was better qualified to render such a "public service," he asked, than himself, the author of many articles on "various commercial" and "manufacturing" subjects and of "other disquisitions which he has submitted to the country since the period of the decline of the old confederation"?[41]

The problem with Coxe's plan was that Philadelphia and the nation at large were already blanketed in newspapers. Although his proposals elicited letters of encouragement and a few subscriptions, Coxe was soon obliged to acknowledge the soundness of the advice offered by a correspondent who lamented that though a paper like Coxe's "was really, if not *absolutely* necessary, . . . there is wanting a sufficient number of honest Patrons . . . to support such a Gazette."[42]

If Coxe could not edit his own newspaper, he could, as he had done for two decades, fill the columns of others. As his fellow publicist Samuel Mitchell remarked, "If Ink and black paint could overpower the enemy, we should give him an unmerciful beating."[43]

Coxe not only supported the war effort through his numerous ar-

---

41. See the *Nat. Intelligencer*, May 13, 1813; William Blair to Coxe, Apr. 23, 1813, Coxe Papers.

42. William Nicholson Jeffers to Coxe, Dec. 7, 1813, Coxe Papers. Coxe's efforts to round up subscribers and their responses can be followed in Hezekiah Niles to Coxe, May 11, 1813, John Langdon to Coxe, May 14, July 19, 1813, Samuel Hammond, Jr., to Coxe, June 1, 1813, John Welch *et al.* to Coxe, June 1, 1813, John Brown to Coxe, June 2, 1813, William Montgomery to Coxe, June 17, 1813, John Dick to Coxe, June 21, 1813, Caesar Rodney to Coxe, June 24, 1813, Elbridge Gerry to Coxe, Aug. 3, 1813, *ibid*.

43. Samuel Mitchell to Coxe, Aug. 3, 1813, *ibid*. For Coxe's articles, see "To the Wise and Good of all Parties and Places Throughout the United States," signed "Juriscola," *Nat. Intelligencer*, Aug. 6, 13, 20, 1812 (for Coxe's authorship, see Coxe to James Monroe, Aug. 22, 1812, Coxe Papers); "To the Government and People of the U. States of America," signed "A Friend to the States," *Demo. Press*, Dec. 15, 20, 1814 (for Coxe's authorship, see John Binns to Coxe, Dec. 18, 1814, Coxe Papers). The latter articles were part of a series of three; number two appeared between Dec. 15 and Dec. 20, though the issue in which it was published has not been found. For Coxe's articles on various phases of the War of 1812, see "Are the British Orders in Council so Modified that they would have ceased to violate our neutral rights, if we had remained in peace," signed "Juriscola," *Demo. Press*, Feb. 15, 1813; "Balance of Naval Power," *Demo. Press*, Sept. 24, 1814; "The Eastern Malcontents," signed "Hosner," *Nat. Intelligencer*, Nov. 21, Dec. 7, 1814. For references to other essays written by Coxe, see C. J. Ingersoll to Coxe, Feb. 21, 1813, Thomas Baiot to Coxe, Apr. 27, 1814, John Mease to Coxe, Mar. 23, 1814, Binns to Coxe, June

ticles but actively contributed by securing commissions in the navy for two of his sons and a place for himself in a corp for the defense of Philadelphia.[44] He still preferred that his own sacrifices be sweetened by a federal job, however, and during the war years he proceeded to reenact the scenario he had staged for two decades, presumably unaware that by this time his audience was weary of the role he had written for himself. Although any job would have done, he applied in July 1813 for that of collector of internal revenues for the Philadelphia district, an office revived in order to collect wartime taxes.[45] Not yet having received the appointment of collector and having heard of the death of General McPherson, naval officer of the port of Philadelphia, Coxe immediately applied for a post that "providence has rendered vacant." The president, persuaded that Coxe had "ever aimed at the public good" and "ever succeeded to promote it," appointed his long-time acquaintance to not only one but both posts, assuming presumably that Coxe would take his pick. Discovering that the post of naval officer paid less than he had supposed, Coxe chose the collectorship and took office on November 26, 1813, his tenure still subject to Senate confirmation.[46]

Coxe's supporters in the Senate could literally have been counted on one hand. His antagonists were influential enough to deny him even a lowly collectorship. "It is with surprise and mortification that I have just been informed that your appointment was this day negativated with only five votes in your favor," William Coxe, Jr., now a member of the House of Representatives, wrote to his brother on February 18, 1814.[47] This rare senatorial rejection of a presidential appointment to a minor post was partly

---

20, 1814, Aug. 11, 1815, John White and others to Coxe, Sept. 26, 1814, Benjamin Reynolds to Coxe, Oct. 3, 1814, Richard Rush to Coxe, Nov. 30, 1814, Jonathan Roberts to Coxe, Dec. 6, 1814, Feb. 5, 1815, Joseph Gales to Coxe, July 22, 1815, Coxe to unknown recipient, Oct. 3, 1815, Coxe Papers. See also Coxe to Madison, 1814 (3 letters), Madison Papers, Lib. of Cong.

44. See Roberts to Coxe, Jan. 9, 1814, Anthony Simons to Coxe, Nov. 5, 1814, Coxe to Monroe, Dec. 27, 1814, Coxe Papers; Coxe to Madison, Dec. 12, 1814, Jan. 4, 1815, Madison Papers, Lib. of Cong.

45. Coxe submitted two letters of application for the post. Coxe to Madison, July 16, 22, 1813, Madison Papers, Lib. of Cong. He renewed his request in a letter of Sept. 2, 1813, ibid. See also "An Act for the assessment and collection of Direct Taxes and Internal Duties," July 22, 1813, U.S. Statutes at Large, III, 22–34.

46. Coxe to Madison, Nov. 6, July 16, 1813, Madison Papers, Lib. of Cong. At Madison's request Gallatin had passed the president's compliment on to Coxe. Madison presumably continued to welcome the advice on public policy that Coxe characteristically freely gave. See Coxe to Madison, Apr. 20, Sept. 2, 1813, Aug. 30, 1814, three letters dated "1814," Apr. 26, 1815, ibid. Coxe's appointment as collector, dated Nov. 8, 1813, is in the Coxe Papers. He was offered the position of naval officer on Nov. 13. Richard Rush to Coxe, Nov. 13, 1813, ibid. His letter to Madison accepting the former was written on Nov. 15, 1813, Madison Papers, Lib. of Cong.

47. William Coxe, Jr., to Coxe, Feb. 18, 1814. Before the actual Senate vote Coxe's nomination had been referred to a Senate committee of which Abner Lacock of Pennsylvania, Coxe's supporter, and Michael Leib were members. Roberts to Coxe, Jan. 31, 1814, Coxe Papers.

owing to the dirty work of Leib, who circulated among his colleagues the rumors that as purveyor of public supplies Coxe had received bribes from a Philadelphia silversmith in return for a lucrative government contract and that his accounts as purveyor were suspiciously unsettled. The Senate's rebuff was also attributable, according to Senator Abner Lacock, who doggedly fought for Coxe's confirmation, to the determination of some senators to resist "the repeated efforts of the President to impose on the Senate a nomination several times rejected for other appointments."[48]

It was a sad but somehow suitable finale to a public career that twenty-five years earlier Coxe had launched with such high expectations. As it was, Coxe at the age of sixty was reduced to the role of a humble supplicant for a minor state job. Governor Simon Snyder came to his rescue in 1815 with an appointment as clerk of the Court of General Quarter Sessions for the city and county of Philadelphia; but even this morsel was snatched from him three years later, reducing him, he lamented, "to real and deep distress, and the most painful prospects."[49] His prospects would have been somewhat less painful had he been willing to part with a portion of the lands he had acquired over the previous thirty years. He might at least then have lived up to the reputation he had earned as a political economist. His writings, not the offices he held or the acres he amassed, were, after all, the basis of his repute in his lifetime and later.

48. Abner Lacock's opinion was quoted in William Coxe, Jr., to Coxe, Feb. 19, 1814, *ibid.* The bribery charge was made by George Armistead, who provided Leib with an affidavit stating that he had given Coxe "a bonus of Plate-silver spoons" and a gold medal. Coxe denied receiving the former and averred that he had accepted the latter only for transmission to the Fine Arts Society. Apropos of the purveyorship, it was asserted that Coxe owed a balance of $2,200. Not content with these accusations, Leib arranged that the proclamation of the Pennsylvania Executive Council in 1778 attainting Coxe of treason be "exhibited in the Senate." Roberts to Coxe, Jan. 31, 1814, Coxe's "Deposition," Feb. 2, 1814, William Coxe, Jr., to Coxe, Feb. 18, 1814, *ibid.* Coxe submitted a memorial, communicated through the president, to the Senate on Feb. 28, 1814 (*Senate Executive Journal*, II, 499), in which he answered the charges leveled against him. An incomplete draft of the memorial is in the Coxe Papers. See also Coxe to Madison, Feb. 24, 1814, Coxe to Elbridge Gerry, Feb. 25, 1814, *ibid.*; Coxe to Madison, Mar. 10, 1814, Madison Papers, Lib. of Cong. According to Roberts, Leib's replacement in the Senate, Coxe's "Memorial was receivd and with some difficulty a reading was obtaind. It could have no effect." Roberts to Coxe, Mar. 22, 1814, Coxe Papers.

49. Coxe to Findley, Oct. 26, 1818, *ibid.* A copy of the appointment is in Miscellaneous I.C. 12, 1812–1816, Dept. of Records, Philadelphia. See also Coxe to Madison, Jan. 14, 1815, Coxe Papers.

25 ⚹

The Defoe of America

During the early decades of the new century, Coxe continued to present the seeming paradox of a staunch Hamiltonian who was also a steadfast Jeffersonian. The "paradox" is resolved, however, when one recalls that the familiar Hamilton-Jefferson duality is primarily the product of American historians who have persisted in personifying economic trends in Hamilton and Jefferson and then have inferred the economic thought of this period from the personification. Coxe himself would have agreed with a recent scholar who cut through the heavy crust of traditional historical wisdom by asserting that both Jefferson and Hamilton "employed the resource of government to promote development" and "bespoke the interests and wishes of a nation anxious to root its political independence in the soil of economic development." Thus it was not inconsistent that Coxe, though an ardent Jeffersonian and holding fast to Republican ideas on foreign policy, remained an advocate of the program that he had helped Hamilton to foster in the 1790s. These policies were, as earlier, the lodestars of his writings during the first two decades of the nineteenth century.[1]

Coxe's writings during the Jeffersonian era added little that was new

---

1. Stuart Bruchey, *The Roots of American Economic Growth, 1607–1861: An Essay in Social Causation* (New York, 1968), 122. The one qualified exception to Coxe's support of Hamilton's economic program was the Bank of the United States. Although Coxe remained its steadfast supporter, he believed that the institution launched in 1791 with his enthusiastic support was now in need of reform. This opinion was expressed in 1810 when Congress first took up the question of renewal of the charter of the Bank of the United States, scheduled to expire in 1812. See "An Inquiry into . . . public and private Banks," *Demo. Press*, Nov. 26, 1810. For Coxe's authorship, see John Binns to Coxe, 1810, Coxe Papers. For an amplification of Coxe's views, see Coxe to Madison, Nov. 10, 1810, *ibid.*; Coxe to Gallatin, Oct. 1810, Gallatin Papers, N.-Y. Hist. Soc., New York.

except for different illustrative and amplificative material. Instead, Coxe tailored familiar policies to the exigencies of a new day when problems, though sometimes dissimilar from those of the past era, could in his view usually be solved by his prescription of economic nationalism. This belief was capsulated in his remark that "it will probably be found much best for the United States to consider, first, the actual general nature, situation and capacities of their own country, and to cultivate, on principle, its great leading interests in concert and harmony."[2]

The means by which Coxe's great object could be obtained were substantially those he had set forth in his debut as a political economist in 1787 and had subsequently embroidered on time and again. He remained steadfast in his faith in national salvation through industrialization, though he emphasized, as previously, that agriculture, manufactures, and commerce were a triad of "intimately interwoven" economic activities—all essential to the general welfare of the state, all worthy of its solicitude. He insisted, however, that agriculture and manufacturing required particular attention. The former was "the collossus of our country," and the latter a *"cluster of arts and trades which minister to its wants."* This emphasis was necessary, Coxe explained, because from its inception the nation had zealously watched over its commerce (by which he meant principally foreign trade and navigation) while comparatively neglecting its *"internal industry."*[3]

Underpinning the tens of thousands of words that Coxe wrote on this subject was his wish to demolish the then-popular argument that in a new and underdeveloped country like the United States agriculture was both inevitably and desirably the principal industry, one not only to be exclusively encouraged but also to be protected against artificially created rivals such as manufacturing. Believing this to be a myopic view, Coxe substituted the goal of a balanced economy made possible by the vast market afforded by an extensive, richly endowed, and economically diversified country. To cement together its interdependent parts, he, like Henry Clay in his famous "American System," recommended tariff protection and large-scale internal

2. Coxe, "Thoughts occasioned by the propositions to convene Congress and for a very considerable exclusion of European Manufactures of all raw materials," signed "A Friend of the National Industry," *Nat. Intelligencer*, June 23, 1819. This was the second in a series of four articles; the others appeared in *Nat. Intelligencer*, June 7, July 3, 19, 1819.

3. Coxe, "Agriculture, Manufactures and Commerce. Circuit Court of the United States, Eastern District of Pennsylvania," Oct. 30, 1819, broadside, Coxe Papers (for a draft of this article in Coxe's hand, see *ibid.*); [Coxe], *Essay on the Manufacturing Interest of the United States . . .* (Philadelphia, 1804), 11; "Franklin," *Aurora*, June 22, 1802. From June through December 1802, Coxe published 23 articles under various titles but all signed "Franklin," *ibid*. They appeared on June 19, 22, 25, July 3, 10, 12, 13, 19, 20, 21, 22, 23, 24, 26, 27, 29, 31, Aug. 3, 21, 27, Nov. 19, 30, Dec. 2, 1802, and are hereafter cited under the appropriate date as "Franklin."

improvements.[4] Once these essential props were provided there were, in Coxe's view, few impediments. Neither the lack of experience and capital nor the vicissitudes of international affairs could thwart the realization of his ambitious plan. It was only necessary to "raise and manufacture American" and to buy American.[5]

Coxe was the more firmly persuaded that his plan would succeed because of his faith in his countrymen's unique inventiveness and industriousness. And to promote these traits, as befitted the spokesman of an underdeveloped but growing economy, he emphasized what later would be termed the "work ethic." "All is the gift of industry," he wrote. "Among individuals it is the supreme virtue; and, when well ordered and duly regulated, it is the only criterion of a good and wise government." Conversely, idleness was the greatest of social vices, an evil that "brings in its train, poverty, ignorance and discontent, the parents of sedition, tumult, and civil war." Given such perfervid fears of sloth, Coxe concluded that its prevention was the supreme test of statesmanship: the greatest statesman was he who banished not only tyranny but also idleness from the land and prevented the nation "from being disgraced by poverty and contempt."[6]

Coxe neither questioned the validity of this linkage between tyranny and idleness, poverty and contempt, nor asked how unemployment would, for the first time in human history, be banished. That he did not was but one aspect of his persistent failure to ask the larger question of *cui bono?*—who was to profit by the eradication of idleness? Who was to benefit by the expansion of business enterprise? Instead, he posited what he termed "a harmony of all interests"—manufacturer and worker, planter and small farmer, international merchant and local shopkeeper.[7] Such a belief stemmed from his conviction that the United States, free of the hereditary distinctions

4. For a particularly far-sighted proposal, see Coxe's plan for more closely connecting the eastern shore of Virginia and Maryland to the rest of the country in Coxe to John Vaughan, Apr. 1, 1806, Coxe Papers. For Coxe's interest in a Dismal Swamp Canal in Virginia, see Thomas Newton to Coxe, May 16, 1820, *ibid.* Since available private capital was unequal to the requisite internal improvements, Coxe considered government aid indispensable, though this might well be supplemented by laws calculated to encourage the large-scale investment of European capital. "Loan Petition and Bill," 1806, *ibid.* Coxe's proposal included the draft of "An Act, the more effectually to secure loans of monies by foreign persons," which provided that citizens of foreign countries might loan money to individuals or to the commonwealth of Pennsylvania on the security of real estate in the state and that they "may and shall be entitled to hold such real estate in trust or by Mortgage or otherwise or to have the same held by trustees for their use and benefit, for the security of the principal and interest."

5. "To the Cultivators, the Capitalists and the Manufacturers of the United States," signed "Juriscola," *Demo. Press*, Aug. 10, 1810. There were seven articles in this series. For the others, see *ibid.*, July 13, Aug. 3, 8, 13, 18, 24, 1810. The series was also published in the *Nat. Intelligencer*, July 27, Aug. 1, 3, 6, 10, 15, 20, 26, 1810.

6. [Coxe], *Essay on the Manufacturing Interest in the U.S.*, 5.

7. "An American Freeholder to the People of the United States," *Demo. Press*, Mar. 15, 1821. There were five articles in this series. For the others, see *ibid.*, Mar. 6, 9, 12, 19, 1812. This series

of European society, had created a society unmarred by class conflict, one characterized instead by a prevailing identity of social and economic interests. Perhaps from the vantage point of a window on Walnut Street in Philadelphia this was indeed the case, but a close inspection of the congested living quarters along the city's waterfront might have dispelled the notion.

Or perhaps Coxe was bedazzled by his shimmering optimism. America remained, as he had said in the 1780s and 1790s, sui generis; it was uniquely progressive, and the accomplishments of the past were harbingers of a future to which he, like his countrymen, looked in brash and racy confidence. These beliefs inspired the familiar formula by which he organized his writings: a comparison of the state of the economy, especially manufacturing, at an earlier date with its present condition—a contrast designed to show both its steady progress and its promise.

Such organization reflected his unchanged faith in the efficacy of discrete facts—his equation of their accumulation with "science" (which thus defined, was to him the paradigm of knowledge)—and his inability to perceive, as one of Pirandello's characters would put it a century later, that a fact is like a sack; it will not stand upright until you put something in it. So it was that there flowed through his essays a current of statistical and other material with which he drifted but that he seldom navigated. As John Binns, editor of the *Democratic Press*, wrote when introducing a series of his friend's essays in 1821: "They are not speculative," but rather "a detail of interesting facts and important suggestions." To Coxe that was as it should be, for to him "all pertinent facts," whether considered as symptoms or as evidence, were "valuable, as indicating the true state of the body politic." Thus persuaded, he paid scant attention to what he once described as "the forms and niceties of literary composition." Instead, he concentrated on "the more solid substance of the pertinent information," convinced that by classifying and tabulating reality he could make a science of it.[8] A master at compiling statistical and other data, he chased his readers with facts and dazed them with computations.

In spite of the flaws in Coxe's discursive style, he remained one of the nation's most consistent and ardent proponents of manufactures, advancing repetitive but persuasive arguments in support of their encouragement. He characteristically ignored impediments and turned alleged handicaps into

---

was reprinted in the *Nat. Intelligencer*, Apr. 6, 10, 12, 14, 1821, with an introductory essay published on Apr. 6 that did not appear in the *Demo. Press*. A second series entitled "An American Freeholder to the landed . . . citizens of the U.S. concerning the prospects of Business . . ." was published in the *Demo. Press*, Apr. 12, 14, 25, May 3, 1821. It was reprinted in the *Nat. Intelligencer*, May 3, 10, 11, 1821. There are drafts of a number of these articles in the Coxe Papers.

8. *Demo. Press*, Mar. 9, 1821; Coxe to William Jones, June 21, 1813, Coxe Papers; "On the Grape Vine," *Nat. Intelligencer*, Nov. 13, 1819 (for full bibliographical information on this series of articles, see n. 15, below).

estimable advantages. He asserted, for example, that the scarcity of workers would lead to the invention and improvement of laborsaving machinery. On other occasions he refused to admit that there was a labor shortage and echoed the contemporary cliché that manufactures would provide employment for women and children, "many of them," as Hamilton once put it, "of a tender age."

To Coxe, who was convinced that "of all other things, the political economist will attend to the proper employment of the fair sex," jobs for the idle young mattered less than opportunities for employable women. Since for millennia the less fortunate women had inhumanely been "put to follow the plough," while the more fortunate had been restricted "to propagating scandal, reading novels, and gaming," they must be rescued from lives as "beasts of burden" or as "fools." Coxe would place women in front of the spinning wheel and the loom, at home or in factories. Such reforms "would contribute greatly" to "manufactures and to the comfort and happiness of the sex," while leaving men free "for the duties of the farm, and other employments, requiring exposure and strength."[9]

Just as the increase of manufactures would expand opportunities for women, so too would it provide jobs for the indigent, whose condition, Coxe wrote, legislators took no constructive steps to ameliorate. Nor could he find validity in the charge that the removal of workers from the farm to the factory doomed them to "wretchedness," as in Great Britain. He argued that "the ingenuity of those employed in the finer arts" allowed them to escape "the iron hand of oppression" to which agricultural laborers were subjugated.[10]

Coxe hoped that the means adopted by the states for encouraging manufactures would be as numerous and varied as the objects to be encouraged; he was also aware that the federal government was highly unlikely to provide any aid other than trade regulations, particularly customs duties. In view of the congressional record, he was by no means confident that adequate assistance of even this kind could be relied upon. The tariff of 1789 had been modified from time to time, but rate increases had been modest, designed chiefly for revenue. There was, moreover, no strong popular mandate for the adoption of a genuinely protective system, largely because the bulk of the nation's available capital was invested in commerce, a far more profitable venture than domestic manufactures. Although this situation appeared to be an inevitable result of seemingly immutable rules of the market-

---

9. [Coxe], *Essay on the Manufacturing Interest of the U.S.*, 15; "To the Cultivators, the Capitalists and the Manufacturers of the United States," *Demo. Press*, Aug. 8, 1810.

10. [Coxe], *Essay on the Manufacturing Interests of the U.S.*, 17.

place, Coxe believed that these rules could be altered by a change in federal impost laws.

Coxe rejected many shibboleths of his day that then passed as economic laws. He repudiated the notion that it was in the best interest of individuals, and thus the nation, "*to buy cheap*"; since it was agreed that this rule did not hold for articles essential to national defense, why, he asked, were items necessary to national prosperity not also exceptions? So too with the commonly accepted rule "*not to enact prohibitions or to impose duties to force manufactures.*" Coxe thought rather that certain industries indispensable to economic growth must be protected against foreign competition either by prohibition or by a high tariff, depending upon the seriousness of the threat from abroad. A consistent protectionist for three decades, he believed that the road to a national economy must be smoothed by carefully calculated customs duties. He also consistently advocated American navigation acts modeled on those of Great Britain and other industrial nations. Such measures would, he believed, not only rescue American ships from the shoals of British navigational policy but also assure smoother sailing for American diplomacy. "An independent and peaceable navigation act," he explained, "would supercede the necessity of a maritime coalition and of an armed neutrality. It is a pacific, precedented and ordinary measure of all governments, to be expected of us."[11]

In his efforts to actualize his vision of a prosperous, industrially advanced, even ideal society, Coxe relied on self-help, as well as governmental paternalism. Reflecting what Tocqueville would later describe as the characteristically American confidence that there is no object unobtainable by the "principle of association, the combined power of individuals united into a society," Coxe believed his pet goal could best be achieved by the organization of societies dedicated to propagating the doctrine of industrialization. He was accordingly instrumental in the revitalization of the Pennsylvania Society for the Encouragement of Manufactures and Useful Arts, as well as the organization of new societies.[12] One, launched in 1803, was the

---

11. "Thoughts on the various departments of the National Industry of the United States," *Analectic Magazine*, XIV (1819), 84–88 (for Coxe's authorship, see Coxe to Gales, Aug. 18, 1819, Coxe Papers); Coxe, *An Addition to the memoir on the subject of cotton culture*, 5–6 (for full citation of this work, see n. 38, below); "The Encouragement of the Most Important Commercial Manufacturers," signed "Juriscola," *Demo. Press*, May 30, 1809.

12. Tocqueville, *Democracy in America*, I, 199. To revitalize this society Coxe wrote a circular entitled *A Communication from the Pennsylvania Society for the Encouragement of Manufactures and the Useful Arts* (Philadelphia, 1804). It also appeared in the *Philadelphia Eve. Post*, Mar. 13, 1804, and in the *Aurora* on the same date. The *Communication from the Pennsylvania Society* included (1) "A Circular Communication" dated Feb. 7, 1804, addressed to manufac-

Philadelphia Society of Artists and Manufacturers, which became one of the country's most influential protectionist lobbies. As its secretary, Coxe was an indefatigable publicist. He also supported the Philadelphia Domestic Society, incorporated in 1805; the Philadelphia Manufacturing Society, organized by himself and Mathew Carey in 1808 for the manufacture of textiles; and the Philadelphia Society for the Promotion of American Manufacturing, founded in 1817 by Coxe, Carey, and others. The last organization was designed, in the words of its constitution, as "a permanent committee on the state of American manufactures," a euphemism for a protectionist pressure group.[13]

In view of Coxe's tireless efforts to demonstrate the interconnection and reciprocity of agriculture and manufacturing, his writings appropriately centered on domestically produced raw materials suitable for manufacture. Tackling even the most pedestrian subject with gusto, Coxe allowed few possibilities to escape his attention, and few inquiries failed to result in an essay. In addition to his crop of articles on cotton cultivation and manufacture, he wrote extensively on many other subjects, particularly wine and wool. That America already manufactured not only all the wool it produced but also all it could import, for instance, was to Coxe an inexhaustibly gratifying theme and proof of the country's industrial progress and boundless potential. The task ahead was to raise more and more sheep, of improved breeds, in more and more sections of the country, thus providing a market at home, free from foreign "injury, insult, and vexation," that would encourage both "the industry of our women and children, and the power of machinery."[14]

Coxe was similarly insistent about the inestimable advantages to be derived from wine-making and related industries. He took particular pride in a series of lengthy essays on this subject, which he planned to expand and

---

turing societies elsewhere, and signed by Coxe as president; (2) a reprint of "The Plan of the Pennsylvania Society for the encouragement of Manufactures and the Useful Arts, Established at Philadelphia in August, 1787"; (3) "A List of the Officers and Members of the Board, Elected on the 20th Day of January, 1804"; and (4) A report of "The Committee appointed to prepare 'a report on the state of Manufactures in the United States generally, and particularly in the State of Pennsylvania, at the time of the establishment of this Society, and of their progressive increase and improvement, to the present time.'" The circular was published by order of the board of the society and signed "Tench Coxe, President."

13. Coxe was vice-president of this society. A printed copy of the constitution is in the Coxe Papers. For Coxe's role in its organization, see Coxe to unknown recipient, Jan. 28, 1817, Alexander S. Coxe to Coxe, Feb. 4, 1817, ibid.

14. "To the Cultivators, the Capitalists and the Manufacturers of the United States," Demo. Press, Aug. 10, 1810. For other articles by Coxe on this subject, see "Thoughts on the Subject of Fine . . . Wool," ibid., May 24, 1809; "Further Thoughts on the Subject of Wool," ibid., May 27, 1809.

publish as a book. "On the Grape Vine," written in 1819, was designed to convince his countrymen that by the cultivation of grapes in extensive areas of the middle states, the West, and the South, "ridges, hills, mountains, . . . gravelly, stony, sandy, and other inferior lands" could be made to resemble "*the vine-covered hills and gay regions of France.*"[15] The matter was "so important, in various points of view, to all the states" that libraries and promotional societies (even philosophical societies) throughout the country should promptly procure "all the treatises" on the subject. Of this literature Coxe provided a liberal sampling. Indeed, his eight articles were, to vary the familiar phrase, a sluggish stream of prose running through a meadow of lengthy quotations—excerpts from Chaptal's standard work *Sur la culture de la vigne*, published in 1801, from l'Abbé Rozier's article on the same subject in his *Dictionary of Agriculture*, from the remarks of "an observing and intelligent young American traveller" on Spanish wines, and from the writings of the English authority on agricultural subjects, Arthur Young. Nevertheless, Coxe's contemporaries presumably delighted in reading his essays and found them important, as he received complimentary letters that were not merely expressions of perfunctory politeness. Henry Johnson, senator from Louisiana, assured him that if his work were published as a pamphlet, "the gentlemen from the South generally will . . . cheerfully subscribe"; Henry Clay, Speaker of the House of Representatives, was so impressed that he promised to have the essays published in Kentucky. Coxe's friend William Lee, who read the essays in draft form, wrote that they demonstrated again that "whatever you write is read with interest," showing "that you are endowed with the spirit of prophecy."[16] And indeed he was, for though his advice was ignored for many decades to come, upper New York state and the Napa Valley in California were to be the fulfillment of his prophecy.

Even more prescient was Coxe's tireless promotion of the cotton industry, which, as he predicted, largely dominated the American economy until the Civil War. His long crusade began in 1787, when "the country did not export a single bale of American cotton," and continued for almost forty years. At the end of this time, the spread of its cultivation throughout the South and the erection of an ever-increasing number of mills in the North

15. "On the Grape Vine, with its wines, brandies, and dried fruits," signed "A Friend to the National Industry," *Nat. Intelligencer*, Nov. 6, 1819. There were eight articles in this series. The others were dated Nov. 10, 13, 16, 20, Dec. 2, 15, 31, 1819. The series was republished in the *National Recorder* (Dover, Del.). See Littell & Henry to Coxe, Dec. 4, 14, 17, 1819, Coxe Papers. Coxe also planned to include the essays in his projected, but never completed, "Manual of Agriculture." The project is described in a broadside, *ibid.*

16. Henry Johnson to Coxe, Feb. 5, May 11, 1820, William Lee to Coxe, June 5, 1819, Coxe Papers. See also Johnson to Coxe, Apr. 4, 1820, *ibid.*

led him to boast without exaggeration that "never did my anticipations of any subject in our affairs issue in a conformity of subsequent events so considerable as in this case."[17]

The results Coxe had foreseen were related, however marginally, to his own promotional activities, but they were also, as he readily admitted, a consequence of the contributions of many other Americans. Chief among these was Eli Whitney's invention of the cotton gin in 1793, which made possible the rapid spread of cotton farming into inland areas of the South, where only the short staple variety to which his invention was particularly suited could grow. The profitability of raising cotton decisively affected the history of the South for decades to come, both by promoting one-crop specialization and by providing an effective excuse for the expansion of slavery in a section where this crop was already entrenched—a development that Coxe, preoccupied with cotton's advantages, persistently refused to acknowledge.

Coxe's personal satisfaction mounted as production of cotton increased, and he energetically sought to accelerate the trend by promoting the growth of cotton manufactures by both the domestic and factory systems. Progress was disappointingly slow, largely because of the flow of capital accumulation into the more profitable area of neutral commerce. By 1800, and in the face of the strenuous promotional activities of publicists like Coxe, the nation's cotton industry consisted merely of eight mills, all located in New England.[18] During the years following, principally due to the enhanced risks of foreign trade and to the reinvestment of profits, this number increased, at first slowly, then sharply. According to Coxe, by 1804 the number of mills had doubled; in 1806 the industry reached a new high; and, following a brief recession, grew rapidly, thanks to the spur of the embargo and nonintercourse.[19] To Coxe there could not be too much of such a good thing, and he continued in good and lean years to share with the American public his virtually messianic vision of the benefits to be derived from what he believed to be the nation's great white hope.

The potentialities of cotton manufacture were, Coxe believed, of incalculable importance to the South. Foreshadowing an argument that would be first on the agenda of advocates of a "New South" seven decades

17. Coxe to James Madison, May 5, 1807, Feb. 2, 1819, Madison Papers, Lib. of Cong.

18. Victor S. Clark, History of Manufactures in the United States, 1607–1860 (Washington, D.C., 1916), 535. Clark estimated that these eight mills probably had less than 2,000 spindles and consumed between 50,000 and 100,000 pounds of cotton annually.

19. Coxe, Report of the Committee appointed to prepare a report on the state of manufactures in the United States . . . and of their progressive increase and improvement . . . (Philadelphia, 1804) (this report was also printed in the Philadelphia Eve. Post, Mar. 13, 1804); Clive Day, "The Early Development of the American Cotton Manufacture," Quarterly Journal of Economics, XXXIX (1925), 463.

later, he called for bringing machinery "into the middle of the *cotton country*, where the raw material is free from every expence of transportation, storeage, damage and agency." Among other inestimable advantages, the rise of cotton mills in the South would diminish the threat "of a certain dangerous description of our laboring inhabitants"; "a numerous white people collected in many villages will facilitate their ability to check any possible irregularities of their men of colour."[20]

The observation made by George Logan in 1802 that Coxe's articles on cotton had "produced a good effect in the Southern States" was verified over succeeding years by prominent southerners who solicited copies of his writings or his advice on cotton manufacture and to whom he sent samples of cloth or drawings of machinery.[21] His advocacy of what he regarded as the panacea for the nation's economy never faltered. He persisted through years of embargoes, blockades, and internal disruptions, in times of comparative peace or imminent war, recession or boom. Indeed, the changing tides in national affairs were seen as yet further evidence of the virtually all-sufficient curative powers of cotton manufacture.

In 1809 Congress took an important step in the direction charted by Coxe when the House Committee on Commerce and Manufactures reported that manufactures should be protected against foreign competition. Specifically proposed were additional duties on cotton manufactures imported from the East Indies. It was a striking departure from the position taken by the same committee five years earlier when, to Coxe's chagrin, it had summarily turned down a similar proposal. The reversal reflected a changed mood. Congress now ordered the reprinting of Hamilton's Report on Manufactures and directed the secretary of the Treasury to submit a report on the same subject, paying due attention to proposals designed to "protect and promote the same."[22]

Gallatin's Report on Manufactures, submitted to Congress in 1810, might, with minor nuances of interpretation and recommendation, have been written by Coxe. Asserting that American manufacturers' use of domestic raw materials and foodstuffs had helped to create a great home

20. "Franklin," *Aurora*, June 22, Aug. 3, June 19, 1802.
21. George Logan to Coxe, Dec. 27, 1802, Coxe Papers. For Southerners requesting Coxe's aid, see James Holland to Coxe, Mar. 16, 1802, Coxe to Waightstile Avery, May 28, Dec. 20, 1802, R. Davison to Coxe, Sept. 28, 1802, George Morgan to Coxe, Nov. 8, 1803, John Roebuck to Coxe, June 16, 1803, William Robinson to Coxe, July 29, 1804, Lawrence Adams to Coxe, May 7, 1805, Joseph Coppinger to Coxe, June 26, 1808, John G. Baxter to Coxe, Jan. 4, 1809, Mar. 14, 1813, Daniel Montgomery to Coxe, Feb. 9, 1809, William Watson to Coxe, Nov. 1, 1809, James Ronaldson to Coxe, June 10, 1809, Mordecai D. Lewis to Coxe, May 4, 1813, *ibid*.
22. *Annals of Cong.*, XX, 702, 363–365.

market, Secretary of the Treasury Gallatin proposed that the laudable progress already made be accelerated by the fostering care of government. In an accompanying letter he further suggested that the third census, scheduled for 1810, might provide a convenient opportunity for the collection of vital statistics on the exact state of the nation's manufactures. Although Congress endorsed the proposal, Gallatin could spare neither the time nor the staff to conduct it.[23] On March 19, 1812, a sympathetic Congress came to his rescue by authorizing him to employ an outsider to prepare "a statement of the number, nature, extent, situation and value of the arts and manufactures of the United States, together with such other details connected with these subjects as can be made." Toward the end of June, Gallatin offered the job to Coxe, who, having just lost the purveyorship, accepted the assignment, which, though congenial, provided him with the rather less-than-handsome reward of $1,500, plus $500 for an assistant.[24]

Although the wording of the congressional resolution of March 19 could have been construed as a call for a document as broad and general as Hamilton's famous report, Gallatin presumably had in mind merely a compilation of statistics based on information already supplied by the United States marshals of the several districts. He allowed Coxe only five months to complete the task. Coxe, however, elated by an opportunity to address Congress on his favorite subject and perhaps to emulate Hamilton's accomplishment, had more ambitious plans. He hastily tabulated and surveyed the marshals' returns in preparation for his own essay on the necessity of manufactures to a balanced economy.[25] When his report was dispatched to Gallatin on December 8, 1812, it included two introductory essays, elaborate tables, and, as he said, "as much as was at all proper of what my life's attention has collected upon the subject." Coxe, certain that the secretary would promptly transmit it to Congress, impatiently awaited the acclaim of which

23. Albert Gallatin's report is printed in *American State Papers, Finance,* II, 425–431. For the law that resulted from this report, see "An Act further to alter and amend 'An act providing for the Third Census, or enumeration of the inhabitants of the United States,'" *U.S. Statutes at Large,* II, 605. This was passed on May 1, 1810, and it authorized the marshals to collect information on manufactures.

24. *Annals of Cong.,* XXIV, 2362–2363; Gallatin to Coxe, June 26, 1812, Coxe Papers.

25. Gallatin to Coxe, June 26, 1812, Coxe Papers. The information from the marshals had been submitted pursuant to Gallatin's circular letter of May 17, 1812, calling for the collection of specified data on manufactures in their districts. A copy of the circular, addressed to John Smith, marshal for Pennsylvania, is in the Coxe Papers. For the correspondence between Gallatin and Coxe on the subject of the latter's report, largely on compensation of the United States marshal for Vermont, see Gallatin to Coxe, June 26, July 6, 7, Oct. 5, Nov. 4, 1812, Coxe to Gallatin, Oct. 9, 1812, *ibid.* For Coxe's efforts to secure information in addition to that supplied by the federal marshals, see John G. Baxter to Coxe, Sept. 25, 1812, William Hirtings to Coxe, Oct. 19, 1812, Jonathan Roberts to Coxe, Nov. 3, 1812, H. Bassett to Coxe, Nov. 26, 1812, R. Dickinson to Coxe, Dec. 28, 1812, *ibid.*

he was confident.[26] Days, then weeks, passed, and no word reached Philadelphia. Finally, on January 23, 1813, he wrote to Gallatin expressing anxiety that his report "may have in some respects or in a general view gone further than you approve," offering to "rectify and amend" it as the secretary might direct.[27] His fears were well grounded, for Gallatin, once he had belatedly read the document, was sharply critical. His comments were appropriate and incisive, but in view of his own failure to supply guidelines he might charitably have softened the language of his critique.

What Coxe had set forth in two essays should have been consolidated into one, Gallatin said. He should have omitted "whatever was extraneous to the subject," such as digressions on climate and geography, and his interpolations from the data should have been confined to "additional *facts* not furnished by the Marshals," notably progress made since the 1810 census. Nor was Coxe's statistical method satisfactory. This defect was most conspicuously apparent in his failure to provide a breakdown of manufactures by counties and his inclusion of agricultural products—wheat, corn, horses, and cattle, for example—under manufactures. What Gallatin detected was his assistant's effort to magnify the nation's industrial progress by slanting the available statistics. Having done precisely this for two decades, Coxe did not see it that way and vigorously defended both his methodology and his premises. But the secretary, engaged in pressing affairs of state, had no intention of participating in a debate on the proper uses of statistics. In a letter of March 13 Gallatin outlined the minimal corrections that had to be made, brusquely adding that if Coxe did not choose to do so he would "immediately employ another person to complete the work under my direction," paying him out of the compensation intended for Coxe.[28]

Forced to acquiesce, Coxe was consoled by confidence that his report, although altered, would nevertheless enhance his standing as one of the nation's top-ranking economists. Three months later he submitted his revised statement to a fellow Philadelphian, William Jones, who had been appointed acting secretary of the Treasury following Gallatin's appointment as one of the commissioners to negotiate the Treaty of Ghent.[29] Jones was no more favorably impressed than his predecessor, but, unlike Gallatin, his

26. Coxe to Gallatin, Jan. 23, 1813, Gallatin Papers. See also Coxe to Gallatin, Dec. 5–6, 8, 18, 1812, Adam Seybert to Coxe, Jan. 2, 1813, Coxe Papers.

27. Coxe to Gallatin, Jan. 23, 1813, Gallatin Papers.

28. Gallatin to Coxe, Jan. 26, Mar. 13, 1813, Coxe Papers. For Coxe's defense, see Coxe to Gallatin, Feb. 27, 1813, *ibid*.

29. Coxe to William Jones, June 21, 1813, *ibid*. Although Coxe retained the two essays to which objections had been made, he did accede to Gallatin's demand that he provide a breakdown of manufacturing returns by counties, a task involving considerable additional labor. Also consonant with Gallatin's demand, he removed statistics on agriculture and extractive industries, only exhibiting them in separate tables.

objections arose more from a personal dislike of the author than from an objective appraisal of Coxe's work. He might have buried it in the files of the Treasury Department had not Coxe's stout congressional ally Dr. Adam Seybert forced his hand by securing on July 9, 1813, House approval of a motion directing the Treasury secretary to "have printed during the ensuing recess . . . one thousand copies of the digest" authorized sixteen months earlier. Perversely uncooperative, Jones found ways of procrastinating. He did not submit Coxe's report until January 1814, and then only because Congress again ordered him to do so.[30]

Personal antagonisms aside, what was there about Coxe's report that stirred such opposition? Of its four parts, two introductory essays and two sections of statistical abstracts, only the former were ever considered exceptionable, and for this there were valid reasons that Gallatin had perceived and Jones had misunderstood.[31] Neither secretary was correct, however, in charging that Coxe had violated the spirit of the resolution authorizing the report. The stipulation that the data collected be presented in whatever "form as shall be deemed most conducive to the interests of the United States" could reasonably have been construed as permission to submit not only facts and figures but also an interpretation of their significance.

The problem lay elsewhere. What Coxe did was to crib from his own numerous articles on the promotion of American manufactures, thus serving up stale fare in a familiar form. He once again attempted, for example, to demonstrate how manufactures were "favorable to the landed interest, . . . beneficial to foreign commerce, . . . advantageous to the business of the fisheries," and closely connected to national defense.[32] Nor could he depart from the formula employed twenty years earlier in A brief examination of

---

30. Seybert to Coxe, June 29, July 9, 1813, *ibid.*; *Annals of Cong.*, XXVI, 413, 573, 935; Jones to Coxe, Aug. 14, 30, Sept. 7, 1813, Coxe to Jones, Dec. 9, 1813, Coxe Papers. The letter of transmittal is in the *Annals of Cong.*, XXVI, 1009–1010. *A Statement of the Arts and Manufactures of the United States of America, for the year 1810: Digested and Prepared by Tench Coxe, Esquire, of Philadelphia* (Philadelphia, 1814) was also printed as an appendix in *Annals of Cong.*, XXVII, 2570–2642, and in *American State Papers, Finance*, II, 666–812. Coxe's covering letter to Jones, dated June 21, 1813, is found in the *Annals of Cong.*, XXVII, 2571.

31. The four parts were as follows: (1) an introductory essay on the advantages of manufactures to agriculture, commerce, navigation, fisheries, and national defense; (2) a second and redundant essay on "the practical foundations, actual progress, condition, and establishment of American arts and manufactures"; (3) statistical tables based on returns of government officials in 1810, setting forth production of the various branches of American manufacturing; and (4) additional tables providing (at Gallatin's request) a breakdown of production by counties. The redundancy of the second part of his report was explained by Coxe as follows: "Some additional information, not reducible into regular columns, has been collected which it is now proposed to submit in the form of statements, concerning several branches and denominations of manufactures and connected machinery." *Annals of Cong.*, XXVII, 2604. Nevertheless, as he admitted, many "facts in the first part of the statement, will be found in this second part." *Ibid.*

32. Coxe, "A Statement of the Arts and Manufactures of the U.S.," *ibid.*, 2573.

lord Sheffield's Observations and many times subsequently. He presented a lengthy discussion on every American manufacture, from cotton stockings to gold leaf, from the fife to the organ, from the processing of hog skins to the making of pig iron. To readers unacquainted with the contemporary literature on the subject, Coxe's essays might have seemed original; to more knowledgeable ones, they must have appeared tediously repetitious. The argument and supportive data on manufactures presented in 1791 by Hamilton, with Coxe's collaboration, may still have been valid, but familiarity rendered what had once been original and bold merely redundant. Perhaps a more creative man—a latter-day Hamilton—could have reshaped the traditional wisdom into a form peculiarly applicable to the exigencies of a new time and situation, but Coxe was not the man.

Whatever the defects of Coxe's report, they should be weighed against the handicaps under which he was obliged to work. As a later student of the subject explained, "this first industrial census was undertaken without even the formality of a schedule, or definite instructions." Moreover, Coxe, as he himself repeatedly pointed out, was forced to rely on faulty and incomplete returns. The collection of information on manufactures was only an incidental feature of taking the census, and the inaccuracies and omissions in many of the returns could not be corrected or supplied because of insufficient time to correspond with officials responsible for collecting the data.[33] The figures furnished him were even less reliable than those that he and Hamilton had used to prepare a similar report twenty years earlier, and his inferences from them, though plausible, were correspondingly less dependable.

In view of such limitations, Coxe merits high rank as a statistician at a time when that discipline was in its infancy—lending substance to the conclusion of a late-nineteenth-century scholar that "whatever utility the figures" in this report "possess was imparted by Tench Coxe."[34] Nor did his defects as a writer seriously detract from the durable significance of his essays on the current state and prospects of American manufactures. They provide still, as he asserted then, "a great number and variety of facts" on the condition of an economy poised for what some scholars of our day (though they disagree on the date, even the decade) term a "takeoff" upon a course of accelerated growth. Coxe was culpable of no more than pardonable

33. S.N.D. North, "Manufactures in the Federal Census," in *The Federal Census: Critical Essays by Members of the American Economic Association* (New York, 1899), 259. Coxe informed Eli Whitney, to cite only one of many possible illustrations, that the returns from Virginia were lamentably imprecise, while only half the districts in South Carolina sent in any returns at all. Eli Whitney to Coxe, Sept. 9, 1812, Whitney Papers, Yale University Library, New Haven, Conn.

34. North, "Manufactures in the Federal Census," in *The Federal Census: Essays*, 259. For a contemporary and critical view of Coxe's *Statement of the Arts and Manufactures*, see *North American Review*, I (1815), 234–247.

exaggeration when he claimed that his report was the "first attempt of an extensive and populous country . . . to ascertain in detail, the facts which constitute and display the actual conditions of its manufactures."[35] From the standpoint of his career as a political economist and publicist on behalf of American manufactures, the report was both the summation and culmination of a quarter-century crusade on behalf of American manufactures.

The renascent nationalism that pervaded the country during the years following the War of 1812 saw the adoption of policies Coxe had tirelessly advocated. Congress endorsed an ambitiously nationalistic program that included a national bank, internal improvements, a protective tariff, and navigation acts. Although on these and many other subjects Coxe would continue to write thousands of words, his essays were no longer adventuresome calls for pioneering programs but rather pleas for the amplification or modification of established policies.

The tariff legislation of 1816 was the harvest, however unrelatedly fortuitous, of a lifetime's work for Coxe. Designed to protect the nation's infant industries, hard-hit by the flood of cheap British goods dumped on the American market following the Treaty of Ghent, and based on Coxe's premise that the desideratum of national self-sufficiency was a balanced economy, this measure imposed duties on various articles. The duties ranged from 7.5 to 30 percent ad valorem and, most gratifying to Coxe, provided protection against the competition of coarse East Indian fabrics by stipulating that all cotton goods, however cheap, would be minimally valued at twenty-five cents a square yard. Not only were the bill's specific schedules a vindication of policies he had consistently advocated, but they also reflected a cardinal tenet of his economic thought—the idea, as John C. Calhoun explained, that the encouragement of manufactures must not depend "on the abstract principle that industry left to pursue its own course, will find . . . its own interest."[36]

Although pleased by congressional endorsement of the principle of protection, Coxe believed that the nation must move swiftly to offer yet firmer security to the industry on which he had long lavished attention. His *Memoir Upon Cotton Cultivation, Trade, and Manufactories*, published in 1817, was designed to alert his countrymen to the rapidly increasing pro-

---

35. Coxe, "A Statement of the Arts and Manufactures," *Annals of Cong.*, XXVII, 2603. For contemporary praise of this work, see C. J. Ingersoll to Coxe, Oct. 22, 1813, Elbridge Gerry to Coxe, Nov. 18, 1814, Roberts to Coxe, Dec. 6, 1814, Seybert to Coxe, Dec. 14, 1814, and Walter Lowrie to Coxe, Feb. 8, 1820, Coxe Papers. The most fulsome praise came from U.S. Atty. Gen. Richard Rush, son of Coxe's estranged friend Benjamin Rush. See R. Rush to Coxe, Nov. 30, 1814, Coxe Papers.

36. Quoted in Dorfman, *Economic Mind in American Civilization*, I, 383.

duction and declining price of that staple in India. Such developments, by glutting the British and Continental markets, seemed likely to cut off an important outlet for the American product, thus undermining southern and, indirectly, national prosperity.[37] This ominous possibility must be obviated, Coxe believed, both by the rapid "diffusion of all the modes and forms of *machine* manufacture" and by congressional action making *"permanent"* the duties imposed by the recent tariff and scheduled for revision in 1819. Returning to the subject a year later in *An Addition to the Memoir of 1817*, Coxe, his anxiety intensified by further discouraging reports on the prices and production of East Indian cotton, recommended more drastic legislation. To prevent the competition of "a people who live without animal food and are hired for a few cents a day," he recommended that Congress promptly prohibit the importation of all foreign cotton goods, a negative form of encouragement to manufactures that had "always excited the attention and prudence of the friends of our public revenue and credit."[38]

Just as the tariff of 1816 embodied a program he had advocated for decades, so the enactment of navigation acts fulfilled a long-cherished feature of his economic program. In response to the shrill demands of American shipowners, Congress in March 1817 adopted a measure, modeled on the English navigation system, that (in the case of nations having similar regulations) limited importations to the vessels of the producing country. The measure also stipulated that all coasting and fishing vessels must have crews with designated percentages of Americans, and it barred all except vessels of the United States from the nation's coastal trade. This was followed in 1818 by an act closing United States ports to vessels of Great Britain arriving from any of its colonial ports that excluded American vessels. Coxe had proposed such a retaliatory measure decades earlier, and it resulted, as he had predicted, in the opening of certain English colonial ports to American vessels. Gratified by the adoption of measures he had persistently recommended, Coxe was confident that "the national industry" had now been "placed upon a broad, deep, and secure foundation."[39]

37. [Coxe], *A Memoir, of February, 1817, Upon the subject of the Cotton Wool Cultivation, the Cotton Trade, and the Cotton Manufactories of the United States of America* (n.d., n.p.). It was printed by order of the Philadelphia Society for the Promotion of American Manufactures and was republished in the Philadelphia edition of E. Chambers and A. Rees's *London Cyclopedia.* Coxe to Madison, Feb. 2, 1819, Madison Papers, Lib. of Cong.

38. [Coxe], *Memoir Upon Cotton Cultivation, Trade, and Manufactories,* 12–13; Coxe, *An Addition, of December 1818, to the memoir, of February and August 1817, on the subject of the cotton culture, the cotton commerce, and the cotton manufacture of the United States* [Philadelphia, 1818], 8, 20.

39. Coxe, "Agriculture, Manufactures and Commerce. Circuit Court of the United States, Eastern District of Pennsylvania," Oct. 30, 1819, broadside, Coxe Papers. Coxe's position as sketched in the paragraph above can be followed in "Thoughts Occasioned by the propositions to convene Congress . . . ," *Nat. Intelligencer,* June 7, 23, July 3, 19, 1819. The navigation acts

Coxe undoubtedly overestimated the effects of these moderate mercantilist measures. Nevertheless, the march of progress seemed to him so steady that it needed only the slightest propellant. This idea of progress illuminating the past and bathing the future in shimmering iridescence continued to inspire Coxe's writings on the economy, as well as on varied aspects of the American past and present. No question intrigued him more than the origins, development, and distinctness of the American character—a subject that has engaged the American imagination from the seventeenth century to the present. His most ambitious contribution to this familiar ethnocentric exercise, appropriately entitled "The New World," took the form of sixteen essays published in 1809 in the *Democratic Press* and republished, though under different titles and in different forms, over the next decade.[40]

This virtually book-length work was described by him as "a profound and faithful enquiry into all the causes, natural, moral and accidental, which have tended to produce our true character."[41] It was primarily an exploration of the American past, which Coxe believed was guided by the law of progress or the hand of Providence (lumped together as causative agents) and was illuminated by the present—it was a morality play addressed to an audience that personified the virtues portrayed. He did not, like many later historians, see history either as a puppet show of the absurd or a drama depicting man's unsuccessful contest with forces beyond his prevention, will, or choice. Coxe was rather the heir of a tradition that eschewed a sense of helplessness for an overriding confidence in the capacity of man to control his own destiny.

Comfortably unaware that his conclusion and premises were the same, Coxe drew a reassuring lesson from his survey of the American past. "At the memorable epoch of the first effectual North American settlements," he wrote, "the monstrous Colossus of *ecclesiastical tyranny* bestrode all Christendom," and the chains of despotism shackled peoples everywhere but in the American colonies. There the oppressions of the Old World

---

that Coxe had advocated for so long and that were finally passed did not, however, become a permanent feature of American commercial policy. Owing largely to southern opposition, the measures were abandoned 12 years later.

40. "The New World: An enquiry into the National Character of the People of United States of America," signed "Columbianus," *Demo. Press*, Oct. 10, 14, 16, 17, 19, 21, 24, 26, 28, Nov. 3, 6, 8, 10, 16, 1809. A revised edition of these articles, entitled "America," appeared in *The American Edition of the New Edinburgh Encyclopædia. Conducted by David Brewster . . . and Now Improved . . . On the People of the United States* (Philadelphia, 1813), I, Pt. II, 586–670. Future cites will be to the *Demo. Press* except when quoting from the additional material that Coxe included in the encyclopedia article.

41. *American Ed. of New Edinburgh Encyclopædia*, I, 655.

melted away in the crucible of freedom—a freedom the colonists preserved in 1776 by "a revolution which has no parallel in the annals of human society." Americans of the Revolutionary generation, unwilling to be "numbered among the melancholy victims of misguided counsels," threw off the weight of traditional forms of government that had "crushed the liberties of the rest of mankind" and pursued, "happily for America, happily . . . for the whole human race," a "new and more noble course." They established their own governments, state and federal, "which have no model on the face of the earth." By this great creative act the Americans at once preserved and permanently guaranteed those conditions of freedom under which a distinctive national character had developed.[42]

What, then, were the unique traits of the Americans? Prefiguring (though surely not atypically so) the frontier thesis developed a century later, Coxe pointed to the influence of the American environment on transplanted Europeans. "The early American settlers," he wrote, "were like a nation of *Crusoes*, who having left their native homes in search of freedom and advancement in life" in a new and virtually unpeopled continent, "had everything to do for their own defence, comfort and prosperity." This situation "toned in fibre" and gave increased "courage and firmness," "ingenuity [and] perseverance" to Americans. The results were "*a high independent personal spirit and resolution*" that "are conceived to be the characteristic of the United Americans." Thus circumstanced and endowed, Americans had produced a society of individualistic, independent freeholders, unmarred by the extreme poverty so common in Europe, a society in which "anxious parents . . . see before them their children's prospects of rising in the world where infant settlements, increasing with our honest labour, pervade the land."[43]

In this New World Garden of Eden there was no sin, neither political inequities nor economic exploitation. There was no racial oppression and no social injustice. The Americans, Coxe boasted, displayed "an *enlightened humanity*," illustrated by their "humane and pious" solicitude for the Indians, their exemplary commitment to "the delicate and serious work of the gradual abolition of slavery," and their liberality toward the members of "the Hebrew nation residing among us." Other characteristics of the Americans included their "*refined humanity*" in the treatment of women, "*the enlightened practical humanity*" of their penal code, and their "intelligent regard and decided attachment" to the rights of property as an object

---

42. "New World," *Demo. Press*, Oct. 14, 1809; *American Ed. of New Edinburgh Encyclopædia*, I, 655.
43. "New World," *Demo. Press*, Nov. 3, 1809; *American Ed. of New Edinburgh Encyclopædia*, I, 656.

"founded in pure morality." Displaying such benevolent characteristics, the Americans had produced the most perfect society the world had ever known. As proof Coxe insisted that "the condition of religious liberty" was "the most favourable on the records of history" and pointed to the sturdy edifice of political freedom that had replaced the shaky establishment of European tyranny. Americans also displayed an uncommon share of "intelligence and exertion" (traits that Coxe implied were in short supply elsewhere), demonstrated most conspicuously in technology and science, journalism and scholarship, and philosophy and literature. All of this had resulted in "the noblest elevation of the public mind" in recorded history.[44]

Thematically dominating this rhapsody in praise of his countrymen were two ideas that have remained central in the interpretation of American history. The first of these was the contrast between America and Europe, by which Coxe implied freedom versus tyranny, innovation versus traditionalism, and innocence versus corruption. The second was the indigenous development of American ideas and institutions—an idea succinctly expressed by Coxe in the remark that "no people . . . have derived the principles and structure of their various institutions in so great a degree from their own will, mind and power, as the united Americans."[45]

In attempting to prove his country's originality, Coxe patently demonstrated that he was actually refracting the past through the lens of the present, a familiar and doubtless inescapable concomitant of historical scholarship. As a historian Coxe has defects that are so glaring, not because he differed substantially from his predecessors, contemporaries, or successors, but because his entrapment in the present was transparently responsible for both the selection and the distortion of his material. His tendency to tie his interpretation of the past to the prejudices of his own day is nowhere more conspicuous than in his strained attempt to show that the history of his country owed little to England, America's foremost antagonist in 1809. Although eschewing an assignment he said would require a separate volume, Coxe confidently asserted that conclusive evidence could easily be "adduced to prove that even the American provinces were rather *the colonies of all Europe*, than of the English kingdom." But even the debt to Europe was slight. The Americans were "the energetic temporal creators of their own . . . goodly country and all the copious blessings it contains," not least of which were their exemplary systems of "morals and religion" and their "own plan of justice and civilization" and "social freedom."[46]

44. "New World," *Demo. Press*, Oct. 24, Nov. 10, Nov. 8, Oct. 26, Nov. 8, 1809; *American Ed. of New Edinburgh Encyclopædia*, I, 625; "New World," *Demo Press*, Nov. 6, Nov. 3, 1809.
45. "New World," *Demo. Press*, Nov. 10, 1809.
46. *Ibid.*, Oct. 17, 1809; *American Ed. of New Edinburgh Encyclopædia*, I, 656.

From this New World paradise no people were excluded except the blacks, whom Coxe consigned to secular purgatory, there to expiate their inferior "natural condition" ("a dispensation of the divine hand") until such time as "the humanity of the white people" should raise them "from their African condition . . . to the knowledge and practice of the salutary arts of civilization, morals and religion." Such a viewpoint was, though susceptible to moral reproach, consistent with the racial bias he had exemplified many times before. The bias was notable only because it was voiced by an avowed abolitionist who had wrestled mightily with his conscience before embracing it.[47]

It was not as a social critic or as a historian, but as a political economist, that Coxe earned his contemporary repute and his claim to posthumous recognition. Coxe was "a man of very handsome talents, fond of political speculation," and "a remarkably ready writer," Joseph Gales of the *National Intelligencer* once commented. "It is probable there are very few men in the country who have written as much on the topics of politics, statistics, and political economy generally." Although his writings were greater in range and volume than subsequently recognized and although they helped to shape the thought of an era, their precise effect is difficult to assess. For one thing, literary or journalistic influence cannot be precisely determined by any known method. For another, it is impossible to say how large an audience Coxe's articles commanded. Nor is it possible to locate the exact niche among Americn economists to which he is entitled. Certainly he was neither an original thinker nor an economic theorist. Although familiar with the writings of Adam Smith, David Hume, James Anderson, and other European political economists, he did not rely on them for verification, amplification, or refutation. (He presumably agreed with Frederich List's comment that "the best book on political economy which one can read in" the United States "is life itself.")[48] Coxe focused on accumulating facts and figures and interpreting them as the progressive unfolding of a grand national destiny that had only the faintest relationship to European practice or theory. It was this virtually messianic impulse that gave Coxe's writings so much of their freshness and vitality. But what he regarded as the inestimable advantage of being a peculiarly American economist was, in fact, a major handicap. That he did not work out of a secure or well-defined intellectual tradition made it difficult for him to achieve reflective depth and profound judgment.

47. "New World," *Demo. Press*, Nov. 10, 1809.
48. *Nat. Intelligencer*, July 20, 1824; Margaret E. Hirst, *The Life of Frederich List and Selections from his Writings* (London, 1909), 37.

Such limitations, however, were also characteristic of most of his fellow American political economists, and Coxe, more than most of them, did have a constructive effect on the economic thought of his time. An appreciative student of his writings has recently remarked that "his claim to our attention rests on two talents: first, a rare empirical bent which led him to make predictions based chiefly upon economic data collected and interpreted by himself, and, second, a master publicist's knack of casting his own aims in the idiom of the dominant ideology." Moreover, his program, which pointed to the essential prerequisites for the country's economic growth, remained viable throughout his long career. Although fortuitous developments were causally more important than his advocacy, many of his recommendations were realized. Whatever their theoretical or stylistic shortcomings, his writings entitle him to a prominent place in the history of American economic thought. He both prefigured and influenced the group of economists known in the decade following the War of 1812 as the American Nationalist School; he was the literary father of the nation's cotton industry —a paternity that had an incalculable effect on succeeding decades; he was the persuasive proponent of industrial mechanization; and he was the country's most tireless advocate of manufactures generally. He surely merited the praise of a contemporary who wrote to him that "your writings on internal manufactures and resources have been of more use than those of any other man." The nation's "foremost exponent of a 'balanced' national economy," Coxe, as a distinguished authority on American economic history has said, "came closest to being the Defoe of America."[49]

49. Marx, *Machine in the Garden*, 151; Roberts to Coxe, Jan. 5, 1809, Coxe Papers; Dorfman, *Economic Mind in American Civilization*, I, 253, 254.

26 🦋

The Last of Life
Is Like the First

If Coxe perceived that posterity would remember him for his accomplishments as a political economist, he nowhere revealed it. He presumably believed instead that if he were remembered at all, it would be by descendants who were grateful for the potentially rich lands he bequeathed them. And as old age withered his long-nurtured political ambition, he increasingly centered attention on his children. When Rebecca died in 1806 there had been ten; seven years later there were only eight. His daughter Sarah Redman died in 1809 at the age of sixteen;[1] more painful yet was the death in 1813 of his eldest son, Tench, then twenty-nine years old.

After graduating from the University of Pennsylvania and qualifying for the bar, Tench, Jr., acquiesced in his father's wishes and in 1807 went south to oversee the sale of Coxe's Rutherford lands and to build up his own law practice. Although sales were sluggish and clients few, Tench remained in lonely exile, barely able to pay for food and lodgings, in a place that Tench, Sr., persisted in viewing as a land of great abundance and opportunity. "The extreme want of money and of a number of absolute necessaries," he complained to his father in January 1809, "has the natural effect of producing despair and despondency in my mind and rendering me almost incapable of thinking of any thing else than my unhappy situation." Had Tench, Sr., possessed the money, he certainly would have shared it; as it was, all he could manage for his son was to round up a postmastership at Rutherford and a county solicitorship. And so the young man stayed on,

---

1. John R. Livingston to Coxe, May 23, 1809, Coxe Papers.

unsuccessful, miserable, and by the summer of 1811 gravely ill. "I am wasting in body daily," he wrote to his father on August 18, 1812. "I do not like it at all, fearful of there being the symptoms of lurking disorder of fatal effect." Subsequent letters made it clear that he was suffering from the disease that had proved fatal to his mother—tuberculosis.[2] Eight months later he died. In a torrential downpour of rain that turned the clay soil into red mud, a handful of acquaintances attended his burial on a hill overlooking a large, elegant orchard on his father's vast North Carolina estate. It was, perhaps, the symbolic burial of the father's impossible dream.[3]

As if aware that he had done for his oldest son rather less than selfless parental devotion might have dictated, Coxe was henceforth a far more solicitous father. He arranged for the transfer of some property to his daughters, Ann Rebecca and Mary Rebecca, who lived with him at the house he rented on Walnut Street. He secured from President Madison commissions as midshipmen for his sons Henry and James, both of whom had graduated from the University of Pennsylvania. He did what he could to assist Charles Sidney, who after his admission to the Philadelphia bar in 1812 was his father's legal counselor and business adviser. He also did his best to further the career of Francis Sidney, who, having joined the Philadelphia firm of Pratt and Kintzing, launched his mercantile career with a three-year European tour that rivaled the commercial exploits of his Uncle Daniel fifteen years earlier.[4] Coxe's closest relationship, however, was with Alexander Sidney, namesake of Coxe's once-esteemed Treasury boss and the son who more than the rest shared his father's broad interests in economics and politics.

Coxe himself, involuntarily freed of official duties except for a minor court clerkship, was a familiar figure in Philadelphia. Tall and erect, though now "of a delicate frame," he seemed the very model of an American aristocrat.[5] And while ambition had led him to consort with rabble-rousers, the commonalty, and strident journalists, he remained at heart a Philadelphia grandee—so much so that his obvious good breeding, his civility, and his

2. Tench Coxe, Jr., to Coxe, Jan. 18, 1809, Aug. 11, 1811, *ibid.* See also Coxe to Francis S. Coxe, July 2, 1809, Tench Coxe, Jr., to Coxe, Sept. 8, 1811, and especially Sept. 8, 1811, *ibid.* For Coxe's efforts to assure adequate medical treatment for his son, see Coxe to Benjamin Rush, Feb. 6, 13, 1813, Rush to Dr. McIntire, Feb. 6, 1813, Rush Papers, Hist. Soc. Pa., Philadelphia.

3. J. M. Eustice to Coxe, Apr. 28, 1813, Coxe Papers.

4. For information on Francis Coxe's European sojourn, see Abraham Kintzing to Coxe, Oct. 19, 21, Nov. 3, Dec. 5, 1809, May 18, Aug. 16, 1810, July 19, 1811, Nov. 13, 14, Dec. 30, 1812, *ibid.* See also a circular letter by Coxe dated 1812, but sent out the following year when he introduced Francis to domestic and foreign merchants. Sometime after his return to the United States, Francis went on a business trip to New Orleans, where he was present at Andrew Jackson's famous military victory in Jan. 1815. See Coxe to James Madison, Jan. 25, 1815, Madison Papers, Lib. of Cong.; Edward Burd to Coxe, Jan. 24, 1815, Coxe Papers.

5. Coxe to James Madison, Jan. 3, 1814, Madison Papers, Lib. of Cong.

impeccable manners obscured to all but his most intimate associates the scars left by political and legal battles. In these he had managed to wound and in turn be wounded by everyone from his father to his favorite brother, Daniel.

It was a tribute to both his extraordinary energy and literary talents that he had managed in the face of such difficulties to turn out pamphlets and essays by the trunkful. Following the War of 1812 he not only continued to do so but took on more ambitious literary projects. Chief among these was the editing of David Ramsay's *History of the United States*. A native of Pennsylvania who had studied medicine under Benjamin Rush, Ramsay had settled in Charleston, South Carolina, where he earned some distinction as a physician and an active public figure, but considerably more as a historian. Ramsay's most influential and enduring work was *The History of the American Revolution*.[6] Despite such limitations as wholesale plagiarism from the British *Annual Register*, this book has been praised by a recent student of American historiography as a remarkable achievement demonstrating that Ramsay, though "an excellent representative of the first generation of Revolutionary War historians," nevertheless "outstrips his contemporaries in the depth and perception of his analyses."[7] Considerably more modest claims must be made for his *History of the United States*, written during the later years of his life and designed as "part of a far more ambitious project that was to contain the 'quintessence' of other histories."[8] As the book was unpublished at the time of Ramsay's death in May 1815, his longtime admirer and friend Mathew Carey proposed to publish it for the benefit of its author's heirs, "much of whose dependence rests on this work." To bring the book, which covered material through 1808, up-to-date, Carey first employed Reverend Samuel Stanhope Smith. Discovering that both Smith's addition and Ramsay's original work were studded with inaccuracies, the publisher hired Coxe, who as ghost-writer and copyeditor was paid $30 a week, "a very high compensation, the highest probably ever given in this country."[9]

6. David Ramsay, *The History of the American Revolution*. The first edition was published in two volumes in Philadelphia in 1789. It was republished as one volume in Dublin in 1793.

7. Page Smith, *The Historian and History* (New York, 1964), 166–167, 176.

8. *Dictionary of American Biography*, "Ramsay, David." Ramsay's work as a whole was entitled *Universal History Americanised . . .* and was finally published in nine volumes in Philadelphia in 1819. Ramsay's *History of the United States* originally constituted volumes X–XIII of this work.

9. Mathew Carey to Coxe, Oct. 30, Nov. 1, 1816, Coxe Papers. The work was finally published between 1816 and 1817. *History of the United States, from Their First Settlement as English Colonies in 1607, to the Year 1808, . . . by David Ramsay, M.D. Continued to the Treaty of Ghent, by S. S. Smith, D.D. and L. L. D. and Other Literary Gentlemen*, 3 vols. (Philadelphia, 1816–1817). A second edition appeared in May 1818. As indicated in the title of the book, Coxe received no credit by name for his contribution except as acknowledged in the phrase, "Other

Neither the editing of Ramsay's history nor other writing projects, like lengthy encyclopedia articles, was of more than marginal financial benefit to Coxe, who was less interested in royalties than in furbishing his literary repute.[10] He was thus particularly gratified by letters from authors soliciting his advice on editorial and publishing matters and from friends requesting that he undertake various projects.[11] Although flattered, Coxe turned down such offers, perhaps because of a dim awareness that he was only an amateur historian and a literary dilettante. But in old age as earlier, he was a more than ordinarily gifted journalist whose writings encompassed virtually the gamut of contemporary American issues.[12] During the last few years of his life, however, he was preoccupied by a problem that had long nagged him: slavery and the related question of race.

Coxe's position on black Americans had always been ambivalent. As a conscientious objector to slavery he had actively participated in the Pennsylvania Abolition Society, but as an unwitting Negrophobe he had time and again expressed his conviction that the black man could not be assimilated into American society. At base, such contrarieties, for him as for other well-intentioned Americans, were the symptom of an inability to resolve the tension between a belief in equal rights and an ineradicable racial prejudice.[13] Since tension is seldom endured patiently, it was in a fragile balance,

---

Literary Gentlemen." "Gentlemen" should have been singular. See also Carey to Coxe, Oct. 23, 24, 31 (two letters), Nov. 2, 5, 6, 9, 19, 21 (two letters), 23 (two letters), 26, 1816, Coxe Papers.

10. The most ambitious of Coxe's encyclopedia articles was the "United States," published in "the Philadelphia Edition of Chambers and Rees's London Cyclopedia . . . in the . . . 39th whole volume of that work." To the same encyclopedia Coxe also contributed "four or five" additional articles. See Coxe to Madison, Feb. 2, 1819, Madison Papers, Lib. of Cong. Coxe, hoping for some financial gain from his writings, proposed publishing a popular book on agriculture. In 1820 or 1821 he drew up a circular containing "Proposals for Publishing by Subscription, A Manual of Agriculture: Designed as a Hand book of System and Reference . . . Collected and Digested, and, in part, composed, by Tench Coxe, Esq. of Philadelphia," Coxe Papers. Coxe said that "this work will be put immediately to press; will contain six or seven hundred pages . . . and will be deliverable in Philadelphia." The work never went beyond the proposal stage.

11. Among the projects was a study of the defense of liberty in early 18th-century Europe, a history of America from the 1760s to the adoption of the Constitution, and an account of the fine arts in the United States. See, for example, Peter S. Du Ponceau to Coxe, July 1, 1814, Coxe to Thomas Barclay, July 31, 1814, John McCall to Coxe, Mar. 12, 1819, Coxe Papers.

12. Coxe obviously wrote many, though unidentified, articles for John Binns's *Demo. Press*, of which he was, in modern parlance, contributing editor. When Binns was obliged to be out of town, moreover, Coxe sometimes took over as editor. See Binns to Coxe, Oct. 2, 1814, Coxe Papers. He was also a frequent contributor to the *Niles' Weekly Register*. See Hezekiah Niles to Coxe, Oct. 7, 28, 1811, Coxe Papers. Coxe also continued to submit opinions on public affairs to prominent statesmen. See, as an example, "An inquiry into the causes of the disorders in the private business of the civilized world; with a *particular view to the case of the United States*, and especially of the *manufacturing branch* of its national industry," enclosed in Coxe to James Monroe, Nov. 28, 1819, Monroe Papers, Lib. of Cong.

13. "New World," *Demo. Press*, Oct. 17, Nov. 10, 1809.

likely to snap at a moment of crisis, and given the prevailing climate of opinion likely also to degenerate into unalloyed racism.

In Coxe's case the precipitant was the Missouri crisis of 1819 to 1821. The controversy surrounding the admission of that territory into the Union as a slave state came to center on the more important problem of what, if any, limits should be set on the future expansion of slavery into the territories. Congressional debate on the subject, rippling out to involve the nation at large, revealed a cancer that for years had been slowly spreading and now threatened American union. To a very few intrepid northerners the time had come at least to oppose (though surely not to offer any radical solutions to) an institution that to many of their countrymen was rather a benign, even a beneficent, manner of obviating the far more terrifying prospect of one and a half million free Negroes. The Missouri controversy, as recent scholars have suggested, involved not merely the expansion of slavery but brought into "premature focus" the principle of equality itself, an issue that "before the weary debates of 1820–21 were over" had "defeated and discredited everyone."[14]

Although Coxe had opposed slavery for well over three decades, he, like many other abolitionists of his day, had only to contemplate fleetingly the notion of equality to be thrown into frenzied terror. As an abstraction, emancipation seemed to him the only solution to a cruel and degrading labor system. Equality was the ultimate desert of black Americans, as long, that is, as its award remained in a future so distant that not even its outlines could be glimpsed. But immediate freedom, much less the granting of equal rights, Coxe believed, could lead only to a bloodbath such as had occurred in Santo Domingo and elsewhere when the blacks had been unshackled.

Thus fearful of immediate emancipation, Coxe exuded terror from virtually every paragraph of his thirteen-part series of articles that had been prompted by the renewal of the dispute over Missouri in the winter of 1820/1821. Entitled "Considerations Respecting the Helots of the United States," his ostensible theme was the importance of mutual forbearance and respect between North and South, but he also offered a disquisition on the historical role and legal status of the Negro in America.[15] He insisted that black men had never been—not in 1776, or in 1789, or in 1819—citizens of

---

14. Dangerfield, *Awakening of American Nationalism*, 114–115.

15. "Considerations respecting the Helots of the United States, African and Indian, native and Alien, and their descendants of the whole and the mixed blood," signed "A Democratic Federalist," *Demo. Press*, Nov. 25, 28, Dec. 2, 5, 9, 13, 22, 25, 28, 29, 30, 1820, Jan. 4, 8, 1821, hereafter cited as "Considerations respecting the Helots." Beginning with the eighth in the series of articles (Dec. 25, 1820), Coxe entitled his articles "To 'The Friends of Truth.'" For Coxe's views on black Americans, see Coxe to Madison, Dec. 28, 1820, Jan. 8, 1821, Madison Papers, Lib. of Cong.

either the United States or the states (an argument Chief Justice Taney and a majority of his Supreme Court associates would write into American constitutional law forty years later in the Dred Scott decision), and Coxe argued that their inferiority precluded any such status or its perquisites until education and the inculcation of higher (or white) morality should amend their innate defects. But Coxe's articles were something more than a mere run-of-the-mill exercise in defamation; they were also an apologia for slaveholders, presenting a defense that not even southern hard liners on the subject could have bettered.

Coxe's historical and constitutional argument, designed to show that Missourians could treat Negroes as they pleased, was a demonstration of the then-familiar allegation that "the black people and their descendants, free or bond, were not parties to the social compacts" made during and after the Revolution and were thus "*excluded . . .* from the rights, qualities and character of citizens." Nor did Coxe believe that Missouri should be criticized for adopting a constitutional ban on the emancipation of slaves without the consent of their owners (an effort, in point of fact, to make slavery irrevocable). The constitutions and laws of the Union and of the several states explicitly recognized slaves as property, and "the rights of property," he reminded fellow northern Republicans, were "the precious keystone of the noble arch of civil society, . . . the *Palladium* of free states."[16]

Had not human bondage and inescapably attendant considerations of morality been involved, Coxe's position, though vulnerable both psychologically and historically, could thus far be set down as merely a narrowly legalistic exercise of a kind that he had engaged in many times before. But he went further. This once redoubtable foe of slavery was now blind to its dehumanizing effects, and the flicker of compassion that had dimly illuminated his earlier views had been snuffed out. The blacks, he now wrote, were "uncivilized or wild men, without our moral sense, . . . our notions of moral character"; at base the fundamental issue was "the important fact of *color* and the prejudice or opinion concerning *faculty*, which no nation . . . has ever surmounted, or ever even attempted." Suppose "untutored black people," ignorant of the white man's religion and morals, "were to become suddenly free in our southern district," he exclaimed. Surely "the effects upon public order and the prostration of everything from the cradle of the infant to the couch of age, the bed of virgin purity, and the half sacred connubial chamber" were too horrible to contemplate, exciting "reflections that torture the sense, and lead to violence and phrenzy." To avert such a ghastly possibility was not only a civic but also a religious duty, one that he pointed out to "*the whole body of ministers of all the churches*" (though

16. "Considerations respecting the Helots," *Demo. Press*, Nov. 25, Dec. 2, 1820.

clearly with Philadelphia Quakers in mind) as a warning that by their misguided zealotry they might bring on the "horror . . . of a *Helot convulsion*." "The best occupation of the friends of liberty and humanity, religion, morals and peace," he admonished "is to render the blacks *amiable*, not terrific."[17] Had the alternatives been unprecedentedly bloody war or docility, the suggestion might have been sound.

Although unable to see that there were other choices, Coxe was at least aware of the injustice and the shameful indignities endured by a people who were oppressed lest they become oppressors. Incapable of resolving the conflict thus engendered, he resorted to a double standard—one for the North and another for the South. His fellow northerners, so adept at hurling stones at southern slaveowners, should take a hard look at their own treatment of the blacks, he impassionately insisted. In most northern states, even in "humane" Pennsylvania, free Negroes were denied the right to attend public schools, to vote, to hold office, to bear arms, and "even to bend their knees with us . . . in the sacraments of the church." "We have," his indictment read, "at strict law, *emancipated* but not really *enfranchised*" them while also denying them all things "necessary for comfort or happiness." Were northerners unwilling ever to grant them "*the whole substance of . . . liberty*"? Were they prepared permanently to deny them rights "which belong to the least qualified portion of the white citizens"? Although the questions were transparently designed to prick the consciences of his fellow northerners, Coxe, in a display of mind-numbing inconsistency, implicitly answered them in the affirmative. Since the blacks could not in his view be assimilated, he proposed that they be segregated. Advocating a variant of the program of the American Colonization Society, which had been founded in 1817 for the purpose of removing free blacks from the United States to Liberia, Coxe proposed to remove them instead to a place he termed "the new Africa," an all black country carved out of the American wilderness, remote from white settlements and policed by the United States government.[18] It was a plan that called on Congress to herd the blacks onto the type of government reservations that would later be set aside for Indians.

Within a year following the publication of this proposal, however, Coxe dropped it as both too expensive and too impractical and reaffirmed a policy he had often advocated. He now called for "the diffusion of the slaves from east to west, within the states . . . into districts numerously populated by white inhabitants." This was an alternative that southern blacks, seeking economic opportunity and relief from Jim Crow laws, would

17. *Ibid.*, Nov. 25, Dec. 25, 22, 1820.
18. *Ibid.*, Dec. 22, 30, 9, 13, 1820; "Civilization," signed "Columbus," *Nat. Recorder*, Feb. 26, 1820.

themselves choose a century or so later, but not until they had endured for many decades the situation that Coxe had recommended in 1820 as an interim policy. Coxe also counseled that until his migration plan should work its magic, the people of the North should show "mutual deference and concession" by allowing "those *authorities* . . . most approximate to the grounds of danger" to handle the blacks in their own way. The southerners, he said, "should be completely facilitated, and by no means *alarmed*, *perplexed*, or *impeded*, in those measures in which they may in their . . . discretion think it proper to lead."[19] There was at least a symbolic personal meaning in his plea. Having reconciled himself in old age to the rebuffs of Jefferson and Madison—the greatest southern Republicans of his time—so he now also resigned himself to the barbaric institution of a section whose economic growth, diversification, and prosperity he had zealously promoted for three decades.

Coxe did not, however, relinquish the political demonology that had long underpinned his democratic faith. Like Jefferson, he believed until the end of his days that the American experiment in free government was threatened from both within and without by secret monarchists. But unlike Jefferson, he continued to insist that the enemy within the gates was personified in those named Adams.

Coxe's renewed outburst against the Adamses was owing to John Quincy's candidacy for the presidency, which according to reports circulating in Philadelphia during the last months of 1822 seemed likely to succeed. Coxe was thunderstruck—how could it be that the son of John Adams, the nation's most notorious monarchist, should seriously be proposed as the Republican nominee for the nation's chief executive? The accuracy of his bold and not very plausible assumption about the senior Adams aside, the answer might well have been that the ideological sins of the father were not necessarily visited upon the child. Coxe entertained no such proposition, even though he would have indignantly dismissed the suggestion that because Tench Coxe was once a tory, his children were tories all. Instead, he remained unalterably persuaded that the national rescue operation he had helped to conduct in 1800 must be repeated in 1824.

He opened his attack upon the Adamses with a series of articles in the *Democratic Press* in January and February 1823, articles that were saturated in repetition and drenched in distortion. But unaware of the flaws in his sinuously semantic argument, Coxe, in what was a somewhat melan-

---

19. "Considerations respecting the Helots," *Demo. Press*, Dec. 29, 30, 28, 1820. Coxe again took up the subject of the blacks in a series of three articles published on Feb. 6, 8, and 12, 1821, and addressed "To the People of the United States of America; concerning the Colored Population" and again signed "A Democratic Federalist." *Ibid.* Yet another article on the subject, entitled "Les Noirs," was published on June 26, 1821, *ibid.*

choly autumnal performance, pursued it for thousands and thousands of words.[20] He did so even though convinced that only the most purblind pro-Adams supporters really needed it. Since to him it was axiomatic that the son shared John Adams's dedication to monarchy, it was redundant to draw up a separate bill of indictment for both. Blithely unaware of the illogicality and the dangers inherent in his own position, Coxe insisted that "when two individuals are partakers in meritorious or demeritorious conduct in the same operation, it is prudent and fair to consider them and their acts together." So considered, it was clear to him that just as the nation had repudiated John Adams in 1800, so it now must be spared another Adams who also insisted "on the beauty, excellence, perfection, and exclusive stability of a foreign rival constitution, full of kingly, baronial, manorial and ecclesiastical powers and influence of a decided hereditary nature and character, around which they desire the American people to rally as their standard."[21]

20. "To the Friends of the Principles of the Constitutions of the United States," siged "Sidney," *ibid.*, Jan. 6, 11, 16, 23, 28, 31, Feb. 11, 1823. There are drafts of these articles in the Coxe Papers. On Feb. 18, 1823, the *Demo. Press* published yet another article signed "Sidney," but this time entitled "Monarchy in the United States." In this essay Coxe turned from the Adamses to Alexander Hamilton. He again accused his former Treasury Department boss of also being a monarchist, offering Hamilton's speech at the Constitutional Convention as his principal evidence.

"Sidney" was the pseudonym Coxe used for one of the three series of articles that he wrote at this time on John Quincy Adams. Coxe described these series to Madison and Thomas Jefferson as follows: "I . . . took up the subject by indicating to two [of] our daily gazettes copies of Publicola's essays in the pamphlet form (as reprinted in London and Dublin with the name 'John Adams Esq're' on the title pages) and in the newspaper form in John Fenno's gazette of the U.S. in 1791 in 11 numbers, from which last authority the whole were reprinted. I prepared six papers under the signature of Greene, for the American Sentinel *here*, which were published after Publicola to shew the predecession [sic] of Mr. Adams senior (in London in 1797–8 [sic] and in N. York in 1790 in his '*defence*' and his Discourses on Davila in 1790) to Mr. Adams Jun'r. in his Publicola's of 1791, and the succession of Mr. Adams junr to his fathers labors, to the same end; the setting up the British, and the undermining the principles and character of our Constitution. While Greene was in the course of publication, I prepared another series under the signature of Sherman, (a name of republican esteem in the East) in five numbers, which will be continued, if I will. These are in Binns's democratic press. At the same time I published another series more strictly on the demerits and evils of Publicola, of which No. 4 has appeared today. They will be continued. I send mine of the Greene's, the Sidney's and the Sherman, all I have by me: also two numbers of Publicola. . . . All these papers have appeared in the Dem. Press and Sentinel since the 5th of January current and were in Washington in 36 hours, and in Boston in 70 hours. But not a syllable has been published in attack, or in explanation, justification, extenuation or reply from either place. . . . The publication, and commentaries (Publicola, and the strictures on him) are so rec'd. as far as I learn, as to leave no doubt that Mr. Adams will be unsupported in Pennsylvania by one electoral vote." Jan. 31, 1823, Jefferson Papers, Lib. of Cong.

There are drafts of seven "Shermans" and eight "Sidneys" in the Coxe Papers. However, the newspaper versions of "Sherman" and "Greene" have not been found because, so far as can be determined, the requisite issues of the *Demo. Press* and the *American Sentinel and Mercantile Advertiser* (Philadelphia) for 1823 have not been preserved.

21. "To the Friends of the Constitutions of the U.S.," *Demo. Press*, Jan. 6, 31, 1823.

Twenty years earlier Coxe's quest for secret enemies of the Union had earned him recognition as the Sir Galahad of the Jeffersonian campaign, but in 1823 his strident evocation of the same issue failed to stir his countrymen, who no longer sniffed a monarchical plot in every breeze. And though he strove to enlist the support of Madison and Jefferson for his campaign, not even these former fellow crusaders were willing to endorse it, much less to enlist in it.[22] For Coxe's part, the crusade must have been more a reflexive than a reflective reaction to the campaign of an Adams—an exercise in what Allen Tate has described as the kind of "demonology" that "attributes to a few persons the calamities of mankind" and that "is perhaps a necessary convention of economy in discourse."

To Coxe it was perhaps also a way of expressing an inchoate anxiety that all was not right in a nation that for forty years he had pictured as well-nigh perfect. That the serpent in the Garden might not be monarchy, but rather the overarching expectations of a people still bound by history and chained to the frailties of common human nature, did not occur to him. Nor, if he considered the possibility that cupidity might be among the frailties undermining the new nation, did he apply that insight to his own activities. Instead, he counted himself the beneficiary of an open society in which, overcoming formidable difficulties, he had acquired extensive property that would afford his children a goodly legacy. And the last few years of his life were spent, more often than not acrimoniously, in assuring that his estate would do just that.

Although shrunk by advantageous sales, his landholdings remained impressively large, and as Coxe had believed for three decades or more, their value would continue to rise, finally yielding a princely income. His lands (some of which were still in the hands of trustees to whom he had consigned them many years earlier) included most of the acreage he had acquired in Pennsylvania, New York, Virginia, Maryland, Kentucky, and, above all, North Carolina.[23] The sale of the North Carolina property at a great profit continued to be an idée fixe, as was the notion that a promotional campaign might accomplish what the experience of others and current market conditions indicated could not be done.

The promotion of land sales was the purpose of his *Proposals for Establishing a Number of Farms*; like those of New England and the middle

22. See Coxe to Madison and Jefferson, Feb. 1, 1823, Madison to Coxe, Mar. 1, Oct. 12, Nov. 3, 1823, Coxe to Madison, Oct. 3, 1823, Madison Papers, Lib. of Cong.; Jefferson to Madison, Oct. 18, 1823, Ford, ed., *Works of Jefferson*, XII, 315.

23. According to figures given by Coxe when in June 1812 he announced the opening of "Coxe's Land Office," he owned 243,000 acres in Pennsylvania, more than 30,000 acres in New York, 48,000 acres in Virginia, smaller acreage in Maryland and Kentucky, and 390,000 acres in Rutherford County, North Carolina. See *Relf's Philadelphia Gazette and Daily Advertiser*, June 9, 1812.

states, the farms in western North Carolina were to be "for the Mutual Benefit of the Settlers." Coxe published the pamphlet in 1816 and distributed it throughout the United States and Europe, concentrating particularly on the South, where "editors of papers from Norfolk to Savannah" were urged as a public service to "publish the whole."[24] As he predictably pictured it, western North Carolina was a New World Promised Land, the Broad and Catawba rivers its Nile and Euphrates, an area affording remarkable natural resources and boundless opportunities, lacking only latter-day Israelites. To him, in brief, the marvels of North Carolina were no less impressive than those of Carolana as depicted by his forebears a century earlier. And though one piece of promotional literature may be rather like another, the similarity between Tench Coxe's *Proposals for Establishing a Number of Farms* and Colonel Coxe's *Description of Carolana* are too striking to be set down as merely fortuitous.

But the expected tide of settlers did not roll in, and Coxe, lacking the financial resources of his forebear, was unable to hold onto virtually virgin lands. In order to safeguard his holdings closer to home, he was by 1819 willing to dispose of his cherished North Carolina estate at considerably less than he had hoped for, but still at a profit. The opportunity was provided by Jacques Donatien Le Ray de Chaumont, the husband of Rebecca Coxe's sister, who rounded up an interested purchaser, Augustus Sackett, a New York speculator eager to buy in the South before the available lands there ran out. On August 12, 1819, after months of negotiation, a contract was signed between Coxe's assignees and the New Yorker. Sackett agreed to buy Coxe's whole Carolina property at fifty cents an acre, to be paid for over a five-year period beginning in 1823.[25] It was for Coxe, whatever his grandiose expectations, an advantageous transaction. The purchase price of $199,978 represented a sum five and one-half times his original investment, though a return commensurate with his worry and care would have bank-

---

24. *Proposals for Establishing a Number of Farms, like those of New England, New York, New Jersey, Pennsylvania, and Delaware, on the South Side of the Western Districts of North Carolina, for the Mutual Benefit of the Settlers, and of The Trade of Charleston, Wilmington, (N.C.), Fayetteville, Georgetown, (S.C.) Augusta, and Savannah; and of The Planters on the Sea-Coast of the two Carolinas Who raise Sugar, Rice, Indigo, Cotton, and Tobacco, and make lumber and Naval Stores, and may not raise Grain or Cattle* (n.p., 1816); Coxe to Joseph Gales, Jan. 17, 1817, Coxe Papers.

25. For information on purchase offers that Coxe declined, see W. S. Hart to Coxe, Nov. 21, 1816, Jan. 6, 1817, May 15, 20, 1818, Coxe to Hart, Jan. 21, 1819, Coxe Papers. The articles of agreement of Aug. 12, 1819, for the sale to Augustus Sackett are in the Coxe Papers. For the negotiations, see Sackett to Du Ponceau, Dec. 29, 1818, Sackett to Coxe, Feb. 4, Apr. 8, 24, May 10, June 4, 1819, Coxe to Sackett, Feb. 23, Mar. 27, 1819, Du Ponceau to Coxe, Jan. 5, 1819 (misdated 1818), *ibid.* The first monies paid by Sackett were to go to Antoine René Charles Mathurin de La Forest, who had purchased Coxe's debt to William Polk of $2,761 and interest after Dec. 27, 1804.

rupt the United States treasury. Nevertheless, the sale must have been a gratifying vindication of an almost twenty-five-year effort to hold onto a half-million acre estate, a battle waged at enormous personal costs—the sacrifice of the physical ease and comfort of his family, the alienation of friends and close relatives, and the humiliating pursuit of minor public offices to provide money to pay mounting taxes. Now that his North Carolina property had been sold at a handsome profit, he need no longer worry about losing his remaining landholdings, which were still sizable, particularly in Pennsylvania. Age did not wither nor did experience stale his lifelong expectation that the peopling of his sparsely settled lands would make his heirs, if no longer himself, rich. And his wishes were in time fulfilled, though anthracite rather than people was responsible. For the time being, Coxe continued to fret and to wrangle over the protection and enhancement of his estate.

After a dispute that would have strained all but the closest family relationship, Coxe persuaded his brothers and William Tilghman to terminate the trusteeship established by his father's will and to vest such proceeds as might be due him in his son Charles Sidney as assignee. He badgered the trustees to whom he had confided his real property twenty years earlier to make a similar arrangement. He quarreled with Augustus Sackett, the purchaser of his North Carolina lands, over the ownership of an additional 40,000 acres of land that, on survey, he claimed his Rutherford property had been found to include. He instituted costly and protracted legal proceedings to assure that his children should receive their rightful share of the estate of their maternal grandfather, Charles Coxe, who died intestate in 1815 and whose property his surviving sons tried to conceal or withhold.[26]

Such negotiations provided a familiar script, and Coxe must have played his role effortlessly. Certainly there was no evidence of strain, although he professed that his was a particularly delicate constitution. "I find a weak body, of my own, kept to a late time of life, in a capacity for action

26. For Coxe's dispute with his brothers and William Tilghman over trusteeship, see "Brief of rights of Wm. Tilghman, W. Coxe Jr., and D. W. Coxe under the codicil to the will of Wm. Coxe Senr.," 1820, "Notes on the Will of Wm. Coxe, Sr.," July 18, 1820, William Coxe, Jr., to Coxe, Sept. 29, Oct. 6, 1818, Jan. 29, Feb. 18, 1820, William and Daniel Coxe to Coxe, July 5, 1820, Coxe to William Coxe, Jr., Oct. 4, 1819, June 21, 1820, *ibid*. For the assignment to Charles S. Coxe, see William Coxe, Jr., to Coxe, Mar. 6, 14, 16, 20, 25, 30, 1820, *ibid*. For the problems with the trusteeship of Coxe's real property, see Coxe to William Coxe, Jr., Sept. 8, 10, 1823, Du Ponceau to Coxe, Jan. 24, Feb. 13, 14, 16, 1824, Coxe to Charles S. Coxe, Feb. 16–17, 1824, *ibid*. Owing to reassignments and trustee changes, the trusteeship of Coxe's property was by the 1820s vested in Du Ponceau alone. For his quarrel with Sackett, see Perkins Nichols to Coxe, Sept. 11, 1821, Coxe to Sackett, Sept. 24, 1821, *ibid*. For the disposition of Charles Coxe's estate, see especially "Tench Coxe's Notes," Aug. 21, 1818, Andrew Allen, Jr., to Coxe, May 15, 1816, Oct. 29, 1823, "Affidavit of children of T and Rebecca Coxe," July 7, 1823, *ibid*.

and thought by regularity in hours, moderation in food, . . . drinking as little as I can," he wrote to Sackett in October 1819.[27] Whether physically weak or not, he retained the inner strength that had always allowed him to accept setbacks—financial, public, and personal—with more than ordinary fortitude. And though he surely had had his share, it was as if fate had decreed that there should be no surcease. Having lost two children only a decade before, his last years were saddened by the deaths of two others. Alexander Sidney, with whom Coxe had lived since 1813, died after a brief illness in October 1821 at the age of thirty-one. Nine months later came yet another blow—the death aboard the United States *Enterprize* of his son James, midshipman and acting naval lieutenant. There were now only six children —Ann, Mary, Francis, Charles, Henry, and Edmund—and to them Coxe, by the terms of a will drawn up in December 1821 and frequently altered in detail, bequeathed his property in six equal shares.[28]

He did not expect his children soon to acquire their legacy, however. Recalling the longevity of his paternal forebears, Coxe at sixty-six believed he had years to go, a confidence expressed in his renewed quest for public office. Once again he sought the aid of Madison and Jefferson, with whom he had continued to correspond. Coxe drew particular gratification from Madison's expressions of esteem and Jefferson's assurances that he considered him to be "a long tried public and personal friend," "*a fellow laborer, indeed, in times never to be forgotten.*" It was in character that after having read such accolades, Coxe should once again ask for a job, not because he now urgently needed the income, but because he wished "a mark of confidence," a token recognition of his "voluntary exertions in politics and *the national œconomy.*"[29] While Jefferson had long since learned to ignore this trait of Coxe's, Madison, a more steadfast friend, gladly obliged by writing letters of recommendation to President Monroe and to Senator James Barbour of Virginia.[30] It came to nothing, as Coxe, who had made it clear that

---

27. Coxe to Sackett, Oct. 2, 1819, *ibid.*

28. Alexander Sidney's obituary appeared in the *Demo. Press*, Nov. 1, 1821, and in the *Nat. Intelligencer*, Nov. 3, 1821. For a description of Alexander Sidney's interest in public affairs and economics, see Coxe to Benjamin W. Crowninshield, Jan. 18, 1818, Coxe Papers. On James's death, see Coxe to Monroe, Sept. 9, 1822, Coxe Papers. Francis's share was somewhat less than the others, as an agreement was reached on May 16, 1822, stipulating that the money Francis S. Coxe had received from the sale of a land patent in North Carolina belonging to Tench Coxe, Jr., should be deducted from Francis's one-sixth share of his father's estate.

29. Coxe to Madison, Nov. 12, 1820, Madison Papers, Lib. of Cong. For Coxe's supplications to Madison and Jefferson, see Coxe to Madison, Mar. 7, Nov. 12, 1820, Madison to Coxe, Nov. 4 [14], 1820, Madison Papers, Lib. of Cong.; Jefferson to Coxe, Oct. 13, 1820, Coxe to Jefferson, Nov. 11, 1820, Jefferson Papers.

30. Madison to Monroe, Nov. 19, 1820, Gaillard Hunt, ed., *The Writings of James Madison . . .*, IX (New York, 1910), 32–33; Madison to James Barbour, Nov. 25, 1820, Barbour to Madison, Dec. 12, 1820, Madison to Monroe, Dec. 28, 1820, Madison Papers, Lib. of Cong.

he would accept no post outside Philadelphia, had certainly known all along. Having typecast himself as a patronage supplicant, he played the role tirelessly and thoughtlessly.

The role was fitting. Nothing in Coxe's life became him more than the manner of his last years. Until the winter of 1823 he was in good though not robust health, filling his days with the activities that had always most fully engaged his attention—the care of his landed property and his writings. His repose may on occasion have been disturbed by shattered dreams of personal riches, but his mind was uncluttered by misgivings about his official and particularly his journalistic career. Always more adept at prescribing for the present than reviewing the past, he remained engrossed in current affairs; still afflicted with the intellectual's occupational vanity, he continued to believe that his writings could mold men's ideas. But though he still turned out articles on economics and politics, his focus now shifted, as it had following the death of his wife fifteen years earlier, to religion.

In 1823 and 1824, as in 1806 and 1807, Coxe's articles on religion were primarily pious invocations of morality—affirmations of traditional Christian beliefs, as well as American secular dogma, notably freedom of conscience and the total separation of church and state. He harped particularly on the theme of separation, demonstrating perhaps that his essential creed centered on democratic good works, not divine revelation. His newfound target in the 1820s was the Roman Catholic church, especially the doctrines of papal supremacy and infallibility. These, Coxe said, "will be found to have a more solemn bearing upon the subject of an external influence, on our internal affairs, than any other in the fixed system of foreign policy." Calling on Pennsylvania communicants of the Roman faith to be good Americans first and Catholics second, he urged them to sever all ties with the pope. While admitting "that I am too prolix on the subject," Coxe allowed his output of articles to grow as his indignation at the Catholic faith in the power of bishops mounted. The monarchist John Adams seemed to have been replaced by the rector of Saint Mary's Church as the American symbol of despotism.[31] That Coxe, like the Philadelphia priest, had once

---

See also Madison to Jefferson, Dec. 10, 1820, *ibid.* Although even Madison's influence was not enough to secure Coxe a federal post, he did not desist. In Sept. 1822 Coxe applied to Monroe for the commissionership of the land office, and in Feb. 1823 he sought the post of Senate clerk. Coxe to Monroe, Sept. 9, 1822, Nathaniel Macon to Coxe, Feb. 27, 1823, John Taylor to Coxe, Mar. 1, 1823, Coxe Papers. He succeeded in neither.

31. "Reflections Occasioned by the Allocution of the *Roman Catholic Pontiff,* and the recent events, in the ancient Congregations, of that Holy Communion, by a friend of religious peace and charity," signed "Pacificus," *Relf's Philadelphia Gaz.,* Mar. 6, 1822. The second of this two part article appeared on Mar. 8. Drafts of the articles are in the Coxe Papers. See also draft of an article endorsed by Coxe "Extract from letter of Coxe—y [ear] 1823. Catholic Church, U.S. and elsewhere," June 7, 1823, *ibid.;* "An Exposition of the Rights of Churches in the United

loyally bowed to the claims of a foreign though secular prince was perhaps all but forgotten. He only remembered the past as it should have been.

"Even in America," Henry Adams once remarked, "the Indian Summer of life should be a little sunny and a little sad, like the season, and infinite in wealth and depth of tone—but never hustled." Perhaps it was so for Coxe, who in so many ways typified the American of his day. In late January 1824 he was "confined for some time by a serious indisposition"; by early spring he was somewhat better but did not venture outside. Sitting in his office-bedroom fronting Pine Street, he day after day sorted the tens of thousands of papers he had accumulated, labeling some, arranging the return of others, and disposing of none; he thus preserved what would be, when finally made available to scholars 150 years later, one of the richest sources for the history of his time. Adding to what already was enough to keep a team of catalogers busy, he kept up his correspondence, now in a handwriting so cramped and spidery that reading it, as Jefferson complained, was like "decomposing and recomposing . . . hieroglyphics."[32]

Although Coxe's correspondence contains no clue to the exact nature of his illness, his strength slowly ebbed, and by late May he was bedridden. His last days, appropriately, mirrored the interests of a lifetime. The last known letter he wrote was to a fellow land speculator;[33] among the last he received was one from a newspaper editor to whom he had only recently sent articles "of a most interesting character as they bear upon our political institutions and public men" and another concerning a federal job in Washington.[34] One of the last pieces he read was on the cultivation of barley.[35]

Coxe died on Thursday morning, July 16, 1824. Funeral services were held on the following "afternoon, at 4 o'clock from his late dwelling, 167 Pine Street."[36] He was buried in Christ Church cemetery, his grave marked by a simple monument. His true monument, long patinaed, was slowly raised by those processes of history that fulfilled his prophecy of a firmly united, industrial, rich, and mighty nation in ways that he could not have imagined.

States," signed "Pacificus," *American Sentinel*, Sept. 2, 7, 1822; "The Christian Church," *American and Commercial Daily Advertiser* (Baltimore, Md.), Oct. 30, 1822.

32. Quoted in John Morton Blum, *The Republican Roosevelt* (Cambridge, Mass., 1954), 142. See also Coxe to Robert Hazelhurst, Jan. 29, 1824, Coxe Papers; Jefferson to Madison, Oct. 18, 1823, Ford, ed., *Works of Jefferson*, XII, 315.

33. Coxe to Samuel Hodgdon, May 13, 1824, Coxe Papers.

34. John Binns to Coxe, May 21, 1824, William Lee to Coxe, May 6, 1824, *ibid*.

35. This took the form of a letter sent to Coxe on Apr. 4, 1824, by Robert Hare, the prominent Philadelphia scientist. *Ibid*.

36. *National Gazette and Literary Register* (Philadelphia), July 16, 1824. See also *Poulson's Daily Adver.*, July 17, 1824; *Nat. Intelligencer*, July 20, 1824.

Bibliography

MANUSCRIPT SOURCES

This biography is principally based on the Tench Coxe Papers in the Historical Society of Pennsylvania. As the provenance and scholarly importance of that collection were described in the Preface, it is unnecessary here to provide a guide. Thanks to a grant from the National Historical Publications and Records Commission, the staff of the Historical Society of Pennsylvania has for the past three years been rearranging, repairing, cataloging, and filming the Coxe Papers. The bulk of the collection, expertly edited by Lucy Fisher West, is now available in a microfilm edition of approximately 122 reels. For this publication the Coxe Papers were divided into four series. Series I (32 reels) consists of bound volumes and printed material. Series II (78 reels) includes correspondence to and from Coxe, along with his general papers. Series III (5 reels) consists of Coxe's books, pamphlets, essays, and writings for newspapers and periodicals. Series IV (7 reels) reproduces Coxe's bills and receipts. Each of the reels is preceded by an introductory note that briefly describes the contents of the manuscripts included thereon. The edition as a whole is described in Lucy Fisher West, *Guide to the Microfilm of the Papers of Tench Coxe in the Coxe Family Papers at the Historical Society of Pennsylvania* (Philadelphia, 1977); this work leads the researcher through the maze of this large collection. There are parts of the Coxe collection that I consulted in the preparation of this biography, and that are accordingly cited in the notes, but that are not included in the microfilm edition. The more important items that were not filmed are, first, over seventy-five document cases of material in the Coxe family manuscripts that consist chiefly of the legal papers of Tench Coxe's sons, Charles S., Alexander S., and Edmund S. Coxe and, second, the papers of Dr. Thomas Ruston, William Harrison, and James McCalley—collections that Coxe either legally seized or became custodian of.

My research in the Coxe manuscripts (for which I primarily consulted photostatic copies made in the 1920s, which were kindly made available to me by the late Daniel M. Coxe) was completed before the microfilm edition was launched. Although the staff of the Historical Society of Pennsylvania had accomplished a preliminary sorting of the collection, the papers with which I worked not only were uncataloged but were organized in a manner quite different from that of the microfilm edition. For this reason the notes to this biography do not include references to volume or box numbers. By using the *Guide to the Microfilm of the Papers of Tench Coxe*, however, one can easily locate the documents cited herein on the appropriate reel of the microfilm edition (excepting, of course, the unfilmed manuscripts described above). I hope that the cojoined text and footnotes of the present biography will themselves serve as a guide to the Coxe Papers, providing a preview of the subjects for which these manuscripts afford so unique a source for examination and re-study.

Rich though this collection may be, I could not—even had I been content to do so—have based my work exclusively on it. As was said in the Preface, Coxe was seemingly incapable of discarding a doodle but was, at the same time, unwilling to go to the trouble of preserving copies of his own letters. To find these, I was obliged to look elsewhere. Some were uncovered in libraries and historical societies throughout the country, and, predictably, the most important of them were found in the papers of Coxe's more prominent correspondents. The single most valuable of these sources was the James Madison Papers in the Library of Congress. The same repository's holdings of the papers of Thomas Jefferson and of Alexander Hamilton are also rich in Coxe letters, and the Stephen Collins Manuscripts there provide revealing information on Coxe's activities as a tory merchant during the Revolution. Other collections in the Library of Congress that include Coxe material are the papers of James McHenry, Robert Morris, the Shippen family, George Washington, and James Monroe.

Other libraries also contain manuscripts that supplement the Coxe Papers. Material on Dr. Daniel Coxe can be found in the Rawlinson and Henry Newman Manuscripts, Bodleian Library, Oxford, in the Colonial Office Papers, Public Record Office, and in the Additional Manuscripts, British Library. Tench Coxe's career as a land buccaneer is illuminated by the Ephraim Kirby Papers, Duke University. His acrimonious relationship with Secretary of the Treasury Oliver Wolcott, Jr., is revealed in the Wolcott Papers at the Connecticut Historical Society. That society's holdings of the papers of William S. Johnson and of Jeremiah Wadsworth also include Coxe documents. The details of his longtime association with Albert Gallatin, Wolcott's successor as Treasury secretary, can be traced in the Gallatin Papers, New-York Historical Society. In the New York Public Library there are a number of manuscript collections that contain Coxe material, notably Nalbro Frazier's letterbooks and Madison's papers. Coxe's connection with Timothy Pickering, his steadfast partner in land speculation and staunch political antagonist, is revealed in the Pickering Papers in the Massachusetts Historical Society, where one may also find interesting Coxe material in the papers of John Adams.

The biographer of a prominent Philadelphian like Coxe will discover at the Historical Society of Pennsylvania a cornucopia of manuscripts. Those including significant Coxe material are the Cadwallader Colden, Dreer, Gratz, Society Miscellaneous, and George M. Dallas collections; the Corroe, Charles Coxe, William Irvine, Thomas McKean, Benjamin Rush, Lea and Febiger, and Tilghman family papers; and the Reed and Forde Business Correspondence. Among other Philadelphia institutions that have relevant material are the Library Company, the American Philosophical Society, Independence Hall, the University of Pennsylvania Archives, and the Philadelphia Department of Records.

Coxe manuscripts of varying numbers and significance are located in the following repositories: Boston Public Library, Houghton Library of Harvard University, the Huntington Library, Library of the Pennsylvania Historical and Museum Commission, Carnegie Library of Pittsburgh, and the libraries of Princeton University, Yale University, the University of North Carolina (Chapel Hill), and Indiana University.

If measured by bulk and not by quality, the most significant source of Coxe material is official records. The outstanding repository of these is the National Archives, where one could (if anyone other than his biographer ever wished to do so) spend a season in the company of Tench Coxe. The record groups that include sizable Coxe material are R.G. 26: Lighthouse Letters; R.G. 58: General Records, 1791–1803, and Letters of the Commissioner of the Revenue, 1794–1797; R.G. 59: Appointment Papers, Miscellaneous Letters, 1790–1799, and General Records of the State Department; R.G. 75: Letters of Tench Coxe, Commissioner of the Revenue, Relating to Procurement of Military, Naval, and Indian Supplies; and R.G. 233: Reports of the Secretary of the Treasury, 1784–1795. Most voluminous of all are the records pertaining to Coxe's purveyorship of the United States. Thousands of letters, for example, are included in the oversize volumes that comprise R.G. 92— Records of the Quartermaster General's Office, Purveyor's Letterbooks, 1800– 1812—and yet hundreds and hundreds more are in the uncataloged Coxe and Irvine Papers in the National Archives. Also indispensable for the history of Coxe's purveyorship are the following collections found in R.G. 107: Secretary of War Letterbook, Miscellaneous Letters Sent by the Secretary of War, Register of Letters Received by the Secretary of War, and Letters Sent by the Secretary of War Relating to Military Affairs.

PRINTED SOURCES

PUBLIC RECORDS

Since historical specialists are familiar with these and the general reader is pardonably uninterested, a comprehensive list seems unnecessary. The official (or quasi-official) federal records on which I most heavily relied were the following: Worthington Chauncey Ford *et al.*, eds., *The Journals of the Continental Congress, 1774–1789*, 34 vols. (Washington, D.C., 1904–1937); [*Annals of the Congress of the United States*]: *Debates and Proceedings in the Congress of the United States, 1789–1824*, 42 vols. (Washington, D.C., 1834–1856); *American State Papers: Documents, Legislative and Executive, of the Congress of the United States*, 38 vols. (Washington, D.C., 1832–1861); volume I of *Journal of the Executive Proceedings of the Senate of the United States from the Commencement of the First, to the Termination of the Nineteenth Congress*, 3 vols. (Washington, D.C., 1828); volume I of *Journal of the House of Representatives of the United States*, 9 vols. (Washington, D.C., 1826); and *The Public Statutes at Large of the United States of America*, 56 vols. (Boston, 1845–1942).

For the sections of this book that deal with Pennsylvania, I frequently referred to public records of the commonwealth (appropriate volumes of *Minutes of the . . .*

General Assembly . . . [usually issued by sessions], *Minutes of the Supreme Executive Council*, and James T. Mitchell and Henry Flanders, comps., *The Statutes at Large of Pennsylvania from 1682 to 1801* . . . [Harrisburg, Pa., 1896–1908], for example), but I would like to single out for tribute one of the most superb documentary collections in the whole field of American history: Samuel Hazard *et al.*, eds., *Pennsylvania Archives*, 1st–9th Ser. (Philadelphia and Harrisburg, Pa., 1852–1935)—containing enough volumes to fill shelf upon shelf.

WRITINGS OF TENCH COXE

The greatest surprise in studying Coxe's career was the discovery that he was among the most prolific writers of his day. Although his major works on political economy are (at least to many historians) well known, his impressive (at least quantitatively) journalistic output has not previously been recognized. Since this subject was discussed in the Preface, it is necessary here only to repeat that drafts and scraps of essays in the Coxe collection provided the initial clues that led to the identification of Coxe's authorship of hundreds of newspaper and magazine articles. Many of them stemmed from his role (as explained in this biography) as silent partner at different times in at least three different Philadelphia newspapers, the *Federal Gazette*, the *Aurora-General Advertiser*, and the *Freeman's Journal and Philadelphia Daily Advertiser*. He also contributed to magazines (particularly the *American Museum*, published in Philadelphia from 1786 to 1792 by Coxe's close friend Mathew Carey) and to other newspapers, among them the *Pennsylvania Packet*, the *American Daily Advertiser* (the title of which varied), the *Gazette of the United States*, the *Democratic Press* (for which he was for a time star columnist), *Poulson's American Daily Advertiser*, and the *American Sentinel and Mercantile Advertiser*. He did not confine himself to Philadelphia journals, however. His essays appeared, for example, in newspapers published in Pittsburgh; Lancaster, Pennsylvania; New York; Baltimore; and Wilmington, Delaware; and also, with especial frequency, in the *National Intelligencer* of Washington, D.C.

I have attributed to Coxe only those articles for which I found concrete proof of his authorship—either a draft (whole, partial, or fragmentary) in the Coxe Papers or an unequivocal imputation of authorship by newspaper editors and correspondents. He almost certainly wrote many, many more (on the basis of the distinctive pen names he used, for example, one might assign hundreds of additional pieces to him), but to try to identify them all would lead one into byways of research from which one might never emerge with a completed book. Nor would any particular point be served by taking such detours. Given the prolixity and redundancy of Coxe's writings, it is highly unlikely that the positive ascription to him of additional essays would alter one's appraisal of his thought. For that there is already an abundance of material.

Coxe's writings that seemed to me of any consequence are cited in the notes to this volume. For the benefit of scholars who may wish a convenient guide to Coxe's major contributions to the literature of political economy and his ideas on the leading issues of his day, I have provided below a highly selective bibliography of his more important writings. They are listed chronologically.

1784

"Proposals for establishing another Bank in the city of Philadelphia, by the name of the Bank of Pennsylvania," Feb. 2, 1784. Broadside, Coxe Papers.

1786

Thoughts concerning the Bank of North America; with some facts relating to such establishments in other countries, respectfully submitted to the honorable General Assembly of Pennsylvania, by one of their constituents ([Philadelphia], 1786).

Cool Thoughts on the Subject of the Bank. Addressed to the Honorable the Representatives of the Freemen of the Commonwealth of Pennsylvania in General Assembly ([Philadelphia], 1786).

Further Thoughts concerning the Bank, respectfully submitted to the Honorable the General Assembly of Pennsylvania, by one of their Constituents ([Philadelphia], 1786).

1787

An Enquiry into the Principles on which a Commercial System For the United States of America should be Founded; to which are added Some Political Observations connected with the subject (Philadelphia, 1787). Also published in the *American Museum*, I (1787), 432–444.

An Address to an Assembly of Friends of American Manufactures, Convened for the Purpose of establishing a Society for the Encouragement of Manufactures and the Useful Arts (Philadelphia, 1787).

Plan of the Pennsylvania Society for the Encouragement of Manufactures and the Useful Arts (Philadelphia, 1787). Also published in the *American Museum*, II (1787), 167–169.

"On the Federal Government," signed "An American Citizen," *American Museum*, II (1787), 303–306, 387–391. Also published in the *Pennsylvania Gazette*, Oct. 24, 1787. Published in 1788 in pamphlet form as *An Examination of the Constitution* . . . (see below).

"A Letter to the Honourable Richard Henry Lee, Esq.," signed "An American," *Pennsylvania Herald*, Dec. 29, 1787. Also published in the *Pennsylvania Packet*, Jan. 2, 1788, and the *American Museum*, III (1788), 78–83.

1788

"Address to the Minority of the Convention of Pennsylvania," signed "A Freeman," *Pennsylvania Gazette*, Jan. 23, 30, Feb. 6, 1788. Also published in the *Pennsylvania Packet*, Jan. 25, 31, Feb. 7, 1788, and in the *American Museum*, III (1788), 158–161, 242–245, 365–367.

"To the People of the United States," signed "A Pennsylvanian," *Pennsylvania Gazette*, Feb. 6, 13, 20, 27, 1788.

"Address to the honourable the members of the Convention of Virginia," signed "An American," *Pennsylvania Gazette*, May 21, 28, 1788. Also published in the *Virginia Gazette and Weekly Advertiser* (Richmond), June 5, 1788, and the *American Museum*, III (1788), 426–433, 544–548.

"Address to the friends of American Manufactures . . . ," signed "An American Citizen," *American Museum*, IV (1788), 341–346. Also published in the *Pennsylvania Gazette*, Oct. 29, 1788.

"Thoughts on the Subject of Amendments to the Federal Constitution," signed "An American Citizen," *Pennsylvania Gazette*, Dec. 3, 10, 24, 31, 1788.

An Examination of the Constitution for the United States of America, submitted to the people by the general convention, at Philadelphia, the 17th. day of September, 1787, and since adopted and ratified by the conventions of eleven states. By an American Citizen. To which is added a speech by the Honorable James Wilson, Esquire, on the same subject (Philadelphia, 1788).

1790

"Address to the Landholders and other Citizens, of New Jersey, showing the practicability, and other advantages, of establishing useful manufactures in that State," *Columbian Magazine* (Mar. 1790), 171–174.

"Notes concerning the united states of America, containing facts and observations relating to that country, for the information of emigrants. Ascribed to Tench Coxe, Esq.," *American Museum*, VIII (1790), 35–42.

1791

"Reflexions relative to the stock of the bank of the United States and to the national funds," signed "A friend to Sober Dealing and Public Credit," *American Museum*, X (1791), 168–171.

A Brief Examination of lord Sheffield's Observations on the Commerce of the United States (Philadelphia, 1791). Also published in the *American Museum*, IX (1791), 121–126, 177–183, 217–226, 233, 241, 289, 295, X (1791), 9–16.

1792

Reflexions on the State of the Union (Philadelphia, 1792). Also published in the *American Museum*, XI (1792), 127–132, 185–192, 253–260, XII (1792), 7–16, 77–80.

"Observations on the preceding letters of 'a farmer' addressed to the yeomanry of the united states," *American Museum*, XII (1792), 167–170, 217–221, 272–278.

1794

A View of the United States of America, in a Series of Papers, Written at Various Times between the Years 1787 and 1794, By Tench Coxe, of Philadelphia; Interspersed with Authentic Documents: The Whole Tending to exhibit the Progress and Present State of Civil and Religious Liberty, Population, Agriculture, Exports, Imports, Fisheries, Navigation, Ship-Building, Manufactures, and General Improvement (Philadelphia, 1794; reprt. London, 1795).

1795

"An examination of the pending Treaty with Great Britain, To the President of the United States," signed "Juriscola," *Philadelphia Gazette*, July 31, Aug. 4, 8, 12, 1795.

1796

The Federalist: Containing Some Strictures upon a Pamphlet, Entitled, "The Pretentions of Thomas Jefferson to the Presidency, examined, and the Charges against John Adams, refuted." Which Pamphlet Was First Published in the Gazette of the United States, in a Series of Essays, under the Signature of "Phocion" (Philadelphia, 1796). The articles also appeared in *Gazette of the United States*, Nov. 9, 11, 14, 15, 16, 17, 18, 21, 24, 25, 29, 30, 1796.

1798

"Neutral Spoliations," signed "An American Merchant," *Philadelphia Gazette* (5 articles): Feb. 3, 5, 16, Mar. 8, 12, 1798; *Aurora* (whole series of 9 articles): Feb. 6, 7, Mar. 7, 8, 9, 10, 25, 27, 28, 1798. Parts of this were reprinted in *Carey's United States' Recorder* (Philadelphia), Mar. 8, 10, Apr. 3, 1798, and the *American Museum for 1798*, 226–260.

1799

"Dissent Of the . . . Members of the House of Representatives . . . of Pennsylvania, from the Address to the President of the United States, adopted by said House," Jan. 1, 1799, *Freeman's Journal*, July 16, 1804.

An Authentic View of the Progress of the State of Pennsylvania since the Establishment of the Independence of the United States of America (Philadelphia, May 1799). Also printed in the *Aurora*, May 14, 1799.

"To the Republicans of Pennsylvania, Tench Coxe *et al.*," Aug. 7, 1799. Broadside, Harvard College Library, Cambridge, Mass. Republished in the *Aurora*, Aug. 15, 1799.

"To the Citizens of the State of Pennsylvania," Sept. 19, 1799, *Aurora*, Sept. 26, 30, 1799.

"Observations on the Cession Proposed in 1797, to be made by Connecticut to the United States, of an alleged jurisdiction, of the Lands in the North-western territory, sometimes called the 'Connecticut reserve,' " signed, "Columbus," *Aurora*, Dec. 28, 1799.

1800

Strictures upon the Letter imputed to Mr. Jefferson, addressed to Mr. Mazzei (n.p., 1800). Also published in the *Freeman's Journal*, June 1804.

To the Republican Citizens of the State of Pennsylvania, Tench Coxe et al. (Lancaster, Sept. 17, 1800). Also published in the *Aurora*, Sept. 27, 1800.

Connecticut Claim. Part I. Jurisdiction and State's Right of Soil (Lancaster, [1800 or 1801]).

1801

An Important Statement of Facts, Relative to the Invalidity of the Pretensions formerly made upon the Pennsylvania Lands, by the unincorporated Companies of Connecticut Claimants, and by those who claimed under those Companies; in a Letter from the Secretary of the Land-office, to the Pennsylvania Commissioners, intended to evince the Liberality of the Government and Land-holders of Pennsylvania, in the Act of the 4th of April, 1799, and the Releases of 120 to 180,000 Acres under the same (Lancaster, 1801).

1802

"Franklin," *Aurora*, June 19, 22, 25, July 3, 10, 12, 13, 19, 20, 21, 22, 23, 24, 26, 27, 29, 31, Aug. 3, 21, 27, Nov. 19, 30, Dec. 2, 1802. The twenty-three articles appeared under varying titles.

1803

"Columbus," *Tree of Liberty* (Pittsburgh), Aug. 13, 20, 27, Sept. 3, 10, 17, Oct. 1, 1803. The seven articles appeared under varying titles.

1804

Since virtually every issue of the Philadelphia *Freeman's Journal* from June to Sept. 1804 carried contributions by Coxe, no listing of those articles is included here. The interested reader should see especially the issues of the *Journal* for June 13, 15, 18, 19, July 7, 10, 11, 12, 16, Aug. 18, 20, 22, 23, 27, Sept. 5, 6, 8, 20, 1804.

A Communication from the Pennsylvania Society for the Encouragement of Manufactures and the Useful Arts, Feb. 7, 1804 (Philadelphia, 1804).

Report of the Committee appointed to prepare a report on the state of manufactures in the United States generally, and particularly in the State of Pennsylvania, at the time of the establishment of this society and of their progressive increase and improvement to the present time. Published by order of the Board, Tench Coxe, President (Philadelphia, 1804). Republished in the *Philadelphia Evening Post*, Mar. 13, 1804.

A Communication from the Pennsylvania Society for the Encouragement of Manufactures and the Useful Arts (Philadelphia, 1804). Republished in the *Philadelphia Evening Post*, Mar. 13, 1804, and the *Aurora*, Mar. 13, 1804.

To the Democratic Republicans of the State of Pennsylvania (n.p. [1804]).

An Essay on the Manufacturing Interest of the United States; with Remarks on Some Passages Contained in the Report of the Committee of Commerce and Manufactures. By a Member of the Society of Artists and Manufacturers of Philadelphia . . . (Philadelphia, 1804).

1805

An Exposition of Some Facts Relative to the Personal Conduct and Business of the Office of Tench Coxe, Purveyor of Public Supplies (Philadelphia, 1805).

1806

Thoughts on the Subject of Naval Power in the United States of America; and on Certain Means of Encouraging and Protecting Their Commerce and Manufactures (Philadelphia, 1806). Republished in the *Democratic Press*, May 27, 29, June 1, 3, 5, 8, 1807.

1807

"A Defence of the conduct of the President of the United States upon the subject of the impressment of Persons from American ships," signed "Juriscola," *Democratic Press*, Mar. 27, Apr. 3, 29, 1807.

An Examination of the Conduct of Great Britain Respecting Neutrals (Philadelphia, 1807; 2d ed., Boston, 1808).

1808

"To the People of the United States," signed "Juriscola," *Democratic Press*, July 25, Aug. 1, 8, Sept. 22, 1808.

An Address to the Citizens of Pennsylvania, on the Situation of our Country; Connected with the Public Conduct of James Ross, a Candidate for the Governmental Chair of Pennsylvania. By a Pennsylvanian (Philadelphia, 1808).

1809

"An Estimate of the Times," *Democratic Press*, Feb. 9, 10, 11, 13, 14, 15, 16, 1809.

A Memoir on the Subject of a Navigation Act, Including the Encouragement of the Manufactory of Boats and Sea Vessels, and the Protection of Mariners (Philadelphia, 1809).

"The New World: An enquiry into the National Character of the People of United States of America," signed "Columbianus," *Democratic Press*, Oct. 10, 14, 16, 17, 19, 21, 24, 26, 28, Nov. 3, 6, 8, 10, 16, 1809.

1810

"To the Cultivators, the Capitalists and the Manufacturers of the United States," signed "Juriscola," *Democratic Press*, July 31, Aug. 3, 8, 10, 13, 18, 24, 1810. Re-published in the *National Intelligencer*, July 27, Aug. 1, 3, 6, 10, 15, 20, 1810.

"An Inquiry into . . . public and private Banks . . . ," *Democratic Press*, Nov. 26, 1810.

1811

Respectful Observations on the subject of the bill in relation to "the establishment of a quartermaster's department," in lieu of the existing military agencies, so far as it may affect the office of the Purveyor of Public Supplies (n.p. [1811]).

"An Examination of the Conduct of Great Britain respecting neutrals since the peace of America in 1803, and before the Fr Berlin decree of 1806," signed "Juriscola," *Democratic Press*, Aug. 6, 13, 17, 21, 1811.

1812

"To the Wise and Good of all Parties and Places Throughout the United States," signed "Juriscola," *National Intelligencer*, Aug. 6, 13, 20, 1812.

1813

"America," *The American Edition of the New Edinburgh Encyclopœdia. Conducted by David Brewster . . . and Now Improved . . . On the People of the United States* (Philadelphia, 1813), I, II, 586–670.

1814

A Statement of the Arts and Manufactures of the United States of America, for the year 1810: Digested and Prepared by Tench Coxe, Esquire, of Philadelphia (Philadelphia, 1814).

1817

A Memoir, of February, 1817, Upon the subject of the Cotton Wool Cultivation, the Cotton Trade, and the Cotton Manufactories of the United States of America (Philadelphia, 1817).

1818

An Addition, of December 1818, to the memoir, of February and August 1817, on the subject of cotton culture, the cotton commerce, and the cotton manufacture of the United States, most respectfully submitting a suggestion, for consideration only, of a specific measure for securing to the planters of cotton a market for their crops (n.d., n.p.)

1819

"Agriculture, Manufactures and Commerce. Circuit Court of the United States, Eastern District of Pennsylvania," Oct. 30, 1819, Broadside, Coxe Papers.

"On the Grape Vine, with its wines, brandies, and dried fruits," signed "A Friend to the National Industry," *National Intelligencer*, Nov. 6, 10, 13, 16, 20, Dec. 2, 15, 31, 1819.

1821

"Considerations respecting the Helots of the U.S., African and Indian, native and Alien, and their descendants of the whole and the mixed blood," signed "A Democratic Federalist," *Democratic Press*, Nov. 25, 28, Dec. 2, 5, 9, 13, 22, 28, 29, 30, 1820, Jan. 4, 8, 1821.

"To the People of the United States of America; concerning the Colored Population," signed "A Democratic Federalist," *Democratic Press*, Feb. 6, 8, 12, 1821.

"An American Freeholder to the People of the United States," *Democratic Press*, Mar. 6, 9, 12, 15, 19, 1821. Republished in the *National Intelligencer*, Apr. 6, 10, 12, 14, 1821.

"An American Freeholder to the landed . . . citizens of the U.S. concerning the prospects of Business . . . ," *Democratic Press*, Apr. 12, 14, 25, May 3, 1821. Republished in the *National Intelligencer*, May 3, 10, 11, 1821.

1822

"An Exposition of the Rights of Churches in the United States," signed "Pacificus," *American Sentinel*, Sept. 2, 7, 1822.

1823

"To the friends of the Principles of the Constitution of the United States," signed "Sidney," *Democratic Press*, Jan. 6, 11, 16, 23, 28, 31, Feb. 11, 18, 1823.

BOOKS AND ARTICLES

As I hope this biography demonstrates, I am greatly indebted to my many fellow historians, past and present, who have depicted in illuminating detail the story of American independence and nation-building. Although I would like to acknowledge my debt in a traditional bibliography, a complete listing of the many books and articles that I consulted is neither feasible nor of any particular scholarly utility. Numerous bibliographical essays and guides are, after all, readily available, rendering superfluous the publication of yet another. My own assessment of the historical literature of the main period covered by this biography can be found in a bibliographical essay that I prepared some years ago ("The Federalist Age: A Reappraisal," in George Athan Billias and Gerald N. Grob, eds., *American History: Retrospect and Prospect* [New York, 1971]). The works there discussed are those on which I principally relied in the preparation of this biography. Coxe's long and multifaceted career, however, obliged me to consult works that are not germane to a bibliographical essay on the early national era or that are too narrowly focused to warrant inclusion. A selective list of such books and articles, as well as a few of the works, described in my bibliographical essay, to which I am most particularly indebted, is given below.

Studies of Tench Coxe: The only previous biographer of Coxe was Harold Hutcheson (*Tench Coxe: A Study in American Economic Development* [Baltimore, Md., 1938]), who did not have access to the Coxe Papers. Despite that limitation, Hutcheson's monograph affords a succinct summary of Coxe's career and an astute appraisal of his ideas. Particularly commendable was Hutcheson's mastery of relevant secondary material, to which his notes and bibliography often pointed me. For the Coxe family genealogy, which even the most patient historian would find tiresome to unravel, I am greatly indebted to Alexander Du Bin's *Coxe Family* (Philadelphia, 1936). For general assessments of Coxe's stature as a political economist and his place in American intellectual history, two books were indispensable: Leo Marx, *The Machine in the Garden: Technology and the Pastoral Ideal in America* (New York, 1964), and Joseph Dorfman, *The Economic Mind in American Civilization, 1608–1865*, 4 vols. (New York, 1946–1959).

The Colonial Background: The best sketch of Dr. Daniel Coxe is G. D. Scull, "Biographical Notice of Doctor Daniel Coxe, of London," *Pennsylvania Magazine of History and Biography*, VII (1883), 317–335. There is also a brief account in [John Oldmixon], *British Empire in America . . .* , 2 vols. (London, 1708). The complicated story of Dr. Coxe's West Jersey proprietorship is related in John E. Pomfret's definitive monographs on colonial New Jersey, *The Province of West New Jersey, 1609–1702* (Princeton, N.J., 1956) and *The New Jersey Proprietors and Their Lands, 1664–1776* (Princeton, N.J., 1964). Pomfret's encyclopedic knowledge of the subject is summarized in *Colonial New Jersey: A History* (New York, 1973). Coxe's own description of his Jersey property is in his pamphlet, "Accounts of New Jersey," located in the Bodleian Library, Oxford. The starting point of any study of Coxe's Carolana claim is Colonel Daniel Coxe, *A Description of the English Province of Carolana. By the Spaniards call'd Florida, and by the French, La Louisiane*, 4th ed. (London, 1741). The best secondary account is Verner W. Crane, *The Southern Frontier, 1670–1732* (Philadelphia, 1929), an exacting example of close scholarship that has seldom been matched. Informative background information and pertinent documents are provided by C. W. Alvord and L. Bidgood, *First Explorations of the Trans-Allegheny Region by the Virginians, 1650–1674* (Cleveland, 1912). A brief account of the subject is supplied by Frank Edgar Melvin in "Dr. Daniel Coxe and Carolana," *Mississippi Valley Historical Review*, I (1914), 257–262. Information on Dr. Coxe's son, Colonel Daniel Coxe, is sparse. Most useful of the few books in which he is briefly discussed are Pomfret, *Colonial New Jersey*, Lewis Townsend Stevens, *The History of Cape May County, New Jersey, from the Aboriginal Times to the Present Day . . .* (Cape May City, N.J., 1897), and Richard S. Field, *Provincial Courts of New Jersey . . .* (New York, 1846). On Tench Coxe's father, William, no account of any use has been published; on the family background of his mother, Mary Francis, sketchy information is offered in [Samuel Alexander Harrison], *Memoir of Lieut. Col. Tench Tilghman, Secretary and Aid to Washington . . .* (Albany, N.Y., 1876); on Tench's brothers and sisters there is nothing in print worth mentioning. The account of Coxe's family that appears in this biography is therefore based on the Coxe Family Papers, Historical Society of Pennsylvania. The same applies to Coxe's childhood and young manhood, though some concrete information about his education is supplied by University of Pennsylvania Archives, as cited in the notes to chapter 1. Conclusions about the milieu in which Coxe was raised can be drawn from any number of books on Philadelphia. The one that I found most informative is, unfortunately, unpublished: Ethel E. Rasmusson, "Capital on the Delaware: The Philadelphia Upper Class in Transition, 1789–1801" (Ph.D. diss., Brown University, 1962). I also found Ms. Rasmusson's study an indispensable source for information on Philadelphia society from 1789 to 1801, the years on which her monograph centers.

The American Revolution: My account of the divided loyalties of the Coxe and related families was inspired by Carl Becker's masterly fictional essay, "The Spirit of '76" (Carl Becker, J. M. Clark, and William E. Dodd, *The Spirit of '76 and Other Essays* [Washington, D.C., 1927]). Specific information on Philadelphia tories and Coxe's loyalist friends elsewhere can be gleaned from Lorenzo Sabine's still definitive *Biographical Sketches of Loyalists of the American Revolution . . .* , 2 vols. (Boston, 1864). As a source of material on Philadelphia during the British occupation, Ellis Paxson Oberholtzer's *Philadelphia: A History of the City and Its People: A Record of 225 Years*, 4 vols. (Philadelphia, n.d.), has not been supplanted by seventy-five years of scholarship. Oberholtzer leaned heavily on Philadelphia newspapers of the time (the *Pennsylvania Evening Post* and the *Royal Pennsylvania Gazette*), as I also did. On British officialdom in occupied Philadelphia I found most useful Edward E. Curtis, *The Organization of the British Army in the American Revolution* (New Haven, Conn., 1926). On economic matters, Willard O. Mishoff's "Business in Philadelphia during the British Occupation, 1777–1778," *PMHB*, LXI (1937), 165–181, is authoritative. The *Pennsylvania Magazine of History and Biography* is an indispensable source of diaries, journals, and memoirs of the occupation period. The standard work on New York City—where most of Coxe's commercial partners were located—during the British occupation is Oscar Theodore Barck, *New York City during the War for Independence, with Special Reference to the Period of British Occupation* (New York, 1931). For Coxe's career during the period of the Revolution following the British evacuation of Philadelphia, I found little in print that was useful except newspapers, particularly *The Pennsylvania Journal and the Weekly Advertiser* and the *Pennsylvania Gazette*.

Confederation and Constitution: Since economic conditions of the 1780s are nowhere more comprehensively depicted than in Coxe and Frazier's voluminous letterbooks, my description of the business cycle and related subjects is based chiefly on that source. I did, however, consult the standard historical literature. Particularly useful as a reference work was Curtis P. Nettels, *The Emergence of a National Economy, 1775–1815* (New York, 1962). I found invaluable Allan Nevins, *The American States during and after the Revolution, 1775–1789* (New York, 1927), and Robert A. East's exemplary monograph on *Business Enterprise in the American Revolutionary Era* (New York, 1938). Also of service was Emory R. Johnson *et al.*, *History of Domestic and Foreign Commerce of the United States*, 2 vols. (Washington, D.C., 1915). I greatly profited from rereading Merrill Jensen, *The New Nation: A History of the United States during the Confederation, 1781–1789* (New York, 1950), though I disagree with many of its conclusions. On the issue of economic growth during the Confederation era, I was the willing student of Stuart Bruchey, *The Roots of American Economic Growth, 1607–1861: An Essay in Social Causation* (New York, 1968), and of Douglass C. North, whose *Growth and Welfare in the American Past: A New Economic History* (Englewood Cliffs, N.J., 1966) also pointed me to significant scholarship that I otherwise might have neglected. On Anglo-American commercial relations, I benefited from the admirably succinct appraisal in Jerald A. Combs, *The Jay Treaty: Political Battleground of the Founding Fathers* (Berkeley, Calif., 1970), as I also did from Francis Armytage's excellent monograph, *The Free Port System in the British West Indies: A Study in Commercial Policy, 1766–1822* (London, 1953). A good starting point for information on the West Indian trade is J. H. Parry and P. M. Sherlock, *A Short History of the West Indies* (London, 1956). On the China trade in the 1780s, the interested reader should consult Foster Rhea Dulles, *The Old China Trade* (Boston, 1930), Samuel W. Woodhouse, "The Voyage of the Empress of China," *PMHB*, LXIII (1939), 24–36, and Eugene S. Ferguson, *Truxton of the Constellation: The Life of Commodore Thomas Truxton, U.S. Navy* (Baltimore, Md., 1956).

In describing aspects of Coxe's career during the 1780s other than his business activities, I relied on the work of historians too numerous to list in entirety here. Robert L. Brunhouse, *The Counter-Revolution in Pennsylvania, 1776–1790* (Harrisburg, Pa., 1942) unraveled for me the knotty tale of Pennsylvania politics. My chief mentor on money and banking was Bray Hammond, *Banks and Politics in America from the Revolution to the Civil War* (Princeton, N.J., 1957), though I relied too on Lawrence J. Lewis, *A History of the Bank of North America: The First Bank Chartered in the United States* (Philadelphia, 1882), Janet Wilson, "The Bank of North America and Pennsylvania Politics, 1781–1787," *PMHB*, LXVI (1942), 3–28, and John Thom Holdsworth, *Financing an Empire: History of Banking in Pennsylvania*, 4 vols. (Chicago, 1928).

On cultural and social matters the first volume of John Bach McMaster, *A History of the People of the United States from the Revolution to the Civil War*, 8 vols. (New York, 1888–1913), affords a mine of information that McMaster culled from contemporary newspapers. Useful too are Nevins, *The American States during and after the Revolution*, and Jensen, *The New Nation*. A splendid guide to the intellectual milieu is Mathew Carey's *American Museum*, a potpourri of literary essays, poetry, current events, economic promotional literature, history, and essays on manners that reveal the flavor and the limited ingredients of American intellectual life of the period. The background requisite to an appreciation of Coxe's instrumental role in promoting American manufactures is in J. Leander Bishop, *A History of American Manufactures from 1608 to 1860*, 3d ed., rev., 3 vols. (Philadelphia, 1868), Victor S. Clark, *History of Manufactures in the United States, 1607–1860* (Washington, D.C., 1916–1928), and George S. White, *Memoir of Samuel Slater, The Father of American Manufactures . . .* (Philadelphia, 1836).

The best way to approach Coxe's contributions to the debate over ratification of the Constitution is to contrast them with the best of the genre, notably the essays of Alexander Hamilton and James Madison in *The Federalist*, as well as with the less distinguished, a number of which are published in Paul Leicester Ford, ed., *Pamphlets on the Constitution of the United States, Published during Its Discussion by the People, 1787–1788* (Brooklyn, N.Y., 1888). The ratification controversy in Pennsylvania, in which Coxe was a principal, can be followed in John Bach McMaster and Frederick D. Stone, eds., *Pennsylvania and the Federal Constitution, 1787–1788* (Philadelphia, 1888). The related activities of Coxe's more important allies in the debate are described in Irving Brant, *James Madison: Father of the Constitution, 1787–1800* (New York, 1950), Broadus Mitchell, *Alexander Hamilton: Youth to Maturity, 1755–1788* (New York, 1957), David Freeman Hawke, *Benjamin Rush: Revolutionary Gadfly* (Indianapolis, Ind., 1971), and Charles Page Smith, *James Wilson: Founding Father, 1742–1798* (Chapel Hill, N.C., 1956).

The Federalist Decade: The principal works on which I relied in writing the chapters of this book that cover the most historically significant phase of Coxe's career are, as I have said, described in my bibliographical essay that covers this period, as well as in many standard works. Particularly valuable are the multivolume biographies of the decade's more prominent statesmen, particularly the appropriate volumes of Douglas Southall Freeman, *George Washington: A Biography*, 7 vols. (New York, 1948–1957), Dumas Malone, *Jefferson and His Time*, 5 vols. (Boston, 1948–1974), Irving Brant, *James Madison*, 6 vols. (Indianapolis, Ind., 1948–1961), Broadus Mitchell, *Alexander Hamilton*, 2 vols. (New York, 1957, 1962), and Page Smith, *John Adams*, 2 vols. (Garden City, N.Y., 1962). To these monuments of American historical scholarship I am greatly indebted. My major reliance, however, was not on biographies of these leaders but on their writings, unpublished and published. Of the latter, I found the *Papers of Alexander Hamilton* (Harold C. Syrett *et al.*, eds., 21 vols. [New York, 1962–1976]) most valuable chiefly because of Coxe's position in the Treasury Department and not, I hope, because I was one of the editors of the pertinent volumes. The *Papers of Thomas Jefferson* (Julian P. Boyd *et al.*, eds., 19 vols. to date [Princeton, N.J., 1950–]) afforded not only essential source material but occasionally challenging interpretations, with some of which I have taken exception in this biography. Indispensable as recent editions of letters and documents are, many older collections remain remarkably valuable historical sources. Those to which I most often referred were George Gibbs, *Memoirs of the Administrations of Washington and John Adams, Edited from the Papers of Oliver Wolcott, Secretary of the Treasury*, 2 vols. (New York, 1846), [Octavius Pickering] and Charles W. Upham, *Life of Timothy Pickering*, 4 vols. (Boston, 1867–1873), Charles R. King, ed., *Life and Correspondence of Rufus King . . .* , 6 vols. (New York, 1894), and Charles Francis Adams, ed., *Works of John Adams, Second President of the United States*, 10 vols., (Boston, 1850–1856).

There are scores of biographies of lesser leaders of the period. By acknowledging only a few of them I do not intend to disparage other excellent ones, many of which I consulted with profit. Particularly useful, however, were Winfred E. A. Bernhard, *Fisher Ames: Federalist and Statesman, 1758–1808* (Chapel Hill, N.C., 1965); George Dangerfield, *Chancellor Robert R. Livingston of New York, 1746–1813* (New York, 1960); and George C. Rogers, *Evolution of a Federalist: William Loughton Smith of Charleston (1758–1812)* (Columbia, S.C., 1962).

My chief source for the history of the national government during this period was, of course, the official records to which I referred above. But I also found a number of scholarly commentaries illuminating, among them these: Kenneth R.

Bowling, "Politics in the First Congress, 1789–1791" (Ph.D. diss., University of Wisconsin, 1968), Bruce W. Bugbee, *Genesis of American Patent and Copyright Law* (Washington, D.C., 1967), and, most especially, Leonard White, *The Federalists: A Study in Administrative History* (New York, 1948), a work of exemplary scholarship that will remain the definitive work on its subject for the foreseeable future.

Dozens of first-rate books and articles expertly describe the varied aspects of the era's history. Every serious student of economic history should pay homage to the scholarly merit of Joseph S. Davis, *Essays in the Earlier History of American Corporations*, 2 vols. (Cambridge, Mass., 1917). To select for honorable mention any of the many excellent studies of the foreign policy of the Federalist decade one must necessarily be arbitrary. To be so: I leaned heavily on Bradford Perkins, *The First Rapprochement: England and the United States, 1795–1805* (Philadelphia, 1955), Merrill D. Peterson, "Thomas Jefferson and Commercial Policy, 1783–1793," *William and Mary Quarterly*, 3d Ser., XXII (1965), 584–610, and, for perhaps pardonable reasons, my own "Country Above Party: John Adams and the 1799 Mission to France," in Edmund P. Willis, ed., *Fame and the Founding Fathers: Papers and Comments* (Bethlehem, Pa., 1967). For developments in national politics I relied primarily on the biographies of leading participants, though I profitably consulted the literature on the subject that has so proliferated over recent decades. To two books I am particularly indebted—the material in Noble E. Cunningham, Jr., *The Jeffersonian Republicans: The Formation of Party Organization, 1789–1801* (Chapel Hill, N.C., 1957), greatly facilitated my research; and William Nisbet Chambers, *Political Parties in a New Nation: The American Experience, 1776–1809* (New York, 1963), gave me fresh insights into the developments of the nation's first political parties. Far and away the best treatment of Pennsylvania politics is Roland M. Baumann, "The Democratic-Republicans of Philadelphia: The Origins, 1776–1797" (Ph.D. diss., Pennsylvania State University, 1970). Still definitive for its larger subject is Harry Martin Tinkcom, *The Republicans and Federalists in Pennsylvania, 1790–1801: A Study in National Stimulus and Local Response* (Harrisburg, Pa., 1950). Superior essays are James Hedley Peeling, "Governor Thomas McKean and the Pennsylvania Jacobins (1799–1808)," *PMHB*, LIV (1930), 320–354; Raymond Walters, Jr., "The Origins of the Jeffersonian Party in Pennsylvania," *PMHB*, LXVI (1942), 440–458; and Roland M. Baumann, "John Swanwick: Spokesman for 'Merchant Republicanism' in Philadelphia, 1790–1798," *PMHB*, XCVII (1973), 131–182.

For information on land speculation, one could turn to the many biographies of prominent Americans of that day, most of whom shared Coxe's enthusiasm for that risky enterprise. Several monographs, however, are especially germane to an understanding of the more grandiose speculative enterprises. Of first importance is Paul O. Evans, *The Holland Land Company* (Buffalo, N.Y., 1924), the merit of which is barely indicated by the term "definitive." Also useful are Helen I. Cowan, *Charles Williamson: Genesee Promoter, Friend of Anglo-American Rapprochement* (Rochester, N.Y., 1941), and C. Peter Magrath, *Yazoo: Law and Politics in the New Republic: The Case of Fletcher v. Peck* (Providence, R.I., 1966). Details about federal land policy can be found in Malcolm J. Rohrbough, *The Land Office Business: The Settlement and Administration of American Public Lands, 1789–1837* (New

York, 1968). A model of clarity and the best account of land speculation in Pennsylvania is Norman B. Wilkinson, "Land Policy and Speculation in Pennsylvania, 1779–1800" (Ph.D. diss., University of Pennsylvania, 1958).

There is no study of Coxe's tenure as secretary of the Pennsylvania Land Office and only one work on that important agency—Wilkinson's "Land Policy and Speculation," which brings the subject up to the mid-1790s. Dr. Wilkinson's first-rate monograph spared me countless hours of research into a complex subject, and I am grateful to him. As for every other position Coxe held, there are mountains of material on his secretaryship in the Coxe Papers. The principal printed matter on the subject is in the *Pennsylvania Archives*, 2d Ser., XVIII. Valuable information also can be culled from *Report of the Case of the Commonwealth vs. Tench Coxe, . . .* (Philadelphia, 1803). In "The Northwestern Lands of Pennsylvania, 1790–1812," *PMHB*, LX (1936), 133–139, Elizabeth K. Henderson expertly unraveled one knotty problem with which Coxe was obliged to deal.

The Age of Jefferson: For this period, as for the Federalist decade, bibliographies abound, including my own, to which I have repeatedly referred. Although when appropriate I used biographies and general histories, my major reliance for this as for previous sections of this biography was on original sources. Since the mid-twentieth-century editions of writings of the Founding Fathers have not gone beyond 1800, I used the still standard, and for most purposes still adequate, earlier editions. I most repeatedly referred to Paul Leicester Ford, ed., *The Works of Thomas Jefferson*, 12 vols. (New York, 1904–1905), and to Gaillard Hunt, ed., *Writing of James Madison*, 10 vols. (New York, 1900–1910). Also helpful was Henry Adams, ed., *Writings of Albert Gallatin*, 3 vols. (New York, 1879). Among other contemporary writings that I found useful were "Memoirs of a Senator from Pennsylvania, Jonathan Roberts, 1771–1854," *PMHB*, LXI (1937), 451–474, LXII (1938), 64–97, 213–248, 366–409, 502–551, and Worthington C. Ford, ed., "Letters of William Duane," Massachusetts Historical Society, *Proceedings*, 2d Ser., XX (1906), 257–394. As a supplement to the official records described earlier in this bibliography, I found the second of Leonard White's administrative histories (*The Jeffersonians: A Study in Administrative History, 1801–1829* [New York, 1951]) invaluable.

No general account of this period rivals (and none is likely to match) Henry Adams, *History of the United States of America during the Administrations of Jefferson and Madison*, 9 vols. (New York, 1889–1891). Although this biography may not mirror the indebtedness, my account of the Jeffersonian era was inspired by this classic—to me the greatest historical work the United States has produced. I also have great admiration for—and have learned much from—Dumas Malone's recounting of Jefferson's presidency (*Jefferson and His Times*, IV and V). Irving Brant's study of Madison's years (*Madison: Father of the Constitution*, VI) is comprehensive, though marred by excessive special pleading. A book to which I repeatedly referred is Marshall Smelser, *The Democratic Republic, 1801–1815* (New York, 1968), the best one-volume history of this era. For the history of the post War of 1812 years, no student should miss George Dangerfield's perceptive and gracefully written books, *The Era of Good Feelings* (New York, 1952) and *The Awakening of American Nationalism, 1815–1826* (New York, 1965).

The political history of the Jeffersonian age can be followed in biographies of its principal politicians, both in works already mentioned and in the many studies of other prominent leaders. The monographs that I found most useful were Noble E. Cunningham, *The Jeffersonian Republicans in Power: Party Operations, 1801–1809* (Chapel Hill, N.C., 1963), and, despite what I consider major flaws, David Hackett Fischer, *The Revolution of American Conservatism: The Federalist Party in the Era of Jeffersonian Democracy* (New York, 1965). On Pennsylvania politics, of which Coxe was for a time the storm center, there is a lamentable shortage of worthwhile books and articles. Sanford W. Higginbotham, *The Keystone in the Democratic Arch: Pennsylvania Politics, 1800–1816* (Harrisburg, Pa., 1952) provides a good deal of useful material but is not up to the standards of its two predecessors in the series, Brunhouse, *Counter-Revolution in Pennsylvania*, and Tinkcom, *Republicans and Federalists in Pennsylvania*. Biographies of the state's party chieftains are also scarce. There are Henry Adams, *Life of Albert Gallatin* (Philadelphia, 1879), and Frederick B. Tolles, *George Logan of Philadelphia* (New York, 1953), but there are no studies of Thomas McKean's governorship or of influential leaders like William Duane and Michael Leib.

The bulky literature on diplomacy of the Jeffersonian years (especially on the causes of the War of 1812) displays a range of interpretations but is otherwise essentially repetitious. The unhurried student could (as I have implied) do no better than to read Henry Adams's massive history. For those whose tastes run to the modern, Bradford Perkins provides two well-written, scholarly, and interpretatively balanced volumes (*Prologue to War: England and the United States, 1805–1812* [Berkeley, Calif., 1963] and *Castlereagh and Adams: England and the United States, 1812–1823* [Berkeley, Calif., 1964]).

For the economic history of this period Coxe's own writings provide a wealth of data. In putting my interpretation of this into proper perspective, I relied on the studies by Curtis Nettels, Stuart Bruchey, and Douglass North, to which I referred above.

Although a subject that deserves a monograph (and there is enough material for several), Coxe's record as purveyor of the United States has been explored only in Erma Risch, *Quartermaster Support of the Army: A History of the Corps, 1775–1939* [Washington, D.C., 1962]), and there only briefly. My own account was drawn almost exclusively from voluminous manuscript sources, principally those in the National Archives. I did benefit, however, from a few works on related subjects, among them: James Ripley Jacobs, *The Beginning of the U. S. Army, 1783–1812* (Princeton, N.J., 1947), George Dewey Harmon, *Sixty Years of Indian Affairs: Political, Economic, and Diplomatic, 1789–1850* (Chapel Hill, N.C., 1941), Edgar B. Wesley, "The Government Factory System among the Indians, 1795–1822," *Journal of Economic and Business History*, IV (1931–1932), 487–511, and Asa B. Gardner, "The Uniforms of the American Army," *Magazine of American History*, I (1877), 461–492.

As background for understanding Coxe's contribution to the intellectual and cultural currents of his day, I owe much to Russel B. Nye's *The Cultural Life of the New Nation* (New York, 1960), to Marcus Cunliffe's perceptive appraisal of American cultural uniqueness in *The Nation Takes Shape, 1789–1837* (Chicago, 1959), and to Louis Hartz's distinguished insights in *The Liberal Tradition in America: An Interpretation of American Political Thought since the Revolution* (New York, 1955). For informative material on the black Americans of this period, I am indebted to Donald L. Robinson, *Slavery in the Structure of American Politics, 1765–1820* (New York, 1970). My interpretation of Coxe as a sincere abolitionist who was also a transparent racist was reinforced and enhanced by Winthrop D. Jordan's *White over Black: American Attitudes toward the Negro, 1550–1812* (Chapel Hill, N.C., 1968), a book that richly deserves the acclaim accorded it.

Index

Compiled by Jean G. Cooke

DATE DUE
